I0894721

# Growth and Emerging Prospects of International Islamic Banking

Abdul Rafay
*University of Management and Technology, Pakistan*

A volume in the Advances in Finance, Accounting, and Economics (AFAE) Book Series

IGI Global
DISSEMINATOR OF KNOWLEDGE

Published in the United States of America by
IGI Global
Business Science Reference (an imprint of IGI Global)
701 E. Chocolate Avenue
Hershey PA, USA 17033
Tel: 717-533-8845
Fax: 717-533-8661
E-mail: cust@igi-global.com
Web site: http://www.igi-global.com



Library of Congress Cataloging-in-Publication Data

Names: Rafay, Abdul, 1973- editor.
Title: Growth and emerging prospects of International Islamic Banking / Abdul Rafay, editor.
Description: Hershey, PA : Business Science Reference, 2020. | Includes bibliographical references and index.
Identifiers: LCCN 2019032858 (print) | LCCN 2019032859 (ebook) | ISBN 9781799816119¬(hardcover) | ISBN 9781799834724¬(softcover) | ISBN 9781799816126¬(ebook)
Subjects: LCSH: Banks and banking--Islamic countries. | Banks and banking--Religious aspects--Islam. | Banking law (Islamic law)
Classification: LCC HG3368.A6 (ebook) | LCC HG3368.A6 G76 2020 (print) | DDC 332.10917/67--dc23
LC record available at https://lccn.loc.gov/2019032858

This book is published in the IGI Global book series Advances in Finance, Accounting, and Economics (AFAE) (ISSN: 2327-5677; eISSN: 2327-5685)

British Cataloguing in Publication Data
A Cataloguing in Publication record for this book is available from the British Library.



For electronic access to this publication, please contact: eresources@igi-global.com.

# Advances in Finance, Accounting, and Economics (AFAE) Book Series

Ahmed Driouchi
Al Akhawayn University, Morocco

ISSN:2327-5677
EISSN:2327-5685

## Mission

In our changing economic and business environment, it is important to consider the financial changes occurring internationally as well as within individual organizations and business environments. Understanding these changes as well as the factors that influence them is crucial in preparing for our financial future and ensuring economic sustainability and growth.

The **Advances in Finance, Accounting, and Economics (AFAE)** book series aims to publish comprehensive and informative titles in all areas of economics and economic theory, finance, and accounting to assist in advancing the available knowledge and providing for further research development in these dynamic fields.

## Coverage

- Accounting Standards
- Economic Indices and Quantitative Economic Methods
- Finance
- Macroeconomics
- Theoretical Issues in Economics, Finance, and Accounting
- Applied Finance
- Banking
- Entrepreneurship in Accounting and Finance
- Interest Rates and Annuities
- Economic Policy



The Advances in Finance, Accounting, and Economics (AFAE) Book Series (ISSN 2327-5677) is published by IGI Global, 701 E. Chocolate Avenue, Hershey, PA 17033-1240, USA, www.igi-global.com. This series is composed of titles available for purchase individually; each title is edited to be contextually exclusive from any other title within the series. For pricing and ordering information please visit http://www.igi-global.com/book-series/advances-finance-accounting-economics/73685. Postmaster: Send all address changes to above address. 

## Titles in this Series

*For a list of additional titles in this series, please visit:*
*https://www.igi-global.com/book-series/advances-finance-accounting-economics/73685*

***Mapping, Managing, and Crafting Sustainable Business Strategies for the Circulr Economy***
Susana Serrano Rodrigues (Polytechnic Institute of Leiria, Portugal) Paulo Jorge Almeida (Polytechnic Institute of Leiria, Portugal) and Nuno Miguel Castaheira Almeida (Polytechnic Institute of Leiria, Portugal)
Business Science Reference • ©2020 • 280pp • H/C (ISBN: 9781522598855) • US $195.00

***Economics, Business, and Islamic Finance in ASEAN Economics Community***
Patricia Ordoñez de Pablos (The University of Oviedo, Spain) Mohammad Nabil Almunawar (Universiti Brunei Darussalam, Brunei) and Muhamad Abduh (Universiti Brunei Darussalam, Brunei)
Business Science Reference • © 2020 • 330pp • H/C (ISBN: 9781799822578) • US $215.00

***Handbook of Research on Theory and Practice of Global Islamic Finance***
Abdul Rafay (University of Management and Technology, Pakistan)
Business Science Reference • © 2020 • 500pp • H/C (ISBN: 9781799802181) • US $445.00

***Challenges and Impacts of Religious Endowments on Global Economics and Finance***
Buerhan Saiti (Istanbul Sabahattin Zaim University, Turkey) and Adel Sarea (Ahlia University, Bahrain)
Business Science Reference • © 2020 • 350pp • H/C (ISBN: 9781799812456) • US $225.00

***Regional Trade and Development Strategies in the Era of Globalization***
Akhilesh Chandra Prabhakar (Lovely Professional University, India) Gurpreet Kaur (Lovely Professional University, India) and Vasilii Erokhin (Harbin Engineering University, China)
Business Science Reference • © 2020 • 325pp • H/C (ISBN: 9781799817307) • US $225.00

***Algorithms for Solving Financial Portfolio Design Problems Emerging Research and Opportunities***
Fatima Zohra Lebbah (Ecole Préparatoire en Sciences et Techniques d'Oran (EPSTO), Algeria)
Business Science Reference • © 2020 • 130pp • H/C (ISBN: 9781799818823) • US $155.00

***Regional Integration and Future Cooperation Initiatives in the Eurasian Economic Union***
Maria Lagutina (Saint Petersburg State University, Russia)
Business Science Reference • © 2020 • 339pp • H/C (ISBN: 9781799819509) • US $245.00

***Impact of Mobile Payment Applications and Transfers on Business***
Thaisaiyi Zephania Opati (Riara University, Kenya) and Martin Kang'ethe Gachukia (Riara University, Kenya)
Business Science Reference • © 2020 • 311pp • H/C (ISBN: 9781799823988) • US $195.00

IGI Global
DISSEMINATOR OF KNOWLEDGE

701 East Chocolate Avenue, Hershey, PA 17033, USA
Tel: 717-533-8845 x100 • Fax: 717-533-8661
E-Mail: cust@igi-global.com • www.igi-global.com

*The heights by great men reached and kept, were not attained by sudden flight, but they, while their companions slept, were toiling upward in the night. – Henry Wadsworth Longfellow in "Ladder of St. Augustine" (1850)*

This handbook of research is dedicated to the memory of (the late) Dr. Hasan Sohaib Murad (1959-2018), a visionary academic activist of extraordinary stature. His sad demise during a tragic accident in 2018 had brought an end of an era. The academic community of Pakistan lost an intellectual of high caliber. In fact, he was an institution in himself and the history of business education in Pakistan is incomplete without him.

He was a creative soul with a flair of writing and reading. His scholarly contribution in the field of management and religion made him a person of great depth and integrity. He is remembered as an educationist in a league of his own. Having devoted all his life for the sake of his vision and mission, his personal and professional integrity reflects in the institution he established in Pakistan, the University of Management and Technology (UMT). He was the founding Rector of UMT. Currently, Ibrahim Hasan Murad, President UMT is the torch bearer for his father's vision. Today in 2020, after three decades, UMT is one of the premier general universities of Pakistan.

Dr. Hasan was a great proponent of Islamic Finance. He decided to establish the Institute of Islamic Banking (IIB) in University of Management and Technology, Pakistan; the first of its kind in this part of the world. The undersigned is one of the graduates of first batch with university distinction.

In order to pay tribute to (the late) Dr. Hasan, the Board of Governors of the University decided to establish Dr. Hasan Murad Institute of Knowledge Futures; Pakistan's first academic research and publishing forum devoted to future studies. Dr. Munawar A. Anees was appointed as the first Director of this Institute.

May Allah rest his soul in peace.

## Editorial Advisory Board

# Table of Contents

# Detailed Table of Contents



This chapter offers a literature review discussing the origin, history, and the growth of Islamic Banking, especially in the GCC countries. It provides detailed information regarding how Islamic Banking evolved throughout the years and what are the current Islamic financial products. Another interesting topic covered in this literature review is the performance comparison of Islamic and conventional banks during different time periods. Accordingly, the chapter explores how the financial standing of Islamic banks altered in comparison to conventional banks before and after the financial crisis of 2008 by presenting earlier studies from various countries. It is concluded that some potential challenges and future opportunities of the Islamic Banking are yet to be explored.



This chapter identifies the internal and external challenges for Islamic banking in Libya. It is a conceptual work using secondary data where relevant concepts in terms of challenges of the conversion process in Libya were demonstrated. Conversion process is surrounded and faced by many challenges. Internal challenges are not less significant than external ones. Trained human resource, lack of awareness in Islamic banking, and resistance to change to Islamic banks are considered as internal challenges which represent the stage of readiness to convert the sector. On the other hand, the economic structure, the political situation, and the regulatory framework hinder the process externally. This implies that stakeholders should come up with comprehensive strategies and plans about the conversion process which will improve the readiness level of the banks, raise the awareness and willingness of their employees, and increase the skills of banks' staff.

The Indonesian banking sector has been stable and generally sound over the past decade, partly through efforts by the Bank of Indonesia as Indonesia's central bank and Otoritas Jasa Keuangan as its financial services regulator. This chapter identifies important issues that remain for both conventional and Islamic banking in Indonesia. Authors suggest the government continue its efforts to reform what remains a geographically concentrated industry, to increase the role of bank credit in the economy, and to widen the provision of banking services through technology. Authors highlight the vulnerability of smaller banks in Indonesia to ongoing competitive market pressures and the necessity of creating larger banks through merger or capital raising and improving credit allocation to small and medium-sized businesses. Islamic banking has an important role to play in these developments, and those relating to Islamic social banking.



Since 1960, after a trial of almost 40 years, the reformation of economy of Pakistan from conventional to Islamic could not be achieved. Since 2000, the government changed the strategy to gradually Islamize the economy and adopted a dual system. In this ambit, the State Bank of Pakistan deliberately announced the vision to make the Islamic banking as first choice for users of banking in Pakistan. This chapter bring insights on the background, current state, issues, challenges, and avenues of future policy regarding Islamic banking of Pakistan. The empirical data about Islamic Banking has been collected from the State Bank of Pakistan for the period 2003-2018. This is to evaluate the current state in terms of market performance, modes of Islamic financing, and financing portfolios of Islamic banking. The findings of this chapter show there is a substantial lack of interest by the government to develop the Islamic banking, and Islamic banking is also deviating from its social and ethical proclaims.



Investors from North Africa are interested in financial products with ethical focus and specific risk profile and are in accordance with their religious convictions. This chapter reviews the status of Islamic banking (IB) in North Africa in which the governments have started introducing fundamental legal and regulatory frameworks to promote the development of Islamic finance. The study also discusses the prospect of Islamic banking in these jurisdictions. To fulfill the objectives of the proposed study, a qualitative research was performed. The empirical approach of this study analyzed the financial position of different banks in North African countries. Overall, Islamic finance can be an ideal opportunity for financing infrastructure and development projects in North Africa.

## Section 2
## Islamic Banking and Finance in Practice



The saying that "history repeats itself" is best manifested in capitalist financial system operating worldwide. It seems people are not learning lessons from the history of financial crises. Leading economists and capitalist gurus are warning about an inherently fragile capitalist financial system and about an urgent need to do something about it before it is too late. After the recent global financial crisis, Kotlikoff proposed the most radical and the most comprehensive reform of the existing financial system. His proposal became known as the Limited Purpose Banking (LPB). Kotlikoff's proposal runs hand in hand with the aspirations of the pioneers of Islamic finance. He envisioned a financial system that is based on risk sharing, cooperation, and overall public interest (maslahah). In short, the idea of the LPB – after certain modifications and minor adjustments – can be applied in developing a true Islamic financial system. Thus, it can be said that the LPB and Islamic finance are two sides of the same coin.



This chapter examines the effect of asset diversification (AD) on the efficiency of Islamic banks using conventional banks as the contrast sample. Data Envelopment Analysis (DEA) is used to generate efficiency score as a proxy of bank efficiency and the Tobit panel data model is estimated. A review of banks in three Asian countries with a dual banking system from 2006 to 2012 indicates that AD positively affects bank efficiency, regardless of bank type. In addition, the positive effect of AD on bank efficiency strengthens with bank size, particularly for Islamic banks. Furthermore, any positive effect of AD on the efficiency of Islamic banks is particularly found among those without foreign ownership, whereas ownership type plays no role in determining AD's effect on the efficiency of conventional banks.



Islamic banks were established as private financial institutions in Turkey based on a law enacted in 1983. Private financial institutions succeeded to have equal rights with commercial banks subject to banking law in 2001. The name of private financial institutions was changed to participation banks in 2005 because of being insufficient in terms of Islamic banking transactions. This chapter includes a performance analysis of participation banks listed in Turkey by considering the efficiency and profitability ratios within the period of 2007-2016 using interval-valued pythagorean fuzzy AHP based fuzzy TOPSIS. Three participation banks, Albaraka Türk, Türkiye Finans, and Kuveyt Turk, were examined for the mentioned period.

Financial Inclusion (FI), a global concern of this decade, has been accepted by development agencies, governments, and policymakers as one of the pre-eminent ways to eradicate worldwide poverty and income inequality. Consequently, authorities are looking for possible ways to include the unbanked in formal financial chain. Islamic finance, specifically Islamic banking, with its welfare-oriented principles and unique products, has been able to capture the attention of policy makers. Moreover, a major portion of the Muslim population still exclude themselves from the formal financial chain due to religious prohibition of interest-based transactions for whom Islamic finance is the only way to inclusion. Bangladesh, one of the major Muslim countries in the world, is still to bring one-fourth of its total population under formal financial chain. At this backdrop, this chapter examines the empirical contribution of Islamic banking sector in financial inclusion condition as well as development scenario of Bangladesh.



The global financial crisis of 2007-2008 depicted that conventional banking has many weaknesses. Hence, there has been much debate on the strength of Islamic banking to confront such crises. There are various advantages of using Shari'ah-compliant financial products pointed out by researches. Moreover, people who abide by their religious belief are mainly those who demand such financial services. But research relating to the determinants of Islamic banking is scant. This chapter examines the determinants of Islamic Banking in Africa over the period 2005-2018. The result shows that if the share of the Muslim population is high compared to other religions, Islamic banking is better diffused. Furthermore, important determinants of Islamic banking obtained from the results are the growth rate of the country and the extent to which the financial system is developed. Interestingly, it is observed that interest rate affects the diffusion of Islamic banking as it represents an opportunity cost.



The unwillingness of contemporary Islamic banks to undertake real business risks has left many to ponder on whether the objectives laid down by the industry's founders have been realized. The need for real risk taking by Islamic banks is critical to justify the profits they earn in the forms of margins, rents, or service charges. This chapter analyzes issues relating to ownership risk (ḍamān al-milkiyyah) in Islamic banking by examining three of its popular products, namely Murabahah (mark-up sale), Ijarah (leasing), and Musharakah Mutanaqisah (diminishing partnership). Following close scrutiny, the chapter concludes that principles of ownership risk as laid down in Fiqh Muamalat (law of transactions) are violated in each of the studied products. Unfortunately, the problem extends beyond these products to include a number of other Islamic financial products. The author calls for closer attention to this important Shari'ah concept of ownership risk in designing Islamic finance products and offers some policy recommendations to improve the current situation.

# Preface

## INTRODUCTION

The desire to edit a book on International Islamic Banking came out of my two decades of experience as a practitioner of conventional finance and few years of experience of dealing with Islamic banking. During financial crises of 2007, the global banking sector faced a serious crisis. As a result, Islamic banking got the chance as an alternative. Since then, Islamic Banking is being considered as a key competitor of conventional Banking in Muslim and non-Muslims countries alike. Islamic banks (IB) have distinct risk profiles and balance sheet structures that differ from conventional banks, with associated implication for financial stability (IMF, 2018). Evidences also show that there exists a link between Islamic banking development and economic growth (Furqani & Mulyany, 2009; Abduh & Azmi, 2012; Imam & Kpodar, 2013; Kassim, 2016).

*Riba*, which is the basis of modern day conventional banking, is forbidden (*haram*) in Islam and this verdict has been passed again and again at various forums by the followers of the four leading and the most prominent *Madhahib* (i.e., *Hanafi, Hanbali, Shafi,* and *Malki*; Wilson, 1995; Usmani, 1999, 2002; Siddiqui, 2004; Hanif & Iqbal, 2010). International Islamic Banking has enabled the growth of financial products which are either *Shari'ah* compliant or *Shari'ah* based.

International Islamic Banking, represented by over 500 full-fledged Islamic Banks, is the major player in Islamic Finance Industry contributing about 71% of the total assets of this industry with a Cumulative Annual Growth Rate (CAGR) of 5% (Thomson Reuters, 2018). Total worth of Islamic finance industry is expected to reach at USD 4 trillion by 2020. (MIFC, 2014; GIFC, 2019). The Islamic Banks of Indonesia, Malaysia, Turkey, Pakistan, UAE, Qatar, Saudi Arabia, Kuwait and Bahrain are contributing over 80% of total assets of International Islamic Banking (CIBE, 2019). Saudi Arabia is enjoying the largest share in Islamic Banking assets followed by Malaysia and UAE. These banks continuously release new *Shari'ah* products and services with a network across the world. Realizing the importance of innovations, these banks are also investing in FinTech and other emerging technologies like Blockchain (Stubing, 2019). Currently the global Islamic banking industry is fragmented with local and international players.

## CONTEXT AND ORGANIZATION OF THIS VOLUME

This volume is organized into three sections that consist of 15 chapters by writers from 15 countries. Twenty-eight authors contributed from disparate parts of the world: UAE (1), Mauritius (2), Libya (1),

Nigeria (1), Taiwan (1), Yemen (1), China (1), Malaysia (5), Tunisia (2), Australia (2), Bosnia and Herzegovina (1), Turkey (4), Saudi Arabia (2), Bangladesh (2), Indonesia (2).

Section 1 addresses the past, present, and future of Islamic banking in developing countries with a set of five chapters authored by writers from UAE, Libya, Malaysia, Nigeria, Australia, and Tunisia. Section 2 addresses the current practices of international Islamic banking with a set of six chapters contributed by authors from Bosnia, Taiwan, Turkey, Bangladesh, China, Mauritius, and Saudi Arabia. Section 3 addresses the role of governance in Islamic banking with a set of four chapters from Yemen, Mauritius, Indonesia, and Malaysia.

In Section 1, the first chapter, "Islamic Banking in GCC: Emergence, Growth, and Prospects," by Eda Orhun, throws light on how Islamic Banking evolved throughout the years in GCC region. The chapter also discusses how the financial standing of Islamic banks altered in comparison to conventional banks before and after the financial crisis of 2008. The second chapter, "Islamic Banking in Libya: Emergence, Growth, and Prospects," by Mahmoud A. S. Abusloum, Khaliq Ahmad, and Nabil Bello, explains that the Libyan government is one of the few countries that has taken the stance to transform all its banks into Islamic banks following the Libyan laws of 2013 and 2015 which postulated that all conventional banks must stop interest-based transactions. The chapter also discusses the challenges being faced by the respective government. The third chapter, "Islamic Banking in Indonesia: Emergence, Growth, and Prospects," by Luthfi Hamidi and Andrew C. Worthington, identifies important issues for both conventional and Islamic banks in Indonesia. The chapter also highlights the vulnerability of smaller banks in Indonesia to ongoing competitive market pressures and the necessity of creating larger banks through merger or capital raising. The fourth chapter, "Islamic Banking in Pakistan: Emergence, Growth, and Prospects," by Muhammad Bilal Zafar and Ahmad Azam Sulaiman, discusses that after a trial of almost forty-years, the results of reformation of Pakistani economy from conventional to Islamic could not be fully achieved. This chapter also highlights the background, issues, challenges and avenues of future policy regarding Islamic banking of Pakistan. The fifth chapter, "Islamic Banking in North Africa: Emergence, Growth, and Prospects," by Yomna Daoud and Aida Kammoun, reviews the status of Islamic banking in North Africa where the governments have started introducing fundamental legal and regulatory frameworks in order to promote the development of Islamic financial industry.

In Section 2, the sixth chapter, "Islamic Finance and Limited Purpose Banking (LPB): Two Sides of the Same Coin," by Edib Smolo, discusses that the idea of the Limited Purpose Banking (LPB) – after certain modifications and minor adjustments – can be applied in developing a true Islamic financial system. LPB is envisioned by Kotlikoff that is based on risk sharing, cooperation and overall public interest. The seventh chapter, "Asset Diversification and Efficiency of Islamic Banks," by Naiwei Chen, examines the effect of asset diversification on the efficiency of Islamic banks using conventional banks as the contrast sample. For practitioners, the results provide useful suggestions on how to engage in diversification strategically to improve the efficiency of Islamic banks. The eighth chapter, "Participative Banking in Turkey: A Performance Analysis," by Serpil Altınırmak, Cumhur Şahin, Çağlar Karamaşa, and Basil Oluch Okoth, discusses the performance analysis of participation banks listed in Turkey by considering the efficiency and profitability ratios within the period of 2007-2016 using interval-valued pythagorean fuzzy AHP based fuzzy TOPSIS. The ninth chapter, "Islamic Financial Inclusion: An Alternative Approach to Reach the Unbanked," by S. M. Sohrab Uddin, Mohammad Zoynul Abedin, and Nahid Afroz, examines the empirical contribution of Islamic banking sector in financial inclusion in Bangladesh. The chapter concludes that there are practical repercussions for the stakeholders in establishing Islamic banking as a potential channel for inclusion in both Muslim and non-Muslim countries. The tenth chapter, "Determinants of Islamic Banking in Africa: An Analysis," by Sheereen Fauzel, examines the determinants of Islamic Banking in Africa over the period of 2005-2018. The result shows that Islamic banking is better diffused if the share of Muslim population is high compared to other religions. The eleventh chapter, "Ownership Risk in Contemporary Islamic Banking," by Alam I. Asadov, analyzes the issues relating to ownership risk in Islamic banking by examining three of its popular products. The chapter concludes that principles of ownership risk as laid down in *Fiqh Mu'amalat* are violated in each of the studied products.

In Section 3, the twelfth chapter, "*Shari'ah* Governance for Islamic Banking: Evidence From Diverse Regulatory Environments," by Naji Mansour Nomran and Razali Haron, highlights some issues related to the differences across jurisdictions in adopting various *Shari'ah* Governance regulatory practices. The findings indicate that Islamic banks demonstrate higher levels of financial performance, on average, while working in regulated jurisdictions. The thirteenth chapter, "Governance and Financial Reporting of Islamic Banks: Evidence From Mauritius," by Ambareen Beebeejaun, intends to discuss the main governance and financial reporting requirements of the offeror of Islamic banking products in Mauritius so the potential investors may be acquainted with the legal and compliance needs of an Islamic bank. The fourteenth chapter, "Banking Governance: Perspective of Islamic Banking," by Mohamad Adam and Muizzuddin Ahmad Tontowi, discusses that the theory and empirical research become the necessary foundation to understand the perspective of governance in Islamic banks, because basically both conventional banks and Islamic banks use governance as a control mechanism in providing value added services. The fifteenth chapter, "*Shari'ah* Governance and Audit Assurance in Islamic Banks," by Nor Faezah Ghazi Ahmad and Aisyah Abdul Rahman, evaluates the role and function of *Shari'ah* audit and *Shari'ah* committee and observes to what extent the *Shari'ah* audit helps in reducing Islamic banks' risk exposure.

I am hopeful that this book will deepen the discourse on the role of International Islamic Banking in a modern day environment. I thank the contributors and also the external reviewers who have patiently critiqued these chapters to meet the minimum acceptable standard.

*Abdul Rafay*
*University of Management and Technology, Pakistan*
*January 2020*

## REFERENCES

Abduh, M., & Azmi, O. M. (2012). Islamic banking and economic growth: The Indonesian experience. *International Journal of Islamic and Middle Eastern Finance and Management*, *5*(1), 35–47. doi:10.1108/17538391211216811

CIBE. (2019). *Al Huda Center of Islamic Banking and Economics*. Retrieved from http://alhudacibe.com

Furqani, H., & Mulyany, R. (2009). Islamic banking and economic growth: Empirical evidence from Malaysia. *Journal of Economic Cooperation and Development*, *30*(2), 59–74.

GIFC. (2019). *Global Islamic Finance Markets Report 2019 "Global Islamic Finance Market - Growth, Trends, and Forecast (2018 - 2024)"*. Retrieved from https://www.globenewswire.com

Imam, P., & Kpodar, K. (2013). Islamic banking: How has it expanded? *Emerging Markets Finance & Trade*, *49*(6), 112–137. doi:10.2753/REE1540-496X490607

IMF. (2018). *IMF Executive Board Adopts Decisions to Formally Recognize the Core Principles for Islamic Finance Regulation (CPIFR) for Banking*. IMF Press Release No. 18/193, Retrieved from https://www.imf.org/

Kassim, S. (2016). Islamic finance and economic growth: The Malaysian experience. *Global Finance Journal*, *30*, 66–76. doi:10.1016/j.gfj.2015.11.007

MIFC. (2014). *Malaysia International Islamic Financial Center (MIFC) Report "2014 – A Landmark Year for Global Islamic Industry"*. Retrieved from www.mifc.com

Siddiqui, M. N. (2004). *Riba, bank interest and the rationale of its prohibition*. Jeddah, Saudi Arabia: Islamic Research and Training Institute.

Stubing, D. (2019). Growth continues for Islamic financial institutions, helped by technology and product innovations. *Global Finance Magazine*. Retrieved from https://www.gfmag.com/magazine/may-2019/best-islamic-banks-world-2019

Thomson Reuters. (2018). *Islamic Finance Development Report 2018 – Building Momentum* (#IFDI2018). Retrieved from https://ceif.iba.edu.pk/pdf/Reuters-Islamic-finance-development-report2018.pdf

Usmani, M. T. (1999). *The Legal Status of Following a Madhab*. Karachi, Pakistan: Durul-Ishaat.

Usmani, M. T. (2002). *An introduction to Islamic finance* (Vol. 20). Brill.

Wilson, R. (1995). *Islamic Development Finance in Malaysia. Leading Issues in Islamic Banking and Finance*. Selangor, Malaysia: Pelanduk Publications.

# Section 1

# Past, Present, and Future of Islamic Banking: Evidence From Developing Countries

# Chapter 1
# Islamic Banking in GCC: Emergence, Growth, and Prospects

**Eda Orhun**
https://orcid.org/0000-0001-7153-4892
*Zayed University, UAE*

## ABSTRACT

*This chapter offers a literature review discussing the origin, history, and the growth of Islamic Banking, especially in the GCC countries. It provides detailed information regarding how Islamic Banking evolved throughout the years and what are the current Islamic financial products. Another interesting topic covered in this literature review is the performance comparison of Islamic and conventional banks during different time periods. Accordingly, the chapter explores how the financial standing of Islamic banks altered in comparison to conventional banks before and after the financial crisis of 2008 by presenting earlier studies from various countries. It is concluded that some potential challenges and future opportunities of the Islamic Banking are yet to be explored.*

## 1. HISTORY OF ISLAMIC BANKING

In the history of Islamic civilization, the notion of partnership and profit-sharing had been always more prominent than interest-based borrowing and lending since *Riba* (interest) is considered as '*Haram*' (prohibited) according to the Islamic principles. However, these Islamic economic principles were forgotten after the rapid rise of the western model of financial intermediation and commercial banking in the post-industrial revolution era. Since the 1850s, almost all Muslim countries accepted laws and legal structures rooted from Western models since they were under direct or indirect pressure from the European countries. After the end of colonial period, although the foreign banks are nationalized in these Muslim countries, they were still run by following the Western style in a 'neo-colonial' system. But especially in rural and religious regions of the Islamic world, the people were skeptical towards these western financial institutions. In this respect, there was a strong need for the formation of a financial institution that watches over the Islamic principles or in other words that is interest-free. The first pioneering

DOI: 10.4018/978-1-7998-1611-9.ch001

initiative for the enlargement of Islamic finance and banking happened in Mit-Ghamr in Egypt. Getting inspired from the German savings banks, the Mit-Ghamr Islamic Savings Bank founded by El-Naggar who eventually took the role as the Secretary-General of the International Association of Islamic Banks in the succeeding years. The Mit-Ghamr project collected savings from the rural sector through savings, investments and *Zakat*[1] accounts. Interest was not given to customers in the saving accounts, but they were authorized to withdraw their deposits when they need. Participants were also qualified to obtain small, short-term interest-free loans for fruitful motives. The money placed in the investment accounts could be withdrawn on a limited basis and were invested based on profit-sharing (Chachi, 2005). Wilson (1983) reported that: "The bank's loans were used for different motives such as house building and repairs … Some loans were used to fund the acquisition of farm animals and fundamental upgrade to the irrigation systems as efficient water provision was absolutely necessary for a society rested solely on cultivation". (Chachi, 2005; Molyneux & Iqbal, 2005) The Mit-Ghamr project that started in 1963 and continued until 1966 gained a big success in these short three years. In three years, the savings deposits increased from 25,000 Egyptian pounds to 125,000 Egyptian pounds. In a similar fashion, investment deposits more than doubled from 35,000 to 75,000 Egyptian pounds. The Mit-Ghamr project also had a zero-default rate by following a stricter and wiser loan lending policy. Despite its success, the Mit-Ghamr project was canceled due to political reasons in the following years. It is said today that this bank would have covered the whole Egypt by now due to its extreme success in its short life period if it was not canceled by the Egyptian authorities. Its extreme success created conflict with the local social authorities because they thought that Mit-Ghamr Islamic Savings Bank started to interfere with their own power. (Chachi, 2005) However, it proved that a financial institution governed by the Islamic principles was longed for and had a strong potential to be successful. After the abolishment of the Mit-Ghamr project, the first interest-free financial institution with the official title of 'bank' that is Nasser Social bank was founded again in Egypt in 1971. (Abedifar et al., 2015)

After observing the success of the Mit-Ghamr project and the government involvement in the establishment of interest-free Nasser Social bank, Muslim businessman who had surplus funds took initiatives to start an Islamic bank in their Muslim countries. Accordingly, the first so-called Islamic bank-Dubai Islamic Bank- got opened in Dubai, UAE in the year of 1975. With the start-up of the Dubai Islamic Bank, worldwide and official Islamic banking practice had started. The seeds of Dubai Islamic bank had been first planted during the First International Conference on Islamic Economics that took place in Saudi Arabia at the beginning of 1970s. The opening of the Dubai Islamic Bank was an important milestone as it was the first role model that other GGC countries would follow in the future. In this respect, the UAE authorities' supportive attitude was very important and had led to a new era in the banking industry. Recently, UAE is the third-largest Islamic banking market by value and deposits held by Islamic banks and as of 2018 this value amounted to AED 392.4 billion with a yearly growth rate of 5%. (World Bank Group, 2018; Sophia, 2015) Following UAE; Kuwait, Bahrain, and Qatar passed legislations to found Islamic banks in 1977, 1979 and 1982 respectively. (Molyneux & Iqbal, 2005; Abdul Alim, 2014)

Despite these developments and its hosting of the First International Conference on Islamic Economics, Kingdom of Saudi Arabia had a skeptical attitude towards Islamic Banking for a very long time. Although Saudi Arabia was very supportive of the international Islamic finance inventiveness and especially the founding of Islamic Development Bank by taking the support of other 56 shareholding member countries, it was reluctant to adopt a national-wide Islamic Banking system that is fully *Shari'ah*-compliant (Wilson, 2009). Following a similar mindset, the authorities had kept the approval of the banking license of Al Rajhi Bank on hold for years until 1987. Before this time, several Al Rajhi establishments that were originally founded in 1957 got merged under the name of 'Al Rajhi trading and exchange corporation' in 1978. Over these long years, the deposits of Al Rajhi trading and exchange corporation increased dramatically and that is why the Saudi Arabian Monetary Agency (SAMA) felt obligated to issue its banking license finally in 1987. The failure of such a big financial institution would create distrust in the overall banking system and especially the smaller but 'regulated' banks would become controversial. (Wilson, 2009)

On the other hand, another GCC country, Bahrain, had been always very supportive of Islamic financial institutions and functioned as a regional financial center since 1976. Bahrain today has the largest number of Islamic banks and *Takaful* companies. Especially, the negative attitude of Saudi Arabia towards Islamic financial institutions pushed Saudi Arabian businessman towards the closest neighboring country, Bahrain. (Wilson, 2009) Bahrain also hosts the Accounting and Auditing Organization for Islamic Financial Institutions (AAOIFI) that was founded in the year of 1991 to maintain and promote financial reporting norms for Islamic financial institutions. As of 2012, Bahrain had 107 registered banks, 27 of which were Islamic banks and this number was the highest of all the countries according to the Bankscope data of 2006. (Vinnicombe, 2012) This is still true for Bahrain as having the highest number of Islamic banks today. (Bahrain Economic Development Board, 2017)

Following the establishment of DIB in 1977, Kuwait was the second country to establish one of the largest Islamic banks in the region, Kuwait Finance House (KFH) that has significant operations also abroad. Especially in 2004, Kuwait enacted an amendment law to the Central Bank Law officially recognizing KFH as the first Islamic Bank of Kuwait and this amendment also opened the way for the establishment of other Islamic Banks in Kuwait, both local and foreign. Following this change, Kuwait Real Estate Bank which is one of the specialized banks in Kuwait transformed into an Islamic Bank and changed its existing name to Kuwait International Bank. New Islamic financial institutions also started to enter to Kuwaiti market after this new legislation which ensured competition for the Islamic finance industry and allowed the entry of new Islamic Banks. In that respect, today there exist four other Islamic Banks in Kuwait in addition to KFH and Kuwait International Bank. One of these banks is Al-Rajhi Bank, the largest Islamic Bank of the world from Saudi Arabia as introduced above (Wilson, 2009; Global Banking and Finance Review, 2013).

Qatar, being another wealthy state of the Gulf region, was a few years late to jump on the bandwagon and duly established the Qatar Islamic Bank (QIB) in 1982. Today QIB holds a market share of 43% of the total Islamic banking assets and is the largest one of the totals of four Islamic Banks existing in the country. QIB is also the fourth largest Islamic Bank of the world and mostly focuses on the domestic market together with its three other competitors. (Bait Al-Mashura Finance Consultations, 2017)

Oman, being the last GCC country, stayed out of the Islamic Banking business for a very long time but could not ignore it anymore as the industry got enormous and very successful regarding the market share. With a new amendment to the banking law in 2012, Oman recognized the inclusion of Islamic Banks as recognized entities either as specialized banks or as independent entities of the existing commercial banks. Following this decree, Nizwa Bank opened its doors as the first Islamic Bank of Oman in 2012. Today there exists around five Islamic Banks in Oman, one of which is the Dubai Islamic Bank (DIB) from UAE. In this short period of time, Oman's Islamic Banking sector has grown significantly that reached to 4.1bn of Omani Rials as of 2018 and it recorded a 14 percent yearly growth rate. (Stubing, 2014; MuscatDaily.com, 2018)

## 2. ISLAMIC FINANCE AND BANKING PRODUCTS

This chapter will provide details regarding the most popular Islamic Banking products and the rationale behind them. As discussed in the previous pages, Islamic banking and its products are highly popular not only in countries where Muslims constitute much of the population but also in non-Muslim countries (Rafay, Sadiq & Ajmal, 2017). Due to its increasing popularity, even global market leaders such as Citigroup, HSBC, and Standard Chartered started to offer these Islamic financing products by establishing Islamic windows in addition to their conventional banking facilities.

- ***Wadiah:*** *Wadiah* is the Arabic term for deposits. According to Muslim scholars, *Wadiah* could be defined as giving authorization to someone to keep the owner's belongings explicitly and implicitly or keeping ownership of personal goods in a certain method. Thus; in the framework of Islamic banking, the bank is considered as a keeper and trustee of funds. One can classify *Wadiah* into two different types: *Wadiah yad Amanah* and *Wadiah yad Damanah*.
    - Safe custody based on trust (*Wadiah yad Amanah*): In this contract, the bank does not gain any profit and is supposed to return the funds at any time when the depositor demands them.
    - Guaranteed Safe Custody (*Wadiah yad Damanah*): In this type of contract, deposits are accepted as the source of funds for the bank and so the bank is entitled to use the deposits for trading and other purposes and has the right to gain profit from these activities. (Qaed, 2014)
- ***Murabahah* (Mark-up / Cost-plus-profit Based Financing):** *Murabahah*, in its original Islamic meaning, is just a sale. Different than a regular sale, in *Murabahah* contract the seller shall inform the purchaser regarding how much cost s/he has incurred and how much extra s/he is charging as the profit. With this logic, *Murabahah* is not a loan lent on interest rather it is a sale of a product for profit. Basically, the bank purchases the product for a client and resells it to the client at a predetermined price that includes the cost that the bank paid plus a negotiated profit. Such contracts are mostly used for working capital and trade financing. (Chong & Liu, 2009) Consumers use *Murabahah* when they purchase cars and household appliances. Similarly, businesses benefit from *Murabahah* when they purchase machinery, equipment or raw materials. *Murabahah* is also used during international trade transactions. In such situations, *Murabahah* contract allows importers to purchase raw materials and any kind of product from foreign countries. The Islamic Bank commits and accepts to pay against the trade documents by issuing a letter of credit and then sells the products imported with a profit margin to the original importer.
- ***Bai muajjal* (Deferred Payment Sale):** The idea of *Bai muajjal* is very similar to the *Murabahah* contract except for the fact that here the customer can make the payment to the Islamic bank for the product on a credit basis. Thus, the bank purchases the product for the customer and sells it to her/him with credit. Of course, the Islamic bank here would ask collateral from the customer to cover the cost of the product. *Bai muajjal* has been applied frequently for house and property financing. Accordingly, the house or the property is taken as the collateral by the bank and if the client fails to make payments, the bank will sell the collateral to cover the initial cost. (Chong & Liu, 2009)
- ***Musharakah* (Partnership Financing):** In Islamic finance, '*Musharakah*' implies a joint enterprise or partnership where two parties split the profits and losses of an enterprise on a pro-rata basis that depends on the initial equity investment of both parties. *Musharakah* derives from the concept of '*shirkah al amwal*' (partnership) in Arabic. *Musharakah* plays a major role in the fi-

nancing of business operations and home financing in accordance with the Islamic principles. For business financing, an entrepreneur who wants to start a business can become a partner with the Islamic bank. Accordingly, they would share the profits on a preset ratio and losses shall be shared according to the initial equity investment of each party. This rule follows the Islamic principle which specifies as one cannot lose more than what s/he contributed. In this way, *Musharakah* contract allows profit and loss sharing. On the other hand, home financing hinges on the declining partnership notion. In the beginning, the customer pays some proportion of the house price to co-own the house and the rest is covered by the Islamic Bank. Afterward, the client will steadily repay the bank's initial investment at an agreed installment rate until the house gets totally possessed by the client. In addition to this periodic installment, the bank charges the customer with *Ijarah*-rental charge for the proportion of the house it owns. When the client pays back the bank's initial investment, the ownership ratio of the bank decreases, and so does the rental charge. (Farooq, 2009; Meera & Razak, 2005)

- ***Mudarabah*** **(Capital Financing):** *'Mudarabah'* is also a very popular type of contact in Islamic financing. In a *Mudarabah* contract, the first partner acts as the financier (the investor-*rabbul mal*) and the second partner manages and uses the financier's investment in an economic activity. *Mudarabah* based products are especially used in two specific situations. The first situation occurs when a customer places an amount of investment in a *Mudarabah* investment account. In this scenario, the customer is *rabbul mal* and the Islamic bank is the *Mudarib* or the fund manager. The customer and the Islamic bank mutually agree on a pre-determined profit-sharing ratio at the start of this contract. However, when it comes to losses, the customer shall bear all the lost since s/he is the financier except the loss occurs due to neglect or misconduct of the Islamic bank. *Mudarabah* contract is also used for project financing cases. Here, the Islamic bank and the customer start a *Mudarabah* venture. Islamic bank provides full financing for the venture and the customer works as the project manager and puts her/his efforts and skills. Again, both parties mutually agree on a profit-sharing ratio. In the case of loss, again the financier-here the Islamic bank- bears it. Considering the fact that the loss is fully borne by the financier, several scholars highlighted the agency problems coming with the *Mudarabah* contract. These scholars argued that *Mudarabah* contract lacks the bonding component of a debt contract and generates wrong incentives, i.e. showing the profits lower than the actual, for the fund manager considering the risk-return framework. (Shaikh, 2011)
- ***Bai Al-Salam / Istisna*** **(Forward Sale):** These Islamic finance products are like futures contracts. *Bai Al-Salam* is used for raw materials, while *Istisna* is used for industrial goods. In *Bai Al-Salam*, an entrepreneur sells some commodities to the Islamic Bank at a specified price. At the start of the contract, Islamic Bank pays the price and the entrepreneur promises the delivery of commodities at a future date. As opposed to *Bai Al-Salam*, in *Istisna* the price does not need to be paid upfront. It can be paid in installments according to the agreement between the parties or some part of the total amount may be paid at the beginning and the remaining balance would be covered later as agreed. (Chong & Liu, 2009; Ebrahim & Joo, 2001; Ali, 2011)
- ***Qard al-hasana*** **(Beneficence Loans):** These are zero-return or interest-free loans extended to needy Muslims by the Islamic banks. Such loans are mainly extended to increase the welfare of the Muslim society and to achieve income redistribution by financing low-income housing, small-scale agro-businesses, and industrial cooperatives. The Islamic bank extending such a loan is only allowed to charge a service charge that is solely related to the administrative costs of issuing such a loan.

- ***Ijarah Sukuk*** **(Lease):** *Ijarah Sukuk* are securities of equal value that represents physical real assets and are related to an *Ijarah* contract. *Ijarah Sukuk* basically represents leased assets and pro-rata ownership on these underlying assets. During the process of *Ijarah Sukuk* issue, there are three parties involved: the issuer, the special purpose vehicle and the investors. First, the issuer transfers the possession of the underlying asset to a special purpose vehicle (SPV). SPV issues *Sukuk* certificates to investors to obtain the amount required to purchase the asset from the issuer. After purchasing the asset from the issuer, SPV rents the asset back to the issuer. The issuer starts paying periodic lease rentals to the SPV and then distributes these rental amounts to the *Sukuk* holders.

## 3. PERFORMANCE COMPARISON OF ISLAMIC AND CONVENTIONAL BANKS

This section will provide a detailed literature review regarding the financial standing comparison of Islamic and conventional banks in different countries. The financial results of Islamic banks have also changed over the years especially in the course of and after the global financial crisis of 2008. Related studies from several countries will be discussed in the following paragraphs:

### 3.1 Islamic vs. Conventional Banks' Performance in the UAE and GCC Countries

One of the first studies that aims to identify the determinants of profitability for Islamic and conventional banks in the GCC region is Alkassim (2005). Return on assets (ROA), return on equity (ROE) and net income margin are employed as profitability measures in this study. The study concludes that larger conventional banks make less profits, higher capital ratios lead to higher profits for Islamic banks and total loans (lending capacity) increase both types of banks' profitability. Furthermore; while the amount of deposits increases the profit levels of conventional banks, deposits decrease the profit levels of Islamic banks according to Alkassim (2005). Al-Tamimi (2010) compares the financial standing of UAE Islamic and conventional banks by using data starting from 1996 till 2008. As performance measures, this paper used ROA and ROE. On the other hand, several internal and external elements including size, GDP per capita, financial development indicator, concentration, liquidity, cost and number of branches are used as explanatory variables affecting the performance. The results indicate that while liquidity and concentration have a positive impact on the financial results of conventional banks, cost and number of branches are more important determinants for the positive performance of Islamic banks. Zeitun (2012) studies a similar issue for all the GCC countries for the time period of 2002-2009. Zeitun (2012) again analyzed the determinants of Islamic versus conventional banks' performance in terms of ROE and ROA by using bank-specific, macroeconomic and ownership structure variables. The results indicate that bank's equity has a notable and positive impact on conventional banks' profitability only. On the other hand, cost has a notable and adverse effect on both Islamic and conventional banks' financial results. Size also has a positive impact on the performance of Islamic banks but has no effect on conventional banks. Another important result from this study is that foreign ownership has no effect on both Islamic and conventional banks' financial standing. Siraj and Pillai (2012) perform a more focused analysis by selecting twelve major Islamic and conventional banks (six from each group) in the GCC zone. Like previous papers, they analyze several financial ratios of these banks measuring profitability, efficiency and capital adequacy levels. Their results show that Islamic banks enjoy higher profitability and are more equity financed.

Another paper that studied GCC countries is Olson and Zoubi (2008). This paper used 26 financial ratios (profitability ratios, efficiency ratios, asset-quality indicators, and cash/liability ratios) to contrast Islamic and conventional banks in the GCC countries between the years 2000 and 2005 that is before the financial crisis of 2008. This study confirmed that Islamic banks in the region are more profitable than conventional banks. However, Islamic banks are not as efficient as conventional banks since they have a lower asset-turnover ratio. The study also finds out that Islamic banks hold more cash relative to deposits than conventional banks.

One other study looking at the financial ratios of Islamic and conventional banks in the GCC region is Khediri et al. (2015). It employs 14 financial ratios for 61 Islamic and conventional banks for the period 2003-2010. This study also agrees with the previous study by concluding that Islamic banks have on average higher profitability, higher capitalization, higher liquidity and face lower credit risk than conventional banks. Moreover, Khediri et al. (2015) report that Islamic banks have less off-balance sheet undertakings and more operating leverage compared to conventional banks. Since the time span of Khediri et al. (2015) covers the credit crisis of 2008, they also indicated that the profitability of both Islamic and conventional banks decreased during this period. On the other hand, Samad (2004) looks at the comparative performance of Bahrain's Islamic and conventional banks in the post-Gulf war period of 1991-2001. This study focuses on nine financial ratios that assess profit levels, liquidity, and credit risk of the banks. The results highlight that there is not a noteworthy distinction between Islamic and conventional banks regarding profitability and liquidity. But Islamic banks are found to have less credit risk in comparison to conventional banks and have credit performance superiority.

## 3.2 Islamic vs. Conventional Banks' Performance in Other Countries

Johnes et al. (2014) present a comprehensive study that includes Islamic and conventional banks from 18 different countries covering the years from 2004 to 2009. By employing a meta-frontier analysis, they decomposed gross efficiency into two constituents as net efficiency and type efficiency. While net efficiency measures managerial competency, type efficiency is a measure for operational efficiency. This paper highlights that Islamic banks are found to be less efficient than conventional banks regarding type efficiency (operational efficiency) but they are found to be more efficient about net efficiency (managerial efficiency). Thus, the paper concludes that conventional banks need to take some lessons from Islamic banks to increase the competency level of their managers. The paper also discusses that this managerial efficiency difference could be related to different manager compensation schemes observed at Islamic and conventional banks. Beck et al. (2013) present a study that is even more comprehensive by contrasting Islamic and conventional banks with worldwide data from Bankscope. Their work shows that Islamic banks are more efficient and have higher capital adequacy ratios. Even though Islamic and conventional banks seem to enjoy almost identical asset quality and stability, this study reports that Islamic banks have lower costs in general with lower operating costs and cost-income ratios.

Jaffar and Manarwi (2011) studied and contrasted the financial standing of Islamic and conventional banks of Pakistan for the years between 2005 and 2009. They looked at the capital adequacy, asset quality, management, earning ability and liquidity positions of 5 Islamic and 5 conventional banks. The study concluded that Islamic banks have higher capital adequacy and liquidity ratios than conventional banks however, they lack management quality and earning ability compared to conventional banks. In addition, the study also noted that Islamic banks have a higher loan loss ratio compared to their conventional peers which is a factor contributing to their lower profitability in Pakistan. Kouser and Saba (2012) is another study on the financial standing of Islamic versus conventional banks in Pakistan covering the years 2006-2010. The results indicate that Islamic banks have stronger capital adequacy and better asset quality compared to conventional banks and Islamic divisions of conventional banks. Furthermore, Islamic banks are found to have better management competency compared to their other types of competitors.

Malaysia is another country where Islamic banking has a history. Accordingly, there are some studies comparing the financial performance and efficiency of two different types of banks. Samad and Hassan (2006) compare profitability, liquidity, risk and solvency ratios of the only existing Islamic bank back then (Bank Islam Malaysia Berhad) in Malaysia with eight other conventional banks for the time period of 1984-1997. Their paper identified the Islamic bank as being more liquid and less risky. Ismail et al. (2013) is a more recent study related to Malaysian banks' efficiency. Their paper examines the efficiency of eight Islamic Banks (seven of which established later in the 2000s) and nine conventional banks for the years 2006-2009. The study finds Islamic banks to be more efficient at allocating resources but less efficient regarding operating costs. Considering their results, Ismail et al. (2013) advise Islamic banks to develop their cost efficiency regarding technical component and conventional banks to focus on efficient allocation and utilization of resources. This paper also highlights that size is an important determinant of efficiency meaning that larger sized banks are found to be more efficient.

Finally, Ahmad and Luo (2010) measure the efficiency of Islamic banks in Europe by studying data from Germany, the UK and Turkey for three years between 2005 to 2008. The study finds out that Islamic banks are technically more efficient even though they need to improve their cost efficiency.

All these studies that are discussed above have some common points regarding the financial performance of banks. Most of these studies agree that Islamic banks make more profits, have higher liquidity and lower risk levels by holding higher capital. That is also why Islamic banks survived the last financial crisis of 2008 with fewer injuries compared to conventional banks. Accordingly, the next chapter will present some interesting studies that focus on how Islamic and conventional banks got affected by the financial crisis of 2008 and whether Islamic banks were more financially sound.

## 3.3 Financial Soundness of Islamic vs. Conventional Banks During the Financial Crisis of 2008

Hasan and Dridi (2010) is the first study looking at the effects of the last financial crisis on Islamic and conventional banks. It examined the profitability levels, credit and asset growths of one hundred twenty Islamic and conventional banks from eight countries. The authors indicated that the business model of Islamic banking limited the loss potential on profitability in 2008. This is due to the fact that Islamic banks are only allowed to invest in *Shari'ah*-compliant financial assets and stayed away from instruments that negatively impacted their conventional peers. However, in the following year, Islamic banks faced a larger decline in their profitability compared to conventional banks due to unsuccessful risk management. Despite this, Islamic banks had a higher rate (almost two times more compared to conventional banks) in their asset and credit growth and are evaluated positively by external credit rating agencies as opposed to conventional banks. Next study following the previous one on this topic is Bourkhis and Nabi (2013). Their paper covers a longer time period from 1998 to 2009 that also includes the crisis period. The authors create a matched sample of 34 Islamic and 34 conventional banks from 16 countries to assess the effects of the crisis on Islamic and conventional banks. The financial soundness indicators of these 64 banks, that are matched in pairs as Islamic versus conventional, are calculated and compared. The results point out that there is no significant difference between the two types of banks regarding financial soundness, liquidity, level of non-performing loans and asset quality during this period. However, it is an undeniable fact that Islamic banks had a significantly higher return on asset ratios during and after the financial crisis and this was mainly thanks to the cost-effective strategies of Islamic banks in 2009.

Besides these mentioned papers, there exist also single-country or single region studies to understand how the financial performance of Islamic and conventional banks changed during the financial crisis of 2007/2008. Kassim and Abdulle (2012) research the answer to this question by studying six Islamic and nine conventional banks from Malaysia for a five-year period from 2006 to 2010. The authors' document two important results: Profitability and credit risk levels of both types of banks were almost identical for the covered time period. However, it is clear that Islamic banks did keep more liquid assets leading to higher liquidity ratios compared to their conventional competitors. Another interesting single country study is performed by Miniaoui and Gohou (2013) for UAE banks for the time period of 1995-2010 covering the financial crisis. They found very interesting results because conventional banks were found to be performing much better compared to Islamic banks based on six different profitability indicators. Islamic banks were found also to have a higher cost to income ratio, but they enjoyed higher asset growth in the study period. A follow-up study by Olson and Zoubi (2016) examined whether the financial crisis of 2008 has led to a convergence in performance of Islamic and commercial banks in the Middle East, Africa, and Southeast Asia (MENASA) region. This study reported that Islamic banks initially performed much better than commercial banks (CBs) in 2007–2008. Then, as the crisis spread to the real economy in 2009, profitability declined substantially for Islamic banks relative to their conventional competitors. A very recent study by Alqahtani, Mayes and Brown (2017) finds that during the crisis, Islamic banks were more cost-efficient in comparison to conventional banks in the GCC region. In addition, Islamic banks approached the profit efficiency level of conventional banks throughout the whole period under investigation.

Finally, IMF analysis from October 2009 reported the resilience of Islamic banks during the inceptive stage of the crisis in 2008. Nonetheless, this positive picture for Islamic banks changed when the financial crisis started to influence the real economy, especially the real estate sector, negatively in 2009. As previous paragraphs discussed, Islamic banks survived the crisis in a better situation because they only invested in *Shari'ah*-compliant financial instruments that are asset-based and are not allowed to invest in financial derivatives that were hit hardest by the crisis. IMF report also highlights that Islamic banks of UAE and Qatar have the highest risk exposure to risky real estate and construction sector within the GCC countries. That is also why the profitability of Islamic banks in the UAE and Qatar decreased more compared to other GCC countries' Islamic banks in 2009. This report also agrees with some other studies mentioned above pointing out that Islamic banks on average hold larger capital and liquidity buffers (except the UAE). Hence, Islamic banks are better positioned in the situation of an adverse market or credit crisis. (Ahmed, 2009)

## 4. THE FUTURE AND CHALLENGES OF ISLAMIC BANKING

The last two decades proved to us that Islamic banking has great potential because the sector witnessed double-digit growth rates that are superior to conventional banks. However, this positive picture started to change with the start of the financial crisis of 2007/2008. Some important deficiencies and problems of the sector came to the surface with the last financial crisis. For instance, Kassim and Abdulle (2012) underline the fact that Islamic banks in Malaysia generally hold excessive amounts of liquid assets which harms the profitability and return levels. Islamic banks need to find more efficient ways to utilize their excess cash in order to sustain their growth and success in the future as well. They should maintain optimal liquidity management in order to create a perfect balance in terms of the liquidity and profitability tradeoff. Hasan and Dridi (2010) assert similar points regarding the deficiencies of Islamic banks by studying international data from 8 different countries. They emphasize that Islamic banks are in a way left with no choice but to hold excessively liquid balance sheet because there is a shallow *Shari'ah*-compliant money market and not enough instruments that could be used as collateral for borrowing in the event of a liquidity shock. Policymakers of GCC and other countries; where Islamic banking sector especially has a big share; are advised to develop *Shari'ah*-compliant money markets and the *Sukuk* market- especially sovereign- in the next years. Another very important point for the policymakers is to ensure having harmonized accounting and regulatory standards within the sector across all the countries. Despite the efforts from Accounting and Auditing Organization of Islamic Financial Institutions (AAOIFI) and the Islamic Financial Services Board (IFSB) to create industry-wide standards, still today Islamic banks' operations and contracts vary from country to country and across jurisdictions. Accordingly; there is a strong need for an international legal framework and efficient regulatory oversight like the Bank for International Settlements working for conventional banks, which will improve the compliance rates and the confidence in the Islamic banking sector. However, achieving this standardization and international regulation for Islamic banks is very difficult because *Shari'ah* scholars from different countries are likely to have different interpretations regarding the acceptability of the same financial product. For that reason, there have been always differences in the availability of some Islamic financial products in Southeast Asia and GCC countries because one *Shari'ah*-compliant product might be unacceptable in the other region.

Another issue that needs to be addressed and developed is limited expertise in the field of Islamic finance. As the Islamic financial products and contracts are becoming more sophisticated every day, there is a strong demand for professionals with dual qualifications both in the field of conventional finance and *Shari'ah*-compliant financial products. The shortage of such specialists damages the potential for product innovation and the effective management of the sector. Thus, there should be more education and graduate programs to up skill the young business professionals and governments-especially GCC countries- might consider subsidizing such international and reputable programs to assist the expansion of the Islamic finance sector and their economy in general.

One big challenge for Islamic banks ahead is the increasing competition and smaller size of them compared to their global conventional competitors, i.e. HSBC, Citibank, etc. Thus, competing in this framework will get harder everyday especially when there are continuously new entrants to the market. As an example, new banking licenses are issued only for Islamic banks recently in the UAE. Moreover, conventional banks are also launching Islamic windows for their interested customers. In order to be able to successfully compete in this framework, Islamic banks need to find ways to attract customers who are indifferent towards *Shari'ah*-compliant or non-compliant products but put weight on the competitiveness of the products and efficiency of the services. In this way, they would be able to allure customers from conventional banks. As mentioned above, product innovation is the key here: Islamic banks could focus more on small and medium-sized enterprises by offering them targeted services and products. Another innovation might be offering ethical banking products such as establishing investment funds that will support sustainable energy projects and green investment. These kinds of green projects and financing will attract non-Muslim customers who are indeed environmentally conscious. Islamic banks should also consider recognizing the hedging needs of their corporate clients and introduce Islamic financial derivatives. The adoption of Islamic financial derivatives is a highly disputed topic because *Shari'ah* scholars argue that derivatives are equivalent to debt exchanges without an underlying asset transfer and are prohibited transactions according to Islamic principles. However, Malaysia became an exception and advocated the introduction of Islamic financial derivatives. Accordingly, the Central Bank of Malaysia (Bank Negara Malaysia) initiated the first global Islamic derivative master agreement and started Islamic derivative transactions in 2007. This initiative might open the way for other Muslim countries soon. (Malaysia World's Islamic Finance Marketplace, 2014)

Despite all these challenges, global Islamic finance assets continue to grow in our decade although its growth rate decreased significantly after 2009. By 2023, the total value of global Islamic finance assets is expected to reach 3.8 billion US dollars. The yearly values of global Islamic finance assets and its future projection are presented in Figure 1. The opportunity for growth always exists for Islamic finance because the sector should also try to penetrate the Western world. Starting from the 2000s, successful initiatives have taken place especially in the UK and this could spread to other European countries and to the US. After the UK government's change in legislation to open the door for Islamic banks, there are recently five fully *Shari'ah*-compliant banks and around sixteen conventional banks that offer specific *Shari'ah*-compliant products and services. Like the UK, Luxembourg also focuses on facilitating Islamic finance products and alluring respective investors to their market since the 2010s. For that reason, the Central Bank of Luxembourg became the first European Central Bank that is accepted as an associate member of the Islamic Financial Services Board (IFSB) and Luxembourg also became the first European country to join the International Islamic Liquidity Management (IILM). Luxembourg tries to become a global hub for Islamic finance especially by establishing Islamic investment funds. Luxembourg already has become the largest Islamic investment fund domicile within the non-Muslim countries by managing assets with a net worth of over five billion Euros. This amount is very likely to increase in the coming years as Luxembourg continues to provide solutions especially for *Sukuk* issuers and sign memoranda of understanding (MoU) with the supervisory authorities of several countries that are already main centers of Islamic finance. In relation to this, the last two agreements that Luxembourg's supervisory authority signed was with Qatar Financial Markets Authority and Abu Dhabi Financial Services Authority (AD Global Markets) which is clearly a positive development for the growth of Islamic finance sector in Luxembourg. (Sidlo, 2017; EY, 2017)

*Figure 1. Yearly values of Islamic finance assets (Source: Islamic Finance Development Report 2018)*

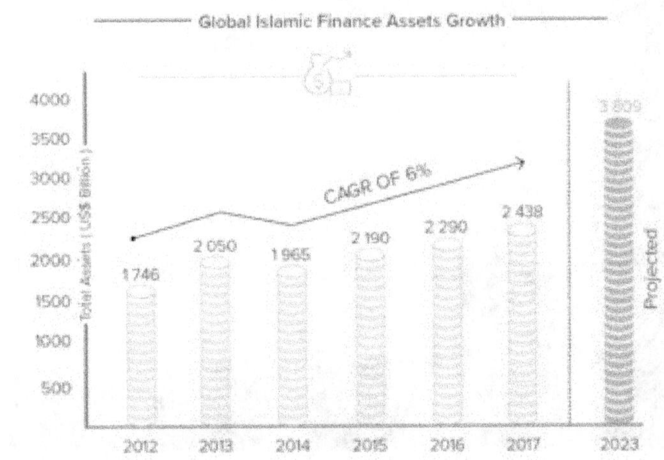

Clearly, the UK and Luxembourg are not the only European countries that have great potential for Islamic finance. Many of the other European and Western countries have large amounts of the Muslim population that would be very interested in Islamic banking and finance products. A few of these countries that would first come to mind and have great potential are Germany and Austria which are home for a significant amount of Turkish people. The first Islamic bank of Germany, KT bank (a subsidiary of Kuwait Turk) got only very recently opened in 2015 despite 4 million Muslims residing in the country. On the other hand, BAWAG, an Austrian bank started to offer very recently an Islamic current account. But there exists still no fully-fledged Islamic bank in Austria. Thus, there is still a lot of potential that waits for exploration by other Islamic banks and finance companies and such new entries will also increase competition in these two countries. Like Germany and Austria, the US is home for over 3 million Muslim people and the Islamic finance industry has not been much explored yet even though there are some existing Islamic financial institutions. The number of existing Islamic banks as of 2016 in different Western countries is provided in Figure 2 for your information.

## 5. CONCLUSION

Islamic banking is the new trend of the finance industry and it has grown so much that even the Western world could not ignore it anymore. It is clear that in the near future Western cities like London, Luxembourg and some others might start competing with the current capitals of the Islamic finance sector such as Dubai, Bahrain, Riyadh, etc. In that respect, those countries with already very developed Islamic finance industries should focus on the development of new products and the adoption of new technologies in order to continue to be the market leaders. As highlighted above, these countries should focus on the endorsement of Islamic financial derivatives and the standardization of Islamic finance products across all the markets. The *Sukuk* market is also open for growth and new investments. Finally, since financial technology has become more important than ever before, the Islamic finance industry also should take the lead in this topic. Related to the development of Islamic financial technology, Dubai International

*Figure 2. Number of Islamic Banks in western countries (Source: UK Embassy Report 2016)*

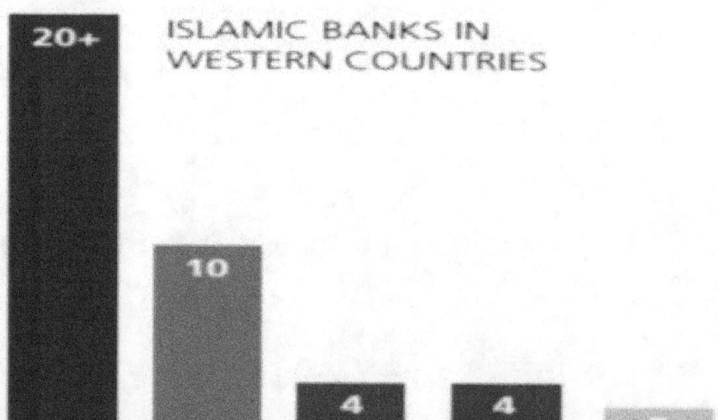

Financial Center is planning to invest $100 million to support Fin-tech startups. In addition, Goodforce Labs that is established in 2018 in Dubai as the first foundry of the MENA region aims to support startups that focus on the Islamic economy. Similarly, Bahrain's Fintech Bay is dedicated to attract and develop Fintech investments and also promote collaboration within the industry. Similar initiatives should also be supported by other countries' governments such as Malaysia, Saudi Arabia, Qatar, and Turkey so that the whole Islamic finance industry shall continue to develop well and compete with its conventional competitors. (DinarStandard, 2018)

## Classifications

JEL Classification: G20, G23, G29
KAUJIE Classification: I2, I3, J33, J41

## REFERENCES

Abdul Alim, E. (2014). *Global leaders in Islamic finance*. Singapore: John Wiley & Sons.

Abedifar, P., Ebrahim, M. S., Molyneux, P., & Tarazi, A. (2015). Islamic banking and finance: Recent empirical literature and directions for future research. *Journal of Economic Surveys*, *29*(4), 637–670. doi:10.1111/joes.12113

Ahmad, W., & Luo, R. H. (2010). Comparison of banking efficiency in Europe: Islamic versus conventional banks. In S. Kim, & M. D. Mckenzie (Eds.), International banking in the new era: Post-crisis challenges and opportunities (International Finance Review, Vol 11) (361-389). Bingley, UK: Emerald Group.

Ahmed, M. (2009, October 14). *Did Islamic banks in the Gulf do better than conventional ones in the crisis*? Retrieved May 23, 2019, from https://blogs.imf.org/2009/10/14/islamic-banking/

Al-Tamimi, H. A. H. (2010). Factors influencing performance of the UAE Islamic and conventional national banks. *Global Journal of Business Research*, *4*(2), 1–11.

Ali, S. S. (2011). *Islamic banking in the MENA region* (The World Bank- Islamic Development Bank Islamic Research and Training Institute Working Paper). Retrieved from http://citeseerx.ist.psu.edu/viewdoc/download?doi=10.1.1.454.2588&rep=rep1&type=pdf

Alkassim, F. A. (2005). *The profitability of Islamic and conventional banking in the GCC countries: A comparative study* (Working Paper). Retrieved from http://upnews.kbu.ac.th/uploads/files/2012/04/04/Profitability_Islamic_B anking.pdf

Alqahtani, F., Mayes, D. G., & Brown, K. (2017). Islamic bank efficiency compared to conventional banks during the global crisis in the GCC region. *Journal of International Financial Markets, Institutions, and Money*, *51*(1), 58–74. doi:10.1016/j.intfin.2017.08.010

Bahrain Economic Development Board. (2017). *Bahrain for Islamic Finance*. Retrieved June 13, 2019, from https://bahrainedb.com/app/uploads/2017/06/IslamicFinance-254x179-Insert-Jun2017.pdf

Bait Al-Mashura Finance Consultations. (2017). *Islamic finance in Qatar (Report 2017)*. Retrieved from http://b-mashura.com/wp-content/uploads/2018/10/Islamic-finance-in-the-State-of-Qatar-Report-2017-1.pdf

Beck, T., Demirguc-Kunt, A., & Merrouche, O. (2013). Islamic versus conventional banking: Business model, efficiency and stability. *Journal of Banking & Finance*, *37*(2), 433–447. doi:10.1016/j.jbankfin.2012.09.016

Bourkhis, K., & Nabi, M. S. (2013). Islamic and conventional banks' soundness during the 2007-2008 financial crisis. *Review of Financial Economics*, *22*(2), 68–77. doi:10.1016/j.rfe.2013.01.001

Chachi, A. (2005). Origin and development of commercial and Islamic banking operations. *Journal of King Abdulaziz University: Islamic Economics*, *18*(2), 3–25.

Chong, B., & Liu, M. (2009). Islamic banking: Interest-free or interest-based? *Pacific-Basin Finance Journal*, *17*(1), 125–144. doi:10.1016/j.pacfin.2007.12.003

DinarStandard. (2018). *Islamic fintech report 2018 current landscape & path forward.* Retrieved May 23, 2019, from https://www.dinarstandard.com/wp-content/uploads/2018/12/Islamic-Fintech-Report-2018.pdf

Ebrahim, M. S., & Joo, T. K. (2001). Islamic banking in Brunei DarusSalam. *International Journal of Social Economics*, *28*(4), 314–337. doi:10.1108/03068290110357708

EY. (2017). *Luxembourg: the gateway for Islamic finance and the Middle East.* Retrieved May 23, 2019 from https://www.ey.com/Publication/vwLUAssets/Luxembourg:_the_ gateway_for_Islamic_finance_and_the_Middle_East__May_2017/$FILE/Islamic%20Finance%20-%20May%202017-LR.pdf

Farooq, M. O. (2009). The *Riba*-interest equation and Islam: Re-examination of the traditional arguments. *Global Journal of Finance and Economics*, *6*(2), 99–11.

Global Banking & Finance Review. (2013). *List of Islamic banks in Kuwait.* Retrieved May 23, 2019 from https://www.globalbankingandfinance.com/list-of-islamic-banks-in-kuwait/

Hasan, M. M., & Dridi, J. (2010). *The effects of the global crisis on Islamic and conventional banks: A comparative study* (IMF Working Paper 10/201). Retrieved from https://www.imf.org/external/pubs/ft/wp/2010/wp10201.pdf

Ismail, F., Majid, M. S. A., & Rahim, R. A. (2013). Efficiency of Islamic and conventional banks in Malaysia. *Journal of Financial Reporting and Accounting*, *11*(1), 92–107. doi:10.1108/JFRA-03-2013-0011

Jaffar, M., & Manarvi, I. (2011). Performance comparison of Islamic and conventional banks in Pakistan. *Global Journal of Management and Business Research*, *11*(1), 1–7.

Johnes, J., Izzeldin, M., & Pappas, V. (2014). A comparison of performance of Islamic and conventional banks 2004-2009. *Journal of Economic Behavior & Organization*, *103*(Supplement), S93–S107. doi:10.1016/j.jebo.2013.07.016

Kassim, S. H., & Abdulle, M. Y. (2012). Impact of global financial crisis on the performance of Islamic and conventional banks: Empirical evidence from Malaysia. *Journal of Islamic Economics. Banking and Finance*, *8*(4), 9–20.

Kearney, A. T. (n.d.). *The future of Islamic banking*. Retrieved May 23, from https://www.atkearney.com/documents/10192/654853/Future+of+Islamic+Banking.pdf/27167edf-a96d-4465-b88a-83beb25ed4bd

Khediri, K. B., Charfeddine, L., & Youssef, S. B. (2015). Islamic versus conventional banks in the GCC countries: A comparative study using classification techniques. *Research in International Business and Finance*, *33*(1), 75–98. doi:10.1016/j.ribaf.2014.07.002

Kouser, R., & Saba, I. (2012). Gauging the financial performance of banking sector using CAMEL model: Comparison of conventional, mixed and pure Islamic banks in Pakistan. *International Research Journal of Finance and Economics*, *82*(1), 67–88.

Malaysia World's Islamic Finance Marketplace. (2014). *Islamic finance ready to finance a greener world*. Retrieved 23 May, 2019 from http://www.mifc.com/index.php?ch=28&pg=72&ac=88&bb=uploadpdf

Meera, A. K. M., & Razak, D. A. (2005). Islamic home financing through *Musharakah Mutanaqisah* and *al-bay' bithaman ajil* contracts: A comparative analysis. *Review of Islamic Economics*, *9*(2), 5–30.

Miniaoui, H., & Gohou, G. (2013). Did Islamic banking perform better during the financial crisis? Evidence from the UAE. *Journal of Islamic Economics. Banking and Finance*, *9*(2), 115–130.

Molyneux, P., & Iqbal, M. (2005). Thirty years of Islamic banking: History, performance and prospect. *Islamic Economics*, *19*(1), 37–39.

MuscatDaily.com. (2018). Oman's Islamic banking assets jump to RO4.1bn. Retrieved May 23, 2019, from https://muscatdaily.com/Archive/Business/Oman-s-Islamic-bankingassets-jump-to-RO4.1bn-5axk

Olson, D., & Zoubi, T. A. (2008). Using accounting ratios to distinguish between Islamic and conventional banks in the GCC region. *The International Journal of Accounting*, *43*(1), 45–65. doi:10.1016/j.intacc.2008.01.003

Olson, D., & Zoubi, T. A. (2016). Convergence in bank performance for commercial and Islamic banks during and after the global financial crisis. *The Quarterly Review of Economics and Finance*, *65*(1), 71–87.

Qaed, I. Q. M. (2014). The concept of *Wadiah* and its application in Islamic banking. *Journal of Research in Humanities and Social Science*, *2*(11), 70–74.

Rafay, A., Sadiq, R., & Ajmal, M. M. (2017). Uniform Framework for Sukuk-Al-Ijara – A proposed model for all *madhahib*. *Journal of Islamic Accounting and Business Research*, *8*(4), 420–454. doi:10.1108/JIABR-09-2015-0042

Samad, A. (2004). Performance of interest-free Islamic banks vis-à-vis interest-based conventional banks of Bahrain. *International Journal of Economics, Management, and Accounting*, *12*(2), 1–15.

Samad, A., & Hassan, M. K. (2006). The performance of Malaysian Islamic bank during 1984-1997: An exploratory study. *International Journal of Islamic Financial Services*, *1*(3), 1–14.

Shaikh, S. A. A. (2011). A critical analysis of *Mudarabah* and a new approach to equity financing in Islamic finance. *Journal of Islamic Banking and Finance*, *28*(3), 1–10.

Sidlo, K. W. (2017). *Islamic finance 2017: State of the art and outlook for the future.* Retrieved from CASE website: http://www.caseresearch.eu/en/islamic-finance-2017-state-of-the-art and-outlook-for-the-future-100498.

Siraj, K. K., & Pillai, P. S. (2012). Comparative study on performance of Islamic banks and conventional banks in GCC region. *Journal of Applied Finance and Banking*, *2*(3), 123–161.

Sophia, M. (2015, March 29). *UAE's Islamic banking assets to reach $263 bn by 2019*. Retrieved June 13, 2019 from https://gulfbusiness.com/uaes-%20islamic-banking-assets-reach- 263bn- 2019/

Stubing, D. (2014, February 22). *Oman: Islamic banking on the rise*. Retrieved May 23, 2019 from https://gulfbusiness.com/oman-islamic-banking-rise/

Vinnicombe, T. (2012). A study of compliance with AAOIFI accounting standards by Islamic banks in Bahrain. *Journal of Islamic Accounting and Business Research*, *3*(2), 78–98. doi:10.1108/17590811211265902

Wilson, R. (1983). *Banking and finance in the Arab Middle East*. Surrey: Palgrave Macmillan UK. doi:10.1007/978-1-349-04817-5

Wilson, R. (2009). *The development of Islamic finance in the GCC* (Working Paper, Kuwait Programme on Development, Governance and Globalization in the Gulf States). Retrieved from http://www.gslb.cima-global.com/Documents/Islamic%20finance/2011/Press%20cuttings/ development-of-IF-in-the-GCC.pdf

World Bank Group. (2018). *Islamic Finance Bulletin*. Retrieved June 13, 2019, from http://www.tkbb.org.tr/Documents/Yonetmelikler/World-Bank- Islamic-Finance-Bulletin-Issue-37-July-2018.pdf

Zeitun, R. (2012). Determinants of Islamic and conventional banks performance in GCC countries using panel data analysis. *Global Economy and Finance Journal*, *5*(1), 53–72.

## ENDNOTE

1 The obligatory contribution of a certain part of one's affluence in support of the poor or needy or for other charitable purposes, considered as one of the duties of Islamic religious practice.

# Chapter 2
# Islamic Banking in Libya: Emergence, Growth, and Prospects

**Mahmoud A. S. Abusloum**
https://orcid.org/0000-0002-4391-2603
*International Islamic University Malaysia, Malaysia & Omar Al-Mukhtar University, Libya*

**Khaliq Ahmad**
*College of Business and Economics, Qassim University, Saudi Arabia*

**Nabil Bello**
*Bayero University Kano, Nigeria*

## ABSTRACT

*This chapter identifies the internal and external challenges for Islamic banking in Libya. It is a conceptual work using secondary data where relevant concepts in terms of challenges of the conversion process in Libya were demonstrated. Conversion process is surrounded and faced by many challenges. Internal challenges are not less significant than external ones. Trained human resource, lack of awareness in Islamic banking, and resistance to change to Islamic banks are considered as internal challenges which represent the stage of readiness to convert the sector. On the other hand, the economic structure, the political situation, and the regulatory framework hinder the process externally. This implies that stake-holders should come up with comprehensive strategies and plans about the conversion process which will improve the readiness level of the banks, raise the awareness and willingness of their employees, and increase the skills of banks' staff.*

## INTRODUCTION

Islamic finance has grown to the extent that it has become a standard norm in the global financial system. At an average growth rate of more than 15% (GIFF, 2016), Islamic financial assets have reached US$ 2.1 trillion as at the end of 2017, even though a bit slower than expected (Damak, 2018). Interestingly, the demand for Islamic financial products is still very high especially with the opening of new markets

DOI: 10.4018/978-1-7998-1611-9.ch002

in unexpected Asian countries such as Japan, South Korea, Hong Kong and China. In Africa, Islamic finance is fast becoming an area of interest in many countries like South Africa, Nigeria, Libya, Senegal, Morocco and many others (MIFC, 2016).

Islamic banking is a significant branch of Islamic finance and therefore the major proportion of the Islamic finance assets operate under the management of full-fledged Islamic banks which was estimated at USD1.286 billion in 2015 (Global Islamic Finance Forum, 2016). In most Muslim countries, the government takes the initiative to introduce and expand Islamic banking (Rafay & Sadiq, 2015). Some Muslim countries like Sudan, Iran, Pakistan and recently Libya imposed Islamic methods of finance to be exclusively the banking system in the country and simultaneously outlawing regular banking practices. To conform with the Islamic principles of banking, the conventional banks were mandated to change their operational system in terms of technology, structure, culture, strategy, processes and infrastructure to operate in accordance to the Shari'ah methods of finance and banking (*mu'amalat*). Even though the adoption of Islamic finance in most of the new markets are restricted to *Sukuk*, there are still moves to convert the whole financial system to Islamic especially in the rich oil countries like Libya.

Libya is a developing Arab country located in North Africa. It has an area of 1.8 million square kilometres and a population of 6,411,776; most of them are Muslims (Libyan General Information Authority, 2013). Libya has an attractive geographical location which is surrounded by African countries such as Egypt from the east and Sudan from the south-east, Chad and Niger from the south and Tunisia and Algieri from the west side. Among these countries, only Egypt, Sudan and recently Tunisia are already practising Islamic methods of finance.

This geographical location makes the country commercially and economically viable given the trade link between these countries. Libya is now seeking to adopt a free market system to encourage investment, especially after the Arab revolution in 2011. This means opening the door for Islamic banks worldwide, especially from neighbouring countries to establish new branches in Libya (Gait, 2009). As a populated Muslim country, Libyan people, in general, expect that the government should adopt the Islamic philosophy of economics which is based upon justice, equity and the prohibition of usurious transactions that involve gambling and excessive speculation (Gath, 2009). This expectation was emphasised by earlier studies that report most Libyans willing to deal with Islamic ways and religion as the significant reason of that (Humaira & Iswusi, 2010; Kumati, 2008).

The Libyan government is indeed one of the few countries that has taken the stance to transform all its bank into Islamic banks following the Libyan law no. 1 of 2013 which postulated that all conventional banks must stop interest-based transactions by the end of 2015. As mentioned, Libya is a 100% Muslim country, which is a factor that significantly proved to facilitate the smooth conversion process to Islamic finance (Gait, 2009). Unfortunately, the process of conversion is deteriorating; in fact, no single bank has yet converted to Islamic banking.

At the beginning of 2015, when Law No. 1/2013 was enforced, the financial system of Libya froze and went into a severe liquidity crisis. Consequently, the government had to extend the enforcement of Law 1/2013 until 2020 by issuing another Law (Law No 7 - 2015, 2015). Of course, there are many challenges at both the bank level and beyond that hinder the successful conversion, which we examine in this chapter. The challenges were classified into internal and external challenges to proffer solutions on the way forward to some of the challenges.

## BACKGROUND

Though the phenomenon of conversion to Islamic finance may take different forms, the main aim of all banks is to meet the needs of customers that choose to take Islamic finance products. Some banks open Islamic windows, subsidiaries or separated branches. The windows and branches are generally categorised as transitional since the parent banks are still interest-based (Yaquby, 2005). In addition, AAOIFI (2015) in its *Shari'ah* standard on conversion to Islamic banking rules that only banks that convert to full-fledged Islamic banks would be considered as Islamic banks. This section contains a description of the phenomenon of the conversion to Islamic banking and the status of the Libyan banking sector.

### The Concept of Conversion to Islamic Banking

Prior literature have used several terms to describe moving from conventional banking to Islamic banking, such as conversion to Islamic banking (Saaid, Shafii, Shahimi, Academic, & Group, 2016), transformation to Islamic banking (Arshad, Yusoff, & Tahir, 2016; El-brassi, Bello, & Alhabshi, 2017), switching to Islamic banking (Abduh, Kassim, & Dahari, 2013), introducing banks to Islamic banking (Sole, 2007), moving banks to Islamic banking (Hallberg & Nettelbladt, 2011), etc. All the terms refer to changing banking practices from the conventional approach to acceptable Islamic approach of banking. The Islamic approach to banking in its basic form takes two features: avoidance of prohibited elements in Islam, such as *Riba* and gharar and replacing them with Islamic acceptable modes of financing that are more into profit and loss sharing, such as *Musharakah* and *Mudarabah*. Thus, from a technical point of view, conversion to Islamic banking means a total change from the present non-*Shari'ah* compliant banking system that is *Riba*-based to an Islamic banking system that complies with its stipulated rules and regulations (Al-Rbaia, 1989).

### Forms of Conversion

Conversion to Islamic banking can take three forms. The first is a complete conversion to full-fledged Islamic banking, which happens instantly and immediately such that all the activities and operations of the bank will fully operate on an Islamic basis. Also, all the interest-based transactions will be disposed of and replaced with *Shari'ah* compliant mode. Secondly, a partial conversion is converting only a section of the bank, such as opening windows, or providing some Islamic banking facilities within the conventional bank. The third is a gradual conversion, where the banks take a long-term strategy of getting rid of non-*Shari'ah* compliant instruments. The bank will not seek for a license to operate as an Islamic bank until the final full conversion of all its assets (Al-Atyat, 2007; Zaki & Hussainey, 2015). However, each of the three forms has advantages and disadvantages. The AAOIFI standard No. 6 on conversion provides the mechanisms and procedures for conversion. While it recognises the first form of conversion, the gradual form of conversion will only be entitled a licence after its fully conversion to Islamic banking operations. Yaquby (2005) further explains that the absence of a *Shari'ah* Supervisory Board to ensure the compliance with the *Shari'ah* is a major component that could not make Islamic windows be considered as Islamic banks.

Several factors are responsible for successful conversion. For example, Saaid and Zurina Shafii (2013) assert that successful conversion will require effective legislation, institutional support and economic stability from a systematic macro level. From the internal external-level Asif, Ahmed, Zahid, & Khan (2017) find that the major factors that motivate banks to convert to Islamic banks in Pakistan are the need to comply with the *Shari'ah*, level of risk and return of Islamic banks and performance of Islamic banks.

## Conversion Phases

Sole (2007) in his study highlighted the necessary prerequisites and phases for conversion to Islamic banking. As a prerequisite, there must be *Shari'ah* compliance by setting a *Shari'ah* board and provision of a legal and regulatory adaptation for Islamic banks by the responsible authorities. Banks will also need to segregate their *Shari'ah*-compliant funds from non-compliant funds. It is also a requirement that they set Islamic standards of accounting and auditing to ensure disclosure, transparency and awareness.

There are three phases of conversion to Islamic banking. In the initial stage, banks commence by offering selected Islamic banking products in preparation for conversion to a full-fledged bank, while the second phase starts by opening windows and subsidiaries to offer products in an Islamic way. In the third phase, the bank will aspire to grow and compete fully with other banks by establishing other branched and introduce a wide range of products and services that will fully meet the requirements of all customers. However, the experiences of countries are different from one country to another. While some countries may take all the three phases, some may be restricted to only two phases. The next section discusses the journey towards Islamic banking in Libya.

## The Status of Islamic Banking in Libya

The first attempt to ban interest from the banking system in Libya was in 1966 during the regime of King Idris who issued a Royal Decree to this effect. The Royal Decree referred to the ban of interest in the National Agriculture Bank, Bank of savings and real estate investment. This came at a time even before the invent of Islamic banking. However, even though the decree was implemented by banning interest, there were no alternative products, and hence, the banks could not survive because no income replaced interest.

The next attempt to consider introducing Islamic banking in Libya was in 1972 at a global Islamic conference was conducted at the Islamic University of Al-Said Mohamed Bin Ali Al-Sanusi in Libya. The conference, attended by eminent *Shari'ah* Scholars in the region, recommended that interest should be banned from the Libyan banking sector. This and other recommendations paved the way to issue of the Libyan Law No 74/1972 that banned interest among individuals and not corporates. Similarly, the law No 86 of 1972 issued in the same year prohibited *gharar* contracts from the Libyan civil code (الجحدة, 1953). However, after 1972, nothing tangible in respect to the introduction of Islamic banking services in the Libyan economy was recorded, not until 2008 where there were few proposals and conferences from the academia and industry that culminated significant initiatives to promote awareness of Islamic banking in Libya (Baej, 2013).

The banking system in Libya is dominated by the Libyan government where it fully or partially owns a significant number of banks (Dempsey, 2013). The banking system is structured based on ownership into three categories.

### State-Owned and Partially State-Owned Banks

This category comprises of the Libyan Foreign Bank and Waha Bank which are fully owned by the Central Bank of Libya (CBL) while state-owned banks with small percentage owned by the private sector comprise: Jumhouria Bank, National Commercial Bank, Wahda Bank, Sahara Bank and North Africa Bank. However, Al-Noran Bank and First Gulf Bank are jointly owned by Libya and Qatar, and UAE respectively. (Research Statistics Department CBL, 2016). The state-owned banks especially Jumhouria Bank, National Commercial Bank are driving the market and owning around 85% of the total Libyan banking assets.

### Private and Partially Private-Owned Banks

These include Al-Ijma Al-Arabi Bank, Assaray Bank, Mutawasit Bank, Arab Trade Bank, Aman Bank, Bank of Commerce and Development, United Bank for Trade and Investment.

### Specialised Banks

Specialised banks are the Agricultural Bank, Development Bank, Saving & Investment Real Estate Bank and Rural bank. These banks are supervised by the government. Figure 1 below shows the classes of banks in Libya based on ownership:

## THE EFFORTS OF CENTRAL BANK OF LIBYA

The Central Bank of Libya (CBL) showed interest in Islamic banking in 2009 where it issued the guideline number A.R.N.M. No. 9 of 2009 which permitted banks to introduce Islamic financial products as an alternative to the conventional products. The Central Bank of Libya also issued guideline number 9/2010 on the rules and regulations to provide alternative banking products compliant with the provisions of *Shari'ah* for the operations of commercial banks in Libya (El-brassi, Bello, & Alhabshi, 2017). The guideline gave the necessary procedures for opening new branches for Islamic window and the requirements for *Shari'ah* supervisory of the respective banks (Khafafa & Shafii, 2013). However, the CBL did not set an implementation plan to be carried out by the commercial banks to introduce Islamic banking even though researchers and bankers asking for such a plan. Humaira & Iswusi, (2010), for instance, found that 73.3% of their sample which was Libyan bankers believed that conversion process requires a comprehensive plan carried out by CBL. Baej (2013) in addition, reported that the absence of a clear and organized plan for implementation of Islamic banking by authorities is one of the main obstacles that hinder the implementation of Islamic banking in the state.

The central bank of libya, on the other hand, mentioned that the task of implementing conversion process is left to banks' management because each bank has its own environment and culture [1]. Besides, the Central Bank of Libya conducted a study to come out with a decision about the best conversion form that banks can follow. The study found that the appropriate form for the Libyan economy is the gradual conversion, where the banks take a long-term strategy of getting rid of non-*Shari'ah* compliant instruments. The bank will hence not seek for a license to operate as an Islamic bank until the final full conversion of all its assets (Central Bank of Libya, 2014b) Instead of CBL, the World Bank Group

*Figure 1. Structure of Libyan banking system*
*Source: Central Bank of Libya (2016) illustrated by the authors*

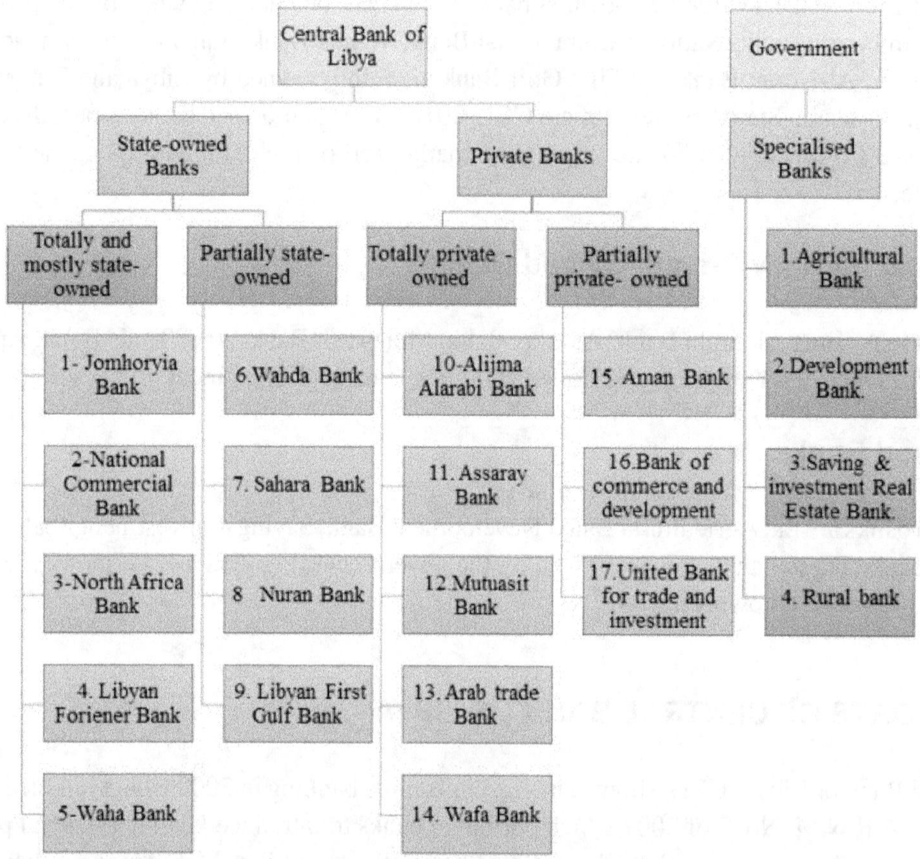


(Finance & Market) suggested a comprehensive plan called Islamic Banking Strategy and Action Plan (IBSAP). The (IBSAP) provides the key elements of developing an Islamic banking system in Libya that is robust, efficient and provides reliable access to *Shari'ah* compliant banking services for a broad spectrum of users, including households, businesses and government (Kipchillis, 2017). It proposed a transition plan for Libyan banking system to move smoothly to Islamic banking in 3 – 5 years. According to the Action plan, the role of CBL is very crucial in ensuring the soundness of the Islamic banking industry in Libya.

According to the CBL, currently, there are only nine banks were given permissions to open Islamic branches and windows to introduce Islamic products. As shown below, Jumhouria bank as the largest share of Islamic banking assets of about 56.78% followed by NCB with 26.46%. Also, there are only two Islamic principles used: *Musharakah* and *Murabahah* with a heavy reliance on *Murabahah*. In fact, only Jumhouria Bank uses *Musharakah*.

*Table 1. Size of Islamic financing in the credit portfolio and market share in Libyan dinar*

| # | Name of Bank | No of Islamic Branches | No of Islamic Windows | Used Islamic Schemes | | Size of Credit Portfolio | Percentage of Islamic Financing vs Credit Portfolio | Market Share |
|---|---|---|---|---|---|---|---|---|
| | | | | *Murabahah* | *Musharakah* | | | |
| 1 | Jumhouria | 15 | 148 | 2,400,432,921.00 | 570,343,784.00 | 8,829,813,052.00 | 33.64% | 56.78% |
| 2 | NCB | 0 | 67 | 1,384,523,818.00 | - | 4,494,726,424.00 | 30.80% | 26.46% |
| 3 | Wahda | 2 | 6 | 551,286,018.00 | - | 2,147,830,693.00 | 25.67% | 10.54% |
| 4 | Sahara | 1 | 6 | 208,981,398.40 | - | 1,847,812,610.00 | 11.31% | 3.99% |
| 5 | NAB | 1 | 48 | 25,610,268.80 | - | 852,953,840.00 | 3.00% | 0.49% |
| 6 | MCIB | 1 | 10 | 80,822,699.00 | - | 119,753,215.00 | 67.49% | 1.54% |
| 7 | Waha | 1 | 0 | 10,447,983.80 | - | 190,674,665.00 | 5.48% | 0.20% |
| 8 | Nuran | 2 | 0 | - | - | – | – | – |
| 9 | Alijma’ | 1 | 0 | - | - | 209,964,954.00 | 0.00% | 0.00% |
| | **Total** | **24** | **285** | **4,662,105,107.00** | **570,343,784.00** | **18,693,529,453.00** | **27.99%** | **100.00%** |

Source: Central Bank of Libya report (30/6/2016)

It should be noted that Jumhouria bank pioneered the introduction of Islamic banking by converting some of its branches to Islamic banking in Libya since 2009 with the intention to convert the whole bank to a full-fledged Islamic bank even before the Law No 1 of 2013.

## THE ROLE OF THE RELEVENT LAWS

The National Transitional Council after the February 2011 revolution amended the Banking Law No 1/2005 to include a chapter with 100 articles to guide the practices of Islamic banking (amendment No 46/2012). To further ensure that interest was stopped, the Libyan government issued law No 1 of 2013 which banned interest totally from the banking sector with effect from 2015. This is considered as the most instrumental law that led to the enforcement of Islamic banking in Libya. However, the implementation of the law was significantly different from one bank to another, as several banks are still yet to respond to the requirements of the law due to several reasons. Saaid (2016) & Abdallah (2016) both investigated some of the reasons why some banks are still yet to implement the law and found several factors responsible for this, such as lack of human resources, inadequate regulations and legislation, lack of *Shari'ah* compliance, resistance to conversion, and lack Islamic banking products and Islamic capital market.

Islamic banking in Libya is still at a very infant stage even with the attempts made by the legislative authority. In fact, in 2015, when the Law No 1 of 2013 was enforced, the financial system in Libya froze, which necessitated the extension of the implementation of the law until 2020. It is still quite unfortunate that until now there are no full-fledged Islamic banks in Libya due to several challenges. These challenges are examined in the next section from both the internal and external levels of the banks.

Before this, there is a need to highlight on the role of Libyan *Shari'ah* scholars with regard to the introduction of Islamic banking. It is worth mentioned that the issuance of Law No 1/2013 was pushed by number of stakeholders, one of them was (*Dar al ifta*) which consists of *Shari'ah* scholars in Libya. In addition, the scholars also had a vital role to clarify and answer some inquiries about the implementation of the conversion process. Furthermore, they participated in the *Shari'ah* committees that established for this purpose.

## CHALLENGES OF CONVERSION PROCESS IN LIBYA

Despite the laws to enforce the transformation to Islamic banking, only two banks out of 17 showed interest in Islamic banking Central Committee for *Shari'ah* advisory (2016). Even the two that showed interest are still yet to finally be celebrated as full-fledged Islamic banks. However, a good number of studies have proven that this lag has been due to several challenges faced by the banks. In this section of the study, these challenges will be studied from the internal and external dimensions of the scenario.

### The Internal-Level Challenges of Conversion

The internal challenges here refer to the obstacles to conversion emanating from individual banks at the firm level. Several factors pose challenges to conversion, which have to do with either organisational barriers or employees' behavioural barriers.

## Organisational Barriers of the Conversion Process

The organisational barriers that affect the conversion process are due to the lack of a clear plan by the banks. The absence of a clear and organised plan by the financial institutions are the main barriers hindering the implementation of the conversion process to Islamic banks in Libya (Baej, 2013). Although the CBL is expected to guide banks with a timeline and phases of conversion to Islamic banking, the individual banks are expected to design a strategic plan for conversion to Islamic banking. The CBL made it mandatory for commercial banks to submit their strategic plan to the CBL before 2015, but no bank submitted its comprehensive transformation plan to the CBL except two banks: Jumhouria and NCB banks.

The denial of banks to develop a strategic plan has been argued that it is due to the inability of banks to convert to full-fledged Islamic banking (CCSA, 2016). On the other hand, Saaid (2016) relates this to the lack of an internal control system, mismanagement and over-employment. Baej (2013) stresses that the staff of the banks lack managerial planning skills for the implementation of Islamic banking.

## Employees' Behavioural Barriers to Conversion Process

Conversion to Islamic banking is a form of the organisational change process (Saaid, 2016), which its success largely depends on the behavioural and human factors (Armenakis, Bernerth, Pitts, & Walker, 2007; Bouckenooghe, Devos, & Broeck, 2009; Holt & Vardaman, 2013). Miller and Peter (2006) confirm that about 70% of organisations failed in implementing organisational change. Studies have demonstrated that this failure is due to employees' resistance to change and lack of employees' readiness for change (Madsen, 2003; Barera, 2008; Cuningham et al., 2002). This, however, illustrates the importance of the human factor in successful change initiatives, which involve various aspects, such as training, awareness and willingness.

1. **Lack of Trained Human Resources:** Literatures have confirmed the importance of human resources in conversion to Islamic banking (Abdalla, 2016; Abdalla, Ridhwan, Johari, & Musbah, 2015; Saaid, 2016; Al-Atyat, 2007; Alani, 2017; Baej, 2013; Gait, 2009; Hasan, 2002; Kumati, 2008; Saaid & Zurina Shafii, 2013). In Libya and Baej (2013) in his study found that there is a lack of skilled human capital, the absence of education and training institutions, the lack of Islamic banking research. Abdalla et al. (2015) went further to address the quality of human resources required to be available for their engagement in Islamic banks. They identified the specifications needed for the staff of Islamic banking and concluded that employees in the Libyan banks are not qualified enough to work in Islamic banks. Using empirical techniques, Abdalla (2016) confirmed that the lack of qualified human resources in Islamic banks scientifically influence the employees' willingness to change to Islamic banks.
2. **Lack of Employees' Awareness in Islamic Banking:** Awareness of Islamic banking is a significant factor in influencing the process of conversion to Islamic banking. Rafay & Sadiq (2015) in a study on far eastern Muslim countries concluded that lack of awareness of Islamic banking is one of the problems that still affects the general acceptability of Islamic banking in several countries. There is a lack of Shari'ah knowledge regarding Islamic finance among the management. Libya is not an exemption to this issue. Awareness of Islamic methods of finance and socioeconomic are key determinants of successful conversion to Islamic banking in Libya (Gait, 2009; Humaira & Iswusi, 2010).

3. **Lack of Willingness to Convert to Islamic Banking:** There is a positive relationship between employees' willingness to change and successful implementation of organisational change (Abdalla & Ridhwan, et al., 2015; Harris & Ogbonna, 1998; Maurer, 1996). Harris & Ogbonna (1998) stresses that willingness to change represents one of the fundamental factors affecting the successful implementation of change in organisations. Abduh & Omarov (2013) and Rammal & Zurbruegg (2007) examine awareness and willingness for Islamic banking products among Kazakhs and Australian Muslims respectively. They found out that about 30% of the Kazakhs respondents and 55.7% of the Australians are not aware of Islamic banking products although their willingness to purchase Islamic products is very high. These results demonstrate that there is no correlation between willingness and awareness. Although Muslims in these countries are unaware and lacking knowledge of Islamic banking products, they are still willing to adopt Islamic banks. Specifically, in the context of Libya and Abdalla (2016) reports that willingness to convert to Islamic banks got only 28% of the effect on the success of the conversion process. In fact, this result indicates that among others, willingness is not a major factor affecting conversion process. This result is inconsistent to some studies which emphasise that willingness to change represent one of the fundamental factors affecting the successful implementation of change in organisations (Harris & Ogbonna, 1998; Maurer, 1996). In contrast, the results of Saaid (2016) reveal that there is no remarkable resistance to the conversion process among bank employees. This means that employees are willing to involve themselves in the conversion process to Islamic banking. These results are consistent with Abo-Homera & Aswaysy (2010) that report that 77% of employees in Jumhouria Bank and Bank of Commerce and Development were willing to convert to Islamic banking. On the other hand, Saaid (2016) confirms that the banks' leaders are playing a negative role and resisting the conversion process. This resistance may be caused through a misunderstanding towards the conversion process among the banks leaders as most study interviewees confirmed. Besides, the study respondents also believed that there are additional reasons for resistance to conversion, such as fear of job loss and loss of some advantages associated with their previous positions (Saaid, 2016). However, resistance to change can be shaped in many ways. In the conversion process to the Islamic banking context, it exists in the negative behaviour that is made by banks leaders which led to delay in the conversion process. Consequently, the free-interest transactions law was postponed from 2015 to 2020.

If transformation is considered as a change process, resistance to change will exist in organisations that undergo radical transformation measures (Abrhiem, 2013). Therefore, lack of careful assessment of an organisation's readiness to change may yield resistance to change (Cunningham et al., 2002). According to Buschmeyer, Schuh, & Wentzel (2016), resistance to change represents one of the critical factors causing the failure of transformational change. This is the result discovered in an empirical study on managing behavioural transformation process. They reported that many transformation managers do not perceive the risk of employee resistance against changes. It should be noted that Libya is a country which has undergone a dictatorial regime since the military coup in 1969 until 2011. In addition, during this period, there was limited religious freedom, violation of human rights and social justice. As a result, the behaviour of citizens has been influenced by this dictatorial form of leadership that does not accommodate flexibility and diversity. Hence, a sudden change in behaviour unfolded in the society. Among these is the inability to accept new ideas, or in other words, the absence of openness for change which yields resistance to change. Similarly, the banking sector was not an exception in this case. Many reasons could be observed merely to show the level of resistance from the banks that underwent radical changes during the conversion process to Islamic banking. According to Saaid et al. (2016), resistance can exist because of the fear of losing jobs and responsibilities if the conversion process succeeds since the employees of banks have several years of working experience in conventional banks and they have a very limited understanding of Islamic banking philosophy. Also, as suggested by Shaikh Nezam Yaquby in an interview conducted by the author confirms that lack of participation among the banking sector is a determinant of resistance. Similarly, Dr Fathi Aqoub [2] also confirmed that in Libya, the imposition of Islamic banking by the legislative authority without banks' consent is another reason for the complication in the conversion process. In addition, lack of proper cooperation and efficient flow of information can cause resistance on one side. Also, communication skills are vital in the change process because the more information passed, the less the expected resistance. Studies have shown that unfamiliarity with details of change can cause resistance to change (Kamarudin, Starr, Abdullah, & Husain, 2014; Simoes & Esposito, 2014).

## The External-Level Challenges of Conversion

External challenges referred to here are those that are beyond the limits and control of the banks and are not related to the behavioural aspect of the phenomenon. These include political instability, insecurity, nature of economic structure, inadequate regulatory and supervisory frameworks, the absence of the vibrant Islamic capital market and so on. As noted by Saaid (2013), these shape the obstacles that face the conversion process.

### Economic Structure

The Libyan economy, like most other Arab countries, is dominated by the oil sector. According to the last annual report of the Central Bank of Libya, the oil industry accounts for more than 60% of the GDP which represents approximately two-thirds of it (Central Bank of Libya, 2014a). Moreover, the oil sector contributes around 96% of government revenue, and hence it covers almost all its trade and foreign exchange earnings. The service sector, however, contributes almost the remaining third of GDP (www.cia.gov).

The contribution of agriculture has remained negligible despite government efforts through its development plans (73-75, 76-80, 81-85, 86-90, 91-95 and 2001-2005) to promote this sector and achieve self-sufficiency in food production. Thus, creating a diversification of income sources and reduction of dependence on the oil industry. However, it could not reach that target. (Central Bank of Libya reports, 1972-2008; (Country Analysis Brief: Libya, EIA, 2015; Muktad, 2011).

Historically, the heavy dependence on the oil industry in addition to socialist policies adversely affected the economy of the country. The policies virtually made all services under state-ownership including banking sector. With this, the central bank exerts full control over the banking sector with an ownership stake in a significant number of the state-owned banks, making up to 85 per cent of Libya's banking assets (Dempsey, 2013). This ownership also created several issues such as independence issues between CBL and banks, introducing low-quality products and services and recently it created a dependency between banks and CBL during the implementation of the conversion process, such that each party is accusing the other of the failure of the conversion process[3].

## Political Challenge

The absence of political stability and security in Libya is the biggest obstacle facing the conventional banks. In his study, Saaid (2016) revealed that banks are not ready to convert to Islamic banking due to the deteriorating political situation in Libya.

Some of the responses of Libyan banks (40%) stressed that unless the government intervenes in implementing Islamic banking, political attitudes that have a clear hand in the development and decision-making in any Libyan banking system will continue to hinder any attempt to introduce Islamic banking services (Kumati, 2008). This Top-down approach of introducing Islamic banking is adopted in several countries such as Malaysia and made very encouraging results. However, in some other countries like UAE and Indonesia for instance, the demand for Islamic banking was taking in a bottom-up approach where people of those communities are pushing their governments in this direction.

## Regulatory Challenge

Referring to 2005, when the General People's Congress (GPC) issued the Law No. 1 of 2005 to reorganise the banking sector Islamic banking was not considered. It was first considered in 2009 where "alternative products" could be introduced such as including Islamic financial products and services. However, the revised Law No. 1 of 2013 was the most significant law that Islamic banking entirely relies on in Libya.

The law was not specific whether banks will have to move to Islamic banking, but practically, the only option they had was to convert to Islamic banking. This kind of ambiguity caused much confusion about the kind of action that the law required the banks to take (Dempsey, 2013). Although the law was generally welcomed by the Libyan people, it was clear that the banks were unable to operate as Islamic financial institutions before the deadline (CCSA, 2016). In fact, there were serious problems when the law was enforced in 2015. This was already predicted by the IMF notes that the action of the government may cause an interruption to the commercial banking sector until a full Islamic finance framework is put in place.

Nevertheless, there was a proposal presented by the CBL of the East of Libya based that proposed the postponement of the enforcement of the law from 2015 to 2020. The legislative authority considered this proposal and approved it in the Law No. 7 of 2015 on the basis that about 70% of the total banking revenues of Libyan public banks come from interest-transactions which were all terminated as a result of the Law 1 of 2013 (Central Bank of Libya, 2014).On the other wing of the CBL in the Western part of Libya, the Law No 1 of 2013 was still the only law that was recognised. However, this itself is another serious drawback because the banks are operating in the entire nation as a single entity and the issue of what law regulates branches in the country will cause confusion.

In this regard, Belal & Hassan (2015) conducted á legal analytical study on the role of regulation to the soundness of Islamic banking in Libya. The study examines four dimensions, namely: regulatory authorities, banking laws, *Shari'ah* governance and dispute resolution. The study notes that there is still no specific and independent law on Islamic finance in Libya as the case for conventional banks which indicates the dire need for a comprehensive regulatory framework for Islamic finance industry. Also, arbitration may be the best method for dispute resolution due to lack of availability of specialised judges.

In another study, Abdalla, Aziz, & Johari (2015) examine the moderating effect of regulation on the relationship between the success of converting conventional banks into Islamic banks in Libya and other factors, which are: relevant experience, willingness to change, Islamic capital market, and qualified human resources. The findings indicate that regulation significantly moderates the effect of the four variables on the success of conversion to Islamic banking. This means that if the regulatory framework is strong enough, the effect of these four variables toward the success of the conversion process will be stronger. From another dimension, the supervisory authorities in the Islamic banking industry face significant regulatory challenges as studied by Rafay and Sadiq (2015). The study reveals that among others, the regulations and legislation have a positive influence on the success of the conversion process.

The previous discussions on the challenges facing the conversion to Islamic banking are studied and confirmed from previous literature. Whether the condition has significantly changed may be interesting for further investigation. However, based on the facts gathered in this study, it will be more beneficial to profound some solutions that may be beneficial to the stakeholders involved in the conversion process, particularly the bank employees and the regulatory authorities as they are the most important agents of this change process.

## ISLAMIC BANKING IN INDONESIA AS A POTENTIAL MODEL FOR LIBYA

Islamic bank in Indonesia was established in 1992 through the establishment of Bank Muamalat Indonesia (BMI) (Sari, Bahari, & Hamat, 2016). In fact, it was considered as a late started of Muslim-majority country like Indonesia. Ariff (1998) stated that delays in the establishment of Islamic banks in Indonesia were due to lack of support from the Muslim community and the government.

According to Sari, Bahari, & Hamat, 2016, phases related to the establishment of Islamic bank in Indonesia can be grouped into three phases. The first phase is the phase of thinking of theoretical phase in the 1930s to 1980, the second phase is the phase of preparation and establishment from 1980 to 1990, and the third phase is the phase after formation (maturation of the concept and setting) 1900 to 2000. They added, the main issues and problems that inhibited the establishment of Indonesian Islamic banks were political issues, lack of government support, legal issues, social problems, economic problems (lack of capital) and the debate among scholars about the legal prohibition of halal-interest conventional banks.

However, the current condition of the Islamic banking in Indonesia still struggling since the official data from 2003 – 2015 revealed that, the assets and shares of Islamic banks in Indonesia was below targets, thus the development of Islamic banks in Indonesia is yet to reach the set targets which is 5% of of the total share of the national bank market (Islamic Banking Statistics 2003-2015, Bank of Indonesia).

At a glance at what has been mentioned in the last sections, the difficulties that faced the Indonesian and Libyan experiences seem to be similar. However, the main obstacle that effected the Indonesian model and made the delay is the fear of Islam term i.e. Islam phobia whether at the level of people or the government due to historical issues regarding this matter. Unlike, Libya is not facing this issue since the government support the conversion process to Islamic banking by issuing the law to prevent interest from the banking system (El-brassi, Bello, & Alhabshi, 2017) but the implementation of this law was delayed due to a mixture of internal and external challenges that demonstrated in this study. In addition, the other difference is that the Indonesian government established new banks to operate without interest as Islamic banks alongside with conventional banks whereas all the Libyan conventional banks were asked to convert to be Islamic by the law. In fact, establishing new banks from scratch is much easier than converting the old ones due to the organizational barriers that discussed earlier. And this what Libyan stakeholders should learn from the Indonesian experience.

## THE WAY FORWARD

The efforts of the Libyan economy towards conversion to a full-fledged Islamic financial system is facing several challenges, both at bank-level and beyond. However, if the right steps are taken, there is much possibility that very soon Islamic finance will see the light of the day. In this section some recommendations are given that will help in the conversion process.

### Recommendations at Bank-Level

#### Human Capacity Development

It is necessary to start by developing the capacity of the employees of Islamic banks before taking the decision to convert to Islamic banking. As a matter of urgency, there is the need to introduce Islamic finance programmes in the Libyan universities, by providing both short courses and full degrees. Short courses on different aspects of Islamic finance, such as banking, capital markets, takaful and wealth management should be introduced. This should be made compulsory to all the employees within a given timeframe. Such courses should have a direct impact on the conversion process by having a direct connection to practical application. This will serve the need for the conversion within the timeframe for conversion.

On the other hand, the full degree programs, starting from undergraduate, should focus on producing students that would be able to work as full Islamic bankers. Students before graduating should be required to undertake industrial training in the banks as a requirement for graduation. At the postgraduate level, the universities may establish institutions to award professional masters programs to train practitioners and students intensively on Islamic finance. With this, the universities can attract scholars from around the world and benefit from their expertise.

#### Job Incentives

The bank managers will need to set a policy to motivate their staff to embrace Islamic finance. Instead of motivating staff only by performance, they can be motivated in terms of their potential in the Islamic finance industry. For example, staff with Islamic finance certification or experience may be given precedence to motivate others.

#### Public Enlightenment

There is the need to raise the awareness of both the public and the bankers. The authorities should take it its responsibility to salvage the economy by optimal utilisation of modern technology: television and radio. Social media is now becoming more common, and this is an excellent platform for increasing awareness among people.

#### Nurturing the Behaviour of Bank Employees

As suggested by studies, the phenomenon of resistance to change is a consonance of willingness to convert to Islamic banking, which mostly happens when there is a failure in the assessment of the organisation's readiness to change. With this, it is highly recommended that there is a need to prepare the employees to accept the conversion process as this will improve their involvement in the process. Many factors that have an impact on making employees ready for change such as context, content, process of change and individual characteristics are important in determining whether there would be resistance or not. Due to the conversion decision imposed in Libya which affected the smooth conversion process, banks should engage their employees at different levels of the conversion process by using participatory management. Another vital component that can enhance the willingness to Islamic banking is adopting communication techniques. Communication must be a strategy existing at two main levels, first between CBL and banks' top management, second; between banks' top management and employees. The communication process should focus on putting the change receivers, i.e. employees and customers in the picture of the conversion process. Without enhancing the readiness level of the banks, the implementation of the Law No 1/2013 may be postponed again.

## Recommendations for the Regulatory Authorities

Regarding the regulatory challenges, few steps can be taken:

### Merging the Monetary Authority is Essential

The central bank of Libya needs to merge its wings in the West of Libya with its wing in the East of Libya to work as a single entity. It will be very difficult or even impossible to introduce Islamic banking in a country with two central bank authorities. Without this step, Islamic banking will suffer, and conversion process cannot be completed.

### Issuing Guidelines

Issuing a separated framework or some set of feasible guidelines that banks must follow to achieve the conversion process. These guidelines should give some requirements that the banks must meet for eligibility. This law should be enforced such that banks that fail to follow the framework will not be considered as Islamic banks. As such, there is a need to embrace a comprehensive plan to implement Islamic banking in the country. Such a plan should not only include issues related to financial issues or the legal framework but should also comprise the institutional aspects to embrace the conversion process.

### Learning From Others' Experiences

There is an important lesson that the Libyan authorities may learn from Malaysia. In 1983, when Malaysia decided to introduce Islamic banking, it started with one bank, Bank Islam and made it a prototype for others to come up. This bank has much support from the authorities, and this was instrumental to its success. Naturally, other banks found Islamic banking interesting, and after ten years other banks started to convert to Islamic banking including some international banks that opened Islamic windows. Libya, however, can take the same step by using one of the banks, such as Jumhouria or NCB and put many efforts into promoting the bank. With time other banks can join.

## The State-Ownership of the Banking System Issue

The Libyan banking system as illustrated before comprises 17 commercial banks. The major state-owned banks in the country which are; Jumhouria, National Commercial Bank, Wahda and Sahara banks are controlled by CBL. The bank has broad control over the banking sector with an ownership stake in a significant number of the state-owned banks, which make up to 85 per cent of Libya's banking assets (Dempsey, 2013). Among the reasons that may hinder the commercial banks from converting is the state-ownership of the major Libyan banks. This ownership creates a dependency between banks and CBL during the implementing of the conversion process, and hence each party accusing the other of the failure of the conversion process. This was hinted by Dr Fathi Aqob in discussion with the authors. To reform this case, Libya needs to engage the private sector as a partner in developing the country (Dempsey, 2013). In his report, Dempsey, (2013) recommended that the Central Bank should see the private sector as a useful source of market information and guidance. Figure 2 below summarises the challenges and recommendations as discussed in this study.

*Figure 2. Summary of challenges and the way forward for conversion to Islamic banking in Libya*

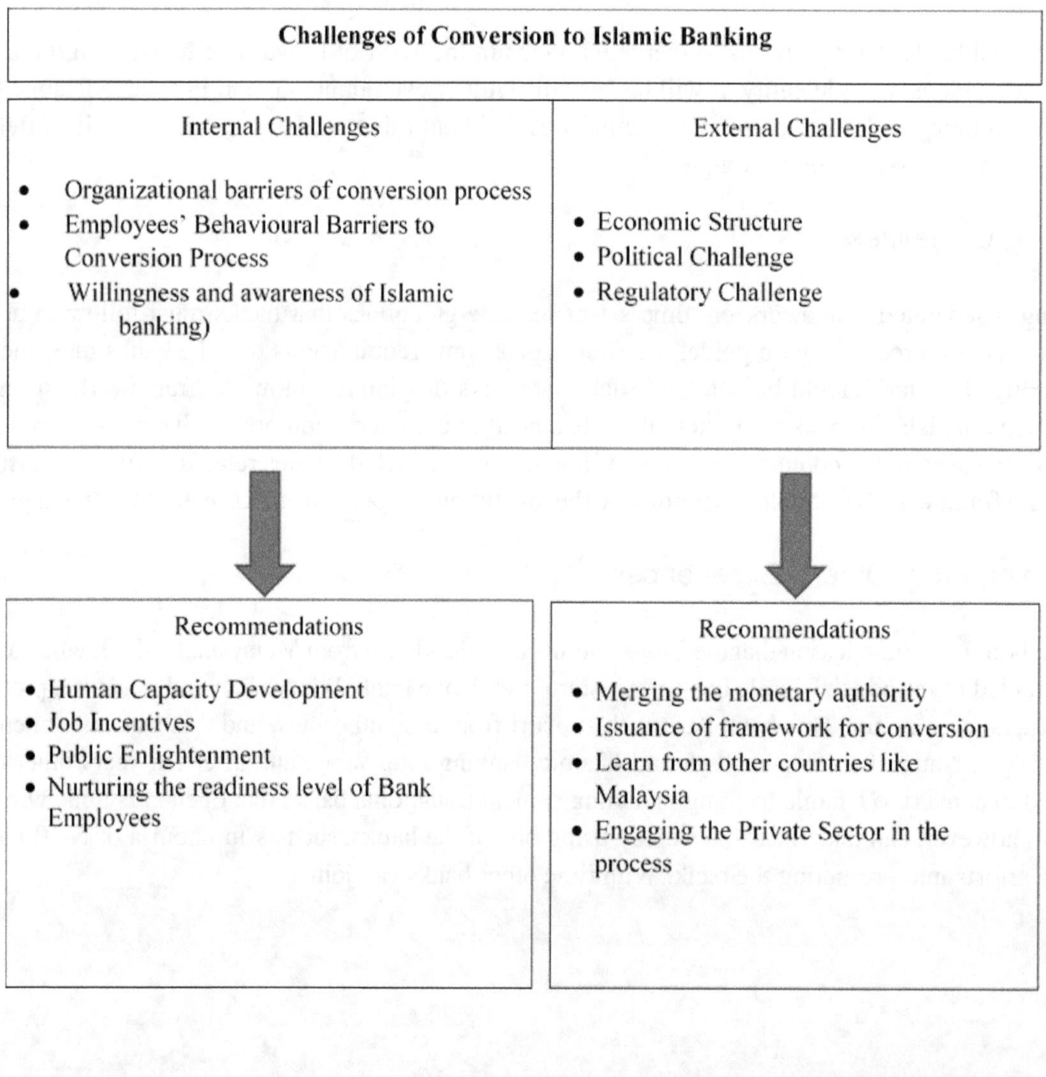

## FUTURE RESEARCH DIRECTIONS

Further studies should proceed by testing the significance of the dimensions discussed in this study using statistical tools. Also, a qualitative study that will explore more issues from the stakeholders involved will give more understanding of the phenomenon. Besides, employees' readiness and resistance to the conversion process in the Libyan context is recommended to explore its determinants since this factor may push or hinder this process.

## CONCLUSION

This study examined the significant internal and external challenges facing the conversion process to Islamic banking in Libya. The major findings of the chapter are that conversion process is surrounded and faced by many challenges. The internal challenges are not less important than the external ones. Trained human resource, lack of awareness in Islamic banking and willingness to convert to Islamic banks are considered as internal challenges which represent the stage of readiness to convert the sector. On the other hand, the economic structure, the political situation and the regulatory framework hinder the process externally. This implies that stakeholders should come up with comprehensive strategies and plans on the conversion process to improve the readiness level of the banks and raise the awareness and willingness of their employees as well as increasing the skills of banks' staff. These are some of the required remedies for the current situation.

In addition, there has also been a new classification of the conversion challenges presented in this chapter which comprises a macro and micro-level point of view. Another issue covered is the significant factors that determine employees' behaviour towards the conversion process to Islamic banking such as awareness and willingness and explaining the link between these factors and organisational behaviour (OB) field in one hand, and conversion process to Islamic banking from the other hand.

### Classifications

JEL Classification: G20, G23, G29
KAUJIE Classification: I2, I3, J33, J41

## REFERENCES

Abdalla, M. A. D. (2016). *Converting Conventional banks to Islamic: A Study on Influencing Factors and the Role of the Central bank, legislation and laws banking in Libya*. (Unpublished doctoral dissertation) Universiti Sains Islam Malaysia.

Abdalla, M. A. D., Aziz, M. R., & Johari, F. (2015). Analyzing the Impact of Banking laws and Legislations on the Converting of Conventional Banks into Islamic in Libya. *International Journal of Management and Applied Research*, *2*(4), 156–171.

Abdalla, M. A. D., & Ridhwan, M. A. Bin, Johari, F. B., & Musbah, A. R. (2015). Human Requirements for the Success of the Islamization of Conventional Banks. *Asian Journal of Management Sciences & Education*, *4*(January), 82–91.

Abduh, M., Kassim, S. H., & Dahari, Z. (2013). Factors Influence Switching Behavior of Islamic Bank Customers in Malaysia. *Journal of Islamic Finance*, *2*(1), 12–19. doi:10.12816/0001113

Abduh, M., & Omarov, D. (2013). Muslim's Awareness and Willingness to Patronize Islamic Banking in Kazakhstan. *Journal of Islamic Banking and Finance, July-Sep*(January 2013), 16–24.

Abrhiem, T. H. (2013). Managing Transformation And Change For The Business Leader. *Business & Management Review*, *3*(2), 14–22.

Adel, A. K. S. (2016). *The Internal Obstacles Facing Conversion Process from Conventional Banks to Islamic Banking: An Empirical Study on Libyan Conventional Banks.* (Unpublished doctoral dissertation) Universiti Sains Islam Malaysia.

Al-Atyat, Y. (2007). *Transforming Conventional Banks to work According to Islamic Shari'a: A Study to show the Viability of Application in Jordan. Aman.* The Arab Academy for Banking and Financial Science.

Al-Rbaia, S. M. (1989). Conversion of Conventional bank to Islamic bank and requirements. *Makkah AL-Mukarramah: Umm AL-Qura.*

Alani, O. (2017). Islamic banking challenges in Libya. *Ijtihad Journal*, *12*, 371–393.

AOIFI. (2015). *Shari'ah Standard.* Manama, Bahrain: AAOIFI.

Armenakis, A. A., Bernerth, J. B., Pitts, J. P., & Walker, H. J. (2007). Organizational Change Recipients ' Beliefs Scale Development of an Assessment Instrument. *The Journal of Applied Behavioral Science*, *43*(4), 481–505. doi:10.1177/0021886307303654

Arshad, M. U., Yusoff, M. E., & Tahir, M. S. (2016). Issues in transformation from conventional banking to Islamic banking. *International Journal of Economics and Financial Issues*, *6*(3), 220–224.

Asif, M., Ahmed, U., Zahid, M., & Khan, A. (2017). Motives Behind the Transfer of a Bank From Conventional Banking to Islamic Banking in Pakistan. *Journal of Business and Tourism*, *3*(2), 225–234.

Baej, Y. M. A. H. (2013). *A Comparison of Key Dimensions in Conventional and Islamic Banking : An International Perspective with Implications for the Bank Transformation Process in Libya.* (Published doctoral dissertation) Griffith University.

Belal, Z., & Hassan, R. (2015). Legal and Regulatory Framework of Islamic Banking in Libya. *Al Mashalih – Journal Of Islamic Law*, 46-58. Retrieved from https://www.researchgate.net/publication/330102366_LEGAL_AND_ REGULATORY_FRAMEWORK_OF_ISLAMIC_BANKING_IN_LIBYA/citation/download

Bouckenooghe, D., Devos, G., & Van Den Broeck, H. (2009). Organizational Change Questionnaire – Climate of Change, Processes, and Readiness: Development of a New Instrument. *The Journal of Psychology*, *143*(6), 559–599. doi:10.1080/00223980903218216 PMID:19957876

Buschmeyer, A., Schuh, G., & Wentzel, D. (2016). Organizational Transformation Towards Product-service Systems – Empirical Evidence in Managing the Behavioral Transformation Process. *Procedia CIRP*, *47*, 264–269. doi:10.1016/j.procir.2016.03.224

Central Bank of Libya. (2014). *Annual-report- Central Bank of Libya 2014*.

Central Bank of Libya. (2014b). *The potential risks of implementing the free - interest law No 1/2013 on the banking sector*. El-Bieda.

Central Committee for *Shari'ah* advisory (Central Bank of Libya). (2016). *Evaluating the conversion process toward islamic banking in the Libyan banking sector. Reality and Prospects*.

Cunningham, C. E., Woodward, C. A., Shannon, H. S., MacIntosh, J., Lendrum, B., Rosenbloom, D., & Brown, J. (2002). Readiness for organizational change: A longitudinal study of workplace, psychological and behavioural correlates. *Journal of Occupational and Organizational Psychology*, *75*(4), 377–392. doi:10.1348/096317902321119637

Damak, M. (2018). Islamic finance 2018: slow growth is the new normal. In *Islamic Finance Outlook (5th Edition)*. S&P Global Ratings.

Dempsey, M. (2013). Libya in Transition: Reforming the financial sector to spur economic growth (Case Study).

El-brassi, M. A. M. A., Bello, N., & Alhabshi, S. M. (2017). Libya's transformation to an Islamic financial ystem: Issues and challenges. *International Review of Management and Business Research*, *6*(3), 976–994.

Gait, A. H. A. (2009). Libyan attitudes towards Islamic methods of finance: An empirical analysis of retail consumers, business firms and banks. (PhD dissertation), Griffith University.

Harris, L. C., & Ogbonna, E. (1998). Employee responses to culture change efforts. *Human Resource Management Journal*, *8*(2), 78–92. doi:10.1111/j.1748-8583.1998.tb00168.x

Holt, D. T., & Vardaman, J. M. (2013). Toward a Comprehensive Understanding of Readiness for Change: The Case for an Expanded Conceptualization. *Journal of Change Management*, *13*(1), 9–18. doi:10.1080/14697017.2013.768426

Humaira, M. A., & Iswusi, N. (2010). Converting conventional banks to Islamic banks: Empirical study on Jomhoryia and Trade & Development banks in Libya. *Islamic finance services conference*.

Information, U. S. E. (2015). *Country Analysis Brief*. Libya.

Kamarudin, M. F., Starr, K., Abdullah, A. N., & Husain, K. (2014). Communicating Change in Organizational Restructuring: A Grounded Theory Case Study. *Procedia: Social and Behavioral Sciences*, *155*(October), 496–501. doi:10.1016/j.sbspro.2014.10.329

Kipchillis, J. K. (2017). *Libya islamic banking strategy and action plan*. Washington, DC: World Bank Group.

Kumati, A. (2008). *Commercial Banking In Libya And The Potential For Islamic Banking*. (Published doctoral dissertation), Durham University.

Law No 7 - 2015. (2015). (قانون 7-2015 المعدل للقانون 1-2013 بشأن منع المعاملات الربوية .

Libyan Civil code (1953).

Maurer, R. (1996). Using resistance to build support for change. *Journal for Quality and Participation, 19*(3), 56.

MIFC. (2016). *Islamic Finance : Development in Non-Traditional Markets*. Kuala Lumpur, Malaysia: Bank Negara Malaysia.

Rafay, A., & Sadiq, R. (2015). Problems and Issues in Transformation From Conventional Banking To Islamic Banking : Literature Review for the Need of a Comprehensive Framework for a Smooth change. *City University Research Journal, 05*(2), 315–326.

Rammal, H. G., & Zurbruegg, R. (2007). Awareness of Islamic banking products among Muslims: The case of Australia. *Journal of Financial Services Marketing, 12*(1), 65–74. doi:10.1057/palgrave.fsm.4760060

Saaid, A., Shafii, Z., Shahimi, S., Academic, I., & Group, P. (2016). The Factors that Influence the Conversion Process from Conventional Banks into Islamic Banking in Libyan Conventional Banks: Proposing Conceptual Framework. *International Journal of Academic Research in Management and Business, 1*(2), 77.

Saaid, A., & Shafii, Z. (2013). The Obstacles Facing Conversion Process From Conventional Banks To Islamic Banking: A Review Of Literature. *The 5th Islamic Economic Conference, Malaysia. 2013. "Sustainable Development Through The Islamic Economics System,"* (September), 4–5.

Sari, M. D., Bahari, Z., & Hamat, Z. (2016). History of Islamic bank in Indonesia: Issues behind its establishment. *International Journal of Finance and Banking Research, 2*(5), 178–184. doi:10.11648/j.ijfbr.20160205.13

Simoes, P. M. M., & Esposito, M. (2014). Improving change management: How communication nature influences resistance to change. *Journal of Management Development, 33*(4), 324–341. doi:10.1108/JMD-05-2012-0058

Sole, J. (2007). Introducing Islamic Banks into Conventional Banking Systems. International Monetary Fund, 1–28.

The world Factbook/Africa/Libya. (2019). Retrieved from https://www.cia.gov/library/publications/resources/the-world-factbook/geos/ly.html

Yaquby, S. N. (2005). *Shari'ah* Requirements for conventional banks. Retrieved from http://www.islamic-banking.com/iarticle_7.aspx

Zaki, F., & Hussainey, K. (2015). Conversion into Islamic banks: Jurisprudence, economic and AAOIFI requirements. *European Journal of Islamic Finance, 3*(June 2016), 1–9.

## KEY TERMS AND DEFINITIONS

**Awareness of Islamic Banking:** It refers to awareness of the general philosophy of Islamic economics and the differences between the Islamic and the conventional banking philosophies.

**Conversion:** A process when a bank transforms its system from conventional to Islamic banking operations.

**Employees' Behavioural Barriers:** It refers to the barriers that relate to human behaviour such as lack of trained human resources, lack of awareness and lack of willingness and so on.

**Organisational Barriers:** It refers to the barriers that relate to the organizational aspects such as structure, strategic plan, internal control system, etc.

**Readiness for Change:** The level of preparedness that an organization or an employee reaches whereby change initiative can be implemented successfully.

**Resistance to Change:** A behaviour taken by employees to reject new changes in their organization.

**Willingness to Convert to Islamic Banking:** This refers to employee' willingness to involve themselves in the conversion process to Islamic banking.

## ENDNOTES

1 Fathi Aqub is the consultant of the CBL's governor for Islamic banking affairs. He explained that in an interview conducted in 2016 with him by the researcher on issues relating to conversion to Islamic banking in Libya.

2 The consultant of the CBL's governor for Islamic banking affairs.

3 Fathi Aqub is the consultant of the CBL's governor for Islamic banking affairs. He explained that in an interview conducted in 2016 with him by the researcher on issues relating to conversion to Islamic banking in Libya.

# Chapter 3
# Islamic Banking in Indonesia: Emergence, Growth, and Prospects

**M. Luthfi Hamidi**
https://orcid.org/0000-0002-1090-923X
*Griffith University, Australia & STEI SEBI, Indonesia*

**Andrew C. Worthington**
https://orcid.org/0000-0003-4113-9036
*Griffith University, Australia*

## ABSTRACT

*The Indonesian banking sector has been stable and generally sound over the past decade, partly through efforts by the Bank of Indonesia as Indonesia's central bank and Otoritas Jasa Keuangan as its financial services regulator. This chapter identifies important issues that remain for both conventional and Islamic banking in Indonesia. Authors suggest the government continue its efforts to reform what remains a geographically concentrated industry, to increase the role of bank credit in the economy, and to widen the provision of banking services through technology. Authors highlight the vulnerability of smaller banks in Indonesia to ongoing competitive market pressures and the necessity of creating larger banks through merger or capital raising and improving credit allocation to small and medium-sized businesses. Islamic banking has an important role to play in these developments, and those relating to Islamic social banking.*

## INTRODUCTION

During the past three decades, Indonesia's banking sector has experienced two major financial crises. In 1997, the Asian financial crisis severely affected the sector and a number of banks collapsed. By early 1999, Bank Indonesia (BI), the Indonesian central bank, had closed 61 banks, and nationalized another 54 (Caprio & Klingebiel, 2002). With a second crisis emanating from the global financial crisis in 2007–08, Indonesian banking was again adversely affected, although not as majorly as countries with more direct links to the US subprime mortgage market. However, among the outcomes, the *Lembaga Penjamin Simpanan* (Deposit Insurance Corporation) bailed out the failed Bank Century, while the Indo-

DOI: 10.4018/978-1-7998-1611-9.ch003

nesian rupiah (IDR) exchange rate weakened to USD/IDR12,650, its lowest level since the 1997/98 crisis (Bank Indonesia, 2009) (as of 11 March 2019 USD/IDR14,298, AUD/IDR10,064 and GBP/IDR18,552).

It was after this second crisis that BI intensified its efforts at transforming what had hitherto been a very risky banking system, including its Islamic banks, into a stronger and more resilient industry able to provide the foundation for sustainable financial development and economic growth. However, these developments are largely unknown outside the country. Accordingly, this chapter has three purposes. First, to review the status of Indonesian banking. Second, to highlight some relevant ongoing challenges to both conventional and Islamic banking in Indonesia. Third, to describe how Islamic banking may be able to address some of the banking challenges present in Indonesia.

The structure of the remainder of the chapter is as follows. The first section examines the profile of the banking sector in Indonesia. The second section discusses its regulation and the third section its supervision. The fourth section considers the performance of the sector and the fifth section entails a critical discussion of current and future challenges and possible remedies. The chapter ends with a brief conclusion in the final section.

## PROFILE AND INDUSTRY STRUCTURE

### Conventional Banks

Banking entities in Indonesia—as per Act No. 10 of 1998 concerning Banking, Chapter III Article 5—are categorised as either commercial or rural banks. Commercial banks are those "…banks that conduct business activities in a conventional manner and/or based on Islamic principles, which within its business activities offer services related to payment flows" (Indonesia Financial Services Authority, 2017, p. 14). In contrast, rural banks provide no payment transaction services. As shown in Table 1, from 2013 to 2018, Indonesia's commercial and rural banks exhibited a significant improvement in almost all growth indicators, except for the number of banks and bank offices.

Since 2013, the total assets of Indonesia's commercial banks have steadily increased from IDR 4,954 to IDR 7,768 trillion, an increase of about 56.8%. Similarly, the total assets of rural banks in the same period increased from IDR 77.4 trillion to IDR 131.5 trillion or by about 67%. The largest bank in

*Table 1. Indonesian banking industry, 2013–18*

| | Indicators | 2013 | 2014 | 2015 | 2016 | 2017 | Sep-2018 |
|---|---|---|---|---|---|---|---|
| Total Assets | Commercial Banks | 4,954,467 | 5,615,150 | 6,095,908 | 6,729,799 | 7,150,388 | 7,768,873 |
| | Rural Banks | 77,376 | 89,878 | 101,713 | 113,501 | 121,583 | 131,508 |
| No. of Banks | Commercial Banks | 120 | 119 | 118 | 116 | 115 | 115 |
| | Rural Banks | 1,635 | 1,643 | 1,636 | 1,633 | 1,622 | 1,598 |
| No. of Offices | Commercial Banks | 31,847 | 32,739 | 32,949 | 32,730 | 32,535 | 31,738 |
| | Rural Banks | 4,678 | 4,895 | 5,982 | 6,075 | 6,157 | 6,242 |

Source: Otoritas Jasa Keuangan (2018a)

Indonesia is Bank Rakyat Indonesia (BRI) with assets of IDR 993 trillion in 2017, and one of the four state-owned banks among the ten-largest banks in Indonesia. The others (asset values in brackets) are Bank Mandiri (IDR 940 trillion), Bank Negara Indonesia (BNI) (IDR 622.9 trillion), and Bank Tabungan Negara (BTN) (IDR 231.9 trillion), together accounting for 38% of the market. Compared with other developing countries, this is a relatively low level of concentration, with the suggestion that Indonesian banking may be less profitable, not as diversified, and less effectively monitored. The remaining top-ten banks are Bank Central Asia (BCA) (IDR 725.5 trillion), Bank CIMB–Niaga (IDR 249.3 trillion), Panin Bank (IDR 156.6 trillion), Maybank (IDR 156.6 trillion), Permata Bank (IDR150.38 trillion), and Danamon Bank (IDR 148.59 trillion).

In addition, since 2013, the number of banks in Indonesia, both commercial and rural, has fallen slightly. In 2013, there were 120 commercial banks, and this fell by 4.16% to 115 banks by September 2018. At the same time, the number of rural banks decreased 2.26% from 1,635 to 1,598. Ultimately, both the BI and *Otoritas Jasa Keuangan* (OJK), the Indonesian financial services authority, forecast that over the next 10–15 years, the number of banks in Indonesia would decline to only 60–70 banks (Ernst & Young, 2015).

In recent years, BI as Indonesia's central bank has paid close attention to creating a robust structure for the banking sector to meet public demand and to support strong and sustainable economic growth. In 2004, BI launched a policy entitled *Arsitektur Perbankan Indonesia* (Indonesian banking architecture), which included several programs and initiatives aimed at enabling the banking sector to run more prudently, soundly, and efficiently (Bank Indonesia, 2004a). Part of this included encouraging banks to significantly increase their capital, either from the injection of new capital from existing shareholders or new investors, merger with other banks, or new share issuance (Bank Indonesia, 2004b). However, this is clearly a challenge, as four of Indonesia's very largest banks remain publicly owned.

## Islamic Banks

In 2002, BI set out a blueprint for Indonesia's Islamic banks to attain a market share of 5% over the next decade (Bank Indonesia, 2002). However, by the end of 2011, the market share of Islamic banking was only 3.2%, suggesting some weakness in the consumer knowledge of Islamic banking services and the low level of commitment of government policy to that objective (Sari, Bahari, & Hamat, 2013). Evidence for the former is ample in that only 8.1% of Indonesians are fully aware of Islamic banking services, compared to 29.5% for conventional banks (OJK, 2017b). Another factor that potentially limits the expansion of Islamic banking generally and in Indonesia is the deficiency in qualified human resources in these banks, and this may serve to discourage both borrowers and depositors (Ismal, 2011). Nonetheless, Indonesia has a massive potential for growth in Islamic banking alongside the halal industry generally, with Indonesia representing about 12.7% of the global Muslim population and around 11% of the global halal industry, particularly foods, fashion, medicaments and cosmetics (Bank Indonesia, 2018).

After remaining at about 4% of market share from 2013 to 2015, Islamic banks finally attained a market share of 6% in September 2018 (Table 2). Under the *Undang-Undang Republik Indonesia Nomor 21 Tahun 2008 tentang Bank Syariah* (Islamic Banking Act), Islamic banks in Indonesia take one of three possible forms: an Islamic commercial bank (ICB) (a fully flagged Islamic bank), an Islamic banking unit (IBU) (where a conventional bank opens an Islamic banking window), and an Islamic rural bank (IRB). The number of Islamic banking entities of all forms has changed slightly over the past five years, with ICBs increasing by two and IRBs by five, but IBUs decreasing by three.

However, one particular factor here is the role of regional development banks (RDB), commercial banks providing financing for regional development. Currently, there are 27 RDBs in Indonesia with total assets of about IDR 618 trillion (8.40% of total commercial bank assets) (Otoritas Jasa Keuangan, 2018b). It was two of these, Bank Aceh and Bank Nusa Tenggara Barat, and their conversion into *Syariah* banks, which accounted for much of the increase in the market share of ICBs during this period.

The conversion of Bank Aceh was enacted by the Aceh provincial government under *Qonun* (local regulation) No. 9 in 2014 leading to the establishment of Bank Aceh Syariah. This marked a new direction in banking policy in Indonesia whereby local government took the lead in encouraging the development of Islamic banking. Other RDBs followed, including Bank NTB (in Nusa Tenggara Barat), Bank Nagari (West Sumatera) and Bank Riau (Riau Kepri) (Kontan, 2017). On 24 September 2018, Bank NTB finally gained approval to operate as Bank NTB Syariah.

Of course, the reasons for the conversion of conventional to Islamic banks differ (Shafii, Shahimi, & Saaid, 2016). However, in the case of Bank Aceh Syariah, *Qonun* No. 5 2016 suggests the primary motivator was religious. This was a similar motivator for Bank NTB Syariah given the majority of its provincial population was Muslim (Rahmatullah, Sudarsono, & Komara, 2018).

The steady expansion of FinTech has also had a major impact on the ways Indonesians bank, with it being largely responsible for decreasing the ICB and IBU branch networks from 2,588 offices in 2013 to 2,202 offices in 2018. In contrast, IRBs increased slightly, from 446 offices in 2015 to 468 offices in 2018, possibly indicating that Islamic bank customers in rural areas of Indonesia have not responded as quickly to technological change as their urban counterparts.

The total assets of ICBs and IBUs increased by 88.5% from IDR 242.3 trillion in 2013 to 456.9 trillion in 2018, while those of IRBs doubled from IDR 5.8 trillion to 11.9 trillion. However, the Islamic banking sector in Indonesia remains highly concentrated, with the five-largest Islamic banks controlling more than 54% of total assets and a corresponding share of the growth in these assets. Three of these are government owned (assets in brackets), being the Bank Syariah Mandiri (IDR 87.94 trillion), Bank Negara Indonesia Syariah (IDR 61.69 trillion), and Bank Rakyat Indonesia Syariah (IDR 31.54 trillion). The remaining largest Islamic banks are Bank Muamalat Indonesia (IDR 61.69 trillion) and BTPN Syariah (IDR 9.15).

*Table 2. Indonesian Islamic banking industry, 2013–18*

| | Indicators | 2013 | 2014 | 2015 | 2016 | 2017 | Sep 2018 |
|---|---|---|---|---|---|---|---|
| Total Assets | ICB+IBU | 242,276 | 273,343 | 292,262 | 356,504 | 401,452 | 456,922 |
| | IRB | 5,833 | 6,573 | 7,739 | 9,157 | 10,840 | 11,894 |
| No. of Banks | ICB | 11 | 12 | 12 | 13 | 13 | 14 |
| | IBU | 23 | 22 | 22 | 21 | 21 | 20 |
| | IRB | 163 | 163 | 163 | 166 | 167 | 168 |
| No. of Offices | ICB+IBU | 2,588 | 2,843 | 2,301 | 2,201 | 2,169 | 2,202 |
| | IRB | 402 | 439 | 446 | 453 | 441 | 468 |
| Islamic banking Market share (%) | | 4.93 | 4.89 | 4.84 | 5.34 | 5.67 | 5.93 |

Source: Otoritas Jasa Keuangan (2018a)

According to the Roadmap of Indonesian Islamic Banking (RISB) 2015–2019, the stated purpose of the Islamic banking sector in Indonesia is to support national economic growth and ensure a sustainable and stable financial system, with sound performance and competitiveness. Seven strategies target these goals. These are: (1) creating synergy between regulators and other stakeholders; (2) improving the capital and scale of banks; (3) enhancing the diversity of funding sources; (4) establishing quality products and services; (5) developing competent human resources and IT infrastructure; (6) developing Islamic literacy and a preference for its services; and (7) harmonising regulations and supervision (Indonesia Financial Services Authority, 2017).

## REGULATION

Banking regulation is an important practical consideration in macro-prudential policy, which along with monetary and fiscal policy establishes the basis for macroeconomic stabilization (Jeanne & Korinek, 2014). Previously, the regulation and supervision of the banking industry in Indonesia was exclusively the domain of BI. However, starting in December 2013, BI progressively transferred the micro-prudential regulation and supervision of banks to OJK, retaining for itself all macro-prudential tasks (Bank Indonesia, 2013a). Consequently, the BI focuses on monetary system, with its main policy objective being the stability of the IDR. For its part, OJK's scope of responsibility includes licensing the establishment of banks and their business activities, providing relevant regulations, conducting bank supervision as well as imposing any sanctions on rule violations (Indonesia Financial Services Authority, 2017). To support these functions, BI and OJK form part of a collaborative platform known as the Joint Decree that covers five aspects of banking regulation. These include: (1) being collaborative in banking regulation, (2) the enhancement of banking efficiency and effectiveness, (3) the avoidance of duplication, (4) complementing regulation of the broader financial sector, and (5) ensuring the smooth implementation of the task of OJK and BI (Indonesia Financial Services Authority, 2017).

For the most part, the banking industry in Indonesia is very highly regulated, with its operations principally governed by *Undang-Undang Nomor 10 Tahun 1998 tentang Perubahan Atas Undang-Undang Nomor 7 Tahun 1992 tentang Perbankan* (Law No. 10 of 1998 on Amendment of Law No. 7 of 1992 on Banking). This firmly states that the Indonesian banking industry is a dual-banking system, comprising both Islamic and conventional banks. In practice, the implementation of banking law is through operational regulation. These regulations are products of the BI and/or OJK. From 2012 to 2017, both BI and OJK stipulated some regulations. In 2012, for instance, BI issued PBI Number 14/18PBI/2012 concerning the capital adequacy requirements for commercial banks stating the minimum capital requirement for commercial banks. This regulation was later renewed by OJK as POJK No. 11/POJK.03/2016. In this, the minimum bank capital is: (a) 8% of risk-weighted assets for a risk profile rating of 1; (b) 9–10% for a risk profile rating of 2; (c) 10–11% for a risk profile rating of 3; and (d) 11–14% for a risk profile rating of 4 or 5. However, this can be set higher where the OJK considers a bank may face a significant shock and potential losses and may then require more capital as a buffer (Otoritas Jasa Keuangan, 2016b).

The minimum bank capital also applies to Islamic banks, with the OJK issuing POJK No. 21/POJK.03/2014 on the capital adequacy requirements for commercial Islamic banking. Both Islamic commercial banks and conventional banks are obliged to provide identical levels of capital as loss buffers. These are (1) a capital conservation buffer amounting to 2.5% of risk-weighted assets; (2) a countercyclical buffer in the range of 0–2.5% of risk-weighted assets; and (3) a capital surcharge particularly for Domestic Systemically Important Bank (D-SIB) in the range of 1 to 2.5% of risk-weighted assets (Indonesia Financial Services Authority, 2017).

In terms of other important components of Indonesian bank regulation, in 2012 BI enacted regulation PBI No. 14/8/PBI/2012 concerning the share ownership of commercial banks, the main purpose being to provide the industry with greater resilience in dealing with the dynamics of regional and global economic development. The BI stated this would be through good corporate governance by limiting shareholdings in Indonesia's banks. The restrictions (maximum shareholding in brackets) are other banks (40%), insurance companies and pension funds (40%), special purpose vehicles, fund management companies, and hedge funds (30%) and (5) individual shareholders (25% for Islamic banks and 20% for conventional banks) (Bank Indonesia, 2012). These are much higher levels of ownership than permitted in many comparable banking systems.

However, under certain conditions, OJK may give banks permission to exceed even their 40% ownership limit. For instance, in 2015, the South Korean Shinhan Bank acquired a 98% share of Bank Metro Express and a 75% share of Bank CNB and subsequently merged these into Shinhan Bank Indonesia. In this case, Shinhan was considered to have a composite risk rating of 1 or 2 and met the capital adequacy ratio as required (Ernst & Young, 2015). Where investors wish to establish a new commercial bank, they have to provide paid-up capital of no less than IDR 3 trillion for a conventional bank and IDR 1 trillion for an Islamic bank. However, only Indonesian citizens and/or legal entities can establish banks either alone or in partnership with foreign individuals and/or legal entities (Indonesia Financial Services Authority, 2017).

Under BI Regulation No. 14/24/PBI/2012, entities can also hold full ownership or be a controlling shareholder in only one commercial bank at a time. Under the legislation, a controlling shareholder owns 25% or more of shares or less than 25% but having effectively direct or indirect control of the bank. There is currently an exemption to this for shareholders controlling two banks where one is a conventional bank and the other is an Islamic or joint venture bank (Bank Indonesia, 2012b). Besides ownership, OJK has issued POJK No. 6/POJK.03/2016 on permitted banking activities and network areas based on core capital. In this, OJK designates the permitted banking activity of banks or BUKU (*Bank Umum berdasarkan Kegiatan Usaha*) according to the level of core capital. These are: (1) BUKU 1 with core capital between IDR 100 billion and IDR 1 trillion; BUKU 2 from IDR 1 trillion to IDR 5 trillion; BUKU 3 from IDR 5 trillion to IDR 30 trillion; and BUKU 4 with core capital exceeding IDR 30 trillion (Otoritas Jasa Keuangan, 2016a). Table 3 details these permitted banking activities for each BUKU, and it is clear that only the very largest banks in Indonesia can engage in the full range of banking activities.

As part of its efforts to strengthen the banking industry, the BI/OJK also actively encourages the banking industry to merge or consolidate according to their BUKU. In particular, banks grouped as BUKU 1 or BUKU 2 are encouraged to either merge or substantially increase their capital. According to OJK Chief Commissioner, Wimboh Santoso, some 62 banks with core capital less than IDR 5 trillion were encouraged to pursue these capital restructurings in light of fierce competition (Yudistira, 2017). In the case of Islamic banks, as of September 2018, none was BUKU 4 and only one BUKU 3. Of the remaining Islamic banks, four were BUKU 1 and eight were BUKU 2 (Otoritas Jasa Keuangan, 2018a). This suggests the significant prospect of consolidation within the Indonesian Islamic banking sector in the near future, particularly as continuing operations as usual may hamper the further expansion of Islamic banking in opening branches, enhancing IT and developing customer services. In this regard, the OJK has consistently encouraged Indonesia's Islamic banks to raise their capital to be at least included in BUKU 2 (Otoritas Jasa Keuangan, 2015).

*Table 3. Permitted banking activities by BUKU*

| Activity Type | Activity | 1 | 2 | 3 | 4 |
|---|---|---|---|---|---|
| Funding | Time deposits, saving accounts, certificate deposits, borrowings and/or debt issuance | Δ | ✓ | ✓ | ✓ |
| | Asset securitization | × | ✓ | ✓ | ✓ |
| Lending | Loans, factoring, purchase of government bonds, placement in NU and/or placement in Other banks | Δ | ✓ | ✓ | ✓ |
| | Purchase of corporate shares and bonds, and acting as lead arranger for syndicate loans | × | ✓ | ✓ | ✓ |
| Trade finance | Domestic letter of credit | Δ | ✓ | ✓ | ✓ |
| | Letter of credit and other trade financing activities | × | ✓ | ✓ | ✓ |
| Treasury activities | Simple and/or complex derivative transactions (i.e. structured products and credit derivatives) | × | ✓ | ✓ | ✓ |
| Foreign currency | Foreign currency dealer | Ö | ✓ | ✓ | ✓ |
| Selling agent and working agreements with other parties | Foreign currency | Δ | ✓ | ✓ | ✓ |
| | Sales agent for mutual funds, government bonds and government Islamic bonds, custodian, trustee, trust and/or banc assurance with distribution business model | × | ✓ | ✓ | ✓ |
| Payment system and electronic banking | Fund transfer, clearing, settlement, ATM, debit card and e-money | Δ | ✓ | ✓ | ✓ |
| | Credit card issuance and internet banking | × | ✓ | ✓ | ✓ |
| Maximum equity participation in financial institutions | As % of core and supplementary capital | – | 15 | 25 | 35 |
| Location for equity participation in financial institutions | Located within Indonesia | ✓ | ✓ | ✓ | ✓ |
| | Located within Asia | × | × | ✓ | ✓ |
| | Located worldwide | × | × | × | ✓ |
| Permitted location for office network expansion | Within Indonesia | ✓ | ✓ | ✓ | ✓ |
| | Within Asia | × | × | ✓ | ✓ |
| | Worldwide | × | × | × | ✓ |
| Minimum loan to productive sector requirement | Minimum loan amount (as % of total loans) | 55 | 60 | 65 | 70 |

Source: Ernst & Young (2017)

In term of networking, OJK stipulates Circular Letter No. 6/SEOJK.03/2015 in relation to OJK Regulation No. 19/POJK.03/2014 on branchless financial services. With this policy, banks may conduct financial transactions without any office branches, but can cooperate with other parties using information technology. In Indonesia, branchless bank products typically include basic saving accounts, microcredit, micro insurance, and other services officially approved by OJK (Ernst & Young, 2015).

The Islamic banking industry in Indonesia has also attracted significant investor interest, both domestic and international. While Bank Muamalat Indonesia, Indonesia's first Islamic bank, began in 1991, it was not until Law No. 21 of 2008 on Islamic Banking that there was specific legislation for these banks. This evidences that Indonesia lags similar developments in neighbouring Malaysia in this respect by about 25 years. In 2016, OJK issued POJK No. 64/POJK.03/2016 concerning the possibility of the change of a conventional bank into an Islamic bank. However, this also stipulated that while a conventional bank in Indonesia could convert into an Islamic bank, it was not possible for an Islamic bank to become a conventional commercial bank (Otoritas Jasa Keuangan, 2016c). This suggests the strict separation of the conventional and Islamic banking systems in Indonesia, and a strong policy intent to expand Islamic banking, possibly at the expense of conventional banking.

Furthermore, the OJK may also assist the merger, consolidation, and acquisition of a conventional and Islamic bank where the resulting entity becomes a fully flagged Islamic bank or a conventional bank with branch offices based on Islamic principles (Indonesia Financial Services Authority, 2018). This policy also applies when conventional rural banks wish to merge with a rural Islamic bank resulting in a new and larger rural Islamic bank. In relation to the accounting standard for Islamic banks, BI issued *Pedoman Akuntansi Perbankan Islamic Indonesia* (PAPSI) 2013 (or Islamic banking accounting guidelines) (Bank Indonesia, 2013b). One of the more important points in PAPSI 2013 is a report on social activities concerning the collection and distribution of *zakat* (alms) and funds for *qard al-hasan* (benevolence loans). This stipulates that *zakat* can be collected either from internal or external sources (including existing bank customers or depositors at their request or non-customers willing to pay zakat via the bank). For their part, the sources of *qard al-hasan* include penalties and non-halal revenue streams.

## SUPERVISION

For a sound and sustainable banking industry, regulations combine with ongoing supervision (Rafay & Gilani, 2016). In terms of supervising banks, OJK has the right to control both on-site and off-site supervision. The first of these relates to the authority of the OJK to conduct both the general and specific examination of banks. The focus of this supervision is to obtain an overall financial picture of the bank and assess the compliance level of the bank pertaining to certain regulations as well as to monitoring the possibility of fraud and other unsound activities that may jeopardise the sustainability of the bank. In contrast, the latter entails supervision based on secondary data such as the reports submitted by the banks (Otoritas Jasa Keuangan, 2017a).

In conducting its supervision of Indonesia's banks, the OJK follows two main approaches. First, it employs compliance-based supervision aimed at compliance with certain regulations. Second, the OJK uses risk-based supervision concerned with identifying early symptoms of banking trouble and actions to tackle and manage any risk. Key risks identified by the OJK include: (1) credit risk; (2) market risk; (3) liquidity risk; (4) operational risk; (5) legal risk; (6) reputational risk; (7) strategic risk; (8) compliance risk; (9) rate of return risk; (10) equity investment risk; and (11) intra-group transaction risk (Indonesia Financial Services Authority, 2017).

In the second quarter of 2017, the OJK conducted general inspection of 1,007 banks (56 commercial banks and 948 rural banks). The OJK also conducted special inspections on specific aspects including paid-up capital, fraud, IT, and corporate governance (Otoritas Jasa Keuangan, 2017a). During the quarter, OJK identified 11 *Penyimpangan Ketentuan Perbankan* or deviations from banking terms, of which it slated three for further investigation.

To manage the soundness of Islamic banks specifically, in 2014, the OJK issued POJK No. 8/POJK.03/2014 Risk-Based Rating for Islamic Commercial Banks and Islamic Business Units. Under this, the ICBs and IBUs are obliged to conduct self-assessment, including that relating to their risk profiles, good corporate governance, earnings, and capital. The OJK also assesses individual half-yearly bank ratings (June and December) based on regular audits, reports submitted by the banks and other relevant information. Where there is a significant difference between each bank's own self-assessment and the OJK's assessment, the OJK will conduct a valuational meeting with the bank.

The OJK also intensively conducts supervision to prevent both conventional and Islamic banks entering and worsening any financial crisis. Based on POJK No. 15/POJK.03/2017 concerning the determination of the status and follow-up of the supervision of a commercial bank, a bank (both conventional and Islamic) will operate under either: (1) normal supervision, (2) intensive supervision, and (3) special supervision. For instance, a bank under intensive as against normal supervision will have a minimum capital adequacy requirement of more or equal to 8%, but a ratio of core (Tier 1) capital less than that proposed by the OJK. If the minimum capital adequacy ratio then also falls below the required level (8%), the OJK would place it under special supervision.

## PERFORMANCE

As shown in Table 4, the total assets of Indonesia's commercial banks grew 8.91% in 2018, slightly slower than the previous year (9.89%). For the most part, this slowing was the result of lower third-party funds (TPF) and capital growth (Otoritas Jasa Keuangan, 2018b). Once again, the results for just a few banks dominate these statistics, with the top-4 banks accounting for 48.47% of assets and the next largest 15 banks only a further 31% of assets. Islamic commercial bank assets also grew, but much more strongly, by 14.54% in 2018, down from 23.5% in 2017.

Total credit in conventional banks gradually expanded by 11.12% from IDR 4,305 trillion in June 2017 to IDR 4,784 trillion in June 2018. In contrast, in Islamic Banks, credit growth increased by 11.20% from IDR 265.3 trillion in 2017 to IDR 341.2 trillion in 2018. Financing by Islamic banks was mostly for consumption (42.34%), followed by working capital (34.60%) and investment (23.06%).

Traditionally, the three largest customers for bank credit in Indonesia are households (23%), wholesale and retail trade (18.82%), and the processing industry (17.47%). However, more recently, the demand for bank credit has been growing strongest in the construction (21.54%), financial (18.10%), and electricity,

*Table 4. Performance of Indonesian commercial banks, 2017–18*

| | Commercial Banks | | | Islamic Banks (ICB+IBU) | | |
|---|---|---|---|---|---|---|
| **Indicators** | **Jun-17** | **Jun-18** | **Δ (%)** | **Jun-17** | **Jun-18** | **Δ (%)** |
| Total assets | 6,754,376 | 7,356,221 | 8.91 | 378,198 | 433,203 | 14.54 |
| Credit | 4,305,803 | 4,784,436 | 11.12 | 265,317 | 295,021 | 11.20 |
| TPF | 4,821,228 | 5,157,744 | 6.98 | 302,013 | 341,216 | 12.98 |
| CAR (%) | 22.74 | 21.91 | –0.83 | 14.72 | 20.59 | 5.87 |
| ROA (%) | 2.47 | 2.55 | 0.08 | 0.73 | 1.37 | 0.64 |
| NIM/NOM (%) | 5.35 | 5.11 | –0.24 | 0.78 | 1.57 | 0.79 |
| BOPO (%) | 79.00 | 79.46 | 0.46 | 95.61 | 88.75 | –6.86 |
| NPL/NPF Gross (%) | 2.90 | 2.63 | –0.27 | 5.68 | 3.83 | –1.85 |
| NPL/NPF NET (%) | 1.35 | 1.19 | –0.16 | 1.61 | 1.43 | –1.85 |
| LDR/LFR (%) | 89 | 93 | 3.45 | 89.32 | 78.68 | –10.64 |

Source: Otoritas Jasa Keuangan (2018a)

gas, and water (14.34%) industries. Part of the explanation for the growth in the construction sector is the Indonesian government directing more than IDR 404 trillion to infrastructure projects in 2018 alone (Jakarta Post, 2018). Of this, small/medium/microenterprises in Indonesia account for about 18.5% of total credit and this exceeds the 15% minimum target stipulated by regulation (No. 14/22/PBI/2012) to be disbursed to small business (Otoritas Jasa Keuangan, 2017a).

*Dana Pihak Ketiga* or third party funds (TPF) also play a significant role in bank financing, with TPF contributing some 87.11% of bank funding (Otoritas Jasa Keuangan, 2018b). Total TPF in conventional banks increased 6.98% from IDR 4,821 trillion in 2017 to IDR 5,157 trillion in 2018, a rate which Islamic banks more than doubled, increasing by 14.54% from IDR 378.19 trillion to IDR 433.2 trillion over the same period. Based on the place of collection, just five provinces account for 77.16% of TPF, being DKI Jakarta (49.54%), East Java (9.65%), West Java (8.47%), central Java (5.22%), and North Sumatera (4.27%).

As shown in Table 4, a sign of improving bank performance in Indonesia is the decline in nonperforming loans/financing (NPL/NPF) in both conventional and Islamic banks. Net NPL/NPF for conventional banks in June 2018 was 1.19%, improving by four basis points from 1.35% in June 2017, while in Islamic banks it was 1.43%, an improvement of 18 basis points from the 1.61% in June 2017, all below the 5% maximum permitted threshold. The profitability of the Indonesian banking industry has also continued to improve according to the return on assets (ROA), which was up by 8 and 27 basis point in June 2018 for conventional and Islamic banks, respectively. In the case of Islamic banks, this significant improvement led to a substantial (40.35%) increase in net income from IDR 2.848 trillion in June 2017 to IDR 3.997 trillion in June 2018, as shown in Figure 1.

*Figure 1. Net income and ROA of Islamic commercial banks, 2017–18*
*Source: Otoritas Jasa Keuangan (2018b)*

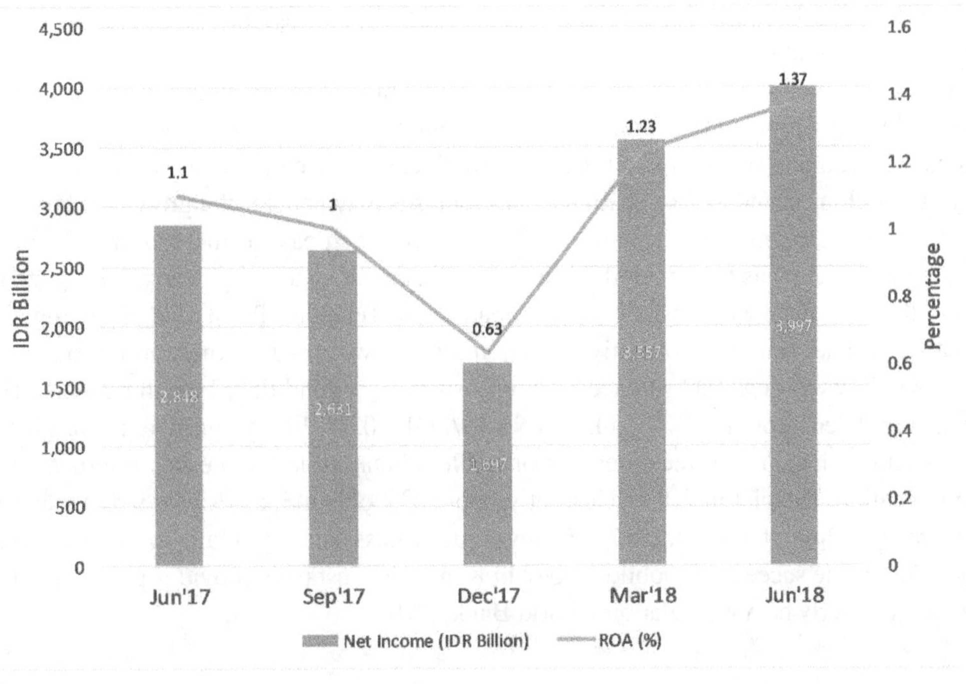

For the most part, Indonesia's Islamic banks have grown faster than its commercial banks in recent years, with assets increasing by 14.54% and TPF by 12.98% in 2018 alone. However, the market share of Islamic banks in Indonesia remains small, being just 5.93% in September 2018. This is a much smaller than in comparable economies like Malaysia. TPF also continues to remain the dominant source of Islamic banking funds, mostly comprising 59.30% *Mudarabah* (partnership) deposits, followed by *Mudarabah* (saving) and *Wadiah* (safekeeping) deposits of 28.79% and 11.91%, respectively. Nevertheless, the profitability of Islamic banks in Indonesia is continuing to increase, sometimes very rapidly. However, Indonesia's Islamic banks continue to lag the commercial banks in ROA (1.37% vs. 2.55%) and net interest/operating margin (NIM/NOM) (1.57% vs. 5.11%). Islamic banks in Indonesia also hold less capital (20.59% vs. 21.91%), and their net NPL/NPF (1.43% vs. 1.19%) is higher. This could be the result, in part, of the smaller scale of Islamic banks and the hesitancy of their shareholders to inject capital. This hints at challenges for Islamic banks in improving their operating efficiency and capital and loan portfolio management.

## DISCUSSION

### On Structure

The core questions for banking structure in Indonesia are whether it sufficiently attracts investment, is under effective supervision, and is sustainable over the longer term. As depicted in Figure 2, Indonesia has a very low level of bank penetration compared with neighbouring countries, some at even lower levels of financial and economic development (PricewaterhouseCoopers, 2017). However, bank margins and profitability remain relatively high. Also according to PricewaterhouseCoopers (2017), 31% of respondents thought Indonesian banking was attractive because of its high profit margin, despite the low level of banking penetration. Accordingly, at a national level, there appears to be considerable scope for future growth in banking.

However, there is also a very low level of concentration in Indonesian banking, and this has particular implications for regulation and sustainability. At present, there are very many small banks, particularly rural banks. The banking sector is also highly geographically concentrated, as shown in Figure 3, albeit on the most populous island of Java, with concern that this may hamper the growth of business growth in other parts of the country, particularly in the less-developed east of the country. Accordingly, the Indonesian government has been undertaking some measures to encourage banks to engage more with business in the regions of Sulawesi, Maluku, Papua, Nusa Tenggara Barat, and Nusa Tenggara Timur in line with a broader economic objective of stimulating new growth in these hitherto less-developed centres. The policy to allow banks to access new customers beyond their branch networks (branchless banking) as stipulated through OJK Regulation No. 19/POJK.03/2014 is a significant policy in this regard.

One particular challenge to the spread of branchless banking is Indonesia's fragmented system of telecommunications (Stapleton, 2013). Currently, about 23% of banking business in Indonesia is through Fintech (PricewaterhouseCoopers, 2017). However, branchless banking entails some risk in this development context, but the success of mobile money in Kenya, for instance, provides good guidelines for its incremental not overly heavy regulation (World Bank, 2010).

*Figure 2. Ratio of bank loans to GDP, Southeast Asia 2016*
*Source: Trading Economics (2017)*

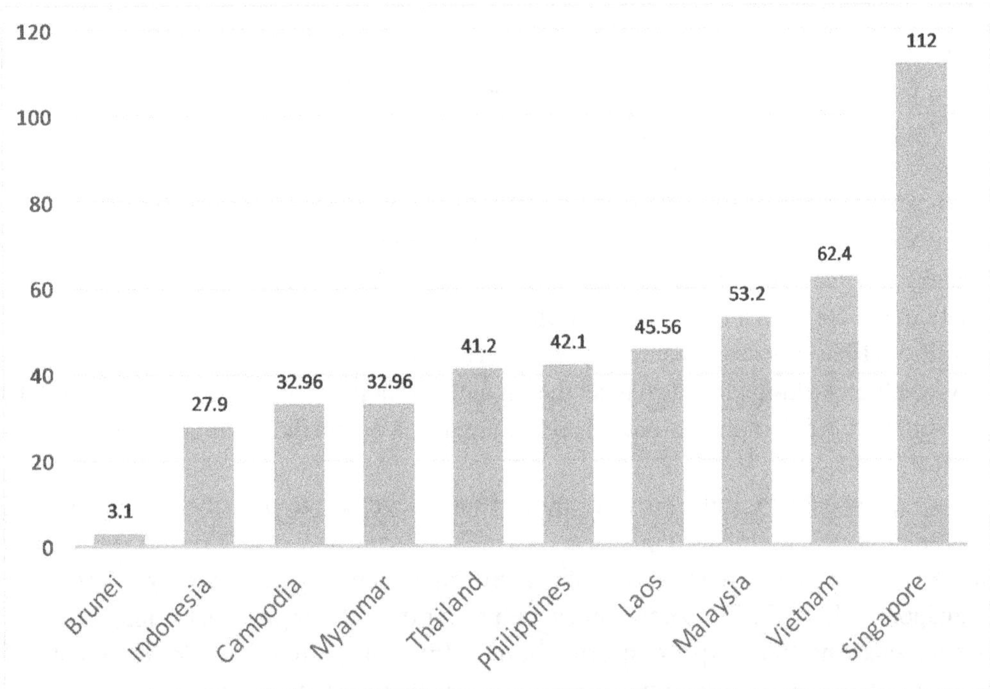


*Figure 3. Regional distribution of Indonesian bank loans, 2016*
*Source: Otoritas Jasa Keuangan (2017b)*

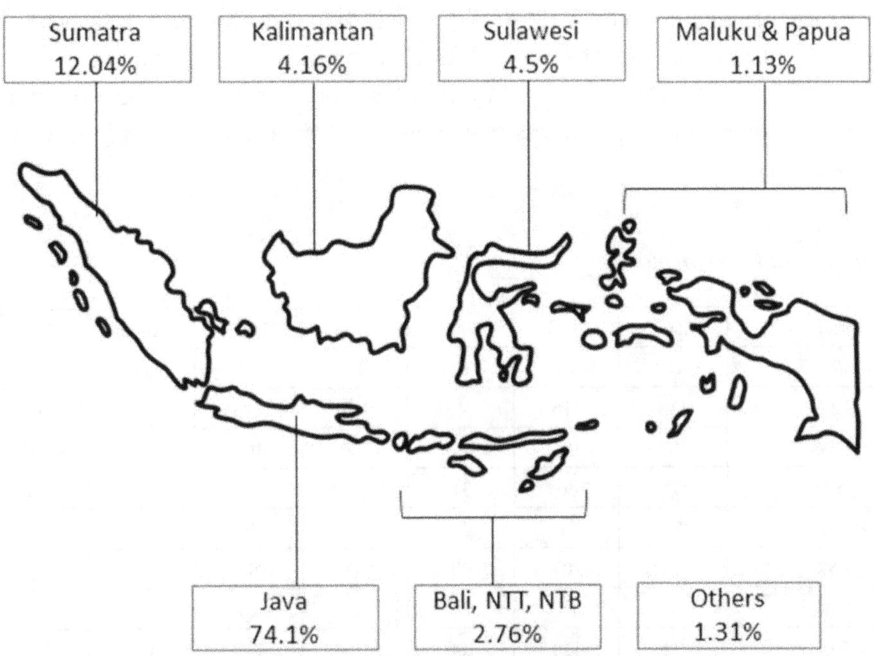

## On Performance

In general, the performance of the banking sector in Indonesia has continued to improve. As shown in Table 5, the ROA on assets in commercial banks has increased, with fewer banks with lower levels of ROA. The number of banks with high levels of NPL has also decreased substantially. The amount of capital held by Indonesia's commercial banks has also increased markedly, suggesting an overall much safer and more stable sector, and one less exposed to severe shocks.

For the most part, Indonesian banks have continued to play an important role in financing small business and now exceed the 15% mandatory allocation for banking credit. While this is nearly double the credit allocation to small business in the nearby Philippines (Asian Development Bank, 2009), whether it is adequate in the context of the some 56 million small business in Indonesia, and their 90% share of business entities (Bhasin & Venkataramany, 2010; Tambunan, 2011) is questionable. It is then worth questioning whether banking alone can meet the financing requirements of Indonesia's huge small business sector without the risk of increased nonperforming loans or whether its mandated level of financing is sufficient.

In terms of a comparison, India provides 40% of total net credit to priority sectors including the financing of small-and-medium-sized business (Asian Development Bank, 2009). As an alternative, the Indonesian government could attempt to replicate Singapore's policy of providing microloans of up to 50,000 Singapore dollars (SGD) to companies with fewer than 10 employees to finance daily business operations and enacting an enterprise investment incentive scheme that provides tax breaks of up to 3 SGD million for those businesses with losses (Asian Development Bank, 2009).

In relation to *akad* (contracts), the most popular product of Indonesian Islamic banking is *Murabahah* (debt-like contracts) rather than *Mudarabah* (partnership contracts) or *Musharakah* (joint ventures). This is important, as the second two contracts are possibly a better representation of a true profit–loss sharing (PLS) contract. In some countries with Islamic banking systems, *Murabahah* financing provides up to 90% of total financing (Vogel 1998; Aggarwal 2000; Ali 2011). In Indonesia, while *Murabahah* contracts account for the largest share (53.23%) it is still much less than elsewhere, followed by *Musharakah* (34.87%) and *Mudarabah* (5.87%). In other words, instead of consumption financing, Islamic banks are increasingly moving towards real economic formation by providing working capital and investment (Figure 4).

*Table 5. Commercial bank performance*

| | Band | 2003 | 2004 | 2005 | 2006 | 2007 | 2008 | 2009 | 2010 |
|---|---|---|---|---|---|---|---|---|---|
| CAR | <12% | 20 | 18 | 12 | 13 | 14 | 11 | 12 | 7 |
| | ≥12% | 118 | 116 | 119 | 117 | 116 | 113 | 109 | 104 |
| NPL | <5% | 101 | 104 | 100 | 100 | 108 | 105 | 107 | 96 |
| | ≥5% | 37 | 30 | 31 | 30 | 22 | 19 | 14 | 15 |
| ROA | <1.5% | 51 | 27 | 41 | 47 | 46 | 41 | 42 | 34 |
| | ≥1.5% | 87 | 107 | 90 | 83 | 84 | 83 | 79 | 77 |
| LDR | <50% | 46 | 24 | 25 | 29 | 20 | 9 | 11 | 5 |
| | ≥50% | 92 | 110 | 106 | 101 | 110 | 115 | 110 | 106 |

Source: Bank Indonesia (2009b, 2010)

*Figure 4. Contracts and distribution of financing of Islamic commercial banks, 2017–18*
*Source: Otoritas Jasa Keuangan (2018d)*

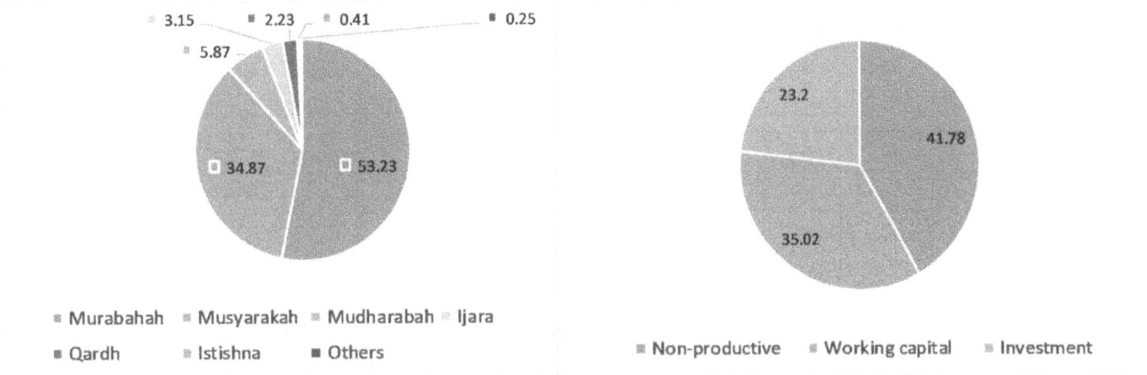


In terms of the performance of Indonesia's Islamic banks, these are much faster growing, but less efficient and profitable than are their conventional counterparts. However, in other respects, including the general types of product, business orientation, and stability, there is almost no difference between them. Elsewhere the evidence suggests that conventional banks are more efficient but less stable (Beck, Demirgüç-Kunt, & Merrouche, 2013) while Islamic banks are better at liquidity management (Ika & Abdullah, 2011) and more readily access equity finance (Siraj & Pillai, 2012).

Although Islamic commercial banks and Islamic banking units in Indonesia are currently less efficient than comparable conventional banks, most of their performance indicators have consistently improved. For example, their CARs increased by 35% from 15.74 in 2014 to 21.25% in 2018; their ROAs increased 244% from 0.41 in 2014 to 1.41% in Sept 2018; and net NPF was 2.35% in 2018, well under the maximum permitted threshold of 5%. Their operating efficiency has also improved, with BOPO (operating expenses to operating revenues) falling from 96.97% in 2014 to 88.08% in 2018. Within Islamic banking, the IRBs outperformed both the ICBs and the IBUs, except in terms of NPL (Table 6).

We more clearly discern the improvement in the financial performance of Islamic banks when we compare very similar banks. For instance, among BUKU 2 banks, there are seven Islamic banks and six conventional banks. Over the period 2015–2018, the CARs for both exceeded the minimum of 8%. However, while the CARs for the conventional banks increased by an average of 11.54%, those for the Islamic banks increased by 54.28% (Table 7). The ROAs of the conventional banks are again better than

*Table 6. Performance of Indonesian Islamic banks, 2017–18*

| Ratio (%) | ICB and IBU | | | | | Islamic Rural Banks | | | | |
|---|---|---|---|---|---|---|---|---|---|---|
| | 2014 | 2015 | 2016 | 2017 | Sep'18 | 2014 | 2015 | 2016 | 2017 | Sep'18 |
| CAR | 15.74 | 15.02 | 16.63 | 17.91 | 21.25 | 22.77 | 21.47 | 21.73 | 20.81 | 19.78 |
| ROA | 0.41 | 0.49 | 0.63 | 0.63 | 1.41 | 2.26 | 2.2 | 2.27 | 2.55 | 2.3 |
| NPF Net | 3.38 | 3.19 | 2.17 | 3.05 | 2.35 | 7.89 | 8.2 | 8.63 | 9.68 | 11.6 |
| FDR | 86.66 | 88.03 | 85.99 | 79.61 | 78.95 | 124.24 | 120.06 | 114.4 | 111.12 | 112.15 |
| BOPO | 96.97 | 97.01 | 96.22 | 94.91 | 88.08 | 87.79 | 88.09 | 87.09 | 85.34 | 86.18 |

Source: Otoritas Jasa Keuangan (2018c)

*Table 7. Comparison of conventional and Islamic bank performance (BUKU 2)*

| Ratio (%) | Commercial Conventional Banks | | | | Δ (%) | Commercial Islamic banks | | | | Δ (%) |
|---|---|---|---|---|---|---|---|---|---|---|
| | 2015 | 2016 | 2017 | 2018 | | 2015 | 2016 | 2017 | 2018 | |
| CAR | 23.05 | 23.72 | 26.47 | 25.71 | 11.54 | 14.96 | 17.78 | 18.68 | 23.08 | 54.28 |
| ROA | 1.62 | 1.66 | 1.57 | 1.55 | –4.32 | 0.48 | 1.08 | 0.94 | 1.62 | 237.50 |
| BOPO | 85.48 | 85.38 | 86.33 | 85.92 | 0.51 | 96.03 | 91.58 | 92.21 | 85.41 | –11.06 |
| LDR | 97.81 | 98.04 | 91.22 | 90.91 | –7.05 | 90.55 | 89.21 | 80.18 | 77.88 | –13.99 |

Source: Otoritas Jasa Keuangan (2018c)

that of the Islamic banks, but these decreased by 4.32% from 2015–2018, while those for the Islamic banks have been steadily improving and more than tripled over the period. As also shown in Table 7, Islamic banks also gradually reduced their costs, cutting their average BOPO from 96% in 2015 to 85.4% in 2018, whereas the average BOPO for the Indonesia's conventional banks remained stable at around 85%.

Clearly, Islamic banking currently accounts for a small share of the Indonesian market. As an infant industry slated for further development by the Indonesian government, there is the possibility of tax incentives to encourage further development. For instance, Malaysia offered an attractive 10-year tax holiday for investors establishing new Islamic banks (Bank Negara Malaysia, 2006; Deloitte, 2016). However, there is also a need to improve their efficiency, especially that relating to scale. Potential options include a program of aggregation aimed at Islamic (and rural) banks and the possible conversion of at least one of the largest state-owned banks into an Islamic bank. In relation to this, the Indonesian government could also pursue a broader program of privatisation aimed at increasing the share of publicly listed banks among Indonesia's largest banks.

## On Regulation and Supervision

Bank regulation and supervision has become a globally important concern, especially in the aftermath of the global financial crisis (Dam, 2009; Lau, 2010; Levine, 2010). Indonesia is not immune to these developments. Following the crisis, both the BI and OJK undertook several improvements through implementing Basel II and III. Since December 2012, Indonesia has fully implemented Basel II through the following three pillars. First, a new minimum capital requirement (PBI No. 10/15/PBI/2008 and PBI No. 15/12/PBI/2013). Second, a refined supervisory review process (PBI No. 14/18/PBI/2012, SE No. 14/37/DPNP, and PBI No. 15/12/PBI/2013). Third, enhanced market discipline (PBI No. 14/14/PBI/2012 and SE No. 14/35/DPNP). Subsequently, Basel III proceeded through three additional new instruments. First, an enhanced capital framework (PBI No. 15/12/PBI/2013), one of the more important points being that banks must have core capital of no less than 6% of risk-weighted asset including main core capital of no less than 4.5%. Second, a more sophisticated liquidity framework (POJK No. 42/POJK.03/2015). Third, a refined leverage framework to cope with excessive leverage (Indonesia Financial Services Authority, 2017).

Figure 5 shows that financial system stability and bank systemic risk in Indonesia have both benefited from these measures. Financial system stability has remained low since the global financial crisis, and is now lower than prior to 2007–08 and continues to trend downwards. Bank systemic stability is also within an acceptable level However, problems remain in Indonesian banking, particularly the limitations

*Figure 5. Indonesian banking (a) financial system stability index (FSSI/ISSK) and (b) banking systemic risk index*
*Source: Bank Indonesia (2017)*

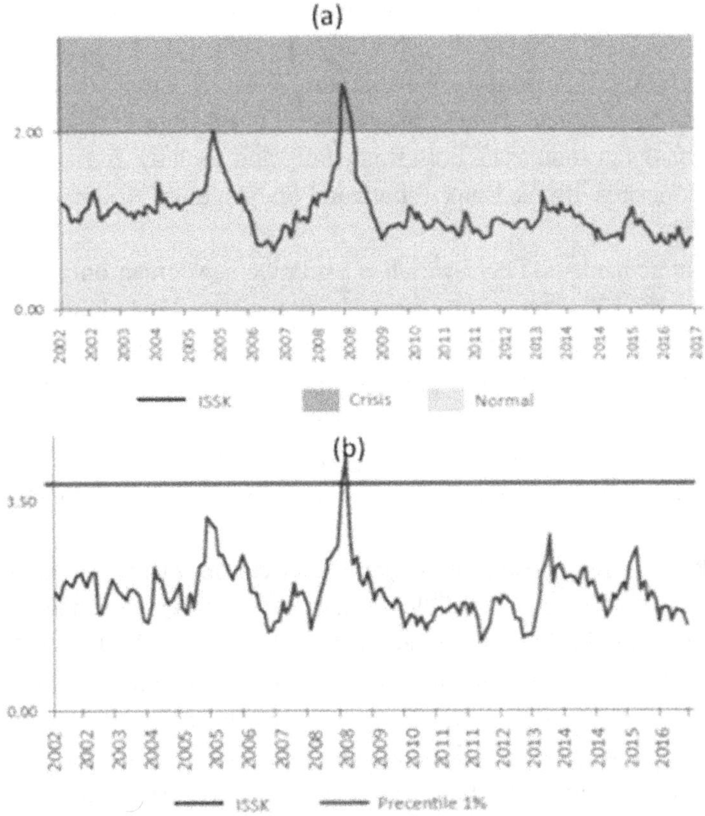


on ownership (PBI Number 14/8/PBI/2012) and sole ownership (PBI bank Number 14/24/PBI/2012). Unlike other developing countries, including China, Indonesia continues to enforce close domestic ownership of its banks and this makes it very difficult for foreign banks to enter the market and for foreign investors to take ownership shares. The dominance of the state-owned banks is also a problem as these are much less efficient than even other domestic commercial banks. Conventionally, reform in this area would follow the line of easing access to the domestic market for foreign banks, which would potentially improve the efficiency and competitiveness of all banks, and entail the privatisation of at least some of the very large state-owned banks (and possible conversion to the fast-growing Islamic banking system).

To date, the existing regulation and supervision seems to be putting Indonesian banking on this track. However, one concern raised is the effectiveness of the monitoring role of the authorities and their close links with the Indonesian government. This suggests reform of the regulation governing these agencies and the possible role of private monitoring and the conduct of supervisory activities, including the supply of comprehensive, accurate, and consolidated documents to obtain certified audits and/or ratings from reputable rating agencies.

## THE NEXT STAGE OF ISLAMIC BANKING

To date, the financial performance of Islamic banks in Indonesia appears less impressive than that of the country's conventional banks. There is also a question about whether the Indonesian Islamic banking industry is meeting its declared social goals, especially in terms of the financially isolated, poor and needy (Asutay & Harningtyas, 2015; Hamidi, Worthington, West, & Ismal, 2018; Mohd Nor, Rahim, & Senik, 2016). This leads to a critical question of whether it is possible for Islamic banks to perform better than conventional banks in Indonesia, both financially and socially. In fact, this kind of Islamic bank already exists in Indonesia, with the Bank Tabungan Pembangunan Nasional (BTPN) Syariah being the best-known example.

Compared to other Islamic banks, BTPN Syariah is a relative newcomer, only commencing in 2010 and thereby becoming only the 12th Islamic commercial bank registered in Indonesia. The most peculiar aspect of this bank is that of its 5 million financing customers, all are women, with a total disbursement fund approaching more than IDR 40.2 trillion. These women contributed 20% of the bank's TPF, with the remainder collected from high-income families. Most of the former are from underprivileged families usually considered 'unbankable', and currently supported by 25 branches, 41 operational offices, and 12,000 staff that actively take part in serving its 3.2 million active member customers (BTPN Syariah, 2018).

Financially, this bank, seemingly despite its strong social commitment, appears to be flourishing. While smaller than most other Islamic banks in Indonesia, its net profit is almost double that of the largest (Table 8). Most of its financial ratios are also remarkable, with its CAR (28.9%), ROA (9%), and ROE (31.7%) also being the highest, even when compared to the three largest conventional banks. Socially, the BTPN Islamic has also succeeded. Among several positive impacts has been a decrease in the percentage of customers' children dropping out of school, down from 17.4% in the first financing cycle (PPI) to 12.5% in the third financing cycle. Elsewhere, and over the same period, customers without proper toilet facilities decreased from 17.4% to 11.1%, while those using firewood for home cooking fell from 10.9% to 6%. This well suggests a suitable model for Islamic social banking, both within Indonesia and elsewhere where there are banking systems including Islamic banks.

In the case of Indonesia's Islamic banking units (*Unit Usaha Syariah*), there is a potential problem regarding their future growth and potential. As a means of accelerating the growth of Islamic banking in Indonesia, the regulator enacted Act No. 21 2008. This includes provisions for the separation of a banking unit once its assets account for 50% of the parent's assets 15 years following the act's ratification (i.e. in 2023). Al Arif (2015) investigated 11 banks (comprising five Islamic banking units, four spin-offs, and two fully flagged Islamic subsidiaries of conventional banks) and found none could possibly exceed this 50% threshold by 2023.

A related concern are the banking units owned by RDBs. Most of these are relatively small, the largest being UUS DKI with just IDR 3.4 trillion in assets and the smallest being UUS BPD Jambi with only IDR 191 billion in assets. In other words, were the act to be strictly applied, many of the Islamic banking units owned by RDBs would fail to meet the asset requirements (Haribowo, 2017). This is problematic in that implementing the 2008 spin-off policy without question could potentially worsen the overall performance of the country's Islamic banking industry.

While facing fierce competition with conventional banks, Indonesia's Islamic banks also face challenges from the growing Fintech industry. The latter offers a new landscape of financial services including cross-border peer-to-peer (P2P) payment, micro-lending, and robo-investment platforms in which the

*Table 8. BTPN Syariah and other Islamic and conventional banks, 2017–18*

| Bank | Asset | TPF | CAR | FDR | ROA | ROE | Net NPL | Net Income |
|---|---|---|---|---|---|---|---|---|
| BSM | 87,940 | 77,903 | 15.89 | 77.66 | 0.59 | 5.72 | 2.71 | 365 |
| BMI | 61,697 | 48,687 | 13.62 | 84.8 | 0.11 | 0.87 | 2.75 | 26 |
| BNIS | 34,822 | 29,379 | 20.14 | 80.21 | 1.31 | 11.42 | 1.50 | 307 |
| BRIS | 31,543 | 26,373 | 20 | 72 | 0.51 | 4.10 | 4.72 | 101 |
| **BTPNS** | **9,156** | **6,545** | **28.9** | **92.5** | **9.00** | **31.70** | **0.10** | **670.18** |
| BCA | 750,320 | 581,115 | 23.1 | 90 | 3.9 | 19.2 | 0.4 | 23,310 |
| BRI | 1,126,248 | 841,656 | 22.96 | 88.13 | 3.69 | 20.03 | 0.88 | 29,044 |
| Bank Mandiri | 1,124,700 | 729,77,529 | 21.64 | 89.25 | 2.72 | 14.53 | 1.06 | 21,443 |

Sources: Annual Reports 2018

majority of processes involve algorithms and less human resource intervention. In this regard, Fintech may advance ahead of both Islamic and conventional banks as they focus on innovation and customer satisfaction, while keeping their overheads at a minimum and cutting the fees currently charged to customers. One way forward would be for Islamic banks to pursue a Fintech-based but *Shari'ah*-compliant strategy, with potentially cheaper and more competitive fees.

## CONCLUSION

Since the 1997 and 2007–08 financial crises, Indonesian banking has gradually improved. Prudential microfinance is now in the control of OJK, while BI focuses on its macro-prudential and monetary tasks. Many reforms have implemented through the Basel II and III accords. However, some challenges remain. First, Indonesia has relatively many banks, particularly rural banks, and many of these are small. Under current Indonesian legislation, most cannot engage in the fullest range of bank activities. This challenges efforts by the regulators to reduce the number of banks through merger and to grow existing banks through capital raisings. Publicly owned banks also dominate Indonesian banking and there are significant restrictions on the ownership and cross-ownership of banks by both foreign and domestic investors. This requires reform.

Second, the performance of Indonesian banking is promising. However, while Indonesia's banks have an important role in national development and growth, including through mandated lending levels to small business, Indonesia has a much lower share of bank credit to GDP than most comparable economies in South-East Asia. Policy needs to encourage the growth of banking, to free up lending to the small business sector, and to encourage banks to expand their markets in Indonesia, at the least through Fintech and possibly regional diversification.

Third, while the market share of Islamic banking in Indonesia remains very small, it is the expectation of the Indonesian government that the sector will continue to grow and compete with conventional banks. However, the performance of Indonesia's Islamic banks generally continues to lag that of its commercial banks, although it is steadily improving. Apart from reforms aimed at Islamic banking, one possibility is the conversion of at least one of the existing (large) publicly owned commercial banks into an Islamic bank, as permitted under current regulations.

Fourth, the banking regulator in the future may consider a model of socially responsible Islamic banking as demonstrated by BTPN Islamic. By achieving both financial and social performance and sustainability, this bank could serve as a model for the future development of Islamic banking, in both Indonesia and elsewhere. Fifth, Indonesia needs to reconsider urgently its spin-off policy relating to Islamic bank units, as almost none of these will meet the required 50% of holding assets by 2023. The rapidly growing Fintech industry is a related challenge, with Islamic banking encouraged to develop a Fintech-based but *Shari'ah*-compliant solution to compete and thrive.

Finally, the Indonesian government needs to review the efficiency of its regulatory and supervisory regime, particularly in light of the quantum of changes made since the global financial crisis and the implementation of Basel II and III, and its capacity to supervise such a large and diverse banking sector, including a significant and growing Islamic banking sector.

## Classifications

JEL Classification: G21, G28
KAUJIE Classification: I33, J32

## REFERENCES

Al Arif, M. N. R. (2015). Impact of spin-off policy on the asset growth on Indonesian Islamic banking industry. *Journal of Islamic Economics, Banking, and Finance*, *113*(3158), 1–12.

Asian Development Bank. (2009). *Key Indicators for Asia and the Pacific 2009: Enterprises in Asia: Fostering Dynamism in SMEs*. Retrieved January 5, 2019, from https://www.adb.org/sites/default/files/publication/27727/special-chapter-06.pdf

Asutay, M., & Harningtyas, A. F. (2015). Developing Maqasid al-Shari'ah index to evaluate social performance of Islamic banks: A conceptual and empirical attempt. *International Journal of Islamic Economics and Finance Studies*, *1*(1), 5–64.

Bank Indonesia. (2002). *Cetak Biru Pengembangan Perbankan Syariah Indonesia*. Retrieved June 6, 2019, from https://www.bi.go.id/id/publikasi/lain/lainnya/pages/blue%20print.aspx

Bank Indonesia. (2004a). *Indonesian Banking Architecture*. Retrieved December 10, 2017, from http://www.bi.go.id/en/perbankan/arsitektur/struktur/Contents/Default.aspx

Bank Indonesia. (2004b). *Structural Reinforcement of the National Banking System Program*. Retrieved December 10, 2017, from http://www.bi.go.id/en/perbankan/arsitektur/struktur/Contents/Default.aspx

Bank Indonesia. (2009). *Peraturan Bank Indonesia Nomor 11/3/PBI/2009*. Retrieved June 6, 2019, from https://www.bi.go.id/id/peraturan/perbankan/Pages/pbi_110309.aspx

Bank Indonesia. (2012). *Peraturan Bank Indonesia Nomor 14/8/PBI/2012 Tentang Kepemilikan Saham Bank Umum.* Retrieved December 13, 2017, from http://www.bi.go.id/id/peraturan/perbankan/Documents/015ad3f77e3846f3a2ea16e18d778ee2pbi_140813.pdf

Bank Indonesia. (2013a). *Bank Indonesia Transferring Regulation and Supervision of Banks to Financial Service Authority.* Retrieved December 13, 2017 http://www.bi.go.id/en/ruang-media/siaran-pers/Pages/SP_155613_DKom.aspx

Bank Indonesia. (2013b). SE/*BI/ No. 15/26/DPbS Perihal Pedoman Akuntansi Perbankan Islamic Indonesia.* Retrieved February, 21 2019, from https://www.ojk.go.id/id/kanal/perbankan/Pages/Pedoman-Akuntansi-Perbankan-Indonesia-(PAPI).aspx

Bank Indonesia. (2017). *Financial Stability Review.* Retrieved January 5, 2019, from http://www.bi.go.id/en/publikasi/perbankan-dan-stabilitas/kajian/Documents/FSR_28_0317.pdf

Bank Indonesia. (2018). *Halal Industry Development To Support National Economic Growth.* Retrieved June 6, 2019, from https://www.bi.go.id/en/ruang-media/info-terbaru/Pages/Pengembangan-Industri-Halal-Dukung-Pertumbuhan-Ekonomi-Nasional.aspx

Bank Negara Malaysia. (2006). *Guidelines on the Establishment of International Islamic Bank.* Kuala Lumpur: Bank Negara Malaysia Retrieved February 7, 2019, from http://www.bnm.gov.my/index.php?ch=57&pg=137&ac=54&bb=file

Beck, T., Demirgüç-Kunt, A., & Merrouche, O. (2013). Islamic vs. conventional banking: Business model, efficiency and stability. *Journal of Banking & Finance*, *37*(2), 433–447. doi:10.1016/j.jbankfin.2012.09.016

Bhasin, B. B., & Venkataramany, S. (2010). Globalization of entrepreneurship: Policy considerations for SME development in Indonesia. *International Business and Economic Research Journal*, *9*(4), 95–103.

Caprio, G., & Klingebiel, D. (2002). Episodes of systemic and borderline banking crises: Managing the real and fiscal effects of banking crises. *World Bank Discussion Paper, 428*, 31-49.

Dam, K. W. (2009). The subprime crisis and financial regulation: International and comparative perspectives. *Chicago Journal of International Law*, *10*(2), 581–638.

Deloitte. (2016). *Taxation and Investment in Malaysia 2016 Reach, Relevance, and Reliability.* Retrieved February 22, 2019, from https://www2.deloitte.com/content/dam/Deloitte/global/Documents/Tax/dttl-tax-malaysiaguide-2016.pdf

Ernst & Young. (2015). *Indonesian Banking Industry: Challenging yet Promising.* Retrieved June 4, 2018, from http://www.ey.com/Publication/vwLUAssets/EY-Indonesian-banking-industry-challenging-yet-promising/%24FILE/EY-indonesian-banking-industry-challenging-yet-promising.pdf

Hamidi, M. L., Worthington, A. C., West, T., & Ismal, R. (2018). *The Prospect of Islamic Social Banking in Indonesia.* Paper presented at the 4th International Monetary Economics and Finance Conference (IIMEFC), Surabaya, Indonesia.

Haribowo, I. (2017). The Indonesian Islamic bank's spin-off: A study in regional development banks. *Al-Iqtishad: Jurnal Ilmu Ekonomi Syariah*, *9*(1), 53–68.

Ika, S. R., & Abdullah, N. (2011). A comparative study of financial performance of Islamic banks and conventional banks in Indonesia. *International Journal of Business and Social Science*, *2*(15), 199–207.

Indonesia Financial Services Authority. (2017). *Indonesia Banking Booklet: Volume 4*. Retrieved June 3, 2018, from http://www.ojk.go.id/en/kanal/perbankan/data-dan-statistik/booklet-perbankan-indonesia/Pages/Indonesia-Banking-Booklet-2017.aspx

Ismal, R. (2011). *Islamic banking in Indonesia: Lessons learned.* Paper presented at Multi-Year Expert Meeting on Services, Development and Trade: The Regulatory and Institutional Dimension, Geneva, Switzerland.

Jakarta Post. (2018, February 21). Government to spend Rp 404t on infrastructure projects in 2018. *Jakarta Post*. Retrieved from https://www.thejakartapost.com

Jeanne, O., & Korinek, A. (2014). Macroprudential policy beyond banking regulation. *Financial Stability Review*, *18*, 163–171.

Kontan. (2017, January 23). Setelah Bank Aceh, 3 BPD minat konversi ke Syariah. *Kontan*. Retrieved from https://keuangan.kontan.co.id

Lau, L. J. (2010*). Financial regulation and supervision post the global financial crisis.* Working Paper No. 2. Institute of Global Economics and Finance, Chinese University of Hong Kong.

Levine, R. (2010). An autopsy of the US financial system: Accident, suicide, or negligent homicide. *Journal of Financial Economic Policy*, *2*(3), 196–213. doi:10.1108/17576381011085421

Mohd Nor, S., Rahim, R. A., & Senik, Z. C. (2016). The potentials of internalising social banking among the Malaysian Islamic banks. *Environment, Development, and Sustainability*, *18*(2), 347–372. doi:10.100710668-015-9651-0

Otoritas Jasa Keuangan. (2015). *Roadmap Perbankan Islamic Indonesia 2015–2019*. Retrieved February 21, 2019, from https://www.ojk.go.id/id/kanal/Islamic/berita-dan-kegiatan/publikasi/Documents/roadmap-pbs_2015-2019.pdf

Otoritas Jasa Keuangan. (2016a). *POJK Nomor 6/POJK.03/2016 tentang Kegiatan Usaha dan Jaringan Kantor Berdasarkan Modal Inti Bank*. Retrieved December 15, 2017, from http://www.ojk.go.id/id/kanal/perbankan/regulasi/peraturan-ojk/Pages/pojk-kegiatan-usaha-dan-jaringan-kantor-berdasarkan-modal-inti-bank.aspx

Otoritas Jasa Keuangan. (2016b). *POJK Nomor 10/POJK.03/2016 tentang Kewajiban Penyediaan Modal Minimum Bank Umum*. Retrieved December, 14, 2017, from http://www.ojk.go.id/id/kanal/perbankan/regulasi/peraturan-ojk/Pages/pojk11-kewajiban-penyediaan-modal-minimum-bank-umum.aspx

Otoritas Jasa Keuangan. (2016c). *POJK Nomor 64/POJK.03/2016 tentang Perubahan Kegiatan Usaha Bank Konvensional Menjadi Bank Islamic*. Retrieved February, 21 2019, from http://www.ojk.go.id/id/kanal/perbankan/regulasi/regulasi-perbankan-Islamic/Pages/POJK-tentang-Perubahan-Kegiatan-Usaha-Bank-Konvensional-Menjadi-Bank-Islamic.aspx

Otoritas Jasa Keuangan. (2017a). *Laporan Profile Industri Perbankan Triwulan II 2017.* Retrieved February, 21 2019, from https://www.ojk.go.id/id/kanal/perbankan/data-dan-statistik/laporan-profil-industri-perbankan/Documents/LPIP%20TW%20II-17%20(Publikasi).pdf

Otoritas Jasa Keuangan. (2017b). *Strategi nasional literasi keuangan Indonesia (Revisit 2017).* Retrieved February 21, 2019, from https://www.ojk.go.id/id/berita-dan-kegiatan/publikasi/Documents/Pages/Strategi-Nasional-Literasi-Keuangan-Indonesia-(Revisit-2017)-/SNLKI%20(Revisit%202017)-new.pdf

Otoritas Jasa Keuangan. (2018a). *Indonesia Banking Statistics*. Jakarta, Indonesia: Otoritas Jasa Keuangan.

Otoritas Jasa Keuangan. (2018b). *Laporan Profil Industri Perbankan Triwulan II 2018.* Retrieved February, 21 2019, from https://www.ojk.go.id/id/kanal/perbankan/data-dan-statistik/laporan-profil-industri-perbankan/Pages/Laporan-Profil-Industri-Perbankan---Triwulan-II-2018.aspx

Otoritas Jasa Keuangan. (2018c). *Sharia Banking Statistics September 2018.* Retrieved March 5, 2019, from https://www.ojk.go.id/en/kanal/perbankan/data-dan-statistik/statistik-perbankan-syariah/Pages/Sharia-Banking-Statistic---September-2018.aspx

Otoritas Jasa Keuangan. (2018d). *Snapshot Perbankan Islamic Indonesia.* Retrieved March 5, 2019, from https://www.ojk.go.id/id/kanal/Islamic/berita-dan-kegiatan/publikasi/Documents/Pages/Snapshot-Perbankan-Islamic-Indonesia-Juni-2018/Snapshot%20Juni%202018%20(final).pdf

PricewaterhouseCoopers. (2017). *Indonesia Banking Survey 2017: Weathering the rise in credit risk. What's next for Banks in Indonesia?* Retrieved February 21, 2019, from https://www.pwc.com/id/en/publications/assets/financialservices/ibs-2017.pdf

Rafay, A., & Gilani, U. J. (2016). Banking Competition and Stability: Evidence from Inter-continental Markets. *DLSU Business and Economics Review*, *25*(2), 24–40.

Rahmatullah, H., Sudarsono, R., & Komara, R. (2018). Business analysis in conversion of regional development bank into Sharia banking: Case study in NTB province, Indonesia. *International Journal of Economics, Commerce, and Management*, *6*(2), 232–339.

Sari, M. D., Bahari, Z., & Hamat, Z. (2013). Perkembangan perbankan syariah di Indonesia: Suatu tinjauan. *Jurnal Aplikasi Bisnis*, *3*(2), 120–138.

Shafii, Z., Shahimi, S., & Saaid, A. (2016). Obstacles and motivation behind conversion of conventional banks to Islamic banks: An overview. *International Review of Management and Business Research*, *5*(3), 1021–1038.

Siraj, K., & Pillai, P. S. (2012). Comparative study on performance of Islamic banks and conventional banks in GCC region. *Journal of Applied Finance and Banking*, *2*(3), 123–161.

Stapleton, T. (2013). Unlocking the transformative potential of branchless banking in Indonesia. *Bulletin of Indonesian Economic Studies*, *49*(3), 355–380. doi:10.1080/00074918.2013.850633

Syariah, B. T. P. N. (2018). *Annual Report 2018.* Retrieved February 22, 2019, from https://www.btpnIslamic.com/images/BTPNS_AR_2018_en.pdf

Tambunan, T. T. H. (2011). Development of small and medium enterprises in a developing country: The Indonesian case. *Journal of Enterprising Communities: People and Places in the Global Economy*, *5*(1), 68–82. doi:10.1108/17506201111119626

World Bank. (2010). *At the Tipping Point? The Implications of Kenya's ICT Revolution: Kenya Economic Update*. Retrieved March 6, 2019, from http://siteresources.world-bank.org/KENYAEXTN/Resources/KEU-Dec_2010_Power-point.pdf

Yudistira, G. (2017). OJK Dorong 62 Bank segera Tambah Modal. *Kontan*. Retrieved March 6, 2019, from http://keuangan.kontan.co.id/news/ojk-dorong-62-bank-segera-tambah-modal

# Chapter 4
# Islamic Banking in Pakistan:
## Emergence, Growth, and Prospects

**Muhammad Bilal Zafar**
https://orcid.org/0000-0001-6329-303X
*Department of Shariah and Economics, University of Malaya, Malaysia*

**Ahmad Azam Sulaiman**
*Department of Shariah and Economics, University of Malaya, Malaysia*

## ABSTRACT

*Since 1960, after a trial of almost 40 years, the reformation of economy of Pakistan from conventional to Islamic could not be achieved. Since 2000, the government changed the strategy to gradually Islamize the economy and adopted a dual system. In this ambit, the State Bank of Pakistan deliberately announced the vision to make the Islamic banking as first choice for users of banking in Pakistan. This chapter bring insights on the background, current state, issues, challenges, and avenues of future policy regarding Islamic banking of Pakistan. The empirical data about Islamic Banking has been collected from the State Bank of Pakistan for the period 2003-2018. This is to evaluate the current state in terms of market performance, modes of Islamic financing, and financing portfolios of Islamic banking. The findings of this chapter show there is a substantial lack of interest by the government to develop the Islamic banking, and Islamic banking is also deviating from its social and ethical proclaims.*

## 1. INTRODUCTION

Islamic banking is considered as a new wave of corporations, whose social goals are as much important as making profits (Haniffa & Hudaib, 2007; Zafar & Sulaiman, 2019). The word Islamic fore mentioned, reflects the real economic activity, social and economic development (Platonova, 2013) and it is an institution having ideology of social welfare and well-being in build (Cebeci, 2012). The social preference and responsibility are regarded as the utmost objective of Islamic banking, regardless of financial consequences, positive or negative (Dusuki, 2008; Dusuki & Abdullah, 2007). This is a real model of

DOI: 10.4018/978-1-7998-1611-9.ch004

banking in modern economy for developing, poor and deprived countries. Pakistan has also a developing economy, having issues of governance, poverty, social and economic developments (Husain, 2018; Zaidi, 2005).

Besides the social and economic significance of Islamic economics, finance and banking for an emerging and developing economy, Pakistan is a country whose constitution also insists on the Islamic social and economic structure (Islamic Research Institute, 2009). Therefore, the government of Pakistan since its foundation, continuously tried to bring the reformations in the economic system, so to make it *Shari'ah* compliant under the state theory. Initially, the government started to bring reformations as a whole, and also declined to be part of dual economy or banking in early 1970's of Islamic banking evolution in the world (Iqbal & Molyneux, 2005, p. 64). But since 1960, after a trial of almost forty-years, the government has badly failed in its strategy (Khan & Bhatti, 2008).

Since year 2000, the government adopted the different strategy, that to bring reformations in the economic system of Pakistan gradually, while explicitly allowing the conventional sector to work along (Saba, 2017). In year 2002, the State Bank of Pakistan issued the first Islamic banking license to the Meezan Bank and captioned the vision, to make the Islamic banking as the first choice for users in Pakistan (State Bank of Pakistan, 2007b). After completion of one-and-a-half decade by Islamic banking in Pakistan, it has overall 13.5% share in banking sector in terms of assets and 15.5% in terms of deposits, with 2851 branches in all around the country (State Bank of Pakistan, 2018a). In addition, State Bank of Pakistan envisioned to increase the share of Islamic banking up to 20% by 2020 (State Bank of Pakistan, 2014b). The rate of growth of Islamic banking is very slow in contrast of vision to transform the economy. In the light of current progress of the Islamic banking and strategic envisioning of government of Pakistan, it will require an entire century to completely transform the economic system. There is a need to study the background and current-state of Islamic banking, point out the issues and challenges, and suggest the avenues of future policy for prompt growth. This chapter therefore intends to do so.

## 2. BACKGROUND OF ISLAMIC BANKING IN PAKISTAN

The background of Islamic banking in Pakistan has three main phases (Table 1), first, the political motives behind the foundation of Pakistan, secondly, the role of government in transformation of economic structure into Islamic during year 1960 to 2000, and third phase involves, the government strategy after year 2000, that to move both sectors parallel, conventional and Islamic.

The history of development of Islamic economic structure in Pakistan can be traced in the political movement behind foundation of Pakistan, which carried the ideology of a state where the Muslims can enjoy their lives under the Islamic principles. In 1948, Muhammad Ali Jinnah, the founder and Governor General of Pakistan inaugurated the State Bank of Pakistan and said:

*I shall watch with keenness the work of your research organization in evolving banking practices compatible with Islamic idea of social and economic life.* [1]

Moreover, the Objective Resolution which is considered as backbone of the constitution of Pakistan was passed on March 12, 1949 by the National Assembly of Pakistan, also elicited the political motive of the country as:

*... the Muslims shall be enabled to order their lives in the individual and collective spheres in accordance with the teachings and requirements of Islam as set out in holy Qur'an and the Sunnah. (see Islamic Research Institute, 2009)*

Under the lens of political motives of the country, that to bring Islamic reformation, the Islamic Commission (later on Council of Islamic Ideology) was formed in 1957 under the article 198 (1-4) of 1956 Constitution of Pakistan.[2] Which was an expert body, aimed to assist the government in *Shari'ah* matters. In 1963 the government referred the matter of interest-based transaction to the council for expert opinion. In response, in 1969 the council resolution stated that, interest is prohibited in all its forms under *Shari'ah*. Furthermore, the council recommended the government to constitute a committee of experts, which may assist the council in further transformation of existing interest-based financial system into *Shari'ah* compliant.

While, the matter faced long pendency in the council. In late 1980's, the major breakthrough in this regard occurred, when General Zia ul Haq, President of Pakistan at that time, expressed his interest in the transformation of economic system, from conventional to Islamic. He directed the council to formulate blueprints for an interest-free economy within three years. In 1977, a panel of economists, bankers and financial experts were formed under the council to examine technical aspects of existing financial sector under the light of *Shari'ah*. In 1980, the council submitted its report to the government. In which, the council laid down the guidelines for operations of commercial banks under *Shari'ah*. In response, to begin with real initiatives, in 1981, several steps were undertaken, and commercial banks were directed to introduce the profit-loss sharing modes of financing. Moreover, commercial banks were also given the leverage to continue the conventional modes as well, but as of July 1985, no bank could accept any interest-bearing deposit except foreign currency deposit. However, number of steps were undertaken to eliminate the interest from economic sector, but the process of transformation was selective and slow (Rafay & Sadiq, 2015). On the other hand, nothing was taken in consideration to eliminate interest from the government sector.

In August 1985, the movement regarding interest-free financial system suffered with delay further. The major disappointing feature was lack of notable progress in the development of assets in profit-loss sharing side of banking. Moreover, there was as well lack of continue mechanism regarding security in operating mechanism of banks from *Shari'ah* point-of-view. In addition, the proposed structure of reformation of banking structure had some loop-holes as well. The major issue was dealing with multiple counter-loans, which was another form of interest, however the council called it temporary tool and allowed under the strict observations of State Bank of Pakistan. But, this was main loop-hole among others, created the unrest in the community, and resultantly several reservations were raised about the transformed system. The central idea of the council behind *Shari'ah* reforms was interest-free economy, and subsequent its recommendation of multiple counter-loan mode of financing, which was an explicit notion of interest, caused even the other major reforms proposed overlooked (Iqbal & Molyneux, 2005; Khan & Bhatti, 2008; Rammal & Parker, 2013; State Bank of Pakistan, 2007b).

This rise of this criticism ended up with 118 petitions before Federal *Shari'ah* Court (FSC).[3] Against these petitions, in 1991, FSC declared the financing on the basis of multiple counter-loan against the *Shari'ah*. In addition, the court directed the government regarding various laws related to banking and finance, that to bring reforms and conclude them according to *Shari'ah*.[4]

Besides, taking reformations, the government went under the appeal with Supreme Court of Pakistan against the FSC judgment.[5] In 1999, after long pendency of the case, the supreme court upheld the FSC judgment, and given a detailed judgment of 1100 pages, longest judgment ever given by any court (Muhammad, 2015). In the judgment, the government was directed to bring several reformations in different laws related to interest. [6] Moreover, the court also directed that, the laws containing interest-based economy would cease to have effect by June 2001 and later on extended the date till June 2002. But again, in a review petition, on June 24, 2002 the appellant bench of Supreme Court of Pakistan set aside the previous verdict of interest, and the case was sent back to FSC for fresh hearing, which is still pending (The Express Tribune, 2017). [7]

Meanwhile, in year 2000, the government initiated to launch dual banking system in Pakistan and adapted the strategy to gradually transform the economy without major disruption (Saba, 2017). Formally, the Islamic banking was introduced in Pakistan in the year 2002, when the Meezan bank was given the first license of Islamic banking (State Bank of Pakistan, 2007b). In this frame, the State Bank of Pakistan adopted the three-point strategy for development and promotion of Islamic banking in Pakistan:[8]

1. Permission to open new full-fledged Islamic banks in the private sector.
2. Permission to the conventional banks to set up Islamic banking subsidiaries.
3. Permission to the existing conventional banks to open stand-alone Islamic banking branches or windows.

*Table 1. Historical background of Islamic banking in Pakistan*

| Phase | Brief Narration |
|---|---|
| Political envision behind foundation of Pakistan | In 1948, formation of State Bank of Pakistan, and visioning as an institution to facilitate the Islamic idea of social and economic life<br>In 1957, foundation of Council of Islamic Ideology for the purpose to assist the government in *Shari'ah* matters |
| Role of government in transformation 1960-2000 | In 1963, government referred the matter of interest-based transaction to Council of Islamic Ideology<br>In 1969, the council pronounced the interest-based transaction as against the *Shari'ah*<br>In 1977, a panel of experts formed under the council to bring reforms in economic system<br>In 1980, the council submitted its recommendations and guidelines of reformations<br>In 1981, several steps of reformations undertaken<br>The banks were directed to accept the deposits on a profit-loss sharing basis along with conventional modes, while at the end of July, 1985 the Islamic mode of financing will be continued only<br>Till 1991, several petitions came before Federal *Shari'ah* Court (FSC) pointing out the issues of Islamic reformations, and likewise FSC declared its verdicts and directed to government to bring several reformations in economic system to completely transform into an Islamic economic system<br>The same judgement of FSC was challenged before the Supreme Court of Pakistan (SCP), after a long pendency, SCP upheld the FSC verdicts and directed the government to bring reforms till June 2001, then extended the date till June 2002<br>While, in a review petition before SCP, the earlier verdict was set aside, and SCP referred the original case back to FSC for fresh hearing, which is still pending before FSC |
| Post-2000 dual-banking strategy | State bank of Pakistan allowed dual banking system, Islamic banking along with conventional sector, and envisioned to make the Islamic banking as first choice<br>In 2002, State Bank of Pakistan issued the first license as Islamic bank to Meezan Bank |

## 3. *SHARI'AH* SUPERVISION OF ISLAMIC BANKING IN PAKISTAN

In Pakistan, under Banking Companies Ordinance, 1962 the banks are allowed to offer the Islamic modes of banking and financing. The central bank i.e. State Bank of Pakistan has *Shari'ah* Board, which has composition of five members, at least two *Shari'ah* scholars, one chartered accountant, one lawyer and one member representing the bankers.

The *Shari'ah* Board of central bank has primary responsibility to review and approve the *Shari'ah* compliance products or instrument. The *Shari'ah* Board of central bank has issued the essential modes of Islamic financing, which are binding for Islamic banking institutions (State Bank of Pakistan, 2008a). While, the Islamic banking institutions are also required to constitute the *Shari'ah* boards, which are responsible to give the opinion and approval regarding the *Shari'ah* compliance of products and operations. However, in case of conflict, the ruling of *Shari'ah* board of central bank is considered the final and binding over the board of an Islamic bank. This implies, the *Shari'ah* board of central bank has final authority regarding the *Shari'ah* verdicts. In nutshell, Islamic banking of Pakistan follows centralized model of *Shari'ah* governance (Hamza, 2013).

In the beginning, State Bank of Pakistan directed the Islamic banks to have at least one *Shari'ah* advisor or member in the *Shari'ah* governance board. In recent years 2014-2015, the number of has been increase to at least three *Shari'ah* members in *Shari'ah* board of every Islamic bank (Statement Bank of Pakistan, 2015).

## 4. PERFORMANCE OF ISLAMIC BANKING IN PAKISTAN

Table 2 shows, the overall current share of Islamic banking in banking sector is 13.5% in terms of assets and 15.5% in terms of deposits, with 2,851 branches in all around the country. There are 5 full-fledged Islamic banks and 17 conventional banks having Islamic windows.

Figure 1 depicts that, there is continue improvement in market share of Islamic banking. However, the average annual change, from 2003-2018, is 0.84% in terms of assets and 0.97% in terms of deposits, that shows the change is under 1%.

Table 2 and Figure 2 depict the market performance of Islamic banking was gradual but consist till 2007-8, but a sudden decrease came in the annual change of assets and deposits of Islamic banking. This decrease however started to recover in coming years, which shows the confidence of customers. The overall trend of post-2010 shows that the Islamic banking of Pakistan is still in process of recovering and regaining of momentum.

Moreover, in 2009-10 the number of branches of Islamic banking also became almost half and one full-fledged Islamic bank withdraw the market. This decrease however started to recover in coming years, which shows the confidence of customers. In 2015, there was a swift increase in number of branches and deposits, this was may be due to inclusion of a new full-fledged Islamic bank in the sector. But, the same withdrew the market in the very next year. The overall trend of post-2010 shows that the Islamic banking of Pakistan is still in process of recovering and regaining of momentum.

The whole ambit elicits the variation in market performance of Islamic banking, it may imply different interpretations. Foremost, the tough competition of conventional banking sector, the conventional banking sector has deep-roots in the economy, operating for 70 years. While, in contrast, Islamic banking is relatively young and has age of just one-and-a-half decade. So, on-and-off pressure from the conventional sector has made the Islamic banking volatile.

*Table 2. Branch network, industry progress and market share of Islamic banking*

| Year | Full-fledge Islamic Banks | Conventional Banks with Islamic Bank Windows | No. of Branches | Annual Increase in No. of Branches | Total Assets Rs. Bn. | Assets % in Banking Industry | Deposits Rs. Bn. | Deposits % in Banking Industry | Annual Change of % in Banking Industry | |
|---|---|---|---|---|---|---|---|---|---|---|
| | | | | | | | | | Assets | Deposits |
| 2003 | 1 | 3 | 17 | 17 | 13 | 0.5 | 8 | 0.4 | 0.5 | 0.4 |
| 2004 | 2 | 7 | 48 | 31 | 44 | 1.4 | 30 | 1.2 | 0.9 | 0.8 |
| 2005 | 2 | 9 | 70 | 22 | 72 | 2.1 | 50 | 1.9 | 0.7 | 0.7 |
| 2006 | 4 | 12 | 150 | 80 | 118 | 2.9 | 83 | 2.8 | 0.8 | 0.9 |
| 2007 | 6 | 12 | 289 | 139 | 206 | 4.3 | 147 | 4.1 | 1.4 | 1.3 |
| 2008 | 6 | 12 | 515 | 226 | 276 | 4.9 | 202 | 4.8 | 0.6 | 0.7 |
| 2009 | 6 | 13 | 649 | 134 | 366 | 5.6 | 283 | 5.9 | 0.7 | 1.1 |
| 2010 | 5 | 13 | 751 | 102 | 477 | 6.7 | 390 | 7.2 | 1.1 | 1.3 |
| 2011 | 5 | 12 | 886 | 135 | 641 | 7.8 | 521 | 8.4 | 1.1 | 1.2 |
| 2012 | 5 | 13 | 1097 | 211 | 837 | 8.6 | 706 | 9.7 | 0.8 | 1.3 |
| 2013 | 5 | 14 | 1304 | 207 | 1014 | 9.6 | 868 | 10.4 | 1 | 0.7 |
| 2014 | 5 | 17 | 1574 | 270 | 1259 | 10.4 | 1070 | 11.6 | 0.8 | 1.2 |
| 2015 | 6 | 17 | 2075 | 501 | 1610 | 11.4 | 1375 | 13.2 | 1 | 1.6 |
| 2016 | 5 | 16 | 2322 | 247 | 1853 | 11.7 | 1573 | 13.3 | 0.3 | 0.1 |
| 2017 | 5 | 16 | 2581 | 259 | 2272 | 12.4 | 1885 | 14.5 | 0.7 | 1.2 |
| 2018 | 5 | 17 | 2851 | 270 | 2658 | 13.5 | 2203 | 15.5 | 1.1 | 1 |
| **Average** | | | | | | | | | **0.84** | **0.97** |

Compiled by the authors

Source: (State Bank of Pakistan, 2007a, 2008b, 2009, 2010, 2011, 2012, 2013, 2014a, 2015, 2016, 2017b, 2018a)

*Figure 1. Market share of Islamic banking*

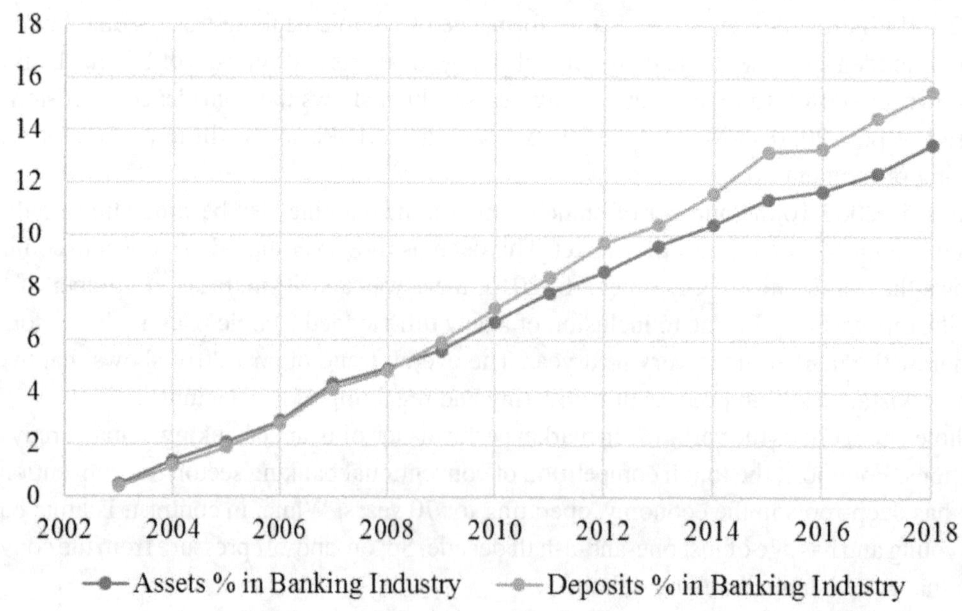

*Figure 2. Annual change in Islamic banking assets and deposits*

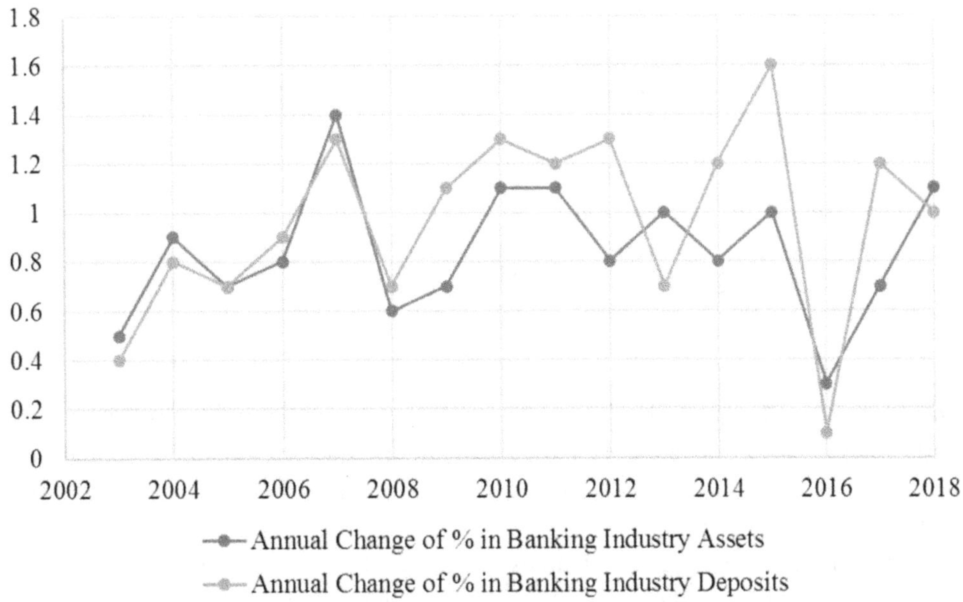


The other interpretation of variations in market performance of Islamic banking can be the political and economic conditions of the country. This is also an empirical fact that GDP significantly effects the performance of Islamic banking in Pakistan (Abbas, Azid, & Hj Besar, 2016). The GDP growth rate during 2007-2010 declined, however post-2010 the same started to recover (The World Bank, 2018), and likewise the market of Islamic banking. During the last decade, Pakistan has faced various economic issues due to in-rush political decisions, including inflation, increase of domestic and foreign debt, corruption and destabilization of national institutions, which has adversely affected the market of Pakistan (Husain, 2018).

Moreover, Pakistan remained in the war-and-terror. During the growth period of Islamic banking the terrorism in the country was relatively high, same started to decrease in the decline phase of Islamic banking (SATP Report, 2019). The terrorism cannot be considered as a good explanation of variations in market performance of Islamic banking. Instead of terrorism, the better interpretation of decline of economic market in Pakistan is bad internal political policies and governance issues (Husain, 2018), which eventually decreased the GDP and market performance of Islamic banking.

## 5. MODES OF ISLAMIC FINANCING

Islamic banking department of State Bank of Pakistan through a Circular No. 2/2008 (2008a) narrated the Islamic financing modes. In which, the modes of financing are divided into four categories (Table 3). The followings are the Islamic financing modes prevailing in the industry:

*Table 3. Modes of Islamic financing in Pakistan*

<table>
<tr><th>Participatory</th><th>Trading</th><th>Debt Based</th><th>Others</th></tr>
<tr><td>Mudarabah</td><td>Ijarah</td><td rowspan="6">Qard-e-Hasana</td><td>Wakalah</td></tr>
<tr><td>Musharakah</td><td>Murabahah</td><td>Assignment of debt</td></tr>
<tr><td>Diminishing Musharakah</td><td>Musawamah</td><td rowspan="4">Kafalah</td></tr>
<tr><td rowspan="3">Equity participation</td><td>Bai Salam</td></tr>
<tr><td>Istisna</td></tr>
<tr><td>Tawarruq (in particular cases on special approval of SBP)</td></tr>
</table>

Source: (State Bank of Pakistan, 2008a)

***Murabahah*:** This is a contract of sale on a mutually agreed profit, and the seller declares the cost and profit prior to sale. As a financing technique, the client requests the bank for purchase of certain goods, in response, the bank purchases the same goods for him for a definite profit over the cost, which is specified in advance.

***Ijarah*:** Literally it means lease, and it denotes the hiring of assets or things which are non-consumable. In *Ijarah*, the corpus of leased commodity remains in ownership of lessor and only the usufruct of commodity is transferred to lessee. Technically, the asset of lease is finally delivered to lessee through periodical payments in account of ownership along with lease. Moreover, until such time that assets to be leased are delivered to the lessee, lease rentals do not become due and payable.

***Musharakah*:** This is a mutual agreement among parties for sharing of profit and loss in a joint business. In this agreement, Islamic banks provide funds to the business enterprise. The profit is shared among parties on pre-agreed ratio, and the loss is borne according to proportion of capital provided.

***Mudarabah*:** This is a form of partnership, in which one party provides the funds and other renders the services or provides the expertise and management. The profits are shared among parties on a pre-agreed basis, and loss is borne only by the provider of the funds.

Diminishing ***Musharakah*:** It is a form of co-ownership in which two or more persons share the ownership of a tangible asset in an agreed proportion and one of the co-owners undertakes to buy in periodic installments the proportionate share of the other co-owner until the title to such tangible asset is completely transferred to the purchasing co-owner.

***Bai Salam*:** This is sale agreement in which payment is made in advance for a specific goods while goods are to be delivered later-on. The objects of this sale are goods and cannot be currencies, gold or silver. *Bai Salam* covers almost everything, which is capable of being definitely described as to quantity and quality.

***Istisna*:** It is a contractual agreement for manufacturing goods and commodities, allowing cash payment in advance and future delivery or a future payment and future delivery. Istisna can be used for providing the facility of financing the manufacture or construction of houses, plants, projects and building of bridges, roads and highways.

***Qard-e-Hasana*:** This is a contract of loan in which the borrower is required to pay back only the principal amount borrowed, and the loan is considered as to be payable on demand.

*Table 4. Modes of Islamic financing prevailing in industry*

| Modes | Financing Mix (% Share) | | | | | |
|---|---|---|---|---|---|---|
| | 2014 | 2015 | 2016 | 2017 | 2018 | Avg |
| *Murabahah* | 30.1 | 24.4 | 15.8 | 13.2 | 13.6 | 19.42 |
| *Ijarah* | 7.7 | 6.6 | 6.8 | 6.4 | 6.2 | 6.74 |
| *Musharakah* | 11 | 14 | 15.6 | 22 | 19.9 | 16.5 |
| *Mudarabah* | 0.1 | 0 | 0 | 0 | 0 | 0.02 |
| Diminishing *Musharakah* | 32.6 | 31.7 | 34.7 | 30.7 | 33.3 | 32.60 |
| *Salam* | 4.5 | 5.3 | 4.4 | 2.8 | 2.4 | 3.88 |
| *Istisna* | 8.3 | 8.6 | 8.4 | 8.2 | 9.1 | 8.52 |
| *Qard/Qard-e-Hasana* | 0 | 0 | 0 | 0 | 0 | 0 |
| Others | 5.6 | 9.3 | 14.3 | 16.7 | 15.5 | 12.28 |
| Total | 100 | 100 | 100 | 100 | 100 | 100 |

Compiled by the authors
Source: (State Bank of Pakistan, 2014a, 2015, 2016, 2017b, 2018a)

Table 4 shows the modes of financing prevailing in Islamic banking, and the financing percentages. In the light of last five years data, the most popular mode of Islamic financing is Diminishing *Musharakah* (32.60%), following the *Murabahah* (19.42%) and *Musharakah* (16.5). This is often argued that most sustainable instruments of Islamic financings are *Musharakah* and *Mudarabah* as compare to *Murabahah*. The *Murabahah*-based financing promotes the individual *Maslaha* or well-being, while *Musharakah* and *Mudarabah*-based financing contribute in the collective well-being due to the nature of instrumentation, and these instruments are considered better for expanding welfare and poverty alleviation (Cebeci, 2012).

In Islamic banking of Pakistan, the popular mode of financing is *Murabahah*, because technically, the Diminishing *Musharakah* is not a pure form of *Musharakah* rather it is mixture of *Ijarah*, *Murabahah* and *Musharakah*. The issue of *Murabahah*-based financing also prevails in the Islamic banking sector of Pakistan likewise in other Islamic banking markets (Cebeci, 2012), which reflects the capitalistic mind-set of banking. This is strange that Islamic banking of Pakistan has totally neglected the *Qard-e-Hasana* instrument, which is a social welfare instrument of Islamic financing.

## 6. FINANCING PORTFOLIOS OF ISLAMIC BANKING

There are diverse financing portfolios of Islamic banking in Pakistan, the most common portfolio is corporate sector (74.74%), followed by consumer finance with share of 10.48% (Table 5).

The total bend towards corporate finance elicits the instrumental behavior of Islamic banking of Pakistan. The corporate finance is considered as more favorable avenue of investment, because it yields the guaranteed profits and having low risks of loss as compare to other sectors e.g. SMEs. This kind capitalistic stance of Islamic banking is neglecting the normative behavior, which is often claimed by the Islamic banking, that is welfare and well-being of at-large regardless of financial consequences and beyond merely the economics interests (Dusuki, 2008; Dusuki & Abdullah, 2007).

*Table 5. Financing portfolio of Islamic banking*

| Sector | Financing Portfolio (% Share) | | | | | |
|---|---|---|---|---|---|---|
| | 2014 | 2015 | 2016 | 2017 | 2018 | Avg |
| Corporate | 76.9 | 74.4 | 77.5 | 70.6 | 74.3 | 74.74 |
| SMEs | 3.6 | 3.1 | 3.4 | 3.3 | 3.7 | 3.42 |
| Agriculture | 0.4 | 0.6 | 0.8 | 0.5 | 0.3 | 0.52 |
| Consumer Finance | 11.9 | 10 | 10.5 | 9.9 | 10.1 | 10.48 |
| Commodity Financing | 5.3 | 8.6 | 5.6 | 13.9 | 10.5 | 8.78 |
| Staff Financing | 1.6 | 1.3 | 0 | 0 | 0 | 0.58 |
| Others | 0.3 | 2 | 2.2 | 1.8 | 1.1 | 1.48 |
| Total | 100 | 100 | 100 | 100 | 100 | 100 |

Compiled by the authors
Source: (State Bank of Pakistan, 2014a, 2015, 2016, 2017b, 2018a)

Pakistan is an agriculture state, 68% population is associated with agriculture (Pakistan Bureau of Statistics, 2011), while agriculture sector has been almost ignored by the Islamic banking. Pakistan has envisioned the development of SMEs sector, while 95% of SMEs cannot survive in first year of their inception (Mubarik, Govindaraju, & Devadason, 2016). This is also astonishing that Islamic banking of Pakistan has also firmly ignored the SMEs sector as well. The Islamic banking proclaims the ethical behavior and promotes the social ideology but same is not reflected in the actions (Kamla & Rammal, 2013), the same dilemma also prevails in the Islamic banking of Pakistan.

## 7. CONCLUSION: KEY CHALLENGES OF ISLAMIC BANKING

Briefly, the central stress of the chapter is on, that after a trail of forty-years the government has been badly failed to transform the economy under the state political theory. While, in year 2000, the government adopted the different strategy to move both Islamic and conventional sector parallel and captioned the vision to make the Islamic banking as first choice. But, after the completion of more than one-and-a-half decade of Islamic banking in Pakistan, it has just captured 15.5% share of the banking market, and the annual rate of change is under 1%, which is extremely low. If Islamic banking goes with this rate, it will require an entire century to transform the economy and translate the state political theory. Under this whole ambit, this chapter reviews the background of Islamic banking, and then it evaluates the sixteen-years journey of Islamic banking of Pakistan. In last, it provides insights into certain challenges, which pave the ways for future policy. The foremost novelty of this piece of work is, that it provides a complete picture of Islamic banking of Pakistan, in a very brief way. Secondly, very gently, it aligns the background and current state with the highlighted challenges.

There are several issues and challenges for Islamic banking, and which also constitute the avenues of future policy. Foremost challenge is related to the ineffective strategies and vague polices of government regarding development of Islamic banking. The development of Islamic banking, economics and finance has long history in Pakistan. Initially, the government has taken the strategy to bring Islamic economic reformation in Pakistan as a whole. But after a trial of around forty years, the same could not achieve.

In the beginning of this century, the State Bank of Pakistan deliberately announced the vision to make the Islamic banking as first choice for users of banking in Pakistan, while adapting the dual banking system in the country. In the second approach, the pace of transformation in very slow, State Bank of Pakistan envisions growth of Islamic banking up to 20% for 2020, at the end of two decades. As in the first-approach strategy, the government was extremely inefficient, growth envisioning up to 20% at the end of two decades, depicts that the government is still reluctant in development and transformation of economic and banking structure according to *Shari'ah* compliant. The state theory of economics has not yet been translated into practice with letter-and-spirit after the seven decades, and still the state ideology is facing the same issues of practical implications on the part of government. There is utmost need of practical envisioning, efficient strategies and concrete policies which may centrally stress to the vision of transformation with a significant pace. Otherwise, the whole ambit and role of the government reflects, that state theory and making Islamic banking the first choice is not more than a myth.

Second challenge is related to the growth of Islamic banking, after completion of around one-and-a-half decade by Islamic banking in Pakistan, it has overall 13.5% share in banking sector in terms of assets and 15.5% in terms of deposits, with 2851 branches in all around the country (Table 2). This is pertinent to mention here that the share of full-fledged Islamic banking is 60% while 40% share is of conventional banking having Islamic windows (Meezan Bank, 2017). The annual rate of change in market growth is under 1% (Table 2), which is very low. Islamic banking of Pakistan requires to revisit its market strategies and deal properly the issues of low market performance. In service industry, such that banking, customer service and quality plays a vital role in performance of bank (Wu, Tzeng, & Chen, 2009). While, the customers of BankIslami, second largest Islamic bank of the country, recently faced the loss of over 6.5 million USD due to cyber-attack (Bhatti, 2018). The empirical evidence also reveals that customer of Islamic banking of Pakistan do not merely relay on the *Shari'ah*-compliance factor of banking, but they also prefer and expect from Islamic banks to be convenient, technologically advance, having high service quality and bank efficiency, and provide the security of their capital (Butt, Ahmad, Naveed, & Ahmed, 2018; Lee & Ullah, 2011; Rehman & Masood, 2012).

Third challenge is related to the competition of conventional banking, the volume of conventional banking as compare to Islamic banking is 4.5/5, such that, there are 28 conventional banks and on the other side, there are 5 full-fledged Islamic banks (State Bank of Pakistan, 2018c). In addition, the market share of conventional banking is 6/7, such that, Islamic banking has market share of 15.5% (Table 2) and reciprocal is share of conventional banking. These ratios suggest that, the conventional banking has strong hold in the market. In addition, the conventional banking is working in Pakistan since seven decades and it has deep roots in the economy and market, while Islamic banking is infant with an age of one-and-a-half decade. Beside this immense competition, full-fledged Islamic banks are less efficient in terms of total technical efficiency and pure technical efficiency than conventional banks (Majeed & Zanib, 2016). The Islamic banking has to increase its capabilities in terms of technology, and as well in term of human capital (State Bank of Pakistan, 2018b), and has to look into other deficiency areas to compete in the market. In addition to work out on the deficiencies, the Islamic banking has to more capitalize the core advantages, such that risk management practices, the Islamic banks are superior to conventional banks in this domain, as *Shari'ah* rules restrict speculation in monetary terms (I. Khan, Khan, & Tahir, 2017).

Forth challenge is related to the portfolios and modes of financing of Islamic banking, which preferences depicts the social ideology of Islamic banking. Unfortunately, the social ideology of Islamic banking is not reflected in its actions. Such that, the 68% population of Pakistan is associated with agriculture

(Pakistan Bureau of Statistics, 2011) while Islamic banking is financing just 0.52% to agriculture sector (Table 5). In addition, the government of Pakistan has adopted the strategy to promote SMEs for economic development, and performance of SME sector is extremely low, almost 95% SMEs cannot survive first year since their inception (Mubarik *et al.*., 2016), but Islamic banking has also ignored the SMEs sector as well by just financing up to 3.42% (Table 5). Moreover, Islamic banking has fully ignored the *Qard-e-Hasana* financing which is one of prime Islamic financing instrument of social welfare (Table 5). In Islamic banking of Pakistan, the popular mode of financing is *Murabahah* (Table 4), which reflects the capitalistic mind-set of Islamic banking (Cebeci, 2012), which is again against the social proclaims of Islamic banking. In this ambit, Islamic banking must sustain its social ideology besides the instrumental gains and interests, which is also being expected by the users of Islamic banking from it.

Fifth challenge is related to the economic conditions, environmental, social and poverty issues of Pakistan and undertaking of social responsibility of Islamic banking. Islamic banking proclaims the ethical institution, so the social responsibility and accountability is an inherent substance of Islamic banking (Zafar & Sulaiman, 2019). Pakistan is the sixth most populated country in the world with an estimated population of 199.71 million, the estimated population growth and fertility rate is 1.86 and 3.0 respectively, there are sever issues of health, education and employment (Ministry of Finance, 2017). According to Global Climate Risk Index (Kreft, Eckstein, & Melchior, 2017), Pakistan is among the top 10 countries which are affected and having long-term climate risk. Beside climate change an important environmental issue in Pakistan, there are as well other, such that pollution, soil erosion, natural disasters, deforestation and land degradation (Kanwal, 2018). Moreover, Pakistan is facing worst economic crises in its history, economic volatility and peaked inflation (Asian Development Bank, 2018). In ambit of environmental issues and sustainable development, the Islamic banking has to meet the expectations of green banking under the guidelines, recently issued by the State Bank of Pakistan (2017a). In addition, the Islamic banking must undertake the social responsibility initiatives to in terms of health, education, poverty and unemployment for the socio-economic development of the country. The ethically and socially responsible behavior of Islamic banking will also enhance the customer loyalty, image and reputation of Islamic banking in Pakistan (Shabbir, Shariff, Yusof, Salman, & Hafeez, 2018), beside its social benefits, it has as well instrumental returns for Islamic banking (Platonova, Asutay, Dixon, & Mohammad, 2018).

Sixth challenge is related to community awareness and exploitation of potential avenues of growth. The key element causing the misperceptions and confusions about the Islamic banking is, the lack of understanding and awareness regarding operating model of Islamic banking. The empirical evidence also supports the same fact, that customers are less agreed and more neutral about the *Shari'ah*-compliant operation at Islamic banking of Pakistan (Majeed & Zainab, 2017), while extent of knowledge plays an important role in selecting Islamic banks as preferred institutions (Salman, Nawaz, Bukhari, & Baker, 2018). The community awareness is one of great challenges, the better awareness can sustain the legitimacy and growth of Islamic banking in Pakistan. The community awareness regarding Islamic banking should be among the foremost important policy of government and as well Islamic banking sector.

In addition, there are several other potential avenues of growth for Islamic banking of Pakistan, such that SMEs, it constitutes nearly 90% of all the enterprises in Pakistan and employs 80% of the non-agriculture labor force (Anas & Zafar, 2018; SMEDA, 2007), while Islamic banking has totally overlooked this sector by giving only 3.42% space in the portfolio (Table 5), the same grievance has also been showed by the State Bank of Pakistan (2014b), that banking sector in general and Islamic banking in particular has ignored the SME sector. Moreover, 68% population of Pakistan is associated with agriculture (Pakistan Bureau of Statistics, 2011) while Islamic banking is financing just 0.52% in agriculture sector (Table 5), there is also great potential of investment in this sector. Moreover, a large population of 80% is untapped market and excluded from the financial sector, containing a significant percentage of faith sensitive community of volunteer exclusion (State Bank of Pakistan, 2014b). The Islamic banking must bring policies, which may increase its network, so it may be assessible to all customers. A large population of the country is rural, mostly is untapped market, so access to Islamic finance in this market may increase the network, one of the options can be Islamic microfinance.

## Classifications

JEL Classification: G18, G20, G28
KAUJIE Classification: F1, J3, S1

## REFERENCES


Abbas, M., Azid, T., & Hj Besar, M. H. A. (2016). Efficiency, effectiveness and performance profile of Islamic and conventional banks in Pakistan. *Humanomics*, *32*(1), 2–18. doi:10.1108/H-09-2015-0058

Anas, M., & Zafar, F. (2018). An Overview of SME sector, Market Access, ISO Certifications and Compliance. *SME Observer, 8*(1), 9–14. Retrieved from https://smeda.org/phocadownload/Publicatoins/SME Observer Jan - Jun 2018.pdf

Asian Development Bank. (2018). *Asian Development Outlook*. Retrieved from https://www.adb.org/sites/default/files/publication/411666/ado2018.pdf

Bhatti, E. (2018, October 29). BankIslami becomes victim of $6.5 million cyber-attack. *Pakistan Todau*. Retrieved from https://profit.pakistantoday.com.pk/2018/10/29/bankislami-becomes-victim-of-6-5-million-cyber-attack/

Butt, I., Ahmad, N., Naveed, A., & Ahmed, Z. (2018). Determinants of low adoption of Islamic banking in Pakistan. *Journal of Islamic Marketing*, *9*(3), 655–672. doi:10.1108/JIMA-01-2017-0002

Cebeci, I. (2012). Integrating the social *Maslaha* into Islamic finance. *Accounting Research Journal*, *25*(3), 166–184. doi:10.1108/10309611211290158

Dusuki, A. W. (2008). What Does Islam Say about Corporate Social Responsibility? *Review of Islamic Economics*, *12*(1), 5–28. doi:10.2190/86QB-KKY1-F27L-3KHK

Dusuki, A. W., & Abdullah, N. I. (2007). Maqasid al-Shari`ah, *Maslahah*, and Corporate Corporate social responsibility. *The American Journal of Islamic Social Sciences*, *24*(1), 25–45. Retrieved from http://irep.iium.edu.my/2209

Hamza, H. (2013). Sharia governance in Islamic banks: Effectiveness and supervision model. *International Journal of Islamic and Middle Eastern Finance and Management*, *6*(3), 226–237. doi:10.1108/IMEFM-02-2013-0021

Haniffa, R., & Hudaib, M. (2007). Exploring the ethical identity of Islamic Banks via communication in annual reports. *Journal of Business Ethics*, *76*(1), 97–116. doi:10.100710551-006-9272-5

Husain, I. (2018). *Governing the Ungovernable: Institutional Reforms for Democratic Governance*. Oxford University Press.

Iqbal, M., & Molyneux, P. (2005). *Thirty Years of Islamic Banking: History, Performance and Prospects*. Basingstoke, UK: Palgrave Macmillan.

Islamic Research Institute. (2009). The Objectives Resolution. *Islamic Studies*, *48*, 89–118. Retrieved from http://www.jstor.org/stable/20839154

Kamla, R., & Rammal, G. H. (2013). Social reporting by Islamic banks: Does social justice matter? *Accounting, Auditing & Accountability Journal*, *26*(6), 911–945. doi:10.1108/AAAJ-03-2013-1268

Kanwal, S. (2018, October 2). The environmental issues in Pakistan. *The Frontier Post*. Retrieved from https://thefrontierpost.com/the-environmental-issues-in-pakistan/

Khan, I., Khan, M., & Tahir, M. (2017). Performance comparison of Islamic and conventional banks: Empirical evidence from Pakistan. *International Journal of Islamic and Middle Eastern Finance and Management*, *10*(3), 419–433. doi:10.1108/IMEFM-05-2016-0077

Khan, M. M., & Bhatti, M. I. (2008). *Developments in Islamic Banking: The Case of Pakistan*. doi:10.1057/9780230582309

Kreft, S., Eckstein, D., & Melchior, I. (2017). *Global Climate Risk Index 2017: Who suffers most from extreme weather events? Weather-related loss events in 2015 and 1996 to 2015*. Retrieved from https://germanwatch.org/sites/germanwatch.org/files/publication/16411.pdf

Lee, K., & Ullah, S. (2011). Customers' attitude toward Islamic banking in Pakistan. *International Journal of Islamic and Middle Eastern Finance and Management*, *4*(2), 131–145. doi:10.1108/17538391111144524

Majeed, M. T., & Zainab, A. (2017). How Islamic is Islamic banking in Pakistan? *International Journal of Islamic and Middle Eastern Finance and Management*, *10*(4), 470–483. doi:10.1108/IMEFM-03-2017-0083

Majeed, M. T., & Zanib, A. (2016). Efficiency analysis of Islamic banks in Pakistan. *Humanomics*, *32*(1), 19–32. doi:10.1108/H-07-2015-0054

Meezan Bank. (2017). *Annual Report*. Retrieved from http://www.sbp.org.pk/stats/Balance/2017/MeezanBankLtd.pdf

Ministry of Finance. (2017). Pakistan Economic Survey: 2016-17. Islamabad.

Mubarik, M. S., Govindaraju, C., & Devadason, E. S. (2016). Human capital development for SMEs in Pakistan: Is the "one-size-fits-all" policy adequate? *International Journal of Social Economics*, *43*(8), 804–822. doi:10.1108/IJSE-02-2015-0033

Muhammad, H. F. (2015, September 10). Report on Riba Case Judgment of Pakistan. *The Lahore Times*. Retrieved from http://www.lhrtimes.com/2015/09/10/report-on-riba-case-judgment-of-pakistan/

Pakistan Bureau of Statistics. (2011). *Agriculture Statistics of Pakistan 2010-11*. Retrieved from http://www.pbs.gov.pk/content/agriculture-statistics-pakistan-2010-11

Platonova, E. (2013). Corporate Social Responsibility from an Islamic Moral Economy Perspective : A Literature Survey. *Afro EUrasian Studies*, *2*(1&2), 272–297.

Platonova, E., Asutay, M., Dixon, R., & Mohammad, S. (2018). The Impact of Corporate Social Responsibility Disclosure on Financial Performance: Evidence from the GCC Islamic Banking Sector. *Journal of Business Ethics*, *151*(2), 451–471. doi:10.100710551-016-3229-0

Rafay, A., & Sadiq, R. (2015). Problems and Issues in Transformation from Conventional Banking to Islamic Banking: Literature Review for the Need of a Comprehensive Framework for a Smooth Change. *City University Research Journal*, *5*(2), 315–326.

Rammal, H. G., & Parker, L. D. (2013). Islamic banking in Pakistan: A History of Emergent Accountability and Regulation. *Accounting History*, *18*(1), 5–29. doi:10.1177/1032373212463269

Rehman, A. A., & Masood, O. (2012). Why do customers patronize Islamic banks? A case study of Pakistan. *Qualitative Research in Financial Markets*, *4*(2/3), 130–141. doi:10.1108/17554171211252475

Report, S. A. T. P. (2019). *Datasheet of Terrorism in Pakistan*. Retrieved from https://propakistani.pk/2018/04/24/terrorism-in-pakistan-declines-by-89-in-8-years/

Saba, I. (2017). Islamic Finance—Local and Global Status. In Developments in Islamic Finance (pp. 1–20). doi:10.1007/978-3-319-59342-5_1

Salman, A., Nawaz, H., Bukhari, S. M. H., & Baker, A. (2018). *Growth analysis of Islamic banking in Pakistan: A qualitative approach. Academy of Accounting and Financial Studies Journal, 22*. Specialiss.

Shabbir, M. S., Shariff, M. N. M., & Yusof, M. S. Bin, Salman, R., & Hafeez, S. (2018). Corporate Social Responsibility and Customer loyalty in Islamic Banks of Pakistan: A Mediating Role of Brand Image. *Academy of Accounting and Financial Studies Journal*, *22*(Special Issue), 1–6.

SMEDA. (2007). *SME Policy*. Retrieved from https://smeda.org/phocadownload/Publicatoins/SME Policy 2007.pdf

State Bank of Pakistan. (2007a). *Islamic Banking Bulletin: December 2007*. Retrieved from http://www.sbp.org.pk/ibd/bulletin/2007/Oct-Dec-Bulletin.pdf

State Bank of Pakistan. (2007b). *Pakistan's Islamic Banking Sector Review*. Retrieved from http://www.sbp.org.pk/departments/ibd/Islamic-Bkg-Review-03-07.pdf

State Bank of Pakistan. (2008a). *Instructions for Shari'ah Compliance in Islamic Banking*. Retrieved from http://www.sbp.org.pk/ibd/2008/C2.htm

State Bank of Pakistan. (2008b). *Islamic Banking Bulletin: December 2008*. Retrieved from http://www.sbp.org.pk/ibd/bulletin/2008/Bulletin-Oct-Dec-2008.pdf

State Bank of Pakistan. (2009). *Islamic Banking Bulletin: December 2009*. Retrieved from http://www.sbp.org.pk/ibd/bulletin/2009/Bulletin-Oct-Dec-2009.pdf

State Bank of Pakistan. (2010). *Islamic Banking Bulletin: December 2010*. Retrieved from http://www.sbp.org.pk/ibd/bulletin/2010/IBB-Dec-2010.pdf

State Bank of Pakistan. (2011). *Islamic Banking Bulletin: December 2011*. Retrieved from http://www.sbp.org.pk/ibd/bulletin/2011/IBB-Dec-2011.pdf

State Bank of Pakistan. (2012). *Islamic Banking Bulletin: December 2012*. Retrieved from http://www.sbp.org.pk/ibd/bulletin/2012/IBB-Dec-2012.pdf

State Bank of Pakistan. (2013). *Islamic Banking Bulletin: December 2013*. Retrieved from http://www.sbp.org.pk/ibd/bulletin/2013/IBB-Dec-2013.pdf

State Bank of Pakistan. (2014a). *Islamic Banking Bulletin: December 2014*. Retrieved from http://www.sbp.org.pk/ibd/bulletin/2014/IBB-Dec-2014.pdf

State Bank of Pakistan. (2014b). *Strategic Plan Islamic Banking Industry of Pakistan*. Retrieved from http://www.sbp.org.pk/departments/pdf/StrategicPlanPDF/Strategy Paper-Final.pdf

State Bank of Pakistan. (2015). *Islamic Banking Bulletin: December 2015*. Retrieved from http://www.sbp.org.pk/ibd/bulletin/2015/IBB-Dec-2015.pdf

State Bank of Pakistan. (2016). *Islamic Banking Bulletin: December 2016*. Retrieved from http://www.sbp.org.pk/ibd/bulletin/2016/Dec.pdf

State Bank of Pakistan. (2017a). *Green Banking Guidelines*. Retrieved from http://www.sbp.org.pk/smefd/circulars/2017/C8-Annex.pdf

State Bank of Pakistan. (2017b). *Islamic Banking Bulletin: December 2017*. Retrieved from http://www.sbp.org.pk/ibd/Bulletin/2017/Jun.pdf

State Bank of Pakistan. (2018a). *Islamic Banking Bulletin: December 2018*. Retrieved from http://www.sbp.org.pk/ibd/bulletin/2018/Dec.pdf

State Bank of Pakistan. (2018b). *Islamic Banking Bulletin: March 2018*. Retrieved from http://www.sbp.org.pk/ibd/bulletin/2018/Mar.pdf

State Bank of Pakistan. (2018c). *Statistics on Scheduled Banks in Pakistan*. Retrieved from http://www.sbp.org.pk/publications/schedule_banks/June-2018/Title.pdf

Statement Bank of Pakistan. (2015). *Shari'ah governance framework for Islamic banking institutions*. Retrieved from http://www.sbp.org.pk/ibd/2015/C1-Annex.pdf

The Express Tribune. (2017, March 14). *FSC agrees to first define 'Riba.'* Retrieved from https://tribune.com.pk/story/1354567/25-years-fsc-agrees-first-define-riba/

The World Bank. (2018). *World Development Indicators: World Bank national accounts data, and OECD National Accounts data files*. Retrieved from https://data.worldbank.org/indicator/NY.GDP.MKTP.KD.ZG

Wu, H.-Y., Tzeng, G.-H., & Chen, Y.-H. (2009). A fuzzy MCDM approach for evaluating banking performance based on Balanced Scorecard. *Expert Systems with Applications*, *36*(6), 10135–10147. doi:10.1016/j.eswa.2009.01.005

Zafar, M. B., & Sulaiman, A. A. (2019). Corporate social responsibility and Islamic banks: A systematic literature review. *Management Review Quarterly*, *69*(2), 159–206. doi:10.100711301-018-0150-x

Zaidi, S. A. (2005). *Issues in Pakistan's Economy* (2nd ed.). Oxford University Press.

## ENDNOTES

1 See history of State Bank of Pakistan, at http://www.sbp.org.pk/about/history/h_moments.htm

2 See history of Council of Islamic Ideology, at http://cii.gov.pk/aboutcii/history.aspx

3 A high court jurisdiction court, which deals the matters regarding Islamic laws.

4 See judgment http://federalshariatcourt.gov.pk/Leading%20Judgements/Judgment%20on%20Riba.pdf

5 Supreme Court is apex court in the judicial hierarchy of Pakistan.

6 See judgment https://www.albalagh.net/Islamic_economics/riba_judgement.shtml

7 See judgment http://www.supremecourt.gov.pk/web/user_files/file/jr_detailed_judgment_in_riba_case.pdf

8 http://www.sbp.org.pk/departments/IBD.asp

# Chapter 5
# Islamic Banking in North Africa:
## Emergence, Growth, and Prospects

**Yomna Daoud**
*Faculty of Economics and Management, University of Sfax, Tunisia*

**Aida Kammoun**
*Higher Institute of Business Administration, University of Sfax, Tunisia*

## ABSTRACT

*Investors from North Africa are interested in financial products with ethical focus and specific risk profile and are in accordance with their religious convictions. This chapter reviews the status of Islamic banking (IB) in North Africa in which the governments have started introducing fundamental legal and regulatory frameworks to promote the development of Islamic finance. The study also discusses the prospect of Islamic banking in these jurisdictions. To fulfill the objectives of the proposed study, a qualitative research was performed. The empirical approach of this study analyzed the financial position of different banks in North African countries. Overall, Islamic finance can be an ideal opportunity for financing infrastructure and development projects in North Africa.*

## INTRODUCTION

Since its inception, Islamic finance has steadily developed in the Muslim and non-Muslim globe. Therefore, its principles, the respective values of Islam, can have a universal vocation. Particularly Muslims customers need financial solutions that are in accordance with *Shari'ah*. After the subprime crisis, the Islamic finance industry has experienced a period of evolution and progress. Several factors positively affect the growth of Islamic finance, which can have a significant effect on a continent's economic trajectory, such as population growth, raised consumer spending power, and the prevailing place of Islam in a continent's demographic.

To date, the Islamic banking continues to be the important sector in the finance industry (Thomson Reuters, 2016b). So including traditional banks with Islamic windows, total Islamic banking represents approximately 75% of total Islamic financial assets.

DOI: 10.4018/978-1-7998-1611-9.ch005

Islamic finance is based on five pillars: three prohibitions and two injunctions.

Briefly, the prohibitions are as follows: (i) *Riba* (interest or usury); (ii) *Gharar* and *Mayssir*, meaning undue uncertainty which refers to excessive risk-taking or hazard (due to asymmetric information); (iii) The banning of funding and trading in transactions and products considered as illegal or impure (such as alcohol, gambling and pork). However, the injunctions (or obligations) included Sharing profits and losses (PLS) between all economic parties and the "Asset-backing" principle according to which financial operation should be associated with real economic operation.

The Islamic financial system operates in ways that are different from the logic of conventional finance and require respect for the ethical principles of *Shari'ah*, which result an Islamic banking intermediation different from conventional ones.

According to Rafik Al Masri (1995): "Islamic banks must not only condemn usury (*Riba*) but must apply Islam in all its orders and prohibitions, in its fields of activity".

The liability and asset structure of an Islamic bank based on different functions and services provides an overview of its activities and intermediation capacities.

Islamic financing instruments are generally structured in two categories: equity techniques founded on the principle of profit and loss sharing (PLS) (*Musharakah* and *Mudarabah*) and trade finance techniques (*Murabahah*, *Istisna*, *Salam* and *Ijara*). Banking activity presents specific risks as a result of the specific structure of banking assets and liabilities (Khan & Ahmed, 2001; Sundarararajan & Errico, 2002; Iqbal & Mirakhor, 2011).

The traditional methods of Islamic finance, namely the *Mudarabah* and *Musharakah*, are similar to the principal-agent model. According to Chapra (2007), financial intermediation based on the PLS principle is a different model from traditional intermediation. According to this structure, Islamic banks act as agents when they collect deposits (investment accounts) and play the role of principal when they lend on a PLS basis.

The Islamic *Shari'ah* does not prevent the existence of intermediaries who collect funds from savers and then place them with the entities that need them. Islamic banks must fully and effectively perform the specific functions assigned to them and maintain the specific characteristics of the Islamic financial system. It is widely perceived as a competing form of financial intermediation.

Actually, Africa represents the second-highest populated part of the globe. Thereby, the mobilization of both natural and economic resources as well as economic diversity is part of the efforts to enhance economic dynamism in the area. The demographic of Africa enables a great need for Islamic financial services and products. The growth momentum of Islamic finance in Africa is synchronized with the growing interest in Islamic finance on a global scale. Islamic financial sector in this region is expected to reach USD 6 trillion in assets in the perspective of 2020 on a global scale. The northern part of Africa covers Egypt, Libya, Tunisia, Algeria, Morocco and Mauritania. Islamic banking in this region has greater developing potential that should drive Islamic finance in Africa. This is due in part to the predominance of the Muslim community, and also to the history of Islamic finance that started in Egypt (Rafay & Farid, 2017). This Arab country has the longest history of modern Islamic bank in the North Africa since 1963, the establishment date of Mit Ghamr Bank, even if this region has an underdeveloped Islamic financial activity compared to the Gulf and Southeast Asia region. The Islamic finance outlooks in North Africa are not restricted to banking sector but also exist in microfinance and *Sukuk*. After Arab countries' spring, development strategies must be amended and focus on the poverty reduction and the promotion of the microfinance. The Islamic finance is being more and more admitted as an alternative financing mode for economic expansion. Overall, Islamic microfinance contributes to satisfying the financing needs of the poorest members of society, while also adapting to the "ethical" aspect of Islamic finance. And actually, the North African country has in fact announced its intention to integrate the *Sukuk* sovereign domain and the governments in Tunisia, Egypt and Morocco are preparing a package of measures to maintain the momentum of development. In general, literature review supports a significant positive association of financial development with economic growth. Kabir, Sanchez and Yu (2011) have concluded that financial development impacts positively on economic expansion in developing state.

In this chapter, the authors examine how Islamic banking can enhance development and prospect in North African countries. First the authors explore the role of Islamic financing industry in ensuring high- quality infrastructure to meet the critical challenges of promoting growth, creating jobs and alleviating poverty, in North Africa, through Islamic project finance. Then, a presentation of the state of Islamic banking services in North African states is developed. Finally, a discussion on the factors that delay Islamic finance growth and the future opportunities for expansion is presented.

## ISLAMIC PROJECT FINANCE IN NORTH AFRICA: A GROWING TREND

The Islamic Development Bank (IDB) represents the principal provider of *Shari'ah* compliant project finance. IDB bank aims to promote economic and social progress of its 57 member countries (MC) and Muslim community in non-Member states in respect to the Islamic legislation. In face to the increasing development needs of its Member Countries (which includes all the countries of North Africa), since inception, total IDB Group *Shari'ah* compliant projects finance attained US$131.3 billion by the end of 2018. The IDB Group's Net Approvals are sourced mainly from IDB Ordinary Capital Resources (IDB-OCR), Islamic Corporation for the Development of the Private Sector (ICD) and International Islamic Trade Finance Corporation (ITFC)[1].

Saudi Arabia is the major financial partner of the IDB with more than a quarter of its paid up capital followed by Libya. Indeed, as Table 1 show, the North African countries represent also important contributors.

Over the recent years, there are a set of conditions participating in the development of Islamic banking and finance, such as (i) consistent high oil prices worldwide, (ii) large consumer request for *Shari'ah*-compliant financial services and products, (iii) regulatory and legal initiatives of the Islamic financial services industry by standard-setting organization (such as IFSB), governments and financial authorities, (iv) diversification and sophistication of Islamic banking instruments and other transitions in the political sphere (Khan & Bhatti, 2008).

*Table 1. The shareholding status of the IDB MC from North Africa*

| Rank | Country | Capital Subscription ($M) | Percentage to Total Capital (%) |
|---|---|---|---|
| 2 | Libya | 4,771.66 | 9.43 |
| 7 | Egypt | 3,579.65 | 7.07 |
| 11 | Algeria | 1,285.59 | 2.54 |
| 16 | Morocco | 256.69 | 0.51 |
| 31 | Tunisia | 36.40 | 0.07 |
| 33 | Mauritania | 35.77 | 0.07 |

Source: IDB annual report, Jeddah 2018

The progress of Islamic finance in North Africa is founded on three main axes: (i) Financial inclusion, (ii) Infrastructure Funding and (iii) SME Funding.

Financial inclusion designed all initiatives that allow providing adequate and qualitative funding services which is available to all segments of the population, especially lower-income and some vulnerable individuals, permitting alleviating poverty and disparities in sharing economic and financial opportunity. In so doing, financial inclusion improves the accessibility of financial services through loans, savings and insurance (Triki & Faye, 2013). On a global scale, 2 billion adults don't have a bank account encompassing 25% in Muslim countries because of religious reasons. The OIC countries where fewer than 10% of adult bank account holders, mainly comprise African members (Shaikh et al. 2017). Financial inclusion via Islamic finance may enhance account ownership and ease financing requirements in these regions. Thus, it is basic to assure that economic growth performance is inclusive and sustained.

Countries such as Tunisia and Egypt have taken significant measures to advance its Islamic finance services while countries such as Libya are currently exploring and developing the system. Among the initiatives to drive Islamic financial services in the country, Morocco also has introduced a law related to Islamic finance products and permit banks to set up units which conform to Islamic law. All these concrete progress of Islamic banking activities in North Africa open wider ways to support financial inclusion in the area.

The second driver of North Africa's Islamic financial services is the infrastructure need, which is becoming increasingly important due to rapid urbanization and special insistence emanating from the political changes of the Arab Spring[2]. Low levels of health and human development, inadequate supplies of roads, restricted availability of safe water and sanitation services and insufficient energy supplies are among the challenges facing the region. Islamic project finance has great importance and is currently extensively utilized to finance, long-term infrastructure and energy generating projects particularly in Middle-East and North Africa (MENA). In developing countries such as North African countries, the majority of Islamic project finance is focused on infrastructure, including energy, transport, water and sanitation and urban services, in addition to agriculture related sectors, human development sectors such as health and education and finance (Microfinance). IDB have launched Islamic infrastructure funds to support infrastructure projects in their member countries (including North African).

Among the top-5 recipients of IDB Group funding there are two countries from North Africa: Egypt (8.7%) and Morocco (5.1%). Project finance is determined on the quality of funding requests and not by the contributions of members. This justifies the merit of Morocco despite its modest contribution to the IDB compared to Libya, Egypt and Algeria (see Table 1), and proves its success in submitting consistent funding request on the basis of robust business models and reasonable cost-and-revenue forecasts.

As the Table 2 shows Energy, others (which comprises "Public Administration" and "Trade related activities") and Finance sectors represented the great part of funding in North Africa countries followed by Transportation sector and Water, Sanitation and Urban Services sector. In terms of IDB Group financing methods, *Istisna* and *Ijara* (Leasing) was often involved for project financing, whereas *Murabahah* is the sole method utilized for commercial funding.

The IDB bank provide support through projects, while concentrating on the need to develop indigenous renewable energy resources and promote energy efficiency enhancement initiatives in generation and distribution in MCs. The IDB Development Effectiveness Review (2017 and 2018) show that the IDB bank has Installed energy generation capacity using renewable sources for only Bangladesh And Turkey. While from the North Africa region Egypt, Mauritania and Tunisia have benefited from the installation of energy generation capacity using non-renewable sources. Table 3 shows that IDB supports MCs in

*Table 2. IDBG approvals by country and sector, in North Africa, from 1976 -2018*

| Sector | Agriculture | Education | Energy | Finance | Health | Industry and Mining | Information and Communications | Real Estate | Transportation | Water, Sanitation & Urban Services | Other Social Services | Others |
|---|---|---|---|---|---|---|---|---|---|---|---|---|
| Number of Projects | | | | | | | | | | | | |
| Algeria | 8 | 1 | 7 | 22 | 3 | 3 | 0 | 0 | 3 | 9 | 7 | 185 |
| Egypt | 7 | 8 | 61 | 50 | 5 | 22 | 3 | 0 | 2 | 8 | 6 | 86 |
| Libya | 2 | 0 | 4 | 6 | 0 | 4 | 1 | 0 | 3 | 1 | 5 | 10 |
| Mauritania | 38 | 21 | 17 | 13 | 7 | 6 | 2 | 5 | 21 | 15 | 7 | 7 |
| Morocco | 18 | 12 | 32 | 21 | 2 | 8 | 2 | 0 | 12 | 20 | 3 | 97 |
| Tunisia | 19 | 10 | 12 | 24 | 4 | 7 | 0 | 0 | 3 | 17 | 3 | 148 |
| US$ Million | | | | | | | | | | | | |
| Algeria | 52.0 | 0.1 | 139.9 | 174.7 | 0.5 | 71.1 | 0.0 | 0.0 | 18.1 | 162.6 | 5.6 | 1,864.9 |
| Egypt | 233.1 | 26.5 | 8,974.8 | 692.20 | 44.0 | 218.5 | 4.6 | 0.0 | 25.6 | 62.1 | 1.7 | 1,364.6 |
| Libya | 22.3 | 0.0 | 104.9 | 20.2 | 0.0 | 114.4 | 22.0 | 0.0 | 58.3 | 0.3 | 5.8 | 299.8 |
| Mauritania | 145.4 | 59.7 | 587.4 | 46.6 | 28.3 | 100.8 | 0.0 | 42.7 | 167.1 | 145.9 | 11.1 | 69.0 |
| Morocco | 241.6 | 14.8 | 3,130.7 | 174.1 | 0.1 | 250.6 | 16.2 | 0.0 | 848.2 | 431.5 | 1.4 | 1,592.4 |
| Tunisia | 184.0 | 92.1 | 1,713.0 | 118.0 | 68.1 | 236.3 | 0.0 | 0.0 | 9.0 | 242.7 | 3.2 | 1,016.7 |
| Total of sector | 878.4 | 193.2 | 14,650.7 | 1,225.8 | 141.0 | 991.7 | 42.8 | | 1,126.3 | 1,045.1 | 28.8 | 6,207.4 |

Source: IDBG operations at a Glance, Q-2 2018, p 2

the North Africa, especially Morocco, through targeted interventions in Education sector for sustained human development. The Bank has also financed projects and grant operations in the agriculture sector in Algeria, Mauritania and Tunisia.

The SME financing is also a main priority of North African countries and IDB. Microfinance is defined as the supply of financial services like savings, deposits, and credit to the poor business persons[3]. Islamic microfinance is the combination of two important sectors: Islamic Finance and Microfinance. It has significant opportunity in North African countries given many Muslims refuse conventional microcredit because of their non-compliance with *Shari'ah* law. In developing countries, many people don't have a bank account and have no guarantees for bank financing. The AMAF (Africa Microfinance Action Forum) report acknowledged that "*the development of Islamic finance products has the potential to bring many unbanked people into the financial sector*"[4].There is unique experience of Islamic microfinance market development in Africa: The Sudanese experience. In 2006, Sudan counted not many institutions providing microfinance services and had a marginal penetration of just 9500 customers. At the end of 2016, Islamic microfinance attained over than 1.5 million customers[5]. The great expansion of the Islamic microfinance industry highlights the government's push to provide financial services to the micro, small, and medium enterprise development sector, through an operating Central Bank that focused on microfinance via a specialized division. The Central Bank of Sudan preceded its efforts in

*Table 3. Results of projects approved by IDB, in North Africa*

| | Core Sector Indicators (CSI) | CSI Name | Results Achieved in 2018 |
|---|---|---|---|
| Tunisia | Employment Generated | People employed (number) | 5,570 |
| | Energy | Installed energy generation capacity using non-renewable sources (MW equivalent) | 400 |
| Mauritania | Agriculture | Area irrigated (hectares) | 124 |
| | | Crop production increased (tons) | 959 |
| | | Crop yield increased (tons/hectare) | 4 |
| | | Livestock (Dairy) production increased (tons) | 1,873 |
| | | Livestock (Meat) production increased (tons) | 31 |
| | | Market centers established, upgraded or rehabilitated (numbers) | 3 |
| | Energy | Installed energy generation capacity using non-renewable sources (MW equivalent) | 60 |
| | Transportation | Expressways and National or Regional highways built, upgraded or rehabilitated (km) | 63 |
| Morocco | Education | Students benefitted (number) | 2,284.174 |
| | | Teachers/Faculty/Staff trained (number) | 12,000 |

Source: Development Effectiveness Report, IDB, 2018

implementing its policies which required that each banks allocate 12% of their portfolio to microfinance through two forms: (i) the direct finance from the banks to the individuals and groups, or (ii) through wholesale funding from the banks to the licensed microfinance institutions[6].

In recent years, the microfinance has experienced high growth in Africa (such as Sudan, Kenya and Ghana) and is becoming an important factor in the expansion of the economies. Agriculture is one of several fields that can be supported by microfinance. African agriculture offers huge investment potential for Islamic financial institutions. Development Effectiveness Report of the IDB bank reveals that expected results from the programs will allow more than a million people to have access to Islamic microfinance, in 2018, as part of the financing of agriculture projects. There are many experiences in Africa that North African countries can take advantage of it. The Sudan experience, cited above, which has emerged as an example of a laboratory for Islamic microfinance transmission new developments may provide insights on successful practices in the field of Islamic microfinance. In fact, setting up similar systems permit the reduction of poverty overcomes financial deprivation and promotes job generation by developing small businesses. A limited number of banks located in North African states have adopted specific *Shari'ah* compliant financing techniques to finance SMEs. There is one Islamic microfinance institution (Zitouna Tamkeen), in Tunisia. The shareholders of this microfinance company are Zitouna Bank, Zitouna Takaful, IDB, World Bank International Finance Corporation, and Tunisian Post[7]. The company provides microfinance services and enables the financial inclusion of both new graduates and disadvantaged people. In Morocco and in Algeria, the majority of Islamic banks and windows incorporated the financing of SMEs into their policies.

## ISLAMIC BANKING SERVICES IN THE NORTH AFRICA CONTEXT

Islam is a dominant religion on North Africa. The impact in terms of the request for Islamic financial products and services will be considerable. There are two types of Islamic banking: a full-fledged Islamic bank or "Islamic finance window" in a traditional bank. The products and services of full-fledged Islamic bank are totally conformed to *Shari'ah*. Islamic banking exists in both forms in North Africa.

The Bahrain-based Al Baraka Banking Group (ABG) is regarded as one of the world's pioneers in the Islam banking industry at the global level and particularly in North Africa (in Algeria, Egypt, Libya and Tunisia). The Group offers its Islamic banking services to almost 1 billion customers in the markets where it functions. It has a large geographic spread that is represented in affiliate banks in three continents in fifteen countries with a network of more than 700 branches.

### Islamic Banking in Egypt

Egypt has 40 banks operators, three of which are fully-fledged Islamic banks and twelve traditional banks operating Islamic windows. By 2017, the assets of Islamic banks had reached 226 billion Egyptian pounds, about 12.8 billion dollars, with an increase of 10.24 percent versus the previous year, as reported by the Egyptian Islamic Finance Association (EIFA). Although Islamic banking makes up 6%[9] of Egypt's overall banking sector and only 1% [10]of global Islamic Banking Assets (in 2016), Egypt is the sixth-largest Muslim nation with more than 95 million residents, which is expected to offer great opportunities for Islamic banks to reach new clients.

Several factors negatively impact the development of the Egyptian Islamic financial sector, including the issue of taxation and the absence of specific regulations governing this sector. Islamic finance is based on real economic operations for example leasing (*Ijara*), sale or purchase (*Murabahah*), all of which are subject to an additional capital gains tax. Despite this, the Egyptian government has not attempted to restrict the constraints on the execution of Islamic financial operations. Currently, there is no explicit regulatory framework for Islamic banking industry, which has restricted the evolution of the sector.

*Table 4. Overview of Islamic finance in North Africa*

| *Country* | *Total Population (million)* | *% Muslim* | *Islamic Banks* | *Banks with Islamic Windows* | *Law Governing Islamic Finance* |
|---|---|---|---|---|---|
| Algeria | 42.55 | 99.75 | 2 | 0 | Yes |
| Egypt | 97.75 | 94.9 | 3 | 11 | Yes |
| Libya | 6.48 | 97 | 0 | 0 | No |
| Mauritania | 4.42[8] | 100 | 5 | 0 | No |
| Morocco | 34.82 | 99.5 | 5 | 3 | Yes |
| Tunisia | 11.45 | 99 | 3 | 0 | Yes |
| Total | 197.27 | | 18 | 14 | |

Source: the authors' calculation from annual reports of Central Bank of each country and Bankscope

Islamic finance has existed in Egypt since decades, but the Egyptian Central Bank (CBE) has not been able to regulate this sector. The first disposal for Islamic finance was passed in 1977 (law N°48), which allowed the constitution of Islamic banks and its regulation by the CBE. Thereby, the Faisal Islamic Bank of Egypt (FIBE) awarded a license from the CBE in 1979, and then Al Baraka Bank of Egypt the latter having obtained its license in 1980.

The regulation was, however, silent on some *Shari'ah* compliance aspects; permitting Islamic banks to incorporate dispositions in their statutes, such as article 3 of the FIBE's statutes concerning the ban of *Riba* and the requirement to pay *zakat*.

The Islamic banking law was amended in 2003, but it did not contain any provisions that could lead growth in Islamic finance. Some of the statutes are unhelpful, especially requirement for Islamic banks to maintain minimum liquidity ratios and adherence to deposit protection clauses similar to their pair conventional. The legitimizing of Islamic political movements in Egypt (the falling of Mubarak and the presidential election of Morsi) could be considered as high expectations from the prospect of Islamic finance. Unfortunately, after removal of Morsi from office by his defense minister, progress of Islamic finance in the country has been slow and disappointing. For the above reasons and others, at present, Egypt has just 3 full-fledged Islamic banks; FIBE, Al Baraka Bank-Egypt, and Abu Dhabi Islamic Bank, as well as 11 banks with Islamic windows.

- **Faisal Islamic Bank of Egypt:** Was established in 1979 as the first Islamic trading bank in Egypt. It offers banking and investment services in accordance with *Shari'ah* principles via its head office and 36 branches in Egypt[11]. Its assets are around EGP 82.57 billion at the end of 2017.

The Faisal Bank provides several types of *Shari'ah*-compliant saving pools in both local and foreign currencies that convenient all the clients and offer attractive benefits and returns. However, numerous Egyptian expatriates in the Gulf or Europe choose to retain portfolios in stronger currencies to prevent depreciation of the Egyptian pound. Total saving accounts and certificates (managed funds) represent 86.1% of total liabilities and shareholders' equity. These balances reached EGP 71 billion by the end of 2017, increasing by EGP 7 billion at the 10.9% rate. Besides the Faisal Bank has proceeded as an investment company and in part invests its resources in the creation of companies, in many sectors (see table 5), by contributing to their capital with other skilled and experienced partners. These businesses have participated to advance national development, afforded several employment opportunities and helped to satisfy a great part of exports and local market requirements.

The assessment of the Bank's performance in 2017 show that the efforts of the FIBE and the financial policies adopted led to achieve total revenues amounted to EGP 6836.7 million.

Revenues generated from *Musharakah*, *Murabahah*, *Mudarabah*, commercial transactions, real estate investments and others reaches EGP 6519.8 million, that is 95% of total incomes. These revenues have sustained the Bank's capacity to generate benefits to the saving pools' clients on an average annual rate of 6.95%, 11.95% per year for investment accounts in local currency and 1.17% for investment accounts in foreign currency. In addition, a part of these is revenues reserved for saving certificated, *Zakat*, income tax and others obligations.

Overall, the favorable macro environment and expediting GDP growth (4.2 percent in 2017) will support an expansion in Islamic banks' business volumes in Egypt.

*Table 5. Sectorial distribution of the Faisal Islamic Bank companies*

| Sector | Number of Companies | Equity Share (EGP Thousand) |
|---|---|---|
| Agriculture and Animal production | 2 | 19885 |
| Industry | 18 | 464402 |
| Local and Foreign Trade | 2 | 18422 |
| Pharmaceuticals and Health Care | 4 | 42100 |
| Investments | 2 | 47833 |
| Housing and Real estate Investments | 6 | 224671 |
| Information Technology | 3 | 17512 |
| Banks and Financial Institutions | 14 | 1350428 |
| Others | 5 | 31356 |
| Total | 55 | 2216609 |

Source: Faisal Islamic Bank Egypt, Annual Report, 2017.

- **Al Baraka Bank Egypt:** Is the tributary of the Bahrain-based Al Baraka Banking Group that run 32 branches. It offers both corporate and retail banking and investment activities in accordance with the principles of Islamic law.

The total Balance Sheet amounted to EGP 50.3 billion representing an increase of 18% compared to the preceding year. In spite of the difficulties it faces, Al Baraka Egypt has run to draw customer deposits of nearly EGP 44.2 billion, up 17% from the year before, as Table 6 shows. Whereas, the inter-bank transactions (with local and foreign banks) are declined compared to last year.

The successful strategy of this bank and the extensive branch network can justify the increase of the total revenues (of which Return on *Murabahah, Mudarabah, Musharakah* represented almost 60%) as by the end of 2017 totaling 5428.3 million EGP, at an approximate 51% increase rate. Al Baraka Bank realized a net profit over the year 2017 of 725.2 million EGP, with an expansion of 42%. This allowed Bank to recommend dividends to its shareholders at a 20% rate for 2017.

*Table 6. Al Baraka Egypt financial statement, 31/12/2017*

| Item | EGP Million | Annual Growth Rates (%) |
|---|---|---|
| Total assets | 50300 | 18 |
| *Murabahah* Transactions, Investment Operations and Financial Investments | 43900 | 17 |
| Total liabilities | 47 646 | 17 |
| Customers deposits | 44 169 | 17 |
| Due to banks | 606 | -34 |
| Net profit | 725.2 | 42 |

Source: Al Baraka Bank, Annual report, 2017.

- **The Abu Dhabi Islamic Bank Egypt (ADIB):** In 2010 the Abu Dhabi Islamic Bank, the Emirates' 2nd largest Islamic bank, bought 51% of the National Development Bank's capital as part of the Egyptian government's privatization process. Thus, the ADIB Egypt represents formerly the National Bank for Development. It offers different *Shari'ah*-compliant banking instruments that respond to the demands of corporate (including SMEs) and retail clients. It is well represented in Egypt with a network of 70 branches throughout the country, much larger than Al Baraka and FIBE Bank. The Bank succeeded in developing a platform to provide retail, SME and corporate customers with both short and long-term financing solutions. ADIB bank offers the best-in-class wholesale banking services represent the principal objective of ADIB Egypt's strategy. During 2017, ADIB's corporate realization reveal the total wholesale assets achieving EGP 11.5 billion, with a 1.6% fall from 2016's. However, wholesale customer deposits rose 7.6% to attain EGP 8.1 billion. In 2017, the Retail Banking division experienced a successful performance with remarkable growth in consumer deposits and assets, remaining competitive in a dynamic banking sector (see Table 7).

ADIB bank Egypt profits increased from EGP 361 million to EGP 435 million in 2017, representing a 21% rise in profits. The bank's balance sheet expanded as well, in which the total financing augmented by 7% to achieves EGP 16.8 billion while total deposits grew 17% to EGP 29.9 billion as at the end of 2017. These results presented above testify the selection of the ADIB for The North Africa awards. Indeed, Banker Africa awarded ADIB Egypt the title *"Best Islamic Bank in North Africa", "Best Islamic SME Bank in North Africa", and "Best Islamic Retail Bank in North Africa",* in 2018.

## Islamic Banking in Libya

Despite the expansion of the Islamic banking system around the world, the financial sector in Libya remains underdeveloped. In Libya the Islamic banking sector is not yet in place, even though there are important steps to develop the Islamic financial industry, including among which:

- In 2009, before the recent crisis, the central bank of Libya (CBL) issued Islamic banking law number 9 (in 2009), authorizing commercial bank to establish Islamic windows or fully-fledged Islamic branches. The CBL has adopted the Islamic regulation based on the purpose of AAOIFI and the IFSB standards to manage Islamic banking sector.
- In 2011, Gumhouria Bank (the Libya's second largest bank) had introduced Islamic banking widows in their network of 150 subsidiaries and 1 fully fledged Islamic subsidiary.

*Table 7. ADIB bank Egypt, business activity, 2017*

| Activity Nature | Assets | | Deposit | |
|---|---|---|---|---|
| | (EGP Billion) | Annual Growth Rates (%) | (EGP Billion) | Annual Growth Rates (%) |
| Wholesale (including SMEs) | 11.5 | -1.6 | 8.1 | 31 |
| Retail | 5.1 | 7.6 | 21.7 | 22 |

Source: ADIB Bank, Annual report, 2017

- In 2013, the General National Congress adopted a law introducing Islamic banking system. As a result, businesses and governmental entities will be banned from both paying and receiving interest starting in 2015. However, this law has been very criticized because a short-term of 2 years to remove total banking sector on fully *Shari'ah*-compliant may caused problems and confusion.
- On the occasion of the 43rd annual meeting of the Islamic Bank, held in Tunis from 1 to 5 April 2018, Libya is again called the Islamic Development Bank to open a local representative office. This request is important for the mobilization of resources for reconstruction and investment by the country.

In Libya, Islamic finance has not expanded until recently despite the efforts of the government and the monetary resources of banking sector in the country.

A Libyan market study carried out in 2018 concluded that Libyan clients are ignorant of Islamic banking and are incapable to decide on choosing Islamic banking services. The study revealed also that both subjective norm and perceived behavioral control affect positively the desire to select Islamic banking. And this implies that Islamic banks should promote an appropriate marketing policy focused on *Shari'ah* services and products (Al Bashir et al. 2018).

There is little data on Islamic financial sector and there are no Islamic banks in Libya which made it impossible the analysis of the Islamic banking market in the country.

Although the context of uncertainty in the management of economic and financial policy following the recent civil war, it seems likely that the system will become more liberal which should favor the inclusion and expansion of Islamic banking in Libya.

## Islamic Banking in Tunisia

Since the Arab Spring, the new political climate of liberty has affected the development of Islamic finance in Tunisia and the government has attached a high priority to the promotion of this industry. The demand for Islamic finance is substantial in Tunisia and a significant part of the Tunisian financial sector tends to adopt products and services that are in conformity with *Shari'ah* law. Ltifi et al. (2016) suggest that clients take into account different considerations when selecting an Islamic bank: the service quality provided by financial entities, confidence and (in particular) respect for the *Shari'ah* law. Their results also show that clients who are better informed about *Shari'ah*-compliant products and services are more likely to frequent Islamic banks. In the same line of research, Echchabi, Azouzi and Abd Aziz (2016) revealed that subjective opinion and norm favorably impacted the decision of Tunisian customers to choose Islamic banking services. In addition, the results have shown that the Tunisian clients are very interested in switching to Islamic financial services.

Table 8 shows, that Tunisian Islamic banking asset represent 5.1% of Tunisian banking assets. Islamic banks in Tunisia provide financing services through a network of 161 branches. And this industry account about 5.6% of total deposits and 4.2% of total loans in the banking sector. The Islamic banking activity has significant growth potential that remains to be explored by Islamic banks or conventional banks through the opening of Islamic windows.

Central bank of Tunisia has emitted new circular on capital adequacy standards including prudential standards specific to Islamic banks[12] as well as the 2016-48 bank legislation which strengthened the Islamic banking system and permitted traditional banks to set up windows providing Islamic financial services.

*Table 8. Indicators of Islamic banks at the end of 2017*

| | 2017 | Share in the Total Sector |
|---|---|---|
| Total assets (MD) | 5709 | 5.1% |
| Staff | 1633 | 7.8% |
| Network | 161 | 8.7% |
| Total Deposits | 3503 | 5.6% |
| Total Credits | 3056 | 4.2% |

Source: Annual report, central Bank Tunisia, 2017

To date, on the Tunisian market, three Islamic banks are operating: Al Baraka bank, Zitouna bank and WIB (Wifak International Bank) known as leasing institution and transformed into a resident bank in 2015. In addition to the banks, there are also a representative office of the UAE's Noor Bank and, recently, an Islamic microfinance institution that are established in Tunisia.

- **Al Baraka Bank Tunisia:** Founded in 1983 and represent the oldest Islamic bank in Tunisia. It is known before 2009 as "BEIT ETTAMWIL TOUNSI SAOUDI – BEST BANK ». In 2013, Al Baraka Bank Tunisia was authorized to transform an Offshore Bank into a Universal Resident Bank. The registered capital of Al Baraka Bank Tunisia is 120 Million Tunisian Dinar. ABG is the main shareholder holding 78.4% of total capital and State Tunisian holds only 10% of total capital. The network has reached a number of thirty-three agencies and four foreign exchange boxes as of December 31, 2016.

As shown in Table 9, Al Baraka bank Tunisia has succeeded in attracting customer deposits exceeding 1000 million dinars. Important interbank transactions are in progress, including those with other banks in the ABG. Client receivables, which 53% is from *Murabahah* operation, are still increasing. The assessment of the Bank performance during 2016 show that the financial policies adopted driven to reach net profit amounted to of 3.2 Million Dinars compared to 8.5 Million Dinars at the end of 2015. This is mainly due to the increase in staff costs under the effect of recruitment and changes in overheads and

*Table 9. Al Baraka bank Tunisia, indicators 2016 (in millions of Dinars)*

| Indicators / Year | 2016 | 2015 |
|---|---|---|
| Customer deposits | 1 032 | 997 |
| Deposits from banks | 236 | 190 |
| Client receivables | 668 | 659 |
| Trading securities | 360 | 345 |
| Total Assets | 1 587 | 1 514 |
| Net profit | 3.2 | 8.5 |
| ROE (%) | 2 | 5,22 |
| ROA(%) | 0.2 | 0,56 |

Source: Annual report, Al Baraka Bank Tunisia, 2016

it will negatively influence the bank's financial performance. The return on Equity (ROE) decreased slightly from 5.22% in 2015 to 2% in 2016. And the return on assets (ROA) fell modestly from 0.56% in 2015 to 0.2% in 2016. This is suggested that the bank's ability to make a profit from their total assets diminished, despite the increase of total assets in 2016, and may transmit a bad signal.

- **Zitouna Bank**: Is the first Islamic bank created by the Tunisian government in 2010. The bank started with nine branches ant actually it runs 114 branches.

Social Capital, at the end of 2016, is distributed as follows: 69.15% held by the Tunisian government (direct and indirect) and 30.84% owned by private and foreign shareholders.

The assessment of the bank's financial position as at 31 December 2017 shows an increase in Customer deposits, Client receivables and Deposits from banks. Zitouna Bank posted in 2017 a net profit of about 20 MD against 12.6 MD in 2016, an increase of 58 percent. And it achieved a successful performance with remarkable growth in ROE and ROA as Table 10 shows.

In line with other Islamic banks, the bank financing practices cover *Murabahah*, *Ijara*, *Musharakah*, *Mudarabah* and *Istisna*. The product financing structure shows that: The share of *Murabahah* and Ijara financing fell slightly, respectively, from 80.9% in 2016 to 80.7% in 2017 and from 15.6% in 2016 to 15.1% in 2017, in favor of other financing elements that increased from 3.5% in 2016 to 4.2% in 2017.

During 2017, Zitouna Bank adopted an ambitious communication plan that is more adapted to new behavioral habits, presenting a proximity communication and a better digital presence. In fact, digitalization is actually an essential leverage of performance; the bank has developed a new High-TECH Agency Concept equipped with the best computer and communication technologies.

- **Al Wifak Bank:** It is "El Wifak Leasing" before 2015 with an initial capital of 5MD, the main purpose of which was to carry out leasing operations on movable and immovable property for professional use. As part of its growth policy, "El Wifak Leasing" was converted in 2015 into a universal Islamic bank, "Wifak International Bank" thus enriching the banking landscape to meet the growing needs of large companies, SME, VSE (very small enterprise) and individuals. Actually, the capital of bank counts 150 MD and it is held at 70% by Tunisian shareholders and the rest by foreign shareholders.

*Table 10. Zitouna Bank Tunisia, indicators at 31/12/2017 (in millions of Dinars)*

| *Indicators / Year* | *2017* | *2016* | *2015* |
|---|---|---|---|
| Customer deposits | 2357 | 1948 | 1532 |
| Deposits from banks | 80 | 57 | 29.5 |
| Client receivables | 2094 | 1707 | 1253 |
| Trading securities | 10 | 10 | 10 |
| Total Assets | 2824 | 2283 | 1799 |
| Net profit | 20 | 12.6 | 9.5 |
| ROE (%) | 12.91 | 10.3 | 8.94 |
| ROA (%) | 0.78 | 0.62 | 0.61 |

Source: Annual report, Zitouna Bank, 2016

In 2016, the bank has chosen to rely on a global banking specialized in Islamic finance, IMAL Path Solutions, making WIFAK BANK the only Tunisian bank adopting this system. *iMAL* is an innovative Islamic banking software package, developed according to AAOIFI standards destined to an innovative Islamic financial institution, traditional banks with Islamic windows and microfinance institutions.

During 2017, Wifak bank began with 9 agencies and predicts a favorable expansion in the future. Despite a difficult economic situation, the Bank succeeded during 2018 in mobilizing a customer deposit around 285 million dinars against 105 million dinars at the end of 2017, an evolution of 172%. On the other hand, Wifak Bank contributed to the financing of the economy for a total of customer financing at the end of 2018 of 402.424 million dinars, an evolution of 60% compared to 2017.

The financial statements closed in 2018 show a net deficit of 3.3 million dinars against a loss of 1.7 million dinars a year earlier. This underperformance is the result of the Bank's investment effort in terms of opening up branches and recruiting staff.

The political climate of liberty that followed the Tunisian revolution is expected to have a positive impact on the long-term expansion of the Islamic financial sector in Tunisia. According to a number of financial experts in Islamic Finance field, the Islamic banks target to retain, by 2022, 15% of bank assets, against 6.5% in 2016, which will support the Tunisian economy and attract more foreign capital.

## Islamic Banking in Algeria

Algeria is another North African country with the highest population (see Table 4) in the region. The market shares of Islamic finance in Algeria exceed saintly 0%. A challenge for the emerging Algerian economy for which the mobilization of savings would represent a significant contribution to its development. Islamic finance could provide, in this context, a response to the part of the population that does not invest for religious considerations.

Islamic finance, still in its infancy in Algeria, was waiting for a legal framework to take off.

The Bank of Algeria has just defined, through a regulation published in the Official Journal (published on December 9, 2018), the conditions of exercise of banking operations in the area of participative finance by banks and financial entities and paves the way for Islamic finance.

"For the purposes of this Regulation are considered banking operations within the participatory finance (...) operations of receipt of funds, investment, finance and investment, which does not result in the receiving or payment of 'interests', explained the Bank of Algeria. These operations include *Murabahah, Musharakah, Mudarabah, Ijara, Istisna, Salam,* as well as deposits in investment accounts, which are part of Islamic finance.

In Algeria, the three Public Banks *"Caisse nationale d'épargne et de prévoyance-Banque"* CNEP, *"Banque De Developpement Local"* (BDL) and *"Banque de l'agriculture et du développement rural"* (BADR) have launched their Islamic Product. At the present time, two Islamic banks are active in Algeria:

- **Al Baraka Bank Algeria:** First mixed-capital institution: public (BADR Algeria, 44%) and private (ABG Bahrain, 56%). Al Baraka Bank of Algeria is created on May 20, 1991, with a capital of 500.000.000 DA. The bank has fifteen branches in Algeria.

  § **Al Salam Bank:** Is certified by the Bank of Algeria in September 2008. The Bank is characterized by its commitment to respect the principles of *Shari'ah* in all its transactions. It has a network of 15 designated Islamic branches throughout Algeria. And in the year 2018, Al Salam Bank-Algeria establishes seven new branches.

*Table 11. Al Baraka Algeria and Al Salam Bank Algeria, Indicators 2017 (in billions of DA)*

| Indicators / Year | Al Salam Bank | | Al Baraka Bank | |
|---|---|---|---|---|
| | 2017 | 2016 | 2017 | 2016 |
| Customer deposits | 64 | 34 | 164.8 | 133.5 |
| Deposits from banks | 0.015 | - | 0.05 | 0.014 |
| Client receivables | 45.4 | 29.3 | 136.5 | 107.5 |
| Trading securities | 12 | 10 | 0 | 0 |
| Total Assets | 85.7 | 53.1 | 248.6 | 210.3 |
| Net profit | 1.18 | 1.08 | 3.5 | 3.9 |
| ROE (%) | 7.3 | 7.2 | 16.6 | 17.7 |
| ROA (%) | 1.37 | 2.03 | 1.4 | 1.85 |

Source: Annual report, Al Baraka Bank Algeria and Al Salam Bank Algeria, 2017

Table 11 shows that the net profit, in 2017, for the two Islamic banks has increased compared to 2016, allowing the growth of banking activities and the increase of their performance.

Thus, the total financial situation of these banks recorded a positive growth in 2017.

Such improvements will be maintained over the next few years, enabling these banks to achieve substantial expansion, reflecting the aspirations of shareholders and other partners overall. The number of clients reflects this expansion, which attained 384.436 clients for al Baraka bank. However, this must be seen in the context of the Algerian community, which exceeds 42 million people.

## Islamic Banking in Morocco

Morocco has almost entirely Muslim (see Table 4). Islamic finance in Morocco is set to take basis. There are attempts, before 2014, to integrate Islamic financial instruments, or so-called alternative financial products in the country, within conventional financial institutions (windows) and no full-fledged Islamic banks would be given licenses. However, this has not made significant impact.

The Kingdom of Morocco took its last steps in introducing participative banking after approving the creation of five participative banks in 2017 by Bank Al-Maghrib. This is in response to the publication in 2015 of a bill regulating participatory financial products in the country. On the Maghreb scale, Morocco has been named as a gateway for Participatory Finance to Africa and Europe.

Indeed, In January 2017, eight banks were licensed to offer Islamic finance products on either a window (three) or affiliate (five) basis. Attijariwafa Bank, BMCE of Africa and *Banque Centrale Populaire* (BCP) obtain licenses and partnered with international entities to settle in Morocco: Attijariwafa collaborates with the IDB which will hold a 10 to 20% shareholding; BMCE is joining forces with Bahrain's Al Baraka Group and BCP is in partnership with Saudi's Guidance Financial.

## Islamic Banking in Mauritania

Mauritania has an entirely Muslim population (see Table 4), disappointingly, up to now, Islamic finance remains underdeveloped in this country. About 90% of the population in Mauritania is considered as unbanked. In the country, the banking sector regroups at least five fully-fledged Islamic banks. The

*"Banque Mauritanienne pour le Commerce International"* (BMCI) represent the oldest Islamic bank in Mauritania. For years, the bank has sought to satisfy its customers, whilst respecting the Islamic *Shari'ah* principles. Actually, retail banking is among BMCI's most developed business divisions. There is little data on Islamic financial sector in Mauritania which hinders the analysis of financial performance of Islamic banks in the country. Four other Islamic banks in the country are presented as follows:

- Among the recent Islamic banks is the *"Banque Mouamalat Assahiha"* (BMS SA), which is a universal and investment bank introduced in Mauritania in 2012. The shareholding of the BMS consists exclusively of Mauritanian businessmen. It operates exclusively in accordance with Islamic *Shari'ah* principles of financial transactions with a network of 16 branches. The analysis of financial data shows a modest change in the total assets, customer deposits and Total Financing and Investments between 2015 and 2016. However, the bank recorded a net loss in 2016 and a return on ROE capital zero.
- The *"Banque Islamique de Mauritani"* (BIM) was created, in 2011, by the "Tamweel Africa" Holding, itself a "joint venture" between two important institutions in the domain of Islamic Finance: the Islamic Society of Private Sector Development (*Société Islamique de Développement du Secteur Privée*, "SID ", Subsidiary of the IDB) and the" Asya Bank "the largest Islamic Bank in Turkey. The bank has a network of 4 designated Islamic branches.
- The "Banque Al Wava Mauritanienne Islamique (BAMIS)" is founded in 1985 and is known as Al Baraka Mauritanian Islamic Bank, with an initial capital of 500 Million Ouguiya owned by al Baraka group (50%), by central bank (10%) and by the Mauritanian businessman (40%). Between 1992 and 2016, several capital restructurings and share transfers between shareholders took place and resulted in a capital of 9000 MRO detained only by Mauritanian companies and businessman.
- The *"Banque Populaire de Mauritanie"* (BPM) is also Islamic bank owned by Groupe Mauritanie Leasing in 1998.

## DILEMMAS AND CHALLENGES OF ISLAMIC BANKING

After more than four decades of Islamic banking and finance experience, the sector does not escape criticisms because of its weaknesses. As highlighted above, stimulating the expansion of Islamic finance in the North African area requires the identification and resolution of obstacles retarding the progress of this industry.

Kaabachi and Obeid (2016) found that, in Tunisia, *"Islamic bank reputation, relative advantage of Islamic banking and its compatibility with consumer religious beliefs, values, lifestyle and banking habits"* all had a positive impact on the intention to adopt Islamic banking services. However, it appears that perceptions of sophistication and risk have a negative influence on the client decision to choose this alternative financing system. The main conclusion of this research is that in Tunisia there is a general absence of consumer awareness of Islamic banking. As a result, the lack of Islamic financial comprehension could hinder the growth of the Islamic banking sector in Tunisia. Some analysts affirm that Islamic finance has deviated from its values and principles; others regard the industry as an imitator of conventional finance. So, the next stage of development in Islamic finance will involve creating *Shari'ah*-based products that have no conventional equivalent.

Until recently, efforts to promote Islamic finance in some country were motivated by prudent political determination, with some believing that Islamic banks in the country were linked to Islamic political parties. In other words, the governments of North Africa have not been great defenders and promoters of Islamic finance, unlike some countries in the Gulf and Asia. This is the case of Egypt, for example, in 2005, religious dignitaries (from *al Azhar*) issued fatwa claiming that the interest is not *Riba*, but it would be considered illegal only if it became excessive. Then, it was rejected because of its political basis.

In addition, the financing costs charged by Islamic banks are generally greater than those of traditional ones, giving the impression that Islamic finance is expensive. These costs certainly include *Shari'ah*-compliance costs, legal fees for product structuring and regulatory costs, which are also higher because if Islamic banks were required to possess conventional treasury bills as part of the central bank's liquidity needs, they had to either renounce or accept interest revenues.

North African authorities and practitioners have become increasingly concerned with Islamic banking and finance. They are convinced by the advantages of Islamic financial intermediation, particularly in terms of the attraction of foreign direct investment.

More importantly, North African countries should prioritize the analysis of constraints to profitability. First, they have to deal with widely inadequate infrastructure for roads, telecommunications and electricity.

The deficit of skilled personnel is another factor that hinders the development of microfinance in this region. In addition to a lack of qualified managers, there are not enough technicians with computer skills, accounting and marketing skills (Al Bashir & Al Amine, 2016).

Improving the use of information and communication technology, can encourage unbanked invidious to manipulate several financial transactions remotely (by mobile banking) which help in developing financial inclusion in North Africa countries.

Innovative Islamic microfinance instruments may lead to advances in SMEs which provides job and benefits the underprivileged.

With the first phase of regulatory changes after the subprime crisis nearing completion (such as in Morocco, Algeria and Tunisia), additional efforts have been launched due to persistent market-related challenges, such as low growth and the lack of equity-based financing and microfinance. Islamic banking sector can allocate its excess liquidity to promote equity-based financing for the benefit of low revenues micro-enterprises (such as Labor-intensive businesses in textile, furniture making, etc.).

The Basel regulations should not be applied systematically but should be adapted to the specificities of Islamic banks. This is the mission of Islamic financial regulators, such as the IFSB. The compliance of Islamic banks with international standards and guidelines, while respecting the principles of Islamic *Shari'ah* law, is the most important challenge. And this is not an easy task, as Islamic banks face different types of risks.

These challenges will continue to influence North African countries' performance despite the recent banking regulation enhancement and the development of Islamic finance in the region.

## CONCLUSION

The development and prospects of Islamic financial institutions in North Africa are linked to the paths they will take in the face of a rapidly changing financial world. Globalization and information technology revolution, contribute to amplifying the list of challenges facing Islamic institutions in this region. They will therefore have to acquire technical management skills to cope with this new environment.

In addition, regulation and supervision of the banking industry is essential to improve the information available to investors and entrepreneurs (Transparency), to guarantee the stability of the financial sector and strengthen the supervision of financial institutions. For Islamic banks, there is an additional dimension for supervision, which corresponds to the supervision of their activities under *Shari'ah* law. Global economic crisis (in Europe, the United States, etc.) seems to be related to financial crises provoked by financial products using interest-rate subsidies and banned by the *Shari'ah*. The principle of PLS and the matching of a financial transaction to real assets are specific features of the Islamic financial system that could introduce more balance into the financial system. The implementation of an honest theory of Islamic finance is potentially capable of avoiding such a crisis since several factors that caused or participated in the creation and spread of the crisis are prohibited under the principles and guidelines of Islamic *Shari'ah* law. Islamic financial products cannot directly repair the international financial system. However, as a first step, Islamic finance must be positioned as an alternative system for traditional finance.

## Classifications

JEL Classification: G21, G24, N27
KAUJIE Classification: I1, J31, J41

## REFERENCES

Abdulsaleh, A. M. (2017). The introduction of Islamic finance in Libya: Capturing the opportunities for SMEs development. *Journal of Emerging Economies and Islamic Research*, *5*(1), 39–48.

African Development Bank. (2018). North Africa Economic Outlook. Retrieved from https://www.afdb.org/fileadmin/uploads/afdb/Documents/Publications/2018AEO/African-Economic-Outlook-2018-North-Africa.pdf

Al Bashir, M., & Al Amine, M. (2016). Islamic Finance in Africa: Current Penetration. *Palgrave Studies*. In *Islamic Banking, Finance, And Economics*. Islamic Finance And Africa's Economic.

Al Bashir, M., & Al Amine, M. (2016). Islamic Finance in Africa: Current Penetration. In *Islamic Finance and Africa's Economic Resurgence: Promoting Diverse and Localized Investment (PP 53-120)*. Palgrave Macmillan.

Al Bashir, W.A., & Zainuddin, Y., & Panigrahi Albashir, S. K. (2018). The Acceptance of Islamic Banking Products in Libya: A Theory of Planned Behavior Approach. *International Journal of Economics and Financial Issues*, *8*(3), 105–111.

Ayachi, R. A., Saidane, D., & Mansouri, F. (2017). Potential of Islamic finance: A survey of Tunisian Northwest companies. *Journal of Emerging Economies & Islamic Research*, *5*(2), 28–42.

Ayadi, R., De Groen, W. P., & Author. (2018). Financial Development and Inclusion in Egypt, Jordan, Morocco And Tunisia. *EMNES Studies, 4*. Retrieved from http://www.euromed-economists.org/wp-content/uploads/2018/05/EMNES_Study_004-Financial_Development_Inclusion-Egypt_Jordan_Morocco_Tunisia-v2.pdf)

Bransdma, J., & Hart, L. (2004). *Making Microfinance Work better in the Middle East and North Africa (English). (Working Paper NO 29657)*. Washington, DC: World Bank; Retrieved from http://documents.worldbank.org/curated/en/889971468774294069/pdf/296570ENGLISH0Microfinance0in0MNA.pdf

Chapra, U. (2007). The Case Against *Riba*: Is It Compelling? *Thunderbird International Business Review, 49*(2), 161–186. doi:10.1002/tie.20138

Echchabi, A., Azouzi, D., & Abd. Aziz, H. (2016). The future prospects of Islamic banking in Tunisia: An empirical survey. *EuroMed Journal of Business, 11*(1), 119–131. doi:10.1108/EMJB-03-2015-0018

GAIT, A.H. (2009). The Impact of Demographic Variables on Libyan Retail Consumers' Attitudes towards Islamic Methods of Finance. *Islamic Economic Studies, 17*(1), 1–18.

Gherbi, E. H. (2018). Factors of Influence in The Establishment of Islamic Banking and Finance in Algeria. *Academy of Accounting and Financial Studies Journal, 22*(1), 1–7.

Global Islamic Finance Report. (2016). Islamic Financial Policy. Islamic Project Finance: A Growing Trend International Bank for Reconstruction and Development / The World Bank (2017). Mobilizing Islamic Finance for Infrastructure Public-Private Partnerships, Report 2017.

Iqbal, Z., & Mirakhor, A. (2011) An Introduction to Islamic Finance: Theory and Practice, 2nd ed. Singapore: John Wiley & Sons (Asia). doi:10.1002/9781118390474

Islamic Development Bank (IDB). (2017). Development Effectiveness Report 2017. Retrieved from http://idbsharedtech1.prod.acquia-sites.com/sites/default/files/2018-10/IsDB%20Develepment%20Effectiveness%20Review%202017.pdf

Islamic Development Bank (IDB). (2018). Development Effectiveness Report 2018. Retrieved from https://www.isdb.org/sites/default/files/media/documents/2019-04/IsDB_DER%202018_31Mar19_Optimized%20for%20Website.pdf

Islamic Development Bank (IDB). Annual Report. (2018). Transformation In A Fast-Changing World: A Road to Sustainable Development Goals. Retrieved from https://www.isdb.org/sites/default/files/media/documents/2019-04/usb%20Annual%20report%20English%202018_softproof.pdf

Islamic Financial Services Board. (2017). Islamic Financial Services Industry Stability Report 2017. Retrieved from https://www.ifsb.org/docs/IFSB%20IFSI%20Stability%20Report%202017.pdf

Kaabachi, S., & Obeid, H. (2016). Determinants of Islamic banking adoption in Tunisia: Empirical analysis. *International Journal of Bank Marketing, 34*(7), 1069–1091. doi:10.1108/IJBM-02-2015-0020

Kabir Hassan, M. (2011). Financial development and economic growth: New evidence from panel data. *The Quarterly Review of Economics and Finance, 51*(1), 88–104. doi:10.1016/j.qref.2010.09.001

Khan, M., & Bhatti, M. (2008). Islamic banking and finance: On its way to globalization. *Managerial Finance, 34*(10), 708–725. doi:10.1108/03074350810891029

Khan, T., & Ahmed, H. (2001). Risk Management –An Analysis of Issues in Islamic Financial Industry. *Islamic Development Bank-Islamic Research and Training Institute*, Occasional Paper, 91, the Islamic Research and Teaching Institute (IRTI).

Ltifi, M., Hikkerova, L., Aliouat, B., & Gharbi, J. (2016). The determinants of the choice of Islamic banks in Tunisia. *International Journal of Bank Marketing, 34*(5), 710–730. doi:10.1108/IJBM-11-2014-0170

Ould Mohamed Mahmoud, L., & Abduh, M. (2014). The Role of Awareness in Islamic Bank Patronizing Behavior of Mauritanian: An Application of TRA. *Journal of Islamic Finance, 3*(2), 030 – 038.

Rafay, A., & Farid, S. (2017). Dynamic Relationship between Islamic Banking System and Real Economic Activity: Evidence from Pakistan. *Journal of King Abdulaziz University. Islamic Economics, 30*(2), 97–114.

Rafik Al Masri. (1995). Les banques islamiques. Centre d'édition scientifique, l'université King Abdulaziz, Jeddah.

Reuters, T. (2016b). State of the Global Islamic Economy 2016/17 (SGIE). Retrieved from https://ceif.iba.edu.pk/pdf/ThomsonReuters-stateoftheGlobalIslamicEconomyReport201617.pdf

Reuters, T. (2017). Islamic Finance Development report 2017. Retrieved from https://islamicbankers.files.wordpress.com/2017/12/icd-thomson-reuters-islamic-finance-development-report-2017.pdf

Saidane, D. (2010). The Regulatory and Institutional Dimension? Consolidation, Privatization, Human Resources and Good Governance. *Multi -Year Expert Meeting On Services, Development, and Trade: The Regulatory Dimension and Institutional Geneva.*

Shaikh, S. A., Ismail, M. A., Shafiai, M. H., Shahimi, S., & Ismail, A. G. (2017). Role of Islamic Banking in Financial Inclusion: Prospects and Performance. In N. Alam, & S.A.R. Rizvi (Eds.), Islamic Banking. Cham, Switzerland: Palgrave Macmillan.

Sundararajan, V., & Errico, L. (2002). Islamic financial institutions and products in the global financial system: key issues in risk management and challenges ahead. (*IMF Working Paper No. WP/02/192*). Retrieved from https://ssrn.com/abstract=1930788

Triki, T., & Faye I. (2013). Financial Inclusion in Africa, *African Development Bank (AfDB).*

## ENDNOTES

1 IDB, annual report, 2017

2 GLOBAL ISLAMIC FINANCE REPORT. (2016). Islamic Financial Policy

3 Bransdma. J., & Hart. L. (2004) .Making Microfinance Work Better in the Middle East and North Africa . World Bank Institute and Private.

4 Diagnostic to Action: Microfinance in Africa . (2008) . Africa Microfinance Action Forum (AMAF) &Women's World Banking

5 Annual Report. (2016). C*entral bank of Sudan*

6 Annual Report. (2016). *Central bank of Sudan, p60*

7 Ayadi, R., De Groen, W.P. & Author. (2018) . Financial Development And Inclusion In Egypt, Jordan, Morocco And Tunisia. *EMNES Studies No 4 / March, 2018.*

8 .https://data.worldbank.org/indicator/SP.POP.TOTL

9 https://www.zawya.com/mena/en/business/story/Huge_potential_for_Islamic_banking_in_Egypt_lack_of_political_will_stymies_growth-ZAWYA20180111064610/

10 Stability Report. (2017). *IFSB*

11 Annual Report. (2017). *Faisal Islamic Bank Egypt*

12 Annual Report. (2017) . Central Bank Tunisia, 2017, p. 8-11

Section 2

# Islamic Banking and Finance in Practice

# Chapter 6
# Islamic Finance and Limited Purpose Banking (LPB): Two Sides of the Same Coin

**Edib Smolo**
https://orcid.org/0000-0002-7645-4581
*SARAYCON - Saray Consultancy for Socially Responsible and Ethical Finance, Bosnia and Herzegovina*

## ABSTRACT

*The saying that "history repeats itself" is best manifested in capitalist financial system operating worldwide. It seems people are not learning lessons from the history of financial crises. Leading economists and capitalist gurus are warning about an inherently fragile capitalist financial system and about an urgent need to do something about it before it is too late. After the recent global financial crisis, Kotlikoff proposed the most radical and the most comprehensive reform of the existing financial system. His proposal became known as the Limited Purpose Banking (LPB). Kotlikoff's proposal runs hand in hand with the aspirations of the pioneers of Islamic finance. He envisioned a financial system that is based on risk sharing, cooperation, and overall public interest (maslahah). In short, the idea of the LPB – after certain modifications and minor adjustments – can be applied in developing a true Islamic financial system. Thus, it can be said that the LPB and Islamic finance are two sides of the same coin.*

## INTRODUCTION

Humans are faced with decision–making processes every day. Regulators, government officials and managers in general are faced with same issue day after day. It is only when we are faced with severe situations that we will try our best to find ways out of the problem. These extreme cases that happen every now and then represent unique opportunities to change the course and take on new roads. The same is true for financial crises. When they happen, and they do happen, more or less, on a regular basis we need to rethink our overall financial system. Even though they represent these unique opportunities to take on different path and make our overall financial system a bit better and sound, we usually fail to do so.

DOI: 10.4018/978-1-7998-1611-9.ch006

In this regard, the global financial crisis of 2007-2009 was unique in many ways and offered a hope that we might rethink the way we do the finance. This is, at least, what Laurence J. Kotlikoff had in mind when writing his book, *Jimmy Stewart is Dead*, and drafting his proposal known as the Limited Purpose Banking (LPB). He offered a completely new blueprint on how we can structure our financial system that would prevent it from entering into similar troubles. This view, however, was not shared by majority of people in the White House and the Wall Street. Obama's administration started bailing out one financial institution after another preserving the existing financial system as it was. By doing so, Kotlikoff believes, they were treating the symptoms, not the disease, making us fiscally and financially weaker.

The Islamic financial system (IFS), although existing since the birth of Islam, is relatively new financial model and offers unique ways for financial intermediation. Original ideas around the IFS are pretty much in line with Kotlikoff's LPB proposal. It is for this reason that we are focusing in this chapter on these two models or proposals. Hence, the main objectives of this chapter are: (i) to discuss briefly anomalies inherently installed within the capitalist financial system (CFS); (ii) to review Kotlikoff's proposal of LPB; (iii) to summarize ideas behind the IFS; and (iv) to relate LPB to IFS.

The rest of the chapter is structured as follows: Section two provides an overview of the global financial crisis that motivated Kotlikoff to propose his LPB model as a viable alternative to the existing financial system. In section three we will briefly discuss the LPB model and the way it is supposed to work in practice. This is followed by section four that will provide an overview of the IFS and elaborate on how the LPB model goes hand in hand with ideas behind the IFS. Finally, section five is reserved for concluding remarks.

## CRITICS OF CFS AND THE GLOBAL FINANCIAL CRISIS: THE EVENT THAT LED TO LPB

Since the starting of the 21st century alone, about 24 economic and financial crises hit economies worldwide.[1] Among these 24 crises, the most severe one is the recent global financial crisis of 2007-2009. In fact, it is so severe that basic tenets of the CFS, such as the notion of *'the invisible hand'*, are questioned openly.

This notion of *'the invisible hand'* was introduced by the 18th century Scottish philosopher and economist Adam Smith in his book *'The Theory of Moral Sentiments'*. He used this phrase in two other places, but with a different meanings (Rothschild, 1994). In this case he refers to some rich landowners who are selfishly interested in their own wellbeing ignoring values such as "humanity" and "justice". They go after precious commodities "from the labours of all the thousands whom they employ". In doing so, *They are led by an invisible hand to make nearly the same distribution of the necessaries of life, which would have been made, had the earth been divided into equal portions among all its inhabitants, and thus without intending it, without knowing it, advance the interest of the society, and afford means to the multiplication of the species* (Smith, 2006, pp. 215-216)

Nowadays, *'the invisible hand'* is considered as the unobservable market force standing behind the demand and supply of goods and services in a free market and bringing about beneficial social and economic outcomes from an individual's self-interested actions. This is, at least, how economists see the notion of *'the invisible hand'*, although this may not be at all Adam's intention – as pointed out by Rothschild (1994).

Generally speaking, capitalism has been criticized from the very beginning until now, from Karl Marx, Paul Krugman, Hyman P. Minsky, to hedge-fund billionaire Ray Dalio – just to name a few. In short, capitalism is seen as anti-democratic, inherently exploitative and unsustainable, leading to economic inequality and an erosion of human rights including but not limited to economic freedom. For example, after the global financial crisis it was obvious that *'the invisible hand'* is not doing what its proponents claimed to do. As a result, experts started questioning the conventional wisdom that the existing financial system is stable. This brought into the limelight Minsky's *'financial instability hypothesis'*. According to this hypothesis financial stability breeds instability (Minsky, 2008).

Recently, the hedge-fund billionaire Ray Dalio criticized the way capitalism is functioning and said that "capitalism is failing" America. Although capitalism has made him a billionaire, knowing the system inside out, he argues that it is no longer functioning well for the majority of Americans as it is "producing self-reinforcing spirals up for the haves and down for the have-nots." According to Dalio, this is due to the following: (i) there has been no real wage growth, adjusted for inflation, for the majority of Americans since 1980; (ii) the income gap is about as high as ever and the wealth gap is the highest since the late 1930s; (iii) most people in the bottom 60% are poor; & (iv) the childhood poverty rate in the US is now 17.5% and America's public-education system is among the worst in the developed world. In order to put capitalism back on track, Dalio recommended the following steps: (i) need for a top leadership that will proclaim the income/wealth/opportunity gap to be a national emergency; (ii) need for a bipartisan and skillful approach to develop policies for restructuring of the system so it works better; (iii) need for clear metrics upon which to hold leaders accountable for their actions; (iv) need for a more equitable redistribution of resources that will benefit the vast majority of Americans; & (v) need for a coordination of monetary and fiscal policies, i.e. a coordination between the Federal Reserve, Congress, and the White House (for details see Dalio, 2019).

Obviously, given a long history of the criticism of CFS, the emergence of the global financial crisis should not be seen as a surprise. In fact, there are numerous studies that questioned the functionality of the CFS and warned us of possibility for such unpleasant scenarios.[2] Although we are relatively aware of end results of the global financial crisis (or perhaps we are still counting the bad effects of it), its causes are less known even to leading experts on the topic. Are the complexity and intensive use of structured financial products, derivatives and other assets with uncertain fundamentals the main culprits for the crisis?[3] Or are we to blame combination of loose monetary policy, lax financial supervision and overall financial deregulations, coupled with low interest rates, excessive leveraging and credit growth for the crisis?[4] According to Dalio, "poor education, a poor culture (one that impedes people from operating effectively together), poor infrastructure, and too much debt cause bad economic results" (Dalio, 2019). This is in line with Fisher's claim that all major crises are initially caused by "too much short-term debt…" that leads to "too great a contraction of the circulating medium" (Fisher, 2009).

In general, every time a financial crisis happens, there are numerous calls for reforms from those suggesting radical changes to those that call for minor or no changes to the existing financial system and its regulations. A sort of minor regulatory changes was proposed by Stiglitz (1993). For instance, addressing the problems related to the savings and loan crisis of the 1980s and 1990s (the S&L crisis),[5] Stiglitz (1993) argues that "some revision of deposit insurance" should be the focal point in most bank reform proposals, including this one. Consequently, his proposed consists of basically four elements: (i) financial institutions interested in deposit insurance should pay premiums on all of its deposits; (ii) the interest rate payable on those deposits need to be regulated; (iii) these institutions would be subjected to a high capital requirement (ratio of net worth plus bonds to deposits); & (iv) similarly, these institutions should satisfy a high net-worth requirement (ratio of net worth to deposits). He proposed 20 percent for the capital requirement and 10 percent for the net-worth requirement (Stiglitz, 1993).

The same is true when the global financial crisis erupted. Experts of all sorts started questioning the existing financial system, especially government bailout actions, and looking for alternative one(s). Today, we can find hundreds and thousands of pages discussing the global financial crisis and evaluating its causes and effects worldwide. Even though these papers indicate many causes of the crisis and highlight many lessons (at least in theory), no serious steps have been undertaken to prevent such crises from happening again. This is because the existing financial system is still functioning in the same way as it was functioning before the crisis. Whatever has been done so far is done in order to preserve the *'status quo'* as no significant changes have been made in any ways.

Again, this should not come as a surprise. The crisis is a result of bad actions and steps taken by people who run financial institutions, governments, regulatory institutions, etc. In other words, those who caused the global financial crisis were invited by the government(s) on a rescue mission to save the global economy. Consequently, we hardly believe that those who led us to this financial crisis can get us out of it, rather they may create additional problems after all. Unfortunately, this is exactly what happened. We ended up with huge fiscal deficits all over the world, bailing out the very same people who lost billions and allowing them to cash out huge bonuses. In short, all the actions taken in the aftermath of the global financial crisis proved that under the CFS profits are privatized while losses are socialized. This left us with the same – inherently unstable – financial system and we can only expect the same outcomes in the near future but their repercussions are expected to be much worse.

Perhaps, the most radical and the most comprehensive reform has been put forward by Laurence J. Kotlikoff. His proposal for overall overhaul of the existing financial system became known as Limited Purpose Banking or LPB (2010). The financial crisis fueled by the wrong prescriptions taken by the governments placed the CFS "in terrible shape." Thus, he argues that this state of the CFS "needs a fundamental overhaul, not an oil change" (Kotlikoff, 2010, p. 189). In the following section, we will discuss LPB in more details.

## LIMITED PURPOSE BANKING (LPB): AN OVERVIEW

According to Kotlikoff, the existing conventional financial system is terminally ill and whatever has been done so far is nothing but a wrongly prescribed medicine that does not represent a long-term solution but rather a postponement of yet another financial crisis that is inevitable. Transferring bad loans and toxic assets from one balance sheet to another one is not going to solve the problem as someone is still going to be faced with default and eventual losses.

In his book *Jimmy Stewart is Dead*, Kotlikoff provides an overall analysis of the financial crisis and offers a way out that would prevent similar episodes in the future. We would not be faced with these crises if the *Efficient Market Hypothesis* (EMH) was correct. In short, he argues that the CFS is "replete with market failure" (Kotlikoff, 2010). While detecting inherent problems with the CFS, Kotlikoff comes with a genuine and possible solution to all problems faced by the current CFS. Although in his analysis he agrees (to some extent) with some authors when it comes to causes that led to the financial crisis, yet Kotlikoff differs significantly when it comes to the way how these problems should be addressed. It is said that 'desperate times call for desperate measures' and this was the time – according to him – that radical changes were needed. In other words, given the global financial crisis the CFS was ripe for major changes, *the overhaul*. Today, about ten years after the global financial crisis, it can be said that no significant changes have been made in the financial world or how we do the business. According to Kotlikoff, there is a need for a transparent financial system with automatic financial firewalls and LPB is the proposal that can take care of these requirements (Kotlikoff, 2010).

## LPB at Glance

The idea behind Kotlikoff's proposal known as LPB stands on three major propositions. First and foremost, all banks and bank-like institutions should be converted into mutual funds. A unique feature of the LPB is that every mutual fund will have *'limited purpose'* as it would hold only what it says it holds and nothing else. For instance, a real estate investment trusts (REITs) mutual fund would only hold REITs certificates; a six-month T-Bill mutual fund would only hold six-month Treasury Bills and nothing else, etc. In other words, funds raised from investors would be placed only in specified asset classes selected and limited by a mutual fund's charter. This way, every investor would know exactly where his/her money is. Through implementation of LPB – Kotlikoff believes – we are limiting banks' functions to the one and the most important function which is the function of intermediation between borrowers and lenders and savers and investors (Kotlikoff, 2010). The banks would simply act as middlemen or as *pass-through* mutual fund companies. For example, if Sara buys, say, $1,000 of shares in a six-month T-Bill mutual fund, that means that Sara literally has $1,000 worth of that mutual fund in an account under her name and under the control of the third-party custodian.

Furthermore, there will be two additional but specific types of mutual funds. The first type would be *cash-only mutual funds* that will be used as the payment system with a 100% reserve requirement. In other words, under the LPB these *cash-only mutual funds* represent the demand deposits (checking accounts) that will be used for writing checks, online payment and ATM withdrawals. By implementing the 100% reserve requirement on checking accounts, the LPB will solve a number of problems faced by the current CFS, namely: (i) a practice of demand deposit will become obsolete removing false sense of security that leads to a *moral hazard*;[6] (ii) there will be no bank runs as money in these demand deposits (*cash-only mutual funds*) will not evaporate from accounts; and (iii) the money supply (M1) would be under the full control by the government and no bank would have any impact on money creation.[7]

The second type would be *insurance mutual funds*. Under the LPB model, all insurance companies will be converted into bank-type mutual funds. Nevertheless, *insurance mutual funds* would differ from conventional mutual funds on two grounds, namely: (i) payments of premiums to purchasers of the insurance, under this model, would be subject to "personal outcomes and decisions" and "economy-wide conditions"; (ii) these *insurance mutual funds* will be closed-end as there will be "no new issues (claims to the fund) to be sold once the fund had launched" (p. 137).[8]

Consequently, banks under the LPB model will not extend credit themselves and since there will be no speculative investments but rather intermediation alone, there will be no-risk banking (Smolo & Mirakhor, 2014). In other words, exclusive rights of gambling and speculative investments would be in the hands of investors only as banks, under LPB, would have no such rights at all. Thus, the existing practice of leveraging that caused disastrous results worldwide would be abandoned. So far, managements of banks and financial institutions leveraged and gambled using our money without our explicit knowledge and consent. Under the LPB, we will be able to leverage with our own money, bearing all risks and consequences, while being fully aware of them. In doing so, a natural financial firewall is created (Kotlikoff, 2010).

Second proposition is that there is a need for a single financial regulatory body that will oversee the financial system. This body is termed as the Federal Financial Authority (FFA) that would oversee the LPB and provide independent government ratings based on full disclosure and transparency. Current system led to practice of insider ratings that misled investors and provided some sort of gateways for the "financial debacle" (p. 128). Given the FFA and full disclosure under the LPB system, people and investors placing their investments within the system will bear all risks and they will be fully aware of them from the very beginning. This mechanism, once in place, will act as built-in firewalls warning protecting us from upcoming financial crises.

Finally, the third proposition of the LPB model foresee that the financing and investment by the mutual funds will be done through online auctions. In particular, the above-mentioned regulator would first ensure transparency and validity of underlying investments, say a mortgage. Once this is done, a particular mutual fund (a bank under the LPB model) would be allowed to buy these investments through this online auction similar to eBay auctions that we are all familiar with.

## LPB and the 100% Reserve Requirement Proposal

Although Kotlikoff's LPB proposal has a certain degree of novelty, some of its features can be traced back to other proposals, in particular to *Narrow Banking*. The *narrow banking*, although known as *Chicago plan*, called for a *100% reserve requirement* on all demand deposits.[9] It was initially originated by Henry C. Simons during the Great depression (Fisher, 2009). During the 1930s, the idea was further developed and advocated by Irving Fisher (2009), Frank Knight (1933) and James W. Angell (1935), among others. Referring to the *100% reserve requirement* proposal, Fisher said that it is the best solution for "the problem of depressions; for it would remove the chief cause of both booms and depressions, namely the instability of demand deposits, tied as they are now, to bank loans" (Fisher, 2009).

Likewise, Frank Knight wrote a memo in 1933 together with seven other economists from the University of Chicago and recommended a proposal for restructuring of the financial system. In short, this proposal called for breaking up of commercial banks into two types of corporations, a *deposit-bank* and a *lending-company*. Similar to the *cash-only mutual funds* under the LPB model, *deposit-banks* would serve exclusively as demand deposits (checking accounts), while *lending-company* would provide short-term lending, discounting, and acceptance (Knight, 1933).

Later on, this idea was endorsed by Milton Friedman (2015) and Robert Litan (1987), among others. Having in place the *100% reserve requirement* would place the control over the money supply (M1) back where it belongs, in the hands of the government. Nowadays, monetary policies have limited impact on economies as they are government tools for partial and indirect control of M1. Here, a money multiplier plays a crucial role and it is part and parcel of the fractional reserve system.

Notwithstanding similarities between *narrow banking* and LPB, Kotlikoff believes that LPB is far more superior and better equipped to deal with complex financial system that we have today. To sum up, LPB has several distinguished features. First, once converted into specific mutual funds, banks are placed back on their original track to do what they were supposed to do originally and that is the intermediation. Second, the principles of LPB are simple and easily understood by common people. For example, these newly created mutual funds would have simple rules and regulations. Third, having a relatively simple structure then the financial market can be served by a single regulatory authority, the Federal Financial Authority. Fourth, LPB would improve corporate governance practices due to its transparency that will help us better evaluate bankers'/managers' performance. Finally, no individual bank would be able to create money as this function will be solely in the hands of the government. All of these are contrary to the features of the existing financial system.

## THE ISLAMIC FINANCIAL SYSTEM: AN OVERVIEW

There are several definitions for Islamic banking and finance.[10] In short, Islamic finance in general and Islamic banking in particular can be defined as business of resource allocation and management as well as financial intermediation based on the principles of *Shari'ah*.

Therefore, the IFS is a system based on a religious worldview. Teachings of Islam and principles of the *Shari'ah* (Islamic law),[11] are the very foundations of and provide legal framework for the IFS. All rules related to Islam are drawn from the four primary sources, namely: The Holy *Qur'an*, the *Sunnah* (tradition),[12] *ijma'* (the consensus of the jurists) and *qiyas* (analogy). These rules provide guidelines on all daily activities, including but not limited to religious rituals. Consequently, a significant portion of the *Shari'ah* is addressing interpersonal relations, be it economic transactions, social, political and international affairs, etc. Over the years, Muslim scholars developed special branch within the *Shari'ah* called *fiqh al-mu'amalat* that is focused primarily on rules about economic transactions and trade related activities.

In general, trade and finance practices did not start, nor did they stop with the advent of Islam. In essence, financial transactions and practices that were in line with the *Shari'ah* principles were approved by the Prophet Muhammad (*peace be upon him*), and those that were against these principles were abolished. Since then these principles of Islamic finance have been practiced not only in the Muslim world but in other parts of the world. For example, the principle of *Mudarabah* (passive partnership)[13] have been used in the Western Europe during the Middle Age. This practice in Europe, however, was known as *commenda* (Brouwer, 2005; Fischel, 1933; Mirakhor, 2003; Udovitch, 1962, 1967, 1970a, 1970b). Nevertheless, the modern day Islamic finance emerged some fifty years ago and gained momentum in the last two decades. Hence, according to the latest report by Thomson Reuters, the global Islamic finance industry grew year-on-year by of 11% to US$ 2.4 trillion in assets in 2017 with a potential to grow to US$ 3.8 trillion in assets by 2023. Iran, Saudi Arabia, Malaysia, Bahrain and the UAE are leading countries in terms of development of the Islamic finance (Thomson Reuters, 2018).

In short, the overall Islamic finance industry attracted worldwide attention due to its relative resilient to the global financial crisis and it attracts Muslims and non-Muslims alike (Smolo & Mirakhor, 2010). As a result, the IFS now encompasses banking, *Takaful* (Islamic insurance), funds, microfinance, capital markets, etc.

## SALIENT FEATURES OF THE ISLAMIC FINANCIAL SYSTEM

In what follows, we will provide a brief note on salient features of the IFS. The idea is to show who these features fit in the LPB model and how these two proposals, i.e. LPB and IFS, are complimentary in many ways. In other words, it should be clear to a reader after getting to know these salient features of IFS that they are overlapping most of the ideas and features that are presented in the LPB model above. Now, let us see what the salient features of IFS are.

In fact, many authors have discussed the salient features of Islamic finance (Rafay & Farid, 2017; Askari, Iqbal, Mirakhor, & Krichenne, 2010; Ayub, 2007; El-Gamal, 2006; Venardos, 2005; Visser, 2009). They are primarily derived from the *Qur'an*, *Sunnah*, *ijma'*, and *qiyas*. Here, we will briefly discuss the most important ones:

- **Prohibition of *Riba* (Interest or Usury):**[14] Payment and receipt of interest (*Riba*) are prohibited in Islam. In this regard, the *Qur'an* says: *Those who devour usury (Riba) will not stand except as one stands whom Satan has driven mad by his touch. That is because they say, 'Trade is like Riba,' whereas Allah (SWT) has permitted trade and forbidden Riba.*[15] The literal meaning of *Riba* is 'excess', 'growth' or 'increment.' Technically, it refers to a predetermined interest collected by a lender, which the lender receives over and above the principal amount he has lent out. One reason, *inter alia*, for the impermissibility of the contract of *Riba* is surely, due to the fact, that this contract transfers all, or at least a major portion, of risk to the borrower. *Riba* is further classified into two types:
  - *Riba al-fadl*: This largely applies to barter transactions. It refers to the trading of one commodity of a category to which the rules of *Riba* apply, for another commodity of the same category, with an increase of one compensation over the other (Al-Zuhayli, 2003, p. 312).[16]
  - *Riba al-nasi'ah*: This is specific to loans. It refers to any excess paid over the principal amount as a compensation for a delay in repayment.
- **Prohibition of *Gharar* (Excessive Risk & Uncertainty):** Literally, the term *Gharar* refers to something with a pleasant appearance and unpleasant reality (Al-Darīr, 1995, p. 48). Consequently, the *Gharar* can be defined as the sale of probable goods whose existence and/or characteristics are not certain. Due to these reasons this trade is akin to gambling. Examples of *Gharar* are the sale of fish in the sea, of birds in the sky, and of unripe fruits on the tree, which cause excessive and avoidable uncertainty.
- **Prohibition of *Maysir* (Gambling/Speculation):** Islam prohibits gambling and games of chance in which there is a possibility of total loss to one party. It is a zero-sum game whereby there is a transfer of wealth from one party to another without creating any new wealth. One of the reasons for prohibiting *Maysir* (gambling) is that it invokes enmity and distracts the faithful from acts of worship.
- ***Shari'ah*-Compliant ACTIVITIES:** Islamic financial institutions may engage in or finance only activities that are in line with teachings of *Shari'ah*. As a result, financing casino activities as well as the production of tobacco, alcohol, pork, pornography, weapons – among others – are strictly disallowed.
- **Risk-and-Return Sharing:** While the *Shari'ah* prohibits earning income through charging interest, it permits income generation through the sharing of risks and rewards between the parties. In other words, Islam encourages and promotes entrepreneurship that builds trust and cooperation between partners.
- **Sanctity of Contracts:** Fulfilling contractual obligations in Islam is considered a sacred duty. Furthermore, disclosure of full information is also required in order to reduce the risk of asymmetric information and moral hazard.
- **Social Justice:** Islam prohibits any transaction that leads to injustice and exploitation. Moreover, Islam gives preference to public interest (*maslahah*) over individual interest.

Thus, by prohibiting *Riba*, *Gharar* and *Maysir* on the one side, and promoting risk-and-return sharing, cooperation and *maslahah* on the other, Islam seeks to foster an environment based on fairness and justice. In short, the focus of Islamic finance is on community banking, ethical banking, and socially responsible investing.

Having this in mind, it is worth noting that pioneers of Islamic finance – such as Uzair (1955, 1978), Siddiqi (1983a, 1983b, 1985), Chapra (1985, 1988), Khan (1986), Kahf and Khan (1992), Mirakhor and Iqbal (1988), and Mirakhor (1993), just to name a few – envisioned a significantly different IFS from the one we have at the moment. They envisioned a model based on the principle of *Mudarabah* (passive partnership) and *Musharakah* (active partnership). As an example, Islamic financial pioneers envisioned financial intermediation based on 'two-tier' or 'two-fold' *Mudarabah*, even though the classical *Mudarabah* is based on bilateral relationship between *Rabb al-mal* (owner of capital) and *Mudarib* (entrepreneur). First-tier is related to a *Mudarabah* between investors as *Rabb al-mal* and banks as *Mudarib*. Subsequently, banks as *Rabb al-mal* invest these funds into projects/businesses who act as *Mudarib* in the second-tier *Mudarabah* (Smolo & Mirakhor, 2014).

In essence, the IFS is supposed to be an equity-based and/or risk-sharing financial system. In case of *Mudarabah*, profits will be shared according to an agreed ratio between *Rabb al-mal* and *Mudarib* while losses are completely borne by *Rabb al-mal* alone. On the other hand, in the case of *Musharakah* profits and losses are to be shared between the partners according to an agreed ratio and capital contribution respectively (Smolo & Mirakhor, 2014).

Nevertheless, although the IFS calls for equity and risk-sharing financing (at least in theory), current model of Islamic banking and finance is far from meeting these objectives. It has been criticized by many due to, among other things, being a replica of the conventional banking, dominated by debt-like and short-term financial instruments, lack of risk-sharing, etc. (Ahmed, 2009; Mirakhor & Smolo, 2011; Smolo, 2010). For example, the contemporary Islamic finance industry has accomplished mainly two things: (i) multilateralize originally bilateral contracts as the latter move from the real sector to the finance sector; and (ii) employ instruments of risk transfer available in conventional finance after making them *Shari'ah*-compatible (Mirakhor & Smolo, 2011).

Finally, having all these that has been said about the salient features of IFS, we can conclude that many of these features (if not all) run hand in hand with features or goals of LPB.[17]

## ISLAMIC FINANCE BASED ON LPB: A PROPOSAL

The original idea behind the IFS is the one envisioned by the above-mentioned pioneers of Islamic finance. As briefly mentioned above, the main financial instruments within the IFS are *Mudarabah* and *Musharakah*. These two instruments are perfect examples of the risk-sharing instruments and completely opposite to the existing debt-based contracts that are dominating the financial area nowadays. Once risk-sharing instruments are in place, then investors' decision-making process will be based on risk characteristics of the underlying assets. Thus, structuring a financial system along the lines described above leads to overall cooperation, economic justice and promotion of public interest (*maslahah*). It follows that in Islam risk plays a fundamental role in determining whether earnings from trade and finance are lawful or not. This view is based on two legal maxims linking returns from trade and finance to risks associated with it. The first one says: *al-ghunm bil al-ghurm* meaning "no risk no gain". And the second states: *al-kharaj bi ad-daman* which means "revenue goes with liability" (ISRA, 2011; Smolo, 2013). Moreover, Islam also recognizes that market participants have different tolerance towards the risk. While some participants are risk-lovers, others are risk-averse.

It should now be clear how Kotlikoff's proposal can contribute to further refine the fundamental ideas in structuring the IFS by allocating the risk to those who are economically more capable to bear it. Similarly, it can be seen that a financial system based on the idea of LPB is similar to the original, *the ideal*, model of the IFS, and vice-versa. Based on the overview of the LPB model, we can see that the risk characteristics of the envisioned mutual funds by Korlikoff are crucial to the model. In particular, under the LPB model, clients (investors) assume risks by investing their money in different funds based on their risk appetite. Identically, this would be similar to the '*Mudarabah* fund' (applied under the LPB model) although it can be broader than Kotlikoff's mutual funds as well as limited to specific purposes as evident from the following example.

*It is reported in Sunnan al-Bayhaqi that Abbas (r.a.)*[18] *would stipulate the following conditions when he was giving his mal (property) to the Mudarib (entrepreneur): (i) not to take property (livestock) on-board a ship; (ii) not to lodge in a valley; and (iii) not to buy any live animals; and if he (Mudarib) were to do so he would be liable for it. Then he referred the matter to the Prophet (May peace be upon him) and he approved it.*

The above example tells us that we can limit our business activities (purposes) when structuring an investment fund. Thus, the IFS could be formulated according the same lines as LPB model having in place two-tier *Mudarabah.*[19] To be precise, initially a bank acts as *Mudarib* on behalf of depositors who are capital providers (*Rabb al-mal*). This is the first *Mudarabah*. Subsequently, banks extend the collected funds to potential entrepreneurs or invest them in projects. This way, these banks become capital providers and the entrepreneurs become their *Mudarib* and this is the second *Mudarabah*. Hence, the overall term for this two-step process is the 'two-tier *Mudarabah*'.

In short, with a minor modification to the Kotlikoff's proposal,[20] we could have the IFS structured along the same lines. In particular, we would have mutual funds based on *Shari'ah*-compliant contracts such as *Mudarabah* mutual fund, *Musharakah* mutual fund, etc. Each and every *Shari'ah*-compliant mutual fund, under this model, will have clear and transparent objectives and investment targets. Similarly, these funds will represent different risk characteristics that would cater for different risk appetites of investors. With full disclosure and transparency in place, as envisioned by LPB, investors will have all information available at their disposal for informed decision-making. As pointed out by Smolo and Mirakhor (2014) these funds could be classified based on underlying *Shari'ah*-compliant instruments. Thus, we would have *Mudarabah, Musharakah, Murabahah*, and similar funds. Otherwise, they could be classified based on financing sector. Having various LPB-based *Shari'ah*-compliant mutual funds, we would be able to provide a more diversified spectrum of products to both investors and borrowers of these funds. All in all, we can see that Islamic finance and LPB are very similar in nature and thus can be considered as *'two sides of the same coin'*.

All of the above, however, represents just a tip of an iceberg when it comes to the implementation of Kotlikoff's LPB model within the Islamic finance industry. It is far from being complete and in any ways flawless as this chapter represents a work-in-progress or a conceptual idea by the author. Thus, it is open to further discussions and improvements. Hopefully this chapter will trigger additional discussion and debate on the proposal and eventually lead to a better ideas and solutions for currently fragile financial system – be it Islamic or conventional.

## CONCLUSION

This chapter represents an attempt on linking Kotlikoff's LPB model with the IFS as envisioned by its pioneers. After reviewing the main ideas and structures behind the LPB model, it is evident that it shares many salient features with of the IFS. Structuring Islamic financial institutions along the lines suggested by Kotlikoff's LPB model, goes hand in hand with the ideal model of the IFS that was and still is advocated by many Muslim scholars and economists. A slightly modified version of Kotlikoff's LPB model, could be used in structuring a better IFS. In fact, Islamic financial instruments such as *Mudarabah* and *Musharakah* are perfect fit for the LPB model. Hence, it can be said that the LPB and Islamic finance are but two sides of the same coin.

Nevertheless, this is still a theoretical proposal that need to be embraced by larger number of scholars and financial professionals to be considered and further elaborated. It is not perfect nor complete. We need to investigate it further in order to identify any possible shortcomings. Finally, although this chapter is limited in scope, it is a good starting point for future debate and discussion on the topic.

### Classifications

JEL Classification: G01, G21, P51
KAUJIE Classification: F12, I11, I24

## REFERENCES

Ahmed, H. (2009). Financial Crisis Risks and Lessons for Islamic Finance. *ISRA International Journal of Islamic Finance*, *1*(1), 7–32.

Al-Darīr, S. M. A.-A. (1995). Al-Gharar wa Atharuhū Fī al-'Uqūd: Fī al-Fiqhi al-Islāmiyyi (2nd ed.). Jeddah, Saudi Arabia: Dallah al-Barakah.

Al-Zuhayli, W. (2003). Financial Transactions in Islamic Jurisprudence (M. A. El-Gamal, Trans. Vol. 1). Damascus, Syria: Dar al-Fikr.

Angell, J. W. (1935). The 100 Per Cent Reserve Plan. *The Quarterly Journal of Economics*, *50*(1), 1–35. doi:10.2307/1882341

Askari, H., Iqbal, Z., Mirakhor, A., & Krichenne, N. (2010). The Stability of Islamic Finance: Creating a Resilient Financial Environment for a Secure Future. Singapore: John Wiley & Sons (Asia). doi:10.1002/9781118390450

Ayub, M. (2007). *Understanding Islamic Finance*. West Sussex, UK: John Wiley & Sons.

Bordo, M. D. (2008). *An Historical Perspective on the Crisis of 2007-2008*. Paper presented at the Central Bank of Chile Twelfth Annual Conference on "Financial Stability, Monetary Policy and Central Banking." Santiago, Chile, November 6-7, Santiago, Chile.

Bossone, B. (2002). Should Banks Be 'Narrowed'? *Public Policy Brief No. 69.*

Brouwer, M. (2005). Managing Uncertainty through Profit Sharing Contracts from Medieval Italy to Silicon Valley. *The Journal of Management and Governance*, *9*(3-4), 237–755. doi:10.100710997-005-7420-4

Chapra, M. U. (1985). *Towards a Just Monetary system: A Discussion of Money, Banking and Monetary Policy in the Light of Islamic Teaching*. London, UK: The Islamic Foundation.

Chapra, M. U. (1988). Towards An Islamic Financial System. *IIUM Journal of Economics and Management*, *1*(2), 1–30.

Chapra, M. U., & Khan, T. (2000). *Regulation and Supervision of Islamic Banks*. Jeddah, Saudi Arabia: IRTI.

Čihák, M., & Hesse, H. (2010). Islamic Banks and Financial Stability: An Empirical Analysis. *Journal of Financial Services Research*, *38*(2-3), 95–113. doi:10.100710693-010-0089-0

Cooper, G. (2008). *The Origin of Financial Crises: Central Banks, Credit Bubles and the Efficient Market Fallacy*. Hampshire, UK: Harriman House.

Dalio, R. (2019). Why and How Capitalism Needs to Be Reformed (Parts 1 & 2). Retrieved from https://www.linkedin.com/pulse/why-how-capitalism-needs-reformed-parts-1-2-ray-dalio/?published=t

El-Gamal, M. A. (2006). *Islamic Finance: Law, Economics, and Practice*. Cambridge, UK: Cambridge University Press. doi:10.1017/CBO9780511753756

Fischel, W. (1933). The Origin of Banking in Medieval Islam. *Journal of the Royal Asiatic Society*, *65*(2), 339–352.

Fisher, I. (2009). *100% Money and the Public Debt*. Pakthongchai, Thailand: ThaiSunset Publications. By Irving Fisher originally published without copyright notice in the *Economic Forum* Spring Number, April-June 1936, pp. 406-420.

Friedman, M. (2015). *A Program for Monetary Stability*. Renenio Books.

FSF. (2008). *Report of the Financial Stability Forum on Enhancing Market and Institutional Resilience*. Retrieved from Basel, Switzerland: http://www.fsforum.org/publications/r_0804.pdf?noframes=1

Garcia, V. F., Cibis, V. F., & Maino, R. (n.d.). Remedy for Banking Crises: What Chicago and Islam Have in Common. (Unpublished). *World Bank and IMF Staffs*.

ISRA. (2011). Islamic Financial System: Principles and Operations. Kuala Lumpur: International Shari'ah Research Academy for Islamic Finance (ISRA).

Jordan, C., & Jain, A. (2009, October). *Diversity and Resilience: Lessons from the Financial Crisis*. Paper presented at the Canadian Law and Economics Association Meeting, University of Toronto, Canada.

Kahf, M., & Khan, T. (1992). *Principles of Islamic Financing: A Survey*. Jeddah, Saudi Arabia: Islamic Research and Training Institute (IRTI), Research Paper No. 16.

Kashyap, A. K., Rajan, R., & Stein, J. (2008). *The Global Roots of the Current Financial Crisis and its Implications for Regulation.* Paper presented at the 5th ECB Central Banking Conference, November. Retrieved from http://www.ecb.int/events/pdf/conferences/cbc5/Rajan.pdf?17bea4624be62b27d96a6a290c65da52

Khan, M. S. (1986). Islamic Interest-Free Banking: A Theoretical Analysis. *Staff Papers - International Monetary Fund. International Monetary Fund, 33*(1), 1–27. doi:10.2307/3866920

Knight, F., Cox, G., Director, A., Douglas, P., Hart, A., Mints, L., ... Simons, H. (1933). Memorandum on banking reform, Franklin D. Roosevelt Presidential Library, President's Personal File, 431.

Kobayakawa, S., & Nakamura, H. (1999). A Theoretical Analysis of Narrow Banking Proposals. *IMES Discussion Paper Series 99-E-19.*

Konstans, P. (2006). Reforming Deposit Insurance. *Public Policy Brief, No. 83.*

Kotlikoff, L. J. (2010). *Jimmy Stewart is Dead: Ending the World's Ongoing Financial Plague with Limited Purpose Banking*. Hoboken, NJ: John Wiley & Sons.

Litan, R. E. (1987). *What Should Banks Do?* Washington, DC: Brookings Institution.

Mersch, Y. (2009). About the Role of Central Bank in Financial Stability and Prudential Liquidity Supervision, and the Attractiveness of Islamic Finance. IFSB 2nd Public Lecture on Financial Policy and Stability, Kuala Lumpur: Islamic Financial Services Board (IFSB).

Minsky, H. P. (1994). Financial Instability and the Decline of Banking: Public Policy Implications. *Working Paper No. 127.*

Minsky, H. P. (2008). *Stabilizing an Unstable Economy*. New York: McGraw Hill.

Mirakhor, A. (1993). Equilibrium in a Non-Interest Open Economy. *Journal of King Abdulaziz University: Islamic Economics, 5*(1), 3–23.

Mirakhor, A. (2003). *Muslim Contribution to Economics*. Paper presented at the Annual Meeting of the South-Western Economic Association, March 1983; reproduced in Essays on Iqtisad; Nur Corp. (1989); republished by Global Scholarly Publication, New York, NY (2003).

Mirakhor, A., & Iqbal, Z. (1988). *Stabilization and Growth in an Open Islamic Economy (IMF Working Paper No. 22)*. Washington D.C.: International Monetary Fund.

Mirakhor, A., & Krichene, N. (2009). The Recent Crisis: Lessons for Islamic Finance. IFSB 2nd Public Lecture on Financial Policy and Stability, Kuala Lumpur: Islamic Financial Services Board (IFSB).

Mirakhor, A., & Smolo, E. (2011). Do Conventional and Islamic Finance Share Common Epistemology? *Global Islamic Finance, August,* 48-53.

Mizen, P. (2008). The Credit Crunch of 2007-2008: A Discussion of the Background, Market Reactions, and Policy Responses. *Federal Reserve Bank of St. Louis Review, 90*(5), 531–567.

OECD. (2009). The Financial Crisis: Reform and Exit Strategies. Paris, France: Organization for Economic Co-operation and Development (OECD).

Phillips, R. J. (1992a). Chicago Plan and New Deal Banking Reform. *Working Paper No. 76.*

Phillips, R. J. (1992b). Credit Markets and Narrow Banking. *Working Paper No. 77.*

Pierce, J. L. (1991). *The Future of Banking: A Twentieth Century Fund Report.* New York: Yale University Press. doi:10.2307/j.ctt1ww3v09

Rafay, A., & Farid, S. (2017). Dynamic Relationship between Islamic Banking System and Real Economic Activity: Evidence from Pakistan. *Journal of King Abdulaziz University. Islamic Economics, 30*(2), 97–114.

Rothschild, E. (1994). Adam Smith and the Invisible Hand. *The American Economic Review, 84*(2), 319–322.

Roubini, N. (2008). Financial Crises, Financial Stability, and Reform: Supervision and Regulation of Financial Systems in a World of Financial Globalization. In J. Bilodeau (Ed.), *The Financial Development Report 2008* (pp. 33-46). New York: World Economic Forum.

Scott, K. E. (1998). Mutual Funds as an Alternative Banking System. *Journal of Institutional and Theoretical Economics, 154*(1), 86–96.

Siddiqi, M. N. (1983a). *Banking Without Interest.* Leicester, UK: The Islamic Foundation.

Siddiqi, M. N. (1983b). *Issues in Islamic Banking (Islamic Economics Series 4).* Leicester, UK: The Islamic Foundation.

Siddiqi, M. N. (1985). *Partnership and Profit-Sharing in Islamic Law.* Leicester, UK: The Islamic Foundation.

Smith, A. (2006). *The Theory of Moral Sentiments (Dover Philosophical Classics).* Cambridge, UK: Cambridge University Press.

Smolo, E. (2010). *Al-Bay' Bithaman Ajil, Musharakah Mutanaqisah and Ijarah Sukuk: A Theoretical Comparison.* Saarbrücken, Germany: Lambert Academic Publishing AG & Co. KG.

Smolo, E. (2013). *Uvod u islamsku ekonomiju i finansije: teorija i praksa.* Sarajevo: Dobra Knjiga.

Smolo, E., & Mirakhor, A. (2010). The Global Financial Crisis and its Implications for the Islamic Financial Industry. *International Journal of Islamic and Middle Eastern Finance and Management, 3*(4), 372–385. doi:10.1108/17538391011093306

Smolo, E., & Mirakhor, A. (2014). Limited Purpose Banking (LPB) and Islamic Finance: Could LPB Model Be Applied to Islamic Finance? *Humanomics, 30*(2), 122–135. doi:10.1108/H-08-2013-0053

Spong, K. (1993). Narrow Banks: An Alternative Approach to Banking Reform. *Working Paper No. 90.*

Stiglitz, J. E. (1993). Perspectives on the Role of Government Risk-Bearing within the Financial Sector. In M. S. Sniderman (Ed.), *Government Risk-Bearing: Proceedings of a Conference Held at the Federal Reserve Bank of Cleveland*, (pp. 109-130), May 1991. Boston, MA: Kluwer Academic Publishers. 10.1007/978-94-011-2184-2_5

Taylor, J. B. (2008, November). The Financial Crisis and the Policy Responses: An Empirical Analysis of What Went Wrong. *Stanford University Working Paper*. Retrieved from http://www.stanford.edu/~johntayl/FCPR.pdf

Thomson Reuters. (2018). *Islamic Finance Development Report 2018: Building Momentum*. Salaam Gateway.

Truman, E. M. (2009). Lessons from the Global Economic and Financial Crisis. Keynote address at the conference "G-20 Reform Initiatives: Implications for the Future of Regulation," cohosted by the Institute for Global Economics and the International Monetary Fund in Seoul, Korea, November 11, 2009. Retrieved from www.iie.com/publications/papers/truman0911.pdf

Udovitch, A. L. (1962). At the Origins of the Western Commenda: Islam, Israel, Byzantium? *Speculum*, *37*(2), 198–207. doi:10.2307/2849948

Udovitch, A. L. (1967). Credit and a Means of Investment in Medieval Islamic Trade. *Journal of the American Oriental Society*, *87*(3), 260–264. doi:10.2307/597719

Udovitch, A. L. (1970a). Commercial Techniques in Early Medieval Islamic Trade. In D. Richards (Ed.), *Islam and the Trade of Asia: A Colloquium* (pp. 37–62). Oxford, UK. doi:10.9783/9781512806021-005

Udovitch, A. L. (1970b). *Partnership and Profit in Medieval Islam*. Princeton, NJ: Princeton University Press. doi:10.1515/9781400820474

Uzair, M. (1955). *An Outline of Interestless Banking*. Karachi, Pakistan: Raihan Publications.

Uzair, M. (1978). *Interest Free Banking*. Karachi, Pakistan: Royal Book Company.

Venardos, A. M. (2005). *Islamic Banking & Finance in South-East Asia: Its Development & Future*. Singapore: World Scientific Publishing Co. Pte. Ltd. doi:10.1142/5751

Visser, H. (2009). *Islamic Finance: Principles and Practice*. Cheltenham, UK: Edward Elgar Publishing Limited.

Wallace, N. (1996). Narrow Banking Meets the Diamond-Dybvig Model. *Federal Reserve Bank of Minneapolis Quarterly Review*, *20*(1), 3–13.

Yellen, J. L. (2009, May). A Minsky Meltdown: Lessons for Central Bankers. *FRBSF Economic Letter No. 2009-15*. May 1, Retrieved from http://www.frbsf.org/publications/economics/letter/2009/el2009-15.pdf

## ENDNOTES

1 For details See https://en.wikipedia.org/wiki/List_of_economic_crises, accessed on 14 May 2019.

2 For some details on this matter see Bossone (2002); Garcia, Cibis, and Maino (n.d.); Kobayakawa and Nakamura (1999); Konstans (2006); Minsky (1994); Phillips (1992a, 1992b); Pierce (1991); Scott (1998); Spong (1993); Wallace (1996).

3 For details see FSF (2008); Jordan and Jain (2009, October); Mersch (2009, p. 14); Mirakhor and Krichene (2009); Mizen (2008); Truman (2009); Yellen (2009, May).

4 See Cooper (2008, p. 171); Kashyap, Rajan, and Stein (2008); Taylor (2008, November). (See also Bordo, 2008; Mirakhor & Krichene, 2009; OECD, 2009; Roubini, 2008).

5 During this crisis, about 747 out of the 3,234 savings and loan associations in the United States collapsed.

6 In economic theory, the term "moral hazard" describes situations in which a party will have a tendency to take risks because the resulting costs will not entirely be incurred by the party taking the risk.

7 This idea was advocated by a number of economists including Milton Friedman.

8 In this section, our goal is to provide a brief overview and introduction of LPB to a reader. Our main focus is banking operations as envisioned by Kotlikoff's LPB. Hence, we avoid detailed elaboration on cash mutual funds, 100% reserves and insurance mutual funds as it goes beyond the scope of this chapter. Note however that the issue of 100% Reserve Requirement Proposal has been discussed further in the next subsection as we believe that this issue is a crucial to any sort of financial reform.

9 The term "*narrow banking*" was coined in Litan (1987).

10 For example, the Islamic Banking Act 1983 of Malaysia (Act A1307) defines Islamic banking business as "*banking business whose aims and operations do not involve any element which is not approved by the religion of Islam*". Similarly, Čihák and Hesse define Islamic or *Shari'ah*-compliant banking as "*the provision and use of financial services and products that conform to Islamic religious practices and laws*" (Čihák & Hesse, 2010). More narrowly, Chapra and Khan define an Islamic bank as a "*depository institution whose core business is financial intermediation on the basis of a combination of profit and loss sharing and sales-based modes of financing*" (M. Umer Chapra & Khan, 2000).

11 Literally, *Shari'ah* means a path to a watering-place, a clear path to be followed. This led to its use for the path which the believer has to tread in order to obtain guidance in this world and deliverance in the next.

12 Sunnah is an Arabic word that means 'habit' or 'usual practice'. Technically, this term refers to whatever was reported that the Prophet Muhammad (May peace be upon him) said, did, or gave his tacit approval.

13 *Mudarabah* or passive partnership is a type of a partnership between *rabb al-mal* (capital owner), who provides the capital and *mudarib* (entrepreneur), who runs the business.

14 Some authors differentiate between usury and interest and say that *Riba* refers to usury only while interest is not included in the prohibition. In this chapter, the term *Riba* refers to both interest and usury.

15 *Al-Qur'an*, 2:275. In fact, the receipt of *Riba* is forbidden in the Holy *Qur'an*, while the payment of *Riba* is prohibited in the *Sunnah* of the Prophet (peace be upon him), and consensus (*ijma'*). In the *Qur'an*, the strongest prohibition is provided in the verses [2:275-279].

16 The following items are mentioned in a *hadith* [a saying of the Prophet (May peace be upon him)] to be *Ribawi* (subject to be usurious items) and as such should be exchanged only in an equal measure or quantity: gold, silver, barley, wheat, salt and dates.

17 For example, by having mutual funds under the LPB model, we are getting into equity-based sort-of financing that is the original idea behind the IFS model. Furthermore, the issue of uncertainty (*gharar*) under the current financial system is one of the reason why Kotlikoff proposed his LPB

model and at the same time, this issue is one of the fundamental prohibitions under the IFS model that needs to be avoided altogether, etc.

18 The acronym (r.a.) stands for '*radiyallahu anhu*' or '*may Allah be pleased with him*'. Abbas is one the companions of the Prophet Muhammad (*May peace be upon him*).

19 In similar way we can have two-tier *Musharakah* funds and so on.

20 For example, Islam does not allow financing of illegal activities such as casinos, production of alcohol, etc.

# Chapter 7
# Asset Diversification and Efficiency of Islamic Banks

**Naiwei Chen**
https://orcid.org/0000-0001-8844-7971
*National Chiayi University, Taiwan*

## ABSTRACT

*This chapter examines the effect of asset diversification (AD) on the efficiency of Islamic banks using conventional banks as the contrast sample. Data Envelopment Analysis (DEA) is used to generate efficiency score as a proxy of bank efficiency and the Tobit panel data model is estimated. A review of banks in three Asian countries with a dual banking system from 2006 to 2012 indicates that AD positively affects bank efficiency, regardless of bank type. In addition, the positive effect of AD on bank efficiency strengthens with bank size, particularly for Islamic banks. Furthermore, any positive effect of AD on the efficiency of Islamic banks is particularly found among those without foreign ownership, whereas ownership type plays no role in determining AD's effect on the efficiency of conventional banks.*

## INTRODUCTION

The existing literature has extensively explored the relationship between diversification and bank performance (Chen,Liang, & Yu, 2018; Gamra & Plihon, 2011; Mercieca, Schaeck, & Wolfe, 2007; Vallascas, Crespi, & Hagendorff, 2012). However, minimal evidence has been provided to support any relationship between diversification and bank efficiency, particularly for Islamic banks. This gap is counterintuitive because banks should enjoy the benefits of diversification, such as risk-diversification and economies of scope (Chen et al., 2018). These benefits should promote bank efficiency in the sense that risk and cost reduction accompanied by diversification facilitates the reduction of the cost involved when converting inputs to outputs. Importantly, the positive effect of diversification on bank efficiency should be particularly found among Islamic banks primarily because they are generally less diversified and smaller than conventional banks. That is, the former is more capable of reaping a net positive effect of diversification on bank efficiency than the latter (Chen et al., 2018). Accordingly, investigating

DOI: 10.4018/978-1-7998-1611-9.ch007

the impact of diversification on the efficiency of Islamic banks is a worthwhile endeavor. The reason is that if the results indicate a positive effect of diversification on bank efficiency, then Islamic banks are recommended to engage in diversification to improve bank efficiency. Such a diversification could improve bank sustainability and performance. In addition, the concerned authorities are recommended to adopt regulations that encourage Islamic banks to engage in diversification to facilitate the improvement of efficiency in the banking industry. Hence, this study is conducted to fill in this research gap.

Despite the abundance of research on the relationship between diversification and bank performance, empirical evidence on such a relationship has remained mixed. Prior studies have generally provided evidence indicating that diversification negatively affects bank performance. This finding suggests that the cost of the accompanied agency problems and diseconomies of management outweighs the benefits of the accompanied risk diversification and economies of scope (Acharya, Hasan, & Saunders, 2006; Chen et al., 2018; DeYoung & Roland, 2001; Laeven & Levine, 2007). In addition, diversification's negative (positive) effect on bank performance is frequently observed among conventional (Islamic) banks (Chatti, Kablan, & Yousfi, 2013; Čihák & Hesse, 2010; Molyneux & Yip, 2013).

Chen et al. (2018) examine the effect of asset diversification (AD) on bank performance in Indonesia, Malaysia, and Pakistan. They find that diversification positively affects asset quality and profitability of banks and that such effects are stronger for Islamic (large) banks than for conventional (small) banks. However, they also determine that diversification has a minimal impact on cost efficiency of conventional banks and no impact on Islamic banks. The possible reason is that the cost-to-income ratio may not be a good proxy for bank efficiency. Tripe (1998) explains that several underlying factors (e.g., structural differences among banks) affect such a ratio, which may not completely reflect bank efficiency.

The current study recognizes the problems with the cost-to-income ratio and extends Chen et al. (2018) by using the data envelopment analysis (DEA)-derived efficiency score as the bank efficiency measure to examine AD's effect on bank efficiency in Indonesia, Malaysia, and Pakistan. DEA's main advantage is its capability to use more than one input and output on the basis of real data to derive the efficiency frontier and evaluate each bank's efficiency. Therefore, the results based on the DEA approach should be more reliable. In addition, the aforementioned three countries are selected primarily because they practice a dual banking system, thereby rendering their banking environment highly competitive.[1] Hence, an analysis should be conducted on AD's effect on bank efficiency and whether and how such effect is influenced by bank size and foreign ownership in Islamic countries with such a unique banking environment. In particular, the role of foreign ownership in modifying AD's effect on bank efficiency in a competitive banking environment has remained unexplored and is worth exploring. Foreign ownership can heighten bank competition and transitively mitigate agency problems caused by diversification given the negative association between competition and agency cost (Ammann, Oesch, & Schmid, 2013; Lee, Hsieh, & Yang, 2016). However, foreign ownership can worsen agency problems accompanied by diversification because of its disadvantages, such as the accompanied ineffective cross-border monitoring, more risk-taking, and informational disadvantage (Albertazzi & Bottero, 2014; Chen, Wu, Jeon, & Wang, 2017). Given these two opposing effects of foreign ownership, whether and how foreign ownership modifies diversification's effect on bank efficiency in a competitive banking environment remain to be seen.

This study proposes three hypotheses. First, AD entails benefits, such as risk diversification and economies of scope (Saunders, Schmid, & Walter, 2014; Vallascas et al., 2012), which should facilitate the efficiency of banks when converting inputs to outputs. Hence, this study posits that AD positively affects bank efficiency. Second, given that large banks are better able to engage in diversification than small banks, AD's positive effect on bank efficiency should increase with bank size (Chen et al., 2018).

Importantly, Islamic banks generally have lower level of diversification and are smaller than conventional banks, such that the room for improvement is larger for the former than the latter. Hence, bank size should play a more important role in modifying diversification's effect on the efficiency of Islamic banks than that of conventional banks (Chen et al., 2018). Third, Islamic banks generally set a lower cap on foreign ownership compared with conventional banks. Government policy also tends to favor domestic investors over foreign investors.[2] Given the entry barrier, foreign ownership is unlikely to strengthen any positive effect of diversification on bank efficiency. Instead, domestic Islamic banks should have home field advantage, such that they are in a better position to maximize diversification's benefits (i.e., risk reduction and economies of scope). Hence, AD's positive effect on bank efficiency should be stronger (weaker) for Islamic banks without (with) foreign ownership.

Using 155 banks in three Asian countries as the study sample, the current research confirms the finding of prior research that Islamic banks are less efficient than conventional banks (Beck, Demirgüç-Kunt, & Merrouche, 2013; Chen et al., 2018). The estimation of the Tobit panel data model indicates that AD positively affects bank efficiency and no differential effect occurs caused by bank types. In addition, bank size plays roles in determining AD's effect on bank efficiency. The positive effect of AD on bank efficiency specifically strengthens with bank size and such a mediating effect of bank size is stronger for Islamic banks than for conventional banks. Furthermore, these results remain robust when foreign ownership is considered. Importantly, foreign ownership weakens AD's positive effect on the efficiency of Islamic banks. By contrast, ownership types do not influence AD's positive effect on the efficiency of conventional banks.

Overall, although bank efficiency is lower for Islamic banks than for conventional banks, the results suggest that AD can assist in promoting bank efficiency for Islamic banks. In addition, size plays a role in determining AD's effect on bank efficiency, particularly for Islamic banks. Although ownership types do not modify AD's effect on the efficiency of conventional banks, foreign ownership weakens AD's positive effect on the efficiency of Islamic banks. Hence, bank size and ownership types should be considered in examining AD's effect on bank efficiency, particularly for Islamic banks in the three Asian countries.

The author's contributions to the existing literature are threefold. First, this study makes an unprecedented attempt to examine whether and how foreign ownership modifies AD's effect on bank efficiency and finds that ownership types matter for Islamic banks. Second, this study uses the DEA approach to derive the efficiency score as the measure of bank efficiency rather than the cost-to-income ratio, which is used in prior studies in examining AD's effect on bank efficiency. Unlike Chen et al. (2018), in which AD is observed to have no effect on Islamic banks' efficiency, the current study results are striking because AD has a positive effect on Islamic banks' efficiency. Third, this study uses different measures of AD in analysis and finds that the results are robust to different measures.

## LITERATURE REVIEW

### Islamic vs. Conventional Banks

Similar to conventional banks, Islamic banks provide lending and borrowing services. However, Islamic banks have to follow the doctrines of Islam and comply with *Shari'ah* law. The main features of Islamic banking are as follows. First, the charging of interest (*Riba*) on loans and deposits is prohibited. Second, money serves as a unit of account and has no intrinsic value. Third, investment in risky financial products is prohibited. Nevertheless, investing in and trading real-asset-linked financial products are permissible. Fourth, Islamic banks stress profit/loss sharing. That is, any profit/loss of Islamic banks is shared with their depositors (Derigs & Marzban, 2008; Hopener, Rammal, & Rezex, 2011; Rafay & Farid, 2019).

In general, Islamic banks have lower profitability and cost efficiency compared to conventional banks. However, Islamic banks have higher stability and asset quality than conventional banks (Beck et al., 2013; Chen et al., 2018; Farook, Hassan, & Clinch, 2014; Masruki, Ibrahim, Osman, & Wahab, 2011). Compared with conventional banks, Islamic banks are less profitable possibly because they have limited methods of external financing and charge lower transaction fees. Cost efficiency is lower for Islamic banks possibly because customers choose to bank with them simply owing to their belief (Chen et al., 2018). Islamic banks are more stable possibly because of the aforementioned features of Islamic banking. However, Beck et al. (2013) find that Islamic and conventional banks resemble each other because they share similar business models.

## Bank Diversification and Performance

The existing literature has shown that income diversification increases the likelihood of bank failures during a financial crisis (Altunbas, Manganelli, & Marques-Ibanez, 2011; Berger, Imbierowicz, & Christian, 2016; Cole & White, 2012; Kayed & Hassan, 2011). This situation is likely because accompanying diversification are ineffective monitoring and adverse selection, thereby resulting in diseconomies and transitively higher risk and lower return for banks (Acharya et al., 2006). Lepetit, Nys, Rous, & Tarazi (2008) use European banks as samples and find that bank risks increase with income diversification. Demirgüç-Kunt & Huizinga (2010) and DeYoung & Torna (2013) use US banks and depository institutions as samples and determine that diversification causes bank failure during a crisis. Mercieca et al. (2007) and Laeven & Levine (2007) use cross-country data as sample and provide evidence indicating the presence of diversification discount. The presence of such a discount can be attributed to the benefit of risk-diversification and economies of scope being overwhelmed by the cost resulting from the severe agency problems accompanied by diversification (Chen et al., 2018).

Despite the aforementioned negative effect of diversification on bank performance, diversification can positively affect bank performance and result in diversification premium. Vallascas et al. (2012) and Saunders et al. (2014) use Italian and US banks, respectively, as study samples and find that banks gain from income diversification. Molyneux & Yip (2013) determine that income diversification positively affects bank performance. Such a positive effect is particularly observed among Islamic banks in Islamic countries that practice a dual banking system. Chatti et al. (2013) use Islamic banks in Malaysia as sample and further confirm that diversification positively affects Islamic banks' performance. Income diversification promotes bank stability for large Islamic banks compared with their small counterparts (Čihák & Hesse, 2010).

In summary, prior studies have generally indicated a negative effect of diversification on bank performance and any positive effect is typically found among Islamic banks (Chen et al., 2018). This result is likely because Islamic banks must be *Shari'ah*-compliant. These banks are specifically required to link financial transaction to real economic activities. They stress risk sharing and are prohibited from charging interests on loans and deposits and engaging in risky investments and speculative financial transactions. These features should mitigate any negative effect of diversification associated with increased agency costs, diseconomies, and risks (Iqbal & Mirakhor, 2011; Magalhães & Al-Saad, 2013).

In addition, diversification level is generally lower for Islamic banks than for conventional banks, such that the former is more capable of reaping a net positive effect of diversification on bank performance than the latter. That is, any diversification's negative (positive) effect is likely overpowered by its positive (negative) effect for Islamic (conventional) banks (Chen et al., 2018).

## Bank Efficiency

Existing literature has documented that bank types and countries matter in determining bank efficiency. For example, Hassan (2006) finds that cost efficiency is generally lower among Islamic banks likely because their regulatory environment hinders bank operations. Beck et al. (2013) also find that Islamic banks are generally less cost efficient than conventional banks. However, cost efficiency varies widely across countries. For example, Pakistan has higher cost efficiency whereas Indonesia and Malaysia have lower cost efficiency, among others. By contrast, using the DEA approach, Yudistira (2004) finds that Islamic banks are more efficient than conventional banks. Efficiency is also lower in the Middle East than in outside Middle East.

In addition to bank types and countries, competition in the banking industry can have bearings on bank efficiency. For instance, Berger & Hannan (1998) find that banks in more concentrated markets are less cost efficient. Casu & Girardone (2006) find that bank efficiency increases with banking competition in EU banking systems. However, Casu & Girardone (2009) subsequently investigate the banking sectors of five EU countries and find that market power positively Granger causes efficiency. Using European banking industries as the sample, Andrieş & Căpraru (2014) find that competition positively affects bank efficiency.

## AD and Bank Efficiency

Diversification's effect on bank performance has been widely examined, but relatively limited research has focused on its effect on bank efficiency. Chen et al. (2018) examine AD's effect on bank performance using three Asian countries as the sample. Although AD has been found to positively affect profitability and asset quality, particularly for Islamic banks, this factor has no bearing on cost efficiency for such banks. The possible reason is that the cost-to-income ratio serves as an inverse proxy for bank efficiency in their study. However, several underlying factors affect such a ratio, thereby rendering it unrepresentative for bank efficiency (Tripe, 1998). If bank efficiency is measured by a better proxy, then AD may prove to positively affect bank efficiency similar to other measures of bank performance (i.e., profitability and asset quality).

Despite minimal evidence indicating AD's effect on bank efficiency, banks should enjoy diversification's benefits of risk-diversification and economies of scope (Chen et al., 2018). Accordingly, these benefits should promote bank efficiency because risk and cost reduction accompanied by diversification facilitate the reduction of the cost involved when converting inputs to outputs. Doan et al. (2018) conduct a cross-country study and show that income diversification promotes bank efficiency. This finding indicates that AD should also promote bank efficiency. Moreover, AD can negatively affect bank efficiency owing to its accompanied diseconomies and agency problems (Laeven & Levine, 2007). However, the negative effect of AD should be minimized because the banking environment is highly competitive in dual-banking countries (Barth, Nolle, Phumiwasana, & Yago, 2003) and the association between competition and agency costs is negative (Ammann et al., 2013). Hence, AD's positive effect should overwhelm its negative effect, such that AD's net effect on bank efficiency is positive. Therefore, the following hypothesis is formulated:

**H1**: AD positively affects bank efficiency.

## Bank Size vs. AD's Effect on Bank Efficiency

The existing literature has directly or indirectly documented that bank size plays roles in determining diversification's effect on bank performance. Mercieca et al. (2007) find a negative effect of income diversification on the performance of small banks compared with large banks. They argue that with diversification, small banks incur more losses and reap fewer gains because they are less specialized and less experienced than large banks. Chen et al. (2018) find a positive effect of AD on bank performance, which is more pronounced among large banks. Altunbas et al. (2011) and Delis & Papanikolaou (2009) find that bank size and efficiency are positively related to each other. Hence, any positive effect of diversification on bank efficiency should increase with bank size because bank efficiency is higher when bank size is larger. Thus, efficiency gain from diversification should increase under such circumstances.

Čihák & Hesse (2010) find that bank size and financial stability are negatively related for Islamic banks. However, they also determine that income diversification positively affects financial stability of Islamic banks when they are large. Hence, the positive effect of income diversification on financial stability can offset or reverse the negative effect of bank size on financial stability. That is, diversification remains beneficial for large Islamic banks in terms of financial stability. Given that higher diversification entails higher financial stability and lower risk when banks are larger, better operating conditions are guaranteed for large Islamic banks. This condition means that diversification's positive effect on bank efficiency should be stronger for large Islamic banks.

Bank size can positively affect the costs resulting from management diseconomies, agency problems, and bureaucracy (Demirgüç-Kunt & Huizinga, 1999; Stiroh & Rumble, 2006). Hence, size can negatively affect AD's positive effect on bank efficiency. However, if the positive effect of size overweighs the negative effect, then size should strengthen AD's positive effect on bank efficiency. In addition, Islamic banks are generally less diversified and smaller, such that the room for improvement is larger. Accordingly, the effect of bank size on AD's positive effect on bank efficiency should be stronger for Islamic banks than for conventional banks. Therefore, the following hypothesis is formulated:

**H2**: Bank size strengthens AD's positive effect on bank efficiency and such a modifying effect is stronger for Islamic banks than for conventional banks.

## Foreign Ownership and Bank Performance

The relationship between foreign ownership and bank performance is mixed based on prior studies. However, the existing literature mostly provides evidence supporting a negative relationship between these two variables. Abbas, Mahmud, & Manan (2017) find a negative relationship between foreign ownership and performance of Islamic banks in Malaysia. Kamarudin, Sufian, Loong, & Anwar (2017) report that DEA-derived efficiency is higher for domestic banks in Southeast Asian countries than for their foreign counterparts. Lee & Hsieh (2014) determine that the financial stability of Asian banks is negatively influenced by foreign ownership. Lensink, Meesters, & Naaborg (2008) conduct a cross-country study and reveal the negative effect of foreign ownership on the efficiency of commercial banks. By contrast, Sufian & Abdul Majid (2008) found that foreign Islamic banks have higher technical efficiency than their domestic counterparts.

Home field advantage theory can explain the negative relationship between foreign ownership and bank performance (Kamarudin et al., 2017). This theory states that foreign banks in host countries incur higher costs and have difficulty competing with local banks. In addition, when foreign ownership is high, banks are inclined to participate in risk-taking behavior, thereby rendering such banks more vulnerable to financial distress during crisis (Angkinand & Wihlborg, 2010; Chen et al., 2017). Consequently, foreign ownership negatively affects bank performance. By contrast, the positive relationship between foreign ownership and bank performance can be explained by global advantage theory. This theory states that banks with foreign ownership have competitive advantages over local banks because of more active corporate control and better technology and human capital in the former than in the latter (Berger, DeYoung, Genay, & Udell, 2000).

## Foreign Ownership and AD's Effect on Bank Efficiency

Given the aforementioned relationship between foreign ownership and bank performance, whether and how foreign ownership modifies AD's effect on bank efficiency should be examined. The underlying reason is that foreign banks can incur higher costs and risks, such that they are outperformed by local banks based on home field advantage theory. Foreign banks can also have competitive advantages over local banks based on global advantage theory. These features (i.e., disadvantages and advantages associated with foreign ownership) should affect agency problems and diseconomies associated with diversification, such that foreign ownership should have a bearing on diversification's effects on bank efficiency.

The current study posits that home field advantage overpowers global advantage in the author's sampled Islamic banks because of the unique features of Islamic banking. Consequently, this situation should result in the failure of foreign ownership to strengthen the positive effect of diversification on bank efficiency (Chen et al., 2018). In particular, Islamic banks have to comply with the *Shari'ah*, which imposes strict requirements and restrictions on bank operations. They also generally set lower foreign ownership limit compared with conventional banks.[3] Furthermore, lack of transparency in government decision-making is highly criticized by foreign investors.[4] Hence, foreign investors experience difficulty in participating in decision-making and exercising corporate control in Islamic banks. Thus, foreign ownership is unlikely to improve agency problems caused by diversification, such that the positive effect of diversification on Islamic banks' efficiency is not strengthened. Following this line of reasoning, any high technology and good human capital accompanied by foreign ownership should be ineffective in promoting the positive effect of diversification on Islamic banks' efficiency.

Foreign ownership should strengthen (weaken) AD's negative (positive) effect on Islamic banks' efficiency because of several disadvantages. First, banks with foreign ownership have severe agency problems because cross-border monitoring is difficult and ineffective (Albertazzi & Bottero, 2014; Goetz, Laeven, & Levine, 2013). Therefore, foreign ownership should aggravate the agency problems and diseconomies brought about by diversification. That is, diversification's negative effect on bank efficiency should strengthen with foreign ownership. Second, banks with foreign ownership tend to take more risks than local banks and more risk-taking incurs cost and reduces efficiency (Chen et al., 2017). Therefore, foreign ownership should increase the costs and risks associated with diversification.

That is, diversification's negative effect on bank efficiency is reinforced. Third, foreign banks have informational disadvantage compared with local banks (Chen et al., 2017), thereby leading to adverse selection and worsen diversification-related agency problems. Therefore, diversification's positive effect on bank efficiency should be weaker for banks with foreign ownership than those without one. These disadvantages associated with foreign ownership should be conspicuous for Islamic banks compared with conventional banks. The reason is that the former is less open to foreign investors and should be more sensitive to the effect of foreign ownership.

The weaker (stronger) positive effect of diversification on the efficiency of Islamic banks with (without) foreign ownership can also be explained by the unique feature of domestic Islamic banks. That is, domestic Islamic banks are less diversified relative to their foreign counterparts.[5] Thus, low diversification level grants domestic Islamic banks a large room to exploit the diversification benefits. This feature should enhance the positive effect of diversification on the efficiency of domestic Islamic banks and counteract any negative effect caused by management diseconomies and increased agency costs that occur with diversification. Hence, the following hypothesis is formulated:

**H3**: AD's positive effect on bank efficiency is weaker among Islamic banks with foreign ownership than those without.

## METHODOLOGY

### Data

The study sample includes 155 banks from three Asian countries (i.e., Indonesia, Malaysia, and Pakistan) and spans the period 2006–2012. Annual bank data are gathered from the Bankscope database. Banks are classified into Islamic and conventional banks based on Bankscope (Chen et al., 2018).[6,7]

Following Chen et al. (2018), these three countries are chosen because they are relatively less explored and have a unique dual banking system. Given high competition in such countries, diversification's negative effect on bank performance owing to the accompanied agency problems should be weaker because competition negatively affects agency costs (Ammann et al., 2013). Moreover, these countries will eventually become the hub of Islamic banking because Islamic assets are concentrated and Islamic population is rapidly increasing. Specifically, Malaysia has been hosting the world's largest *Sukuk* (i.e., Islamic bond) market and is the center of Islamic finance (Gelbard, Hussain, Maino, Mu, & Yehoue, 2014; Sy, 2007). As of 2010, Indonesia has the world's largest Muslim population (12.7% of the total global Muslim population), whereas Pakistan is second (11.1%). The Muslim population of Pakistan is expected to exceed that of Indonesia by 2030 (Lugo & Cooperman, 2011). Large Muslim populations in these two countries will create high demand for Islamic banking. Therefore, whether diversification's negative effect widely observed in other countries also exists in these dual banking countries should be examined.

Bank efficiency is measured by the average of the efficiency scores (E) derived from DEA with varying returns to scale. Total customer deposits and debt (loans and securities) are used as the inputs (outputs). Guarda, Rouabah, & Vardanyan (2013) follow a similar approach. More specifically, E is directly measured by the average of the DEA-generated efficiency scores based on four combinations (i.e., (input(s); output(s)): (total customer deposits; securities), (total customer deposits; securities and loans), (total customer deposits and debt; securities), and (total customer deposits and debt; securities and loans)).

Following the approach of prior studies (Chen et al., 2018; Doumpos, Gaganis, & Pasiouras, 2016; Elsas, Hackethal, & Holzhäuser, 2010), the asset-based diversity or AD is used to measure diversification in this study. Three kinds of AD are calculated as follows:

$$AD1 = 1 - \frac{NL}{TEA} \tag{1}$$

$$AD2 = 1 - \left(\frac{NL}{TEA}\right)^2 - \left(\frac{TEA - NL}{TEA}\right)^2 \tag{2}$$

$$AD3 = AD1 + AD2 \tag{3}$$

where NL and TEA denote net loans and total earning assets, respectively.[8]

Following Laeven & Levine (2007), control variables are selected as follows: deposits divided by liabilities (DL), equity divided by assets (EA), growth in assets (GIA), and log of total assets (TA), which are used to measure bank intermediation, capitalization, growth opportunities, and bank size, respectively. To avoid the effect of extreme values, 1% and 99% winsorization rule is applied for these variables.

Dummy variables are generated to indicate different bank types, countries, years, and ownership types. Specifically, *Islam* is a dummy variable that equals one if some bank is an Islamic bank; zero otherwise. *Country* and *Year* are dummy variables used to represent different countries and years, respectively. *Foreign* is a dummy variable that equals one if some bank has foreign ownership; zero otherwise.

Table 1 gives the descriptive statistics for the variables used in the study. The median values for AD1, AD2, and AD3 are lower for Islamic banks than for conventional banks, indicating that asset diversity is lower for the former than for the latter.[9] The mean and median values for E are lower for Islamic banks than for conventional banks, indicating that bank efficiency is lower for the former than for the latter. Results are consistent with prior studies (Beck et al., 2013; Chen et al., 2018; Srairi, 2010). The results on control variables are like those of Chen et al. (2018). Specifically, Islamic banks have lower mean and median values of EA and log (TA) than conventional banks, indicating that capitalization is lower and bank size is smaller for the former than for the latter. Islamic banks have higher mean and median values of GIA than conventional banks, indicating that growth opportunities are greater for the former than for the latter. Islamic banks have higher median value of DL than conventional banks, thereby indicating higher bank intermediation for the former than the latter.[10] Conventional banks have higher mean value of Foreign than Islamic banks, thereby indicating higher percentage of banks with foreign ownership for the former than for the latter.

Prior to model estimation, the variance inflation factors (VIFs) for the benchmark model are calculated. The VIFs are low, ranging from 1.05 to 1.46. Hence, multicollinearity is not a concern.

*Table 1. Descriptive statistics for the variables used in the study*

| Bank Type | Variable | Mean | Min | p25 | p50 | p75 | Max | sd | N |
|---|---|---|---|---|---|---|---|---|---|
| Conventional | E | 0.331 | 0.028 | 0.189 | 0.275 | 0.419 | 1.000 | 0.206 | 520 |
| | AD1 | 0.388 | 0.000 | 0.257 | 0.348 | 0.487 | 0.977 | 0.183 | 541 |
| | AD2 | 0.408 | 0.000 | 0.359 | 0.436 | 0.486 | 0.500 | 0.097 | 541 |
| | AD3 | 0.795 | 0.000 | 0.638 | 0.802 | 0.987 | 1.125 | 0.221 | 541 |
| | DL | 0.867 | 0.097 | 0.836 | 0.917 | 0.956 | 0.995 | 0.150 | 541 |
| | EA | 14.509 | -3.300 | 8.110 | 10.620 | 16.440 | 68.130 | 11.167 | 541 |
| | GIA | 23.295 | -41.110 | 7.560 | 16.230 | 29.110 | 234.230 | 35.847 | 541 |
| | Log(TA) | 9.154 | 6.985 | 8.647 | 9.155 | 9.623 | 10.784 | 0.705 | 541 |
| | Foreign | 0.809 | 0.000 | 1.000 | 1.000 | 1.000 | 1.000 | 0.394 | 460 |
| Islamic | E | 0.265 | 0.067 | 0.149 | 0.236 | 0.358 | 0.703 | 0.145 | 77 |
| | AD1 | 0.413 | 0.048 | 0.215 | 0.313 | 0.556 | 1.000 | 0.259 | 88 |
| | AD2 | 0.352 | 0.001 | 0.271 | 0.392 | 0.475 | 0.500 | 0.133 | 88 |
| | AD3 | 0.766 | 0.140 | 0.552 | 0.743 | 1.039 | 1.102 | 0.253 | 88 |
| | DL | 0.830 | 0.037 | 0.918 | 0.946 | 0.960 | 0.996 | 0.267 | 88 |
| | EA | 12.840 | 3.520 | 7.280 | 9.490 | 15.610 | 53.510 | 9.330 | 88 |
| | GIA | 44.374 | -26.930 | 13.575 | 26.005 | 46.200 | 820.060 | 94.844 | 88 |
| | Log(TA) | 8.884 | 7.317 | 8.428 | 9.030 | 9.365 | 10.376 | 0.758 | 88 |
| | Foreign | 0.577 | 0.000 | 0.000 | 1.000 | 1.000 | 1.000 | 0.497 | 78 |

Notes: This table gives the descriptive statistics for the variables used in the study, including mean, minimum (Min), first quartile (p25), second quartile or median (p50), third quartile (p75), maximum (Max), standard deviation (sd), and number of observations (N). E is the average of DEA-generated efficiency scores based on four combinations (input; output): (total customer deposits; securities), (total customer deposits; securities and loans), (total customer deposits and debt; securities), and (total customer deposits and debt; securities and loans).

$\mathrm{AD1} = 1 - \frac{\mathrm{NL}}{\mathrm{TEA}}$; $\mathrm{AD2} = 1 - \left(\frac{\mathrm{NL}}{\mathrm{TEA}}\right)^2 - \left(\frac{\mathrm{TEA} - \mathrm{NL}}{\mathrm{TEA}}\right)^2$; $AD3 = AD1 + AD2$, where NL and TEA denote net loans and total earning assets, respectively. DL denotes the ratio of deposits to liabilities. EA denotes the ratio of equity to total assets. GIA denotes growth in assets. Log (TA) denotes the logarithm of total assets. Foreign is a dummy variable that returns a value of one if a given bank has foreign ownership and zero otherwise.

## Model

The author's estimation model is like that of prior studies (Beck et al., 2013; Chen et al., 2018; Laeven & Levine, 2007). However, since the DEA-generated efficiency scores are bounded by 0 and 1, the limited dependent variable approach (e.g., Tobit) is considered appropriate (Wooldridge, 2010). Given that the data are longitudinal, different specifications of the following random-effects Tobit panel data model is estimated.

$$\begin{aligned} E_{i,t} &= \beta_0 + \beta_1 AD_{i,t} + \beta_2 AD_{i,t} \times Islam_i + \beta_3 DL_{i,t} + \beta_4 EA_{i,t} + \beta_5 GIA_{i,t} + \beta_6 \log(TA)_{i,t} \\ &+ \sum_{j=1}^{3} \sum_{t=2006}^{2011} \gamma_{j,t} Country_j \times Year_t + \mu_i + \nu_{i,t} \end{aligned} \tag{4}$$

All variables are as defined above. *Country* is a dummy variable that equals one if some country is *j* (Indonesia, Malaysia, or Pakistan); zero otherwise. *Year* is a dummy variable that equals one if some year is *t*; zero otherwise. *Country* and *Year* are included to capture country-year effects. $\mu_i$ is the unobservable random effect for bank *i* whereas $v_{it}$ is the remainder disturbance for bank *i* and year *t*.

## EMPIRICAL RESULTS

### AD's Effect on Bank Efficiency

Table 2 shows the results of whether and how AD affects bank efficiency (E). The coefficients of AD1 and AD3 are significantly positive in columns 1 and 3, respectively, whereas that of the interaction variable is insignificant in all columns, thereby indicating that AD positively affects bank efficiency regardless of bank types. Given that the magnitude of the coefficients obtained from the Tobit model estimation cannot be interpreted similar to an OLS regression, the author further calculates the average effects of AD on E. The results in Columns 1 and 3 indicate that the average effect of AD on E is significantly positive and no differential effect occurs caused by bank types. Hence, the results support H1. Any differences in results can be attributed to different measures of AD, as documented by Elsas et al. (2010).

*Table 2. AD's effect on bank efficiency*

| **Dependent Variable = E** | | | |
|---|---|---|---|
| **Independent Variable** | (1) | (2) | (3) |
| AD1 | 0.269*** | | |
| | (0.030) | | |
| AD1×Islam | -0.045 | | |
| | (0.067) | | |
| AD2 | | 0.023 | |
| | | (0.055) | |
| AD2×Islam | | -0.043 | |
| | | (0.076) | |
| AD3 | | | 0.157*** |
| | | | (0.023) |
| AD3×Islam | | | -0.028 |
| | | | (0.037) |
| DL | -0.031 | -0.036 | -0.039 |
| | (0.040) | (0.043) | (0.042) |
| EA | 0.004*** | 0.005*** | 0.005*** |
| | (0.001) | (0.001) | (0.001) |
| GIA | -0.000 | -0.000 | -0.000 |
| | (0.000) | (0.000) | (0.000) |

*continues on following page*

*Table 2. Continued*

| Dependent Variable = E | | | |
|---|---|---|---|
| Log(TA) | 0.216*** | 0.214*** | 0.211*** |
| | (0.017) | (0.017) | (0.017) |
| Constant | -1.754*** | -1.613*** | -1.717*** |
| | (0.159) | (0.160) | (0.159) |
| *N* | 598 | 598 | 598 |
| *Wald chi2(26)* | 519.41*** | 399.33*** | 467.03*** |
| *Log-likelihood* | 604.098 | 567.273 | 588.797 |
| *(a)Average effect of AD on E (Islam=0)* | 0.269*** | 0.023 | 0.157*** |
| *(b)Average effect of AD on E (Islam=1)* | 0.225*** | -0.020 | 0.130*** |
| $\chi^2(1)$ *for (a)-(b)* | 0.44 | 0.33 | 0.56 |

Notes: E is the average of DEA-generated efficiency scores based on four combinations (input; output): (total customer deposits; securities), (total customer deposits; securities and loans), (total customer deposits and debt; securities), and (total customer deposits and debt; securities and loans).

$AD1 = 1 - \frac{NL}{TEA}$; $AD2 = 1 - \left(\frac{NL}{TEA}\right)^2 - \left(\frac{TEA - NL}{TEA}\right)^2$; $AD3 = AD1 + AD2$. Islam is a dummy variable that returns a value of one if a given bank is an Islamic bank and zero otherwise. DL denotes the ratio of deposits to liabilities. EA denotes the ratio of equity to total assets. GIA denotes growth in assets. Log (TA) denotes the logarithm of total assets. In all columns, country and year dummy variables are included to capture country- and year-specific effects respectively, but the results are saved for brevity. *N* represents the number of bank-year observations. The numbers in the parentheses are standard errors. ***, **, and * stand for 1, 5 and 10% significant, respectively

For the results on control variables, the coefficient of EA is significantly positive in all columns, thereby indicating that capitalization positively affects bank efficiency. This result is likely because equity serves as a buffer to absorb any future losses. The coefficient of log (TA) is also significantly positive across columns, thereby indicating that bank size positively affects bank efficiency because of economies of scale. These results concur with those of prior studies (Chen et al., 2018; Rosman, Wahab, & Zainol, 2014). However, the coefficients of DL and GIA are not significant, thereby indicating that bank intermediation and growth opportunities have no effect on bank efficiency.

## Bank Size vs. AD's Effect on Bank Efficiency

Given that diversification's effect on bank performance can be influenced by bank size (Mercieca et al., 2007), the author re-estimates the model for Islamic and conventional banks by including AD×Q1 and AD×Q4, where AD is AD1, AD2, or AD3; and Q1 (Q4) is a dummy variable that equals one if bank size is in the bottom 25% (top 25%) range and zero otherwise. The objective is to examine whether and how bank size modifies the effect of AD on bank efficiency for different types of banks. Table 3 presents the results. Columns 1 to 3 (4 to 6) present the results for the Islamic (conventional) banks. Given the bank size, the results are more revealing than those in Table 2. In Column 1, the coefficient of AD1 is significantly positive and the coefficients of AD1×Q1 and AD1×Q4 are significantly negative and significantly positive, respectively. These results indicate that the positive effect of AD on bank efficiency increases with the sizes of Islamic banks. A similar pattern is observed when AD is measured using AD3 in Column 3. That is, AD continues to have a positive effect on the efficiency of Islamic banks and such a positive effect strengthens with bank size. The results are slightly different when AD is measured using AD2. In Column2, the coefficient of AD2 is insignificant. However, the coefficients of AD2×Q1 and AD2×Q4 are significantly negative and significantly positive, respectively. These results indicate that the positive effect of AD on bank efficiency is observed for large Islamic banks only.

To be precise, the author calculates the average effect of AD on the efficiency of banks with different sizes (i.e., bottom 25% (small), middle 50% (medium), and top 25% (large)) (Table 3). The figures in Columns 1 to 3 indicate no effect of AD on the efficiency of small Islamic banks. In addition, AD positively affects the efficiency of medium and large Islamic banks and such a positive effect is stronger for large Islamic banks.

*Table 3. Bank size vs. AD's effect on bank efficiency*

| Dependent Variable = E | Islamic | Islamic | Islamic | Conventional | Conventional | Conventional |
|---|---|---|---|---|---|---|
| Independent Variable | (1) | (2) | (3) | (4) | (5) | (6) |
| AD1 | 0.264*** | | | 0.258*** | | |
| | (0.078) | | | (0.033) | | |
| AD1×Q1 | -0.164** | | | -0.025 | | |
| | (0.064) | | | (0.034) | | |
| AD1×Q4 | 0.382*** | | | 0.233*** | | |
| | (0.140) | | | (0.037) | | |
| AD2 | | 0.075 | | | -0.023 | |
| | | (0.106) | | | (0.061) | |
| AD2×Q1 | | -0.216*** | | | 0.041 | |
| | | (0.069) | | | (0.040) | |
| AD2×Q4 | | 0.326*** | | | 0.143*** | |
| | | (0.112) | | | (0.040) | |
| AD3 | | | 0.114** | | | 0.151*** |
| | | | (0.047) | | | (0.026) |
| AD3×Q1 | | | -0.090*** | | | -0.006 |
| | | | (0.033) | | | (0.019) |
| AD3×Q4 | | | 0.165*** | | | 0.095*** |
| | | | (0.062) | | | (0.020) |
| DL | -0.236*** | -0.229*** | -0.235*** | 0.060 | 0.047 | 0.049 |
| | (0.064) | (0.068) | (0.066) | (0.045) | (0.050) | (0.048) |
| EA | 0.005*** | 0.006*** | 0.006*** | 0.004*** | 0.006*** | 0.005*** |
| | (0.001) | (0.001) | (0.001) | (0.001) | (0.001) | (0.001) |
| GIA | -0.000* | -0.000 | -0.000* | -0.000 | 0.000 | -0.000 |
| | (0.000) | (0.000) | (0.000) | (0.000) | (0.000) | (0.000) |
| Log(TA) | 0.079* | 0.061 | 0.075* | 0.174*** | 0.201*** | 0.179*** |
| | (0.043) | (0.045) | (0.045) | (0.021) | (0.022) | (0.021) |
| Constant | -0.391 | -0.139 | -0.336 | -1.444*** | -1.543*** | -1.495*** |
| | (0.377) | (0.394) | (0.398) | (0.194) | (0.203) | (0.199) |

*continues on following page*

*Table 3. Continued*

| Dependent Variable = E | Islamic | Islamic | Islamic | Conventional | Conventional | Conventional |
|---|---|---|---|---|---|---|
| *N* | 77 | 77 | 77 | 521 | 521 | 521 |
| *Wald chi2(27)* | 387.44*** | 347.82*** | 375.79*** | 489.88*** | 352.14*** | 420.78*** |
| *Log-likelihood* | 120.941 | 118.749 | 119.403 | 538.780 | 494.324 | 517.633 |
| *Average effect of AD on E (Q1=1,Q4=0)* | 0.100 | -0.141 | 0.024 | 0.233*** | 0.017 | 0.145*** |
| *Average effect of AD on E (Q1=Q4=0)* | 0.264*** | 0.075 | 0.114** | 0.258*** | -0.023 | 0.151*** |
| *Average effect of AD on E (Q1=0, Q4=1)* | 0.646*** | 0.401*** | 0.279*** | 0.492*** | 0.120* | 0.246*** |

Notes: E is the average of DEA-generated efficiency scores based on four combinations (input; output): (total customer deposits; securities), (total customer deposits; securities and loans), (total customer deposits and debt; securities), and (total customer deposits and debt; securities and loans).

$AD1 = 1 - \frac{NL}{TEA}$; $AD2 = 1 - \left(\frac{NL}{TEA}\right)^2 - \left(\frac{TEA - NL}{TEA}\right)^2$; $AD3 = AD1 + AD2$. DL denotes the ratio of deposits to liabilities. EA denotes the ratio of equity to total assets. GIA denotes growth in assets. Log (TA) denotes the logarithm of total assets. In all columns, country and year dummy variables are included to capture country- and year-specific effects respectively, but the results are saved for brevity. *N* represents the number of bank-year observations. The numbers in the parentheses are standard errors. ***, **, and * stand for 1, 5 and 10% significant, respectively.

For conventional banks, the coefficient of AD1 in Column 4 is significantly positive; the coefficient of AD1×Q1 is insignificant, whereas that of AD1×Q4 is significantly positive. These results indicate that AD positively affects bank efficiency and such a positive effect is stronger for large conventional banks. When AD is measured using AD2 in Column 5, the coefficients of AD2 and AD2×Q1 are insignificant, whereas the coefficient of AD2×Q4 is significantly positive. These results indicate that AD positively affects the efficiency of large conventional banks. The results in Column 6 are similar to those in Column 4. In particular, the coefficients of AD3 and AD3×Q4 are significantly positive, whereas the coefficient of AD3×Q1 is insignificant. These results indicate that AD positively affects the efficiency of conventional banks and such a positive effect is stronger for large conventional banks.

The results of the average effects of AD on the efficiency of conventional banks concur with those previously discussed. The figures particularly indicate that either AD's positive effect on the efficiency of conventional banks increases with bank sizes or any positive effect of AD is observed for large conventional banks.

In summary, the results indicate that any positive effect of AD on the efficiency of Islamic banks is found when banks are medium- or large-sized. By contrast, AD's positive effect on bank efficiency appears to be more common among conventional banks. The reason is that such an effect can be observed for conventional banks with different sizes. Hence, H2 is supported.

The results related to the control variables indicate that the full sample results in Table 2 are driven by conventional banks. Moreover, the coefficients of EA and log (TA) remain significantly positive for Islamic and conventional banks, thereby indicating that capitalization and bank size positively affect the efficiency for both types of banks. However, DL and GIA have significantly negative coefficients for Islamic banks only, thereby suggesting that bank intermediation and growth opportunities negatively affect the efficiency for such banks.

## Foreign Ownership vs. AD's Effect on Bank Efficiency

The results in Table 4 are used to examine whether and how foreign ownership modifies the effect of AD on the efficiency of Islamic and conventional banks. In Columns 1 to 3, the coefficient of AD is significantly positive, whereas that of AD×Foreign is significantly negative. These results indicate that AD positively affects the efficiency of Islamic banks. However, AD's positive effect is weaker for Islamic banks with foreign ownership than those without one. By contrast, the results for conventional banks indicate that AD positively affects bank efficiency, although AD enters the regression insignificantly in Column 5. Given that the coefficient of AD×Foreign is insignificant in Columns 4 to 6, AD exerts no differential effect on bank efficiency considering ownership types for conventional banks.

*Table 4. Foreign ownership vs. AD's effect on bank efficiency*

| Dependent Variable = E | Islamic | Islamic | Islamic | Conventional | Conventional | Conventional |
|---|---|---|---|---|---|---|
| **Independent Variable** | **(1)** | **(2)** | **(3)** | **(4)** | **(5)** | **(6)** |
| AD1 | 0.591*** | | | 0.302*** | | |
| | (0.089) | | | (0.049) | | |
| AD1×Foreign | -0.359*** | | | 0.019 | | |
| | (0.077) | | | (0.052) | | |
| AD2 | | 0.477*** | | | -0.039 | |
| | | (0.142) | | | (0.087) | |
| AD2×Foreign | | -0.403*** | | | 0.001 | |
| | | (0.113) | | | (0.079) | |
| AD3 | | | 0.313*** | | | 0.187*** |
| | | | (0.060) | | | (0.038) |
| AD3×Foreign | | | -0.211*** | | | -0.012 |
| | | | (0.047) | | | (0.034) |
| DL | -0.234*** | -0.258*** | -0.247*** | -0.045 | -0.044 | -0.054 |
| | (0.058) | (0.062) | (0.059) | (0.052) | (0.057) | (0.054) |
| EA | 0.008*** | 0.008*** | 0.008*** | 0.004*** | 0.005*** | 0.005*** |
| | (0.001) | (0.001) | (0.001) | (0.001) | (0.001) | (0.001) |
| GIA | -0.000* | -0.000 | -0.000 | -0.000* | -0.000 | -0.000 |
| | (0.000) | (0.000) | (0.000) | (0.000) | (0.000) | (0.000) |
| Log(TA) | 0.174*** | 0.095** | 0.134*** | 0.246*** | 0.246*** | 0.245*** |
| | (0.030) | (0.039) | (0.033) | (0.022) | (0.022) | (0.021) |
| Constant | -1.300*** | -0.438 | -0.894*** | -2.022*** | -1.861*** | -2.029*** |
| | (0.270) | (0.343) | (0.297) | (0.207) | (0.208) | (0.207) |
| *N* | 67 | 67 | 67 | 443 | 443 | 443 |
| *Wald chi2(26)* | 428.79*** | 364.45*** | 405.58*** | 431.97*** | 318.57*** | 375.19*** |
| *Log-likelihood* | 112.806 | 103.357 | 108.784 | 456.617 | 420.897 | 439.526 |

*continues on following page*

*Table 4. Continued*

| Dependent Variable = E | Islamic | Islamic | Islamic | Conventional | Conventional | Conventional |
|---|---|---|---|---|---|---|
| *(a)Average effect of AD on E (Foreign=0)* | 0.591*** | 0.477*** | 0.313*** | 0.302*** | -0.039 | 0.187*** |
| *(b)Average effect of AD on E (Foreign=1)* | 0.232*** | 0.074 | 0.102** | 0.321*** | -0.038 | 0.175*** |
| $\chi^2$ *(1) for (a)-(b)* | 21.93*** | 12.69*** | 20.17*** | 0.14 | 0.00 | 0.12 |

Notes: E is the average of DEA-generated efficiency scores based on four combinations (input; output): (total customer deposits; securities), (total customer deposits; securities and loans), (total customer deposits and debt; securities), and (total customer deposits and debt; securities and loans).

$AD1 = 1 - \frac{NL}{TEA}$; $AD2 = 1 - \left(\frac{NL}{TEA}\right)^2 - \left(\frac{TEA - NL}{TEA}\right)^2$; $AD3 = AD1 + AD2$. Foreign is a dummy variable that returns a value of one if a given bank has foreign ownership and zero otherwise. DL denotes the ratio of deposits to liabilities. EA denotes the ratio of equity to total assets. GIA denotes growth in assets. Log (TA) denotes the logarithm of total assets. In all columns, country and year dummy variables are included to capture country- and year-specific effects respectively, but the results are saved for brevity. *N* represents the number of bank-year observations. The numbers in the parentheses are standard errors. ***, **, and * stand for 1, 5 and 10% significant, respectively.

The results related to the average effect of AD on bank efficiency also reveal that AD has a positive effect on the efficiency of Islamic banks. However, such a positive effect is weaker for Islamic banks with foreign ownership than those without one because the average effect of the former is significantly smaller than that of the latter. By contrast, AD positively affects the efficiency of conventional banks. However, given that the difference in the average effect between conventional banks with foreign ownership and those without one is insignificant, foreign ownership plays no role in modifying AD's effect on conventional banks' efficiency.

In summary, the results in Table 4 concur with those in Tables 2 and 3, in which AD positively affects bank efficiency. However, foreign ownership weakens such a positive effect for Islamic banks and has no bearing for conventional banks in this regard. Hence, the results support H3. Overall, the results in Tables 2 to 4 suggest the importance of considering bank size and ownership types in determining AD's effect on bank efficiency, particularly for Islamic banks.

## Foreign Ownership vs. AD's Effect on Bank Efficiency – Additional Tests

The next issue that naturally arises is why AD's positive effect on bank efficiency is weaker for Islamic banks with foreign ownership than those without one. Another issue worth exploring is how to counteract foreign ownership's negative effect on the positive effect of AD on the efficiency of Islamic banks. To address these questions, the author restricts the sample to Islamic banks and examine the channels through which AD affects bank efficiency, including DL, EA, GIA, and log (TA). Table 5 presents the results. In each column, AD interacts with one of the control variables (i.e., DL, EA, GIA, and log (TA)) and foreign ownership (Foreign).

The coefficients of the three-way interaction variables (i.e., Foreign×AD1×DL, Foreign×AD1×EA, Foreign×AD1×GIA and Foreign×AD1×log(TA)) are all significantly negative. This result indicates that an increase in DL, EA, GIA, or log (TA) weakens any positive effect of AD on the efficiency of Islamic banks with foreign ownership. For Islamic banks with foreign ownership, AD's positive effect on bank efficiency decreases with bank intermediation, capitalization, growth opportunities, or bank size. That

*Table 5. Foreign ownership vs. AD's effect on bank efficiency – additional tests*

| Dependent Variable = E | (1) | (2) | (3) | (4) |
|---|---|---|---|---|
| **Independent Variable** | | | | |
| AD1 | 0.584** | 0.350*** | 0.497*** | -0.124 |
| | (0.292) | (0.127) | (0.060) | (0.787) |
| DL | -0.229** | -0.269*** | -0.352*** | -0.238*** |
| | (0.100) | (0.057) | (0.045) | (0.058) |
| EA | 0.008*** | 0.010*** | 0.008*** | 0.007*** |
| | (0.001) | (0.002) | (0.001) | (0.001) |
| GIA | -0.000* | -0.000* | 0.000 | -0.000* |
| | (0.000) | (0.000) | (0.000) | (0.000) |
| Log(TA) | 0.178*** | 0.212*** | 0.197*** | 0.143*** |
| | (0.035) | (0.030) | (0.018) | (0.049) |
| AD1×DL | -0.004 | | | |
| | (0.362) | | | |
| Foreign×AD1×DL | -0.343*** | | | |
| | (0.118) | | | |
| AD1×EA | | 0.021*** | | |
| | | (0.008) | | |
| Foreign×AD1×EA | | -0.027*** | | |
| | | (0.005) | | |
| AD1×GIA | | | 0.001 | |
| | | | (0.002) | |
| Foreign×AD1×GIA | | | -0.004*** | |
| | | | (0.001) | |
| AD1×log(TA) | | | | 0.083 |
| | | | | (0.092) |
| Foreign×AD1×log(TA) | | | | -0.043*** |
| | | | | (0.010) |
| Constant | -1.340*** | -1.665*** | -1.499*** | -1.003** |
| | (0.361) | (0.274) | (0.163) | (0.447) |
| *N* | 67 | 67 | 67 | 67 |
| *Wald chi2(26)* | 411.01*** | 426.43*** | 711.50*** | 436.86*** |
| *Log-likelihood* | 110.86164 | 113.64271 | 107.66624 | 112.34358 |
| *(a)Average effect of AD on E (Foreign=0)* | 0.580*** | 0.510*** | 0.482*** | 0.663*** |
| *(b)Average effect of AD on E (Foreign=1)* | 0.260*** | 0.269*** | 0.335*** | 0.231*** |
| $\chi^2$ *for (a)-(b)* | 11.04*** | 17.26*** | 2.85* | 11.90*** |

Notes: E is the average of DEA-generated efficiency scores based on four combinations (input; output): (total customer deposits; securities), (total customer deposits; securities and loans), (total customer deposits and debt; securities), and (total customer deposits and debt; securities and loans). $AD1 = 1 - \frac{NL}{TEA}$. Foreign is a dummy variable that returns a value of one if a given bank has foreign ownership and zero otherwise. DL denotes the ratio of deposits to liabilities. EA denotes the ratio of equity to total assets. GIA denotes growth in assets. Log (TA) denotes the logarithm of total assets. In all columns, country and year dummy variables are included to capture country- and year-specific effects respectively, but the results are saved for brevity. *N* represents the number of bank-year observations. The numbers in the parentheses are standard errors. ***, **, and * stand for 1, 5 and 10% significant, respectively.

is, bank intermediation, capitalization, growth opportunities, or bank size is less effective in enhancing AD's positive effect on the efficiency of Islamic banks with foreign ownership than those without. To counteract the negative effect of foreign ownership on AD's positive effect on bank efficiency, Islamic banks should decrease bank intermediation, capitalization, growth opportunities, or bank size.

The magnitude of the coefficients in Tobit regression cannot be interpreted similarly as in linear regression. Hence, the author further derives the average marginal effects of AD on bank efficiency for Islamic banks with foreign ownership and those without one. The results are summarized in the bottom of Table 5. Evidently, the average effects of AD on bank efficiency are all significantly lower for Islamic banks with foreign ownership than those without one.[11]

In summary, the results in Table 5 suggest that AD affects the efficiency of Islamic banks through bank intermediation, capitalization, growth opportunities, and bank size. The results further confirm the data obtained in Table 4. That is, the observation of the weaker positive effect of AD on the efficiency of Islamic banks with foreign ownership than those without is robust to different model specifications that consider the interaction between AD, Foreign and control variables.[12]

## CONCLUSION

This chapter investigates whether and how AD influences bank efficiency. Using the banks in three dual banking Asian countries from 2006 to 2012 as the sample, results indicate that AD positively affects bank efficiency. Considering the effect of bank size, results indicate that AD's positive effect on bank efficiency is especially observed among large banks. Such a positive effect is also especially found among Islamic banks as opposed to conventional banks. Moreover, considering the effect of foreign ownership, results reassure AD's positive effect on bank efficiency. More importantly, foreign ownership weakens such a positive effect for Islamic banks. By contrast, ownership type does not modify the effect of AD on the efficiency of conventional banks. Furthermore, the weaker positive effect of AD on the efficiency of Islamic banks with foreign ownership can be explained by the finding that bank intermediation, capitalization, growth opportunities, and bank size appear to counteract AD's positive effect on the efficiency of such banks.

Implications are provided for researchers, practitioners, and policymakers. For researchers, results suggest that AD positively affects bank efficiency. In addition, bank size and ownership type matter in determining AD's effect on bank efficiency, particularly for Islamic banks. Hence, future studies on bank efficiency should take these findings into account.

For practitioners, the results provide useful suggestions on how to engage in diversification strategically to improve efficiency. Results generally suggest that banks should diversify their assets to reap the efficiency gain. However, caution has to be exercised when diversifying their assets. This is because large banks are more likely to gain from AD, particularly for Islamic banks. However, diversification can do more harm than good for small banks. In addition, Islamic banks should be aware that AD's positive effect on bank efficiency can weaken when they have foreign ownership. Hence, Islamic banks with foreign ownership are recommended to pursue AD in moderation. By contrast, the concern about the negative effect of foreign ownership can be alleviated for conventional banks because foreign ownership plays no roles in determining AD's effect on these banks' efficiency.

For policymakers, given that AD's effect on bank efficiency varies with bank size and ownership type, authorities should implement policies to encourage AD on a case-by-case basis. Specifically, given that AD's positive effect on bank efficiency is stronger when bank size is large particularly for Islamic banks, policy should be implemented to encourage AD for large banks only, especially for Islamic banks. Moreover, AD is more effective in improving the efficiency of domestic Islamic banks than that of Islamic banks with foreign ownership. Hence, AD is encouraged particularly for Islamic without foreign ownership because it results in higher efficiency for such banks than Islamic banks with foreign ownership.

The results and implications of this study should be applicable to the three dual banking Asian countries or other Islamic countries with similar institutional environments. Future research should include a more comprehensive set of Islamic countries to provide better insights into the research question. However, given that the countries examined in this study are characterized by rapid growth of Islamic population and relatively high Islamic assets in their banks, these countries serve as the model in the Islamic world. Hence, the results are also meaningful for other Islamic countries that will eventually become more Islamized. Specifically, these countries may want to improve bank efficiency through AD when their Islamic banking becomes more mature in the future. However, they should be cautious of the potential effects of bank size and foreign ownership when engaging in AD to promote bank efficiency.

## Classifications

JEL Classification: G21, G29
KAUJIE Classification: J32, L25

## ACKNOWLEDGMENT

The author would like to thank Dr. Yu, M.-T. and Dr. Liang, H.-Y. for their assistance with the collection of my data.

## REFERENCES

Abbas, S. Z. M., Mahmud, R., & Manan, N. S. A. (2017). Foreign ownership and performance of Islamic banks. *Journal of Computational and Theoretical Nanoscience*, *23*(8), 7594–7596.

Acharya, V. V., Hasan, I., & Saunders, A. (2006). Should banks be diversified? Evidence from individual bank loan portfolios. *The Journal of Business*, *79*(3), 1355–1412. doi:10.1086/500679

Albertazzi, U., & Bottero, M. (2014). Foreign bank lending: Evidence from the global financial crisis. *Journal of International Economics*, *92*, S22–S35. doi:10.1016/j.jinteco.2014.01.002

Altunbas, Y., Manganelli, S., & Marques-Ibanez, D. (2011). Bank risk during the Great Recession: Do business models matter? *ECB Working Paper* 1394.

Ammann, M., Oesch, D., & Schmid, M. M. (2013). Product market competition, corporate governance, and firm value: Evidence from the EU area. *European Financial Management*, *19*(3), 452–469. doi:10.1111/j.1468-036X.2010.00605.x

Andrieş, A. M., & Căpraru, B. (2014). The nexus between competition and efficiency: The European banking industries experience. *International Business Review*, *23*(3), 566–579. doi:10.1016/j.ibusrev.2013.09.004

Angkinand, A., & Wihlborg, C. (2010). Deposit insurance coverage, ownership, and banks' risk-taking in emerging markets. *Journal of International Money and Finance*, *29*(2), 252–274. doi:10.1016/j.jimonfin.2009.08.001

Barth, J. R., Nolle, D. E., Phumiwasana, T., & Yago, G. (2003). A cross-country analysis of the bank supervisory framework and bank performance. *Financial Markets. Institutions & Instruments*, *12*(2), 67–120. doi:10.1111/1468-0416.t01-2-00001

Beck, T., Demirgüç-Kunt, A., & Merrouche, O. (2013). Islamic vs. conventional banking: Business model, efficiency and stability. *Journal of Banking & Finance*, *37*(2), 433–447. doi:10.1016/j.jbankfin.2012.09.016

Berger, A. N., DeYoung, R., Genay, H., & Udell, G. (2000). Globalization of financial institutions: Evidence from cross-border banking performance. Brookings–Wharton Papers on Financial Services, 2000(1), 23–72.

Berger, A. N., & Hannan, T. H. (1998). The efficiency cost of market power in the banking industry: A test of the "quiet life" and related hypotheses. *The Review of Economics and Statistics*, *80*(3), 454–465. doi:10.1162/003465398557555

Berger, A. N., Imbierowicz, B., & Christian, R. (2016). The roles of corporate governance in bank failures during the recent financial crisis. *Journal of Money, Credit and Banking*, *48*(4), 729–770. doi:10.1111/jmcb.12316

Casu, B., & Girardone, C. (2006). Bank competition, concentration and efficiency in the single European market. *Manchester School*, *74*(4), 441–468. doi:10.1111/j.1467-9957.2006.00503.x

Casu, B., & Girardone, C. (2009). Testing the relationship between competition and efficiency in banking: A panel data analysis. *Economics Letters*, *105*(1), 134–137. doi:10.1016/j.econlet.2009.06.018

Chatti, M. A., Kablan, S., & Yousfi, O. (2013). Are Islamic banks sufficiently diversified? An empirical analysis of eight Islamic banks in Malaysia. *Islamic Economic Studies*, *21*(2), 23–54. doi:10.12816/0001557

Chen, M., Wu, J., Jeon, B. N., & Wang, R. (2017). Do foreign banks take more risk? Evidence from emerging economies. *Journal of Banking & Finance*, *82*(C), 20–39. doi:10.1016/j.jbankfin.2017.05.004

Chen, N., Liang, H.-Y., & Yu, M.-T. (2018). Asset diversification and bank performance: Evidence from three Asian countries with a dual banking system. *Pacific-Basin Finance Journal*, *52*, 40–53. doi:10.1016/j.pacfin.2018.02.007

Čihák, M., & Hesse, H. (2010). Islamic banks and financial stability: An empirical analysis. *Journal of Financial Services Research*, *38*(2-3), 95–113. doi:10.100710693-010-0089-0

Cole, R. A., & White, L. J. (2012). Déjà vu all over again: The causes of U.S. commercial bank failures this time around. *Journal of Financial Services Research*, *42*(1-2), 5–29. doi:10.100710693-011-0116-9

Delis, M. D., & Papanikolaou, N. I. (2009). Determinants of bank efficiency: Evidence from a semi-parametric methodology. *Managerial Finance*, *35*(3), 260–275. doi:10.1108/03074350910931771

Demirgüç-Kunt, A., & Huizinga, H. (1999). Determinants of commercial bank interest margins and profitability: Some international evidence. *The World Bank Economic Review*, *13*(2), 379–408. doi:10.1093/wber/13.2.379

Demirgüç-Kunt, A., & Huizinga, H. (2010). Bank activity and funding strategies: The impact on risk and returns. *Journal of Financial Economics*, *98*(3), 626–650. doi:10.1016/j.jfineco.2010.06.004

Derigs, U., & Marzban, S. (2008). Review and analysis of current Shariah-compliant equity screening practices. *International Journal of Islamic and Middle Eastern Finance and Management*, *1*(4), 285–303. doi:10.1108/17538390810919600

DeYoung, R., & Roland, K. P. (2001). Product mix and earnings volatility at commercial banks: Evidence from a degree of total leverage model. *Journal of Financial Intermediation*, *10*(1), 54–84. doi:10.1006/jfin.2000.0305

DeYoung, R., & Torna, G. (2013). Nontraditional banking activities and bank failures during the financial crisis. *Journal of Financial Intermediation*, *22*(3), 397–421. doi:10.1016/j.jfi.2013.01.001

Doan, A. T., Lin, K. L., & Doong, S. C. (2018). What drives bank efficiency? The interaction of bank income diversification and ownership. *International Review of Economics & Finance*, *55*, 203–219. doi:10.1016/j.iref.2017.07.019

Doumpos, M., Gaganis, C., & Pasiouras, F. (2016). Bank diversification and overall financial strength: International evidence. *Financial Markets. Institutions & Instruments*, *25*(3), 169–213. doi:10.1111/fmii.12069

Elsas, R., Hackethal, A., & Holzhäuser, M. (2010). The anatomy of bank diversification. *Journal of Banking & Finance*, *34*(6), 1274–1287. doi:10.1016/j.jbankfin.2009.11.024

Farook, S., Hassan, M. K., & Clinch, G. (2014). Islamic bank incentives and discretionary loan loss provisions. *Pacific-Basin Finance Journal*, *28*, 152–174. doi:10.1016/j.pacfin.2013.12.006

Gamra, S. B., & Plihon, D. (2011). Revenue diversification in emerging market banks: Implications for financial performance. *CEPN Working Papers hal-00598136*, HA.

Gelbard, M. E., Hussain, M. M., Maino, M. R., Mu, M. Y., & Yehoue, M. E. B. (2014). Islamic finance in sub-Saharan Africa: Status and prospects (No. 14-149). International Monetary Fund.

Goetz, M. R., Laeven, L., & Levine, R. (2013). Identifying the valuation effects and agency costs of corporate diversification: Evidence from the geographic diversification of U.S. banks. *Review of Financial Studies*, *26*(7), 1787–1823. doi:10.1093/rfs/hht021

Guarda, P., Rouabah, A., & Vardanyan, M. (2013). Identifying bank outputs and inputs with a directional technology distance function. *Journal of Productivity Analysis*, *40*(2), 185–195. doi:10.100711123-012-0326-7

Hassan, M. K. (2006). The X-efficiency in Islamic banks. *Islamic Economic Studies*, *13*(2), 49–78.

Hopener, A. G. F., Rammal, H. G., & Rezex, M. (2011). Islamic mutual funds' financial performance and international investment style: Evidence form 20 countries. *European Journal of Finance*, *17*(9-10), 829–850. doi:10.1080/1351847X.2010.538521

Iqbal, Z., & Mirakhor, A. (2011). An introduction to Islamic finance. *Theory into Practice*, *687*. John Wiley & Sons.

Kamarudin, F., Sufian, F., Loong, F. W., & Anwar, N. A. M. (2017). Assessing the domestic and foreign Islamic banks efficiency: Insights from selected Southeast Asian countries. *Future Business Journal*, *3*(1), 33–46. doi:10.1016/j.fbj.2017.01.005

Kayed, R. N., & Hassan, M. K. (2011). The global financial crisis and Islamic finance. *Thunderbird International Business Review*, *53*(5), 551–564. doi:10.1002/tie.20434

Laeven, L., & Levine, R. (2007). Is there a diversification discount in financial conglomerates? *Journal of Financial Economics*, *85*(2), 331–367. doi:10.1016/j.jfineco.2005.06.001

Lee, C. C., & Hsieh, M.-F. (2014). Bank reforms, foreign ownership, and financial stability. *Journal of International Money and Finance*, *40*, 204–224. doi:10.1016/j.jimonfin.2013.09.001

Lee, C. C., Hsieh, M. F., & Yang, S. J. (2016). The effects of foreign ownership on competition in the banking industry: The key role of financial reforms. *Japan and the World Economy*, *37*, 27–46. doi:10.1016/j.japwor.2016.02.002

Lensink, R., Meesters, A., & Naaborg, I. (2008). Bank efficiency and foreign ownership: Do good institutions matter? *Journal of Banking & Finance*, *32*(5), 834–844. doi:10.1016/j.jbankfin.2007.06.001

Lepetit, L., Nys, E., Rous, P., & Tarazi, A. (2008). Bank income structure and risk: An empirical analysis of European banks. *Journal of Banking & Finance*, *32*(8), 1452–1467. doi:10.1016/j.jbankfin.2007.12.002

Lugo, L., & Cooperman, A. (2011). *The future of the global Muslim population*. USA: Pew Research Center.

Magalhães, R., & Al-Saad, S. (2013). Corporate governance in Islamic financial institutions: The issues surrounding unrestricted investment account holders. *Corporate Governance: The International Journal of Business in Society*, *13*(1), 39–57. doi:10.1108/14720701311302404

Masruki, R., Ibrahim, N., Osman, E., & Wahab, H. A. (2011). Financial performance of Malaysian founder Islamic banks versus conventional banks. *Journal of Business and Policy Research*, *6*(2), 67–79.

Mercieca, S., Schaeck, K., & Wolfe, S. (2007). Small European banks: Benefits from diversification? *Journal of Banking & Finance*, *31*(7), 1975–1998. doi:10.1016/j.jbankfin.2007.01.004

Molyneux, P., & Yip, J. (2013). Income diversification and performance of Islamic banks. *Journal of Financial Management, Markets, and Institutions*, *1*(1), 47–66.

Rafay, A., & Farid, S. (2019). Islamic Banking System: A Credit Channel of Monetary Policy – Evidence from an Emerging Economy. *Economic Research*, *32*(1), 742–754.

Rosman, R., Wahab, N. A., & Zainol, Z. (2014). Efficiency of Islamic banks during the financial crisis: An analysis of Middle Eastern and Asian countries. *Pacific-Basin Finance Journal*, *28*, 76–90. doi:10.1016/j.pacfin.2013.11.001

Saunders, A., Schmid, M. M., & Walter, I. (2014). *Non-Interest income and bank performance: Is banks' increased reliance on non-interest income bad?* School of Finance, University of St. Gallen.

Srairi, S. A. (2010). Cost and profit efficiency of conventional and Islamic banks in GCC countries. *Journal of Productivity Analysis*, *34*(1), 45–62. doi:10.100711123-009-0161-7

Stiroh, K. J., & Rumble, A. (2006). The dark side of diversification: The case of US financial holding companies. *Journal of Banking & Finance*, *30*(8), 2131–2161. doi:10.1016/j.jbankfin.2005.04.030

Sufian, F., & Abdul Majid, M. Z. (2008). Bank ownership, characteristics, and performance: A comparative analysis of domestic and foreign Islamic banks in Malaysia. *Journal of King Abdulaziz University: Islamic Economics*, *21*(2), 3–38.

Sy, A. (2007). Malaysia: An Islamic capital market hub. *IMF Survey Magazine: Countries & Regions*.

Tripe, D. (1998). *Cost to income ratios in Australasian banking*. Department of Finance, Banking and Property, College of Business, Massey University.

Vallascas, F., Crespi, F., & Hagendorff, J. (2012). Income diversification and bank performance during the financial crisis. Available at SSRN 1793232.

Wooldridge, J. M. (2010). *Econometric analysis of cross section and panel data*. Cambridge, MA: The MIT Press.

Yudistira, D. (2004). Efficiency in Islamic banking: An empirical analysis of eighteen banks. *Islamic Economic Studies*, *12*(1), 1–19.

## ENDNOTES

1. According to Chen *et al.* (2018), "these three countries are above the world average in terms of bank competition level, with Malaysia being the most competitive among them."
2. Please visit the following website for details: https://www.state.gov/e/eb/rls/othr/ics/2015/241648.htm
3. It is not until recently that Islamic banks started to ease the limit of foreign ownership. In fact, conventional banks have higher percentage of foreign ownership than Islamic banks in the author's study sample. Specifically, the percentage of conventional banks with foreign ownership is 80.9% whereas that of Islamic banks with foreign ownership is 57.7% (Table 1).
4. Please refer to the following website for details: https://www.state.gov/e/eb/rls/othr/ics/2015/241648.htm

5 The author finds that the level of AD is higher for Islamic banks with foreign ownership than those without. The results are not reported for brevity.

6 Conventional banks include cooperative banks, depository institutions, investment banks, and savings banks.

7 The sample consists of 127 conventional banks and 28 Islamic banks. Due to data homogenization, banks with data that cannot be converted to common international standards are excluded from Bankscope. This explains why Bankscope covers fewer Islamic banks than expected.

8 The AD measure is slightly different from that of Chen *et al.* (2018). In addition, since the results of estimation based on different measures of diversification can be different (Doumpos *et al.*, 2016; Elsas *et al.* 2010), the author creates another measure of diversification (i.e., AD3) by summing up the simple measure and the Herfindahl-type measure (i.e., AD1 and AD2 respectively) to average out the respective effects of AD1 and AD2.

9 The mean values for AD2 and AD3 are also lower for Islamic banks than for conventional banks.

10 Since the distributions of these variables are asymmetric, median values are considered more appropriate than mean values when comparing variables between these two types of banks.

11 AD2 and AD3 are also used to estimate the model. The results resemble those based on AD1 and are therefore saved for brevity.

12 The potential impact of government ownership is also considered. However, the author fails to provide more sophisticated analysis because there are only 8 government-owned banks (i.e., banks with government ownership exceeding 50%). Notwithstanding this, the author reestimates the model by excluding government-owned banks and finds that major results remain.

# Chapter 8
# Participative Banking in Turkey: A Performance Analysis

**Serpil Altınırmak**
*Anadolu University, Turkey*

**Cumhur Şahin**
https://orcid.org/0000-0002-8790-5851
*Bilecik Şeyh Edebali University, Turkey*

**Çağlar Karamaşa**
*Anadolu University, Turkey*

**Basil Oluch Okoth**
*Anadolu University, Turkey*

## ABSTRACT

*Islamic banks were established as private financial institutions in Turkey based on a law enacted in 1983. Private financial institutions succeeded to have equal rights with commercial banks subject to banking law in 2001. The name of private financial institutions was changed to participation banks in 2005 because of being insufficient in terms of Islamic banking transactions. This chapter includes a performance analysis of participation banks listed in Turkey by considering the efficiency and profitability ratios within the period of 2007-2016 using interval-valued pythagorean fuzzy AHP based fuzzy TOPSIS. Three participation banks, Albaraka Türk, Türkiye Finans, and Kuveyt Turk, were examined for the mentioned period.*

## INTRODUCTION

The concept of interest-free banking extends to the beginning of human history. The literature shows that even the first men conducted interest-free borrowing and lending transactions among themselves. It has been shown that people borrowed what they needed gave them back when they were due, interest-free. This system has continued in the same way after the introduction of money, as it was before money.

DOI: 10.4018/978-1-7998-1611-9.ch008

The concept of Islamic banking became known to the world in the 20th century. As a result of the widespread use of classical banking in western countries and the avoidance of this kind of banking by the Muslim world due to religious requirements, the idea of Islamic banking was introduced by Muslim scholars in the 20th century to make good use of the savings of the Muslim community that was left outside the economic system.

Islamic banking or the non-interest banking system could be defined as a system that collects funds and conducts its operations based on the principle of profit/loss sharing (Rafay & Farid, 2019; Tenekeci, 2017). The main difference between Islamic banking and the classical banking system is interest. Therefore, Islamic banking is a banking system that performs its funds collection and use on the basis of profit/loss participation as opposed to on interest. With regard to banking services, it generally offers its customers similar services to those offered by classical banking.

As in other countries, Turkey also has a number of institutions that offer Islamic banking. The Turkish government, which was one of the founding members of the Islamic development bank in 1975, became one of major partners of the bank by increasing its share of capital in 1984, thereby earning itself a permanent position in the bank's board of directors. The first interest-free banking service in Turkey was first offered by the Investment Bank for Public Industrial Workers (DESİYAB) which was established in 1975 to provide services to citizens and SMEs who wanted to evaluate their savings in accordance with the interest-free system. DESİYAB, which operated until 1978 earned Turkey significant experience in the field of interest-free banking. At the establishment of bank, the board of directors was given the mandate to choose between interest and interest-free banking, and thus the bank chose to go interest-free in 1978. In 1988, DESİYAB changed its name development bank of Turkey. Another important development with regard to the interest-free banking in Turkey was the decree on "Profit / Loss Partnership (KZOB)" which was included in the decree that formed DESİYAB. The details of the system were prepared on February 24, 1984 by the Ministry of the Treasury and Foreign Trade and in March of the same year they were published by the notification of the Central Bank of Turkey (Canbaz, 2012). After this decree, the activities of the Islamic banks in Turkey have continued under special finance institutions.

Six Islamic banks were established in Turkey between 1984 and 1996 and these include, *Al Baraka Türk* and *Faisal Finans* private finance institutions which were established in 1984 and started operations a year later in 1985. *Kuveyt Türk* special finance institution was established in 1989 followed by *Anadolu Finans*, *İhlas Finans* and *Asya Bankası* private finance institution in 1991, 1995 and 1996 respectively. While the first three of these banks are mostly foreign capital based, the remaining three banks are mostly domestic capital based (Canbaz, 2014).

The interest in the products and services offered by the Turkish Islamic banking is increasing by the day. In 2014 *Ziraat* participation bank entered the Turkish participation banking sector, followed by *Vakıf* participation bank in 2015. However, with the closure of one of the banks in 2016, the number of participation banks in Turkey became five. The future of Islamic banking in Turkey is promising and this number is only expected to rise.

The aim of this study was to analyze the financial performances of participation banks listed in BIST within the period between 2010 and 2016 using interval-valued Pythagorean fuzzy AHP based fuzzy TOPSIS. Pythagorean fuzzy sets was chosen in order to better express the decision makers' judgments related to performance evaluation of participation banks in indeterminate, ambiguous and vague environment due to mathematical complication. To the best of our knowledge, this is the first study to evaluate the participation banks using Pythagorean fuzzy sets. The literature review regarding participation banks is given in background section. The Pythagorean fuzzy sets, interval-valued Pythagorean fuzzy AHP and fuzzy TOPSIS are then explained in the methodology section. The results of the study are given in solutions and recommendations sections. Finally, the conclusion of the study is given and recommendation for future studies provided in the conclusion section.

## BACKGROUND

Akın and Ece (2010) evaluated the performance and the increasing share of participation banks operating in Turkey between 2003 and 2009. The study discussed the basic principles of Islamic finance system, its increasing importance and the comparison of Islamic banking and traditional banking. Moreover, the development of participation banks over the years and its increasing share of the Turkish financial system were presented using various banking indicators.

Ada and Dalkılıç (2014) used the set of indicators obtained from the balance sheet data of 22 Islamic banks to examine the effects of scale efficiency, efficiency changes, and total factor productivity change. During the study, data from 4 Islamic banks operating in Turkey and 18 Islamic banks operating in Malaysia for the period 2009-2011 were used. Data envelopment analysis, efficiency changes and total factor were used in the measurement of efficiency, while malmquist total factor productivity index was used to determine the productivity change. The study observed that participation banks in Turkey had a high average of scale activity compared to banks in Malaysia in 2009 and a low rate in 2010 – 2011. The change in total productivity was found to be low for Turkey in the period of 2009 - 2010 compared to 2010 – 2011, and in Malaysia, there was a general increase except for 3 banks.

Toraman et al. (2015) analyzed the performance of traditional and participation banks using a comparative method. Within the scope of the study, the financial ratios of the traditional and participation banks operating in Turkey were calculated from the financial statements for the period 2006-2014. Independent samples using the t - test method, it was found that the total assets and liquid assets of traditional banks were higher than participation banks and they were stronger than participation banks in terms of capital adequacy. Further, they used the two-stage generalized method of moments to influence bank profitability and found the bank profitability to be positively related to the operational efficiency and capital adequacy. There is a negative correlation between the ratio of non-performing loans to total loans, which is an indicator of credit quality.

Bayramoğlu and Başarır (2018) used CAMELS-based TOPSIS model to determine the risk ratings of participation banks listed in Turkey using financial ratios in 2016. They found *Vakıf* participation bank with the lowest risk compared to other participation banks. However, considering that the *Vakıf* participation only started its activities recently, *Kuveyt Türk* was considered to have performed better in terms of risk management.

Samad (1999) compared the relative performances of full-fledged Islamic banks and conventional banks in Malaysia during 1992-1996. The study found the administrative efficiency of conventional banks to be higher than that of full-fledged Islamic banks.

Hussein (2001) investigated the cost-effectiveness of Islamic banks in Sudan during the 1990- 2000 period. In the study, the cost-effectiveness of 17 banks was investigated by applying the stochastic frontier approach. As a result, small banks were determined to be more efficient than large banks.

Mokhtar et al. (2006) compared the activities of Islamic banks listed in Malaysia between 1997 and 2003 using the stochastic frontier approach. In this study, they concluded that the assets, deposits and financing bases of Islamic banks were rapidly growing compared to conventional banks and that Islamic banks were more efficient than local banks in this period.

Srairi (2011) examined the impact of financial liberalization on the increase in banking productivity in the Gulf Cooperation Council countries during the 1990-2007 period. In the study, both the Islamic and conventional banks were analyzed using DEA and malmquist total factor productivity index. The results showed that the banks of Gulf countries had a change in productivity during the liberalization period rather than a rise in productivity. It was also concluded that conventional banks performed better than Islamic banks in terms of productivity.

As a result, literature gap related to studies of Islamic and participation banking includes 1999 and 2018.

## METHODOLOGY

### Pythagorean Fuzzy Sets

Pythagorean fuzzy sets (PFS) is developed by Yager (2013) in order to better represent vague and imprecise environment. PFS as an extension of IFS can handle indeterminate and uncertain judgments of human beings more efficiently. PFS can be expressed such as:

Let X be a fixed set. A PFS M is a mathematical object having the form as below:

$$M:\left\{\left\langle x,\mu_M\left(x\right),v_M\left(x\right)\right\rangle;x\in X\right\} \tag{1}$$

where the function $\mu_M(x)$: $x\rightarrow[0,1]$ represents the degree of the membership and $v_M(x)$: $x\rightarrow[0,1]$ symbolizes the degree of non-membership of the element $x\in X$ to M respectively, for every $x\in X$,

$$0\leq\left(\mu_M\left(x\right)\right)^2+\left(v_M\left(x\right)\right)^2\leq 1 \tag{2}$$

PFS is characterized by membership and non-membership degrees whose sum of squares is less than or equal to 1.

Additionally the hesitant degree of $x\in X$, ($\pi_M(x)$) is calculated as follows:

$$\pi_M\left(x\right)=\sqrt{1-\left(\mu_M\left(x\right)\right)^2-\left(v_M\left(x\right)\right)^2} \tag{3}$$

Let $C_1=M\left(\mu_{C_1},v_{C_1}\right)$ and $C_2=M\left(\mu_{C_2},v_{C_2}\right)$ be two pythagorean fuzzy number (PFNs) and $\lambda>0$, then the operations on these two PFNs are described as below:

$$C_1 \oplus C_2 = M\left(\sqrt{\mu_{C_1} + \mu_{C_2} - \mu_{C_1}\mu_{C_2}},\ v_{C_1}v_{C_2}\right) \tag{4}$$

$$C_1 \otimes C_2 = M\left(\mu_{C_1}\mu_{C_2},\ \sqrt{v_{C_1} + v_{C_2} - v_{C_1}v_{C_2}}\right) \tag{5}$$

$$\lambda C_1 = \left(\sqrt{1-\left(1-\mu_{C_1}^2\right)^{\lambda}},\ v_1^{\lambda}\right) \tag{6}$$

$$C_1^{\lambda} = \left(\mu_{C_1}^{\lambda},\ \sqrt{1-\left(1-v_{C_1}^2\right)^{\lambda}}\right) \tag{7}$$

Let $D=M(\mu_D, v_D)$ be a PFN, then the score and accuracy functions of D is computed as follows:

$$s(D) = (\mu_D)^2 - (v_D)^2 \tag{8}$$

$$h(D) = (\mu_D)^2 + (v_D)^2 \tag{9}$$

The larger score and accuracy functions of $s(D)$ and $h(D)$, the better and higher accuracy of PFN D.

The euclidean distance of two PFNs such as $C_1 = M\left(\mu_{C_1}, v_{C_1}\right)$ and $C_2 = M\left(\mu_{C_2}, v_{C_2}\right)$ can be obtained as below:

$$d\left(C_1, C_2\right) = \sqrt{\frac{1}{2}\left[\left(\left(\mu_{C_1}\right)^2 - \left(\mu_{C_2}\right)^2\right)^2 + \left(\left(v_{C_1}\right)^2 - \left(v_{C_2}\right)^2\right)^2 + \left(\left(\pi_{C_1}\right)^2 - \left(\pi_{C_2}\right)^2\right)^2\right]} \tag{10}$$

## Interval-Valued Pythagorean Fuzzy AHP

Criteria and alternatives are evaluated by taking weighting scale into the account under pythagorean information shown as Table 1. Interval-valued pythagorean fuzzy AHP can be summarized as below (İlbahar, Karaşan, Çebi & Kahraman, 2018, p.127; Gül & Ak, 2018, pp.656-657):

1. Compromised pairwise comparison matrix $A=(a_{ij})_{n\times m}$ is obtained by taking experts' opinions into the account via weighting scale seen as Table 1.
2. Difference matrix $D=(d_{ij})_{n\times m}$ is constructed by considering lower and upper values of the membership and non-membership functions as Eqs. (11) and (12):

$$d_{ijL} = \mu_{ijL}^2 - v_{ijU}^2 \tag{11}$$

$$d_{ijU} = \mu_{ijU}^2 - v_{ijL}^2 \tag{12}$$

*Table 1. Weighting scale used for evaluating criteria and alternatives under pythagorean information*

| Linguistic Terms | Interval Valued Pythagorean Fuzzy Numbers | | | |
|---|---|---|---|---|
| | $\mu_L$ | $\mu_U$ | $v_L$ | $v_L$ |
| Certainly low importance | 0 | 0 | 0.9 | 1 |
| Very low importance | 0.1 | 0.2 | 0.8 | 0.9 |
| Low importance | 0.2 | 0.35 | 0.65 | 0.8 |
| Below average importance | 0.35 | 0.45 | 0.55 | 0.65 |
| Average importance | 0.45 | 0.55 | 0.45 | 0.55 |
| Above average importance | 0.55 | 0.65 | 0.35 | 0.45 |
| High importance | 0.65 | 0.8 | 0.2 | 0.35 |
| Very high importance | 0.8 | 0.9 | 0.1 | 0.2 |
| Certainly high importance | 0.9 | 1 | 0 | 0 |
| Exactly equal | 0.1965 | 0.1965 | 0.1965 | 0.1965 |

3. Interval multiplicative matrix $P=(p_{ij})_{n\times m}$ is obtained by using Eqs. (13) and (14):

$$p_{ijL} = \sqrt{1000^{d_L}} \tag{13}$$

$$p_{ijU} = \sqrt{1000^{d_U}} \tag{14}$$

4. Determinacy value $\tau_{ij}$ of the elements for compromised pairwise comparison matrix $a_{ij}$ is calculated according to Eq. (15):

$$\tau_{ij} = 1 - \left(\mu_{ijU}^2 - \mu_{ijL}^2\right) - \left(v_{ijU}^2 - v_{ijL}^2\right) \tag{15}$$

5. The matrix of weights $Y=(y_{ij})_{n\times m}$ is constructed by multiplying determinacy degress with $P=(p_{ij})_{n\times m}$ matrix as Eq. (16):

$$y_{ij} = \left(\frac{p_{ijL} + p_{ijU}}{2}\right)\tau_{ij} \tag{16}$$

6. Finally normalized priority weights are calculated according to Eq. (17):

$$w_i = \frac{\sum_{j=1}^{n} y_{ij}}{\sum_{i=1}^{n}\sum_{j=1}^{n} y_{ij}} \tag{17}$$

## Fuzzy Topsis

Hwang and Yoon (1981) developed the TOPSIS method to select the alternative with the shortest euclidean distance from the positive ideal solution (PIS) that maximizes benefit and minimizes cost, and the farthest distance from the negative ideal solution (NIS) that maximizes cost and minimizes benefit (Behzadian, Otaghsara, Yazdani & Ignatius, 2012). Fuzzy TOPSIS has been applied by researchers in many areas under inconsistent, indeterminate and inaccurate environment.

Fuzzy TOPSIS can be explained as below (Wang & Chang, 2007; Jahanshahloo, Hosseinzadeh & Izadikhah, 2006):

1. A fuzzy decision matrix $\tilde{B}$ including k alternatives $(A_1, A_2, \ldots, A_k)$, l criteria $(C_1, C_2, \ldots, C_l)$ and fuzzy values $\tilde{y}_{ij}$ which shows the rating of alternative $A_i$ with respect to criterion $C_j$ is formed and presented as Eq.(18):

$$\tilde{B} = \begin{bmatrix} \tilde{y}_{11} & \tilde{y}_{12} & \cdots & \tilde{y}_{1l} \\ \tilde{y}_{21} & \tilde{y}_{22} & \cdots & \tilde{y}_{2l} \\ \vdots & \vdots & \vdots & \vdots \\ \tilde{y}_{k1} & \tilde{y}_{k2} & \cdots & \tilde{y}_{kl} \end{bmatrix}_{kxl} \quad i = 1, 2, \ldots, k \quad j = 1, 2, \ldots, l \tag{18}$$

2. Fuzzy decision matrix is normalized via linear scale transformation and presented as Eq.(19):

$$\tilde{N} = \begin{bmatrix} \tilde{n}_{11} & \tilde{n}_{12} & \cdots & \tilde{n}_{1l} \\ \tilde{n}_{21} & \tilde{n}_{22} & \cdots & \tilde{n}_{2l} \\ \vdots & \vdots & \vdots & \vdots \\ \tilde{n}_{k1} & \tilde{n}_{k2} & \cdots & \tilde{n}_{kl} \end{bmatrix}_{kxl} \quad i = 1, 2, \ldots, k \quad j = 1, 2, \ldots, l \tag{19}$$

Elements of normalized fuzzy decision matrix $\tilde{n}_{ij}$ are acquired via equation (20) for benefit criteria (*G*), it is valid for cost ones (*M*) via Eq. (21).

$$\tilde{n}_{ij} = \left( \frac{d_{ij}}{f_j^*}, \frac{e_{ij}}{f_j^*}, \frac{f_{ij}}{f_j^*} \right), \quad f_j^* = \max_i c_{ij} \quad j \in G \tag{20}$$

$$\tilde{n}_{ij} = \left( \frac{d_j^-}{f_{ij}}, \frac{d_j^-}{e_{ij}}, \frac{d_j^-}{d_{ij}} \right), \quad d_j^- = \min_i d_{ij} \quad j \in M \tag{21}$$

3. Weighted normalized decision matrix $\left(\tilde{H}\right)$ is formed by using Equation (22):

$$\tilde{H} = \begin{bmatrix} \tilde{h}_{11} & \tilde{h}_{12} & \cdots & \tilde{h}_{1l} \\ \tilde{h}_{21} & \tilde{h}_{22} & \cdots & \tilde{h}_{2l} \\ \vdots & \vdots & \vdots & \vdots \\ \tilde{h}_{k1} & \tilde{h}_{k2} & \cdots & \tilde{h}_{kl} \end{bmatrix}_{kxl} \quad i = 1,2,\ldots,k \quad j = 1,2,\ldots,l \tag{22}$$

Elements of weighted normalized fuzzy decision matrix $\tilde{h}_{ij}$ are acquired according to Equation (23).

$$\tilde{h}_{ij} = \tilde{n}_{ij} \otimes \widetilde{ag}_j \tag{23}$$

where $\widetilde{ag}_j$ denotes the weight of criterion $C_j$.

4. Fuzzy pozitive ideal solution ($FPIS, Z^*$) and fuzzy negative ideal solution ($FNIS, Z^-$) are described as below:

$$Z^* = \left(\tilde{h}_1^*, \tilde{h}_2^*, \ldots, \tilde{h}_l^*\right) = \left\{\left(\max_i \tilde{h}_{ij} \middle| j \in J\right), \left(\min_0 \tilde{h}_{ij} \middle| j \in J'\right)\right\} \tag{24}$$

$$Z^- = \left(\tilde{h}_1^-, \tilde{h}_2^-, \ldots, \tilde{h}_n^-\right) = \left\{\left(\min_i \tilde{h}_{ij} \middle| j \in J\right), \left(\max_0 \tilde{h}_{ij} \middle| j \in J'\right)\right\} \tag{25}$$

$$\tilde{h}_j^* = (1,1,1), \tilde{h}_j^- = (0,0,0), \; j = 1,2,\ldots,l \tag{26}$$

5. Distances of each alternative from $Z^*$ and $Z^-$ are calculated via Eq.(27) and (28):

$$u_i^* = \sum_{j=1}^{l} u\left(\tilde{h}_{ij}, \tilde{h}_j^*\right), \quad i = 1,2,\ldots,k \tag{27}$$

$$u_i^- = \sum_{j=1}^{l} u\left(\tilde{h}_{ij}, \tilde{h}_j^-\right), \quad i = 1,2,\ldots,k \tag{28}$$

6. Closeness coefficient ($YK_i$) of each alternative is computed according to Eq.(29):

$$YK_i = \frac{u_i^-}{u_i^* + u_i^-}, \quad i = 1,2,\ldots,k \tag{29}$$

The alternatives are ranked according to the values of $YK_i$ in descending process. If the value of $YK_i$ approaches to 1 alternative $A_i$ having this value closes to FPIS. On the other hand if the value of $YK_i$ approaches to 0 alternative $A_i$ having this value closes to FNIS.

## SOLUTIONS AND RECOMMENDATIONS

In this study, 12 financial ratios (identified as criteria) were considered for evaluating the performance of the 3 participation banks (identified as alternatives) listed in BIST within the period between 2010 and 2016. The ratios were identified based on in-depth literature review and classified into two groups, namely efficiency and profitability. The ratio groups can be seen in Table 2.

The ratio of non-performing loans / (loan + leasing) is essential for the bank's operational performance and quality of bank assets. Effective operations of the bank favor this ratio to be as low as possible. The ratio of (loan + leasing)/total assets is one of the important indicators of the bank's asset quality and structure. The rise and fall of this ratio affect the reserves and asset quality of banks in different ways. For this reason, it is desired to have a higher rate for bank activity. The ratio of dividend expenses / (collected funds+ loans obtained) shows the amount paid in dividends by the banks on the loans and funds they obtain. A lower rate is preferred. The dividend income/dividend expenses ratio is used to compare the earnings from the use of funds and the dividends paid to the sources of the funds. A ratio greater than one is preferable as it shows that the income earned by the bank from the use of the funds is more than the expenses paid in dividends to the sources.

The ratio of shareholder's equity/total risk weighted items is the necessary capital requirement that the bank is required by law (No. 5411) to maintain. The sum of risk weighted items constitutes the risk associated with credit risk, market risk, operational risk, structural interest rate risk and concentration. A higher ratio is an indicator of a strong capital structure.

Dividend income/shareholder's equity is an important indicator for measuring the bank's effectiveness and may also be used to indicate the sustainability of bank operations. A higher ratio indicates the effective use of the bank's capital. A higher ratio for earnings before tax/total assets is desirable as it indicates the effective use of the bank's capital. Net income for the period/shareholder's equity represents the returns from banks' equity and is used in efficiency analysis. A higher ratio indicates the efficient use of the bank's equity. (Credits+ leasing)/number of branches is a measure of efficiency that shows

*Table 2. Ratio groups for the study*

| Ratio Groups | Explanation |
|---|---|
| Efficiency ratios | Non-performing loans/(loan+ leasing) |
| | (Loan+ leasing)/total assets |
| | Dividend expenses/(collected funds +loans obtained) |
| | Dividend income/dividend expenses |
| | Shareholders' equity/total risk weighted items |
| | Dividend income/shareholders' equity |
| Profitability ratios | Earnings before tax/total assets |
| | Net income for the period/shareholders' equity |
| | (Credits+ leasing)/number of branches |
| | (Credits+leasing)/(collected funds+loans obtained +shareholders' equity) |
| | Net income from fees and commissions /total assets |
| | Total assets/number of personnel |

whether the bank branches are operating efficiently. At the same time, this figure shows the amount of credit per branch. (Credits + leasing)/ (collected funds+ loans obtained + shareholder's equity) shows how much of the resources on the liabilities side of the bank's balance sheet turned into resources on the assets side. A higher ratio is desirable. Net income from fees and commissions/total assets shows the assets of the bank and the shares of these assets within the volume of the bank's operations. A higher ratio shows higher efficiency by the bank. The ratio of total assets/number of personnel shows the amount of assets per employee. A higher ratio indicates that the per capita efficiency and the quality of the personnel is high.

The criteria were evaluated by nine experts using interval valued Pythagorean fuzzy AHP. Authors assumed equal weights for nine experts. Pythagorean fuzzy numbers are chosen to show good and bad specifications of criteria and evaluate the alternatives under various factors. Then the decision matrix is formed by handling the mean of opinions of the nine decision makers related to criteria and alternatives. The decision matrix is given in Table 3.

The elements in parenthesis seen as Table 3, represent the membership and non-membership degree of measuring the performance of alternative in terms of criteria respectively. After applying interval valued Pythagorean fuzzy AHP method, weights of financial ratios are obtained shown as Table 4.

According to the results of Table 4, while the ratio of shareholders' equity/total risk weighted items was found as the most important one with a weight of 0.102374, total assets/number of personnel was found to be the least important with 0.067343.

The participation banks are then evaluated by fuzzy TOPSIS. For this purpose crisp data are transformed to triangular fuzzy numbers according to Wang's (2014) method seen as eq. (30):

*Table 3. Decision matrix for Pythagorean fuzzy AHP*

| Banks<br>Ratios | *Albaraka Türk* | *Kuveyt Türk* | *Türkiye Finans* |
|---|---|---|---|
| Non-performing loans/(loan+leasing) | (0.725,0.275) | (0.4,0.6) | (0.85,0.15) |
| (Loan+ leasing)/total assets | (0.95,0) | (0,0.95) | (0.95,0) |
| Dividend expenses/(collected funds +loans obtained) | (0.85,0.15) | (0.275,0.725) | (0.85,0.15) |
| Dividend income/dividend expenses | (0.95,0) | (0.275,0.725) | (0.95,0) |
| Shareholders' equity/total risk weighted items | (0.85,0.15) | (0.275,0.725) | (0.95,0) |
| Dividend income/shareholders' equity | (0.85,0.15) | (0.15,0.85) | (0.95,0) |
| Earnings before tax/total assets | (0.85,0.15) | (0.15,0.85) | (0.85,0.15) |
| Net income for the period/shareholders' equity | (0.85,0.15) | (0.15,0.85) | (0.85,0.15) |
| (Credits+ leasing)/number of branches | (0.725,0.275) | (0.275,0.725) | (0.85,0.15) |
| (Credits+ leasing)/(collected funds+loans obtained +shareholders' equity) | (0.85,0.15) | (0.15,0.85) | (0.85,0.15) |
| Net income from fees and commissions/total assets | (0.95,0) | (0.15,0.85) | (0.95,0) |
| Total assets/number of personnel | (0.95,0) | (0,0.95) | (0.95,0) |

*Table 4. Weights of financial ratios*

| Financial Ratios | Weights |
|---|---|
| Non-performing loans/(loan+ leasing) | 0.080898 |
| (Loan+ leasing)/total assets | 0.075294 |
| Dividend expenses/(collected funds +loans obtained) | 0.081162 |
| Dividend income/dividend expenses | 0.080535 |
| Shareholders' equity/total risk weighted items | 0.102374 |
| Dividend income/shareholders' equity | 0.096704 |
| Earnings before tax/total assets | 0.097861 |
| Net income for the period/shareholders' equity | 0.088124 |
| (Credits+ leasing)/number of branches | 0.079312 |
| (Credits+ leasing)/(collected funds+loans obtained+shareholders' equity) | 0.078387 |
| Net income from fees and commissions /total assets | 0.072004 |
| Total assets/number of personnel | 0.067343 |

Let $y_{ij}(d)$ present the value of related criteria $j$ for alternative $i$ on period $d$ and $O_{ij}$ be the performance rating value for alternative $i$ on criterion $j$, where $i=1,2,\ldots,k;$ $j=1,2,\ldots,l;$ $d=1,2,\ldots,p$.

$$O_{ij} = \left(o_{1ij}, o_{2ij}, o_{3ij}\right) \text{where,}$$

$$o_{1ij} = \min_{1 \le d \le p} \left\{y_{ij}\left(d\right)\right\},\ o_{2ij} = \frac{1}{p}\sum_{d=1}^{p} y_{ij}\left(d\right),\ o_{3ij} = \max_{1 \le d \le p} \left\{y_{ij}\left(d\right)\right\} \tag{30}$$

Performance rating values of $[O_{i1},O_{i2},\ldots,O_{il}]$ describe the performance matrix of alternative $A_i(i=1,2,\ldots,k)$ on all criteria. Following that the normalized fuzzy decision matrix is constructed and can be shown as Table 5.

After that the weighted normalized fuzzy decision matrix is formed and presented as Table 6.

Distances of each alternative from $Z^*$ and $Z^-$ are calculated and demonstrated as Table 7.

As a result, $YK_i$ values of each alternative are computed and alternatives are ranked as Table 8 in descending manner.

According to the findings presented in Table 8 while *Türkiye finans* places first by value of 0.213496, *Kuveyt türk* places last by value of 0.207640.

## CONCLUSION

This study evaluated the performances of three participation banks listed in BIST using financial ratios. For this purpose, twelve financial ratios classified under effectiveness and efficiency dimensions were determined. The three participation banks traded in BIST were evaluated as alternatives. Firstly, weights

*Table 5. Normalized fuzzy decision matrix*

| Banks<br>Ratios | *Albaraka türk* | *Kuveyt Türk* | *Türkiye finans* |
|---|---|---|---|
| Non-performing loans/(loan+ leasing) | (0.33,0.58,0.81) | (0.49,0.70,1) | (0.32,0.51,0.69) |
| (Loan+ leasing)/total assets | (0.86,0.91,0.97) | (0.80,0.86,0.94) | (0.92,0.96,1) |
| Dividend expenses/(collected funds +loans obtained) | (0.58,0.65,0.77) | (0.73,0.82,1) | (0.5,0.6,0.78) |
| Dividend income/dividend expenses | (0.78,0.82,0.92) | (0.91,0.96,1) | (0.85,0.9,0.96) |
| Shareholders' equity/total risk weighted items | (0.68,0.76,0.84) | (0.76,0.85,1) | (0.68,0.78,0.94) |
| Dividend income/shareholders' equity | (0.73,0.85,1) | (0.64,0.72,0.8) | (0.75,0.78,0.82) |
| Earnings before tax/total assets | (0.33,0.67,0.83) | (0.55,0.65,0.87) | (0.36,0.68,1) |
| Net income for the period/shareholders' equity | (0.43,0.79,1) | (0.58,0.72,0.84) | (0.39,0.69,0.9) |
| (Credits+ leasing)/number of branches | (0.53,0.71,1) | (0.46,0.6,0.73) | (0.41,0.69,0.95) |
| (Credits+financial leasing)/(collected funds+loans obtained +shareholders' equity) | (0.74,0.78,0.81) | (0.69,0.74,0.81) | (0.84,0.9,1) |
| Net income from fees and commissions /total assets | (0.44,0.7,1) | (0.32,0.41,0.62) | (0.37,0.54,0.78) |
| Total assets/number of personnel | (0.39,0.6,0.89) | (0.35,0.6,0.89) | (0.32,0.65,1) |

*Table 6. Weighted normalized fuzzy decision matrix*

| Banks<br>Ratios | Albaraka türk | Kuveyt Türk | Türkiye finans |
|---|---|---|---|
| Non-performing loans/(loan+ leasing) | (0.02,0.04,0.06) | (0.03,0.05,0.08) | (0.02,0.04,0.05) |
| (Loan+ leasing)/total assets | (0.06,0.06,0.07) | (0.06,0.06,0.07) | (0.06,0.07,0.07) |
| Dividend expenses/(collected funds +loans obtained) | (0.04,0.05,0.06) | (0.05,0.06,0.08) | (0.04,0.04,0.06) |
| Dividend income/dividend expenses | (0.06,0.06,0.07) | (0.07,0.07,0.08) | (0.06,0.07,0.07) |
| Shareholders' equity/total risk weighted items | (0.07,0.07,0.08) | (0.07,0.08,0.1) | (0.07,0.08,0.09) |
| Dividend income/shareholders' equity | (0.07,0.08,0.09) | (0.06,0.07,0.07) | (0.07,0.07,0.07) |
| Earnings before tax/total assets | (0.03,0.06,0.08) | (0.05,0.06,0.08) | (0.03,0.06,0.09) |
| Net income for the period/shareholders' equity | (0.03,0.06,0.08) | (0.05,0.06,0.07) | (0.03,0.06,0.07) |
| (Credits+ leasing)/number of branches | (0.04,0.05,0.07) | (0.03,0.04,0.05) | (0.03,0.05,0.07) |
| (Credits+ leasing)/(collected funds+loans obtained +shareholders' equity) | (0.05,0.06,0.06) | (0.05,0.05,0.06) | (0.06,0.07,0.07) |
| Net income from fees and commissions /total assets | (0.03,0.05,0.07) | (0.02,0.02,0.04) | (0.02,0.03,0.05) |
| Total assets/number of personnel | (0.02,0.04,0.05) | (0.02,0.04,0.06) | (0.02,0.04,0.06) |

*Table 7. Distances of each alternative from $Z^*$ and $Z^-$*

| Participation Banks | $u_i^*$ | $u_i^-$ |
|---|---|---|
| Albaraka türk | 9.465280 | 2.552832 |
| Kuveyt türk | 9.517205 | 2.494010 |
| Türkiye finans | 9.454126 | 2.566324 |

*Table 8. $YK_i$ values and ranking of participation banks in descending manner*

| Participation Banks | $YK_i$ values | Rank |
|---|---|---|
| Albaraka türk | 0.212415 | 2 |
| Kuveyt türk | 0.207640 | 3 |
| Türkiye finans | 0.213496 | 1 |

of criteria were calculated using interval-valued Pythagorean fuzzy AHP. The ratio of shareholders' equity/total risk weighted items was determined to be the most essential. After that, the participation banks were evaluated according to fuzzy TOPSIS. To the best of our knowledge, there are no studies based on evaluating the performance of participation banks via interval-valued Pythagorean fuzzy AHP based fuzzy TOPSIS. For further studies, different hybrid-based methods under various financial ratios could be applied to evaluate the performance of participation banks listed in Turkey or other countries.

## Classifications

JEL Classification: G17, G21
KAUJIE Classification: H25, L25

## REFERENCES

Ada, A. A., & Dalkılıç, N. (2014). Efficiency Analysis In Islamic Banks: A Study For Malaysia And Turkey. *BDDK Bankacılık ve Finansal Piyasalar*, *8*(1), 9–33.

Akın, F., & Ece, N. (2010). İslami Finans Sistemi İçerisinde İslami Bankacılığın Yeri ve Türkiye'de Katılım Bankacılığının Gelişimi. *Mevzuat Dergisi*, *13*(151), 4–5.

Bayramoğlu, M, F. & Başarır, Ç. (2018). Türk Katılım Bankalarının Risk Derecelendirmesi: CAMELS Tabanlı TOPSIS Modeli Uygulaması, *İşletme & Ekonomi Yazıları*, *5*(2), 390-399.

Behzadian, M., Otaghsara, S. K., Yazdani, M., & Ignatius, J. (2012). A State of Art Survey of TOPSIS Applications. *Expert Systems with Applications*, *39*(17), 13051–13069. doi:10.1016/j.eswa.2012.05.056

Canbaz, M. (2012). Katılım Bankacılığı ve Türkiye'deki gelişimi. In F. Kaya (Ed.), *Bankacılık giriş ve ilkeler* (pp. 137–198). İstanbul, Turkey: Beta Basım.

Canbaz, M. (2014). Katılım Bankacılığı ve Türkiye'deki gelişimi. In F. Kaya (Ed.), *Bankacılık giriş ve ilkeleri* (pp. 149–252). İstanbul, Turkey: Beta Basım.

Gül, M., & Ak, M. F. (2018). A comparative outline for quantifying risk ratings in occupational health and safety risk assessment. *Journal of Cleaner Production*, *196*, 653–664. doi:10.1016/j.jclepro.2018.06.106

Hussein, K. A. (2001). Operational Efficiency. In *Islamic Banking: The Sudanese Experience, Islamic Research And Training Enstitute*. Islamic Development Bank.

Hwang, C. L., & Yoon, K. (1981). *Multiple Attribute Decision Making: Methods and Applications*. Berlin, Germany: Springer-Verlag. doi:10.1007/978-3-642-48318-9

İlbahar, E., Karaşan, A., Çebi, S., & Kahraman, C. (2018). A novel approach to risk assessment for occupational health and safety using Pythagorean fuzzy AHP & fuzzy inference system. *Safety Science*, *103*, 124–136. doi:10.1016/j.ssci.2017.10.025

Jahanshahloo, G. R., Hosseinzadeh, L. F., & Izadikhah, M. (2006). Extension of the TOPSIS method for decision-making problems with fuzzy data. *Applied Mathematics and Computation*, *181*(2), 1544–1551. doi:10.1016/j.amc.2006.02.057

Mokhtar, H. S. A., Abdullah, N., & Al-Habshi, S. M. (2006). Efficiency of Islamic banks in Malaysia: A stochastic frontier approach. *Journal of Economic Cooperation*, *27*(2), 37–70.

Rafay, A., & Farid, S. (2019). Islamic Banking System: A Credit Channel of Monetary Policy – Evidence from an Emerging Economy. *Economic Research Journal*, *32*(1), 742–754.

Samad, A. (1999). Comparative Efficiency of the Islamic Bank Vis- A - Vis Conventional Banks in Malaysia. *IIUM Journal of Economics And Management*, *7*(1), 1–27.

Srairi, S. A. (2011). Productivity Growth In GCC Banking Industry: Conventional Versus Islamic Banks. *Journal of Knowledge Globalization*, *4*(2), 59–90.

Tenekeci, M. (2017). *Katılım Bankacılığın finansal istikrara etkisi: Türkiye örneği* (Unpublished master's thesis). Karatay University, Konya, Turkey.

Toraman, C., Ata, H. A., & Buğan, M. F. (2015). İslami Bankacılık Faaliyetlerine Yönelik Müşteri Algısı Üzerine Bir Araştırma, *Gaziantep University*. *Journal of Social Sciences*, *14*(4), 761–779.

Wang, T. C., & Chang, T. H. (2007). Application of TOPSIS in evaluating initial training aircraft under a fuzzy environment. *Expert Systems with Applications*, *33*(4), 870–880. doi:10.1016/j.eswa.2006.07.003

Wang, Y. J. (2014). The evaluation of financial performance for Taiwan container shipping companies by fuzzy TOPSIS. *Applied Soft Computing*, *22*, 28–35. doi:10.1016/j.asoc.2014.03.021

Yager, R. R. (2013). Pythagorean fuzzy subsets, In *Proceedings of the Joint IFSA World Congress and NAFIPS Annual Meeting* (pp. 57-61). Edmonton, Canada. 10.1109/IFSA-NAFIPS.2013.6608375

# Chapter 9
# Islamic Financial Inclusion:
## An Alternative Approach to Reach the Unbanked of Bangladesh

**S. M. Sohrab Uddin**
*University of Chittagong, Bangladesh*

**Mahmoud A. S. Abusloum**
*International Islamic University Malaysia, Malaysia & Omar Al-Mukhtar University, Libya*

**Nahid Afroz**
*Credit Rating Agency of Bangladesh, Bangladesh*

## ABSTRACT

*Financial Inclusion (FI), a global concern of this decade, has been accepted by development agencies, governments, and policymakers as one of the pre-eminent ways to eradicate worldwide poverty and income inequality. Consequently, authorities are looking for possible ways to include the unbanked in formal financial chain. Islamic finance, specifically Islamic banking, with its welfare-oriented principles and unique products, has been able to capture the attention of policy makers. Moreover, a major portion of the Muslim population still exclude themselves from the formal financial chain due to religious prohibition of interest-based transactions for whom Islamic finance is the only way to inclusion. Bangladesh, one of the major Muslim countries in the world, is still to bring one-fourth of its total population under formal financial chain. At this backdrop, this chapter examines the empirical contribution of Islamic banking sector in financial inclusion condition as well as development scenario of Bangladesh.*

## INTRODUCTION

Financial Inclusion (FI), a global concern of this decade, has been accepted by development agencies, governments and policymakers as one of the preeminent ways to eradicate worldwide poverty and income inequality. Consequently, authorities are looking for possible ways to include the unbanked in formal financial chain. Islamic finance, specifically Islamic banking, with its welfare-oriented principles and unique products, has been able to capture the attention of policy makers.

DOI: 10.4018/978-1-7998-1611-9.ch009

Moreover, a major portion of Muslim population still excludes themselves from the formal financial chain due to religious prohibition of interest-based transactions for whom Islamic finance is the only way to inclusion. Bangladesh, one of the major Muslim inhabited country in the world, is still to bring one-fourth of its total population under formal financial chain. Despite a significant number of studies are conducted focusing on alternative FI mechanism, very few of them addressing *Shari'ah* mechanism from individual country perspective.

Starting from the early eighties, Islamic banking in Bangladesh has been able to capture one-fourth of the banking share of the country within a few decades and offers every potential to grow beyond that. At these circumstances, this chapter endeavors to examine the empirical contribution of Islamic banking sector in FI condition as well as development scenario of Bangladesh.

The current study employs four dependent variables and seven independent features to examine the extent of Islamic FI on development as well as inclusion. The dependent variables are the GDP Growth Rate (GDP_grt), Financial Development Index (FDI), Savings (% of GDP) and Consumption Growth (Cons_Grt). Then, seven independent features are Consumer Price Index (CPI), amount of deposits, amount of investment, number of branches, number of (Automated Teller Machines) ATMs, amount of *Waqf* (Charitable endowment) deposits and amount of *Qard* (Welfare loan) investment. The datasets span over 2009 to 2017 covering six full-fledged Islamic banks in Bangladesh. Nevertheless, employing fixed effects panel regression, the datasets are regressed applying both fixed and variable independent set to capture the contribution of Islamic FI on various development indicators as well as on inclusion condition.

Unlike the existing studies on FI, this chapter establishes Islamic FI as potential channel for inclusion in developing economies with majority of Muslim habitats. The study has practical implications to policymakers, development agencies and Islamic banking authorities in both Muslim and non-Muslim countries in introducing a viable FI mechanism directed to sustainable development of the targeted unbanked populace. Moreover, the study particularly addresses the case of Islamic FI situation of Bangladesh which can be of great use in reducing the access gap and obstacles in Islamic FI.

## BACKGROUND

FI can be defined as the process of extending minimum financial services (deposit, low cost credit, fund transfer and insurance) to the unbanked at an affordable cost and within formal financial system. As a high policy priority concern of the current century and enabler of seven of sustainable development goals, academicians, practitioners, and policymakers are showing growing interest in FI in recent decades. After recognition as a political issue in the UK in 1997, FI has come into discussion in different meetings like G20 Summit 2010 where FI action plan was endorsed followed by formation of Global Partnership for FI (Kabakova & Plaksenkov, 2018). Moreover, the United Nations Development Program (UNDP) has launched several projects with different banks to design suitable plans for FI of the underserved from 2009. However, in most of the cases, initiatives for FI are not self-initiated rather undertaken to fulfill regulatory compliance imposed by public entities or lead by development agencies and civil activist agency through the establishment of non-government organizations (NGOs), microfinance institutions (MFIs), and co-operatives. In spite of the growing concern and collective efforts, the worldwide formal institutional network covers only 69 percent of the total adult population which is even lower in case of disadvantaged segments of population.

Nevertheless, authorities are looking for possible ways to include the unbanked in formal financial chain. Development agencies and governments are working in alliance to provide basic financial services for all. Most of the banks around the globe currently offer No-Frills Account (NFA) opening and maintenance services for the underserved at minimum or no charges. Though supported and regulated by the authorities, such provisions fail to attract a large portion of the unbanked who lack financial literacy or identity to operate an account. Also, NFAs are not adequate to include the gender based or area based excluded strata. Besides conventional banks, MFIs and in some cases, co-operatives are recognized as possible channels of inclusion. Though successful in offering deposit and collateral free lending to the underserved, especially women, the irregularities and very high cost of credit along with profit oriented focus make these institutions infeasible for mass FI. Furthermore, conventional FI mechanisms fail to attract Muslims who constitute about 23.9% of global population and are religiously prohibited to involve in interest-based transactions. Accordingly, the loopholes of conventional FI channels and voluntary exclusion of a vast population of 40 million for religious purposes (Zulkhibiri, 2016) create vacuum for *Shari'ah* based or Islamic FI mechanism.

Islamic finance, specifically Islamic banking, with its welfare-oriented principles and unique products, has been able to capture the attention of policy makers as a potential FI mechanism. Within next decade the total value of assets of Islamic finance institutions is expected to grow by14% exceeding the threshold of USD 1.8 trillion with control over 50% of savings in all Islamic countries (Earnest & Young, 2016; AL-Hersh, 2016). Moreover, study reveals (Demirguc-Kunt, Klapper and Randall, 2013) that the Muslims are most likely to cite religion as the first reason for financial exclusion. A major portion of Muslim population excluding themselves from the formal financial chain for religion reason consider Islamic finance as the only way to inclusion. Further studies (Demirguc-Kunt et al., 2015) gather empirical evidence to the fact that Islamic banking is likely to rise the level of FI in Asia by 5%. The unique products of Islamic banking, for example: *Qard, Waqf, Zakat* (donation), etc. make Islamic banks more competent than other financial institutions in reaching the financially excluded populace. Also, *Mudarabah* (profit-loss sharing) and *Musharakah* (partnership) based financing (Rafay, Sadiq, & Ajmal, 2016) encourage entrepreneurship of low-income excluded strata, and accordingly include them in formal financial network. Islamic banks around the globe are also involved in welfare based micro-finance program which opens up an avenue for offering affordable credit and minimum savings, two basic provisions in inclusion parameters for the unbanked who either exclude them for religious purposes or fail to afford the cost of credit.

Bangladesh, one of the major Muslim inhabited country in the world, is still to bring one-fourth of its total population under formal financial chain. Chronological initiatives in post-liberation periods from both public and private sector, for instance: nationalization of banking industry, government supported co-operatives, mushrooming of MFIs, etc., have been unable to include a significant portion of religiously concerned rural populace in conventional financial chain.

Besides, FI can be measured using different indicators of financial services usage such as the percentage of account ownership or number of bank accounts, access to ATMs per 1000 square kilometers or per 100000 adult population, domestic credit, savings, and insurance (World Bank, 2013; Kim et al., 2018; Neaime & Gaysset, 2018). Moreover, financial innovations, like: mobile banking, internet banking and agent banking, are generating digital measurement factors of FI, for instance: number of mobile banking account, number of agent banking account, agent outlets per 100000 people/per 1000 square kilometers, etc. Due to differences of conventional financial mechanism from that of Islamic finance, some unique factors of inclusion such as the *Waqf* deposit and *Qard* investment are included in current study as Islamic FI variable. Then, the FDI and several country specific macro-variables are used in the current study to assess the development condition of Bangladesh. The FDI is developed by the International Monetary Fund (IMF) experts applying weighted-geometric functional aggregator which ranks a state from zero to 100, from the least financially developed state to the highest level of development. Besides, the term 'loan' or 'credit' is replaced by 'Investment' which refers to credit disbursement rather than investment in any other assets. Such substitution is made to match the reporting convention of Islamic banks. The current study uses log transformed value of amount of deposit and investment, number of branches and ATMs, amount of *Waqf* and *Qard* as measurement factors of FI, as any other usage statistics is not available for all sample banks.

## LITERATURE REVIEW

With growing interest on development and its relationship with FI, academicians and practitioners are thriving towards identifying proper inclusion mechanisms along with their measurement. A rising body of research studies are focused on FI among which a significant part is employed in discussing conventional FI mechanism and its relationship with economic development.

For instance, Iqbal and Sami (2017) investigate the impact of FI on economic growth and bank's role in such procedure. Using multiple correlations, the study concludes that impact of FI is more evident on traditional development indicators like GDP growth and less significant on impact of ATMs on GDP. Similarly, Loyaza and Ranciere (2006) and Kim et al. (2018) have identified positive correlation between FI and economic growth. However, the study of Loyaza and Ranciere (2006) identify contrasting short-run impact of financial intermediation on economic activity. Developing a mean group estimator model, the authors draw conclusion that long run impact of FI on output growth is mostly positive with encompassing mostly negative short-run relationship. Nevertheless, for examining the impact of FI upon the diffusion of Shari'ah-complaint financial systems of inclusion on economic growth of 55 Organization of Islamic Cooperation (OIC) countries, Kim et al. (2018) employ dynamic panel estimation, panel VAR, IRFs, and panel Granger causality tests. The study reveal positive impact of FI on economic growth of OIC countries. Furthermore, Neaime and Gaysset (2018) investigate the effect of inclusion in reducing income inequality, poverty and financial instability of MENA (Middle East and North African) region. Using the Generalized Moment Method and Generalized Least Squared Method, the study identify FI decreases income inequality, has no effect on poverty and contributes positively to financial stability. Swamy (2014) has also found significant correlation of income growth in economic scenario of different states in India with particular focus on gender dimension. The study reveal gender of participating poor affects the outcome of poverty reduction programs reflected in income growth after considering the net inflation effect. In an extensive empirical study of eleven south-Asian countries Sehrawat and Giri (2016) examines the causal relationship between financial sector development and poverty reduction in South East Asian countries employing Pedroni's panel co-integration test. The test results confirm presence of a long run relationship between financial development, trade openness, inflation and poverty reduction.

Apart from the above studies, a few literature present Islamic finance as possible FI channel. In order to explore the reasonable solution to voluntary exclusion of Muslims of Middle East and sub-Saharan Africa from conventional financial chain, Zamer (2018) identify Islamic banking specifically as potential alternative to conventional FI mechanism. The study summarizes existing literature on Islamic FI and tries to find out the answer of five fundamental questions of barriers to inclusion of Muslim population from previous studies. The author suggests Islamic banks for collaboration with mobile operators in improving product structure, access channel and service quality.

Abdu et al. (2018) ferreted out the impact of introducing Islamic finance and Islamic banking in enhancement of FI in Sub Saharan Africa. Employing binary probit regression model, Tobit regression model and Juhn-Murphy-Pierce decomposition, their study finds the empirical evidence for positive impact of introduction of Islamic banking and finance on FI in countries of sub-Saharan Africa. Of specific interest is the conclusion that suggests that introducing Islamic finance and Islamic banking in OIC countries is necessary but not sufficient for overall FI of Muslim households. Moreover, Zulkhibiri (2016) also examine the relationship between FI and Islamic financial services industry in Muslim inhabited countries. The study identifies cost, distance, documentation, trust and religious requirements in reaching the excluded strata in Muslim nations. The author recommends income redistribution through Islamic instruments such as, *Awqaf, Qard-e-Hasana, Sadaqa* (donation) and *Zakat* for including 40 million religiously excluded population in formal financial network.

Furthermore, using documented evidences, Usman and Tasmin (2016) reveal human empowerment and increased financial services can be obtained if Islamic FI mechanisms are employed. The study also suggests the contribution of *Zakat* and *Awqaf* institutions in generating community assets, capacity building, wealth creation, skill enhancement of entrepreneurs and accelerate inclusion in formal financial chain. The study basically addresses the development oriented and ethical stand of Islamic finance in inducing human development in Muslim society.

Studies on Islamic FI mechanism basically identify either Islamic banking (Zamer, 2018; Mohieldin et al., 2012; Leon & Weill, 2016; Naceur et al., 2015) or Islamic micro-finance (Ali, 2015) as potential channels for inclusion while some other studies (Demirguc-Kunt, Klapper & Randall, 2013; Usman & Tasmin, 2016) broadly report Islamic finance as potential FI mechanism. Consequently, Leon and Weill (2016) find the contribution of Islamic banks to be positive only when the number of conventional banks is limited. Contrarily, the study of Mohieldin et al. (2012) suggest Islamic banking and finance contribute significantly in FI, income redistribution and building stronger economy of OIC countries. Naceur et al. (2015), on the other hand, suggest weak and tentative evidence from regression analysis of contribution of Islamic banking and finance in inclusion. The study uses country-level data of OIC countries on inclusion and usage of Islamic financial services in said territory. Again, Ali (2015) examine the role of Islamic microfinance in social and economic inclusion. The study reveal Islamic microfinance plays substantial role in FI of initially excluded segment of population in Muslim countries. However, before granting microcredit, the disadvantaged population should be supplemented by Islamic social tools, for instance *Sadaqa, Waqf,* and *Zakat.*

However, most of the studies on Islamic FI mechanism are conducted on Middle Eastern or African countries where *Shari'ah* compliant financing mechanism is already existent. Very limited number of quality research are found to deal with the Islamic FI mechanism from Bangladesh perspective. As part of research studies into conventional FI mechanism, Khalily (2016) investigates the structure of the financial market, financial regulation, and financial literacy along with its impact on conventional FI in Bangladesh. The study employs the logit regression technique on household level data and finds the level of financial literacy in Bangladesh is moderate with the positive impact on inclusive finance. Moreover, the study of Siddik et al. (2014) particularly focuses on factors influencing behavioral intention to adopt or continue using mobile banking in Bangladesh. The study identifies perceived financial cost, perceived risk and subjective norm as the most influential factor in shaping people's behavior towards mobile banking.

No studies are found to deal particularly with Islamic Finance as potential chain for inclusion though Muslims constitute major portion of population and Islamic banks cover 20% of formal banking network of the country. The current study concentrates on country specific perspective with special reference to contribution of *Shari'ah* based FI mechanism on FI condition of Bangladesh where the *Shari'ah* mechanism is yet to assume a mature shape.

## DATA AND METHODOLOGY

### Data Instances and Features

The current study is performed to explore the contribution of Islamic banking in FI condition of Bangladesh which constitute one-fourth of the banking share of the country. Data used in this chapter are compiled from different authentic archives like World Bank databases, IMF development databases and respective Islamic bank websites. FI variables both Islamic (*Waqf* and *Qard*) and traditional inclusion variables (Deposit, Investment, Branches, and ATMs), are retrieved from annual reports of respective banks. Measures of Financial development such as GDP growth (*GDP_grt*), savings (% of GDP), consumption growth (*Cons_Grt*), are extorted from World Development Indicators database of World Bank (https://datacatalog.worldbank.org/dataset/world-development-indicators). One development index of IMF, namely the *FDI* obtained from the IMF database, is employed in this study. The Islamic banking industry of Bangladesh consists of eight full-fledged Islamic banks: Islami Bank Bangladesh Limited, Al-Arafah Islami Bank Limited, Social Islami Bank Limited, Export Import Bank of Bangladesh Limited, First Security Islami Bank Limited, Shahjalal Islami Bank Limited, ICB Islamic Bank Limited, and Union Bank Limited. The dataset covers six Islamic banks out of eight. ICB Islamic bank and Union Bank are kept out of the purview of this study due to missing data and inconsistent reporting. The study covers 2009 through 2017 compiled in stacked panel time series. Table 1 lists an overview of sample banks used in this chapter.

However, the current study analyzes four explanatory macro-economic variables such as *GDP Growth Rate* (Model 1), *FDI* (Model 2), *Savings (% of GDP)* (Model 3), and *Consumption Growth* (Model 4). Moreover, another experimentation taking one of the variables as dependent and others as independent variable each time, six models are constructed. The explanatory variables are *Deposit* (Model 5), *Investment* (Model 6), *Branches* (Model 7), *ATMs* (Model 8), *Waqf* (Model 9) and *Qard* (Model 10). FSIBL is excluded from the experimentation of Model 9 because of data unavailability. Table 2 provides summary statistics of analyzed features.

Nonetheless, the GDP growth rate (*GDP_grt*) indicates the annual growth rate of total marketable goods and services produced in a particular period in a specific country. The mean *GDP_grt* of Bangladesh for the assessment period is 6.29 (0.71). Besides, *savings* factor applied in this study refers to the percentage of savings in terms of GDP. The maximum value of *savings* is 25.33 with mean value of 22.18 (1.82) for Bangladesh. The *Cons_Grt* parameter applied in this study measures the annual percentage change in household consumption. The standard deviation of consumption growth is 1.84 and mean value is 4.76.

The *FDI* as shown in Table 2 is a composite index developed by IMF to assess the financial development position of a particular region. The mean value for FDI is 0.16 (0.06) while the index value of 2017 for Bangladesh is unavailable. Moreover, a control variable for inflation is attached in the first set of experimentation. The *CPI* or CPI has maximum value of 11.33 (in 2011) with standard deviation of 1.87.

*Table 1. Overview of sample Islamic banks*

| Name of Bank | Year of Establishment | FI Variables | Operating Income | Paid-up Capital |
|---|---|---|---|---|
| Islami Bank Bangladesh Limited (IBBL) | 1983 | Amount of deposit, amount of investment, number of branches, number of ATMs, amount of cash *Waqf* deposit and amount of *Qard.* | BDT 35979.56 million | BDT 16099.91 million |
| Al-Arafah Islami Bank Limited (AIBL) | 1995 | Amount of deposit, amount of investment, number of branches, number of ATMs, amount of cash *Waqf* deposit and amount of *Qard.* | BDT 12264.19 million | BDT 9943.06 million |
| Social Islami Bank Limited (SIBL) | 1995 | Amount of deposit, amount of investment, number of branches, number of ATMs, amount of cash *Waqf* deposit and amount of *Qard.* | BDT 10984.48 million | BDT 7382.99 million |
| Export Import (EXIM) Bank of Bangladesh Limited | 1999 | Amount of deposit, amount of investment, number of branches, number of ATMs, amount of cash *Waqf* deposit and amount of *Qard.* | BDT 11022.81 million | BDT 14122.51 million |
| First Security Islami Bank Limited (FSIBL) | 1999 | Amount of deposit, amount of investment, number of branches, number of ATMs, and amount of *Qard.* | BDT 9925.24 million | BDT 7840.99 million |
| Shahjalal Islami Bank Limited (SJIBL) | 2001 | Amount of deposit, amount of investment, number of branches, number of ATMs, amount of cash *Waqf* deposit and amount of *Qard.* | BDT 7305.81 million | BDT 7714.22 million |

Source: Constructed by the authors based on annual reports of respective banks.
*Notes*: Operating income and paid-up capital are reported based on updated citations available in respective bank websites.

In addition to CPI, another six independent features are applied to study the factors of Islamic FI. The first proxy is *Ln.deposit* which is log transformed measure of amount of deposits in particular banks which offers insight as to contribution of Islamic banks in deposit mobilization of Bangladesh. The mean value of this feature is the highest for IBBL (12.92) with highest volatility of SIBL (standard deviation of 0.66). Again, *Ln.investment*, a proxy for credit measures the amount of investment by particular Islamic bank. In terms of investment feature, AIBL has the minimum share (10.50) and FSIBL has the maximum volatility (standard deviation of 3.01) among the sample banks. The third measure *Ln.branches is* a measure of account penetration that covers the outreach of particular Islamic banking institutions. The mean value for this parameter is the lowest for EXIM bank 4.38 with standard deviation of 0.29. Fourth, *Ln.ATM* is also a measure of account penetration as ATMs are usually issued against accounts at financial institutions and enhances the ability to access financial services. The highest mean (5.33) and maximum value (6.33) for this parameter is recorded for IBBL. However, all sample banks except IBBL has minimum value of 0.00 for this feature as none of them started this service from the beginning of the study period. The *Waqf* or cash *Waqf* deposit refers to a special kind of deposit whose profit earned is distributed in any welfare activities and indirectly influences inclusion. The mean value for *Ln.Waqf* is the highest for IBBL (6.01) and minimum (0.00) for EXIM bank since it started *Waqf* deposit from 2011. No reported *Waqf* deposit has been found in financial statements of FSIBL.

*Table 2. Summary of descriptive statistics, 2009-2017*

| | IBBL | | AIBL | | SIBL | | SJIBL | | EXIM | | FSIBL | |
|---|---|---|---|---|---|---|---|---|---|---|---|---|
| | Mean (St. Dev.) | MinV. (MaxV.) | Mean (St. Dev.) | MinV. (MaxV.) | Mean (St. Dev.) | MinV. (MaxV.) | Mean (St. Dev.) | MinV. (MaxV.) | Mean (St. Dev.) | MinV. (MaxV.) | Mean (St. Dev.) | MinV. (MaxV.) |
| Ln.deposit | 12.92 (0.44) | 12.33 (13.53) | 11.66 (0.62) | 10.55 (12.41) | 11.48 (0.66) | 10.36 (12.34) | 11.43 (0.34) | 10.77 (11.89) | 11.96 (0.46) | 11.21 (12.56) | 14.33 (3.06) | 10.66 (17.21) |
| Ln. investment | 13.00 (0.44) | 12.28 (13.53) | 11.60 (0.62) | 10.50 (12.37) | 11.32 (0.70) | 10.19 (12.26) | 11.37 (0.37) | 10.69 (11.97) | 11.85 (0.44) | 11.14 (12.45) | 14.16 (3.01) | 10.56 (17.12) |
| Ln. branches | 5.64 (0.12) | 5.44 (5.81) | 4.65 (0.30) | 4.09 (5.04) | 4.50 (0.32) | 3.95 (4.93) | 4.42 (0.25) | 3.93 (4.73) | 4.38 (0.29) | 3.95 (4.77) | 4.67 (0.41) | 3.95 (5.12) |
| Ln.ATM | 5.33 (1.16) | 3.18 (6.33) | 3.15 (1.92) | 0.00 (5.09) | 2.52 (1.55) | 0.00 (4.33) | 3.17 (1.32) | 0.00 (4.30) | 3.07 (1.86) | 0.00 (4.65) | 2.86 (2.21) | 0.00 (4.85) |
| Ln.*Waqf* | 6.01 (0.60) | 5.07 (6.81) | 2.10 (0.74) | 1.17 (3.24) | 4.52 (0.78) | 3.32 (5.63) | 1.97 (2.75) | 0.58 (9.28) | 2.16 (1.39) | 0.00 (3.62) | NaN (Missing) | NaN (Missing) |
| Ln.*Qard* | 9.06 (0.81) | 7.65 (9.90) | 7.28 (0.54) | 6.44 (7.95) | 8.61 (0.57) | 7.50 (9.20) | 5.45 (1.76) | 2.88 (9.10) | 6.14 (0.61) | 5.34 (7.32) | 6.26 (0.36) | 5.85 (6.92) |
| GDP_grt | 6.29 (0.71) | 5.05 (7.28) | 6.29 (0.71) | 5.05 (7.28) | 6.29 (0.71) | 5.05 (7.28) | 6.29 (0.71) | 5.05 (7.28) | 6.29 (0.71) | 5.05 (7.28) | 6.29 (0.71) | 5.05 (7.28) |
| Savings | 22.18 (1.82) | 20.33 (25.33) | 22.18 (1.82) | 20.33 (25.33) | 22.18 (1.82) | 20.33 (25.33) | 22.18 (1.82) | 20.33 (25.33) | 22.18 (1.82) | 20.33 (25.33) | 22.18 (1.82) | 20.33 (25.33) |
| FDI | 0.16 (0.06) | 0.00 (0.19) | 0.16 (0.06) | 0.00 (0.19) | 0.16 (0.06) | 0.00 (0.19) | 0.16 (0.06) | 0.00 (0.19) | 0.16 (0.06) | 0.00 (0.19) | 0.16 (0.06) | 0.00 (0.19) |
| Cons_Grt | 4.76 (1.84) | 2.29 (7.43) | 4.76 (1.84) | 2.29 (7.43) | 4.76 (1.84) | 2.29 (7.43) | 4.76 (1.84) | 2.29 (7.43) | 4.76 (1.84) | 2.29 (7.43) | 4.76 (1.84) | 2.29 (7.43) |
| CPI | 7.00 (1.87) | 5.42 (11.33) | 7.00 (1.87) | 5.42 (11.33) | 7.00 (1.87) | 5.42 (11.33) | 7.00 (1.87) | 5.42 (11.33) | 7.00 (1.87) | 5.42 (11.33) | 7.00 (1.87) | 5.42 (11.33) |

Source: Authors' calculations.

Notes: Macroeconomic variables are same for all banks within the economy.

The last measure is *Qard,* another Islamic banking parameter indicating welfare loan at low or zero cost with minimal restrictions for repayment. Usually, such lending is provided to low-income strata and indirectly induces their involvement to formal financial sector. Among the sample banks, SJIBL has the lowest (2.88) share of investment in *Qard* with the highest level of volatility (1.76) among the sample banks.

The independent features are all popular measures of basic FI services. The *Ln.deposits* and *Ln.ATM* are measures of account penetration; where the first one assess the deposit mobilization and the latter fund transfer facility to account holders. Again, *Ln.investments* offers insight to second basic provision for FI, access to credit. Moreover, *Ln.branches* is another indicator of account penetration which also measures area based access to financial services. Lastly, *Ln.Waqf* and *Ln.Qard* are respectively two unique Islamic FI measures of welfare deposit and credit.

All investigated units of the sample banks and macro variables except a few cases have a common feature of having the minimum value at the beginning of sample period and maximum value at the end. Such pattern indicates data used in this study follows normal trend of progression. Among the sample banks, IBBL holds the highest share in almost all features, while SJIBL and FSIBL have the most volatile results owing to their late entry to the industry.

## RESEARCH METHOD

In order to capture the contribution of Islamic banking institutions in FI in Bangladesh, the study employs fixed effects panel regression. According to Hasan et al. (2018), panel data captures both the benefits of time series and cross-sectional data, hence empirical analysis with panel data generates the robust estimations with minimized multicollinearity and missing data problems. Accordingly, the static model applied in this study has no serious problems with heteroskedasticity. The panel regression model takes the followingform of basic function in Eq. (1),

$$Y_{it} = \alpha + X_{it}\beta + u_{it},\ i = 1, 2, \ldots, N;\ t = 1, 2, \ldots, T \tag{1}$$

In Eq. (1) the subscript *i* represents cross-sectional element and *t* implies time, $Y_{it}$ indicates dependent variable for the cross-sectional unit in period *t*, $X_{it}$ is a $X_k$ vector of independent variables for unit *i* in time *t*, $\alpha$ is the common intercept, and $u_{it}$ is the error term of the equation. The study uses two sets of experimentation. In first set, a fixed set of independent variables are regressed to capture the impact of Islamic FI on development condition of Bangladesh. One control variable, *CPI* is included in this set of regression. The latter, on the other hand, assumes one variable as dependent variable in each time and takes others as independent. This set excludes macro variables and covers only bank specific factors. The following model in Eq. (2) applies to execute the regression statements in first set of experimentation:

$$Y_{it} = \alpha + \beta_1(CPI_{it}) + \beta_2(Ln.deposit_{it}) + \beta_3(Ln.investment_{it}) + \beta_4(Ln.branches_{it}) + \beta_5(Ln.ATM_{it}) + \beta_6(Ln.Waqf_{it}) + \beta_7(Ln.Qard_{it}) + u_{it} \tag{2}$$

In Eq. (2) $Y_{it}$ is the *i*th cross-sectional element in period *t*, $\beta_k$ is the regression coefficient of dependent variables. *CPI* is the Consumer Price Index, *Ln. deposit* is log transformed amount of deposits, *Ln.investment* is log transformed amount of investment, *Ln.branches* is log transformed number of branches, *Ln.ATM* is log transformed number of ATMs, *Ln.Waqf* is log transformed amount of cash *Waqf* deposits and *Ln.Qard* is log transformed amount of *Qard* investment. The equations take following forms:

$$GDP\_grt_{it} = \alpha + \beta_1(CPI_{it}) + \beta_2(Ln.deposit_{it}) + \beta_3(Ln.investment_{it}) + \beta_4(Ln.branches_{it}) + \beta_5(Ln.ATM_{it}) + \beta_6(Ln.Waqf_{it}) + \beta_7(Ln.Qard_{it}) + u_{it} \ldots \quad (3)$$

$$FDI_{it} = \alpha + \beta_1(CPI_{it}) + \beta_2(Ln.deposit_{it}) + \beta_3(Ln.investment_{it}) + \beta_4(Ln.branches_{it}) + \beta_5(Ln.ATM_{it}) + \beta_6(Ln.Waqf_{it}) + \beta_7(Ln.Qard_{it}) + u_{it} \ldots \quad (4)$$

$$Savings_{it} = \alpha + \beta_1(CPI_{it}) + \beta_2(Ln.deposit_{it}) + \beta_3(Ln.investment_{it}) + \beta_4(Ln.branches_{it}) + \beta_5(Ln.ATM_{it}) + \beta_6(Ln.Waqf_{it}) + \beta_7(Ln.Qard_{it}) + u_{it} \ldots \quad (5)$$

$$Cons\_grt_{it} = \alpha + \beta_1(CPI_{it}) + \beta_2(Ln.deposit_{it}) + \beta_3(Ln.investment_{it}) + \beta_4(Ln.branches_{it}) + \beta_5(Ln.ATM_{it}) + \beta_6(Ln.Waqf_{it}) + \beta_7(Ln.Qard_{it}) + u_{it} \ldots \quad (6)$$

The second set of experimentation takes all independent variables used in first set of experimentation except *CPI* as dependent variable in each model. Following regression statements are generated in this process:

$$Ln.deposit_{it} = \alpha + \beta_1(Ln.investment_{it}) + \beta_2(Ln.branches_{it}) + \beta_3(Ln.ATM_{it}) + \beta_4(Ln.Waqf_{it}) + \beta_5(Ln.Qard_{it}) + u_{it} \quad (7)$$

$$Ln.investment_{it} = \alpha + \beta_1(Ln.deposit_{it}) + \beta_2(Ln.branches_{it}) + \beta_3(Ln.ATM_{it}) + \beta_4(Ln.Waqf_{it}) + \beta_5(Ln.Qard_{it}) + u_{it} \quad (8)$$

$$Ln.branches_{it} = \alpha + \beta_1(Ln.deposit_{it}) + \beta_2(Ln.investment_{it}) + \beta_3(Ln.branches_{it}) + \beta_4(Ln.Waqf_{it}) + \beta_5(Ln.Qard_{it}) + u_{it} \quad (9)$$

$$Ln.Waqf_{it} = \alpha + \beta_1(Ln.deposit_{it}) + \beta_2(Ln.investment_{it}) + \beta_3(Ln.branches_{it}) + \beta_4(Ln.ATM_{it}) + \beta_5(Ln.Qard_{it}) + u_{it} \quad (10)$$

$$Ln.Qard_{it} = \alpha + \beta_1(Ln.deposit_{it}) + \beta_2(Ln.investment_{it}) + \beta_3(Ln.branches_{it}) + \beta_4(Ln.ATM_{it}) + \beta_5(Ln.Waqf_{it}) + u_{it} \quad (11)$$

Furthermore, the Schwarz criterion, popularly known as the Bayesian information criterion (*BIC*) in Eq. (12), partially based on likelihood function, is employed for identifying the best model among a finite set of classifiers. Under this criterion, the lower the value of the *BIC* of a specific model, the more the model is preferred than the others. The likelihood of the model fitness can be increased by adding additional parameters to the model; however, such attempts may cause over fitting. Besides, the Akaike information criterion (*AIC*) or Akaike criterion in Eq. (13) is another test of goodness fit of models which deals with the problem of both under fitting and over fitting. *BIC* and *AIC* are calculated as follows,

$$BIC = l_n(n)k - 2\, l_n(\hat{L}) \quad (12)$$

$$\text{AIC} = 2k - 2\, l_n\, (\hat{L}) \tag{13}$$

In Eqs. (12)-(13), $\hat{L}$ indicates the maximized value of the likelihood function of the model, *n* refers to the sample size, and *k* stands for the number of parameters estimated by the model. Among several models with same parameters, the one with the lowest *BIC* is preferred. Since Akaike reduces the chance of information loss to the minimum, the model with the lowest AIC is preferred over a set of models.

Moreover, the Spearman's rank correlation coefficient (*Rho*) in Eq. (14) is a monotonic function of measuring the statistical dependence or association between two variables. The model with higher value of rho represents a similar or identical rank of variables over other models. *Rho* is calculated as follows,

$$\rho_{rgx,\, rgy} = Rho = \frac{cov\left(rgx, rgy\right)}{\left(\sigma rgx\right)\left(\sigma rgy\right)} \tag{14}$$

In Eq. (14), $2cov(rgx,rgy)$ represents the covariance of rank variables, $(\sigma_{rgx})\,(\sigma_{rgy})$ stands for the standard deviation of rank variables. A positive *Rho*'s value indicates positive association between the features and reverse indication is for the negative values. Conversely, *R*-squared ($R^2$) in Eq. (15) is a popular statistical measure of determining the capacity of the independent variable to explain the sensitivity of response variable. The following formula is applied to calculate *R*-squared:

$$R^2 = 1 - \frac{SS_{rs}}{SS_{tot}} \tag{15}$$

In Eq. (15), $SS_{rs}$ refers to the sum squared of residuals; $SS_{tot}$ indicates the total sum squared proportional to the variance of dataset. The higher value of $R^2$of a model represents better capacity of independent variable to explain the percentage change of the response variable. Besides, the Durbin-Watson (*DW*) test is performed in this study to ascertain the presence of any autocorrelation in residuals. The *DW* value of 1.5 to 2.5 is considered as acceptable. The *DW* is calculated as follows,

$$DW = \frac{\sum_{t=2}^{T}\left(e_t - e_{t-1}\right)^\wedge 2}{\sum_{t=1}^{T} e_t^2} \tag{16}$$

In Eq. (16), $e_t$ refers to the value of the residuals associated in time *t*, and *T* is the number of observations. Lastly, the *F*-statistic is a robustness test to assess the capacity of a model to capture the effect of a change in dependent variables for variation in estimators. The acceptable levels of robustness indicator evidences of the structural validity of a particular model. *F*-statistic in Eq. (17) is exercised for multiple hypotheses testing in a linear regression model by comparing the error term in a regression model estimated under the null hypothesis ($H_0$) to that of a model under the alternative ($H_1$) proposition. The *F*-statistic assuming the null hypothesis is true can be calculated as,

$$F = MSR\,/\,MSE \tag{17}$$

In Eq. (17), the *MSR* is the regression mean squared and *MSE* is the mean squared error. If *FÎ* I, the null hypothesis is accepted, and if *FÏ* I, the null hypothesis rejected, here *I* is the confidence interval.

## EMPIRICAL RESULTS AND FINDINGS

The current study inspects the contribution of Islamic Banks in FI condition of Bangladesh. As mentioned earlier the current study deals with ten explanatory variables such as *GDP Growth Rate* (Model 1), *FDI* (Model 2), *Savings (% of GDP)* (Model 3), *Consumption Growth* (Model 4), *Deposit* (Model 5), *Investment* (Model 6), *Branches* (Model 7), *ATMs* (Model 8), *Waqf* (Model 9) and *Qard* (Model 10). Therefore, Tables 3-4 exhibit the results of regression inspecting the effect of Islamic FI on development and Inclusion from Bangladesh perspective.

### Regression Results and Analysis

Table 3 examines the impact of Islamic inclusion parameters on different development indicators, for instance: *GDP Growth*, *FDI*, *Savings* and *Consumption Growth*. As expected, the results indicate all inclusion parameters (except *Deposit* and *Qard)*, both traditional and Islamic, have positive impact on *GDP*_grt; while CPI and Ln.branches have positive significant impact on the said development parameter at 1% level of significance.

On the other hand, opposite direction of *Ln.deposit* and *Ln.Qard* parameter with *GDP*_grt, from that of the other independent features offers some indication of contribution of Islamic Banks in domestic production growth, to be precise on development. Though Islamic banks constitute one-fourth of the banking industry in Bangladesh, the regression results reflect their deposit as well as *Qard* investment is still not sufficient to contribute positively towards economic development of the country. Nevertheless, the model fits the data very well as the value of R-squared is 76.65%. However, DW test value of 1.1000 suggests that there is existence of autocorrelation in the model, though no serious concern is required as long as DW value is within the threshold of 1.00-3.00.

For *FDI* the test results exhibit both positive and negative impact of independent variables. While CPI, *Ln.deposit*, *Ln.ATM* and *Ln.Qard* show positive effect on dependent variable, *Ln.investment*, *Ln.branches* and *Ln.Waqf* suggest negative impact of inclusion factors on development. The test results are significant for *Ln.branches* at 1% level of significance, for CPI and *Ln.Waqf* at 5% level of significance, and for *Ln.ATM* at 10% level of significance, respectively.

Overall test results suggest the presence of significant impact of Islamic banks on development condition of Bangladesh reflected by the *FDI* parameter. Even though the inclusion parameters have both positive and negative relationship with the index, a significant positive coefficient indicates the aggregate contribution is directed in a positive stream. Moreover, the DW value is 1.2641 indicating no serious case of autocorrelation exists. The R-squared of 30.25% also indicate the model explains the dependent variable well.

In case of *Savings,* all estimators except *Ln.investment* and *Ln.branches* show negative impact, while the results of *Ln.branches* is significant at 1% confidence level. Among other indicators, only CPI has significant negative effect on Savings at 1% level of significance.

Taking into consideration the relationship of common intercept with the *Savings* parameter, as well as the negative effect of other inclusion parameters on said indicator, it can be said that the Islamic banks are so far unable to make notable positive contribution towards deposit mobilization of the country. *Ln.investment* and *Ln.branches* parameters, on the contrary, stand against the trend and contribute in inducing public savings. However, the model is good fit with satisfactory DW of 1.3839 and R-squared of 75.52%.

For Consumption Growth, the test results are significant with positive impact of CPI, *Ln.investment*, *Ln.branches*, and *Ln.Waqf* factor and negative impact of *Ln.deposit*, and *Ln.Qard* indicator, respectively. The combined effect of independent variables on the said dependent feature is negatively significant at 1% level of confidence. Interestingly, the parameters choose both positive and negative direction in their relationship with development factor. Again, the aggregate effect reflected in the common intercept imply the involvement of Islamic banks are still to make any significant contribution in household consumption growth. The model exhibits satisfactory DW (2.2213) with high R-squared (above 50%).

As expected, CPI has negative significant impact on only Savings parameter. *Ln.deposit* and *Ln.Qard* have negative impact on all dependent variables except FDI and significant impact on Consumption growth only. Conversely, *Ln.investment* has positive impact on all parameters except FDI and significant impact on consumption growth also. The *Ln.ATM* parameter indicate significant result for FDI parameter, with positive impact of GDP growth and FDI and negative impact on Savings and Consumption Growth. Lastly, Ln.*Waqf* parameter has significant effect with positive results on Consumption growth and negative results on FDI factor. The test results establish significant link of inclusion parameters of Islamic banks with development factor. While the Islamic banks of Bangladesh are yet to reflect significant contribution towards socio-economic development of the country, the regression results reveal the probability of establishment of stronger link among variables.

Table 4 inspects the impact of each FI parameters on others. In case of *Ln.deposit*, only *Ln.investment* has significant result with positive effect; while *Ln.branches*, *Ln.ATM* and *Ln.Qard* have negative impact and *Ln.Waqf* has positive impact on savings. Similarly, *Ln.deposit* has positive effect on *Ln.investment*. As expected, the results show all other indicators have the opposite impact on *Ln.investment* compared to *Ln.deposit* parameter.

For *Ln.branches*, all features except *Ln.deposit* exhibit positive effect. The *Ln.ATM* has significant positive impact on *Ln.branches* parameter at 1% level of significance. Moreover, the constant factor also suggests significant positive effect of FI features on said indicator.

Conversely, in case of *Ln.ATM*, *Ln.branches* solitarily has positive significant effect at 1% level of significance. The *Ln.deposit* and *Ln.Qard* have negative impact on assessment variable reflected by the significant result of constant factor with negative effect.

For *Ln.Waqf* parameter only *Ln.Qard* has significant positive effect, while the opposite is observed for *Ln.Qard*. The other indicators also mirror reflect the results in both factors. The *Ln.branches*, however, has positive impact on both indicators. All the models have good fit with satisfactory R-squared (from 41.02% to 98.62%) and DW value (from 1.2876 to 1.9810) indicating no serious case of autocorrelation is faced.

*Ln.deposit* has positive effect on *Ln.investment* and *Ln.Waqf*, while negative effect on *Ln.branches* and *Ln.ATM*, as the deposits does not grow proportionately with increasing facility. Nevertheless, *Ln.investment* has positive impact on all features except *Waqf* deposits. As expected, *Ln.branches* has positive effect on all indicators except *Ln.deposit* due to fundamental nature of banking. Again, *Ln.branches* and *Ln.ATM* have similar impact on other factors. However, in case of *Ln.Qard*, the said estimators have reverse effect. *Ln.Waqf* and *Ln.Qard,* on the other hand, exhibit contrasting effect on other indicators except in case of *Ln.branches*, for which both exhibit positive effect.

*Table 3. Regression results -dependent variable GDP Growth, FDI, Savings (% of GDP), Consumption Growth Model (1-4)*

| Independent Variables | GDP_grt | FDI | Savings | Cons_Grt |
|---|---|---|---|---|
| Constant | -1.9376<br>(0.2378)*** | 0.7025<br>(0.0014)*** | -1.9871<br>(0.4089) | -12.0112<br>(0.0068)*** |
| CPI | 0.0571<br>(0.0021)*** | 0.0047<br>(0.0280)** | -0.2499<br>(0.0033)*** | 0.5385<br>(2.19083E-06) *** |
| Ln.Deposit | -0.4533<br>(0.2077) | 0.0298<br>(0.6112) | -0.9427<br>(0.5025) | -1.9017<br>(0.0017) *** |
| Ln.Investment | 0.3060<br>(0.3834) | -0.0248<br>(0.6757) | 0.7626<br>(0.5880) | 1.7374<br>(0.0032) *** |
| Ln.Branches | 2.0393<br>(0.0070) *** | -0.1653<br>(0.0006)*** | 6.3085<br>(0.0002)*** | 3.9350<br>(0.0024) *** |
| Ln.ATM | 0.0907<br>(0.3112) | 0.0122<br>(0.0947)* | -0.1889<br>(0.2671) | -0.0287<br>(0.8767) |
| Ln.Waqf | 0.0648<br>(0.1071) | -0.0083<br>(0.0381)** | -0.0032<br>(0.9832) | 0.2376<br>(0.0088)*** |
| Ln.Qard | -0.0597<br>(0.5427) | 0.0169<br>(0.1011) | -0.1244<br>(0.5926) | -0.5525<br>(0.0243)** |
| Schwarz criterion | 82.9557 | -124.3601 | 187.2394 | 205.0033 |
| Akaike criterion | 57.0989 | -150.2169 | 161.3826 | 179.1465 |
| Rho | 0.3917 | -0.0722 | 0.1790 | -0.8077 |
| R-squared | 0.7665 | 0.3025 | 0.7552 | 0.5832 |
| Durbin-Watson | 1.1000 | 1.2641 | 1.3839 | 2.2213 |
| Robustness<br>P-value | 0.9674<br>(0.4587) | 0.3180<br>(0.8969) | 0.7804<br>(0.5743) | 0.8152<br>(0.5515) |

*Notes*: ***significant at 1%, **at 5%, *at 10%, FDI = Financial Development Index; Rho = Spearman's rank correlation.

## Findings

The study deals with the contribution of Islamic FI by investigating significant parameters being measured access to the financial products and services in sample banks. The empirical results and interpretations can be summarized in following points:

Islamic FI features are moderately associated with the development features with potential to grow more. All independent features except deposit and *Qard* have positive effect on GDP growth of Bangladesh, indicating that among all FI elements of Islamic banks, deposit and *Qard* are failing to contribute significantly towards GDP growth of the country. Taking *FDI* as a dependent variable, the model suggests combined significant positive impact of inclusion parameters with mixed results for independent features. Negative results of Savings parameter indicate failure of Islamic banks to induce savings of the country. On the contrary, the investment and branches indictor reflects positive impact of Islamic FI on development. Consumption growth as a dependent variable indicates the presence of significant contribution of Islamic FI on development condition of the country with fluctuated results. CPI and *Ln.branches* have significant impact on all four development indicators presenting strong force of inflation and enhancement of banking facility on development. Taking variable independent set, the

*Table 4. Regression results-Dependent variable Deposit, Investment, Branches, ATMs, Waqf and Qard (Model 5-10)*

| Independent Variables | Ln.Deposit | Ln.Investment | Ln.Branches | Ln.ATM | Ln.*Waqf* | Ln.*Qard* |
|---|---|---|---|---|---|---|
| Constant | 0.0510 (0.9324) | -0.0591 (0.9155) | 3.6459 (0.0001)*** | -20.5342 (0.0003)*** | -3.8520 (0.3389) | 5.5587 (0.2379) |
| Ln.Deposit | | 0.9483 (1.43E-06)*** | -0.0020 (0.9828) | -0.1598 (0.7530) | 0.1059 (0.8101) | -0.3723 (0.3601) |
| Ln.Investment | 1.0171 (2.38214E-09)*** | | 0.0493 (0.5987) | 0.2886 (0.5963) | -0.3059 (0.5895) | 0.3333 (0.4463) |
| Ln.Branches | -0.0043 (0.9825) | 0.0997 (0.3462) | | 4.6956 (0.0001)*** | 0.5010 (0.6156) | 0.2081 (0.8400) |
| Ln.ATM | -0.0095 (0.8085) | 0.0161 (0.7208) | 0.1295 (0.0005)*** | | 0.2626 (0.3749) | -0.0194 (0.9387) |
| Ln.Waqf | 0.0028 (0.8310) | -0.0075 (0.6912) | 0.0061 (0.6756) | 0.1159 (0.4627) | | 0.4173 (0.0078)*** |
| Ln.Qard | -0.0192 (0.6009) | 0.0161 (0.6235) | 0.0050 (0.8470) | -0.0168 (0.9387) | 0.8187 (0.0620)* | |
| Schwarz criterion | -9.2214 | -13.0054 | -50.9691 | 142.9446 | 187.1324 | 150.7451 |
| Akaike criterion | -31.1002 | -34.8842 | -72.8479 | 121.0658 | 165.2535 | 128.8662 |
| Rho | -0.0150 | -0.0116 | 0.2444 | 0.0569 | -0.0861 | 0.1618 |
| R-squared | 0.9862 | 0.9868 | 0.8694 | 0.8587 | 0.4921 | 0.4102 |
| Durbin-Watson | 1.9415 | 1.9161 | 1.2876 | 1.6712 | 1.9810 | 1.4291 |
| Robustness P-value | 3.1656 (0.0271)** | 1.7422 (0.1678) | 8.5626 (0.0001) | 2.1621 (0.0950)* | 4.2586 (0.0073)*** | 5.2563 (0.0025)*** |

*Notes*: ***significant at 1%, **at 5%, *at 10%, FDI = Financial Development Index; Rho = Spearman's rank correlation.

results indicate that the features all pair up, (for instance: *Ln.deposits* and *Ln.investment*, *Ln.branches* and *Ln.ATM*, *Ln.Waqf* and *Ln.Qard*) and each has significant impact singularly on their peer and not on others. Again, the results of such pairs reversely match to their peer.

All experimented models produce statistically robust results (except a few) along with both positive and negative impact of Islamic FI variables, which suggests the presence of significant association among variables coupled with scope for growth.

## CONCLUSION AND RECOMMENDATIONS

Enlisted as one of the emerging nations of Asia as well as the world, Bangladesh is pacing rapidly towards its journey to economic growth and self-sufficiency. However, to reach such height the country is required to overcome obstacles like financial exclusion of its one-fourth population. Moreover, worldwide digital financial integration through mobile banking, agent banking and internet banking is offering challenges as well as opportunities for the country to join the rally. At one side these innovations are making it easier, cheaper and more convenient to reach the unbanked, however, on the other hand, they are threatening to emerge another form of exclusion, digital financial exclusion, if failed to keep pace with the world.

At this background, this chapter tried to assess the potential of Islamic banking as alternative FI channel through focusing on the contribution of Islamic banking institutions on inclusion and development condition of Bangladesh. Accordingly, the study employed fixed effects panel regression of Islamic FI parameters on inclusion and development indicators applying two sets of experimentation with fixed and variable set of independent features. The empirical results evidenced the combined effect of inclusion parameters on FDI, Consumption growth, branches and ATM parameters is strongly significant; CPI and branches parameter have significant impact on all development indicators. Moreover, the presence of paired effect is established from variable set of experimentation.

However, weak to moderate association along with mixed impact of inclusion parameters on development indicators present scope for Islamic banking institutions to contribute more in inclusion. Broad based product offering coupled with appropriately designed unique package for the financially excluded population is suggested to reach the unbanked. Islamic micro-finance can be the proper mechanism for mass inclusion of the excluded segment. Moreover, sufficient digital integration can be considered coupled with financial literacy initiatives.

This study is one of the first in line to investigate Islamic FI as alternative FI channel along with its contribution to development from Bangladesh perspective. Firstly, it appends to the existing literature by offering an overview of Islamic FI scenario of Bangladesh along with its potentials and challenges; and secondly, by establishing the connection of inclusion to development along with individual Islamic bankwise perspective. The study also contributes towards existing Islamic banking wings through focusing the gaps in channelizing inclusion efforts to development. Moreover, this research provides insights for the stakeholders in assessing *Shari'ah* mechanism as an alternative to reach excluded strata who exclude themselves voluntarily from formal financial network due to religious prohibition of interest-based transaction. The policy makers as well as the Islamic banking institutions in developing Muslim and non-Muslim countries are offered with the intellectual perspective required for establishing Islamic banking products as potential instruments for FI.

## FUTURE RESEARCH DIRECTIONS

Nevertheless, despite the wide acceptability of account usage and account ownership statistics, this study does not cover them due to inconsistent reporting convention of Islamic banks in Bangladesh. Also, a major portion of these banks are engaged in micro-finance program through group lending though not reported chronologically, therefore kept outside the purview of this study. Digital financial integration issue is also not addressed for the same reason. Subsequently, further study can be performed covering the said issues which might be of great interest to the academics.

## Classifications

JEL Classification: G21, O21
KAUJIE Classification: E33, H15, N6

## REFERENCES

Abdu, M., Jibir, A., Abdullahi, S., & Rabi'u, A. A. (2018). Can Islamic Banking and Finance Spur Financial Inclusion? Evidence from Sub-Saharan Africa. *CBN Journal of Applied Statistics*, *9*(1), 77–104.

AL-Hersh, N. F. (2016). The Impact of Jordan's Conventional and Islamic Banking Development Factors on Economic Growth. *International Journal of Economics & Finance*, *8*(9), 148. doi:10.5539/ijef.v8n9p148

Ali, A. S. (2015). Islamic Micro-finance: Moving beyond Financial inclusion. *European Scientific Journal*, *11*(10), 297–310.

Demirguc-Kunt, A., Klapper, L., & Randall, D. (2013). Islamic Finance and Financial Inclusion: Measuring Use of and Demand for Formal Financial Services among Muslim Adults (Policy Research Working Paper: 6642) [PDF File]. Retrieved from http://documents.worldbank.org/curated/en/611351468337493348/pdf/WPS6642.pdf

Demirguc-Kunt, A., Klapper, L., Singer, D., & Van, O. P. (2015). The Global Findex Database 2014: Measuring Financial Inclusion around the World. (Policy Research Working Paper: WPS 7255) [PDF File]. Retrieved from http://documents.worldbank.org/curated/en/187761468179367706/

Earnest & Young. (2016). *World Islamic Banking Competitiveness Report 2016*. Retrieved from Earnest and Yong Website: https://www.ey.com/em/en/industries/financial-services/banking---capital-markets/ey-banking-in-emerging-markets

Hasan, M. B., Islam, S. M. N., & Wahid, A. N. M. (2018). The Effect of Macroeconomic Variables on the Performance of Non-life Insurance Companies in Bangladesh. *Indian Economic Review*, *53*(1-2), 369–383. doi:10.100741775-019-00037-6

Iqbal, B. A., & Sami, S. (2017). Role of Banks in Financial Inclusion in India. *Contaduría y Administración*, *62*(2), 644–656. doi:10.1016/j.cya.2017.01.007

Kabakova, O., & Plaksenkov, E. (2018). Analysis of factors affecting financial inclusion: Ecosystem view. *Journal of Business Research*, *89*, 198–205. doi:10.1016/j.jbusres.2018.01.066

Khalily, M. A. B. (2016). Financial Inclusion, Financial Regulation, and Education in Bangladesh (ADBI Working Paper 621. Tokyo: Asian Development Bank Institute). Retrieved from https://www.adb.org/publications/financial-inclusion-financial-regulation-and-educationbangladesh

Kim, D.-W., Yu, J.-S., & Hassan, M. K. (2018). Financial Inclusion and Economic Growth in OIC Countries. *Research in International Business and Finance*, *43*, 1–14. doi:10.1016/j.ribaf.2017.07.178

Leon, F., & Weill, L. (2016). Islamic Banking Development and Access to Credit (University of Strasbourg Working paper, No. 2016/02). Retrieved from https://ideas.repec.org/p/lar/wpaper/2016-02.html

Loyaza, N., & Ranciere, R. (2006). Financial Development, Financial Fragility, and Growth. *Journal of Money, Credit, and Banking*, *38*(4), 1051–1076. doi:10.1353/mcb.2006.0060

Mohieldin, M., Iqbal, Z., Rostom, A., & Fu, X. (2012). The Role of Islamic Finance in Enhancing Financial inclusion in Organization of Islamic Cooperation (OIC) Countries. *Islamic Economic Studies*, *20*(2), 55–120.

Naceur, S. B., Barajas, A., & Massara, A. (2015). Can Islamic Banking Increase Financial inclusion? (IMF Working Paper WP/15/31). Retrieved from IMF Website: https://www.imf.org/en/Publications/WP/Issues/2016/12/31/Can-Islamic-Banking-Increase-Financial-Inclusion-42710

Neaime, S., & Geaysset, I. (2018). Financial Inclusion and Stability in MENA: Evidence from Poverty and Inequality. *Finance Research Letters*, *24*, 230–237. doi:10.1016/j.frl.2017.09.007

Rafay, A., Sadiq, R. & Ajmal, M. M. (2016). Fragmentation of Islamic Financial Products – An Exploratory Study of Islamic Schools of Thought. *Abasyn Journal of Social Sciences, Special Issue*, 48-61.

Sehrawat, M., & Giri, A. K. (2016). Financial Development and Poverty Reduction: Panel Data Analysis of South Asian Countries. *International Journal of Social Economics*, *43*(4), 400–416. doi:10.1108/IJSE-04-2014-0069

Siddik, M. N. A., Sun, G., Yanjuan, C. U. I., & Kabiraj, S. (2014). Financial Inclusion through Mobile Banking: A Case of Bangladesh. *Journal of Applied Finance & Banking, 4*(6), 109-136. ISSN: 1792-6580 (print version), 1792-6599 (online) Scienpress Ltd, 2014.

Swamy, V. (2014). Financial Inclusion, Gender Dimension, and Economic Impact on Poor Households. *World Development*, *56*, 1–15. doi:10.1016/j.worlddev.2013.10.019

Usman, A. S., & Tasmin, R. (2016). The Role of Islamic Micro-finance in Enhancing Human Development in Muslim Countries. *Journal of Islamic Finance*, *5*(1), 53–62. doi:10.12816/0027652

World Bank. (2018). The Global Findex Database 2017: Measuring Financial Inclusion and the Fintech Revolution. Doi:10.1596/978-1-4648-1259-0

Zamer, K. Z. (2018). Islamic Banking: A New Approach for Financial inclusion. *International Journal of Economics and Finance, 10*(7), 118-124.

Zulkhibiri, M. (2016). Financial Inclusion, Financial Inclusion Policy and Islamic Finance. *Macroeconomics and Finance in Emerging Market Economies*, *9*(3), 1–18.

## KEY TERMS AND DEFINITIONS

**Financial Inclusion:** The process of including the unbanked within formal financial system through extending minimum financial services at an affordable cost.

**Islamic Banking:** An alternative form of ethical banking that replaces interest with profit and adheres to Islamic *Shari'ah*.

**Islamic Finance:** The alternative form of interest-free financing activities that comply with the rulings of Islamic *Shari'ah*.

***Qard*:** Also called *Qard-al-hasana*, a special form of loan offered by Islamic financing institutions disbursed in specific welfare sector at zero or low cost with no urgency for repayment.

***Waqf*:** A form of deposit product offered by Islamic financing institutions whose profit are distributed for welfare purposes and not entitled to depositors.

***Zakat*:** A form of obligatory donation of Muslims based on income and possessions and disbursed in certain specified sectors for welfare purposes.

# Chapter 10
# Determinants of Islamic Banking in Africa:
## An Econometric Analysis

**Sheereen Fauzel**
*University of Mauritius, Mauritius*

## ABSTRACT

*The global financial crisis of 2007-2008 depicted that conventional banking has many weaknesses. Hence, there has been much debate on the strength of Islamic banking to confront such crises. There are various advantages of using Shari'ah-compliant financial products pointed out by researches. Moreover, people who abide by their religious belief are mainly those who demand such financial services. But research relating to the determinants of Islamic banking is scant. This chapter examines the determinants of Islamic Banking in Africa over the period 2005-2018. The result shows that if the share of the Muslim population is high compared to other religions, Islamic banking is better diffused. Furthermore, important determinants of Islamic banking obtained from the results are the growth rate of the country and the extent to which the financial system is developed. Interestingly, it is observed that interest rate affects the diffusion of Islamic banking as it represents an opportunity cost.*

## 1. INTRODUCTION

In 2017, there are at least 1,389 full-fledged Islamic financial institutions and windows offering in the Islamic finance industry. Also, out of the industry's total assets, Islamic banking accounted for 71%, or US$ 1.7 trillion in the same year. This share is seen to keep growing as there are major mergers and acquisitions which is being formed in the major markets such as Malaysia and the Gulf countries (GCC). Another innovation in this field is the application of technology to renovate the Islamic banking sector. Several digital-only Islamic banks are being launched which is seen as a major breakthrough in this sector. Such innovation will definitely help the basic traditional Islamic banks to enter other countries mainly in the regions of Europe or Africa.

DOI: 10.4018/978-1-7998-1611-9.ch010

*Figure 1. Global Islamic finance assets growth from 2012-2023*
*Source: Salaamgateway.com*

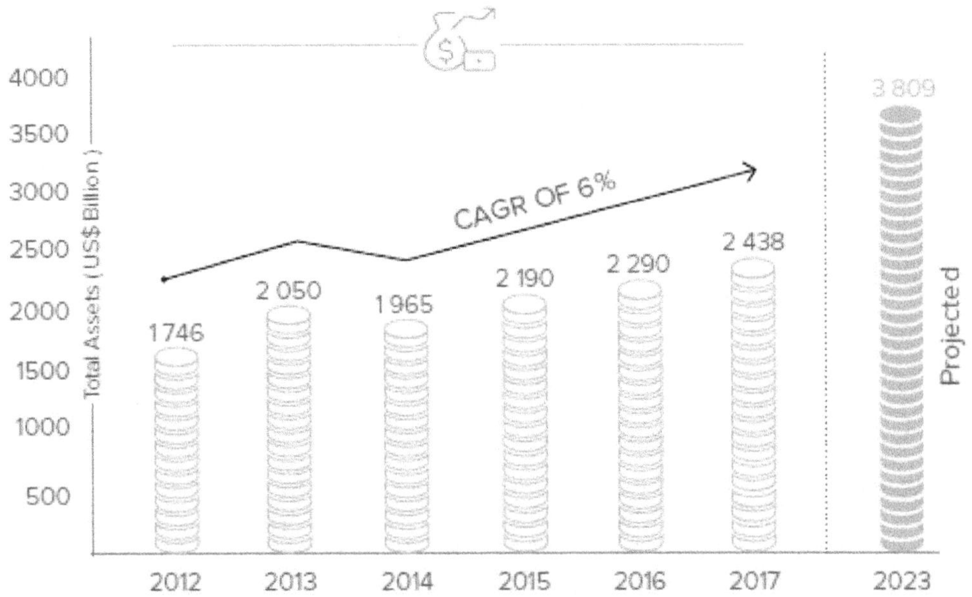


The diagram in Figure 1 clearly shows the increasing growth in global Islamic finance assets.

Given favorable economic conditions, the global IFSI has grown significantly and the industry's assets have exceeded USD 2 trillion. Consider Table 1.

Referring to Africa, it is recognized to be a region that will record tremendous growth in Islamic banking, as many conventional banks are opening Islamic windows. More so, such development is supported by the different African countries government[1]. One of the fastest growing segments of the financial market industry comprises of Islamic finance and the *Shari'ah*-compliant financial products that form the core of Islamic banking. More so, these products also form the important part of Islamic Banking. (Čihák & Hesse, 2010).

While both Islamic banking and conventional banking are important, Islamic banking is now expanding on a larger scale to become a market that could compete with the conventional banking in many countries. Islamic banks are highly considered as a substitute to conventional banks in Islamic countries and countries with a percentage of Islamic population. Many countries are adopting full fledge Islamic banks and if not, the conventional banks have launched Islamic windows with important amount of *Shari'ah*-compliant financial assets.

Islamic banking is seen to grow massively in Africa. Assets related to Islamic banking is seen to increase by 10 percent in the future in total African banking assets (Moody's). For instance, Sudan register 100 percent Islamic banking assets while Djibouti has 20 percent of Islamic banking assets. In total there are at least 80 Islamic financial institutions in Africa with the greatest number in the north of Africa mainly in Sudan. Nigeria, Senegal and Kenya have implemented banking, legal and regulatory frameworks to boost growth in their Islamic banking sectors. Moreover, there are a number of well-established conventional banks across Africa which have Islamic windows in which *Shari'ah*-compliant products are provided. These include Absa Bank of South Africa, Ecobank Chad and Sterling Bank Plc of

*Table 1. Breakdown of global IFSI by sector and region (USB billion, 2017*)*

| Region | Banking Assets | *Ṣukūk* Outstanding | Islamic Funds' Assets | *Takāful* Contributions | Total | Share (%) |
|---|---|---|---|---|---|---|
| Asia | 232.0 | 239.5 | 24.8 | 3.3 | 499.6 | 24.4 |
| GCC | 683.0 | 139.2 | 26.8 | 12.6 | 861.6 | 42.0 |
| MENA (ex. GCC) | 569.0 | 17.8 | 0.1 | 9.5 | 596.4 | 29.1 |
| Africa (ex-North) | 27.1 | 2.0 | 1.6 | 0.7 | 31.4 | 1.5 |
| Others | 46.4 | 1.5 | 13.3 | 0.0 | 61.3 | 3.0 |
| Total | 1,557.5 | 399.9 | 66.7 | 26.1 | 2,050.2 | 100.0 |

**Data for ṣukūk outstanding and Islamic funds' assets are for the full year 2017; data for Islamic banking are for the six months ended June 2017 (1H2017); and data for takāful are as at end 2016.*
*Source: IFSB Secretariat Workings*
*Note: Data are mostly taken from primary sources (regulatory authorities' statistical databases, annual reports and financial stability reports, official press releases and speeches, etc. and including IFSB's PSIFI database). Where primary data are unavailable, third-party data providers have been used, including Bloomberg. Takāful contributions are used as a basis to reflect the growth in the takāful industry. The breakdown of Islamic funds' assets is by domicile of the funds, while ṣukūk outstanding is broken down by domicile of the obligor.*

Source: Islamic Financial Services Industry (IFSI), 2018

Nigeria[2]. Several African countries such as South Africa, Nigeria, Kenya, Senegal, Djibouti and Uganda have introduced legal and regulatory frameworks to promote the development of Islamic finance products in their respective jurisdictions. Examples include recent changes to Kenya's stamp duty and VAT regulation to create a more level playing field between *Shari'ah*-compliant and conventional products. Nigeria and South Africa are now home to Islamic banks and *Takaful* (Islamic insurance) companies[3].

The diagram in Figure 2 shows the prevalence of Islamic banking in different parts of Africa.

It is noted that there are very few studies which have been conducted on Islamic banking. There are not many analyses done on the determinants of Islamic banking in Africa so far. Hence, the aim of the present chapter is to analyze the factors determining Islamic banking in selected African countries over the period 2005-2018. Static panel data analysis is being used for investigation purposes.

## 2. LITERATURE REVIEW

While Islamic banks are seen to be demanded mainly by Muslim customers, they are not representing any religious organization. Similar to other financial intermediaries they are also profit-maximizing bodies. Just like the key function of a conventional bank is to channel funds from surplus to deficit economic unit and also offer other services like safeguarding the valuables of customers among many other services, Islamic banks also have the same functions. But it should be noted that Islamic financial institution bears their principles from Islamic law and the authentic hadiths which incorporates a set of obligations that need to be applied while conducting their financial operations.

*Figure 2. Islamic banking in different parts of Africa*

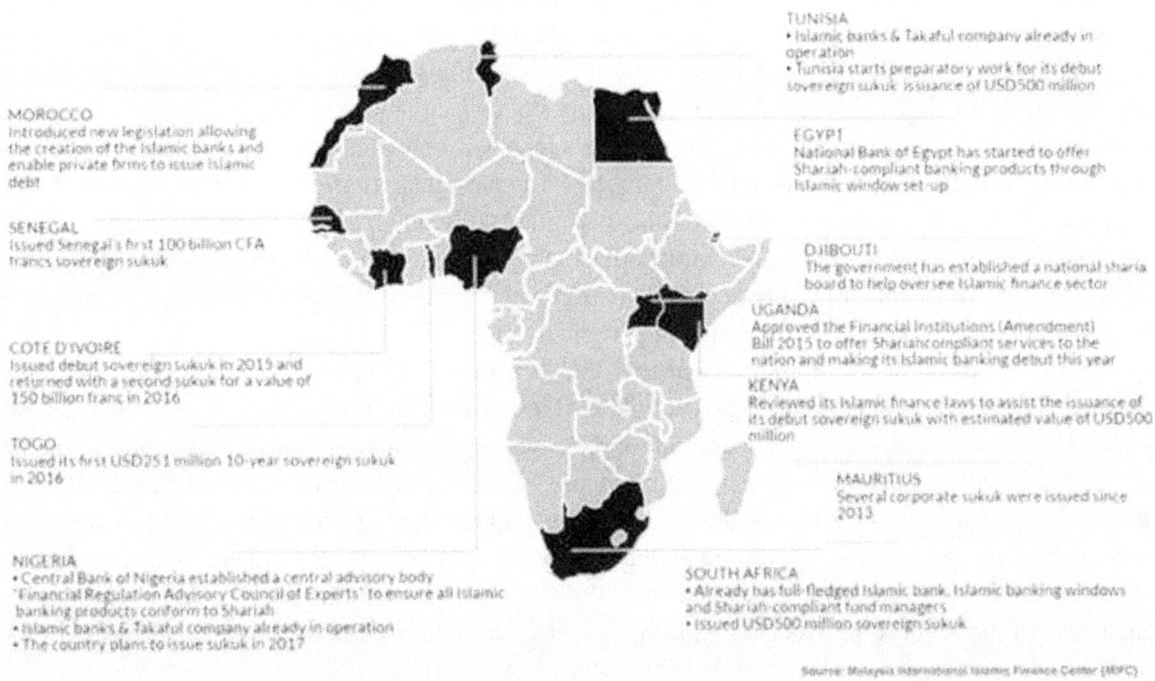


Islamic law is considered to affect the traditional functions of the banking system (El-Gamal, 2006). Four factors in particular are unique to Islamic banking. These are outlined below:

The first factor is the prohibition of interest (*Riba*). Unlike the conventional banking system, the Islamic banking system does not function on the sole premise of paying a fixed and predetermined rate of interest on deposits nor does it permit charging of a fixed rate of interest on monies advanced to borrowers. The system does not treat money as a lendable commodity for the price of interest. Referring to Kamran, the simplest and widely used meaning of *Riba* is inconsistent profit. This refers to the fact that fair profit is allowed, and inconsistent profit is prohibited. The query which arises however relates to the problem of finding the one who will determine the difference between fair and unfair profit. *Riba* is further viewed as the main factor that differentiate between Islamic and conventional banking. All forms of *Riba* is not permissible in Islam given that interest rates are indeed a form of exploitation, which is completely against fairness. It hence means that Islamic law prohibit to calculate a return on a loan in advance and expect a reward for this transaction. The debate is based on the fact that *Riba* implies an inappropriate seizure of the property of other people and is considered as detrimental for growth. (El-Gamal, 2006)

The *Qur'an*, the holy scripture of Muslims and the last revealed text expressly prohibits giving and taking of interest referred to as *Riba*[4] or usury and directs that all financial transactions should be free of usury which should be eliminated from the economic lives of people. This prohibition as revealed in four *Surahs* under various contexts, along with the traditions of the Holy Prophet *(May peace be upon him)* set forth guidelines which were refined and elaborated by the four schools of Islamic thought by which was evolved the Islamic jurisprudence on the subject of economics, banking and finance which is a full-fledged discipline of study.

The Muslim community under the above directions and stipulation is averse to all interest-bearing transactions including conventional banking and its operations. This necessitates evolving a financial and banking system which could cater not only to the needs of this group but also offers to the world economy a system which is technically viable in the modern times fulfilling most of the present-day requirements.

Another factor is the prevention of *Maysir*[5] (games of chance) and of *Gharar*[6] (chance). Speculation is prohibited by Islamic banking whereby a person's money is being increased solely because of chance instead of working for it. It should not be confused with investment as *Maysir* refers to needless doubts, such as gambling in a casino. Inevitable risk is permitted (El-Gamal, 2006). More so *Gharar* contracts are prohibited. It refers to uncertain contracts like embarking on businesses with excessive risk or lack of information. It is similar to imperfect information whereby there are lack of information, misunderstanding and conflicts between the different parties.

Thirdly we have the Prohibition of *haram* (illegal) activities as another factor. Islamic laws allow Islamic banks to fund only *halal* (legal) activities. These banks are not supposed to give loans to any party whose aim is to use the money for haram purposes such as investing in gambling houses, selling of pork and alcoholic products. One constraint identified here however is the fact that pure halal investments are difficult to find. *Zakat* or the Islamic tax is another factor which is essential to consider for Islamic banking. *Shari'ah* laws prescribed that the poor should be provided a share of wealth. *Zakat* is also one of the five doctrines of Islam and normally it is 2.5 percent of the assets held. However, where the banks do not collect the Islamic tax, same is collected by institutions which establish *Zakat* funds and later direct it to the deprived people (Shah, Raza & Khurshid, 2012).

Referring to Islamic finance we quote the work of Naser and Moutinho (1997) which highlighted the fact that financing of projects which were interest free was practiced by Arabs prior to the advent of Islam, and same was adopted by Muslims as an acceptable form of trade financing. It started on a small scale for centuries, and then its commercial application began in 1970. Warde (2000) in his paper defines Islamic finance as Islamic financial institutions based on the principles of the *Qur'an*. Islamic banks have as task to come up with financial products which are in line with the *Shari'ah* principles. Furthermore, as stated by Ali and Ali (1994), this concept has resulted in transforming the way traditional deposit and lending products to be in line with the *Shari'ah*. In order to attain this, a number of financial products were developed which satisfy the *Shari'ah* law. Mostly, there is more a partnership relationship between lenders and borrowers instead of debtor-creditor relationship and risk are shared. Both parties get a return which is based on the profit and performance of the investment or project rather than on the interest which is at a pre-determined rate.

It is noted that Islamic banking has achieved great growth and, in many countries, today the aspect of Islamic banking is present. If full fledge Islamic banks are not found, there is however Islamic windows. According to Sheik (2007), Islamic Banking is expected to capture 12% of the deposit market by 2012. Also, during the 2008 financial crisis, Islamic banks have been able to grow and many people in the non-Muslim countries are interested in Dual Banking system. However, apart from the benefits, there are certain controversies and challenges which Islamic banks face (Shah, Raza & Khurshid, 2012).

One problem identified is the fact that each Islamic bank has their own *Shari'ah* Supervisory Board (SSB) having their own perspective of finance and religion (Rafay & Farid, 2018). The trial facing Islamic bank is the diversion in opinion among the *Shari'ah* scholars, and as a result consumers and investors are confused as this creates a lot of uncertainties regarding the extent to which the products are Shari'ah compliant or not. According to Malik et al. (2011), another problem is the issue of fatwa whereby scholars interpret and issue rulings based on their own understanding of the *Shari'ah* rulings. In many cases it is seen that the interpretation on certain *Shari'ah* issues are different by one group of scholars to another which complicates matters more.

Another strand of the literature identified the fact that not all Islamic banks are compliant to *Shari'ah* principles even though they claim in their annual reports that they comply with *Shari'ah* rules and principle. (Patel, 2010) On the other hand, there is a lack of skilled *Shari'ah* scholars who can advise the Islamic banks. According to Ainely et al., 2000, there is shortage of knowledgeable *Shari'ah* Scholars with banking experience and knowledge. Referring to the survey of Khaleej Times (2008), there is about 250-300 *Shari'ah* scholars around the world. Moreover, the *Shari'ah* scholars serve more than one board and they are also providing the advisory services to direct competitors and earning millions of dollars. This is a major critic here. Also, conventional bankers can understand the operation of Islamic banks with ease, but they need knowledge on *Shari'ah* laws and principles to be able to develop Islamic products.

Referring to the determinants of Islamic banking in the literature, it is noted that economic growth is quoted as a main macroeconomic indicator affecting the profitability of Islamic banks. Bashir (2003), used data from 14 Islamic banks in 8 countries and used return on asset (ROA) and return on equity (ROE) as dependent variables for measuring profitability of Islamic banks, found that economic growth has a significant and positive relationship in the study. Same was discussed by Srairi (2009) and Wasiuzzaman and Tarmizi (2010) whose studies was based on the determinants of profits based by Islamic banks in the GCC countries and in Malaysia respectively. The result shows a positive relationship between economic growth and profit of Islamic banks. However, Ramadan et al. (2011) studied the determinants of profitability of Jordanian banks over the period of 2001-2010 and their studies could not find a direct and significant relationship with GDP growth and profitability. Also, Demirgüç-Kunt and Huizinga (2000) and Vong and Chang (2009) found that there is an insignificant relationship between profitability of banks and economic growth.

Analyzing the work of Asutay & Izhar (2007), inflation was seen to affect banks' profitability. Similar results were obtained by Wasiuzzaman and Ahmed Tarmizi (2010), Bashir (2003), Athanasoglou et al. (2008), Asutay & Izhar (2007), Vong and Chang (2009), Kunt and Huizinga (2000). However, Sriari (2009) and Naceur (2003) found no significant link between the profitability of banks and inflation. Financial development is another determinant of Islamic banking quoted in literatur2e. Referring to the work of Srairi (2009) analyzed the extent to which bank characteristics, macroeconomic indicators and financial structure influences the profitability of retail as well as Islamic banks operating in the GCC countries over the years 1999–2006. They found that financial development proxies by the growth in money supply has a significant positive link with profitability of Islamic bank and also with that of retail commercial banks. More so, interest rates and unemployment are seen to be other macroeconomic indicators of profitability.

Several studies have been using primary data to investigate the adoption of Islamic Banking in each country. Most of the studies have used the theory of Planned Behavior, diffusion of Innovation theory and customer innovativeness theory in their research. For instance, Obeid and Kaabachi (2016), investigated the factors influencing the adoption of Islamic banking by conventional bank customers in Tunisia. The results showed that religious commitment, the amount of information held by consumers about Islamic finance, the relative advantage of Islamic banking and its compatibility with consumer values, lifestyle, and banking habits are among the factors influencing the adoption of Islamic banking. On the other hand, the study by Yahaya et al., (2014) came up with a theoretical framework involving the study of Islamic banking products and services adoption among the Nigerian bank customers. The study laid importance on the relevance of Innovation Diffusion Theory. Importance is set on customer involvement as a variable amongst the perceived attributes. Also, there is the investigation by Possumah et al., (2018) who studied the determinants of Islamic banking adoption across different religious groups in Ghana and found that perceived knowledge, perceived benefit, perceived innovativeness, perceived religious promotion, customer's attitude and readiness to comply with sharia were significant determinants of Islamic banking adoption for the Muslims, Christians and Africa Traditional Religion (ATR) sub-groups. However, perceived threat of violence was a significant negative determinant of Islamic banking adoption for the Christians and ATR sub-groups but insignificant for the Muslims sub-group.

The same concept was investigated for the case of Malaysia by Mahdzan et al., (2017) based on Rogers' (1983; 2003) Diffusion of Innovation. Precisely, the impact of perceived attributes and variables like understanding, consumer innovativeness and bank personnel's professionalism on Islamic banking adoption was studied. Their results showed that the understanding of Islamic banking concepts and perceived advantage significantly influences the adoption of Islamic banking services. Another strand of literature by Lalip et al., (2017) analyses the influential factors that are associated with Islamic banking adoption between the Muslim and non-Muslim populations in Malaysia. They identified four attributes of innovation, namely; relative advantage, compatibility, observability and complexity, and three additional variables namely; perceived risk, perceived trust and customer innovativeness. Their results showed that compatibility, relative advantage/observability and complexity have a significant relationship with customers' adoption of Islamic banking products and services. Investigating the relationship between consumer innovativeness and customers' intention to adopt Islamic banking as well as the role of consumer innovativeness in relationship between attitudes, social influence, perceived behavioral control and intention to adopt Islamic banking in Nigeria, Othman (2016) came up with a theoretical framework as depicted in Figure 3.

*Figure 3. Consumer intention to adopt Islamic banking in Nigeria*
*Source: Othman (2013)*

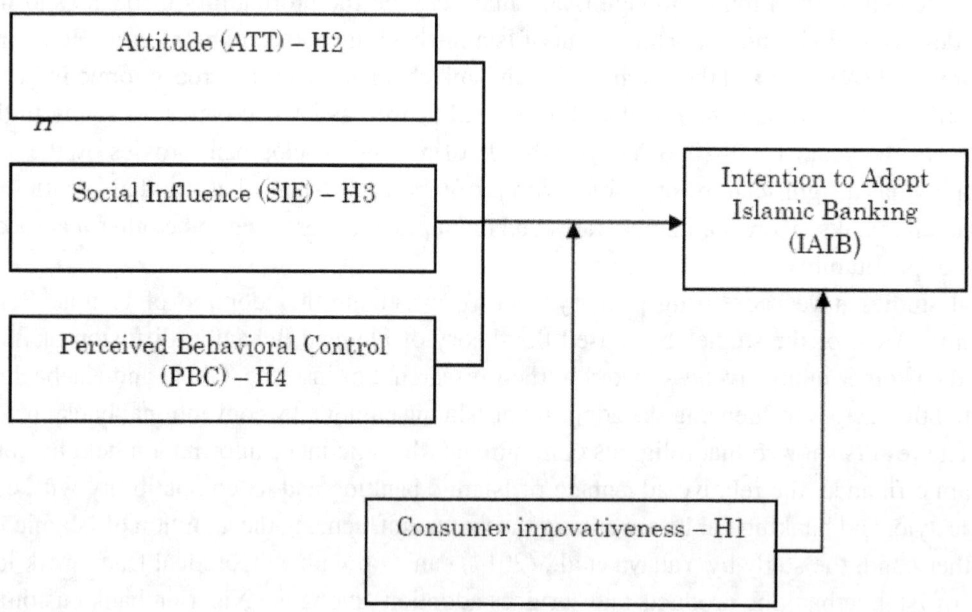

Hence, intention to adopt Islamic banking is related to consumer innovativeness, attitude, social influence and perceived behavioral control. While most studies have been using a survey approach to determine the adoption of Islamic banking, the present chapter uses secondary data to do the investigation. Also, analyzing the literature, there is no consensus on the factors determining Islamic banking. Unlike previous studies, the objective of this chapter is hence to investigate the likely determinants of Islamic banking in Africa by using innovation secondary data approach.

## 3. METHODOLOGY AND RESULTS FINDINGS

In this study, the aim is to investigate the determinants of Islamic Banking in selected African countries[7]. The sample size used in the study is from 2005-2018. Drawing on the work of Patrick Imam and Kangni Kpodar (2010), the following regression equation is used

$$\text{IB} = f\,(ISPOP,\ GDP,\ FINDEV,\ CPI,\ IR) \quad (1)$$

### Dependent Variable

Since data on Islamic banking is very limited mainly for African countries, the number of Islamic banks (IB) has been used as a proxy to measure the extent of Islamic banking presence in the countries. Data was collected individually from the central bank of each country and from reports on the individual Islamic banks for the selected countries.

### Independent Variables

Islamic population (ISPOP) in a country does influence the establishment of Islamic banking. Hence, this variable was included as a possible determinant in the regression equation. Here, it is expected that the higher the Islamic population in a country, the more importance will Islamic banking hold in that economy. Current estimates suggest there are an estimated 1.6 billion Muslims worldwide, with high concentrations in the Middle East, North Africa, and South-East Asia but otherwise spread across the globe.

Another control variable included is the level of growth in the country. In this study, GDP per capita has been used to account for the growth rate prevailing in the countries. Indeed, the higher the growth rate of a country, the more well off the population will be. Hence, with rising income, it is expected that countries will experience more development in their financial activities and thus this will lead to the diffusion of Islamic banking.

Another variable included is financial system development (FD) proxies by domestic credit to the private sector as a percentage of GDP. Financial system development is a crucial factor affecting the flow of Islamic banking in a country. As highlighted by Imam and Kpodar (2010), a more innovated and refined banking system could act as an alternative for Islamic banks. Hence, this fact may make the flow and growth of Islamic banks more difficult. But on the other hand, with an innovated banking system, it can give Islamic bank the opportunity to spread and grow better as it will provide better infrastructure, such as human capital which are needed by Islamic banks. Hence, in this way Islamic banks would act as a supplement to the retail banks.

Interest rate is the benefits obtain from savings with conventional banks. Hence, the population of a country will compare the interest rate from savings with that obtained from Islamic banks to decide on their savings plans. Hence, interest rate represents the opportunity cost of using Islamic banks rather than conventional banks. If it is low, the opportunity cost foregone is low, and Islamic banking should be stimulated. IR is the proxy used for interest rate.

In order to account for macroeconomic stability of the country the inflation rate is included as another exogenous variable. Normally, the more an economy is stable, there is more financial intermediation. Hence, it is expected that Islamic banks will flow better in more stable economies. CPI is used as a proxy for inflation rate. Data for the independent variables have been extracted from the World Bank Database.

Because of the variance stabilizing properties of log transformation, the log values of the variables are used. In fact, logged variables yield a more clear-cut interpretation of the coefficients in terms of percentage change. The econometric specification can be written as follows:

$$\ln IB_{it} = \alpha_{it} + \beta_1 \ln ISPOP_{it}, + \beta_2 \ln GDP_{it}, \beta_3 \ln FINDEV_{it} + \beta_4 \ln CPI_{it\,+}\ \beta_5 \ln IR_{it} + \varepsilon_{it} \quad (2)$$

where i is the respective countries in the sample and t denotes the years and ε refers to the error terms.

## Estimation Issues

To begin with, a panel analysis is carried forward. Statistical models such as the Fixed Effect (FE) model and the Random Effect (RE) model are used in order to account for the individuality of each country. As is well known, both the FE and RE statistical models differ in their main assumptions concerning the intercept and the error terms. The assumption is that the error term can be decomposed into two independent elements:

$$\varepsilon it = \mu it + vit$$

where μit, is time-invariant and accounts for any unobservable country specific effects not included in the regression. The vit, term represents the remaining disturbances, and varies over time and by country. It can be thought of as the usual disturbance in a regression.

Both the FE and RE accommodates unobservable heterogeneity. While the Ui's are fixed parameters to be estimated in the FE model, the Ui's are assumed to be random in the RE model, independent and identically distributed, ie. Ui ~ IID (0, σ2μ). Hence, it can be seen that the RE model is more efficient than the FE model mainly due to the loss of freedom. Also, the RE model transfers the unobservable effects into the error term which is not done by the FE model. The RE model also assumes that they are uncorrelated with regressors.

## Empirical Results

The first part of the analysis involves testing equation (2) using the full sample. Equation (2) is estimated using the fixed effect (FE) and the random effect (RE) models.

Column 1 & 2 of Table 2 shows estimations of equation (1) using the FE and RE models respectively.

*Table 2. Panel data (Fixed & Random Effects findings)*

| Variables | FE(1) | RE(2) |
|---|---|---|
| C | -0.544768 | **-2.276333***** |
| LMPOP | 0.124092*** | **0.126799***** |
| LFD | -0.054979 | **0.004212*** |
| LGDP | 0.034289 | **0.037885**** |
| LIR | -0.143794** | **-0.116432*** |
| LCPI | -0.135427 | **0.163997** |
| Number of observations | 110 | 110 |
| Prob F | 0.000 | 0.000 |
| Test | Hausman Test | Hausman Test |

Dependent variable is = ln (IB)
*significant at 10%, ** significant at 5%, ***significant at

## Hausman Specification Test

The main problem encountered with panel data is the choice of using a random effects or fixed effects estimation approaches. Hence, to determine which of these estimators should be used for our investigation, the Hausman specification test was carried forward.

$$HS = [b_{fe} - b_{re}]^{1} \text{ VAR } [b_{fe} - b_{re}]^{-1} [b_{fe} - b_{re}] \sim X^{2}(k)$$

From the results obtained, the Hausman test favours the random effects approach. The investigation is in logarithm form to test the elasticity of the explanatory variables to the dependent variable and the results are shown in the table above.

Hence, the random effect results are being discussed below.

Referring to column 3 of table 2, it is noted that indeed Muslim population is an important determinant of Islamic banking in Sub Saharan African countries. Hence, the higher the Muslim population in a country, the better is the diffusion of Islamic Banking. Looking at the random effect findings, it is noted that the relationship between interest rate and Islamic banking is negative and highly significant as expected, implying that the higher the rate of interest, the population will prefer to use conventional banking thus reducing the diffusion of Islamic banking and vice versa. This relationship therefore shows that Islamic banking and conventional banking are substitutes. Hence, consumers compare the benefits from saving with either bank in their savings decisions. Consumers save more money in Islamic banks when opportunity costs fall and save more money in conventional banks when opportunity cost rises.

The elasticity of Islamic Banking with respect to gross domestic product per capita is positively and statistically significant at the 5% level. This result is consistent with the hypothesis that the growth of an economy increases the diffusion of Islamic banking. It shows that holding other variables constant, Islamic banking will increase by 0.04% when GDP per capita of the country increases by 1%. Indeed, referring to existing literature, banking and financial institutions have also related to economic growth. There are three likely links between financial development and economic growth. The first arguments relate to the fact that financial development is a factor influencing economic growth. The second argument is based on the fact that financial development follows economic growth, and thirdly there is bidirectional causality between finance and growth (Furqani 2009). Also, since it is problematic to segregate banking as an exogenous variable, attempts to do so have yielded results that show financial development having an impact on growth and vice versa. The results also show that the more developed the financial system is, the higher will be Islamic diffusion.

The rate of inflation has been included to account for the impact of macroeconomic instability on Islamic banking. Review of the literature shows that with more inflation in a country, financial intermediation is affected whereby people prefer to dis save and invest rather in hard assets. In this way both conventional banks and Islamic banks are negatively affected. However, our result does not support this view. An insignificant result is obtained. This result is in line with the findings of Kaminsky and Reinhart (1996).

## 4. CONCLUSION

This paper investigates the determinants of Islamic Banking in Africa over the period 2005-2018. The exogenous variables included are the Muslim population, the inflation rate, the interest rate, GDP per capita, and financial development. It is observed that after the financial crisis of 2008, countries have started to adopt Islamic banking and finance in the financial structure of their economies. The result shows that in countries where the share of Muslim population is high compared to other religions, Islamic banking is better diffused. Furthermore, important determinants of Islamic banking obtained from the results are the growth rate of the country and the extent to which the financial system is developed. Interestingly, it is observed that interest rate affects the diffusion of Islamic banking as it represents an opportunity cost in saving with Islamic banks. Thus, Islamic banking and conventional banking are substitutes. The result also shows that financial development encourages the diffusion of Islamic banking. It should be noted that Islamic countries can build up the banking system even if a country makes little progress at reforming institutions as its foundation are built on *Shari'ah* laws. This is different from conventional banking systems.

## Classifications

JEL Classification: G21, B23, B41
KAUJIE Classification: A1, H11, I2

## REFERENCES

Ainley, M., Mashayekhi, A., Hicks, R., Rahman, A., & Ravalia, A. (2007). *Islamic finance in the UK: Regulation and challenges. The Financial Services Authority*. London, UK: FSA.

Ali, S., & Ali, N. (1994). *Information Sources on Islamic Banking and Economics: 1980-1990*. London, UK: Kegan Paul International.

Asutay, M., & Izhar, H. (2007). Estimating the profitability of Islamic banking: Evidence from bank Muamalat Indonesia. *Review of Islamic Economics*, *11*(2), 17–29.

Athanasoglou, P. P., Brissimis, S. N., & Delis, M. D. (2008). Bank-specific, industry-specific and macroeconomic determinants of bank profitability. *Journal of International Financial Markets, Institutions and Money*, *18*(2), 121–136. doi:10.1016/j.intfin.2006.07.001

Bashir, A. H. M. (2003). Determinants of profitability in Islamic banks: Some evidence from the Middle East. *Islamic Economic Studies*, *11*(1), 31–57.

Čihák, M., & Hesse, H. (2010). Islamic banks and financial stability: An empirical analysis. *Journal of Financial Services Research*, *38*(2-3), 95–113. doi:10.100710693-010-0089-0

Demirgüç-Kunt, A., & Huizinga, H. (2000). Financial structure and bank profitability. *World Bank Policy Research Working Paper*, (2430).

El-Gamal, M. (2006). *Islamic Finance: Law, Economics and Practice*. Cambridge, UK: Cambridge University Press. doi:10.1017/CBO9780511753756

Furqani, H., & Mulyany, R. (2009). Islamic banking and economic growth: Empirical evidence from Malaysia. *Journal of Economic Cooperation & Development*, *30*(2), 59–74.

Kaminsky, G. L., & Reinhart, C. M. (1999). The twin crises: The causes of banking and balance-of-payments problems. *The American Economic Review*, *89*(3), 473–500. doi:10.1257/aer.89.3.473

Kamran, R. (no date). *Interest (Riba) Religion and Spirituality*. Retrieved from http://www.booksie.com/all/allkamranrifat/interest-(*Riba*)-the-myth-and-reality

Kpodar, K., & Imam, P. A. (2010). Islamic banking: how has it diffused? *IMF Working Papers*, 1-29.

Latip, M., Yahya, M. H., & Junaina, M. (2017). Factors Influencing Customer's Acceptance of Islamic Banking Products and Services. *Ikonomika*, *2*(1), 1–18. doi:10.24042/febi.v2i1.681

Levine, R. (1997). Financial Development and Economic Growth: Views and Agenda. *Journal of Economic Literature*, *35*, 688–726.

Mahdzan, N. S., Zainudin, R., & Au, S. F. (2017). The adoption of Islamic banking services in Malaysia. *Journal of Islamic Marketing*, *8*(3), 496–512. doi:10.1108/JIMA-08-2015-0064

Malik, M. S., Malik, A., & Mustafa, W. (2011). Controversies that make Islamic banking controversial: An analysis of issues and challenges. *American Journal of Social and Management Sciences*, *2*(1), 41–46. doi:10.5251/ajsms.2011.2.1.41.46

Naceur, S. B. (2003). The determinants of the Tunisian banking industry profitability: Panel evidence. *Universite Libre de Tunis working papers*, *11*(3), 317-319.

Naser, K., & Moutinho, L. (1997). Strategic marketing management: The case of Islamic banks. *International Journal of Bank Marketing*, *15*(6), 187–203. doi:10.1108/02652329710184424

Nienhaus, V. (1983). Profitability of Islamic Banks Competing with Interest Banks. *Journal of Research in Islamic Economics*, *1*(1), 37–47.

Obeid, H., & Kaabachi, S. (2016). Empirical investigation into customer adoption of Islamic banking services in Tunisia. *Journal of Applied Business Research*, *32*(4), 1243–1256. doi:10.19030/jabr.v32i4.9734

Othman, M. A. (2013). Reflecting customers' innovativeness and intention to adopt Islamic banking in Nigeria/Ahmad Muhammad Gumel and Mohammad Azmi Othman. *Business & Management Quarterly Review*, *4*(3&4), 27–37.

Patel, I. (2010). *Islamic Banks need restructuring*. Retrieved from www.accountancy.com

Possumah, B. T., Appiah, M. K., & Hilmiyah, N. (2018). Determinants of Islamic banking adoption across different religious groups in Ghana: A panoptic perspective. *Journal of International Studies*, *11*(4), 138–154. doi:10.14254/2071-8330.2018/11-4/10

Rafay, A., & Farid, S. (2018). *Shari'ah* Supervisory Board Report (SSBR) in Islamic Banks: An experimental study of Investors' perception and behaviour. *International Journal of Islamic and Middle Eastern Finance and Management*, *11*(2), 274–296. doi:10.1108/IMEFM-07-2017-0180

Ramadan, I. Z., Kilani, Q. A., & Kaddumi, T. A. (2011). Determinants of Bank Profitability: Evidence from Jordan. *International Journal of Academic Research*, *3*(4), 180–191.

Shah, S. F., Raza, M. W., & Khurshid, M. R. (2012). Islamic banking controversies and challenges. *Interdisciplinary Journal of Contemporary Research in Business*, *3*(10), 1018–1026.

Sheikh, S. A. (2007). *Critical analysis of current Islamic Banking system*. Retrieved from www.accountancy.com.pk

Srairi, S. A. (2009). Factors Influencing the Profitability of Conventional and Islamic Commercial Banks in GCC Countries. *Review of Islamic Economics*, *13*(1), 5–30.

Times, K. (2008). *Islamic banks enjoy double digit growth*. Khaleej Times.

Vong, A., & Chang, H. (2009). Determinants of Bank Profitability in Macao. University of Macao Working Paper.

Warde, I. (2000). *Islamic Finance in the Global Economy*. Edinburgh, Scotland: Edinburgh University Press. doi:10.3366/edinburgh/9780748612161.001.0001

Wasiuzzaman, S., & Tarmizi, H. A. (2010). Profitability of Islamic Banks in Malaysia: An Empirical Analysis. *Journal of Islamic Economics, Banking, and Finance*, *6*(4), 51–68.

Yahaya, S., Yusoff, W. S. B. W., Idris, A. F. B., & Haji-Othman, Y. (2014). Conceptual framework for adoption of Islamic banking in Nigeria: The role of customer involvement. *European Journal of Business and Management*, *6*(30), 11–24.

## ENDNOTES

1. https://repository.salaamgateway.com
2. http://www.africanreview.com/finance/banking-a-finance/islamic-banking-set-to-grow-in-africa
3. https://www.whitecase.com/publications/insight/islamic-finance-africa-opportunities-and-challenges
4. Refer to Appendix
5. Refer to Appendix
6. Refer to Appendix
7. Botswana, Kenya, Gambia, Ghana, Guinea, Liberia, Djibouti, Nigeria, Senegal, Tanzania

# APPENDIX

*Table 3. Islamic Banking Basic Terminology*

| Term | Definition |
|---|---|
| ***Riba*** **(Interest)** | Defined as an unearned or unequally distributed income, forbidden in Islamic economic jurisprudence |
| ***Maysir*** | Gambling (*Maysir*, رسيْمَلأو or Qimar, رامق) as a game to spend money and expect larger outcomes was widespread practiced in the pre-Islamic time of the Arabs. The *Qur'an* prohibited gambling alongside alcoholics in *Sura Al Baqarah* (Sura 2), Verse 219 |
| ***Gharar*** | An Islamic finance term describing a risky or hazardous sale, where details concerning the sale item are unknown or uncertain. *Gharar* is generally prohibited under Islam, which explicitly forbids trades that are considered to have excessive risk due to uncertainty. |

# Chapter 11
# Ownership Risk in Contemporary Islamic Banking

**Alam I. Asadov**
https://orcid.org/0000-0003-0805-6482
*Prince Sultan University, Riyadh, Saudi Arabia*

## ABSTRACT

*The unwillingness of contemporary Islamic banks to undertake real business risks has left many to ponder on whether the objectives laid down by the industry's founders have been realized. The need for real risk taking by Islamic banks is critical to justify the profits they earn in the forms of margins, rents, or service charges. This chapter analyzes issues relating to ownership risk (ḍamān al-milkiyyah) in Islamic banking by examining three of its popular products, namely Murabahah (mark-up sale), Ijarah (leasing), and Musharakah Mutanaqisah (diminishing partnership). Following close scrutiny, the chapter concludes that principles of ownership risk as laid down in Fiqh Muamalat (law of transactions) are violated in each of the studied products. Unfortunately, the problem extends beyond these products to include a number of other Islamic financial products. The author calls for closer attention to this important Shari'ah concept of ownership risk in designing Islamic finance products and offers some policy recommendations to improve the current situation.*

## INTRODUCTION

The rapid growth of Islamic banking industry within the last several years signifies an important achievement. Total assets of the Islamic finance industry was estimated at US$2.4 trillion in 2017 and is expected to increase to reach US$3.8 trillion by 2023. As of 2017, market share of Islamic banking was equal to 71% of the entire industry, or US$1.7 trillion with an annual growth rate of 5% (Reuters, 2018). The current state of Islamic banking, however, does not match the original expectation of its founding fathers, where Islamic banking was initially envisioned to be the catalyst of economic growth and prosperity through its engagement in mainly profit and loss sharing based financing.

DOI: 10.4018/978-1-7998-1611-9.ch011

When one undertakes careful observation of the majority of product structures offered by contemporary Islamic banks, striking similarities are found with the financing products of conventional banks in terms of operations. The fundamentals of Islamic banking products are supposed to align with *Shari'ah* principles, and financing provided to businesses and individuals must be based on the principles of true sale, partnership and provision of genuine services in order to earn profits. Nevertheless, the current structures of most Islamic banking products leave room for suspicion as to whether such transactions are done in reality. One critical issue to remember in this line of reasoning is the need for risk taking by Islamic banks to justify their earnings in the forms of margins, rents or service charges. True risk taking should be reflected in various aspects of Islamic banking products, such as the possibility of loss in partnership-based contracts; and exposures to market risk in sales transactions and ownership risk which arise when there are elements of transfer of ownership and its related benefits within the products.

In this chapter, the author analyzes only one of such risks, namely ownership risk. The chapter begins with a brief introduction of the concept of ownership in Islam, followed by description of ownership related risk and liabilities in *Shari'ah* (*ḍamān al-milkiyyah*). Once the reader obtains clear understanding of the ownership risk concept, the author continues with an analysis of some popular products offered by Islamic banks and specifically investigates whether the risk and liability related to ownership *(ḍamān al-milkiyyah)* are correctly assigned in the structuring of those products in contemporary Islamic banks. The investigation and analysis focus on Islamic banking products such as *Murabahah* (mark-up sale), *Ijarah* (leasing) and *Musharakah Mutanaqisah* (diminishing partnership). The chapter also examines issue of ownership risk in some other Islamic finance products such as *Takaful* and *Sukuk*. Thereafter, it looks into some real court cases directly related to violation of ownership risk principles in Islamic finance industry. The chapter concludes with some policy recommendations.

## GENERAL OVERVIEW OF OWNERSHIP AND OWNERSHIP RISK CONCEPT

### Concept of Ownership in Islam

In Islam, the notion of ownership somewhat differs from the Western view of this concept. The differences are mainly in two aspects, namely in terms of the concept of absolute ownership and the liberty of the owner in utilizing his or her property. For instance, based on the views of the extreme right 'libertarian' philosophies of the West such as those advocated by Rothbard (1978) and Narveson (1988) which reflect the general position of capitalism, the ownership of property is solely founded on the individual who owns it, and no one else has the right to utilize or benefit from it. Their views on ownership can be summarized as "Agents may appropriately use, or even destroy whatever natural resources they want (as long as they do not violate anyone's self-ownership)"[1]. On the other hand, the extreme left views such as of Marx's and of supporters of communist philosophy argue against private property as they support collective ownership. To them, private property is the cause of class clashes in society and therefore should be totally abolished. In a communist society which they are in favor of, labor is deemed to be the main source of livelihood. Therefore, Marx argues that "nothing can pass to the ownership of individuals except individual means of consumption (i.e. earned directly by their labor)" (McLellan, 2000). Accordingly, it is observed that in communism, individuals do not possess any rights of ownership and such rights are assigned to decision makers of collective property.

Islam takes the middle path in many circumstances and the same is true when it comes to the concept of property ownership. Unlike the capitalists' or communist philosophers' views, in Islam, the concept of ownership is fundamentally different. First of all, Muslims believe that the ultimate ownership of all things belongs to *Allah (SWT)* alone and humans are considered merely as vicegerents (trustees) of such ownership. There are several evidences from main sources of *Shari'ah*[2] that support the belief that ultimate ownership belongs to *Allah (SWT)*. In the Holy *Qur'an*, *Allah (SWT)* announces: "*To Him belongs what is in the heavens and what is on the earth and what is between them and what is under the soil*" (Q20:6)[3].

Therefore, in Islam, the possession of properties in this world is only considered as a trust from *Allah (SWT)*. One of the evidences from the *Qur'an* that confirms the principle of vicegerency (trusteeship) that is delegated from *Allah (SWT)* to humans read as follows: "*And He has subjected to you whatever is in the heavens and whatever is on the earth – all from Him. Indeed in that are signs for a people who give thought*" (Q45:13). Thus, as Allah's vicegerent on Earth, the property owner is considered just as a trustee or custodian and therefore he/she is obliged to utilize the property only in matters described by the Almighty Creator[4].

There are many definitions of private ownership provided by Muslim scholars throughout Islamic history. A comprehensive Islamic definition of ownership is given by Al-Qarafi as "A ruling of *Shari'ah* (*hukm shar'i*) or a juridical attribute (*wasf shar'i*), which is specified in a real object (*'ayn*) or usufruct (*manfa'a*), and enables a person to control, dispose, or exchange it in any manner he wishes provided that there is not legal impediment against it"[5]. Even though this definition of ownership seems to be very similar to the one offered by Western libertarians quoted above, there is at least one major difference. While the former places emphasis on 'violate no one's self-ownership', the latter highlights the requirement of 'there is no legal impediment against it'. Legal impediment refers to any sort of prohibitions imposed by primary or secondary sources of *Shari'ah*, which indirectly means managing one's property according to Allah's (SWT) will.

According to the Mejelle (Ottoman Code on Islamic Civil Law), everyone has the liberty to dispose his property in any way he thinks is fit. However, if there are the rights of another attached to it, this could prevent the owner from making an independent disposition. Additionally, any type of excessive harm that can be caused to others from the disposal of a property could be prevented by limiting full or partial utilization of such property rights (The Mejelle, n.d., Articles 1192 & 1200). In this context, only legal limits are imposed on the ownership given that the Mejelle is a compilation of legal codes by the Ottomans. Based on the definitions of Al-Qarafi, legal impediment could also be in the form of any morally prohibited acts.

In *Shari'ah*, there are two types of ownership, namely complete ownership (*al-milk al-tamm*) and deficient ownership (*al-milk al-naqis*). Another classification includes private ownership (*al-milk al-khas*) and public (collective) ownership (*al-milk al-fardi*) (Kamali, 2013b). As the second categorization has no direct relation to the scope of this chapter, there will be no discussion on its nuances.

The complete ownership of a property (*al-milk al-tamm*) comprises both ownership of the object and its usufruct. This is permanent and the most common type of ownership in *Shari'ah*. The deficient type of ownership (*al-milk al-naqis*) also exists but less frequently in *Shari'ah*. It is however still possible to have ownership of either the object or the usufruct only. In most cases, the deficient type of ownership would be a temporary arrangement and limited to a certain time period or other provisional conditions (Kamali, 2013b).

Any property in *Shari'ah* could either be owned or not. Property that is owned by a human being is termed as *mal mamluk* (owned property), and one that is not owned by anyone is called *mal mubah* (permissible property). There are definite protections provided for ownership of the owned property and its owner's rights. Ownership of the un-owned property could be acquired through *istila* (domination), which is performed by demonstration of possession or occupation (*al-hayaza*) and any other activity which is an indication of a person's intent to own that property. In the case of a property which is already owned (*mal mamluk*), the ownership can only be transferred through methods of sale (or exchange), gift and inheritance (Kamali, 2013b, pp. 268-69.).

Once a property is owned either through *istila* or other permissible means, there are certain restrictions placed on its owner. The main restrictions that the *Shari'ah* imposes on ownership aim to prevent harm to others, to protect public interest (*maslahah*), to be concerned on the utilization of barren land, and the pre-emption rights and inheritance. In the case of either complete or deficient ownership, the owner is always liable for any risk related to ownership. Ownership of property could expose the owner to some risks, which are specifically termed as ownership risks (*ḍamān al-milkiyyah*)[6].

## Concept of Ownership Risk (*ḍamān al-milkiyyah*) from *Shari'ah* Perspective

There are many types of ownership risks, such as risk of damage to properties, risk of hurting others, risk of loss (theft or destruction), price risk etc. One of the significant benefits that come with ownership is the entitlement for usufruct of property and profiting from such ownership through sales, lease or any other legitimate means. It is important to note that the notion of profit could not be considered separately from the notion of risk or liability in Islam. Therefore, in Islam, gains or profits are always accompanied with liability and risk of loss.

In Islamic finance, there are two main legal maxims which are used to express ownership risk (*ḍamān al-milkiyyah*) that accompanies any gain or benefits. The legal maxims are "*al-kharāj bi al- ḍamān*" (benefit goes with liability) and "*al-ghurm bi al-ghunm*" (liability accompanies gain). Fundamental principles such as justice and fairness to all parties in Islamic finance transactions are laid down in these maxims (Laldin et al., 2013). Thus, to understand the concept of ownership risk, it is important to also understand the meaning of these legal maxims.

The meaning of the first maxim, "*al-kharāj bi al- ḍamān*" is that a person who takes liability of any loss to the asset has the right to benefit from it. For instance, according to *Shari'ah*, a buyer can ask a seller to give him an option or *khiyār* to return the purchased good within a specified period in case of any defects. At the same time, the buyer will be entitled to benefit from the purchased asset during the holding period because he also takes liability for any damage caused to the good during that time. As opposed to the seller who has provided that option, the seller is not entitled to any fee or lease charge from the sale in case the good is returned. This is because all liabilities for the damage or loss of the sold goods are temporarily transferred to the buyer during the option period, therefore the seller cannot benefit from something for which he does not carry any liability (Abdul Razak & Saupi, 2017; Laldin et al., 2013).

The second maxim, "*al-ghurm bi al-ghunm*" (liability accompanies gain) in general means that the owner of the asset is liable for bearing all costs and losses associated with such ownership since he is also entitled to benefits coming from the ownership right (Laldin et al., 2013). A ruling which can be derived from the legal maxim is such that sole or part ownership of an asset cannot shift all risks or liabilities associated with the ownership to another party or partner, while still maintaining the right to benefit or profit from such ownership. The two maxims are interconnected and can be considered as two sides of the same coin (Abdul Razak & Saupi, 2017).

Both maxims are based on a hadith narrated by Imam Shafiʿī, Imam Ahmad and al-Hakim in their hadith compilations. In the hadith recorded through ʿUrwah fromʿĀʾishah (may Allah be pleased with her), she states that during the time of the Prophet (May peace be upon him), a slave was purchased by a man of whom the slave remained with for some time. Thereafter, the slave was returned to the previous owner due to a defect that was found on him. The case was brought to the Prophet (May peace be upon him) whose judgment was in favor of the return. The previous owner however objected by saying, "But he benefited from him". The Prophet (May peace be upon him) then replied: "*Al-kharāj bi al- ḍamān*" (Elgari, 2003). The hadith is supported by a majority of jurists despite some disagreements arising from either its chain of transmission or legal interpretation (Abdul Razak & Saupi, 2017).

Generally, the two maxims demonstrate the significance of ownership risk (*ḍamān al-milkiyyah*) which can be directly applied to all contracts of Islamic banking and finance. In summarizing the conclusion of these maxims in one sentence, it can say as 'benefit of ownership cannot be enjoyed without taking respective liability and risk'. If one insists on separating the benefits of ownership from the liability attached to it, especially by trying to guarantee profit without taking risk of ownership, it would be akin to insisting on *Riba* (usury)[7]. *Riba* which is literally translated from Arabic as the excess or increase, is defined in *Shari'ah* as an increase which is acquired by one party from another without giving an equivalent counter-value or recompense (*'iwad*) in return (Khan, 2005). Therefore, if one is enjoying the benefit or profit deriving from his ownership of certain assets in the forms of rent, gains from sale or in any other form, then that person should also take respective liability by bearing all the risks associated with such ownership.

## Importance of Ownership Risk from *Maqasid al-Shari'ah* Perspective

'*Maqasid al-Shari'ah*' stands for Objectives of *Shari'ah*, which gives general description of objectives in *Shari'ah* rulings intended by the Law Given (i.e. *Allah (SWT)*). Execution or omission of the rights and obligations as stated in *Maqasid al-Shari'ah* has major implication on the life of the servants of Allah, both in this worldly life and the hereafter. According to Imam al-Shatibi, there are two parts to the objectives of *Shari'ah*. The first part relates to the objectives which refer to the Law Giver (Allah) and to His servant. The second part refers to objectives related to *Shari'ah* restrictions on what the servants of Allah can and cannot do (Kamali, 1999).

Imam al-Shatibi further divided the second part into three sub-parts: first is *darruriyyat* (essentials), second is *hajiyyah* (complementaries), and the last is *tahsiniyyah* (embellishments). The essentials (*darruriyyat*) are indispensable because of their vital role in sustaining and preserving the five objectives of *Shari'ah*. In a sense, if they are disrupted, the stability of the society will be at stake. The five essential objectives of *Shari'ah* include essential interests that need to be preserved, namely faith, life, lineage, intellect and property[8]. The complementary objectives are needed in order to remove hardship and impediments, hence complement the essential interests (Kamali, 1999).

*Darruriyyat* could also pertain to the rights and responsibilities of a servant. *Darruriyyat* are objectives which are essential for the lives of people and its abandonment can lead to total disorder to their lives. Therefore, these objectives must be fulfilled to ensure harmony is achieved both in this life and in the hereafter. Failure to comply may cause misconduct and corruption in this life and eternal disappointment in judgment day. The preservation of *darruriyyat* is evident in all aspects of *Shari'ah*, be it for worship (*ibadah*) or human interaction (*muamalat*). *Al-Taklif* is fulfilled by performance of rights and responsibilities as stated in the *Shari'ah* (Azli et al., 2011).

In general, ownership risk can be considered as one of the *darruriyyat* (essentials). Correct allocation of ownership risk would result to the assurance that at least two out of the five essential objectives would be preserved, i.e. life and property. A basic example would illustrate this point. Assume that a farmer has some cattle which he uses for milk production and supply of beef. If one of his cattle is left loose and cause damages to the wall of a neighbor's house or injures a person, then the farmer who is the owner of the cattle should be liable to compensate for the property damage or bodily injuries caused. Since the farmer is benefiting from the milk and meat of the cattle, he should also bear the ownership risk. Risk related to ownership is however broader than this simple example, especially when it comes to financial transactions where correct assignment of rights and responsibilities will assure true allocation of ownership risk.

Islamic Commercial Law requires the preservation of the objective of welfare in any business transactions. For instance, all parties to a contract should strictly follow the requirements stated in the *Shari'ah*. It is in this manner that compliance to the *darruriyyat* objectives of *Shari'ah* will result in fulfilment of peoples' responsibilities towards each other and in reduction of crime and disputes in society. Thus, if the pillars and conditions of Islamic contract, or the rights and responsibilities of contracting parties in any transaction are not property clarified, then the discussion of *Maqasid al-Shari'ah* will be incomplete (Azli et al., 2011).

## OWNERSHIP RISK IN ISLAMIC BANKING

When it comes to financial transactions, the role of ownership risk is more evident. According to the principles of Islamic Law of Contracts, the level of risk will vary depending on whether ownership is transferred or not under the given contract. Let's take an example of two very similar contracts of Islamic bank deposits, i.e. *Wadiah* (trust) and *Qard* (loan) deposit contracts for a certain amount of money. Both contracts look very similar in form, i.e. in both contracts the first party gives some money to the second party for safe keeping under the condition that it will be returned on demand. However, the two are completely different in terms of ownership risk borne by the borrower or the lender. If in *Wadiah*, the contract is mainly in the form of trust (or safekeeping) where ownership is not transferred, while under *Qard*, the contract is in the form of loan where ownership of the asset (i.e. money) is transferred completely. Thus, if money is lost without any negligence from the second party (i.e. Islamic bank), under *Wadiah* contract there is no duty on the trustee to return the amount[9], while under *Qard* contract there is full duty on the borrower to return the loaned amount to the first party. The difference in ruling comes from transfer of ownership, and the privileges and responsibilities carried with it, which also includes ownership risk.

It has been argued that full application of ownership risk has been lacking in contemporary Islamic banking, and compliance to this concept has in a way been missed by *Shari'ah* boards that are responsible in approving Islamic banking products (Abdul Razak & Saupi, 2017; Asadov et al., 2018; Azli et al., 2011; Boon Ka, 2009; Kamali, 2007). When it comes to *Shari'ah* compliance, in most cases there is no problem in the form of Islamic banking products. This indicates that most Islamic banking products are not at fault of not complying with *Shari'ah* principles based on form. Nevertheless, when it comes to the essence of these products, there is not a great deal of difference from the products of conventional banks. The author suspects that one of the culprits for such deviation is lack of attention on meeting the requirement of ownership risk during the product development process in modern Islamic banking.

As mentioned earlier, according to the Islamic legal maxims *al-kharāj bi al- ḍamān* and *al-ghurm bi al-ghunm*, it is not permissible to claim entitlement for benefits of an asset without taking complete liability of ownership. However, the current practice of Islamic banks may have been lacking in terms of meeting the requirement of these legal maxims. In this regard, the current chapter aims to answer the research question of whether the concept of ownership risk has been properly applied in contemporary Islamic banking. If there is any misapplication of ownership risk concept in contemporary Islamic banking and if it is theoretically supported, the next objective will be to demonstrate whether such violation can be proven in practice.

The following sections will delve deeper into analyzing the application of ownership risk concept in contemporary Islamic banking. It will investigate the burning question of whether contemporary Islamic banks have indeed been trying to avoid ownership related risks and liabilities in their products. The preceding sections will focus on current practices by analyzing some specific Islamic banking products such as *Murabahah*, *Ijarah* and *Musharakah Mutanaqisah* and investigate a number of real court cases pertaining to the matter.

## Avoidance of Ownership Risk by Islamic Banks and Issue of *Shari'ah* Compliance

Conventional banking practices are based on the principle of risk shifting where all business risks are shifted to the shoulders of borrowers while banks enjoy riskless profits[10]. Therefore, such profits without taking risk are considered prohibited (haram) in Islam. This is the essence of *Riba*, which is generally defined as an unjustified increment in borrowing or lending of money. Interest or any other profit which is obtained from using one's capital could not be considered just in Islam if it does not involve sharing of relevant business risk. For instance, if a person makes profit from the sale of a particular item but does not take responsibility of any defects in the sold item, then this makes his profit unlawful (*haram*) and the contract void (*batil*) according to *Shari'ah* principles.

Overall, it is important to note that Islamic banks should not behave or operate like conventional banks in terms of risk taking and avoiding sharing of business risks with their clients. This is particularly important in terms of taking ownership risk simply because Islamic banking products are based on sales or partnerships. For example, in the case of *Murabahah* (mark-up sale), it is not reasonable to shift all risks to the client only by appointing him as an agent of the bank to perform certain transactions such as selecting and accepting delivery of the good.

Additionally, in lease transactions, all risks and responsibilities of damage not caused due to negligence from the lessee should be borne by the lessor. But in modern practice, most *Ijarah* (leasing) agreements by Islamic banks shift such risks to the lessee either directly (by specifying additional clause in the contract) or indirectly (by obliging the client to purchase *Takaful* insurance that would cover such risks). However, such methods used by Islamic banks are either prohibited or discouraged under *Shari'ah* principles.

Finally, *Musharakah Mutanaqisah* has been offered as one of the *Shari'ah* compliant products in real estate or enterprise financing. Nevertheless, when contemporary contracts of *Musharakah Mutanaqisah* home financing are closely scrutinized, clear traces of conventional housing mortgage contracts are easily traceable. Indiscriminate use of *Wad* (unilateral promise) in several instances in this Islamic banking home financing product totally shifts almost all risks related to the home ownership from one partner (i.e. Islamic bank) to the other (i.e. the client) in a so-called partnership. Thus, the chapter continues with an investigation of details relating to handling of ownership risk by Islamic banks for the above three mentioned products.

## Issue of Ownership Risk (*ḍamān al-milkiyyah*) in *Murabahah* Contract

*Murabahah* contracts correspond to mark-up sale, where the bank purchases a commodity and sells it to the client with additional mark-up over the cost. Such contracts belong to contracts of fiduciary sales (*Buyu' al-amanah*) where the buyer totally depends on the integrity of the seller, given that both the cost and the profit margin are disclosed to him. The sale of a commodity based on *Murabahah* is allowed in Islam. In fact, it is a pre-Islamic practice and can either be done for spot transaction with immediate, instalment or deferred payment.

In general, for sale (*bai'*) contracts, there is plenty of evidence from main sources of *Shari'ah* about its permissibility. *Allah (SWT)* grants full permission to *bai'* (trading) and prohibits *Riba* (usury) in the following verse of the *Qur'an*:

*Those who devour usury will not stand except as stand one whom the Evil one by his touch hath driven to madness. That is because they say: "Trade is like usury," but Allah hath permitted trade and forbidden usury. Those who after receiving direction from their Lord, desist, shall be pardoned for the past; their case is for Allah (to judge); but those who repeat (the offence) are companions of the Fire: They will abide therein (forever)" (Q 2: 275).*

However, Rosly (2001) states that the injunction to observe *bai'* instead of *Riba* in business transactions has led *Shari'ah* scholars and banking practitioners to adopt Islamic commercial contracts as a mode of financing rather than adopting them in the original way. For this reason, they have been acutely selective in applying specific Islamic commercial contracts that can best suit their role as banks. An example of this could be heavy employment of *Murabahah* credit sale by most Islamic banking practitioners. Given that it is the most popular Islamic banking product, *Murabahah* accounts for up to 90% of total portfolio for some banks. It is mainly because the mark-up concept provides easy profiting without taking much risk (Kahf, 2006).

According to Ibn al-Arabi, there are three types of sales; namely an exchange of material substances (regular sale), advance payment for a good (*Salam* or *Istisna*), and exchange material substance for a usufruct (*Ijarah*). He continued to say that *Riba*, on the contrary, is an increase (*ziyadah*) which does not bring (in exchange) an equivalent counter value. *'Iwad* (an equivalent counter value) is an essential requirement of a lawful sale transaction in *Shari'ah*. In a sale, it is compulsory to have equivalent consideration both in terms of the subject matter and the price. Many authors list three essential elements of *'iwad*, namely the existence of risk (*ghurm*), the existence of work and effort (*ikhtiar*), and taking of liability (*ḍamān*) (Rosly, 2001 and Azli et al., 2011). Shifting of ownership risk (*ḍamān al-milkiyyah*) under some practices of Islamic banking can also raise serious doubts about the existence of *'iwad* in such contracts.

Regular trade often involves risk of loss (*ghurm*) either due to some damages or just changes in market conditions. This is not the case for Islamic banks that get involved in sale contracts such as *Murabahah* to purchase order (MPO) as they do not want to take such risk. Therefore, they require advance promise (*wa'd*) from the client to purchase the required good and appoint him as an agent for the good selection and sale performance. This automatically shifts all risks and responsibilities of the ownership to the client and as a result, the client would be denied of all privileges as a buyer (such as option for defect) which are assigned by rules of *Fiqh al-Muamalat* (law of commercial transactions) in *Shari'ah*.

During a sale transaction, as a *Shari'ah* requirement, the bank should hold ownership of the property and be responsible for all liabilities arising from such ownership. This issue was clearly explained in the analysis of the *Shari'ah* legal maxim *'al-ghurm bil-ghunm'* (any risk must be followed by any reward). An observation of practiced documentations however demonstrates that Islamic banks merely act as conventional banks rather than sellers and exclude themselves of all liabilities. By ignoring the concept of *'iwad*, some practiced *Murabahah* contracts such as *Bai' Bithaman Ajil* (BBA) house financing will not be following the *Maqasid al-Shari'ah*. It is especially true of the objectives of *Shari'ah* relating to removal of hardship (*raf' al-haraj*) and prevention of harm (*daf' al-dharar*) (Meera & Abdul Razak, 2005).

Another important point to note is when the sale structure is compromised in some types of *Murabahah* such as Commodity *Murabahah* (CM). This can even lead us to question the permissibility of such a contract in *Shari'ah*. This arises due to the existence of *bai' al-inah* (sell and buy back) and *tawarruq manazzam* (pre-arranged *tawarruq*) in CM. The operating mechanism of CM is such that the Islamic bank agrees with the client to buy a commodity and then sells it to him or her based on deferred payment. The client appoints the bank as his agent to act on his behalf to sell the bought commodity to another third party. The second sale takes place in the case of a price being lower than the deferred price. This is against the economic objective of a sale transaction, which takes possession of a product to benefit from it. CM is thus a combination of facade sale and agency contracts to generate liquidity for the client and the bank benefits from provision of such cash. With its pre-arranged nature, a CM contract is only used for making money out of money which defies the realism concept of the *Shari'ah* (Azli et al., 2011).

In summary, in *Murabahah* to purchase order (MPO) and *Bai' Bithaman Ajil* (BBA), Islamic banks avoid ownership risk by shifting all liabilities to the shoulders of clients and under Commodity *Murabahah* (CM), neither the banks nor the clients carry any risk of ownership. Thus, if the existence of *'iwad* (equivalent counter value) was doubtful under MPO or BBA, there is not much doubt that under CM, *'iwad* does not exist. In fact, it is questionable if CM can be regarded as a sale contract, as alternatively it would be more qualified as a loan or financing contract. There is indeed some clear violation of ownership risk concept (which is part of *'iwad* concept) which could lead to serious issues about the *Shari'ah* compliance of some types of *Murabahah*.

## Issue of Ownership Risk in *Ijarah* Contract

*Ijarah* (leasing) is considered a type of *bai'* (sales) contract in *Shari'ah*. However, the main difference between the two is that in the latter, whole asset ownership is transferred while in the former, only partial ownership of the asset's usufruct is transferred from the lessor to the lessee. Therefore, the lessor should have complete ownership of the asset so that he or she is able to transfer the entitlement for the usufruct to the lessee (Kamali, 2007). Therefore, precise determination of the ownership risk and liabilities for the lessor is instrumental in this regard.

In classical *Fiqh* literature, reference to *Ijarah* usually implies the so-called operating lease. Modern *Ijarah* agreements however mostly correspond to the type of financial leasing that is considered as an extension of the operating lease contract. The main difference between operating and financial lease is that in the former, the option of purchasing the leased asset at the end of the lease period is not provided, while this is not the case for financial lease (Securities Commission Malaysia, 2007).

Despite financial lease being widely accepted and practiced by Islamic banks, there are still some *Shari'ah* compliance concerns surrounding it. One concern relates to the case of the lessor assigning the lease to the lessee without obtaining full ownership of the asset. Such assignment of lease without proper establishment of ownership for the leased asset is prohibited in *Shari'ah*. More specifically, the issue is problematic when the financer (i.e. Islamic bank) starts receiving payments for the asset's rental prior to the transfer of full ownership to its name. The only case that such assignment is allowable in *Shari'ah* is when the original owner of the asset transfers his or her right for rental collection to another party without any monetary consideration (Usmani, 2007).

In *Shari'ah*, the lessor in the *Ijarah* agreement carries all risks and liabilities of ownership, and in the event the asset is damaged during the lease period, the lessor should bear all losses. Likewise, if the leased asset stops providing the intended usufruct which is not due to the lessee's negligence, the lessor's entitlement for receiving the rentals should also stop. This is one of the differences between *Ijarah* and conventional leasing, as the latter entitles the lessor to receive rent even if the lessee could not obtain any benefit from the leased asset (Kamali, 2007). Similarly, in some practices of contemporary Islamic financial lease, most risks and costs associated with ownership of the leased asset are transferred to the lessee. For instance, the lessee is usually made responsible for payment of *Takaful* or the lessee would bear sole responsibility for majority of damages to the leased asset. Even worse, in some cases, the client continues paying rental or instalment payments to the Islamic bank despite the usufruct of the rented asset being unavailable due to force majeure situation. Generally, in such situation the lessor should provide the lessee either with a replacement asset or the client should be allowed to stop paying rentals (Mohamad, 2014).

In summary, one can observe that in contemporary practice of *Ijarah*, the risk of ownership is shifted away from the lessor to the lessee. For an *Ijarah* contract to be valid, the bank as the lessor must bear the risk related to the ownership of the leased asset as stated in *Shari'ah* requirements of the contract. Whether it is a sale contract or lease contract, the rules of *'al-kharāj bil-ḍamān'* and *'al-ghurm bil-ghunm'* apply to all situations. However, it is unfortunate that when it comes to bearing ownership risks and liabilities, contemporary *Ijarah* contracts behave very similarly to conventional financial lease.

## Issue of Ownership Risk in *Musharakah Mutanaqisah* Contract

A *Musharakah Mutanaqisah* (MM) agreement is an Islamic banking facility that involves the usage of the concepts of *Musharakah* (partnership), *Al-bai'* (sale) and possibly *Ijarah* (lease), depending on the subject of partnership. In general, the partnership begins with two parties (i.e. the Islamic bank and the client) purchasing an asset such as a house. After the purchase, the client starts renting or utilizing the whole asset. In return, the client pays periodic rentals or profit shares to the Islamic bank according to the agreed ratio. However, if there is any loss, it should be shared in line with the partner's share in the asset (Asadov et al., 2018).

In addition to sharing profit or loss (or renting) from the asset, the client starts to gradually acquire his partner's share in the asset by making additional payment over the bank's profit share (the rental payment) during each period (e.g. every month). By every subsequent payment, the profit (rental) part of the instalment decreases since the bank's share decreases in the shared asset. The partnership ends when the client makes his last payment to the bank which covers both its profit (rental) and amount equal to the last share of the bank in the asset. Even though the concept appears straight forward, there are some detailed *Shari'ah* principles which make the facility very complicated.

In the current versions of MM that are being practiced, ownership risk is totally borne by the client, even though the bank is theoretically considered as a partner. In the case of properties under construction, a developer's default is a major risk and huge lost. Boon Ka (2009) described events in the case of 'abandoned properties' or 'winding up of developers' that are not the fault of the clients. In such cases, the clients are still obligated to buy the banks' shares in the assets because of the *wa'd* (unilateral promise) component of the MM agreement. This practice is like conventional loans where clients are required to pay installments to the banks until proceeds from insurance coverage are received by the banks.

However, if there is no *Takaful* protection available to cover such risks in the MM agreement, the situation will worsen. The question about which party would be responsible for the cost of *Takaful* would arise, if *Takaful* protection must be purchased for the property against certain risks. Based on the analogy and argument presented earlier, *Musharakah* (partnership) terms would require both partners to share the *Takaful* cost in line with their shares in the property. Unfortunately, in practice, Islamic banks tend to oblige their clients to pay for such costs (Asadov et al., 2018).

According to *Ijarah* terms, the owner (lessor) should bear the cost of basic and structural maintenance, and the lessee is responsible for the routine and operational maintenance of the property. Some *Shari'ah* scholars however argue that since the client's ultimate objective is to own an asset and not merely to rent it for a certain period of time, then the client should bear all ownership related risks and costs. This somewhat controversial argument is in favor by Islamic banks. This is evident by a sample of MM contract that was scrutinized where its results indicate that 'the client shall pay 100 percent of the amount of taxes due in relation to or associated with the property, notwithstanding the client being the partial owner of the property until the end of the co-ownership" (Boon Ka, 2009).

Furthermore, in a *Musharakah* contract, one of the partners could not be held responsible for the damage cause to the partnership property because of a natural calamity or a third-party action. This is particularly true if it is not due to the client's negligence or fault. In Al-Zuhaili's words, it is defined as "...partnership property in the possession of one partner is considered a trust, since the partner is not holding the partnership property to collect a price or to guarantee some other payment as in pawning, he is not responsible for the perishing of what is kept in his possession" (Al-Zuhaili, 2003). Defining such costs and risks of ownership as the sole responsibility of the client runs against the concept of risk sharing under a *Musharakah* agreement.

Additionally, Meera and Abdul Razak (2005) have argued on the fairness of benchmarking rental rate under MM house financing as it does not represent true economic value of the rent. Therefore, the authors advocated the use of rental rate as either benchmarked to some specific rental index or periodically valued by an independent party that would represent rent like one under an actual *Ijarah* contract. The authors also mentioned some proposals made by others who suggested the need to revalue the property before its share is transferred to the client. In this manner, both client and bank would absorb the true risk of ownership through any gains or losses in the value of the property over time. In contrary, if the price is fixed at the original cost and rental is benchmarked to the market interest rate, and the client is obliged to purchase the property and instalment continues as currently practiced under MM, this will make it very similar to a conventional housing loan[11] (Asadov et al., 2018).

## Issue of Ownership Risk in Other Islamic Finance Products

Misallocation of ownership risk does not only arise in Islamic banking products, but also occurs in several other Islamic finance products. Such products could be related to *Sukuk*, which is often referred as Islamic bond, and *Takaful*, which is generally referred as Islamic insurance. Both representations are misleading, because for Islam bond which has predetermined returns, fix or floating rates cannot exist and similarly, insurance is considered not *Shari'ah* compliant due to its violation to many *Shari'ah* principles.

Bonds are debt certificates issued either by a firm, municipality or national government which provides some predetermined returns in the forms of coupons or discount from its face value. Since there are clear elements of *Riba* present in bond issuance, such form of certificate cannot exist in Islamic finance. As such, an investment certificate called *Sukuk* was introduced close to the end of the past century which represents ownership share in an underlying asset which generates income for the *Sukuk* holder. Unlike bonds, the returns on *Sukuk* cannot be predetermined since business returns can only be predicted and not predetermined, as the case with interest paid on bonds. *Sukuk* could be based on different *Shari'ah* contracts, such as *Musharakah, Mudarabah, Ijarah* or *Murabahah*. Depending on the type of contract used, the returns and structuring of *Sukuk* may vary to some extent. However, in general, firms or sovereigns interested in the issuance of *Sukuk* would set up a Special Purpose Vehicle (SPV) to raise funds for *Sukuk* subscription and the funds raised would be used to purchase part or whole of an underlying asset (Rafay, Sadiq & Ajmal, 2017). Once ownership is obtained, the *Sukuk* holders have the right to benefit from this ownership either by selling it back on a deferred basis, leasing it or contributing to a partnership with the firm. Thus, during the holding period, the *Sukuk* holder will benefit from the ownership in the forms of profit margins, rentals or partner's share of the profit earned by the owned asset. Upon maturity, the underlying asset would be purchased back by the firm at market price.

In reality, there are several violations of the above assumptions in the issuance of *Sukuk*. In one of his speeches in 2007, Sheikh Taqi Usmani announced that 85 percent of all outstanding *Sukuk* were not *Shari'ah* compliant (Usmani, 2008). He brought several reasons for such announcement, some of which could have existed in most of the *Sukuk* outstanding at that time. Most of the issues listed related to inappropriate allocation or shifting of ownership risk to guarantee riskless profit to *Sukuk* investors. For instance, some *Sukuk* had company shares as the underlying assets but did not resemble true ownership of those shares. In the case of several *Sukuk*, profits to be distributed were linked to certain interest rates such as LIBOR, which had nothing to do with ownership of the underlying asset. It was also observed that for most *Sukuk*, returns of the invested principal were guaranteed which would not be possible if firms bought back the underlying asset at market price (Abdul Razak & Saupi, 2017). Vague specification of true ownership of the underlying asset to *Sukuk* holders has thus raised doubts on *Shari'ah* compliance of such certificates.

Issue of ownership risk is also a concern in the practice of *Takaful*. *Takaful* could be defined as an Islamic model of insurance, which is free from *Riba* (usury), *gharar* (ambiguity) and *maisir* (gambling) elements of conventional insurance. In a way, it is like insurance, but rather than having companies insuring the clients, it is the mutual pool of contributors to the '*Takaful* fund' that covers the losses occurring to members. *Takaful* fund is the result of a contributory arrangement in which members contribute to the total on the basis of mutual help and sacrifice (Ayub, 2007). It is a concept of mutual cooperation to assist mutual protection of *Takaful* members.

*Takaful* is a joint guarantee, whereby a group of participants agree to jointly guarantee among themselves against a defined loss. In other words, participants in a *Takaful* scheme agree to donate a certain proportion of the premium (*tabarru'*) into a *Takaful* pool to assist other *Takaful* participants suffering from defined loss or damage. *Tabarru'* can be defined as a gift, donation, or contribution. *Takaful* scheme recognizes the elements of shared liability, joint indemnity and mutual assistance. Making the uncertainty element allowable under the *Takaful* contract is the core of *Takaful* system (Mortuza Ali, 2006).

As *Takaful* is founded on the basis of voluntary contribution to the *Takaful* fund, *Takaful* participants would lose their money once it is donated to the fund. The donation made cannot be conditional on terms of re-compensating, which is violated in most *Takaful* schemes. Making the contribution conditional makes it similar to an exchange contract and akin to the problems of conventional insurance. Similarly, *Takaful* operators using the surplus of *Takaful* fund for increasing the wealth of shareholders of *Takaful* companies are similar to profiting without having true ownership of the fund (Habib & Shaukat, 2016).

*Takaful* fund is considered as a trust or *Waqf* in most of *Takaful* models, as such it is no one's property. This alludes that both *Takaful* operators and participants do not have legal rights to profit from the funds. Therefore, as long as *Takaful* companies are operating as profit minded corporations, it is difficult to achieve the true underlying objectives of *Takaful*. This can only be achieved if *Takaful* funds are managed by non-profit minded organizations and the operators hired to manage the fund would not profit from it. Furthermore, as no one has ownership and carries the risk of the *Takaful* fund, no one has the right to benefit from it (Abdul Razak & Saupi, 2017).

As seen from the above examples, misallocation of ownership risk in the case of *Sukuk*, or non-existence of ownership as in the case of *Takaful* will determine when one has the right to claim any related profit or capital gain, and when one does not have such right. Even though a number of Islamic financial institutions do not pay much attention to the concept of ownership in current times and consider it as a secondary decision criterion at the time of product development, the analysis shows that this should not be the case. There are many barriers which prevent true application of ownership risk (*ḍamān al-milkiyyah*) such as institutional, legal and physiological at individual, institutional and state level. Thus, there is a need to have resolution on some policy considerations to ensure correct allocation of all risks related to ownership and to prevent such liabilities being shifted without true transfer of ownership.

## POLICY AND LEGAL CONSIDERATION REGARDING OWNERSHIP RISK IN ISLAMIC BANKING

### Economic Implications of Ownership Risk for Society

The given examples illustrate that there may be several dimensions in which risk shifting by Islamic banks and other financial institutions to the shoulders of clients may occur in economic terms. Firstly, such risk shifting weakens the relationship between financial and real sectors of the economy. Given that the general notion is that Islamic finance is based on linking and strengthening ties between financial and real sectors, this founding inspiration may not be achieved by resorting to risk shifting. Risk sharing based on partnership and trade is a crucial element of the distinguishing characteristics of Islamic banks. If Islamic banks continue to operate like conventional banks that transfer risk through debt instruments along with high leverage, it may result to a weakening of the link between the financial and real sector, thus posing a threat to financial sector stability. The latest financial crisis of 2008 which still has its traces in the economy of most countries could be a good example of catastrophic results that can follow if such situation remains unaddressed (Mirakhor, 2010).

Secondly, risk shifting will limit possibilities of large profit and loss sharing. This may hurt growth potentials by limiting investment opportunities and discouraging risk taking by entrepreneurs. Some good opportunities of innovation and product development may be forgone because of downsized risk possibilities. Cizakca (2014) nicely illustrates in his work on how the shift from true Islamic principles of risk sharing to risk shifting brought large damage to the economy of the Ottoman Empire during its last few centuries of existence. On the contrary, he also demonstrates how adoption of true risk sharing principles by the United States and some European countries have benefited their economies substantially.

## Some Cases Related to Ownership Risk

As highlighted earlier, one of the extreme cases of avoiding risk of ownership under the current practice of Islamic banking is the use of BBA (deferred payment sale) contract which has been widely practiced for Islamic home financing in Malaysia until recently. Since *Bai' bithaman ajil* (BBA) is a type of *Mudarabah* contract with deferred payment, the bank should first gain ownership of the asset before selling it the client. However, under BBA home financing as practiced by Malaysian Islamic banks, the bank does not purchase any property at all. Instead, the client identifies the property and makes a down payment to the developer prior to approaching an Islamic bank. Once the terms are agreed upon, the bank uses either *Bai' al-'inah* or *Tawarruq* contracts to finance the remaining obligation of the client to purchase the house from the developer. Some of the famous court cases are proofs of how burdensome such a contract could be on clients.

One of the cases relating to BBA in Malaysia is that of Dato' Haji Nik Mahmud bin Daud vs Bank Islam Malaysia Berhad (BIMB). This occurred in 1998 and is one of the earliest cases which represents a dispute between an Islamic bank and its client under BBA home financing. The client claimed that the executed BBA contract was incompliant and void in Islam, since there was no actual ownership transfer of the concerned land that took place. However, the court's ruling was in favor of the bank as to assist the bank to recover its profit under BBA. The ruling also aimed to safeguard the reputation of the Islamic banking industry in Malaysia, given that the usage of BBA instrument was widely practiced by Islamic banks for home financing in Malaysia at that time.

Another infamous Malaysian court case is that of Affin Bank Bhd vs Zulkifli bin Abdullah which took place in 2006. The case was also ruled in favor of the bank and the client was ordered to pay the remaining instalments. The underlying reason of the ruling was a default by the client in the payment of instalments in a home financing facility. The client bought a house under BBA for a sum of RM 346,000 where a charge was registered against the title and the financing repayment was for a tenure of 18 years. Later in December 1997, the client resigned from the agreement at his request and the financing facility was restructured. Under the new restructured facility, the selling price of the house increased to become RM 992,363.40 and the financing tenure was extended to a period of 25 years. New documents were also executed following the restructuring.

Nevertheless, after making several payments, the defendant defaulted again in June 2001. The bank then filed for two actions – first was an order for sale, and second was an order to recover the full sum in the event of a deficiency in the sale proceeds. The above information indicates that the bank did not elaborate the details of the contract to the client, which caused the client to pay more due to the bank's restructuring of the financing facility. The situation was not in favor of the client who had less legal power.

One of the early court cases also in Malaysia involves the Ijarah contract between Tinta Press Sdn. Bhd. and Bank Islam Malaysia Berhad (BIMB) that was brought to the Supreme Court in Kuala Lumpur on 23 December 1986. In this case, the respondent (BIMB) had leased certain printing equipment to the appellants (Tinta Press) under the lease (*Ijarah*) agreement initiated with a letter of credit. After making an initial deposit and some rental payments, Tinta Press defaulted on its monthly rentals for several months. This resulted on BIMB taking action on making an *ex parte* application for a mandatory injunction to recover ownership of the leased equipment, where BIMB managed to obtain the injunction. Tinta Press then applied to dissolve the case and set aside the mandatory injunction, claiming that the contract was of a loan type and the Bank did not have the right to possess the property as the lessor. Following the refusal of this application, Tinta Press proceeded with an appeal and lost the case at the Supreme Court as well. Base on the terms of the letter of credit, the court concluded that the factual agreement was of a leasing (*Ijarah*) contract and not of a financing contract.

As such, the Supreme Court upheld the decision of the courts, which was that the printing equipment was owned by the respondent (as lessor). Therefore, it ruled that the appellant does not have the right of ownership for the equipment until it makes full payment of the lease rentals to the bank. In this case, we can clearly see that even if it is supposed to be an Islamic lease (*Ijarah*) contract, there was no clear transfer of ownership from the supplier of the equipment to the bank's name. In fact, the documents relating to the equipment were under the name of Tinta Press. This fact, together with some other issues relating to avoidance of ownership responsibilities probably provided a justification or an excuse for Tinta Press to claim that contract was of a loan type, and the bank did not have right to possess the property as the lessor.

In the case of *Musharakah Mutanaqisah* (MM) home financing, there are no related court cases yet, since this contract is relatively new and uncommon in the practice of Islamic banks. However, there were some case studies which investigated the legal aspects of MM home financing. For instance, a study by Nor et al. (2019) found numerous legal concerns in the implementation of MM as a property financing product in Malaysia. The main legal concerns relate to documentation, ownership of properties, issues with properties under construction, certain legal restrictions in cases involving foreign partner(s), some properties being subjected to Malay-reserved status, and some issues relating to maintenance and major repairs to the properties. As a result, the authors recommend some improvements to the country's legal framework, as well as various laws and documentations relating to implementation of MM financing in general, and also pertaining to ownership, maintenance and major repairs of MM properties (Nor et al., 2019).

Another work by Ali, Hassan & Othman (2017) which also investigates MM home financing contract in Malaysia argues that the terms and conditions of legal documentation of MM home financing prepared by solicitors of Islamic financing institutions (IFIs) favor IFIs over their clients. Since clients have no choice but to abide by the terms stipulated by IFIs, their welfare is seriously affected. This would also be the case when the client's ownership rights are violated or ownership risk of the IFI as a partner in MM home financing are shifted off to its the client in the MM agreement drafted by the IFI itself. The authors' examination of the existing legislations in Malaysia found them to be insufficient to regulate unfair terms of contract in MM home financing in the country. Thus, they suggest that the present legislation should be reformed by making required changes in the Consumer Protection Act and Contract Act to ensure consumer protection in any MM agreement (Ali et al., 2017).

Finally, a more recent and infamous case relates to ownership risk in *Sukuk* issuance. This is the case of Dana Gas PJSC v. Dana Gas *Sukuk* ruled by Mr. Justice Leggatt of the UK's High Court of Justice in 17 November 2017. In brief, Dana Gas PJSC, which is incorporated under the UAE law raised financing worth US$1 billion through an issuance of certificates in 2007. The transaction was however later restructured as *Mudarabah Sukuk* in 2013 when *Sukuk* certificates with US$850,080,000 aggregate face value were issued. The *Sukuk* certificates with maturity date of 31 October 2017 are traded and listed on the Irish Stock Exchange.

The certificates were issued by Dana Gas *Sukuk* (the Trustee) and the proceeds of the issuance and assets derived from the proceeds are held by the Trustee on behalf of the certificate holders on declaration of trust, which is governed by English law. *Mudarabah* assets are supposed to generate cash flows to fund the payment of the periodic distribution amounts specified in the terms of *Mudarabah*. The *Mudarabah* agreement also provides for the liquidation of *Mudarabah* assets and the return of capital to the Trustee at the end of the contract. As security for the *Mudarabah Sukuk,* Dana Gas PJSC also signed a Purchase Undertaking to irrevocably buy all the Trustee's rights, benefits and entitlements in the *Mudarabah* assets at the stated exercise price. This is done in case Dana Gas fails to pay the agreed periodic payments or if there is failure to liquidate the *Mudarabah* assets at an agreed price.

As can be seen from the structuring of Dana Gas' *Mudarabah Sukuk*, there was no real ownership transfer of the so-called *Mudarabah* assets. Firstly, the *Sukuk* included some assets situated in Egypt and a fixed charge over shares of Dana LNG Ventures Ltd, a company registered in the British Virgin Islands as security. Company shares, as stated earlier, could not be used as an underlying asset since no real ownership is being transferred. Secondly, the fixed percentage of periodic return and guarantee of the principle which is backed by purchase undertaking virtually guarantees riskless return that defies the principles of *Mudarabah* and eliminated any risk of ownership. However, when Dana Gas DJSC rejected *Shari'ah* compliance of the *Sukuk* agreement and tried to void the contract, the ruling of the English court was against it. Irrespective of *Shari'ah* compliance of the original *Mudarabah* agreement in the original *Sukuk* certificate, the purchase undertaking was a valid contract under the English law and was a requirement to be performed by Dana Gas which signed the contract.

The above cases give clear indication of how incorrect assignment of ownership and its risk could result to disastrous outcomes for regular members of the society. Even though the cases only analyzed three products as well as a *Mudarabah Sukuk* agreement, the implications could be generalized for other Islamic banking and finance products. Unless ownership rights are correctly assigned, new Islamic banking and finance products could bring harm to society, even more so than conventional ones. Some authors have also demonstrated that in some examples, the terms and conditions of BBA contract are more unfavorable than conventional housing loans in cases of default by clients[12]. We have also seen in the case of MM home financing contracts that welfare of the clients may be jeopardized and it is a concern that the existing legal system does not provide adequate consumer protection for Islamic banking customers. Based on the last case, one can observe that the problem is not only limited to three Islamic banking products examined in this chapter, but it also relates to the misallocation of ownership risk and liabilities that violated the *Shari'ah* principles governing Islamic finance contracts.

## Recommendations for Re-Establishment of Ownership Risk in Islamic Banking

Rosly (2001) recommends considering three additional parameters in addition to default checking of contracts (*aqad*) for *Shari'ah* compliance while developing new Islamic banking products. Those parameters are *Maqasid al-Shari'ah*, financial reporting, and legal documentation of contracts for true product compliance with *Shari'ah* requirements. He believes that the consistency and stability of form and substance in all the four methods are important. The author provides an example of *Murabahah* contract, which is validated via the *aqad* approach, and the financial reporting approach would be used to indicate if the bank has initially held ownership prior to the *Murabahah* sale. In a true *Murabahah* sale, the object of trade should be recorded as a fixed asset in the balance sheet of the bank, prior to its disposal. The bank should also hold *Murabahah* receivables once the *Murabahah* sale is executed. The transfer of ownership from the vendor to the bank, and from the bank to the client via proper registration of ownership should serve as basis of the legal documentation approach.

The sale contract should also provide legal protection to the client if there are any defects in the delivered asset. Similarly, in the case of default by the client on his *Murabahah* debt obligation, the bank would be provided with protection by the court, resulting in fair dispute settlement. The *Maqasid* approach could thus provide insights that the *Murabahah* contract is free of *Riba*. Usually, the *aqad* approach mainly resorts to screening of the contract to ensure absence of *Riba* (usury), *maisir* (gambling) and *gharar* (ambiguity) elements in it, as well as verifying permissibility of traded commodities. It may however fail to verify proper assignment of ownership risk to the parties involved. Thus, it is imperative for *Shari'ah* scholars at IFIs' *Shari'ah* boards to understand the importance of legal and financial reporting approaches to verify true *Shari'ah* compliance of the products they approve. The social impact of those products should also be understood and their alignment with the *Maqasid al-Shari'ah* should also be verified while drafting various products for Islamic banks (Rosly, 2001).

In addition to the above recommendations by Rosly (2001), considerations should also be given to the requirement for institutional and legal changes. For instance, in the case of Malaysia which is considered as one of the leading countries in terms of implementing Islamic finance, there are still some legal barriers in the country that prevent full implementation of *Shari'ah* contracts. These include difficulty of joint ownership of a partnership asset between the bank and the client, unfavorable tax treatments of equity compared to debt, and excessive paperwork and fees required for true transfer of ownership from the seller to the bank's and to the client's names. Those are some of the areas where improvements can be considered. Therefore, prior to requesting Islamic banks to undertake full risk of ownership in order to make their products more *Shari'ah* compliant, there must be an enabling environment which will not burden the banks with additional legal and administrative costs.

## CONCLUDING REMARKS

This chapter has looked at the issue of ownership risk (*ḍamān al-milkiyyah*) involved in contemporary Islamic banking and tried to answer the question of whether the concept has been properly applied. Analysis was done by investigating three contracts that are often used by the industry, namely *Mudarabah* (mark-up sale), *Ijarah* (leasing) and *Musharakah Mutanaqisah* (diminishing partnership). The findings indicate that the current state of Islamic banking with respect to compliance with ownership requirement of *Shari'ah* is not justifiable. This points to the need for serious consideration to improve the current situation as to ensure that the functioning of Islamic banks is more *Shari'ah* compliant.

At a glance, it may seem to require significant amount of additional legal and administrative costs. Nevertheless, it is important to note that bearing of ownership risk should not always be associated with additional costs. There are numerous examples of business practices in both distant and recent history that show superiority of risk sharing to that of risk shifting, and the former being much simple in structure compared to the latter in most cases. A simple example is the comparison of stocks versus bonds issuance. Unlink bonds, stocks do not oblige companies for imbursement of any periodic payments and even principals of raised capital at maturity. Since stocks do not have any fixed obligations attached, firms are as safe as before issuance of equity and cannot go bankrupt for not paying any dividends.

In the original objectives, contracts approved by *Shari'ah* should suit the diverse needs of people (e.g. investors and investees). Nevertheless, defective structuring and indiscreet use of these contracts without considering other important aspects of *Shari'ah*, such as attention to risks and liabilities of ownership, can make Islamic banking products more exploitative and more akin to the conventional system. The elements of fairness and justice which are even more important than economic benefit should not be forgotten. *Maqasid al-Shari'ah* (Objectives of *Shari'ah*) aims to achieve the justice that the Law Giver (*Allah (SWT)*) intended by detailed guidance provided in sources of *Shari'ah*. Therefore, the more important objectives of justice and ethics in true *Shari'ah* compliant financing practices must be kept in mind. Of importance, is to have an enabling and conducive environment before expecting significant response from the industry.

An important consideration that authorities should keep in mind is that the philosophical shift towards the importance of risk sharing should be engrained in the designing of every new regulation for the Islamic finance industry. All Muslims believe that the *Shari'ah* is a complete and perfect system of life prescribed upon humanity by Allah Almighty. Thus, any deviation from *Shari'ah* guidelines in developing Islamic banking and finance products will jeopardize the reputation of the entire industry and shadow its authenticity. Paying closer attention to the issue of ownership risk in designing Islamic finance products is therefore a crucial step towards showcasing the true value proposition of Islamic finance.

## Classifications

JEL Classification: G21, L21, P40
KAUJIE Classification: B4, K1, M9

## REFERENCES

Abdul Razak, L., & Saupi, M. N. (2017). The concept and application of ḍamān al-milkiyyah (ownership risk): Islamic law of contract perspective. *ISRA International Journal of Islamic Finance*, *9*(2), 148–163. doi:10.1108/IJIF-06-2017-0002

Al-Zuhaili, W. (2003). *Financial Transactions in Islamic Jurisprudence* Vol. 1-2, (M. A. El-Gamal, Ed.). Damascus, Syria: Dar al-Fikr al-Muaasir.

Ali, S. A. M., Hassan, R., & Othman, A. A. (2017). Inadequacy of Consumer Protection from Unfair Contract Terms in Musharakah Mutanaqisah Home Financing in Malaysia. *Journal of Islamic Finance*, *6*(Special Issue), 231–241. doi:10.12816/0047351

Asadov, A., Muhamad Sori, Z. B., Mohamad Ramadilli, S., Anwer, Z., & Shamsudheen, S. V. (2018). Musharakah Mutanaqisah home financing: Issues in practice. *Journal of Islamic Accounting and Business Research*, *9*(1), 91–103. doi:10.1108/JIABR-08-2015-0036

Ayub, M. (2007). *Understanding Islamic finance*. Chichester, UK: John Wiley & Sons.

Azli, R. M., Othman, R., Sahri, M., Aris, N. A., Arshad, R., & Yaakob, A. R. (2011). Implementation of Maqasid Shari'ah in Islamic house financing: A study of the rights and responsibilities of contracting parties in Bai' Bithaman Ajil and Musharakah Mutanaqisah. *Journal of Applied Business Research, 27*(5), 85–96. doi:10.19030/jabr.v27i5.5595

Boon Ka, A. N. (2009). Shari'ah and legal issues of Musharakah Mutanaqisah. *New Horizon, Oct–Dec*(173), 46–48.

Cizakca, M. (2014). Risk sharing and risk shifting: An historical perspective. *Borsa Istanbul Review, 14*(4), 191–195. doi:10.1016/j.bir.2014.06.001

Elgari, M. A. (2003). Credit risk in Islamic banking and finance. *Islamic Economic Studies, 6*(2), 1–25.

Habib, F., & Shaukat, M. (2016). Shariah appraisal of the *Takaful* model based on 'tabarru' (donation). *Journal of Islamic Banking & Finance, 33*(3), 65–83.

Kahf, M. (2006). Maqasid al Shari ' ah in the Prohibition of *Riba* and their Implications for Modern Islamic Finance. In *IIUM International Conference on Maqasid al Shari'ah* (pp. 184–203).

Kamali, M. H. (1999). "Maqāṣid al-sharī'ah": The objectives of Islamic law. *Islamic Studies, 38*(2), 193–208.

Kamali, M. H. (2007). A Shari'ah Analysis of Issues in Islamic Leasing. *J.KAU: Islamic Econ., 20*(1), 3–22.

Kamali, M. H. (2013a). *Principles of Islamic Jurisprudence* (2nd ed.). Kuala Lumpur, Malaysia: Ilmiah Publishers Sdn. Bhd.

Kamali, M. H. (2013b). *The Right to Life, Security, Privacy and Ownership in Islam*. Kuala Lumpur, Malaysia: Ilmiah Publishers Sdn. Bhd.

Khan, M. A. (2005). *Islamic Economics and Finance: A Glossary (2nd editio)*. London, UK: Routledge.

Laldin, M. A., Bouheraoua, S., Ansary, R., Khir, M. F. A., Ali, M. M., & Mustafa, M. M. (2013). Islamic Legal Maxims & Their Applications in Islamic Finance. Kuala Lumpur, Malaysia: International Shariah Research Academy for Islamic Finance (ISRA).

McLellan, D. (Ed.). (2000). *Karl Marx: Selected Writings*. Oxford, UK: Oxford University Press; doi:10.12681/grsr.651

Meera, A. K. M., & Abdul Razak, D. (2005). Islamic home financing through musharakah mutanaqisah and al-bay bithaman ajil contract: A comparative analysis. *Review of Islamic Economics, 9*(2), 5–30.

Mirakhor, A. (2010). Whither Islamic Finance? Risk Sharing in An Age of Crises. *Munich Personal RePEc Archive (MPRA)*. Retrieved from http://mpra.ub.uni-muenchen.de/56341/

Mohamad, M. H. (2014). The concept of "no risk, no gain" in Islamic finance. *The Star*. Retrieved from http://www.thestar.com.my/Opinion/Columnists/IKIM-Views/ Profile/Articles/2014/02/25/The-concept-of-no-risk-no-gain-in-Islamic-finance/

Mortuza Ali, K. M. (2006). *Introduction to Islamic Insurance*. Dhaka, Bangladesh: Research Publications.

Narveson, J. (1988). *The Libertarian Idea*. Philadelphia, PA: Temple University Press.

Nor, M. Z. M., Mohamad, A. M., Azhar, A., Latif, H. M., Khalid, A.-H. M., & Yusof, Y. (2019). Legal Challenges of Musharakah Mutanaqisah as an Alternative for Property Financing in Malaysia. *Journal of Legal, Ethical, and Regulatory Issues*, *22*(3), 1–8.

Rafay, A., Sadiq, R., & Ajmal, M. M. (2017). Uniform Framework for Sukuk-Al-Ijara – A proposed model for all *Madhahib*. *Journal of Islamic Accounting and Business Research*, *8*(4), 420–454. doi:10.1108/JIABR-09-2015-0042

Reuters, T. (2018). *Islamic Finance Development Report 2018: Building Momentum*. Retrieved from http://bit.ly/IFDatabase

Rosly, S. A. (2001). Iwad As a Requirement of Lawful Sale: A Critical Analysis. *IIUM Journal of Economics and Management*, *9*(2), 187–201.

Rothbard, M. (1978). *For a New Liberty, The Libertarian Manifesto* (Revised ed.). New York: Libertarian Review Foundation.

Saheeh International. (Ed.). (2010). *The Qur'an: With Surah Introductions and Appendices*. Birmingham, UK: Maktabah Booksellers and Publishers.

Securities Commission Malaysia. (2007). *Resolutions of the Securities Commission Shariah Advisory Council*. Kuala Lumpur, Malaysia: Securities Commission.

Smolo, E., & Hassan, M. K. (2011). The potentials of musharakah mutanaqisah for Islamic housing finance. *International Journal of Islamic and Middle Eastern Finance and Management*, *4*(3), 237–258. doi:10.1108/17538391111166476

Stanford Encyclopedia of Philosophy. (2012). Libertarianism. Retrieved from https://stanford.library.sydney.edu.au/archives/sum2012/entries/libertarianism/

The Mejelle. (2003). *Being An English Translation of Majallah el-Ahkam-I-Adliya and A Complete Code on Islamic Civil Law* (C. R. Tyser, D. G. Demetriades, & I. Haqqi Effendi, Eds.). Kuala Lumpur, Malaysia: The Other Press.

Usmani, M. T. (2007). *An Introduction to Islamic Finance*. Karachi, Pakistan: Maktaba Ma'rifatul Quran. Retrieved from http://muftitaqiusmani.com/en/books/PDF/An Introduction To Islamic Finance/An_Introduction _to_Islamic_Finance.pdf

Usmani, M. T. (2008). Sukuk and their contemporary applications. In Translated from the original Arabic by Sheikh Yusuf Talal DeLorenzo, AAOIFI Shari'a Council meeting, Saudi Arabia.

## ADDITIONAL READING

Ahmed, A. (2010). Global financial crisis: An Islamic finance perspective. *International Journal of Islamic and Middle Eastern Finance and Management*, *3*(4), 306–320. doi:10.1108/17538391011093252

Iqbal, M. Ahmad, A., & Khan, T. (1998). Challenges Facing Islamic Banking. Jeddah: Saudi Arabia: Islamic Research and Training Institute.

Iqbal, M., & Llewellyn, D. (2002). *Islamic banking and finance: new perspectives on profit sharing and risk*. Cheltenham, UK: Edward Elgar Publishing. doi:10.4337/9781843765318

Meera, A. K. M., & Abdul Razak, D. (2009). Home Financing through the Musharakah Mutanaqisah Contracts: Some Practical Issues. *J.KAU: Islamic Econ.*, *22*(1), 121–143.

Mohamed Ali, W. A. R. K. (Ed.). (2012). *Shariah rulings and opinions on ijarah, musharakah, and mudharabah*. Petaling Jaya, Selangor, Malaysia: Sweet & Maxwell Malaysia.

Rosly, S. A. (1999). Al-Bay' Bithaman Ajil financing: Impacts on Islamic banking performance. *Thunderbird International Business Review*, *41*(4–5), 461–480. doi:10.1002/tie.4270410410

Sairally, B. S. (2002). Murabahah Financing: Some Controversial Issues. *Review of Islamic Economics*, *12*(12), 73–86.

## KEY TERMS AND DEFINITIONS

***Bai Bithaman Ajil* (BBA):** A type of *Murabahah* (mark-up) sale where payment is generally made on a deferred basis. *Bai Bithaman Ajil* is also called with different names in some countries such as *Bai' al Muajjal* in Pakistan or *Bai' Muazzal* in Bangladesh.

***Ijarah* (Leasing):** It is an agreement which refers to hiring of labor for a wage or a durable good's usufruct for a rental payment. However, in modern term, *Ijarah* generally refers to operating or financial lease where one party (lessor) agrees to the sale of the usufruct of his or her durable goods to another party (lessee) for an agreed fee and specified period.

***'Iwad* (An Equivalent Counter Value):** An essential requirement of a lawful sale transaction in *Shari'ah*. Three essential elements of *'iwad* are the existence of risk (*ghurm*), the existence of work and effort (*ikhtiar*), and taking of liability (*ḍamān*).

***Maqasid al-Shari'ah*:** It stands for Objectives of *Shari'ah*, which gives general description of objectives in *Shari'ah* rulings intended by Law Given (i.e. Allah). The objectives are divided into three parts in terms of their priority, namely *darruriyyat* (essentials), *hajiyyah* (complementaries), and *tahsiniyyah* (embellishments), respectively.

***Mudarabah*:** A joint venture agreement in which one party (capital provider or *rabb al-mal*) invests with capital and the other party (entrepreneur or *mudarib*) invests with his skill or labor. The profit of the venture is shared according to a pre-agreed ratio, while the entire loss is born by the capital provider unless it was due to negligence of the entrepreneur.

***Mudarabah*** **(Mark-up Sale):** A contracts correspond to mark-up sale, where the bank purchases a commodity and sells it to the client with additional mark-up over the cost. Such contract belongs to contracts of fiduciary sales (*Buyu' al-amanah*) because the seller is supposed to disclose both the cost and the profit margin to the buyer.

***Musharakah Mutanaqisah*** **(MM):** A mode of Islamic financing, where the bank and the client enter into a contract of joint property ownership. Throughout the financing period, the client will rent the bank's share in the property and increase his ownership through gradual acquisition of the bank's share through payment of periodic instalments.

**Ownership Risk** (*ḍamān al-milkiyyah*)**:** Risk and liabilities that the owner of a certain asset should carry for profits and benefits associated with ownership of the given asset could be justified as *Shari'ah* compliant or *halal* (permissible) in Islam.

***Sukuk*:** A *Shari'ah* compliant investment certificate with certain underlying asset which represents contribution into an investment pull organized by a Special Purpose Vehicle (SPV) which was established to finance a certain project of the issuing company. It can be based on different *Shari'ah* contracts, such as *Musharakah*, *Mudarabah*, *Ijarah* or *Murabahah*. Depending on the type of contract used, the returns and structuring of *Sukuk* may vary.

***Takaful*:** An Islamic alternative to conventional insurance where participant in a *Takaful* scheme agree to donate a certain proportion of the premium (*tabarru'*) into a *Takaful* pool to assist other *Takaful* participants suffering from defined loss or damage. *Takaful* scheme recognizes the elements of shared liability, joint indemnity and mutual assistance. *Takaful* fund is generally managed by a *Takaful* operator for a fee or a share of the investment profit.

## ENDNOTES

1 See Definition of Self-ownership in Libertarianism at Stanford Encyclopedia of Philosophy (2012).

2 *Shari'ah* is considered as set of laws related all aspects of human life in Islam. *Shari'ah* principles are derived mainly from its primary sources, which are the *Qur'an* (Muslims' holy book) and the *Sunnah* (practices and sayings of the Prophet Muhammad (peace be upon him)) and secondary sources which are *Ijma* (consensus) and *Ijtihad* (exercise of reasoning to come up with *Shari'ah* rules base on certain principles of *Qiyas* (analogy)), *Istihsan* (juristic preference), *Maslahah Mursalah* (public interest), *Istishad* (continuity) and others. See (Kamali, 2013a) for more details.

3 All of the English translations of *Qur'anic* verses are taken from Saheeh International's (2010) English translation of The *Qur'an*: With Surah Introductions and Appendices.

4 For more details see Chapter Four on "The Rights of Ownership" in Islam in (Kamali, 2013b), p. 243-267.

5 For more details see (Kamali, 2013b), p. 259.

6 Translation of *ḍamān al-milkiyyah* as ownership risk would be somewhat misleading, and a more appropriate translation would be liability that comes from ownership. Since the term *ḍamān* relates more to liability than risk and *al-milkiyyah* means ownership, the second phrase would be more descriptive. However, in order to be consistent with conventional literature, the term ownership risk is used in this chapter to refer to *ḍamān al-milkiyyah.* One can refer to the paper by Abdul Razak & Saupi (2017) for more details.

7 *Riba* (usury) is one of the major three prohibited *(haram)* elements that would make any business transaction invalid *(batil)* in Islam. Other two elements are *Gharar* (ambiguity) and *Maisir* (gambling).

8 Almost all Islamic scholars, both historical and current agree about those five necessities in *Maqasid*. Imam al-Ghazali was the first one to categorize and list many classifications of the *Maqasid al-Shari'ah*.

9 In general, *Wadiah* can be of two types: *Wadiah yad amanah*, which refers to trust-based deposits, and *Wadiah yad damanah*, which refers to guaranteed savings or safe-keeping. In the latter type, the bank guarantees the deposited principal amount and will bear responsibility for any incurred losses. This deviation is due to breach of original contractual obligations of trust, since the bank is utilizing the deposited money (Abdul Razak & Saupi, 2017). In our example, reference is made to the former type, *Wadiah yad amanah*, which has features historically attached to *Wadiah* contract in the *Fiqh* literature.

10 Riskless profit means profit without taking real business risk. On the contrary, some may argue that conventional banks are still taking risk of default by the client (i.e. credit risk). However, it is apparent that conventional banks are not sharing any of the business risk while advancing the loan to the same client, and the credit risk does not justify the profit earned since such risk is present in any other financial transactions involving delayed payments.

11 In its 136th Resolution taken during the 15th session, the International Fiqh Academy of OIC has specifically mentioned about impermissibility of any right given to either parties involved in a *Musharakah Mutanaqisah* contract to acquire the shares of others at the cost price.

12 See Meera & Abdul Razak (2005) or Smolo & Hassan (2011) for detailed discussion.

# Section 3
# Governance for Islamic Banks

# Chapter 12
# *Shari'ah* Governance for Islamic Banking:
## Evidence From Diverse Regulatory Environments

**Naji Mansour Nomran**
*Department of Finance and Banking, Faculty of Administrative Sciences, Thamar University, Yemen*

**Razali Haron**
https://orcid.org/0000-0003-0415-4093
*Institute of Islamic Banking and Finance, International Islamic University Malaysia, Malaysia*

## ABSTRACT

*Due to the rapid global growth in Islamic banking and finance industry, supervisory authorities in many countries have developed different Shari'ah governance (SG) regulatory systems to regulate this industry. However, the current SG practices across jurisdictions still suffer from some drawbacks. This chapter highlights some issues related to the differences across jurisdictions in adopting various SG regulatory practices and supports the discussion using descriptive analysis. The findings indicate that Islamic banks (IBs) demonstrate higher levels of financial performance, on average, when located in regulated jurisdictions, in jurisdictions that restrict cross-membership of scholars in Shari'ah Supervisory Boards (SSBs), and in jurisdictions adopting Centralized supervision model (CSGM). The findings also show that IBs in jurisdictions adopting Reactive regulatory model report the worst performance in comparison with the other models (Passive, Pro-active, Interventionist and Minimalist).*

DOI: 10.4018/978-1-7998-1611-9.ch012

## 1. INTRODUCTION

In recent years, the regulations, supervision and corporate governance (CG) practices of banking systems have attracted attention from researchers and businesses especially after the global financial crises of 1997 and 2008 since many considered the weakness of these practices, especially CG mechanisms, as among the main reasons causing the world financial collapse (Minton, Taillard, & Williamson, 2010; Alam, 2013). Basically, sound CG practices play an important role in enhancing financial institutions' performance with most of the studies confirming that good governance improve institutions' profitability, productivity, competitiveness and decreases risk (Todorovic, 2013). This impact would be reflected in improving the financial system and then the economies especially for the developing economies (Abdurrouf, 2011).

In the current practices, conventional banks (CBs) are not operating alone in the market. This is because Islamic banks (IBs) have become their most competitive rival. The Islamic banking industry has grown rapidly in the recent decades due to many reasons, led by the religious aspect that increases the demand on *Shari'ah* compliant products particularly in a Muslim majority country (Ashraf, Robson, & Sekhon, 2015; Ullah & Khanam, 2018). Unlike CBs, IBs are prohibited from charging or paying of interest, therefore they offer profit-sharing investment accounts, such that investors' return depends on the return on the assets financed by the investors' funds (Karim, 2001). In general, Islamic business should bring benefits to the society and the welfare of the people as well in align with the goal of Islamic economics which is to achieve economic well-being (Mohammed & Muhammed, 2017; Safiullah & Shamsuddin, 2018). Therefore, a sound *Shari'ah* governance (SG) framework helps in achieving sustainable development with equitable distribution of both opportunities and wealth, which are the main objectives of the concept of economic development in Islam (Ruzlan, 2018).

Further, the Islamic financial system has become a viable alternative to the conventional one after the series of failures of several conventional financial institutions as the result of the 2008 crisis[1] (Kassim & Majid, 2010). According to Zeineb and Mensi (2014), the principles of interest-based transactions and risky investments which the CBs is based on, may perhaps be the cause of the crisis. In addition, many CBs collapsed due to the weak nature of internal wealth (Hussien, Alam, Murad, & Wahid, 2019). In contrast, IBs is proposed to be more resilient to the financial shocks compared to CBs due to their distinctive nature in which all the financial transactions must be trade based and asset linked (Kassim & Majid, 2010). During the crisis of 2008, while CBs was in crisis due to banking failures, IBs were said to have remained resilient (Zeineb & Mensi, 2018). Despite this, Zeineb and Mensi (2014) indicated that some IBs were affected negatively by the crisis. For example, the performance of GCC IBs has been indirectly affected during the crisis, despite their strong resilience in resisting the direct impact of the crisis (Hussien *et al.*, 2019). This is due to some reasons especially the CG weakness as will be shown later in this study.

The differences between IBs and CBs in the functions and structure have resulted in the IBs having additional agency problem besides the common agency problems that occur between managers and shareholders, e.g., in any case managers deviate from their duty to ensure *Shari'ah* implementation (Zainuldin, Lui, & Yii, 2018). Hence, IBs have additional internal governance mechanism i.e., *Shari'ah* Supervisory Board (SSB) besides the Board of Directors (BoD) with both aiming at moral and legal monitoring, respectively and consequently mitigate agency problems (Abdelsalam, Dimitropoulos, Elnahass, & Leventis, 2016).

Generally, many observers identify CG and supervision weaknesses of financial institutions as among the main causes of the financial crises (Minton et al., 2010). This CG weakness was not limited to the CBs, but IBs also suffered from this problem because their implementation of CG practices is still weak (Dusuki, 2006). The fall of Ihlas Finance House of Turkey in 2001, the South Africa's IB in 1997, and the Dubai Islamic IB's losses at between 2004 and 2007 are the clearest evidences of the IFI's poor governance (Dusuki, 2006; Rahman & Bukair, 2013; Grassa, 2015). In this context, Zeineb and Mensi (2018) claim that although the CG structure of IBs may have helped in protecting them from the problems faced by CBs during the crisis of 2008, it is believed that IBs are not immune to CG failures due to potential conflicts between the BoDs and management, audit failure and excessive risk-taking by management (Zeineb & Mensi, 2018).

According to a recent report of CIBAFI (2017), the weakest CG practices in IBs are found in risk governance, followed by SG and the BoD e.g., there is a lack of independent board directors, and of involvement by independents in key areas such as Audit Committee and Risk Committee. In addition, BoD and SSB are not meeting as frequently as supposed to be. Further, there is a lack of diverse experience of the members on the SSB. Regarding the SG weakness, the report indicated that many factors may cause it, but one key reason is likely to be whether there are regulatory standards governing SG, and supervisory oversight of them. Therefore, regulations and strict monitoring of banking operation and higher supervisory power of the authorities is crucial in enhancing the efficiency of IBs (Alam, 2013).

## 2. BACKGROUND

Recently, Islamic banking and finance industry is experiencing rapid growth globally and parallel with this growth many challenges and issues have arisen related to the effectiveness of regulation and governance of IBs and Islamic Financial Institutions (IFIs) across jurisdictions. As a response to that, supervisory authorities in many countries in which IBs operate have developed different SG regulatory systems to regulate the Islamic banking and finance activities (Karim, 2001). Generally, IBs across jurisdictions still have weak regulatory and legislative frameworks (Ben Bouheni & Ammi, 2015). This lack of regulatory environment is one of the most significant issues influencing SG in IBs (Alkhamees, 2013). In fact, the existence of proper legal regulation is necessary to avoid a total erosion of trust in the entire Islamic finance industry (Oseni, 2017). Regulators should have provisions related to legal and regulatory issues for IBs in order to protect the rights of depositors (Ahmed, 2011). However, these different SG regulation practices across jurisdictions still require further evaluation in order to be improved.

From the stakeholder theory (SKT) perspective, Mohammed and Muhammed (2017) depicts that regulation is among the external stakeholders influencing IBs' performance. The differences in the SG practices across jurisdictions may affect bank performance via variations in regulatory models which regulate the SSB's characteristics, roles, and duties, and then affect SSB effectiveness in conducting its roles[2]. Grassa (2013b) claims that such differences have revealed many gaps which raise new issues related to the roles, duties and the effectiveness of the SSBs. The current SG practices across jurisdictions still suffer from some drawbacks especially in the regulatory frameworks relating to the SSB's duties and characteristics (Grassa, 2015).

In practice, each jurisdiction adopts its suitable SG practices based on its own circumstances, when there is no one fits all SG practices recommended by researchers. However, studies concerning many important issues arisen from the SSB function and SG in IBs are still lacking. For example, IBs are subject to different regulations under which they operate, and this resulted in different resolution. For instance, some jurisdictions restrict the SSB cross-membership while some others give allowance to it. Therefore, it is still questionable whether such resolution is beneficial in enhancing the SSB effectiveness and IBs performance or not. In an attempt to find the best SG practices for IBs, this chapter aims to highlight the current different SG regulatory practices that regulate the Islamic banking across jurisdictions to explore their strengths and drawbacks points. Yanīkkaya and Pabuçcu (2017) assert that neglecting such issues by researchers further aggravates them.

The following section discusses the literature relating to the CG of IBs particularly the SG practices. This includes the SG features, SG issues, SG models and the diversity across jurisdictions in the SG regulatory environments.

## 2.1 Corporate Governance Features in Islamic Banks

The CG system of IBs is more complicated than that of the CBs (Matoussi & Grassa, 2012). The reason is that the operation mechanisms of IBs are mainly based on the Islamization in all their activities and operations (Grassa, 2013a; Grassa, 2013b). For this, IBs operate based on a profit and loss and (risk-sharing) model instead of interest-based (*Riba*) as in the CBs (Mollah & Zaman, 2015). CG of IBs derives from two principles, namely, the faith-based principle which implies conducting the operations based on *Shari'ah* and profit-motive principle (Grassa, 2013a). Accordingly, IBs have two types of regulation; the first one is that which applies to CBs while the second one is the form which ensures that all their activities are compliant with *Shari'ah* by the SSBs (Ghayad, 2008).

Based on this, IBs are subject to two internal structures of CG (dual board), BoD and SSB (Lewis, 2007). This means that the CG structure of IBs differs from their conventional counterparts due to the existence of *Shari'ah* compliant activities and the SSBs. These two unique features of the IBs provide another layer of governance besides the usual boards such as the BoD. This extra layer of governance in the IBs modifies their governance structure from "single-layer" as in the conventional ones into "multi-layer" governance (Mollah & Zaman, 2015; Safiullah & Shamsuddin, 2018).

## 2.2 *Shari'ah* Governance Mechanism in Islamic Banks

The main feature of IBs is to ensure *Shari'ah* compliance in all their operations (Grassa, 2013a; Ben Bouheni & Ammi, 2015). Any failures to guarantee such condition can have negative effects on the growth of IBs and subsequently the growth of the Islamic financial system (Grassa, 2013a). For this reason, SSB is the most important governance mechanism that ensures compliance with *Shari'ah* rules in the IBs (Besar, Sukor, Muthalib, & Gunawa, 2009). It is an independent board which includes *Shari'ah* scholars who are selected by the IBs (Matoussi & Grassa, 2012; Grassa & Matoussi, 2014) to answer any inquiries that may arise (Grassa, 2013a). Despite SG being relatively new, it was known during early modern Muslim societies as the institution of *Hisbah*[3]. Currently, SSB is therefore the ideal institution to play the role of *Hisbah* in IBs (Hakimi, Rachdi, Ben Selma Mokni, & Hssini, 2018).

The main function of the SSB is to guarantee that all the operations and activities of the IBs are based on *Shari'ah* (Grassa & Matoussi, 2014). SSB is responsible for checking the contracts and procedures, and it must withdraw any products against the *Shari'ah* and convert them to a charity (Grassa, 2013a). The board must guarantee that there is enough transparency in the *Shari'ah* proceedings (Matoussi & Grassa, 2012; Grassa & Matoussi, 2014). The roles of SSB is summarized in certifying allowable financial products and verifying that transactions comply with the *fatawa*, approving calculation of Zakat, and disposing of prohibited return (Nathan & Pierce, 2009).

As Garas and Pierce (2010) state, the significance of *Shari'ah* supervision in IBs comes from different sides, religious, social, economic, legal and governance. The religious importance lies in the religious position of *Shari'ah* scholars, who issue *fatawa* to guide the management. The social importance stems from the good reputation of *Shari'ah* scholars in the Muslim societies, which plays an important role in providing confidence to stakeholders about the activities of IBs. The economic power is derived from the fact that the profitability of IBs depends on the performance of SSB while the legal power stems from the regulators, the law, and the policies of IBs. Finally, the governance importance lies in the articles of association which consist of the appointment of SSB, the hierarchical position of SSB, and the relationship between the SSB and the other governance organs (Garas & Pierce, 2010).

## 2.3 Issues of the *Shari'ah* Governance Mechanism (SSB) Function

There are six issues of CG resulted from the SSB function, which are the independence, confidentiality, competence, consistency, the disclosure (Grais & Pellegrini, 2006a; Grassa, 2013a; Ben Bouheni & Ammi, 2015) and the reputation (Grassa, 2013a). The following part discusses these issues:

### 2.3.1 Independence of SSB

This issue concerns with the independence of SSB from the management especially when IBs management and shareholders appoint SSB members and suggest their reward. This in turn may have a negative effect on the SSBs independence. Under such circumstances, IBs management may affect SSBs decisions (*fatawa*) by using the management authority, thereby promoting "*fatwa* shopping"[4] (Grais & Pellegrini, 2006a; Grassa, 2013a; Ben Bouheni & Ammi, 2015). The concern is that SSB members may approve suspicious activities to guarantee their position on the board (Grassa, 2013a).

### 2.3.2 Confidentiality of SSB

Most SSB scholars are members in different IBs i.e., they have cross-membership, which may pose negative reflection on their independence where confidentiality issue may intertwine with the independence (Grais & Pellegrini, 2006a; Ben Bouheni & Ammi, 2015). There are concerns over confidentiality when inside information from one bank is manipulated by another (Grassa, 2013a).

### 2.3.3 Competence of SSB

This issue is related to the nature of SSB qualification in IBs as it is important for the scholars to have enough knowledge in both *Shari'ah* and financial and accounting fields (*Fiqh al-Muamalat*) (Grais & Pellegrini, 2006a; Ben Bouheni & Ammi, 2015). The lack of SSB scholars who have such qualifications in both fields has become a serious issue regarding the SSB competency (Grais & Pellegrini, 2006a; Grassa, 2013a). Thus, it is argued that the SSB member who has a doctorate degree in a relevant field is surely better versed in Islamic finance and banking fields (Farook & Lanis, 2007; Farook, Hassan, & Lanis, 2011; Rahman & Bukair, 2013). Nevertheless, there are scholars who do not have any academic qualification or degree whatsoever even in *Shari'ah*-related studies (Bakar, 2016).

### 2.3.4 Reputation of SSB

The success of IBs depends on investor confidence in SSB members, and then each member must be reputed and have noble characteristics such as honesty, integrity and fairness. If the SSB members do not have good reputation, the activities of IBs may be negatively affected (Grassa, 2013a).

### 2.3.5 Consistency of *Fatawa*

This issue is related to the uniformity of *fatawa* issued by SSB scholars across IBs, time and across countries (Grais & Pellegrini, 2006a; Grassa, 2013a; Ben Bouheni & Ammi, 2015). *Fatawa* issued can change due to different conditions, which in turn lead to a conflict of opinion among scholars about some products (Grassa, 2013a). In parallel with the rapid growth of the IFIs, there is an expected increase in the number of conflicting *fatawa*, which may decrease the confidence of customers in the Islamic financial system (Grais & Pellegrini, 2006a; Grassa, 2013a). Additionally, *Shari'ah* interpretation is diverse due to differences in Islamic jurisprudence schools (i.e. *Hanafi, Hanbali, Maliki* and *Shafi'i*), and such conflicts foster different perceptions of ineffectiveness for IBs (Rafay, Sadiq & Ajmal, 2017; Almutairi & Quttainah, 2017).

### 2.3.6 Disclosure

This issue is related to the disclosure of all information about the SSB. In order to enhance stakeholders' trust in SSB, IBs should provide clear information about their SSB responsibilities, *fatawa*, their competence and board composition (Grais & Pellegrini, 2006a; Grassa, 2013a).

To sum up the above discussion, the six issues can be classified into two main groups. First, issues related to the characteristics of SSB scholars, namely, SSB cross-membership and its impact on the SSB confidentiality, SSB qualification and experience, and SSB reputation[5]. Second, issues related to the SSB structure and task, namely, SSB independence from the management and shareholders, the consistency of *fatawa* issued by SSB and meeting the required disclosure about SSB activities.

However, dealing with these issues is reflected in the SG regulatory framework for each country. Again, many jurisdictions adopt different regulatory models which regulate the SSB's characteristics, roles, and duties. Oseni et al. (2016) assert that the SG models and Islamic finance legislations adopted across jurisdictions play a significant role in regulating the dynamics and duties of SSBs. Similarly, SG regulation deals with the issues related to the SSB structure and task such as adopting the suitable model that ensures more consistency of *fatawa*. In the current practice, some jurisdictions adopt Centralized SG model (CSGM) as such model would provide more standardization, consistency and enhance SSBs independence by eliminating any conflicts of interest that may arise between SSBs members and management of IBs (Grais & Pellegrini, 2006a; Grais & Pellegrini, 2006b; ICLR, 2016). In contrast, some other jurisdictions adopt Decentralized SG model (DSGM)[6]. However, there is no specific SG model that can fit all (Hasan & Sabirzyanov, 2015). Due to that each SG approach has its own advantages and disadvantages, and there are many differences between countries in the provisions, rules and circumstances related to the governance structure. Given all of that, the differences across jurisdictions in adopting various SG regulatory practices and its impact on the SSB characteristics will be discussed and analysed in this chapter.

## 3. *SHARI'AH* GOVERNANCE AND REGULATORY ENVIRONMENTS FOR ISLAMIC BANKING

The development of Islamic banking industry is influenced by the legal and regulatory environment which differs across jurisdictions. IBs are not free to choose any manner to finance their products, because the legal and regulatory systems restrict their selections. Hence, any issues related to the IBs operations are determined by the laws that vary across jurisdictions (Ahmed, 2014). IBs activities are subject to the *Shari'ah* rules and the bank regulatory authorities (Naser & Pandlebury, 1997). This discussion requires us to understand the meanings of legal and regulatory environments; therefore, the definition of legislation and regulation terms should be understood. According to the Guide to Making Federal Acts and Regulations (2001):

*Regulations are a form of law, often referred to as delegated or subordinate legislation. Like Acts, they have binding legal effect and usually state rules that apply generally, rather than to specific persons or situations.*

Generally, IBs across jurisdictions still have weak regulatory and legislative frameworks (Ben Bouheni & Ammi, 2015). This lack of regulatory environment regarding SSB's function is one of the most significant issues that influence SG in IBs (Alkhamees, 2013). Most of "*fatwa* shopping" cases, for example, occurs in jurisdictions with lack of regulatory framework (Oseni et al., 2016). More specifically, the current SG practices across jurisdictions still suffer from some drawbacks especially in the regulatory frameworks that are related to the SSB's duties and characteristics (Grassa, 2015). Restriction on cross-membership of SSB scholars and adopting different SSB size and SSB qualifications are examples of the aforementioned regulated elements that differ across jurisdictions based on their regulatory environments. In this context, several jurisdictions e.g., Malaysia, Pakistan and the UAE, have explicit legal provisions regarding the mandatory nature of SSBs decisions for IBs management while in several other jurisdictions such provisions are not available (Malkawi, 2013) e.g., Saudi Arabia (Alkhamees, 2013).

In fact, SG practices are unregulated in some jurisdictions, whilst in some other jurisdictions the practices are regulated (Nomran et al., 2018). This situation raises concerns regarding the feasibility of the SG practices as well as the independence and qualification of SSBs in IBs across jurisdictions that have different regulatory environments (Alkhamees, 2013). One of the main challenges facing the SSBs in IBs is the lack of SG regulation framework in some jurisdictions and then concerns are raised about the efficiency of SSBs performance in the unregulated jurisdictions (Grassa, 2013a; Nomran et al., 2018).

In this regard, however, jurisdictions can be classified into regulated and unregulated (Alkhamees, 2013), thereby it is expected that IBs will demonstrate higher levels of performance when they are in regulated jurisdictions as opposed to those in unregulated jurisdictions. Table 1 provides a summary for the regulated and unregulated[7] jurisdictions. In some countries SG is generally unregulated such as

*Table 1. Regulated and unregulated jurisdictions*

| Country | Regulated/Unregulated |
|---|---|
| Saudi Arabia | Unregulated |
| Malaysia | Regulated |
| Kuwait | Regulated |
| UAE | Regulated |
| Bahrain | Regulated |
| Pakistan | Regulated |
| Palestine | Regulated |
| Egypt | Unregulated |
| Jordan | Regulated |
| Morocco | Unregulated |
| Qatar | Regulated |
| Syria | Regulated |
| Tunisia | Unregulated |
| Libya | Unregulated |
| Yemen | Regulated |
| Brunei | Regulated |
| Indonesia | Regulated |
| Iraq | Regulated |
| Bangladesh | Regulated |
| Lebanon | Regulated |
| United Kingdom | Unregulated |
| United States | Unregulated |
| Turkey | Unregulated |
| Thailand | Unregulated |
| Kazakhstan | Unregulated |
| Nigeria | Regulated |

Source: (See, Grais & Pellegrini, 2006a; Alkhamees, 2013; Grassa, 2015b).

in Saudi Arabia, Egypt, Turkey and the United Kingdom, whilst in some other countries like Malaysia, Pakistan, the UAE, Kuwait, Jordan and Lebanon, there are clear provisions regarding SSBs and their power, as well as the regulatory authorities in these countries impose on IBs to establish their SSBs before starting their operations (Alkhamees, 2013).

The following section highlights the differences across jurisdictions that have IBs in terms of their SG practices under different regulatory environments and some selected key issues resulted from such diversity.

## 3.1 *Shari'ah* Governance Regulatory Models (Degree of Regulatory Interference)

While extreme SG intervention of regulatory agencies is preferred by some jurisdictions, it is not preferred by some others. So far, it is still controversial if the extreme or slight intervention is better to be applied (Hasan, 2009, Nomran et al., 2018). Hence, the performance of SSB continues to be a matter of concern especially for IBs across countries that have different regulatory environment (Nomran et al., 2018). Based on this, Hasan (2009) and Hasan (2012) classified SG models from regulatory perspective (degree of regulatory interference) into five models as the following (see Table 2):

### 3.1.1 Reactive Model

Under this model, the regulators are silent upon the SG framework and there is no particular legislation to govern the IFIs. This model is more common in jurisdictions that adopt western legal regimes such as the United Kingdom and Turkey (Hasan, 2009; Hasan, 2012). As such, jurisdictions that are classified as western legal regimes as Table 2 shows, will be classified under this model like the United States, Thailand, Tanzania, Sri Lanka, South Africa, Kazakhstan and Singapore.

### 3.1.2 Passive Model

This model is exclusive to Saudi Arabia in which the current SG system is a product of self-initiative instead of the regulatory requirement or regulator's direction[8] (Hasan, 2009; Hasan, 2012). Saudi Arabia does not have any framework for SG (Alkhamees, 2013). The main reason is that Saudi Arabia was formed to be an Islamic country practicing Islamic law only; therefore, all banks should be consistent with *Shari'ah* (AI-Abdullatif, 2007). Indeed, Saudi Banks have to follow the Saudi Arabian Monetary Agency (SAMA) regulations and requirements which do not consider AAOIFI accounting standards as one of the accounting standards that should be adopted in Saudi Arabia (AI-Abdullatif, 2007).

### 3.1.3 Minimalist Model

This model is adopted by four GCC countries namely, Bahrain, Kuwait, Qatar and the UAE. It gives slight intervention on the part of regulatory authorities and the regulators expect IBs to have proper SG system without identifying the requirements in detail. For example, under this model there is no restriction on cross-membership of the SSB members (Hasan, 2009; Hasan, 2012).

### 3.1.4 Pro-Active Model

This model which is only applied in Malaysia is also called a regulation-based approach (Hasan, 2011). Malaysia has a comprehensive SG framework from regulatory and non-regulatory sources. The Malaysian parliament has passed and improved several laws such as the Islamic Banking Act 1983, the Takaful Act 1984, the Banking and Financial Institutions Act 1984 and the Securities Commission Act 1993 (Hasan, 2009; Hasan, 2012).

### 3.1.5 Interventionist Model

This model is exclusive to SG system in Pakistan. It gives third party institution the authority to take decision on *Shari'ah* issues related to the Islamic finance. In Pakistan, the *Shari'ah* Federal Court is the highest authority although there is national SSB at the State Bank of Pakistan level (Hasan, 2009; Hasan, 2012).

It is argued that comparing the SG practices among countries adopting different intervention models, may provide a better view of the best SG intervention practices for the IBs (Nomran et al., 2018). However, Nomran et al. (2018) provide empirical evidence on the relationships between SSB characteristics and IBs performance in Malaysia being a country that applies the most extreme intervention of regulatory

*Table 2. Shari'ah governance models based on the degree of regulatory interference across jurisdictions*

| Country | Model |
|---|---|
| Saudi Arabia | Passive |
| Malaysia | Pro-active |
| Kuwait | Minimalist |
| UAE | Minimalist |
| Bahrain | Minimalist |
| Qatar | Minimalist |
| Pakistan | Interventionist |
| United Kingdom | Reactive |
| Turkey | Reactive |
| Singapore | Reactive |
| United States | Reactive |
| Thailand | Reactive |
| Tanzania | Reactive |
| Sri Lanka | Reactive |
| South Africa | Reactive |
| Kazakhstan | Reactive |

Source: Adapted from literature (see, Grais & Pellegrini, 2006a; Hasan, 2009; Hasan, 2011; Hasan, 2012; Hassan, Abdullah, Hassan, Ibrahim, Sawari, Aziz, & Triyanta, 2013; Alkhamees, 2013; Grassa, 2015b).

agencies (Pro-active model). To date, it seems that the study of Nomran et al. (2018) is among the rare studies that empirically highlight this issue.

It seems important to mention that some jurisdictions have introduced new regulations and guidelines besides their existing SG frameworks (SGFs) for IFIs to strengthen the SG practices. In Malaysia, for example, the regulators issued a comprehensive SGF in 2010 to govern the practice of the Islamic finance industry and cover stakeholders' scope of duties and responsibilities, and recently in 2017, they updated the SGF in order to enhance the existing regulatory requirements and expectations on SG for IFIs[9] (Laldin & Furqani, 2018).

Lastly, it should be indicated that IBs operate in some countries that have parallel legal systems in which Islamic law plays a direct part in the legal system i.e. Iran, Saudi Arabia, and Sudan (CIBAFI, 2017). Alkhamees (2013) claims that it is not necessary for IBs in the jurisdictions of *Shari'ah* legal regimes to have any SSBs; as such legal environment should provide all the wanted opinions *fatawa*. Regarding this, CIBAFI (2017) compared the aggregate CG practices of 77 IBs across the different legal systems, and found that IBs operating in the common law system have the highest average CGI, followed by banks in the civil law systems, while the countries operating in parallel legal systems (Islamic law), have the lowest aggregate CG practices.

## 3.2 Legal Restrictions Across Jurisdictions on Scholars Cross-Membership

One of the most crucial issues facing the SSB is the repetition of names of *Shari'ah* scholars in several SSBs across IFIs (Grassa, 2013b). Out of 280 scholars, the top 20 scholars having 621 board membership while the remaining 260 scholars having 520 board membership for more than fourteen countries including the GGC countries, Malaysia, Pakistan, UK and Sudan (Ünal, 2011). In the GCC countries, three popular names sit on 26% of all the SSBs (Grassa, 2013a). The reason is that qualified *Shari'ah* scholars are too limited to meet the growing demand of the IFIs (Nathan Garas, 2012).

However, there are mixed findings in the literature regarding whether the costs or the benefits outweigh from numerous and simultaneous board memberships (Alman, 2012). Some researchers believe that cross-membership of SSB would have a good implication for IBs (Farook & Lanis, 2007; Farook et al., 2011; Abdullah, Percy, & Stewart, 2014) while some others argue that the opposite implication is right as cross-membership of SSB may lead to the conflicts of interest and then decreases the SSB effectiveness (Nathan & Pierce, 2009; Hasan, 2011; Nathan Garas, 2012; Alman, 2012; Grassa, 2013a). Unfortunately, there is a lack of empirical studies that investigate the impact of this resolution. Hence, it is still questionable whether the restrictions on the SSB cross-membership are beneficial in enhancing the SG supervision effectiveness and the performance in IBs or not.

In general, the concentration of a few *Shari'ah* scholars in the SSB may pose some problems. The least of these problems is the concentration risk among a few scholars (Bakar, 2016). The majority of IBs have SSB members with cross-memberships and this may lead to conflicts of interest and may raise concern for SSB members maintaining confidentiality particularly when there are no applied mechanisms to reduce such conflict (Hasan, 2011). The main issue of multiple memberships is the duty of confidentiality (Bakar, 2016). Hence, it is argued that the regulators should control the cross-memberships for each *Shari'ah* scholar and the privacy of keeping the information when a member sits in many SSBs (Garas & Pierce, 2010).

To control this issue, few jurisdictions have restricted the numbers of membership of scholars in SSBs whereas others do not have any restriction regarding this issue (Grassa, 2013b; Grassa, 2015). The regulatory authorities in some jurisdictions restrict SSB scholars from serving on multiple boards in order to implement a good SG system (Mollah & Zaman, 2015). Table 3 provides a summary of the jurisdictions that impose restriction on the cross-membership of SSB scholars.

Given that, any restrictions on the SSB cross-membership would diminish the conflict of interest and enhance the SSB effectiveness. Therefore, it is expected that the performance of IBs will be higher for IBs in jurisdictions that have restrictions on the SSB cross-membership as compared to those in jurisdictions that do not have such restrictions.

*Table 3. Jurisdictions that restrict the cross-membership of SSB scholars*

| Country | Restriction |
|---|---|
| Malaysia | "Member of SC cannot be member in SC of another IFI in the same industry". |
| Oman | "Member of SSB cannot be member of SSB of more than 1 competing IFI in Oman but can be member of SSB on more than one non-competing IFI". |
| Nigeria | "SAC member should not be member in more than one SAC of IFIs in the same category". |
| Sudan | "SB members cannot have the same position in more than two IFIs in the same category". |
| Indonesia | "Members of the Board may only hold concurrent positions as SB members at not more than 2 other banks and 2 IFIs". |
| Pakistan* | No details |

Source: (Grassa, 2013b; Grassa, 2015b; Grassa & Matoussi, 2014). *(Alkhamees, 2013).

## 3.3 *Shari'ah* Governance Structure Models (Centralized vs. Decentralized)

From different angle, currently IBs operate across jurisdictions under various SG structure (Hasan, 2009), which refers to the structures and processes that ensure IBs compliance with *Shari'ah* rules (Ahmed, 2011). Several studies classified SG structure models into two main models which are the Centralized and Decentralized (CSGM and DSGM) (Grais & Pellegrini, 2006a; Grais & Pellegrini, 2006b; Alman, 2012; Hassan et al., 2013; Hamza, 2013; Abd Razak, 2018). DSGM reflects the *Shari'ah* supervision at the institutional level where each IB should establish its SSB; while in contrast, CSGM reflects *Shari'ah* supervision at both the institutional and the national levels by having a national SSB at the Central Bank or the Securities Commission besides the SSBs of IBs (Grassa, 2015; Hakimi et al., 2018). Under the DSGM, SSB at the institutional level has the ultimate decision on the products but under the CSGM, there is also a national SSB that have the highest *Shari'ah* authority (Rafay, Sadiq, & Ajmal, 2017). Figure 1 shows the difference between the two models (CSGM and DSGM).

Given this, SG supervision/structure models across jurisdictions can be either CSGM or DSGM (Grais & Pellegrini, 2006a; Hassan et al., 2013; Hamza, 2013; Abd Razak, 2018). While some jurisdictions adopt CSGM, some others adopt DSGM. This diversity appears to be even among those jurisdictions that apply the same legal regime. For example, although jurisdictions such as Saudi Arabia and Sudan are classified within those jurisdictions that apply *Shari'ah* law regime, Saudi Arabia adopts the DSGM while Sudan adopts the CSGM. Similarly, the law regime of Malaysia and Kuwait is classified as mixed legal regime, but the SG in Malaysia is the CSGM while in Kuwait is the DSGM.

According to Hasan and Sabirzyanov (2015), there is no specific SG model that can fit all. Due to that each SG approach has its own advantages and disadvantages, and there are many differences between countries in the provisions, rules and circumstances related to the governance structure. Absence of SG either CSGM or DSGM can have a negative impact on IBs governance infrastructure (Shaffaii, 2008). IFIs is still in its early stages of expansion around the world, particularly in the western countries, hence, any attempt to adopt a rigid, rule-based approach hastily for the purpose of enhancing the SG of these institutions might impede its development (Hasan & Sabirzyanov, 2015).

*Figure 1. Shari'ah governance models based on supervision structure (CSGM & DSGM)*

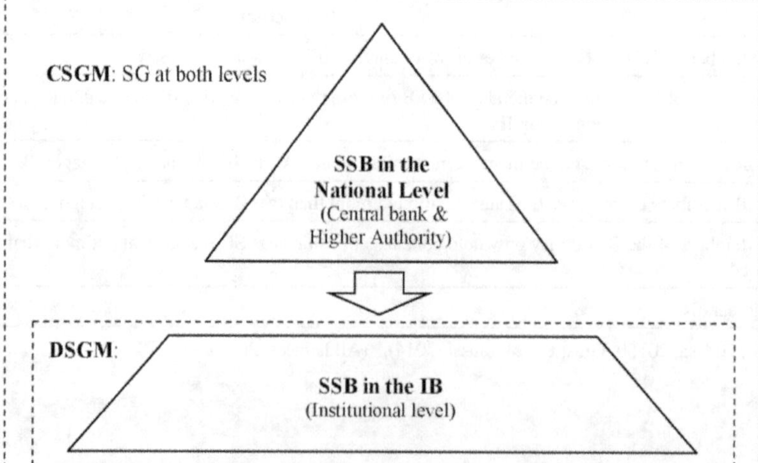

There are no uniform criteria for the above classifications between studies. While Alman (2012), Hamza (2013), and Abd Razak (2018) classified SG models into two and Hasan and Sabirzyanov (2015) classified them into three based on the existence of central *Shari'ah* board with SSBs or only SSBs (governance structure), Ahmed (2011), on the other hand, adopted four standards to classify them into four models, which are the existence of IB law and regulation, regulatory requirements for SSB, national *Shari'ah* authority and SSBs at the institutional level.

Due to the absence of uniform standards for the SG models classification, there appears to be a disagreement among researchers regarding which countries adopt each model. This difference seems to appear even among those researchers who adopted the same standard such as Alman, (2012), and Hamza (2013). Although they classified SG models into two based on the same criteria which is the existence of central *Shari'ah* board with SSBs or only SSBs, they classified jurisdictions such as Jordan, Yemen and Indonesia in the opposite manner. To examine how the impact of SSB on risk-taking varies between the DSGM vs. CSGM models, Alman (2012) divided the entire sample into GCC and Non-GCC countries to reflect countries that adopt the DSGM vs. CSGM respectively. This implies that countries such as Jordan, Yemen and Indonesia have been among those countries that adopt CSGM. In contrast, Hamza (2013) classified the same countries among those that adopt the DSGM.

According to Hamza (2013), the CSGM reflects SG at both central level and IB level, whilst in the DSGM; SG is limited to IB level. It is found that most the above-mentioned classifications included at least the CSGM and DSGM. As an example, Ahmed (2011) classified the SG models into four including the robust and passive models, whereas Ginena and Hamid (2015) classified them into four including SSB at CB/IB and SSB at IB models. The robust and SSB at CB/IB models seem to be like the CSGM as it reflects SG at the national and institutional levels, while the passive and SSB at IB models look like the DSGM in which SG is applied at institutional level. However, there are still many differences between the different classification regarding some standards such as whether SSB at the national level with or without the final authority. According to Ahmed (2011), and Hamza (2013), Malaysia and Pakistan are examples of the countries that adopt CSGM or robust models, while Kuwait is an example of those that adopt DSGM or passive models.

Consequently, jurisdictions can be classified within those who adopt either CSGM or DSGM. In fact, there appears to be a consensus among researchers regarding countries that adopt each model, while there is still disagreement about the adopted model in some other countries. Based on many studies (Hassan et al., 2013; Quttaina et al., 2013; Hamza, 2013; Kammer, Norat, Pinon, Prasad, Towe, & Zeidane, 2015), there are some countries that adopt CSGM e.g., Malaysia, Morocco, Nigeria, Brunei, Bangladesh, Pakistan, Palestine, Sudan and Iran. In contrast, Hassan et al. (2013), Hamza (2013), Grassa (2015), and ICLR (2016) indicated that there are many countries adopting DSGM e.g., Saudi Arabia, Qatar, Singapore, the United Kingdom, Jordan, Yemen and Gambia. Despite this, there are some countries that are still controversial such as Bahrain, Kuwait, Oman, UAE and Indonesia. While some consider these five countries among those that adopt the CSGM (Grais & Pellegrini, 2006a; Hassan et al., 2013; Kammer et al., 2015), some others classify them within those countries that adopt the DSGM (see, e.g., Alman, 2012; Hamza, 2013).

As mentioned earlier, the disagreement between researchers is due to the absence of uniform criteria. Nevertheless, there is a reasonable justification for these differences in literature regarding the above-mentioned countries. Hassan et al. (2013) argue that countries such as, Bahrain and UAE, have national *Shari'ah* advisory committees which are responsible only to advise the Central Bank, while the *Shari'ah* committees in the others countries, such as Malaysia, Indonesia and Pakistan, are the final authority for any *Shari'ah* decisions. Hence, they considered countries with and without the final authority to be within those who adopt CSGM. In addition, Hassan et al. (2013) indicated that Kuwaiti IBs follow the *fatwa* Board of the Ministry of *Awqaf*, but there is no centralized *Shari'ah* committee, and hence Kuwait is among those countries that adopt DSGM.

The present chapter follows the classification of Hasan and Sawari (2011) and Hassan et al. (2013), in which jurisdictions such as Indonesia, Bahrain and UAE are within those jurisdictions that adopt the CSGM, while Kuwait with those jurisdictions that adopt the DSGM. Figure 2 depicts the top jurisdictions that adopt CSGM which are Malaysia, UAE, Bahrain, Indonesia, Bangladesh, Pakistan, Sudan, Brunei and Oman. It presents that approximately 59% of jurisdictions adopt DSGM, while almost 41% of them adopt CSGM.

Based on the above discussion, this study classifies jurisdictions based on the CSGM and DSGM following many studies (Grais & Pellegrini, 2006a; Hassan et al., 2013; Hamza, 2013). This classification adopts a specific criterion which is the existence of central *Shari'ah* board with SSB (CSGM) or only institutional SSB (DSGM) (Alman, 2012; Hamza, 2013). For those jurisdictions with or without the final authority, they will be classified within those that adopt CSGM such as Bahrain and UAE following the study of Hassan et al. (2013). Table 4 presents the SG models classification across jurisdictions based on SG structure (CSGM and DSGM).

However, there has been much debate regarding the issue of whether the IBs need CSGM or only DSGM (Abd Razak, 2018). In practice, there is no specific model can be of preference by all jurisdictions (Hasan & Sabirzyanov, 2015; Oseni et al., 2016). Even among researchers, some of them believe that the CSGM approach is better for IBs than the DSGM (Hamza, 2013; Kammer et al., 2015; Oseni et al., 2016; Abd Razak, 2018), while there are some others who believe that DSGM is better than CSGM (Grais & Pellegrini, 2006a; Alman, 2012; Quttainah, Song, & Wu, 2013) as each model has its advantages and disadvantages (Hasan & Sabirzyanov, 2015).

*Figure 2. Top countries with centralized SSBs based on Islamic finance assets (US$ billion), 2014*
*Source: Islamic Commercial Law Report (ICLR) 2016*

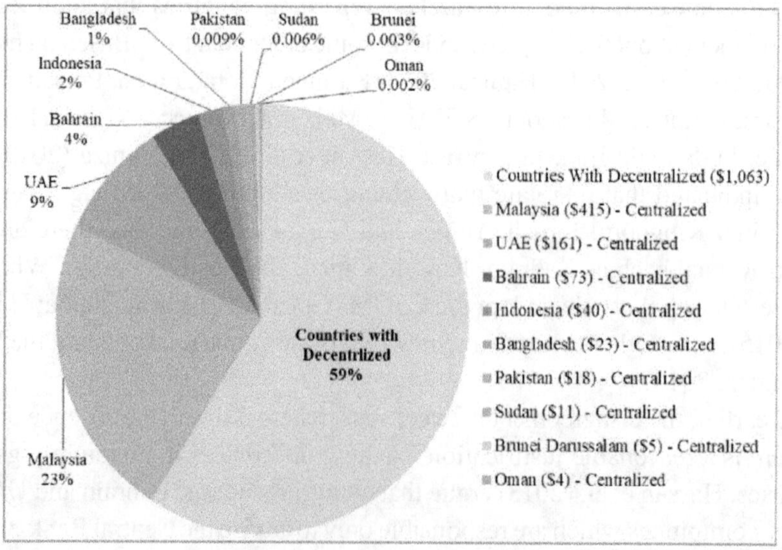

*Table 4. Shari'ah governance structure models classification across jurisdictions (CSGM vs. DSGM)*

| Country | Model |
|---|---|
| Sudan | Centralized (CSGM) |
| Malaysia | Centralized (CSGM) |
| UAE | Centralized (CSGM) |
| Bahrain | Centralized (CSGM) |
| Pakistan | Centralized (CSGM) |
| Palestine | Centralized (CSGM) |
| Morocco | Centralized (CSGM) |
| Brunei Darussalam | Centralized (CSGM) |
| Indonesia | Centralized (CSGM) |
| Iran | Centralized (CSGM) |
| Bangladesh | Centralized (CSGM) |
| Afghanistan | Centralized (CSGM) |
| Nigeria | Centralized (CSGM) |
| Oman | Centralized (CSGM) |
| Saudi Arabia | Decentralized (DSGM) |
| Kuwait | Decentralized (DSGM) |
| Jordan | Decentralized (DSGM) |
| Qatar | Decentralized (DSGM) |
| Yemen | Decentralized (DSGM) |
| United Kingdom | Decentralized (DSGM) |
| Singapore | Decentralized (DSGM) |
| Gambia | Decentralized (DSGM) |
| Thailand | Decentralized (DSGM) |

Source: (see, Grais & Pellegrini, 2006a; Hassan *et al.*, 2013; Hamza, 2013; Bakar, 2016; ICLR, 2016).

The main benefit of the CSGM is to avoid having different opinions about any *Shari'ah* issues that may arise regarding the Islamic banking products, operations and activities. This would make the Islamic banking sector to be in harmony with each other, thereby enhancing the regulatory environment in this industry (Hamza, 2013). Accordingly, several jurisdictions adopt CSGM as such model would provide more standardization, consistency and enhance SSBs independence by eliminating any conflicts of interest that may arise between SSBs members and management of IBs (Grais & Pellegrini, 2006a; Grais & Pellegrini, 2006b; ICLR, 2016). CSGM is the practicable model that can reduce the "*fatwa* shopping" problem as it is more efficient in monitoring the SSBs function (Oseni et al., 2016). Using a dummy variable to reflect the existence of CSGM in countries, Alam, Zainuddin, and Rizvi (2019), and Mezzi (2018) examined the impact of CSGM on IBs' performance and efficiency, respectively, and they found positive and significant impacts.

Under DSGM, IBs may suffer from a lack of harmonization or the variation in the *Shari'ah* rules interpretations, which in turn may be reflected negatively on the confidence in the Islamic banking sector (Kammer et al., 2015). One of the issues resulted from the SSBs function is the consistency of opinions (*fatawa*) across IBs, time, and across countries (Grais & Pellegrini, 2006a; Grassa, 2013b; Ben Bouheni & Ammi, 2015). The inconsistencies on opinion may emerge under DSGM as there are many scholars across IBs and they may come out with many different opinions on the same issue (Grais & Pellegrini, 2006a; Grais & Pellegrini, 2006b). Al-Amine (2011) asserts that most scholars do not have the same opinions about IBs' products. He provides an example of this issue as in the case of Japan Bank for International Cooperation (JBIC) when it has decided to issue its first sovereign *Sukuk*. The bank selected Citibank from Dubai and CIMB of Malaysia to arrange a deal but the SSBs scholars of the two selected banks disagreed on whether *Sukuk* was *Shari'ah* compliant. The deal will need to be restructured adding to cost, time and frustration for the issuer, which in turn cannot be beneficial to the market (Al-Amine, 2011).

On the other hand, for those who claim that DSGM is better for IBs than CSGM, they believe that DSGM provides the opportunity for innovation more than the CSGM (Grais & Pellegrini, 2006a; Al-man, 2012). IBs under CSGM are exposed to delay in order to receive *fatawa* on specific issues from the central *Shari'ah* board, thereby this processing takes a lot of time until the central authority respond and provide the required *fatwa* for IBs. The waiting time until a bank receives the *fatwa* may lead to loss of opportunities thus a negative impact on IBs performance (Quttainah et al., 2013).

However, as there is lack of empirical studies that have analyzed the above-mentioned issues, the current chapter supports the discussion by utilizing descriptive analysis approach following the study of Grassa and Matoussi (2014) that has employed descriptive statistics rather than regression-based analysis.

## 4. SAMPLE AND METHODOLOGY

### 4.1 Sample Construction

The study sample consists of 68 IBs located in 14 countries over the period 2007-2015. Data related to internal SG mechanism attributes (SSB characteristics) are hand collected from the annual reports of IBs while data on financial performance is sourced from the BankScope (bank data). The sample distribution is presented in Table 5.

*Table 5. Sample distribution*

| Country | No of Islamic Banks | No of Observations |
|---|---|---|
| Bahrain | 6 | 49 |
| Indonesia | 6 | 42 |
| Jordan | 3 | 22 |
| Kuwait | 6 | 45 |
| Malaysia | 10 | 79 |
| Oman | 3 | 9 |
| Pakistan | 10 | 75 |
| Qatar | 5 | 33 |
| Saudi Arabia | 4 | 33 |
| Sudan | 5 | 40 |
| Thailand | 1 | 9 |
| UAE | 3 | 26 |
| United Kingdom | 4 | 33 |
| Yemen | 2 | 18 |
| Total | 68 | 513 |

**Notes**: IBs in Oman started operations in 2013; therefore, the data for Omani IBs are only for the years (2013-2015); UAE: United Arab Emirates.

## 4.2 Methodology

Using independent t-*test* and ANOVA analysis, the authors test for differences in means of selected SG mechanism attributes (SSB characteristics) and financial performance between samples of IBs across 14 countries that reflect diverse regulatory environments related to the discussed following issues:

- IBs that operate in regulated vs. unregulated jurisdictions.
- IBs that operate in jurisdictions adopting the five SG regulatory models.
- IBs that operate in jurisdictions restrict the SSB cross-membership vs. those with no restriction.
- IBs that operate in jurisdictions adopting CSGM vs. DSGM.

Table 6 provides a summary of the sample distribution based on these diverse regulatory environments.

### 4.2.1 Variables Measurement

There are two types of variables used in this research. First, variables related to internal SG mechanism in IBs (SSB characteristics) namely, size, cross-membership, educational qualification[10], reputation and expertise. These variables are the most intensely studied SSB characteristics which determine the effectiveness of SSB in conducting its tasks. Further, the differences in the SG practices across jurisdictions may affect bank performance via variations in regulations related to these characteristics. Second, variables related to financial performance of IBs, namely, ROA, ROE, ROIAA, and ROIAE. Table 7 summarizes the measurements of the variables.

*Table 6. Summary of Shari'ah governance practices classification across jurisdictions of the study sample*

| Country | Regulated/Unregulated | SG Regulatory Models | Restriction on the Cross-Membership | CSGM vs. DSGM Models |
|---|---|---|---|---|
| Bahrain | Regulated | Minimalist | Not restricted | CSGM |
| Indonesia | ---- | ---- | Restricted | CSGM |
| Jordan | ---- | ---- | Not restricted | DSGM |
| Kuwait | Regulated | Minimalist | Not restricted | DSGM |
| Malaysia | Regulated | Pro-active | Restricted | CSGM |
| Oman | ---- | ---- | Restricted | CSGM |
| Pakistan | Regulated | Interventionist | Restricted | CSGM |
| Qatar | Regulated | Minimalist | Not restricted | DSGM |
| Saudi Arabia | Unregulated | Passive | Not restricted | DSGM |
| Sudan | ---- | ---- | Restricted | CSGM |
| Thailand | Unregulated | Reactive | Not restricted | DSGM |
| UAE | Regulated | Minimalist | Not restricted | CSGM |
| United Kingdom | Unregulated | Reactive | Not restricted | DSGM |
| Yemen | ---- | ---- | Not restricted | DSGM |

*Table 7. Measurement of Variables*

| *Variables* | *Definitions and Coding* | *Measurement* | *References* |
|---|---|---|---|
| *SSB Characteristics & Effectiveness:* | | | |
| SSB-SIZE | SSB size | N of scholars on the SSB | Farook *et al.* (2011)<br>Nomran *et al.* (2018)<br>Almutairi and Quttainah (2017) |
| SSB-CRMEMB | SSB cross-membership | % of scholars who sit on other SSBs | |
| SSB-DQ | SSB educational qualification | % of scholars who have PhD degree | |
| SSB-REPUT | SSB reputation | % of scholars who sit on SSB of AAOIFI & at least two SSBs | |
| SSB-EXPER | SSB expertise | % of scholars with accounting/economic/ finance knowledge | |
| *Financial Performance:* | | | |
| ROA | Return on assets | Net income divided by average total assets | Mollah and Zaman (2015)<br>Nomran *et al.* (2018) |
| ROE | Return on equity | Net income divided by average total equity | |
| ROIAA | Operational efficiency (assets) | Operating profit divided by average total assets | |
| ROIAE | Operational efficiency (equity) | Operating profit divided by average total equity | |

**Note:** SSB reputation is measured by the percentage of the SSB members who sit on the board of the AAOIFI (see, e.g., Nomran *et al.*, 2018). This is because the *Shari'ah* board of the AAOIFI is the highest *Shari'ah* board in the world, and a scholar with affiliation to AAOIFI is considered a scholar with higher reputation. It is comprised of highly reputable *Shari'ah* scholars who represent, to a large extent, the best *Shari'ah* minds of both the Islamic world and Islamic Finance (Bakar, 2016).

## 5. EMPIRICAL FINDINGS

Tables 8, 9, 10, 11 and 12 provide summary descriptive statistics of the SSB characteristics and financial performance for the used samples of IBs.

### 5.1 Descriptive Statistics for IBs with Full Sample

Table 8 provides summary statistics for selected variables describing the SSB characteristics and financial performance of the full sample of IBs. Tables 8 shows that the mean of variables related to the SSB characteristics (SSB-SIZE, SSB-CRMEMP, SSB-DQ, SSB-REPUT, and SSB-EXPER) for the full sample IBs are (3.7310, 0.5731, 0.7212, 0.2365, and 0.3593), respectively.

The average number of SSB size is almost four, which ranges from one to nine scholars. This seems to be consistent with Mollah and Zaman (2015) who find similar mean size of the SSB (4.17) but ranging from 1 to 14. In general, it is noticed that the SSB characteristics that have high percentages are cross-membership and educational qualification which have mean values of 0.5731 and 0.7212 respectively. This indicates that SSBs in IBs have more scholars with educational qualification and with cross-memberships. Most of IBs have SSB members with cross-memberships (Hasan, 2011). Grassa and Matoussi (2014) found, on average, Southeast Asia IBs exhibit SSB cross-membership (0.5460), while GCC IBs exhibit higher cross-membership (0.9320). Regarding educational qualification, Nomran, Haron, and Hassan (2017) found the mean of SSB-DQ is 0.7670. In contrast, SSB reputation and expertise show modest mean values of (0.2365 and 0.3593), respectively.

*Table 8. Descriptive Statistics of SSB Characteristics and Performance Variables for IBs with Full Sample*

| *Variable* | *N* | *Mean* | *Median* | *Std. Dev.* | *Minimum* | *Maximum* |
|---|---|---|---|---|---|---|
| **SSB Characteristics:** | | | | | | |
| SSB-SIZE | 513 | 3.7310 | 3.0000 | 1.4354 | 1.0000 | 9.0000 |
| SSB-CRMEMB | 513 | 0.5731 | 0.6700 | 0.3445 | 0.0000 | 1.0000 |
| SSB-DQ | 513 | 0.7212 | 0.7500 | 0.2771 | 0.0000 | 1.0000 |
| SSB-REPUT | 513 | 0.2365 | 0.1700 | 0.2802 | 0.0000 | 1.0000 |
| SSB-EXPER | 513 | 0.3593 | 0.3300 | 0.3155 | 0.0000 | 1.0000 |
| **Financial Performance:** | | | | | | |
| ROA | 513 | 0.7313 | 0.9100 | 2.7701 | -14.2700 | 7.9700 |
| ROE | 513 | 7.3497 | 7.2500 | 12.7403 | -41.5700 | 63.1500 |
| ROIAA | 513 | 0.9813 | 1.1800 | 2.9124 | -14.5400 | 12.9400 |
| ROIAE | 513 | 9.3077 | 9.3600 | 15.0930 | -51.3200 | 64.2900 |

**Notes**: N = Number of observations; Number of IBs = 68; SSB-SIZE = SSB size; SSB-CRMEMB = SSB cross-membership; SSB-DQ = SSB educational qualification; SSB-REPUT = SSB reputation; SSB-EXPER = SSB expertise; ROA = Return on asset; ROE = Return on equity; ROIAA = Operational efficiency in terms of assets; ROIAE = Operational efficiency in terms of equity.

As shown in Table 8, the mean of the financial performance variables (ROA, ROE, ROIAA, and ROIAE) are 0.7313, 7.3497, 0.9813, and 9.3077, respectively. These findings are almost in support of Nomran *et al.* (2018) who report that the mean values of the ROA, ROE, and ROIAE are 0.6036, 9.0985 and 12.5780.

## 5.2 Independent t-*Test* of IBs in Regulated vs. Unregulated Jurisdictions

Table 9 presents the independent t-*test* results of the comparison of the research variables average for the IBs in regulated vs. unregulated jurisdictions.

Table 9 suggests that IBs in regulated jurisdictions have exhibited mean SSB size of 3.83, slightly and significantly lower compared to mean of 4.25 for its counterparts in unregulated jurisdictions. Table 9 also shows that, on average, the presence of the scholars with cross-membership of IBs in regulated jurisdictions (0.64) is significantly higher than those observed in unregulated jurisdictions IBs (0.54). This observed behaviour can be explained by the presence of 4 GCC countries as regulated jurisdictions, namely, (Bahrain, Kuwait, Qatar, and UAE) (see Table 6). While some countries restrict the cross-memberships of SSB scholars e.g., Indonesia and Malaysia, no specific regulation in the matter exists for IFIs of GCC countries (Grassa & Matoussi, 2014). In the GCC countries, the three popular names sit on 26% of all the SSBs (Grassa, 2013a). Grassa and Matoussi (2014) found that IBs in the GCC countries have higher SSB cross-membership (0.93) than the IBs in Southeast Asia (0.54).

Similarly, Table 9 presents that IBs in regulated jurisdictions have exhibited mean SSB expertise (SSB-EXPER) of 0.43, slightly and significantly higher compared to mean of 0.32 for IBs in unregulated jurisdictions. In contrast, it is shown that IBs in regulated jurisdictions have exhibited mean SSB reputation (SSB-REPUT) of 0.27, slightly and significantly lower compared to mean of 0.36 for IBs in unregulated jurisdictions. However, as Table 9 shows, IBs in regulated and unregulated jurisdictions have almost similar mean of 0.72 and 0.70 for SSB educational qualification, respectively.

*Table 9. Independent t-test of SSB characteristics and performance variables for IBs in regulated vs. unregulated jurisdictions*

| Variables | Mean | | |
|---|---|---|---|
| | **IBs in Regulated Jurisdictions** | **IBs in Unregulated Jurisdictions** | **t-statistics (p-value)** |
| **SSB Characteristics:** | | | |
| SSB-SIZE | 3.8339 | 4.2533 | -2.1920 (0.0290)** |
| SSB-CRMEMB | 0.6413 | 0.5451 | 2.2291 (0.0264)** |
| SSB-DQ | 0.7243 | 0.7018 | 0.6294 (0.5294) |
| SSB-REPUT | 0.2743 | 0.3698 | -2.5491 (0.0112)** |
| SSB-EXPER | 0.4386 | 0.3273 | 3.3892 (0.0009)*** |
| **Financial Performance:** | | | |
| ROA | 0.8576 | -0.3366 | 2.7077 (0.0080)*** |
| ROE | 7.3084 | 1.5743 | 2.9943 (0.0035)*** |
| ROIAA | 1.0338 | 0.1907 | 1.7434 (0.0845)* |
| ROIAE | 8.5678 | 4.4874 | 1.6672 (0.0990)* |

**Notes:** *p*-value for the coefficient is within parentheses; ***, ** and * are significant at 1%, 5%, and 10% respectively.

Importantly, Table 9 provides evidence that all the financial performance variables (ROA, ROE, ROIAA, and ROIAE) of IBs in regulated jurisdictions are significantly much more (average: 0.8576, 7.3084, 1.0338, and 8.5678) than those in unregulated jurisdictions IBs (average: -0.3366, 1.5743, 0.1907, and 4.4874).

## 5.3 ANOVA Test of IBs Under *Shari'ah* Governance Regulatory Models

Table 10 presents ANOVA one-way test results of the comparison of the research variables average for IBs in different SG regulatory models. The sample IBs were grouped into five and their average of SSB characteristics and performance variables were compared.

As shown in Table 10, the ANOVA test reported an *F*-statistic of 58.31 with a *p*-value of 0.00 and a Welch (*p*-value) of 0.00 by comparing the average SSB size for the five models. This revealed a significant difference in SSB size for the five regulatory models and, hence, is concluded that differences across jurisdiction in their adopted regulatory framework can affect SSB size. It is noticed that the highest SSB size, on average, is almost five which were adopted by IBs in jurisdiction adopting Pro-active and Passive models. Generally, many jurisdictions such as Malaysia, UAE, Bahrain, Saudi Arabia, Syria, Oman, Jordan, Palestine, Nigeria, Libya, Indonesia and Kuwait regulate the required SSB size that should be adopted by IBs (Hasan, 2009; Grassa, 2015). In practice, IBs adopt different SSB size based on their different regulations across jurisdictions. Nevertheless, it is still questionable whether small or large SSB size is beneficial in enhancing performance of the IBs.

Similarly, the ANOVA test exhibited an *F*-statistic of 41.97 with a *p*-value of 0.00 and a Welch (*p*-value) of 0.00 by comparing the average SSB cross-membership for the five models. The highest SSB cross-membership, on average, is 0.81, adopted by IBs in jurisdictions adopting Minimalist model (Bahrain, Kuwait, Qatar, and UAE). This is in support of the findings of Table 9 which shows that these 4 GCC countries suffer from high SSB cross-membership concentration. The ANOVA test also exhibited an

*Table 10. ANOVA one way test of SSB characteristics and performance variables for IBs under different SG regulatory models*

| SG Regulatory Model | SSB Characteristics | | | | | Financial Performance | | | |
|---|---|---|---|---|---|---|---|---|---|
| | SSB-SIZE | SSB-CRMEMB | SSB-DQ | SSB-REPUT | SSB-EXPER | ROA | ROE | ROIAA | ROIAE |
| Pro-active | 5.1646 | 0.5425 | 0.7374 | 0.0926 | 0.6082 | 0.8100 | 11.7789 | 1.0846 | 15.8129 |
| Minimalist | 3.7908 | 0.8188 | 0.7925 | 0.4318 | 0.2668 | 0.8067 | 6.0492 | 0.9046 | 5.5872 |
| Interventionist | 2.5200 | 0.3830 | 0.5715 | 0.1444 | 0.6104 | 1.0022 | 5.3645 | 1.2257 | 7.3152 |
| Passive | 5.1212 | 0.3540 | 0.7667 | 0.3076 | 0.2010 | 1.9578 | 11.1572 | 2.8827 | 17.9467 |
| Reactive | 3.5714 | 0.6952 | 0.6508 | 0.4187 | 0.4266 | -2.2485 | -6.8107 | -2.0417 | -7.2462 |
| *F*-statistic | 58.3135 | 41.9754 | 9.7502 | 32.8588 | 34.4205 | 13.0382 | 19.7991 | 14.1864 | 25.0186 |
| (*p*-value) | (0.0000)*** | (0.0000)*** | (0.0000)*** | (0.0000)*** | (0.0000)*** | (0.0000)*** | (0.0000)*** | (0.0000)*** | (0.0000)*** |
| Welch (*p*-value) | (0.0000)*** | (0.0000)*** | (0.0001)*** | (0.0000)*** | (0.0000)*** | (0.0000)*** | (0.0000)*** | (0.0000)*** | (0.0000)*** |

**Notes**: *p*-value for the coefficient is within parentheses; ***, ** and * are significant at 1%, 5%, and 10% respectively; Pro-active is applied in Malaysia; Minimalist is applied in Bahrain, Kuwait, Qatar and UAE; Interventionist is applied in Pakistan; Passive is applied in Saudi Arabia; Reactive is applied in UK and Thailand. As the sample sizes were unequal and most of Levene's tests were significant, robust tests of equality of means (Welch) were conducted.

*F*-statistic of 9.75 with a *p*-value of 0.00 and a Welch (*p*-value) of 0.00 by comparing the average SSB educational qualification for the five models. The highest SSB educational qualification, on average, is 0.79 adopted by IBs in jurisdictions adopting Minimalist model, followed by 0.76 and 0.73 for IBs in jurisdictions adopting Passive and Pro-active models.

As shown in Table 10, the ANOVA test reported an *F*-statistic of 32.85 with a *p*-value of 0.00 and a Welch (*p*-value) of 0.00 by comparing the average SSB reputation for the five models. This implies a significant difference in SSB reputation for the five models. Therefore, the conclusion drawn is that the SG regulatory framework does have a significant impact on SSB reputation at 1 per cent level of confidence. Table 10 shows that Pro-active model exhibited the lowest SSB reputation of 0.09 as compared to the other models supporting the findings of Nomran *et al.* (2018) who report that the percentage of reputable SSBs scholars for IBs under Pro-active model is very small, which is only 0.07 on average. This huge gap in the modest appearance of reputable scholars in the SSBs of IBs under Pro-active model can be justified as a result of the effective and strict restriction of cross-membership of scholars by the respective authorities in Malaysia, the country that adopts this extreme model, which may prevent having more external reputable scholars.

The ANOVA test also exhibited an *F*-statistic of 34.42 with a *p*-value of 0.00 and a Welch (*p*-value) of 0.00 by comparing the average SSB expertise for the five models. The highest SSB expertise, on average, is 0.61 and 0.60 adopted by IBs in jurisdictions adopting Interventionist and Pro-active models. In contrast, the lowest SSB expertise is 0.20 and 0.26 adopted by IBs in jurisdictions adopting Passive and Minimalist models i.e., GCC countries with the exception of Oman.

Finally, the ANOVA test reported a *p*-value of 0.00 and a Welch (*p*-value) of 0.00 by comparing the average performance in terms of all the four measurements (ROA, ROE, ROIAA, and ROIAE) for the five models. As shown in Table 10, IBs in jurisdictions adopting Reactive model report the lowest performance (negative) as compared to the other models. However, from Table 10, the highest performance, on average, is reported by IBs in jurisdictions adopting Passive model followed by Pro-active and Interventionist models, respectively.

## 5.4 Independent t-*Test* of IBs in Jurisdictions with Restriction on SSB Cross-Membership

Table 11 shows the independent t-*test* results of the comparison of the research variables average for the IBs in jurisdictions that restrict the SSB cross-membership vs. those with no restriction.

As Table 11 presents, IBs in jurisdictions that restrict the SSB cross-membership have exhibited mean SSB size and educational qualification of 3.57 and 0.66, slightly and significantly lower compared to mean of 3.87 and 0.77 for its counterparts in jurisdictions with no restriction. Table 11 also suggests that, on average, the presence of the scholars with cross-membership of IBs in jurisdictions that restrict the SSB cross-membership (0.47) is significantly lower than those observed for IBs in jurisdictions with no restriction (0.66). Similarly, on average, the presence of SSB reputable scholars of IBs in jurisdictions that restrict the SSB cross-membership (0.09) is significantly lower than those observed for IBs in jurisdictions with no restriction (0.36). This is not surprising as the restriction resolution on the SSB cross-membership in some jurisdictions also indirectly poses restricting the appearance of reputable scholars in SSBs across IBs as the SSB cross-membership is common among reputable scholars. The top 20 scholars have 621 board membership for more than 14 countries including the GGC countries, Malaysia, Pakistan, UK and Sudan (Ünal, 2011).

In contrast, Table 11 presents that, on average, the presence of the scholars with expertise for IBs in jurisdictions that restrict the SSB cross-membership (0.46) is significantly higher than those observed for IBs in jurisdictions with no restriction (0.26). This may indicate that jurisdictions that restrict the SSB cross-membership also encourage IBs to give the priority of SSB scholars' selection to those with expertise.

*Table 11. Independent t-test of SSB characteristics and performance variables for IBs in jurisdictions that restrict the SSB cross-membership vs. those with no restriction*

| Variables | Mean | | |
|---|---|---|---|
| | IBs with restriction on the SSB cross-membership | IBs with no restriction on the SSB cross-membership | t-statistics (p-value) |
| **SSB Characteristics** | | | |
| SSB-SIZE | 3.5714 | 3.8769 | -2.3710 (0.0182)** |
| SSB-CRMEMB | 0.4729 | 0.6642 | -6.5393 (0.0000)*** |
| SSB-DQ | 0.6665 | 0.7707 | -4.2638 (0.0000)*** |
| SSB-REPUT | 0.0919 | 0.3687 | -13.0991 (0.0000)*** |
| SSB-EXPER | 0.4644 | 0.2635 | 7.5221 (0.0000)*** |
| **Financial Performance** | | | |
| ROA | 0.9367 | 0.2479 | 1.6153 (0.1070) |
| ROE | 9.8041 | 7.7683 | 0.8179 (0.4140) |
| ROIAA | 1.3592 | 0.5581 | 1.9512 (0.0518)* |
| ROIAE | 12.8026 | 9.6444 | 1.1630 (0.2454) |

**Notes**: *p*-value for the coefficient is within parentheses; ***, ** and * are significant at 1%, 5%, and 10% respectively.

Table 11 also shows that all the financial performance variables (ROA, ROE, ROIAA, and ROIAE) of IBs in jurisdictions that restrict the SSB cross-membership are much more (average: 0.9367, 9.8041, 1.3592, and 12.8026) than those in jurisdictions with no restriction (average: 0.2479, 7.7683, 0.5581, and 9.6444). However, the difference is only significant in terms of ROIAA at the 10 per cent level of confidence while the differences in ROA, ROE, and ROIAE are not significant.

## 5.5 Independent t-*Test* of IBs Under CSGM vs. DSGM *Shari'ah* Governance Structure Models

Table 12 depicts the independent t-*test* results of the comparison of the research variables average for the IBs in jurisdictions adopting CSGM vs. those adopting DSGM.

Table 12 shows that IBs in jurisdictions adopting CSGM have exhibited mean SSB size, educational qualification and reputation of 3.56, 0.68 and 0.19, slightly and significantly lower compared to mean of 4.00, 0.78 and 0.30 for its counterparts in jurisdictions adopting DSGM. Apparently, it is logical for IBs under CSGM to have lower SSB size compared to those operating under DSGM due to the fact that CSGM provides external additional *Shari'ah* supervision, and then the demand for more scholars in SSBs for IBs in jurisdictions adopting this model would decrease. In contrast, IBs in jurisdictions adopting CSGM have exhibited mean SSB expertise of 0.47, significantly much higher compared to mean of 0.16 for those in jurisdictions adopting DSGM.

Finally, Table 12 also shows that the financial performance variables (ROE and ROIAE) of IBs in jurisdictions adopting CSGM are significantly much more (average: 8.2765 and 10.3155) than those in jurisdictions adopting DSGM (average: 5.8183 and 7.6332). Similarly, the financial performance variables (ROA and ROIAA) of IBs in jurisdictions adopting CSGM are much more (average: 0.7769 and 1.0041) than those in jurisdictions adopting DSGM (average: 0.6571 and 0.9449) but not significant.

*Table 12. Independent t-test of SSB Characteristics and performance variables for IBs under CSGM vs. DSGM models*

| Variables | Mean | | |
|---|---|---|---|
| | **IBs under CSGM** | **IBs under DSGM** | **t-statistics (p-value)** |
| **SSB Characteristics** | | | |
| SSB-SIZE | 3.5656 | 4.0052 | -3.6779 (0.0003)*** |
| SSB-CRMEMB | 0.5665 | 0.5833 | -0.5372 (0.5913) |
| SSB-DQ | 0.6833 | 0.7834 | -4.2840 (0.0000)*** |
| SSB-REPUT | 0.1968 | 0.3023 | -4.3718 (0.0000)*** |
| SSB-EXPER | 0.4740 | 0.1694 | 13.1207 (0.0000)*** |
| **Financial Performance** | | | |
| ROA | 0.7769 | 0.6571 | 0.4878 (0.6259) |
| ROE | 8.2765 | 5.8183 | 2.1826 (0.0295)** |
| ROIAA | 1.0041 | 0.9449 | 0.2247 (0.8223) |
| ROIAE | 10.3155 | 7.6332 | 1.9814 (0.0481)** |

**Notes**: *p*-value for the coefficient is within parentheses; ***, ** and * are significant at 1%, 5%, and 10% respectively; CSGM: Centralized SG model; DSGM: Decentralized SG model.

## 6. CONCLUSION AND IMPLICATIONS

Unlike CBs, IBs operate based on *Shari'ah* and profit-motive principle therefore they must ensure that all their activities are compliant with *Shari'ah.* As a result of this, the CG structure of IBs differ from that of CBs as IBs have additional internal governance mechanism i.e., SSB besides the BoD. Parallel with the rapid growth of Islamic banking, supervisory authorities across jurisdictions in which IBs operate have developed different SG regulatory systems to regulate the Islamic banking. However, these different SG regulation practices across jurisdictions still require further evaluation in order to be improved. Given this, the current chapter discusses four key issues related to the differences across jurisdictions in adopting various SG regulatory practices. The discussion is supported by descriptive analysis in which the authors test for differences in means of selected SSB characteristics and financial performance between samples of IBs across 14 countries that reflect diverse regulatory environments related to the following issues.

First, literature shows that jurisdictions in which IBs operate are classified into regulated and unregulated, thereby it is argued that IBs will demonstrate higher levels of performance when they are in regulated jurisdictions as compared to those in unregulated jurisdictions. As expected, the descriptive analysis provides evidence that IBs demonstrate higher levels of performance, on average, when they are in regulated jurisdictions as compared to those in unregulated jurisdictions. In terms of SSB characteristics, the analysis shows that the presence of the scholars with cross-membership of IBs in regulated jurisdictions is significantly higher than those observed in unregulated jurisdictions IBs. A possible reason is that the SSB cross-membership is common among reputable scholars in many countries especially GCC countries. Although Bahrain, Kuwait, Qatar, and UAE are regulated countries, their SG regulatory frameworks do not have any restriction on the cross-memberships of SSB scholars.

Second, from regulatory perspective (degree of regulatory interference), SG models are classified into five models (Reactive, Passive, Minimalist, Pro-active, and Interventionist). It is still controversial as to whether the extreme or slight SG intervention of regulatory agencies is better to be applied by IBs. The descriptive analysis suggests that IBs in jurisdictions adopting Reactive regulatory model (unregulated) report the worst performance (negative) as compared to the other models (Passive, Pro-active, Interventionist and Minimalist). Under Reactive model which is applied more in jurisdictions adopting western legal regimes, there is no particular legislation to govern the IFIs. However, the analysis shows that IBs demonstrate positive levels of performance, on average, when they are in jurisdictions adopting the other models (Passive, Pro-active, Interventionist and Minimalist), respectively. Further, it is found that the differences across jurisdiction in their adopted regulatory framework affect the SSB characteristics of IBs such as board size, educational qualification, reputation, and expertise. Importantly, the differences across jurisdiction in their adopted regulatory framework also affect the SSB cross-membership. The existence of highest SSB cross-membership, on average, is found in IBs operating in jurisdictions adopting Minimalist model i.e., Bahrain, Kuwait, Qatar, and UAE, in support with the above findings. In addition, the lowest SSB expertise, on average, is found in IBs operating in jurisdictions adopting Passive and Minimalist models i.e., Saudi Arabia, Bahrain, Kuwait, Qatar, and UAE.

Third, some jurisdictions have restricted the numbers of membership of scholars in SSBs whereas others do not have any restriction regarding this issue. However, it is still questionable whether this resolution is beneficial in enhancing the effectiveness of SG supervision and the performance in IBs or not. The analysis shows that the performances of IBs with restriction on the SSB cross-membership are much more than those in jurisdictions with no restriction. Nonetheless the differences are not significant for most of the performance measurements. The descriptive analysis also suggests that, on average, the presence of the scholars with reputation besides cross-membership of IBs in jurisdictions that restrict the SSB cross-membership is significantly lower than those observed for IBs in jurisdictions with no restriction. The reason is that the restriction resolution on the SSB cross-membership in some jurisdictions also indirectly restricts the appearance of reputable scholars in SSBs across IBs.

Finally, literature classifies SG models across jurisdictions based on the supervision structure into two main models, namely, CSGM and DSGM. However, there have been extensive debates on whether the IBs need CSGM or only DSGM. The analysis suggests that the performance of IBs in jurisdictions adopting CSGM is much more than those in jurisdictions adopting DSGM. In addition, it is found that the differences across jurisdiction in their adopted SG structure model (CSGM vs. DSGM) affect the SSB characteristics of IBs such as size, educational qualification, reputation, and expertise. The analysis shows that the mean of SSB size in jurisdictions adopting CSGM is slightly lower than those in jurisdictions adopting DSGM. This difference in SSB size across the two models can be explained because CSGM provides external additional *Shari'ah* supervision, and then the demand for more scholars to sit in SSBs for IBs in jurisdictions adopting this model would decrease.

Turning to the implications of this research, it is a useful source of information that provides relevant guidelines for improving SG practices and regulations for Islamic banking across diverse regulatory environments. First, for unregulated jurisdictions in which IBs operate, they should adopt suitable SG regulatory framework as an important element to enhance the performance of IBs, and then the prosperity of Islamic banking industry. To adopt a suitable SG regulatory model, they may benefit from the existing three regulated models (Pro-active, Interventionist, and Minimalist) either by adopting the most extreme intervention of regulatory agencies i.e., Pro-active model or creating a new model that benefits from the strengths and drawbacks points of the three regulated models.

Second, for both regulated and unregulated jurisdictions, they should restrict the cross-membership of SSB scholars across IFIs at the same time, and this is required more for jurisdictions adopting Minimalist model i.e., Bahrain, Kuwait, Qatar, and UAE. Third, for jurisdictions adopting Passive and Minimalist models i.e., Saudi Arabia, Bahrain, Kuwait, Qatar, and UAE, they should give the priority of SSB scholars' selection to those with expertise in accounting/economic/finance knowledge besides *Shari'ah*. Fourth, in terms of *Shari'ah* supervision model, for both regulated and unregulated jurisdictions, it is better for them to adopt CSGM as a suitable model to enhance the performance of IBs as compared to DSGM.

However, no regression analysis has been provided in this research to examine the relationships between SG mechanism and the performance of IBs across diverse regulatory environments, including the discussed issues, as suggested by literature (Nomran et al., 2018), therefore this is the main limitation of this research. Besides this limitation, the analysis did not use non-financial performance due to the lack of data. Further, consistency of *Fatawa* and disclosure issues were not examined in the analysis. Thus, further research works should take these points into consideration.

## Classifications

JEL Classification: G21, G34, G38
KAUJIE Classification: L22, L33, T4

## REFERENCES

Abd Razak, A. H. (2018). Centralisation of corporate governance framework for Islamic financial institutions: Is it a worthy cause? *ISRA International Journal of Islamic Finance*, *10*(1), 36–51. doi:10.1108/IJIF-08-2017-0020

Abdelsalam, O., Dimitropoulos, P., Elnahass, M., & Leventis, S. (2016). Earnings management behaviors under different monitoring mechanisms: The case of Islamic and conventional banks. *Journal of Economic Behavior & Organization*, *132*(1), 155–173. doi:10.1016/j.jebo.2016.04.022

Abdullah, W. A. W., Percy, M., & Stewart, J. (2014). Corporate governance disclosure practices of Islamic banks: the case of Islamic banks in the Southeast Asian and the Gulf cooperation council region. In *Journal of International Accounting Research (JIAR) Conference proceedings*, The Hong Kong Polytechnic University, Hong Kong.

Abdurrouf, M. A. (2011). The relationship between corporate governance and value of the firm in developing countries: Evidence from Bangladesh. *The International Journal of Applied Economics and Finance*, *5*(3), 237–244. doi:10.3923/ijaef.2011.237.244

Ahmed, H. (2011). *Shari'ah* Governance Regimes for Islamic Finance: Types and Appraisal-I regimi di governance conformi alla *shari'ah* nella finanza islamica: tipologia e valutazione. *Economia Internazionale/International Economics, 64*(4), 393-412.

Ahmed, H. (2014). Islamic Banking and *Shari'ah* Compliance: A Product Development Perspective. *Journal of Islamic Finance*, *3*(2), 15–29. doi:10.12816/0025102

AI-Abdullatif. S. A. (2007). *The application of the AAOIFI accounting standards by the Islamic banking sector in Saudi Arabia* (Doctoral dissertation). Durham University, UK.

Al-Amine, M. A. B. M. (2011). *Global Sukūk and Islamic Securitization Market: Financial Engineering and Product Innovation*. Boston, MA: Brill.

Al-Nasser Mohammed, S. A. S., & Muhammed, J. (2017). The relationship between agency theory, stakeholder theory and Shari'ah supervisory board in Islamic banking: An attempt towards discussion. *Humanomics*, *33*(1), 75–83. doi:10.1108/H-08-2016-0062

Alam, N. (2013). Impact of banking regulation on risk and efficiency in Islamic banking. *Journal of Financial Reporting and Accounting*, *11*(1), 29–50. doi:10.1108/JFRA-03-2013-0010

Alam, N., Zainuddin, S. S. B., & Rizvi, S. A. R. (2019). Ramifications of varying banking regulations on performance of Islamic Banks. *Borsa Istanbul Review*, *19*(1), 49–64. doi:10.1016/j.bir.2018.05.005

Alkhamees, A. (2013). The impact of *Shari'ah* governance practices on *Shari'ah* compliance in contemporary Islamic finance. *Journal of Banking Regulation*, *14*(2), 134–163. doi:10.1057/jbr.2012.12

Alman, M. (2012). *Shari'ah* Supervisory Board Composition Effects on Islamic Banks' Risk-Taking Behavior. *Journal of Banking Regulation*, *14*(1), 134–163.

Almutairi, A. R., & Quttainah, M. A. (2017). Corporate governance: Evidence from Islamic banks. *Social Responsibility Journal*, *13*(3), 601–624. doi:10.1108/SRJ-05-2016-0061

Ashraf, S., Robson, J., & Sekhon, Y. (2015). Consumer trust and confidence in the compliance of Islamic banks. *Journal of Financial Services Marketing*, *20*(2), 133–144. doi:10.1057/fsm.2015.8

Bakar, M. D. (2016). *Shari'ah Minds in Islamic Finance*. Kuala Lumpur, Malaysia: Amanie Media.

Ben Bouheni, F., & Ammi, C. (2015). Banking Governance: What's Special About Islamic Banks? *Journal of Applied Business Research*, *31*(4), 1621–1630. doi:10.19030/jabr.v31i4.9341

Ben Zeineb, G., & Mensi, S. (2018). Corporate governance, risk and efficiency: Evidence from GCC Islamic banks. *Managerial Finance*, *44*(5), 551–569. doi:10.1108/MF-05-2017-0186

Besar, M. H. A., Sukor, M. E. A., Muthalib, N. A., & Gunawa, A. Y. (2009). The practice of Shari'ah review as undertaken by Islamic banking sector in Malaysia. *International Review of Business Research Papers*, *5*(1), 294–306.

CIBAFI. (2017). *Corporate Governance Practices in Islamic Banks 2017* (General Council for Islamic Banks and Financial Institutions and The World Bank Group). Retrieved June 04, 2019, from http://cibafi.org/ControlPanel/Documents/Library/Pdf/CorporateGovernancePracticesinIslamicBanks2017.pdf

Dusuki, A. W. (2006). Corporate governance and stakeholder management: An Islamic perspective. In *National Seminar in Islamic Banking and Finance,* KUIM, Nilai, Aug. 20-30.

Farook, S., Hassan, K., & Lanis, R. (2011). Determinants of corporate social responsibility disclosure: The case of Islamic banks. *Journal of Islamic Accounting and Business Research*, *2*(2), 114–141. doi:10.1108/17590811111170539

Farook, S., & Lanis, R. (2007). Banking on Islam? Determinants of corporate social responsibility disclosure. *Advances in Islamic Economics and Finance*, *1*, 217–247.

NathanGaras, S. (2012). The conflicts of interest inside the *Shari'a* supervisory board. *International Journal of Islamic and Middle Eastern Finance and Management*, *5*(2), 88–105. doi:10.1108/17538391211233399

Ghayad, R. (2008). Corporate governance and the global performance of Islamic banks. *Humanomics*, *24*(3), 207–216. doi:10.1108/08288660810899368

Ginena, K., & Hamid, A. (2015). The Shari'ah Supervisory board. In *Foundations of Shari'ah Governance of Islamic Banks*. Chichester, UK: John Wiley & Sons.

Grais, W., & Pellegrini, M. (2006a). *Corporate governance and Shari'ah compliance in institutions offering Islamic financial services*. (4054), World Bank policy working paper.

Grais, W., & Pellegrini, M. (2006b). *Corporate governance in institutions offering Islamic financial services: issues and options. (4052)*. World Bank Publications. doi:10.1596/1813-9450-4052

Grassa, R. (2013a). *Shari'ah* Governance System in Islamic Financial Institutions: New Issues and Challenges. *Arab Law Quarterly*, *27*(2), 171–187. doi:10.1163/15730255-12341254

Grassa, R. (2013b). *Shari'ah* supervisory system in Islamic financial institutions: New issues and challenges: a comparative analysis between Southeast Asia models and GCC models. *Humanomics*, *29*(4), 333–348. doi:10.1108/H-01-2013-0001

Grassa, R. (2015). *Shari'ah* supervisory systems in Islamic finance institutions across the OIC member countries: An investigation of regulatory frameworks. *Journal of Financial Regulation and Compliance*, *23*(2), 135–160. doi:10.1108/JFRC-02-2014-0011

Grassa, R., & Matoussi, H. (2014). Corporate governance of Islamic banks: A comparative study between GCC and Southeast Asia countries. *International Journal of Islamic and Middle Eastern Finance and Management*, *7*(3), 346–362. doi:10.1108/IMEFM-01-2013-0001

Guide to Making Federal Acts and Regulations. (2001). Government of Canada, Privy Council Office, 2nd Edition. Retrieved from https://www.canada.ca/en/privy council/services/publications/guide-makingfederal-acts-regulations.html

Hakimi, A., Rachdi, H., Ben Selma Mokni, R., & Hssini, H. (2018). Do board characteristics affect bank performance? Evidence from the Bahrain Islamic banks. *Journal of Islamic Accounting and Business Research*, *9*(2), 251–272. doi:10.1108/JIABR-06-2015-0029

Hamza, H. (2013). Sharia governance in Islamic banks: Effectiveness and supervision model. *International Journal of Islamic and Middle Eastern Finance and Management*, *6*(3), 226–237. doi:10.1108/IMEFM-02-2013-0021

Hasan, A., & Sabirzyanov, R. (2015). Optimal *Shari'ah* Governance Model in Islamic Finance Regulation. *International Journal of Education and Research*, *3*(4), 243–258.

Hasan, A., & Sawari, Md., M. F. (2011). Analysis on Shari'ah governance in Islamic banking: a comparative perspective. In *International Conference on Shari'ah Governance in Islamic Banking Across Jurisdiction*, Dec. 3, 2011, Inna Garuda Hotel, Yogyakarta, Indonesia.

Hasan, Z. (2011). A survey on *Shari'ah* governance practices in Malaysia, GCC countries and the UK: Critical appraisal. *International Journal of Islamic and Middle Eastern Finance and Management*, *4*(1), 30–51. doi:10.1108/17538391111122195

Hasan, Z. (2012). *Shari'ah Governance in Islamic banks*. Edinburgh University Press.

Hasan, Z. B. (2009). Regulatory framework of *Shari'ah* governance system in Malaysia, GCC Countries and the UK. *Kyoto Bulletin of Islamic Area Studies*, 3-2.

Hassan, R., Abdullah, N. I., Hassan, A., Ibrahim, U., Sawari, M. F., Aziz, A. A., & Triyanta, A. (2013). A Comparative Analysis of *Shari'ah* Governance in Islamic Banking Institutions Across Jurisdictions. *ISRA Research Paper*, 50, 1-63.

Hussien, M. E., Alam, M. M., Murad, M. W., & Wahid, A. N. (2019). The Performance of Islamic Banks during the 2008 Global Financial Crisis: Evidence from the Gulf Cooperation Council Countries. *Journal of Islamic Accounting and Business Research*, *10*(3), 407–420. doi:10.1108/JIABR-01-2017-0011

Islamic, C. L. R. (2016). *An Annual Publication Assessing the Key Issues and Trends in Islamic Commercial Law for the Broader Islamic Finance Industry*. Produced by ISRA & Thomson Reuters.

Kammer, M. A., Norat, M. M., Pinon, M. M., Prasad, A., Towe, M. C. M., & Zeidane, M. Z. (2015). *Islamic Finance: Opportunities, Challenges, and Policy Options (No. 15)*. International Monetary Fund.

Karim, R. A. A. (2001). International accounting harmonization, banking regulation, and Islamic banks. *The International Journal of Accounting*, *36*(2), 169–193. doi:10.1016/S0020-7063(01)00093-0

Kassim, S. H., & Majid, S. A. (2010). Impact of financial shocks on Islamic banks: Malaysian evidence during 1997 and 2007 financial crises. *International Journal of Islamic and Middle Eastern Finance and Management*, *3*(4), 291–305. doi:10.1108/17538391011093243

Laldin, M. A., & Furqani, H. (2018). Islamic Financial Services Act (IFSA) 2013 and the Sharīʿah-compliance requirement of the Islamic finance industry in Malaysia. *ISRA International Journal of Islamic Finance*, *10*(1), 94–101. doi:10.1108/IJIF-12-2017-0052

Lewis, M. K. (2007). Islamic banking in theory and practice. *Monash Business Review*, *3*(1), 1–8.

Malik, M. S., Malik, A., & Mustafa, W. (2011). Controversies that make Islamic banking controversial: An analysis of issues and challenges. *American journal of social and management sciences*, *2*(1), 41-46.

Malkawi, B. H. (2013). *Shari'ah* Board in the Governance Structure of Islamic Financial Institutions. *The American Journal of Comparative Law*, *61*(3), 539–578. doi:10.1093/ajcl/61.3.539

Matoussi, H., & Grassa, R. (2012). Is Corporate Governance Different for Islamic Banks? A Comparative Analysis Between the Gulf Cooperation Council Context and The Southeast Asia Context. In the Economic Research Forum, 734, 2-28.

Mezzi, N. (2018). Efficiency of Islamic banks and role of governance: Empirical evidence. *Managerial Finance*, *44*(5), 590–603. doi:10.1108/MF-05-2017-0171

Minton, B. A., Taillard, J., & Williamson, R. (2010). Do independence and financial expertise of the board matter for risk taking and performance? Working paper, Ohio State University, Oct. 14.

Mollah, S., & Zaman, M. (2015). Shari'ah Supervision, Corporate Governance and Performance: Conventional vs. Islamic Banks. *Journal of Banking & Finance*, *58*(1), 418–435. doi:10.1016/j.jbankfin.2015.04.030

Naser, K., & Pendlebury, M. (1997). The influence of Islam on bank financial reporting. *International Journal of Commerce and Management*, *7*(2), 56–83. doi:10.1108/eb047349

Nathan, S., & Pierce, C. (2009). CSR in Islamic financial institutions in the middle east. In C. A. Mallin (Ed.), *Corporate Social Responsibility: A Case Study Approach*. London, UK: Edward Elgar. doi:10.4337/9781849802192.00022

Nathan Garas, S., & Pierce, C. (2010). *Shari'a* supervision of Islamic financial institutions. *Journal of Financial Regulation and Compliance*, *18*(4), 386–407. doi:10.1108/13581981011093695

Nomran, M. N., Haron, R., & Hassan, R. (2017). Bank performance and Shari'ah supervisory board attributes by Islamic banks: does bank size matter? *Journal of Islamic Finance*, Special Issue (2017), 174–187.

Nomran, M. N., Haron, R., & Hassan, R. (2018). Shari'ah supervisory board characteristics effects on Islamic banks' performance: Evidence from Malaysia. *International Journal of Bank Marketing*, *36*(2), 290–304. doi:10.1108/IJBM-12-2016-0197

Noordin, N. H., & Kassim, S. (2019). Does Shari'ah Committee composition influence Shari'ah governance disclosure? Evidence from Malaysian Islamic banks. *Journal of Islamic Accounting and Business Research, 10*(2), 158–184. doi:10.1108/JIABR-04-2016-0047

Oseni, U. A. (2017). *Fatwa* shopping and trust: Towards effective consumer protection regulations in Islamic finance. *Society and Business Review, 12*(3), 340–355. doi:10.1108/SBR-03-2017-0016

Oseni, U. A., Ahmad, A. U. F., & Hassan, M. K. (2016). The Legal Implications of '*Fatwa* Shopping' in the Islamic Finance Industry: Problems, Perceptions and Prospects. *Arab Law Quarterly, 30*(2), 107–137. doi:10.1163/15730255-12341319

Quttainah, M. A., Song, L., & Wu, Q. (2013). Do Islamic banks employ less earnings management? *Journal of International Financial Management & Accounting, 24*(3), 203–233. doi:10.1111/jifm.12011

Rafay, A., Sadiq, R., & Ajmal, M. (2017). Uniform framework for *Sukuk al-Ijarah* a proposed model for all *Madhahib. Journal of Islamic Accounting and Business Research, 8*(4), 420–454. doi:10.1108/JIABR-09-2015-0042

Rahman, A. A., & Bukair, A. A. (2013). The influence of the Shari'ah supervision board on corporate social responsibility disclosure by Islamic banks of Gulf Co-operation Council countries. *Asian Journal of Business and Accounting, 6*(2), 65–104.

Ruzlan, M. (2018). The role of law and Sharia governance in Islamic finance towards social justice in diversity. Thomson Reuters Islamic finance development report 2016. *Diponegoro Law Review, 3*(2), 142–153.

Safiullah, M., & Shamsuddin, A. (2018). Risk in Islamic banking and corporate governance. *Pacific-Basin Finance Journal, 47*, 129–149. doi:10.1016/j.pacfin.2017.12.008

Saiti, B., Ardo, A. A., & Yumusak, I. G. (2019). Why non-Muslims subscribe to Islamic banking? *Qualitative Research in Financial Markets*, QRFM-01-2018-0005. doi:10.1108/QRFM-01-2018-0005

Shaffaii, S. (2008). How *Shari'ah* Governance Empowers Islamic Finance. *Islamic Finance News, 5*(36), 1–3.

Todorovic, I. (2013). Impact of corporate governance on performance of companies. *Montenegrin Journal of Economics, 9*(2), 47–53.

Ullah, M. H., & Khanam, R. (2018). Whether Shari'ah compliance efficiency is a matter for the financial performance: The case of Islami Bank Bangladesh Limited. *Journal of Islamic Accounting and Business Research, 9*(2), 183–200. doi:10.1108/JIABR-01-2016-0001

Ünal, M. (2011). *The small world of Islamic finance—Shari'ah scholars and governance—a network analytic perspective*. Retrieved from Funds@Work website, www. funds-atwork. com/uploads/media/Sharia-Network_by_Funds_at_Work_ AG. pdf

Yanīkkaya, H., & Pabuçcu, Y. U. (2017). Causes and solutions for the stagnation of Islamic banking in Turkey. *ISRA International Journal of Islamic Finance*, *9*(1), 43–61. doi:10.1108/IJIF-07-2017-005

Zainuldin, M. H., Lui, T. K., & Yii, K. J. (2018). Principal-agent relationship issues in Islamic banks: A view of Islamic ethical system. *International Journal of Islamic and Middle Eastern Finance and Management*, *11*(2), 297–311. doi:10.1108/IMEFM-08-2017-0212

Zeineb, G. B., & Mensi, S. (2014). Does the PLS Paradigm Spur the Islamic Banks Vs Conventional Banks Soundness: Case of the Global Financial Crisis. *Journal of Economics and Development Studies*, *2*(3), 177–192. doi:10.15640/jeds.v2n3a13

## ENDNOTES

1 According to Saiti, Ardo, and Yumusak (2019), the stability in the performance of IBs during the crises confirmed the inherent resilience of the Islamic banking system as an alternative financial system that ensures synergy between fiscal and economic activities; therefore these unique facets are largely liable for the pursuit of Islamic financial services among Muslims and non-Muslims.

2 No doubt that the SG models and Islamic finance legislations adopted across jurisdictions play a significant role in regulating the dynamics and duties of SSBs (Oseni, Ahmad, & Hassan, 2016).

3 "*Hisbah* is referred to enjoining of evidently abandoned good and forbidding what is indecent and evil. The *Hisbah* system is run by *Muhtasib* (supervisor) whose responsibilities are to control the unethical actions in society's economic affairs. Thus, board members who are the trustees of shareholders might play important roles as *Muhtasib* by monitoring and instructing the bank's management in ensuring that the business activities are parallel with *Shari'ah*" (Zainuldin *et al.*, 2018, p. 306).

4 "*Fatwa* shopping "refers to seeking opinion and rulings by Islamic scholars on matters where there is ambiguity that a certain product or banking activity is in line with *Shari'ah* or not" (Malik, Malik, & Mustafa, 2011, p. 42).

5 For this, the effectiveness of a SSB in conducting its tasks are determined based on its members' characteristics e.g., size, doctoral qualification, reputation, cross-membership and expertise (see, e.g., Farook *et al.*, 2011; Nomran, Haron, & Hassan, 2018).

6 CSGM reflects *Shari'ah* supervision at both the institutional (bank) and the national levels. DSGM reflects *Shari'ah* supervision only at the institutional level.

7 "Regulated" means the existence of a regulatory framework (clear provisions) that regulates SG practices in a country while "unregulated" means the absence of such framework.

8 In this model, *Shari'ah* compliance is perceived at best as a reputational issue, therefore, this more flexible SG model may require the IFIs to construct their own ways of ensuring *Shari'ah* compliance and mitigating *Shari'ah* risks. Consequently, different IFIs may have different approaches of handling *Shari'ah* non-compliance issues with no final authority to decide on *Shari'ah* matters (Noordin & Kassim, 2019).

9 The amendments include: strengthened board oversight on accountability and responsibilities over SG; enhanced requirements for the SSBs in providing objective and sound advice to IFIs; enhanced expectations for the board and senior management to promote a *Shari'ah* compliant culture and further integrate SG considerations in business and risk strategies; and enhanced regulatory expectations on the quality of internal control functions to ensure effective management of *Shari'ah* non-compliance risks.

10 SSB scholars with doctoral qualifications could improve their ability to operationalize Islamic principles into banking practices (Safiullah & Shamsuddin, 2018). Further, they can have greater analytical capabilities, be richer sources of innovative ideas and policy development, and then the strategic choice of appointing such scholars improves decision-making (Almutairi & Quttainah, 2017).

# Chapter 13
# Governance and Financial Reporting of Islamic Banks:
## Evidence From Mauritius

**Ambareen Beebeejaun**
*University of Mauritius, Mauritius*

## ABSTRACT

*While Islamic finance continues to evolve at a fast pace across the globe, the government of Mauritius is undertaking various initiatives to encourage and facilitate the conduct of Islamic banking activities in the country. Examples are the admission of the Bank of Mauritius as an associate member of the Islamic Financial Services Board in 2007, the enactment of the guidelines for Islamic banking in 2008, and the hosting of the 11th Islamic Financial Services Board Summit in 2014. Consequently, through these endeavors, several stakeholders offering Islamic finance products are expressing interest to set up their business infrastructures in Mauritius. Hence, this chapter discusses the main governance and financial reporting requirements of the offeror of Islamic banking products such that potential investors are acquainted with the legal and compliance needs of an Islamic bank operating in Mauritius.*

## INTRODUCTION

Mauritius is a developing country that is located in the Indian Ocean and the Gross Domestic Product of Mauritius is USD 14 billion as at 31st December 2018 (Mauritius Chamber of Commerce and Industry, 2018). Since the country's independence in 1968, Mauritius has transitioned from a poor sugar economy into one of the most remarkable flourishing economies in Africa. This economic development is attributed mainly to a long history of political stability and good governance in addition to the growing corporate, information and telecommunication technology and tourism sectors in Mauritius. As of 31st December 2018, the tertiary economic sector comprises of 63.9% of the entire Mauritian economy as compared to the secondary sector being 19.1% and the primary sector being 17% of the Mauritian economy (Mauritius Chamber of Commerce and Industry, 2018). In essence, Mauritius is recognised

DOI: 10.4018/978-1-7998-1611-9.ch013

as an international financial centre for conducting business and acts as a gateway to Africa and Asia (BOI, 2017). Furthermore, following the collaboration of the London Court of International Arbitration, the country is well-known to be an international and regional jurisdiction for arbitration in commercial matters (MIAC, 2014).

Moreover, Mauritius is now striving to be a centre for Islamic business activities. This is because Islamic finance is evolving at a fast pace across the globe which is evidenced by the expectation that total assets involved in Islamic finance are likely to surpass US$ 4 trillion in the year 2020 (Mauritius National Investment Promotion Agency, 2014). Having recognised the potential of Islamic banking, various initiatives have been undertaken by the Mauritius government in order to develop the reputation of Mauritius as a jurisdiction for structuring Islamic banking structures such as *Sukuk* through the establishment of sharia-compliant trusts. Amongst such endeavours are the the admission of the Bank of Mauritius as an associate member of the Islamic Financial Services Board in 2007, the enactment of the guidelines for Islamic banking in 2008 and the hosting of the 11th Islamic Financial Services Board Summit in 2014. Another notable incentive of the Mauritius government is the amendment of the Banking Act 2004 of Mauritius in the year 2007 to enable existing banks licensed in the country to carry out Islamic banking business through window operations and to grant banks a specific Islamic banking licence to conduct Islamic banking business exclusively. Hence, the aim of this research is to explore and discuss the governance and financial reporting requirements of Islamic banks in Mauritius with the view of bringing transparency for potential investors that would like to establish an Islamic bank in the country and also to shed light to existing Islamic banks on their legal and compliance obligations.

With respect to the methodologies adopted, this chapter has made use of secondary data to illustrate the research work carried out. For this purpose, online materials, existing laws and regulations, newspaper and journal articles and existing studies on Islamic banking have been extensively referred to. In addition, while the introductory part of this chapter has briefly portrayed the ambition of Mauritius to develop Islamic banking in the country, the other parts of the chapter are structured as follows: the background section sets out the historical background underlying the emergence of Islamic banks in Mauritius, the literature review part illustrates the importance of having an appropriate governance and financial reporting framework to ensure the good functioning of Islamic banking activities and existing researches on this topic will be discussed, the governance structures section highlights various governance practices of different countries such as Malaysia, Bahrain, Saudi Arabia and Mauritius, the section on financial reporting distinguishes the internationally accounting standards from standards established by the Accounting and Auditing Organisation for Islamic Financial Institution (AAOIFI) and will provide the various reporting requirements for Islamic banks operating in Mauritius. Lastly, this chapter will discuss the challenges facing Islamic banks in Mauritius and the appropriate recommendations will be set out.

## BACKGROUND

The history of Islamic finance in Mauritius dates back to the year 1998 whereby a society under the name of Al Barakah Cooperative Society Limited which is an Islamic cooperative credit union, started offering Islamic financing. However, only members forming part of this society could avail of these facilities which comprise of tailor-made *Murabahah* schemes, *Hajj* savings accounts and *Istisna* financing (Gerlbard et al., 2014). Given the growing demand for Islamic finance products both from the Muslim community and the non-Muslim community, a Steering Committee was set up in October 2005 by the

Mauritius Government. Accordingly, the mandate of the Steering Committee geared at reviewing existing laws and regulations and proposing the necessary amendments to cater for a business environment conducive to Islamic finance. Consequently, proposals were made by this Committee which led to the amendment of the Banking Act 2004 and the Bank of Mauritius Act 2004 in the year 2007. As such, it is now possible for banks to conduct Islamic banking business solely or to offer Islamic banking services through window operations (Rassool, 2011).

Following the amendments made to the laws of Mauritius in 2007, the Islamic finance sector experienced the need to have its own tailor-made supervisory and regulatory regime due to its particularities which differ from conventional banking activities or financial services. Hence, a working group was established to design this regulatory framework and this has resulted in the issuance of the Bank of Mauritius Guidelines for Institutions Conducting Islamic Banking Business in 2008 (BOM Guidelines) under Section 100 of the Banking Act 2004. Furthermore, in 2009, the amendments made to the Value Added Tax Act 1998 and the Public Debt Management Act 2008 now empowers the government of Mauritius to issue sovereign *Sukuk* and to exempt *Murabahah* transactions from double taxation (Rassool, 2018). Also, the Bank of Mauritius issued an exclusive Islamic banking licence to Century Banking Corporation in 2011 and HSBC and recently, the State Bank of Mauritius has started offering Islamic financial products to its global clients through window operations. Consequently, all these Islamic Banking Institutions (IBIs) and other potential IBIs have to follow certain prescribed requirements especially in terms of governance and financial reporting.

## LITERATURE REVIEW

This part of the chapter will emphasise on the importance of having a sound and appropriate governance and financial reporting framework and mechanism to ensure the smooth running of Islamic banking activities. For this purpose, existing studies on this topic are referred to in this section.

Good governance is the underlying foundation for the success of any institution, and it is a key element on which banks and financial institutions are built on (Rahahleh et al., 2019). In this regard, the establishment of a proper governance system for IBIs is a vital attempt that ensures the protection of these IBIs and also to ensure that their business activities are in accordance with Islamic principles or *Shari'ah* law. Consequently, *Shari'ah* governance in the Islamic financial sector encompasses two elements, the first one being a formal system of accountability from senior management to shareholders and the second one relates to the formal and informal interactions and dealings that involve the IBIs and various stakeholders such as the society (Hassan, 2019). Furthermore, Malekian and Daryaei (2018) highlight that a good system of governance encourages stability in the sense that a robust management framework helps to prevent corporate scandals, fraud, civil and criminal liability of the organisation. This will in turn guarantee justice, accountability, truthfulness, transparency and protection of minorities.

While *Shari'ah* governance includes ethical principles which are taken from corporate governance practices, it goes a step further in order to entrench Islamic principles such as the prohibition of *Riba* (interest). Yet, there are a few critics that *Shari'ah* governance for IBIs is inspired by the western system and does not emanate from sound Islamic practices (Siswantoro, 2012). As such, there is a dire need for a *Shari'ah* governance framework to comprise of *Shari'ah* law supervision by highly qualified individuals specialised in this domain who will be able to advise the board, carry out *Shari'ah* audit and review the implementation of *Shari'ah* law as well. As a result, this will ensure proper practice within an IBI since it is imperative to safeguard the interests and rights of stakeholders generating satisfaction and boosting customers' confidence (Zain & Shafii, 2018).

Given that *Shari'ah* governance comprises of values such as responsibility, accountability, transparency, fairness and justice, this begs the question as to whether *Shari'ah* governance helps in enhancing the performance of firms. In this respect, Mollah and Zaman (2015) conducted a study on the relationship between *Shari'ah* supervision which includes the *Shari'ah* Committee's supervisory or advisory role, on firm's performance. The authors made use of accounting ratios to conclude that *Shari'ah* supervision boosts the profitability of the company. This result concurs with the findings of Musibah (2014) who found that the Return on Assets and Return on Equity were each found to be a significant mediating factor for the relationship between capital employees' efficiency, structure capital efficiency and corporate social responsibility in Islamic banks.

Once a system of *Shari'ah* governance is in place, it is vital to continuously review this system for further enhancement. In other words, *Shari'ah* auditing is imperative to ensure good governance. In this regard, Zain and Shafii (2018) investigated on the impact of *Shari'ah* audit on firm's performance. The findings were derived from the bank's financial statements, organisational structures, systems and processes and it was concluded that there is a positive correlation between *Shari'ah* audit and firm performance. The results imply that internal audit is important because it is closely associated with the financial report which illustrates firm's performance. Likewise, *Shari'ah* audit provides signal to management as to whether the work is being carried out as initially planned and whether amendments are required. Contrarily, a lack of *Shari'ah* audit may cause loss of confidence in IBIs.

In addition to *Shari'ah* auditing, risk management is also perceived to be a crucial factor for the performance and success of banks (Khalid & Amjad, 2018). Essentially, several studies conducted in the past reveal that the most common risk in IBIs relate to the risk of non-compliance with *Shari'ah* principles (Ginena, 2017). In fact, *Shari'ah* risk is defined as a form of operational risk because there is always the risk of financial losses that IBIs may experience due to their involvement in such activities that do not follow the norms of Islamic principles which are determined by either the *Shari'ah* committee of the respective IBIs or the relevant authority of each country (Samah & Hassan, 2016). Consequently, *Shari'ah* risk entails the risk of financial loss since this reflects the integrity level of the organisation. In fact, Rosman and Rahman (2018) conducted a research on the link between *Shari'ah* risk and the theory of financial intermediation. The results showed that failure to manage risk would reduce confidence among stakeholders and tarnish the reputation of the Islamic financial institution on the market. This in turn decreases profitability and customer base of the respective IBIs.

While *Shari'ah* governance ensures that Islamic principles are being complied with, it is also imperative to communicate to shareholders and other stakeholders the manner in which governance is carried out. Hence, some scholars such as Bahari and Baharudin (2016) support the view that the harmonisation of *Shari'ah* governance rules is necessary in order to ensure a high level of transparency as well as to increase confidence and protect the rights and interests of both the IBIs and stakeholders. Basically, a proper system of reporting reduces the information asymmetry between shareholders and executives. For instance, shareholders, the government and the public are always concerned regarding the use of their funds by IBIs and on the results of their investment decisions (Haqqi, 2014). Additionally, the concept of reporting and transparency lies at the core of Islamic principles and to attain this transparency, IBIs have to report true and accurate information on transaction or activities carried out by the organisation as well as on the cost of capital, reputation, investors' decision and share prices. In this regard, Lahrech et al. (2017) analysed the relationship between transparency level and the profitability of investment account holders. The result indicated that there is a significant positive effect of transparency on financial performance. In other words, a high level of disclosure contributes to better governance and eventually, this boosts the profitability level of IBIs and investor's confidence.

In brief, this literature review part provides an overview of existing researches carried out on the importance of having an appropriate *Shari'ah* governance and reporting framework. It is noted that the majority of studies demonstrate that *Shari'ah* governance and reporting each have a positive impact on the IBI's financial performance, as illustrated in Figure 1 below:

The above Figure 1 shows that by establishing a *Shari'ah* committee which comprises of highly qualified professionals and a constant review or monitoring of an IBI's activities, the profitability level of the IBI increases. Also, it is imperative to manage *Shari'ah* risks to maintain investor's confidence in Islamic financial institutions. Moreover, a proper system of financial reporting and disclosure to relevant parties ensures profitability and by harmonising both *Shari'ah* rules and reporting standards, there is enhanced transparency which in turn reassures investor's confidence in Islamic banking activities. The following section aims at analysing in depth the various parties and concepts involved in the governance structure and financial reporting framework of an IBI.

## GOVERNANCE STRUCTURES

Governance is a concept which is not new to Islam. In fact, over the years, in various parts of the *Qur'an* and *Hadiths*, Islamic principles are found to underlie the basics of accountability, transparency and trustworthiness (Shanmuguam et al., 2006). Basically, statutory governance in Islam obliges Islamic financial institutions to abide by a set of rules derived from the *Qur'an* and *Hadith* known as the Islamic law or *Shari'ah*. For instance, it is an Islamic principle not to engage in *Riba* (interest) in any form and ensure that the banking operations do not exploit or do injustice to the bank's shareholders. As such, IBIs have a crucial role in ensuring their banking activities comply with the principles of *Shari'ah* as well as in the monitoring and supervision of the roles of all stakeholders concerned.

*Figure 1. Impact of Shari'ah governance and reporting on performance of IBIs and investors*

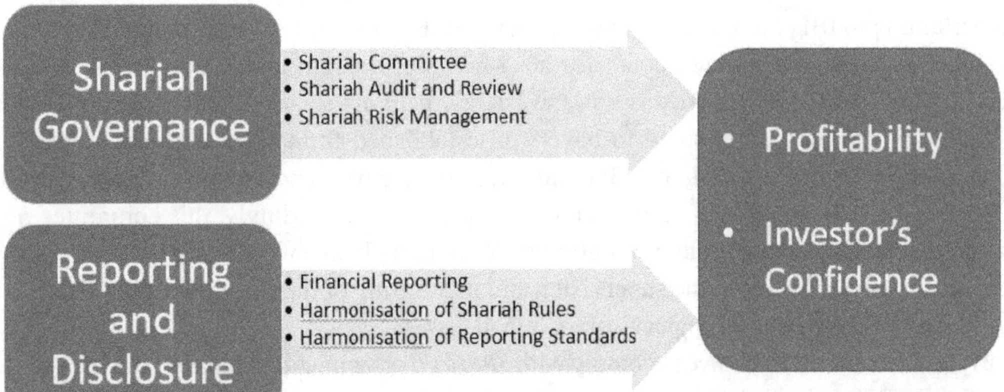

In principle, banks being governed by the *Shari'ah* laws have to abide by the rulings of the AAOIFI and the Islamic Financial Services Board (IFSB). While the AAOIFI is an Islamic international institution that establishes accounting, auditing, ethical and *Shari'ah* standards for the Islamic financial sector, the IFSB is an international body that caters for the stability and soundness of the Islamic financial services industry. Also, it is a matter of good governance to appoint Islamic scholars known as *Ulama* on the advisory board of IBIs or to employ these people for consultancy purposes (Rafay & Saqib, 2018). Indeed, the *Ulama* are playing a vital role in encouraging Islamic finance and they inspire an element of trust and confidence from the stakeholders concerned. This is because they are qualified to apply and observe *Shari'ah* principles in commercial matters. Usually, the advisory board that comprises of *Ulama* has the mandate to ensure that *Shari'ah* laws are observed by the IBIs. Hence, they do so in two steps. While, the first step concerns the review of the business activities of the IBIs to ensure compliance with Islamic laws, the second phase involves responding to queries regarding potential transactions or products that are in line with the *Shari'ah*. Furthermore, it is common practice for the advisory board to provide recommendations in all matters concerning Islamic law within the business organisation. Apart from the *Ulama*, the services of professional persons such as economists and bankers are often sought at the advisory committee's level in order to develop the existing business or to expand in new financial horizons provided that these comply with the *Shari'ah*. As such, governance within an IBI implies the collaboration of each and every one including *Ulama* and financial or marketing experts as well as an appropriate monitoring and supervisory framework to observe compliance with Islamic principles.

## Governance Practices of IBIs in Selected Countries

The agency theory lies at the core of Islamic banking and the main stakeholders involved in Islamic banking comprises of shareholders, account holders, *Musharakah* financing partners, *Mudarabah* investment account holders, employees and customers (Shanmuguam et al., 2006). As such, given the involvement of various stakeholders at the level of the IBI, agency problems are likely to crop up since the economic interests of one group of stakeholder may differ from the other and this is usually the case for the agent being the bank management and the principal being the bank's investors. Fortunately, the Islamic principles embodied in *Shari'ah* laws help in mitigating the agency problems and in turn, this helps in boosting investor's confidence and in encouraging the establishment of a sound legal and regulatory framework.

In the light of the above, this chapter will portray briefly the existing governance principles of some countries pertaining to IBIs though it is widely recognised that there is no single recognised best model of governance. As such, the selected countries are Malaysia, Bahrain and Saudi Arabia. Principally, the reason for choosing these countries is that the Islamic banking sector exists since the late nineties in these countries and they are reputed to have well-established framework of Islamic finance. For instance, in Malaysia, under the Islamic Banking Act 1983, governance requires IBIs to establish a Religious Supervisory Council including three to seven *Ulama*. Accordingly, this committee operates under the three principles mainly: the prohibition of *Riba*, compliance with *Shari'ah* and avoidance of contradictory activities. Moreover, the supervision and monitoring of the activities of the IBIs are under the responsibility of the Religious Supervisory Council.

Similarly, in Bahrain, all IBIs have to comply with *Shari'ah* principles and monitor the IBIs' activities, the board of each IBI has to conduct annual reviews and produce reports to shareholders. These reports in turn allow shareholders to express their satisfaction level regarding their investments and on the manner in which operations are carried out by the IBIs. In addition, Bahrain functions on a system of sanctions in the event that an IBI breaches an Islamic law. In principle, breaches of *Shari'ah* principles require the board of the respective IBI to find alternatives to transactions that comply with *Shari'ah* and if no alternative is found, then the existing transaction is put to an end (Shanmuguam et al., 2006). Also, if a transaction is already carried out and a breach is detected afterwards, then the income received from this particular activity is transferred to a charity account. Furthermore, the country has in place an AAOIFI that examines Islamic financial products and establishes accounting standards. In fact, the AAOIFI aims at harmonising the applications and concepts of various Islamic financial instruments across different IBIs in order to mitigate and avoid inconsistences between related practices.

With regards to Saudi Arabia, being a pioneer in the Islamic finance, the Islamic Development Bank (IDB) established by the country largely dominates this particular sector. In essence, the IDB operates like the World Bank to the effect that its main task is to encourage Islamic finance activities among member countries and the Muslim communities in order to foster Islamic economic development. As such, the IDB offers various facilities such as participation in equity capital and granting of loans for projects that are in line with Islamic principles. Accordingly, the governance of IBIs in Saudi Arabia is based on the following *Shari'ah* principles: prohibition of *Riba*, policy of non-wastage of resources, equitable sharing of risk and gains, securing due benefits or income to owners, benevolent loans and ethical and moral investments. It is noteworthy to highlight that the IDB requires commitment not only from the IBIs but also from their clients. In other words, the IDB encourage IBIs to hold training and coaching sessions with their existing or prospective clients to deal with their banks in an ethical manner while providing full and honest disclosures of their business dealings.

Hence, a study of the governance structures for the above-mentioned countries reveals that it is not the sole responsibility of IBIs to practice ethical Islamic banking but a collaboration of all stakeholders involved is also vital.

## Governance Requirements of IBIs in Mauritius

As part of the governance strategy, it is a mandatory requirement under Section 20 of the Banking Act 2004 for IBIs operating under the laws of Mauritius to maintain at all times a paid up or assigned capital of not less than 200 Million Mauritius Rupees or an equivalent amount in any other currency that is approved by the Bank of Mauritius. For this purpose, the BOM Guidelines have highlighted the need for IBIs to consider the *Shari'ah* principles when dealing with financial instruments for deriving their minimum capital requirements. Accordingly, IBIs in Mauritius have to establish a governance policy framework for the conduct of its business activities. This governance policy is inter alia responsible for setting up the appropriate mechanism that ensures strict compliance with *Shari'ah* rules which is vital to ensure the integrity and sustainability of an IBI.

In addition, the BOM Guidelines make it compulsory for IBIs to adopt a code of best practices in view of upholding ethical values within the organisation while simultaneously, safeguarding the interests of its various stakeholders. Along the same lines, the governance requirements impose on the board of an IBI to clearly define lines of responsibility and accountability within the business organisation and to establish an internal control system that ensures the existence of ethical values of Islamic finance. Also, for a proper dissemination of these information, the BOM Guidelines require the board of an IBI to incorporate the internal control system in a written manual to be shared across each level of operation and to review the appropriateness of this framework in the light of current market, legal or regulatory developments.

Similar to other countries that have well-established systems of Islamic finance, the governance requirements set out by the BOM Guidelines impose on every IBI either the establishment of a *Shari'ah* advisory board or the appointment of a *Shari'ah* advisor. In principle, the *Shari'ah* advisory board or the *Shari'ah* advisor will have to approve financial instruments offered by the IBI that conform to *Shari'ah* principles and also, review the internal procedures before launching any new Islamic products or services by the IBI. In fact, the BOM allows several IBIs to constitute a common *Shari'ah* advisory board with the consent of the BOM itself. In appointing a member of the *Shari'ah* advisory board or a *Shari'ah* advisor, the following criteria have to be considered:

- The person needs to be a scholar based either in Mauritius or abroad.
- The individual needs to demonstrate high integrity, honesty and ethical reliability.
- The person needs to prove experience and knowledge in matters concerning Islamic law.

## Risk Management of IBIs in Mauritius

Risk management is of utmost importance for an entity that intends to enhance its corporate governance. Basically, the principles of corporate governance imply that risks should be kept at a tolerable level, if not completely eliminated. Consequently, banks in Mauritius are bound to follow risk management guidelines set out in the *Core Principles for Effective Banking Supervision* of the Basel Committee on Banking Supervision. In addition to the Basel Committee's requirements, the BOM Guidelines provide that an IBI has to follow the principles established by the IFSB.

Essentially, an IBI has to establish risk management techniques that conform to *Shari'ah* principles. For instance, an appropriate framework is required in order to prevent profit generation on the basis of *Riba* or transacting without any bearing of risks. Hence, a comprehensive risk management is needed which is relevant to the modes of financing which are either asset-based, profit-and-loss sharing in a partnership or joint-venture relationship or profit-sharing and loss-bearing under *Mudarabah* contracts. Alongside with managing the risks related to business operations, an IBI is required to implement a sound investment strategy while taking into consideration its objectives and interests of investment account holders. This strategy comprises of the following principles:

- A feasibility assessment of projects and Customer Due Diligence on projects' partners.
- Implementation of appropriate valuation methods for each project.
- Constant monitoring and evaluation of risks at each level of the project.
- Application of *Shari'ah* principles in projects' development.

In addition to risk management and investment strategy, the BOM Guidelines require IBIs to have recourse to *Shari'ah* compliant funds. This is because an IBI like any conventional bank needs to have an efficient system of liquidity management in order to meet withdrawal demands from clients, which is a fiduciary duty of the IBIs towards the investment account holders. In other words, the IBI will invest clients' monies in investment funds that comply with Islamic principles such as *Sukuk* (Islamic bonds) or *Ijarah* (Islamic leasing).

## Transparency of IBIs in Mauritius

Likewise, the principles of good governance, transparency lies at the core of Islamic principles which strongly prohibit and condemn concealment of evidence. Usually, lack of transparency implies the existence of unfair advantage which explains the need to hide related information. However, the BOM Guidelines makes it compulsory for an IBI to make accurate, meaningful and timely disclosure regarding the investment accounts held by clients while at the same time ensuring the confidentiality of information. These disclosures are vital since they enable investment account holders to monitor the performance of their investments and to take further actions accordingly. Viewed from the perspective of market discipline, the disclosure obligations on IBIs aim to prevent excessive risk-taking by the IBIs in carrying out their commercial activities. As such, transparency on the financial and non-financial activities benefits the stability and sustainability of the Islamic finance sector.

## Financial Reporting of IBIs

Coupled with the principle of transparency, IBIs are expected to produce high quality financial information and for this purpose, IBIs need to observe accounting principles that are globally acceptable. As such, IBIs have to develop the appropriate conceptual framework to meet their reporting obligations. Some major accounting standards setters such as the International Accounting Standard Board (IASB) has established a conceptual framework that provides guidance on both the quantitative and qualitative aspects of financial information as well as the form and particularities of financial statements with the objective of ensuring consistent existing and future standards. Hence, on one hand, while the aim of the IASB conceptual framework enables preparers of financial statements to communicate the financial information in an effective and efficient manner, on the other hand, users of these financial statements are able to avail of the necessary information in order to make informed investment decisions.

Similarly, in the context of Islamic finance, the standard setter being the AAOIFI has issued its own conceptual framework for IBIs to report their financial information. This conceptual framework differs to some extent from the International Financial Reporting Standards (IFRS) issued by the IASB and from other local General Accounting and Auditing Practices which are developed based mostly on conventional products or practices. Hence, the AAOIFI aims at setting standards that cater for the specificities of Islamic financial products and activities to enable IBIs report their transactions in a manner that complies with *Shari'ah* principles (Sori et al., 2017). Basically, the rationale behind establishing the AAOIFI conceptual framework is to produce financial statements that illustrates the rights and obligations of the relevant parties and to ensure high quality information. Indeed, the various scandals concerning human opportunistic behaviours among senior executives in business organisations have urged investors to verify the authenticity and reliability of financial information concerning their monies. As such, accounting and financial reporting standards are used as benchmark for assessing financial statements.

# DIFFERENCES BETWEEN IASB AND AAOIFI STANDARDS

To ensure the sustainability of the Islamic finance sector, it is of utmost importance to continuously attract investors and capital providers. For this reason, financial information of IBIs has to be easily understood by investors and these should be comparable across geographical areas. In particular, the restriction on interest (*Riba*) in commercial transactions is the primary reason for distinction between IFRS and the standards of the AAOIFI. Hence, while IFRS are most commonly applied across business enterprises globally, this chapter will assess the differences of the conceptual framework surrounding IFRS and the standards issued in the context of Islamic finance by the AAOIFI. Since it is not practical to illustrate all the differences between the standards of the IASB and AAOIFI, this chapter will emphasise only on the following distinctions: objectives, revenue recognition, recognition of deposits and investment account holders, classification of leasing arrangement, reserves from clients' accounts, treatment of *Zakat* and the consolidation of special purpose vehicles.

Principally, one of the fundamental differences between IFRS and the Islamic financial accounting standards is the basic objectives of accounting set by the IASB and the AAOIFI. In fact, the IASB has published its "framework for the preparation and presentation of financial statements" in 2001 and according to Paragraph 12 of the framework, the objective of financial statements is to provide information about the financial position, performance and changes in financial position of an entity that is useful to a wide range of users in making economic decisions. In other words, the IASB deems it vital for information to be reliable and to faithfully represent transactions and events that support the figures reported as assets, liabilities and equity of the reporting entity. In contrast, as illustrated under Paragraph 3.1 of the "conceptual framework for financial reporting by Islamic financial institutions" issued by the AAOIFI, the objective behind financial accounting is to determine the rights and obligations of all parties involved in accordance with the *Shari'ah* and the principles of fairness, clarity and compliance with ethics. Also, another objective established by the conceptual framework is to provide financial information that will work towards the enhancement of the managerial and productive capabilities of IBIs and encourage compliance with Islamic principles in all commercial transactions undertaken by the IBIs. Hence, it is noted that IFRS focuses on reporting the economic substance of transactions whereas the AAOIFI requires the accounting standards to demonstrate compliance with *Shari'ah* principles.

Moreover, another notable difference between the IASB and the AAOIFI standards lies in the recognition of revenue. In essence, for the IASB, the recognition of revenue standard (International Accounting Standard - IAS 18) unlike the corresponding AAOIFI standard, relies on the underlying principles of substance over form and the time value of money. To better understand the differences, a practical case scenario is illustrated here. For instance, if a bank buys a house at US$ 100,000 and sells the property to a customer at US$ 150,000, it can be said that this transaction is a sale of goods with a profit of US$ 50,000. The customer has the possibility to pay in monthly instalments over a period of 10 years. Hence, under the Financial Accounting Standard (FAS) 2 issued by the AAOIFI which is on *Murabahah* and *Murabahah* to the Purchase ordered, the profit of US$ 50,000 is recognised proportionately over the repayment period or as and when instalments are received which is contrary to the accruals concept of accounting. However, under IAS 18, the concept of time value of money is crucial to report financial information. The profit of US$ 50,000 is recognised as interest revenue using the effective method under IAS 39 which is on Financial Instruments: Recognition and Measurement. Consequently, the effective interest method amortises the cost of the financial asset being US$ 150,000 and allocated the interest income of US$ 50,000 over the 10-year period based on the effective interest rate obtained by using a calculator. Usually, under FAS 2, the AAOIFI refers to the fair value of an asset as the value that is agreed between the parties to the transaction. Uncertainty prevails as to how this fair value is determined especially in the absence of active markets or whether this can be derived from the net present value of future cash flows.

Furthermore, the IFRS and the AAOIFI accounting standards differ as to the recognition of deposits from investment account holders. Under IFRS, deposits of conventional banks are classified as liability while the AAOIFI categorise deposits of Islamic banks as equity of investment accounts and their equivalents. In this light, the AAOIFI differentiates between unrestricted investment accounts and restricted investments. The former refers to money received from investors and the IBI is free to investment those funds without the consent of the account holder which also includes the mixture of clients' monies with those of the Islamic banks. Restricted investments, in contrast, require the prior consent of the investors before the bank can mix its own funds with those of investors. Also, the investment account holders may request the IBI not to invest their monies in certain industries or sectors. Yet, under IFRS, this treatment is not recognised since the balance sheet comprises only of three elements being assets, liabilities and equity. In addition, IFRS does not attach importance to investment mandate in the sense that irrespective of how broad or narrow the mandate is, an investment account is only reported if it gives rise to a liability under IAS 37 (Provisions, Contingent Liabilities and Contingent Assets) or a financial liability under IAS 32 (Financial Instruments: Presentation).

Differences also exist as the recognition of leasing arrangement. In particular, IFRS and AAOIFI standards differ with respect to accounting for hire purchase agreement. Under IFRS, this is treated as a finance lease since the risks and rewards associated with owning the assets are in substance transferred to the lessee. Indeed, IAS 17 requires that the property be categorised as an asset while the lessor will classify the arrangement as a receivable for the rent and interest. However, under FAS 8 issued by the AAOIFI, the legal ownership of the asset is crucial and this principle relies on the fact that the legal title is transferred to the lessee only at the end of the lease period. Accordingly, the AAOIFI requires the lessor being the legal owner to record the asset on its balance sheet at the book value and account for the interest received in its profit and loss statement which is similar to the treatment of an operating lease. Therefore, depending on any of the four recommended ways the underlying asset is transferred to the lessee, the transfer is accounted for in the following manner. It is possible to account for the lease either as a transfer through gift whereby the leased assets are depreciated according to the lessor's normal depreciation policy according to FAS 8, Paragraph 27 or as a transfer through sale for a token consideration at the end of the lease term whereby this consideration is subtracted in determine the depreciable cost of the leased asset as per FAS 8, Paragraph 34.

Another difference between the IFRS and the AAOIFI standards lies in the accounting treatment for provisions and reserves. In fact, the AAOIFI FAS 11 (Provisions and Reserves) sets out some rules concerning Profit Equalisation Reserve (PER) and Investment Risk Reserve (IRR). PER refers to the amount taken by IBIs from the *Mudarabah* (capital provider) income prior to allocating the *Mudarib* (labour provider) share and this practice is done so as to maintain a certain level of return on investment for investment account holders and to increase owners' equity. In other words, the PER is a reserve built from profits before proceeding to the distribution of profits. IRR, on the other hand, refers to the amount taken by the IBIs from the income of investment account holders after allocating the *Mudarib* share. This is done in order to cater against future losses for investment account holders since under *Shari'ah* laws, if there is a loss from a *Mudarabah* investment, it is the capital provider who bears the full loss. Nevertheless, in practice, during circumstances of losses, it is witnessed that IBIs have forgone their own profits share in favour of their customers. While these PER and IRR are accounted for as reserves under the AAOIFI standards, the accounting for these reserves under IFRS differs as to whether the IBI is under an obligation to pay the investment account holders from the reserves. Also, the establishment of the PER implies that IBIs are effectively creating an expected loss provision which does not accord with the principles under IAS 39.

Regarding the accounting treatment of *Takaful*, two main and opposing practices exist. *Takaful* is a contact that collects a sum of money from a particular group of persons who agree to share risks. In case of loss to any group member, the money collected is given to that particular individual. However, to prevent any shortfall in the participant's funds, several IBIs are required to advance funds also known as *Qard*. One accounting practice is to present *Qard* as a loan measured at cost. Yet, under IFRS, there is no such thing as a loan measured at cost and it is more likely that *Qard* be classified as a financial instrument under IAS 39. Accordingly, a financial instrument is measured either at amortised cost or at fair value only.

Amongst the main objectives of financial reporting put forward by the AAOIFI is to present financial information in a manner that will help in determining the *Zakat* payable. *Zakat* refers to a compulsory sum of money that has to be given to the less well-off ones of the society in accordance with *Qur'an* and *Hadith*. Consequently, AAOIFI FAS 9 requires that *Zakat* should be treated as expenses and *Zakat* is computed on the current fair value of the entity's assets. In contrast, IAS 2 (Inventories – Measurement of Inventories) requires inventories to be measured at the lower of cost and net realisable value. Basically, under IAS 2, the fair value of inventories are not disclosed to stakeholders unlike FAS 9.

Usually, IBIs engage in some partnership agreements such as *Mudarabah* or *Musharakah* to provide funding to an entity. By structuring the arrangement through a *Sukuk*, the asset is transferred by the originator into a special purpose vehicle and the holder of interests in the vehicle assumes all the rights and obligations pertaining to the underlying asset. As such, it may be relevant for the IBI to consolidate the special purpose vehicle if the IBI has significant influence over the vehicle (IAS 28 – Investments in Associates), or joint control over the entity (IAS 31 – Interests in Joint Ventures), or control over the entity (IAS 27 – Consolidated and Separate Financial Statements). Accordingly, an IBI's assets has a different nature compared to those of a conventional bank since IBIs concentrate mostly on asset-based investments which are backed by a real asset. Conversely, a conventional bank has the tendency to keep a fixed income with very low credit risk debt securities. This results in the lending capacity of IBIs tied to the availability of tangible assets in the economy and as such, there is no leveraged credit creation.

Although each of the IFRS and the AAOIFI standards aim at presenting useful financial information, the above differences undeniably affect comparability of financial data especially in the context of today's globalisation. So as not to discourage investors and the flourishing of the Islamic finance industry, it is vital for stakeholders to work in collaboration to establish a common set of principles for financial reporting.

## Financial Reporting of IBIs in Mauritius

In Mauritius, the BOM Guidelines impose a compulsory obligation on IBIs to produce quarterly and annual financial statements in accordance with the Guideline on Public Disclosure of Information issued by the BOM. Also, the IBI is required to publish a formal disclosure that is in line with the aforementioned guideline and that provides the basis for financial reporting in terms of content and transparency. The BOM Guidelines expressly state that the IBI has to follow the principles of AAOIFI and in the case of conflicts between the Guideline on Public Disclosure of Information and the AAOIFI standards, the latter shall prevail.

Furthermore, the form of income statements of banks holding an Islamic banking licence is provided in one of the annexures of the BOM Guidelines. As for IBIs offering Islamic banking through window operations, the form of income statement still applies except that the relevant details have to be provided for in the Notes to the Accounts. It is also mandatory for IBIs to describe in the Notes to the Accounts the methods used to ensure *Shari'ah* compliance in the operations of the entity that supports the services and products being offered by the Islamic bank. Basically, the explanatory notes to the financial statements aims at enhancing transparency and improving accounting in relation to the performance of the IBIs, on the manner in which profits are calculated and distributed and on the amount set aside as PER and IRR. As for IBIs operating through a window, there is an additional requirement on them to establish a system of strong firewalls so that funds relating to conventional banking activities are kept separate from funds for Islamic banking. This is important to ensure compliance with *Shari'ah* since there can be potential intermingling of funds that include *Riba* and also to maintain the trust and confidence of investors.

Among the disclosure requirements lies the obligation of an IBI to report the payment of *Zakat*. According to Paragraph 24 of the BOM Guidelines, an IBI has to fulfil this obligation in compliance with the requirements of the AAOIFI and for an IBI operating through window operations, *Zakat* is determined based on the net assets held by the respective windows.

Due to the particularities of Islamic finance, an IBI needs to have an internal audit function in place which ensures an independent assessment of control procedures addressed to Islamic banking activities. In this respect, the terms of reference of the internal audit function has to incorporate *Shari'ah* compliance audits to be carried out with the help of the *Shari'ah* advisory board or the *Shari'ah* advisor as the case may be. For this purpose, the internal audit function will need to be comprised of professional individuals with experienced skills and knowledge to conduct the reviews. In brief, the internal audit has to cover the review of the efficiency of firewalls established, the record-keeping requirement of accounts and compliance with Islamic law. In the event that any discrepancy is found during the review, the matter needs to be reported to the Audit Committee of the IBI and the board of directors will take remedial actions as deemed necessary. External auditors, on the other hand, are appointed by the IBI in accordance with the Guideline on Transactions or Conditions Respecting Well-being of a Financial Institution Reportable by the External Auditor to the BOM. Once appointed, external auditors have the duty to work in collaboration with the Audit Committee and shall follow internationally recognised accounting standards relevant to Islamic banking activities.

## Challenges for IBIs

Despite the various endeavours which have succeeded in promoting Islamic finance across the globe, this sector is not free from the challenges. Islamic banking services are available to everyone, both Muslim and non-Muslim communities and also to the Small and Medium Enterprises (SMEs). Yet, it is witnessed that in non-Muslim countries, the penetration of Islamic banks has been slow due to regulatory and *Shari'ah* complication issues (Qureshi, 2017). Furthermore, the evolving nature of global banking puts continuous pressure on Islamic banks to develop new product or indulge in new economic activities so as to remain competitive with the conventional banks.

Basically, the issue of uncertainty is most blatant in Islamic finance. This is because IBIs are governed by their *Shari'ah* advisory board or a *Shari'ah* advisor who has the responsibility to ensure compliance with *Shari'ah* laws. While these persons are Islamic scholars that operate on an individual basis, it is noted that disputes often arise regarding practices that is permissible and those that are not allowed. This problem is accentuated due to an absence of a central authority regulating the affairs and conduct of Islamic scholars and the absence of an authority that promulgates *Shari'ah* law. Hence, the differences of opinion of Islamic scholars threaten the stability of the Islamic finance industry. For instance, some

Islamic scholars disagree with the *Bai-al-dain* practice which pertains to the sale of debt whereas in Malaysia, some scholars allow this practice. Issues also arise with respect to compliance with *Shari'ah* concerning *Sukuk* since a study conducted by a Sharia scholar has revealed that around 85% of *Sukuk* on the market are not in line with *Shari'ah* principles (Qureshi, 2017).

One of the major challenges facing IBIs is the source of finance that ensures liquidity. Compared to conventional banks that can avail of long-term finance through the issue of bonds, investment in mutual funds, contracts with insurance companies or pension funds, IBIs cannot deal with these investments since they carry interest. As such, Islamic banks find themselves in the obligation to increase their equity funds. Also, the issue of liquidity is increased due to the fluctuating nature of the prices of goods and commodities. Fundamentally, products that are offered by IBIs are based on goods and commodities and hence, any change in the price or exchange rate of these items may create a risk for the banks.

In addition to the uncertainty and liquidity issues, IBIs face legal issues since the commercial, banking or corporate laws are at times too narrowly defined and this may prohibit the scope of Islamic banking activities. For instance, in the absence of Islamic banking laws at the national level, the enforcement of contracts in courts of law may be costly and require extra efforts (Karimi, 2017). This is because firstly there is no special court that deals with disputes concerning *Shari'ah* law and secondly, courts are likely to apply the legal regimes under Common law and Civil law as opposed to *Shari'ah* law. In turn, the court's ruling may contradict the underlying basis of an Islamic financial agreement which requires the contract to be *Shari'ah* compliant.

## Challenges for IBIs in Mauritius

Considerable efforts are being made by the Mauritius government to promote Islamic finance in the country. However, these endeavours do not free IBIs from the imperfections underlying the Islamic finance industry. Lallmahamood (2014) has conducted a comprehensive study on the challenges that an IBI may face in Mauritius. According to the study, IBIs in Mauritius are likely to encounter liquidity problems which in turn will enable them to fulfil their financing commitments and meet withdrawal of deposits demands from investment account holders. This is due to the fact that apart from investments through *Sukuk*, there is a shortage of *Shari'ah*-compliant liquidity instruments or inter-bank deposits and Lallmahamood (2014) states that the Islamic banking infrastructure is less developed in Mauritius as compared to other countries.

Moreover, IBIs need Islamic scholars to sit on their advisory boards or to act as a *Shari'ah* advisor. There is undeniably a lack of qualified Islamic scholars that are well-acquainted with *Shari'ah* laws in Mauritius, which impacts adversely on the development of the Islamic finance industry. As of date, no locally based university in Mauritius offers a course or module on *Shari'ah* principles and training as well is lacking in this discipline.

On the legal front, Mauritius law is governed by the Common and Civil law. Accordingly, the enforceability of Islamic finance contracts is governed by the Mauritius Code Civil which differs from *Shari'ah* law principles. Moreover, as of date, there is no case law precedent on how an Islamic finance issue is dealt by Mauritius courts.

Furthermore, in the context of the growing Financial Technology (FinTech) industry, customers' demands are increasing in terms of faster, cheaper and more convenient and innovative services from banks. In this respect, the IFSB states that only a few Islamic banks offer Islamic FinTech services but this number is expected to grow in the near future (IFSB, 2017). As of date, no study has yet been conducted regarding the use of FinTech in Islamic banking in Mauritius, which may be a potential avenue for further research.

## CONCLUSION AND RECOMMENDATIONS

The Islamic banking industry is still at an early stage of its development in Mauritius. Various incentives and initiatives are being developed to enable existing and potential IBIs to conduct their banking activities with much ease. For instance, the entry in force of the BOM Guidelines has brought much clarity as to what is being required from IBIs in Mauritius. In terms of governance, this chapter has set out the fundamental elements that is needed to enable Islamic banks operate in a *Shari'ah*-compliant environment. This includes the establishment of a governance policy framework, adoption of code of ethics, the setting up of a *Shari'ah* advisory board or the appointment of a *Shari'ah* advisor by each IBI, the need for IBIs to abide by risk management principles put forward by the Basel Committee on Banking Supervision, the IFSB and *Shari'ah* principles, and the establishment of a framework for disclosure of information. In addition, the governance structures of some selected countries being Malaysia, Bahrain and Saudi Arabia, have been discussed.

This chapter has also illustrated the need to produce high quality financial information in the context of Islamic banking and differences between the accounting standards put forward by the IASB and AAOIFI. In particular, notable differences are found regarding the objectives of financial reporting, recognition of revenue, treatment of deposits and investment account holders, accounting for leasing arrangement, reserves from clients' account, treatment of *Zakat* and consolidation of special purpose vehicles. The chapter has also highlighted the supremacy of the AAOIFI standards for IBIs as stipulated by the BOM Guidelines, the determination of *Zakat*, the form of income statements for IBIs and the requirement of an internal audit function.

Finally, the challenges underlying the Islamic banking industry have been discussed with a specific section emphasising on particular problems being encountered by IBIs in Mauritius. It is found that there is a need to develop *Shari'ah*-compliant products in the country in order to improve liquidity of IBIs. Also, to ensure the sustainability and growth of Islamic banking, it is vital for education and training providers based in Mauritius to start offering courses related to *Shari'ah* law. Moreover, to reduce or eliminate legal interpretation issues on IBIs matters, it is advisable that a separate *Shari'ah* court be constituted with qualified personnel and the governing law for disputes concerning Islamic finance activities should be changed from Common and Civil law to *Shari'ah* law. Nevertheless, these recommendations are long-term initiatives which are costly and time-consuming and as such, the appropriate feasibility study has to be conducted while considering the particularities of Islamic finance prior to embarking on these projects.

### Classifications

JEL Classification: K10, K20, K29
KAUJIE Classification: I1, I2, L11

## REFERENCES


Bahari, N. F., & Baharudin, N. A. (2016). *Shari'ah* Governance Framework: The role of *Shari'ah* review and *Shari'ah* auditing. *International Journal of Management, 3*(1), 15–18.

BOI. (2017). *Board of Investment Mauritius.* Retrieved from www.investmauritius.com

Gelbard, E. A., Hussain, M., Maino, R., Mu, Y., & Yehoue, E. B. (2014). *Islamic finance in Sub-Saharan Africa: status and prospects.* IMF working paper WP/14/149, International Monetary Fund, Washington, DC, 1-28.

Ginena, K. (2017). *Shari'ah* risk and corporate governance of Islamic banks. *Corporate Governance: The International Journal of Business in Society, 1*(14), 25–40.

Haqqi, A. R. (2014). *Shari'ah* governance in Islamic Financial Institution: An Appraisal. *The Journal of Risk Finance, 13*(1), 13–20.

Hassan, Z. (2019). Corporate governance: Western and Islamic perspectives. *International Review of Business Research Papers, 5*(1), 2–3. Retrieved from http://industry.govmu.org/English/Documents/4_Financial%20Services_web.pdf

IFSB. (2017). *Islamic Financial Services Stability Report 2017.* Kuala Lumpur, Malaysia: Islamic Financial Services Board Publishing.

Karimi, A. J. (2017). *Challenges facing Islamic banks.* Retrieved from https://pdfs.semanticscholar.org/6ca7/fe7cd4303f716e0a54ea3fd5ad41e8e68aa3.pdf

Khalid, S., & Amjad, S. (2018). Risk management practices in Islamic banks of Pakistan. *The Journal of Risk Finance, 2*(13), 8–10.

Lahrech, N., Lahrech, A., & Boulaksil, Y. (2017). Transparency and performance in Islamic Banking. *International Journal of Islamic and Middle Eastern Finance and Management, 7*(1), 5–10.

Lallmahamood, M. (2014). Islamic finance in Mauritius: Prospects and Challenges. *Journal of Islamic Business and Management, 4*(1), 25–35. doi:10.12816/0019137

Malekian, E., & Daryaei, A. (2018). Islamic values forward into better corporate governance systems. *International Journal of Business and Economics, 2*(8), 6–9.

Mauritius National Investment Promotion Agency. (2014). *Global Assets under Management by product.* Retrieved from MCCI. (2017). *Economic Data.* Retrieved from https://www.mcci.org/en/publications/economic-data/

MIAC. (2014, January). *The litmus test: challenges to awards and enforcement of awards in Africa.* Paper presented at Mauritius International Arbitration Conference, Moka, Mauritius

Mollah, S., & Zaman, M. (2015). *Shari'ah* supervision, corporate governance and performance: Conventional vs Islamic banks. *Journal of Banking & Finance, 25*(8), 1–28.

Musibah, A. S. (2014). The mediating effect of financial performance on the relationship between *Shari'ah* supervisory board effectiveness. *Intellect Capital, 17*(10), 45–60.

Qureshi, S. (2017). *The challenges facing Islamic banking*. Retrieved from https://www.changeboard.com/article-details/15380/the-challenges-facing-islamic-banking/

Rafay, A., & Farid, S. (2018). *Shari'ah* Supervisory Board Report (SSBR) in Islamic Banks: An experimental study of Investors' perception and behaviour. *International Journal of Islamic and Middle Eastern Finance and Management*, *11*(2), 274–296. doi:10.1108/IMEFM-07-2017-0180

Rahahleh, N. A., Bhatti, I. M., & Nisman, F. N. (2019). Developments in Risk Management in Islamic Finance: A review. *Journal of Risk and Financial Management*, *12*(37), 10–15.

Rassool, N. H. (2011). Mauritius: An emerging Centre for Islamic finance. *New Horizons (Baltimore, Md.)*, *25*(180), 100–120.

Rassool, N. H. (2018). Towards establishing an Islamic retail bank in a Muslim-minority country: Prospects and challenges in Mauritius. *ISRA International Journal of Islamic Finance*, *10*(1), 35–50. doi:10.1108/IJIF-11-2017-0048

Rosman, R., & Rahman, A. R. (2018). The practice of IFSB guiding principles of risk management by Islamic banks. *Journal of Islamic Accounting and Business Research*, *6*(2), 60–75.

Samah, Z., & Hassan, R. (2016). Empirical study on the understanding of *Shari'ah* review by Islamic banks in Malaysia. *Intellectual Capital*, *8*(1), 8–18.

Shanmugam, B., & Perumal, V. (2006). Governance Issues and Islamic Banking. *Islamic Finance News*, *3*(37), 12–15.

Siswantoro, D. (2012). A critique of Islamic banks' good corporate governance report in Indonesia. *Journal of Islamic Business and Management*, *2*(2), 10–13. doi:10.12816/0004980

Sori, M. Z., Abdul Wahab, S., & Yaacob, A. S. (2017). Financial Reporting of Islamic Financial Institutions – Contemporary Issues. *Journal of Islamic Finance*, *4*(2), 4–8.

Zain, S., & Shafii, Z. (2018). The impact of *Shari'ah* governance to financial and non-financial reporting in Islamic financial institutions: A literature survey. *International Journal of Islamic Business*, *3*(2), 1–40.

## KEY TERMS AND DEFINITIONS

**BOM:** The Central Bank of Mauritius which is the regulatory body responsible for banking matters in the country.

**BOM Guidelines:** The Bank of Mauritius Guidelines for Institutions Conducting Islamic Banking Business which are issued in 2008 under Section 100 of the Banking Act 2004 and that concern the regulation of Islamic banks licensed by the BOM.

**IBI:** An Islamic banking institution to which the BOM issues an exclusive Islamic banking licence or which offers Islamic financial products to its global clients through window operations.

**IFSB:** The Islamic Financial Services Board which is an international body that caters for the stability and soundness of the Islamic finance industry.

***Ijarah***: A form of leasing arrangement which permits one party to use an asset or property owned by another party over an agreed sum for a specified time period.

***Mudarabah***: A contract between a capital provider and a skilled entrepreneur whereby the former will contribute capital to an enterprise which is managed by the entrepreneur.

***Mudarib***: An entrepreneur or a labour provider that provides technical skills and know-how to a capital provider under a *Mudarabah* transaction.

***Murabahah***: A contract under which an IBI agrees to sell an asset that is in its possession to a customer at an agreed selling price which includes a profit margin.

***Musharakah***: A contract between an Islamic bank and a customer to inject capital to an entity or to own an asset either on a temporary or permanent basis.

***Qard***: A form of loan or debt.

*Riba*: Interest accrued.

***Takaful***: A contract that collects a sum of money from a particular group of persons who agree to share risks.

***Ulama***: A person who is qualified as an Islamic Scholar.

***Zakat***: A compulsory sum of money that has to be given to the less well-off ones of the society in accordance with the principles of the *Qur'an* and *Hadith*.

## ACRONYMS AND ABBREVIATIONS

**AAOIFI:** The Accounting and Auditing Organisation for Islamic Financial Institution.
**FAS:** The Financial Accounting Standard.
**IAS:** The International Accounting Standard.
**IASB:** An International Accounting Standard Setter.
**IDB:** The Islamic Development Bank.
**IFRS:** The International Financial Reporting Standards issued by the IASB.
**IRR:** The Investment Risk Reserve.
**PER:** The Profit Equalisation Reserve.
**SMEs:** The Small and Medium Enterprises.

# Chapter 14
# Banking Governance:
## Perspective of Islamic Banking

**Mohamad Adam**
https://orcid.org/0000-0002-3984-6391
*Universitas Sriwijaya, Indonesia*

**Muizzuddin**
*Universitas Sriwijaya, Indonesia*

## ABSTRACT

*This chapter discusses governance in the context of Islamic banking. The discussion begins with various theories that underlie the concept of governance and empirical research in the application of governance. The theory and empirical research become the necessary foundation to understand the perspective of governance in Islamic banks. Both conventional banks and Islamic banks use governance as a control mechanism in providing some value addition by increasing protection of depositors' and investors' rights, facilitating access to finance, reducing capital costs, improving operational performance, and also improving the health of institutions against external/market shocks. This concept is basically in line with Chapra and Ahmed (2002), in that the primary concern in Islamic law is closely related to the idea of fair protection of the rights of all stakeholders, regardless of shareholders.*

## INTRODUCTION

A series of failures by giant global companies gave shocks to stakeholders to increase their attention on corporate governance issues. After the global financial crisis, this attention led to an increase in corporate transparency in general, especially financial institutions (Setiyono & Tarazi, 2014). Furthermore, Setiyono and Tarazi (2014) explained that disclosure is expected to reduce asymmetric information, and therefore stakeholders can control bank management risk-taking. Disclosure of governance in the annual report is an indicator of the extent to which the company tries to ensure that stakeholders have high confidence in the management of the company. Bhat, Hope, and Kang (2006) show that knowledge of corporate governance practices is a tool to assess the credibility and quality of financial information and facilitate users in estimating future conditions.

DOI: 10.4018/978-1-7998-1611-9.ch014

Corporate governance is basically about responsibilities and fulfillment to shareholders and stakeholders. Good governance is a critical element of building banks and financial institutions. Similar to conventional banks, proper governance in Islamic banks is also an urgent priority, one of the alternatives and complementary business models that has experienced significant growth, especially after the presence of the Islamic Development Bank (IDB) in 1975, this then triggered the presence of Islamic banks in several countries in the world (Rafay & Farid, 2017), for example, Dubai Islamic Bank (Dubai) in 1975, Faisal Islamic Bank (Egypt & Sudan) in 1977 and Kuwait Finance House (Kuwait) in 1977. Until 2017, global Islamic bank assets in the whole world reaches US$ 1.72 trillion, 505 Islamic banks, and 6% share of Islamic banks to total global banking assets (IFDI, 2018).

Islamic banks are, in principle, different from conventional banks. Various economic and financial policies refer to Islamic law (*Shari'ah*) which have an impact on the business model and transactions of the Islamic banking industry, some of these things such as excessive risk-taking (*Gharar*), gambling (*Maysir*), investing in "unethical business" (for example, pornography), investing in something that does not have underlying economic assets or activities, and receiving or paying interest (*Riba*). Furthermore, Islamic legal principles provide limits for banks not to invest in specific sectors (conventional banks), transfer risk, or speculate through derivatives (for example, credit default swaps-CDS) or provide or receive regular credit (for example, bonds and traditional loans).

Farag, Mallin, and Ow-Yong (2018) state is adding that the principles of finance and Islamic banks depend on two basic Islamic laws and principles: that all transactions must contain an element of risk-sharing, and that all purchases must be supported by (or based on) tangible assets. The first principle requires the parties involved in the transaction to carry proportional risks related to the business or assets to be financed; the second principle avoids the risk of establishing a debt-based relationship, where only the exchange of money for money is happening. In this way, it will promote equity-based finance and finance into activities to support real economic activity.

Accurately for Islamic banking, various parties will observe the proactive attitude of regulators so that it challenges them to improve the regulatory and supervisory framework in support of higher Islamic financial institution governance standards. Therefore, it requires a better structure in corporate governance for these institutions. The uniqueness of Islamic banks requires governance standards following their nature, and several related organizations issued such guidelines and regulations, such as the central banks of each country, the Islamic Financial Services Board (IFSB) and the Accounting and Auditing Organizations of Islamic Financial Institutions (AAOIFI).

This chapter will discuss governance based on the perspective of Islamic banks. The discussion will begin with various theories that underlie the concept of governance and empirical research in the application of governance. The theory and empirical research become the necessary foundation to understand the perspective of governance in Islamic banks, because basically both conventional banks and Islamic banks make governance as a control mechanism in providing added value by increasing protection against depositors and investor rights, facilitating access to finance, reduce capital costs, improve operational performance, and improve the health of institutions against external / market shocks. This conception is basically in line with what was stated by Chapra and Ahmed (2002), that the primary concern in Islamic law (*Shari'ah*) is closely related to the idea of fair protection of the rights of all stakeholders regardless of shareholders or vice versa, whereas, from the perspective of the Islamic financial institution. Compliance with Islamic law (*Shari'ah*) is a matter of priority (Sulaiman, Abd Madjid, & Moh Arifin, 2015).

## THEORETICAL PERSPECTIVES OF GOVERNANCE

The rapid and dynamic development of the business environment spurred various companies to undertake multiple business expansions to achieve optimal profits. Of course, to carry out these activities, the owner offers the public ownership of the company.

This concept then becomes the beginning of agency theory, where there are principals (shareholders) who delegate the authority to manage the company to the agent (management) and to act on behalf of the principal's interests. This separation raises agency problems, namely the existence of differences in interests between owners and management. The owner expects his company to grow in the long term, while management in carrying out its duties is more oriented to the short time, following the contract of the work period, and abuse of authority for personal interests charged to the company. Agency theory is the embryo of corporate governance. In general, corporate governance is the mechanism of a company managed and implemented as well as studying the relationships between various parties related to the company. Then based on this concept, multiple arrangements emerge for companies known as "good corporate governance" to protect the interests of shareholders and stakeholders. The theory explains that people or employees are responsible for their duties and responsibilities, requires good governance (Abdullah & Valentine, 2009).

Farag et al. (2018) explain that three theoretical perspectives become the foundation of corporate governance, including agency theory, legitimacy theory, and resource dependence theory. Agency theory is the relationship between two parties that have different interests related to the management of the company; for example, the owner (principal) and the executive (agent). Both parties may have different preferences. Owners may expect a high return on their investment, while company executives may expect flexibility in running the company. Owners may expect company executives not to take high-risk projects so as not to reduce their potential profits, while company executives want to take high-risk projects so that when successful, they will get an award worth it.

Differences in interests and perceptions underlie the desire of company owners to obtain enough information regarding their assets. The definition of corporate governance is a system of rules, practices, and processes carried out by the company as a framework for achieving company goals by considering the stakeholders in the company: owners, management, clients, suppliers, capital providers, the government and the general public. This system includes many things, including internal control, transparency, and disclosure.

### 1. Agency Theory

Agency theory dominates corporate governance, where good governance is often interpreted solely oriented towards maximizing value (Daily, Dalton, & Cannella Jr., 2003). The focus on value maximization means adapted to the first layer of agency theory that is often described by the benefits and desires of self-interest (Jensen, 2002). Agency problems arise because of the relationship between owner and management. Scandals in corporate governance make scientists (scholars) define corporate governance based on the perspective of problem-solving or the standpoint of corporate affairs (the problem-solving perspective or corporate affairs perspective). Also, most definitions state that internal governance mechanisms involve the board of directors and external temporary ownership structures involving market takeovers and legal systems.

Focusing on describing what good governance looks like has helped obscure the second layer of agency theory; shareholders (community agents). The second layer recognizes that companies enter into contracts with communities to create positive and mutually beneficial relationships, which, if violated, can lead to adverse social actions against the company (Walsh & Seward, 1990).

Although it can apply the main aspects of corporate governance to banks, the relevance of banks in the economic system and the nature of banking businesses make the problems involved in corporate governance particular such as the mechanisms available to deal with issues such as ownership monitoring and regulatory monitoring. The complexity of a banking business increases information asymmetry and reduces the capacity of stakeholders to monitor bank managers and activities.

## 2. Resource Dependence Theory

The next theory, resource dependence theory, was put forward by Aldrich and Pfeffer in 1976. This theory was initially developed to provide an alternative perspective for economists regarding mergers and board interlocks, and to understand the types of inter-organizational relations that have played a significant role in market failure lately. The basis of this theory is Emerson's statement in 1962 stating that power A above B came from control of the resources needed B (other places do not have these sources). So that company managers have the motivation to ensure the survival of the company and increase the autonomy of the companies they manage. The emphasis on power and careful study of the tactics available to company managers is a feature of the theory of resource dependence that distinguishes it from other approaches.

Pfeffer and Salancik (1978) developed their theory of resource dependence based on an open system perspective, which states that the environment is an essential part of determining the level of organizational effectiveness. One suggestion that they offer to control the setting is by appointing outside representatives to fill positions in the organization, primarily through the board of commissioners. Pfeffer (1973) states that changes in membership in the board of commissioners are a direct reaction to environmental change. According to Baysinger and Butler (1985), an independent board of commissioners is a crucial element of the board of commissioners crucial, which provides a source of "managerial wisdom" regarding external relations that allows the company to achieve dividend performance targets.

## 3. Legitimacy Theory

Legitimacy theory shows that companies try to harmonize their social values with the norms and boundaries set in the communities in which they operate (Deegan & Blomquist, 2006). Legitimacy can describe as a resource that a business needs to work. Legitimacy is the process of equating perceptions or assumptions that actions taken by an entity are actions that are desirable, appropriate, or per a system of norms, values, beliefs, and definitions that are developed socially (Suchman, 1995), it becomes necessary because people's legitimacy to companies, especially banks, is a strategic factor for the company's future development. Legitimacy is giving the community to the company and is the hopes and desires of the company. Thus, legitimacy has benefits to support the survival of a company. Legitimacy is a company management system, that is oriented towards the community (society), individual governments and community groups.

## RESEARCH ON BANKING GOVERNANCE

Post-crisis, many banks experienced a decline in financial performance due to the severe Asian financial crisis in East Asian countries, so various strategies were put in place by regulators to oversee bank activities. Many cases are related to weak corporate governance. Various studies were developed to evaluate bank risk-taking and become an interesting topic because of the high leverage and opacity, especially post-crisis (Chen & Lin, 2016), but many aspects have not been resolved to answer the evaluation. The empirical evidence refers to institutional problems that question the adequacy of corporate governance and regulatory frameworks for banks, even then the Organization for Economic Co-operation and Development reports that financial crises are related to failures and weaknesses in corporate governance arrangements (Kirkpatrick, 2009).

Banks as asset transformation and essential entities in the economy of a country must be able to manage capital allocation in supporting productive activities, because proper management of these allocations contributes to economic growth and stability, while governance acts as a mechanism control through a series of related activities (Laeven, 2013): a) ensure bank capital providers (depositors, debtholders, and shareholders) get a return on their investment, and; b) preventing bank managers from investing in risky projects.

Governance is a series of mechanisms that have an impact on companies to facilitate access to domestic and foreign investments, obtain lower capital costs, provide better decisions in improving the company's economic performance, increase stakeholder trust and trust in the company and protect directors and commissioners from lawsuits. Of course, based on these objectives, companies that implement governance are expected to be more efficient and their competitiveness increase, so that in the end, it becomes a sustainable company that is trusted to improve company performance as a control mechanism consists of two series, namely internal and external. Weir, Laing, and McKnight (2002) explain internal mechanisms include board structure variables such as duality and proportion of non-executive directors, debt financing, and executive director share ownership, while external mechanisms are market control mechanisms as stated by Jensen (1986) as a last resort mechanism.

Sierra, Talmor, and Wallace (2006) and Adams and Mehran (2012) investigate the relationship between governance mechanisms and their effect on company performance and value, indicating that a current board can improve bank performance, the same as research results. Adams & Mehran (2012) showed similar findings for board size but failed to identify the relationship between independent directors and financial performance. In addition to its implications for business performance, several studies also argue that weak governance leads to higher risk-taking in banks (Fama & Jensen, 1983), resulting in a higher risk of failure. Peni and Vähämaa (2011) state that studies related to governance refers to the mechanism of dealing with agency problems and risk control, the concept of which refers to motivational and constraint devices. The motivational tool is related to company executives and compensation, while the restriction mechanism refers to the role of shareholders or board of directors in the company.

Positively various studies have evaluated the influence of corporate governance factors (e.g., manager incentives, executive compensation, ownership structure, and board characteristics) on bank performance and risk-taking. These studies show different results and all focus on individual performance and risk, so it does not provide a consensus regarding the role of bank governance mechanisms specifically for risk-taking (Chen & Lin, 2016).

Several studies elaborate on the relationship between governance and financial performance. Most of these studies support the idea that there is a positive relationship between effective corporate governance. The seminal paper (Jensen & Meckling, 1976) explores the theoretical relationship between corporate governance and company performance with the approach of elements of agency theory, property cost theory, and financial theory, to develop the theory of corporate ownership structure. In particular, agency theory suggests that better-governed companies have better performance and higher valuation because of lower agency costs. Several empirical studies support these predictions. Gompers, Ishii, and Metrick (2003) found that better corporate governance was associated with higher corporate valuations as measured by Tobin's q.

Erkens, Hung, and Matos (2012) show that corporate governance has a substantial impact on company performance during a crisis through company management decisions that dare to take risks and finance policies. Furthermore, empirical findings provide clues that companies with more independent boards and higher institutional ownership experience worse stock returns during the crisis period. Even when further explored the results show that a) companies with higher institutional ownership take a more significant risk before the crisis, resulting in higher shareholder losses during the crisis period, and b) companies with more independent boards increase more capital equity during the crisis, causing the transfer of wealth from existing shareholders to debtholders.

Sami, Wang, and Zhou (2011), in their study, showed that corporate governance had a positive impact on ROA, ROE, and Tobin's q. Therefore, the regression results support the central hypothesis, which predicts that companies with overall better corporate governance will have better organizational performance and higher corporate value. Also, the regression results indicate that company size has a positive relationship with company performance and a negative association with firm value.

The global financial crisis requires a re-examination of the practices of corporate governance in banks. How secure are managerial entrenchment and the failure of the board to monitor the executive that might be the cause of excessive risk-taking and financial instability? Theoretically, there is no clarity regarding the implementation of good governance (such as the existence of an independent board), which leads to a reduction in risk-taking. However, of course, corporate governance that aligns managerial incentives with the interests of shareholders can potentially lead to excessive risk-taking, because shareholders face payments that are limited by limited obligations.

John, Sauders, and Senbet (2000) explains that CEO compensation has negatively related to bank risk. In contrast, Guo, Jalal, and Khaksari (2014) believe that the relationship between executive compensation and risk is positive and significant. Levine (2004) clarifies that ownership concentration is associated with high-risk taking, while dispersed ownership can reduce risk. In other studies, several empirical results indicate that banks with a high level of ownership have a low risk of assets and insolvency. Spread ownership and limitation of shareholders' rights in the form of voting and ownership ceilings cause banks to be ineffectively monitored by their shareholders and disciplined by the market and thus direct the bank's CEO to be stable.

According to the research discussed above, bank classification is a bank that is controlled by owners and managers through a series of corporate governance variables related to shareholders and management. Manager-controlled banks tend to have dispersed ownership and large boards, whereas owner-controlled banks tend to have concentrated ownership, small boards, and many independent directors. If the majority of shareholders manage the bank, he may suffer an increase in risk-taking. However, when banks are weak, the controllers are shareholders who may face risk reduction.

Governance is a concept that refers to agency theory, the implementation of which is expected to provide confidence to investors in their investments. The assumption is that when the company's management refers to the voting system, the results are expected to be in line with investor expectations. Furthermore, governance is a system that regulates and controls the company, which is expected to influence its resilience to risk, which in turn has an impact on financial stability.

## ISLAMIC BANKING GOVERNANCE

Along with the development of the Islamic banking industry, good corporate governance in the Islamic banking industry is becoming increasingly important to implement. Corporate governance considers the balance between economic and social goals and the balance between individual and community goals. Governance is needed to build community trust because governance is designed to protect the interests of all stakeholders. It is also in line with the primary concern in *Shari'ah* closely related to the idea of civil protection of the rights of all stakeholders regardless of shareholders or vice versa.

The Islamic system believes that the absolute and eternal owner of everything on earth and in heaven belongs to *Allah (SWT)*, and humans are only caliphs (*Khalifah*) of it. The *Shari'ah* code of ethics encourages every Muslim to apply fair, justice, and honest to everyone involved in business transactions. In other words, Islamic law provides lessons to maintain high moral behavior that prohibits betrayal, deceives, or exploits other people or natural resources and gains business profits while maintaining moral values in business. Muslims are required to work honestly to increase productivity rather than being slow and unproductive. So, whatever the system requires an ethical and moral climate, out of the climate, it is challenging to be able to influence the proper governance system.

Islamic corporate governance always links all concepts and behaviors in business governance by connecting them with *Shari'ah* rules. It is a consequence of a Muslim's faith in *Allah (SWT)*. So, from here, we know the value of monotheism as the basis for all the beliefs, thoughts, and behavior of a Muslim, including in understanding corporate governance. One of the principles which are the most significant derivative of monotheism is the principle of justice. Islamic teachings always encourage the ummah to be fair in every way, both in matters of *Aqidah*, *Shari'ah*, and *Akhlaq*[1] because of the faith and to achieve the degree of loyalty. One of the principles in implementing corporate governance is fairness, which is intended to present proper company management for each party. If it is related to *Shari'ah*, then justice must include spiritual and material aspects. Then the meaning of fair can be extended to every principle contained in Corporate Governance and other values that can raise for the implementation of justice.

The best practice in implementing good governance is to comply with applicable laws and regulations. Besides, it also continuously makes improvements and improvements in GCG management to realize the company's vision and mission. Good corporate governance (GCG) is an essential component in the banking industry, given the increasing risks and challenges faced by the banking industry. The implementation of GCG will consistently strengthen the company's competitive position, maximize company value, manage resources and risks more efficiently and effectively, which in turn will strengthen the trust of shareholders and stakeholders. The Islamic Financial Services Board (IFSB) defines corporate governance in relation to Islamic financial institutions as a set of relationships between company management, the board of directors, shareholders, and other stakeholders that provide a structure in which: 1) sets the goals of the company; 2) ways to achieve this goal and monitor the specified performance. IFG-IFDI-Team (2018) describes the governance of institutions offering *Shari'ah* financial services:

*Table 1. AAOIFI's government principles*

| Effective *Shari'ah* Compliance Structures | Fair Treatment of Equity Holders | Equitable Treatment of Fund Providers and Other Significant Stakeholders | Fit and Proper Conditions for Board and Management |
|---|---|---|---|
| Effective oversight | Audit and governance committee | Risk management | Avoidance of conflicts of interest |
| Appropriate compensation policy oversight | Public disclosures | Code of conduct and ethics | Proper enforcement of governance principles and standards |

Source: (IFG-IFDI-Team, 2018)

1) A set of organizational rules that align with stakeholders.
2) Providing appropriate incentives for government organs such as the board of directors, SSB, and management to achieve objectives that are following the interests of stakeholders and facilitate effective monitoring to use resources more efficiently.
3) Compliance with Islamic *Shari'ah* rules and principles.

Furthermore, it explains the AAOIFI governance concept, which states that there is no single measure suitable for all structures that will guarantee effectiveness or health in governance. In this case, good governance is not only a matter of determining specific structures or problems obeying predetermined rules. Besides, AAOIFI stated several government principles which include:

Central banks or financial authorities in several countries (in more than 45 countries support AAOFI) adopt AAOIFI standards to carry out Islamic finance either in full adoption (mandatory) or as a basis of guidelines. In more. One of the objectives of AAOIFI is to disseminate relevant accounting and auditing standards in Islamic financial institutions whose application is through training, seminars, publishing periodicals, conducting research, and other means. AAOIFI carries out this goal to adapt to the teachings of the Islamic *Shari'ah*, which are comprehensive in all aspects of life and following the environment in each Islamic financial institution's location. Some countries differ in adopting standards issued by AAOIFI. The countries of Bahrain, Oman, Pakistan, Sudan, and Syria have made *Shari'ah* standards and AAOIFI accounting standards as part of mandatory regulatory requirements. The Islamic Development Bank (IDB) also adopted it in full. The implementation of good governance in the Islamic banking industry refers to five basic principles:

1) **Transparency**: Openness in presenting material and relevant information and transparency in the decision making the process.
2) **Clarity**: The clarity of functions and the responsibility of bank organs so that their management is useful.
3) **Suitability**: The suitability of bank management with applicable laws and regulations, and the principles of sound bank management.
4) **Professional**: The competence and capable of acting objectively and free from influence/ pressure from any party (independent) and has a high commitment to develop Islamic banks.
5) **Fairness**: Fairness and equality in fulfilling the rights of stakeholders based on agreements and applicable laws and regulations.

Discussion regarding governance structures in Islamic banking is still small, although rapid growth has occurred in this industry since the mid-1970s (Hasan, 2009). Bibliometric analysis using Harzing software shows that there is 101 research related to the topic when entering the keyword "*Shari'ah* banking governance." However, among these articles, only 47 items have affiliations with specific journals. Of course, this shows that the amount of research on the topic of *Shari'ah* banking governance is relatively small and still needs further exploration.

Like other civilizations and religions, Islamic culture has also instilled good corporate governance since the beginning of Islamization. Islamic societies have different views and values compared to the non-Islamic outside world (Abu-Tapanjeh, 2009). Belief in the importance of implementing accountability not only in the world but after this life has implications for the lives of every Muslim. This rule becomes a way to regulate a broader scope than conventional principles. A strong belief in accountability in this world and beyond has substantial implications in every Muslim's life and governs the full range and expanded obligations of corporate governance with that compared to conventional principles.

In Islamic banking governance, there are additional items on the *Shari'ah* bank balance sheet, for example, *Zakat*[2]. Also, Islamic banks need a *Shari'ah* board. Thus, the governance structure is different. Furthermore, Islamic banks require the suitability of investment and financing to be in line with Islamic law (*Shari'ah*) and the expectations of the Muslim community. Banks are the main economic element of a country; this then makes it one of the essential players in economic growth. Islamic banks do impose special requirements on organizations dealing under the surface of Islamic transactions. One of the most critical elements is related to the existence of the *Shari'ah* council, which is responsible for ensuring that operational activities comply with Islamic rules, principles, and laws.

Governance in Islamic banking is more complex and presents more enormous challenges because of the additional risks compared to conventional banking. Hasan (2009) explains the problems, and for example, depositors will become exposed to various types of risk when Islamic banks begin to move into a risk-sharing model, namely *Mudarabah* and *Musharakah*. Therefore, every Islamic company, especially Islamic financial institutions need to have an appropriate governance framework to ensure its growth and success.

The governance structure in Islam is indeed different from general corporate governance in standardizing rules that must comply with *Shari'ah* law stated in the Qur'an, where the governance structure must meet the expectations of the Muslim community by providing an acceptable mode of Islamic financing (Abu-Tapanjeh, 2009).

Islamic corporate governance must obey a set of Islamic rules. *Shari'ah* regulates bank operations and transactions under Islamic principles derived from the *Qur'an* and *Hadith*. *Shari'ah* in Islamic banking has an important role not only in managing bank transactions and processes but also in monitoring and overseeing the function of all players in the banking system. *Shari'ah* is a blueprint and to ensure that banking procedures do not exploit or injustice the bank's shareholders.

The paradigm offered by Islamic banking is different from conventional banking and the perspective of corporate governance; it manifests some exciting features because of the participation of capital (capital participation), risk-sharing arrangements. Islamic banking offers a different paradigm from conventional banking, and corporate governance, it has several attractive features because of equity participation, risk, and profit-sharing arrangements that form the basis of Islamic financing. This arrangement has implications for relations between different stakeholders because depositors have direct financial interests in bank investment and equity participation. Besides, Islamic banking is subject to an additional layer of governance carried out by the *Shari'ah* Supervisory Board (SSB). The issue of a general agency that arises is the possibility of management carrying out their duties to maximize shareholder wealth, and the separation between depositors and investor control rights is an issue.

The Islamic governance system in Islamic banks is the structure and process adopted by stakeholders in institutions that offer Islamic Financial Services to ensure compliance with Islamic rules and principles (IFSB, 2009). Also, a fundamental feature of *Shari'ah* governance in Islamic banks is the presence of the *Shari'ah* Supervisory Board (SSB), which plays an essential role in convincing stakeholders about bank compliance with Islamic law (Grais & Pellegrini, 2006). The part of *Shari'ah* supervisors is crucial in the context of the development of the Islamic financial institution industry. Its functions and responsibilities are not only pleasing with the accountability of an Islamic financial institution, but also in terms of its management which is not only accountable to the community, but also *Allah (SWT)* as the owner of everything. Some argue that SSB influences the performance of Islamic banks; a similar idea applies to BOD because the roles of BOD and SSB are the same (Hanefah, 2018).

SSB, which consists mainly of scholars, is responsible for ensuring that financial institutions comply with *Shari'ah* rules by carrying out their functions at two stages. In the first phase, SSB reviews the operations of financial institutions to ensure *Shari'ah* compliance. The second phase discusses whether a transaction proposal or a new product is under *Shari'ah*. The Board also offers constructive and creative recommendations in all matters relating to *Shari'ah* and, besides, establishing a dialogue with economists and bankers in developing new financial products that are following *Shari'ah*. These dialogues are essential to make Islamic banking in line with market demands. Strict adherence to *Shari'ah* and conversation with funders will also help minimize agency problems, as discussed earlier. The existence of SSB makes *Shari'ah* bank governance unique. There is a dual board structure that is likely to affect the performance of Islamic banks. Research conducted by Farag et al. (2018) using a sample of 90 Islamic banks in 13 countries during the period 2006-2014 shows that the higher the SSB, the better financial performance will be. These results reinforce the fundamental role of the SSB to authorize permitted financial instruments and products. Further exciting findings also explained that a larger SSB size could result in lower agency costs, and the greater the unrestricted contract size, the higher the agency costs, this according to them, implies that open revenue sharing contracts are one of the primary sources of relationship unique agency in Islamic banks.

The governance mechanism of Islamic banks is different from conventional banks because of the nature and characteristics of the Islamic banking industry. As a result, we believe that Islamic banks have a unique agency relationship. Hasan (2009) states that the design model of corporate governance in Islam has its unique features and presents different characteristics compared to the western concepts of Anglo-Saxon and European models. Furthermore, in his study, it was stated that the elements of Islamic corporate governance became four aspects, namely episteme, organizational objectives, nature of management, management board, and ownership structure related to capital.

In the aspect of the epistemological method, Islam places monotheism as episteme while the company's goals based on the protection of all stakeholders' interests and rights in line with the principle *of Maqasid Shari'ah.* The nature of management of the Islamic corporate governance model is center on two fundamental principles of *shura* and interactive, integrated and evolutionary processes, and the highest level of control is the *Shari'ah* council, which is responsible for overseeing and overseeing the overall activities of the company to comply with *Shari'ah* principles.

*Table 2. Corporate governance from Islamic prospective*

| OECD Principles and Annotation | Islamic Principles |
|---|---|
| The right of shareholders and essential ownership functions | Property as a trust from *Shari'ah* rules |
| Promotion of transparent and efficient markets with the rule of law and division of responsibility Basic shareholder rights | Sole authority is *Shari'ah* |
| Basic shareholder rights | Society as stakeholders |
| Participation of decision making at the general meeting | Accountability not only to stakeholders but also to god, the ultimate owner |
| Structure and arrangement for corporate control | Just and fairness of value |
| Ownership rights: all shareholders, including institutional shareholders | Equitable distribution of wealth |
| The consultative process between shareholders and institutional shareholders | In the form of *Zakat* and *Sadaqah*[3] |
| The equitable treatment of shareholders | Social and individual welfare (spiritual and moral obligation) |
| Protection to minority and foreign shareholders Sensation of equality | Sensation of equality |
| The role of stakeholder in corporate governance | Islamic accountability to *Falah* and social welfare orientation |
| Creating wealth, jobs and sustainability of the financially sound enterprise | *Haram/ halal* in transaction |

Sources: (OECD, 2004); (Abu-Tapanjeh, 2009).

## CONCLUSION

As with conventional banks, good Islamic banking governance is an urgent priority, one of the alternatives and complementary business models that has experienced significant growth. Islamic banks are in principle different from conventional banks, various economic and financial principles refer to Islamic legal rules (*Shari'ah*) and have an impact on business models and transactions in the Islamic banking industry, some of which include excessive risk-taking (*Gharar*), gambling (*Maysir*), change rather than risk-sharing, invest in "unethical" businesses.

Various parties will observe the proactive attitude of the regulator towards the existence of Islamic banks, which is, in principle, different from the conventional bank business model. These observations will provide a challenge for the relevant regulators to improve the regulatory and supervisory framework in support of higher Islamic financial institution governance standards, so better structures in corporate governance for these institutions are urgently needed.

The uniqueness of Islamic banks requires governance standards that are under their nature so that they require various guidelines and standards. Some institutions issue such things as the Accounting and Audit Organization of Islamic Financial Institutions (AAOIFI), Islamic Financial Services Board (IFSB), and the central banks of each country. *Shari'ah* governance systems in Islamic banks are structures and processes adopted by stakeholders in institutions that offer Islamic financial services to ensure compliance with *Shari'ah* rules and principles (IFSB No.10, 2009). Besides, a fundamental feature of governance in Islamic banks is the presence of SSB, which plays a significant role in convincing stakeholders about bank compliance with Islamic law (Farag et al., 2018). He further explained that Islamic banks have a unique dual board structure.

Finally, proper corporate governance practices in financial institutions both conventional and Islamic banks must provide added value by increasing the protection of depositors and investor rights, facilitating access to finance, reducing capital costs, increasing operational performance, and improving the health of institutions against external shocks. Ensuring strong corporate governance standards is essential for the stability of all financial institutions worldwide. Good governance is an essential priority for Islamic finance, an aspect of international finance that has enjoyed significant growth stages over the past decade.

## Classifications

JEL Classification: G30, G21
KAUJIE Classification: I22, L24

## REFERENCES


Abdullah, H., & Valentine, B. (2009). Fundamental and Ethics Theories of Corporate Governance. *Middle Eastern Finance and Economics*, *4*(4), 88–96.

Abu-Tapanjeh, A. M. (2009). Corporate governance from the Islamic perspective: A comparative analysis with OECD principles. *Critical Perspectives on Accounting*, *20*(5), 556–567. doi:10.1016/j.cpa.2007.12.004

Adams, R. B., & Mehran, H. (2012). Bank board structure and performance: Evidence for large bank holding companies. *Journal of Financial Intermediation*, *21*(2), 243–267. doi:10.1016/j.jfi.2011.09.002

Baysinger, B. D., & Butler, H. N. (1985). Corporate Governance and the Board of Directors: Performance Effects of Changes in Board Composition. *Journal of Law Economics and Organization*, *1*(1), 101–124.

Bhat, G., Hope, O.-K., & Kang, T. (2006). Does corporate governance transparency affect the accuracy of analyst forecasts? *Accounting and Finance*, *46*(5), 715–732. doi:10.1111/j.1467-629X.2006.00191.x

Chapra, M., & Ahmed, H. (2002). *Corporate Governance in Islamic Financial Institution*. Occasional Paper. Islamic Research and Training Institute/ Islamic Development Bank.

Chen, H.-J., & Lin, K.-T. (2016). How do banks make the trade-offs among risks? The role of corporate governance. *Journal of Banking & Finance*, *72*(Supplement), S39–S69. doi:10.1016/j.jbankfin.2016.05.010

Daily, C. M., Dalton, D. R., & Cannella, A. A. Jr. (2003). Corporate Governance: Decades of Dialogue and Data. *Academy of Management Journal*, *28*(3), 371–382.

Deegan, C., & Blomquist, C. (2006). Stakeholder influence on corporate reporting: An exploration of the interaction between WWF-Australia and the Australian minerals industry. *Accounting, Organizations, and Society*, *31*(4-5), 343–372. doi:10.1016/j.aos.2005.04.001

Erkens, D. H., Hung, M., & Matos, P. (2012). Corporate governance in the 2007–2008 financial crisis: Evidence from financial institutions worldwide. *Journal of Corporate Finance*, *18*(2), 389–411. doi:10.1016/j.jcorpfin.2012.01.005

Fama, E. F., & Jensen, M. C. (1983). Separation of Ownership and Control. *The Journal of Law & Economics*, *26*(2), 301–325. doi:10.1086/467037

Farag, H., Mallin, C., & Ow-Yong, K. (2018). Corporate governance in Islamic banks: New insights for dual board structure and agency relationships. *Journal of International Financial Markets, Institutions, and Money*, *54*, 59–77. doi:10.1016/j.intfin.2017.08.002

Gompers, P. A., Ishii, J. L., & Metrick, A. (2003). Corporate Governance and Equity Prices. *The Quarterly Journal of Economics*, *118*(1), 107–155. doi:10.1162/00335530360535162

Grais, W., & Pellegrini, M. (2006). *Corporate Governance and Shari'ah Compliance in Institutions Offering Islamic Financial Services*. World Bank Policy Research Working Paper. World Bank.

Guo, L., Jalal, A., & Khaksari, S. (2014). Bank executive compensation structure, risk taking and the financial crisis. *Review of Quantitative Finance and Accounting*, *45*(3), 609–639. doi:10.100711156-014-0449-1

Hanefah, M. H. (2018). *Corporate and Shari'ah governance in public listed companies and public trust entities. Bandar Baru*. USIM Press.

Hasan, Z. (2009). Corporate Governance: Western and Islamic Perspectives. *International Review of Business Research Papers*, *5*(1), 277–293.

IFDI. (2018). *Islamic Finance Development Report 2018*. Retrieved from http://www.bitly/IFDatabaase

IFG-IFDI-Team. (2018). *Islamic Finance Development Indicator*. ICD-Thomson Reuters. Thomson Reuters. Retrieved from https://www.zawya.com/islamic-finance-development-indicator/files/IFDI-Rulebook.pdf?v2

IFSB. (2009). *Guiding Principles on Shari'ah Governance Systems for Institutions offering Islamic Financial Services*. Islamic Financial Services Board.

Jensen, M. C. (2002). Value Maximization, Stakeholder Theory, and the Corporate Objective Function. *Business Ethics Quarterly*, *12*(2), 235–256. doi:10.2307/3857812

Jensen, M. C., & Meckling, W. H. (1976). Theory of The Firm: Managerial Behavior, Agency Costs and Ownership Structure. *Journal of Financial Economics*, *3*(4), 305–360. doi:10.1016/0304-405X(76)90026-X

John, K., Sauders, A., & Senbet, L. W. (2000). A Theory of Bank Regulation and Management Compensation. *Review of Financial Studies*, *13*(1), 95–125. doi:10.1093/rfs/13.1.95

Kirkpatrick, G. (2009). The corporate governance lessons from the financial crisis. *OECD Journal: Financial Market Trends*, *2019*(1). Retrieved from https://www.oecd-ilibrary.org/content/paper/fmt-v2009-art3-en

Laeven, L. (2013). Corporate Governance: What's Special About Banks? *Annual Review of Financial Economics*, *5*(1), 63–92. doi:10.1146/annurev-financial-021113-074421

Levine, R. (2004). *The Corporate Governance of Banks: A Concise Discussion of Concepts and Evidence*. World Bank Policy Research Working Paper. World Bank.

OECD. (2004). *OECD Principles of Corporate Governance*. OECD.

P3EI-UII. (2018). *Ekonomi Islam*. Jakarta: PT Rajagrafindo Persada.

Peni, E., & Vähämaa, S. (2011). Did Good Corporate Governance Improve Bank Performance during the Financial Crisis? *Journal of Financial Services Research*, *41*(1-2), 19–35. doi:10.100710693-011-0108-9

Pfeffer, J. (1973). Size, Composition, and Function of Hospital Boards of Directors: A Study of Organization Environment Linkage. *Administrative Science Quarterly*, *18*(3), 17. doi:10.2307/2391668

Pfeffer, J., & Salancik, G. R. (1978). *The External Control of Organizations: A Resource Dependence Perspective*. New York: Harper & Row.

Rafay, A., & Farid, S. (2017). Dynamic Relationship between Islamic Banking System and Real Economic Activity: Evidence from Pakistan. *Journal of King Abdulaziz University. Islamic Economics*, *30*(2), 97–114.

Sami, H., Wang, J., & Zhou, H. (2011). Corporate governance and operating performance of Chinese listed firms. *Journal of International Accounting, Auditing, & Taxation*, *20*(2), 106–114. doi:10.1016/j.intaccaudtax.2011.06.005

Setiyono, B., & Tarazi, A. (2014). *Disclosure, ownership structure and bank risk: Evidence from Asia*. Paper presented at the 27th Australasian Finance and Banking Conference, Sydney. 10.2139srn.2395315

Sierra, G. E., Talmor, E., & Wallace, J. S. (2006). An Examination of Multiple Governance Forces within Bank Holding Companies. *Journal of Financial Services Research*, *29*(2), 105–123. doi:10.100710693-006-5921-1

Suchman, M. C. (1995). Managing Legitimacy: Strategic and Institutional Approaches. *Academy of Management Journal*, *20*(3), 571–610.

Sulaiman, M., Abd Madjid, N., & Moh Arifin, N. (2015). Corporate Governance of Islamic Financial Institutions in Malaysia. *Asian Journal of Business and Accounting*, *8*(1), 65–93.

Syaltut, M. (1966). *Al-Islam 'Aqidah wa Syari'ah*. Cairo, Egypt: Dar al-Qalam.

Walsh, J. P., & Seward, J. K. (1990). On the efficiency of internal and external corporate control mechanisms. *Academy of Management Review*, *15*(3), 421–458. doi:10.5465/amr.1990.4308826

Weir, C., Laing, D., & McKnight, P. J. (2002). Internal and External Governance Mechanisms: Their Impact on the Performance of Large UK Public Companies. *Journal of Business Finance & Accounting*, *29*(5&6), 579–611. doi:10.1111/1468-5957.00444

## ENDNOTES

1 *Aqidah* is faith in *Allah* and not to his condemnation with anything. *Shari'ah* is a variety of rules and wisdom that has been established by *Allah* or appointed by principles, and He told the Muslims to hold fast to the decree in conducting daily activities in relation with *Allah* and man (Syaltut, 1966). These rules or laws govern humans in dealing with *Allah* (*hablun minallah-ibadah*) and in dealing with others (*hablun minannas-muamalah*), this relationship is the scope of *Shari'ah*. *Ibadah* regulates how humans can relate to *Allah*, while *muamalah* is a form of human activity in dealing with each other, the kinds of relationships can be in the form of marital relations, division of inheritance, economy, criminal law (*Jinayah*), politics, international relations, and justice. *Akhlaq* is the norm in behaving, and ethics, which is a behavior that is born of a man deliberately, genuine, and has become customary.

2 Certain assets that must be issued by people who are Muslim and are given to groups who are entitled to receive it (poor people and so on).

3 Giving a Muslim to others voluntarily and sincerely without being limited by a certain amount of time and amount.

# Chapter 15
# *Shari'ah* Governance and Audit Assurance in Islamic Banks

**Nor Faezah Ghazi Ahmad**
https://orcid.org/0000-0001-7245-8510
*Universiti Kebangsaan Malaysia (UKM), Malaysia*

**Aisyah Abdul-Rahman**
*Universiti Kebangsaan Malaysia (UKM), Malaysia*

## ABSTRACT

*This chapter is about two major components namely Shari'ah audit (SA) and Shari'ah compliance (SC). The chapter evaluates the role and function of Shari'ah audit and Shari'ah committee and observes to what extent the Shari'ah audit helps in reducing Islamic banks' risk exposure. Five banks were chosen to answer the research questions; and five Shari'ah officers from different groups of respondents, who are involved directly in the process of Shari'ah compliance/auditing in Malaysian Islamic Financial Institutions (IFIs), were interviewed. Findings of the in-depth interviews revealed that the Shari'ah Governance Framework (SGF) positively impacts SA. The research shows that the functions of Shari'ah audit are more specific and covers all aspects. It should possess good knowledge, both of Shari'ah and accounting/auditing. The majority of the respondents agreed that Shari'ah non-compliance risk in IFIs is minimal.*

## 1. INTRODUCTION

The strength and stability of the Islamic financial system has gained worldwide attention especially during the global financial crisis that took place in 2008. After the crisis, the growth of Islamic financial institutions (IFI) was boosted and the total assets of Islamic financial institutions (IFIs) rose 19% in 2011 and 21% in 2012 as compared to less than 10% in the conventional banking system around the world .Contributions to corporate social responsibility (Abdelsalam, Duygun, Matallín-Sáez, & Tortosa-Ausina, 2014; Platonova, Asutay, Dixon, & Mohammad, 2018) and the improvement of financial development can be seen as the achievement and development of IFIs (Gheeraert, 2014; Gheeraert & Weill, 2015).

DOI: 10.4018/978-1-7998-1611-9.ch015

With the improvement and rapid growth in the finance industry, Malaysia is documented as the third largest country in the world after Iran and Saudi Arabia to contribute to the overall assets of domestic banks at approximately 21.9%, while there was a 9.6% contribution to global Islamic banking in the year ending 2014. The outstanding achievement shown by Malaysia has placed the country within the world as having developed an Islamic banking system. This progress is due to the comprehensive and efficient governance framework embodied in the *Shari'ah* governance framework (SGF) which was enforced in 2011 (IMF, 2017). *Shari'ah* principles, which are the backbone of Islamic finance, are crucial for the confidence of stakeholders in IFIs. Therefore, the strength of governance practiced by IFIs is seen as promoting stakeholder confidence and enhancing the credit rating of IFIs (Ginena, 2014; Grassa, 2016; Ullah, Harwood, & Jamali, 2018).

In order to safeguard the interests of stakeholders, *Shari'ah* audit is compulsory for every IFI in Malaysia (Ghani & Rahman, 2015) and it is performed as an internal audit function. This function is responsible to provide assurance of risk management (Zakaria, Nurazalia, & Noraini Mohd Ariffin, 2016). Organisations that have an effective audit function are better and more stable in terms of risk exposure to fraud and mismanagement (Omar & Bakar, 2012). *Shari'ah* audit has become the main aspect of research interest in recent years. However, little is known about the roles and responsibilities of *Shari'ah* audit practice especially in mitigating *Shari'ah* Non-Compliance Risk (SNCR) in IFIs (Ghani & Rahman, 2015). The lack of knowledge and proper training regarding *Shari'ah* audits has led to the occurrence of *Shari'ah* SNCR in IFIs (Endaya & Hanefah, 2013, 2016). In addition, mistakes in understanding the terms, and wrong interpretation of fatwa by the *Shari'ah* audit staff is the cause of the occurrence of SNCR. Previous studies have focused on *Shari'ah* audit issues such as the aspect of separation between conventional and *Shari'ah* audit (Karim, 1990), human capital in implementing *Shari'ah* audit (Shafii, Abidin, Salleh, Jusoff, & Kasim, 2013) and the gap between the actual and the desired outcomes in implementing *Shari'ah* audit (Kasim, Mohamad Ibrahim, & Sulaiman, 2009) and research into *Shari'ah* audit effectiveness (Endaya & Hanefah, 2016). Even though many studies have been implemented, it is indeed difficult to find field studies concerning a review of *Shari'ah* audit after implementation of SGF 2011. Therefore, this area of study is worth exploring and to narrow the gap between theoretical and field study research.

This research aims to explore the quality of audit assurance provided by *Shari'ah* audit during a performance review of the risk management process in the light of the new implementation of SGF 2011 in helping to reduce the risk exposure of Islamic banks. This study uses semi-structured interviews with five respondents from five Islamic banks in Malaysia to gather valuable insight into the role of *Shari'ah* audit in mitigating *Shari'ah* non-compliance risk.

## 2. BACKGROUND

### 2.1 Concept of *Shari'ah* Governance

Islamic Financial Institutions (IFIs) are different from conventional financial institutions whereby the IFIs have the responsibility of ensuring their products, instruments, operations, and activities are in compliance with *Shari'ah* principles. Failure to meet the necessary requirements related to these principles will expose the IFIs to *Shari'ah* non-compliance risk. *Shari'ah* non-compliance risk (SNCR) is the risk that arises from the failure of a bank to comply with *Shari'ah* rules and principles as determined by the relevant *Shari'ah* regulatory councils. Compliance with *Shari'ah* principles is best achieved by having a proper *Shari'ah* governance framework. Guidelines regarding the *Shari'ah* governance system for Institutions Offering Islamic Financial Services are stated in the IFSB-10 guideline principles defined as:

*A set of institutional and organisational arrangements through which Islamic financial institutions ensure that there is an effective independent oversight of Shari'ah compliance over the issuance of relevant Shari'ah pronouncements, dissemination of information and an internal Shari'ah compliance review.*

In Malaysia, *Shari'ah* governance has been introduced by Bank Negara Malaysia (BNM) to ensure the business operations of all Islamic financial institutions in Malaysia comply with *Shari'ah* principles (Ahmed & Khatun, 2013; Hashim, Mahadi, & Amran, 2015; Safiullah & Shamsuddin, 2018). In October 2010, BNM issued a guideline regarding the *Shari'ah* governance framework for Islamic Financial Institutions (IFIs) with an effective implementation date in January 2011 by all IFIs. There are three important organs in this guideline, namely the board, the management, and the *Shari'ah* Supervisory Board (Rafay & Farid, 2018). Each of these organs is interdependent in ensuring the IFI is *always Shari'ah compliant.* These three main organs are supported by the *Shari'ah* risk management control function, *Shari'ah* review, *Shari'ah* research, and *Shari'ah* audit. The roles of *Shari'ah* risk management are to identify all possible *Shari'ah* non-compliance risks and take remedial measures to reduce the risk. The *Shari'ah* review is to review the business operations and activities of the institution on a regular basis in accordance with *Shari'ah* principles. The *Shari'ah* research function is responsible for conducting in-depth research into *Shari'ah* matters prior to submission to the *Shari'ah* committee. Lastly, the *Shari'ah* audit is to provide independent assessment and objective assurance designed to be value added and to improve the compliance of IFIs with *Shari'ah* principles. This is to ensure adequate internal control (formulated by the IFIs themselves) and to undergo the assessment of adequacy of the *Shari'ah* governance process

The compliance of IFIs with the *Shari'ah* principles will be reached by having an appropriate *Shari'ah* governance framework (Hamza, 2013). The main objective of the *Shari'ah* governance framework is to strengthen the role of the board, the *Shari'ah* Committee or *Shari'ah* Supervisory Board and the management in relation to *Shari'ah* matters. This includes improving the significant key organs that have the responsibility of ensuring *Shari'ah* compliance as well as a research function to achieve a *Shari'ah* - based operating environment. Compliance with *Shari'ah* rules and principles can have a significant impact on IFIs to avoid the failure of IFIs to fulfil the *Shari'ah* law which could lead to a negative perception and damage the image of the industry (Ahmad & Al-Aidaros 2015)

The common corporate governance practice of conventional banks is that they are governed by a Board of Directors. However, for IFIs they have an additional organ which is the *Shari'ah* Committee. The main function of the *Shari'ah* committee is to oversee the accountability of *Shari'ah* related matters. The *Shari'ah* committee plays two important roles, not only an advisory role but also as a monitoring role as well. This is to safeguard that all the transactions and activities of the IFIs are following *Shari'ah* law. IFSB-10 and BNM SGF have laid out the guiding principles of *Shari'ah* governance based on the established principles of corporate governance. This includes oversight, accountability and responsibility, independence, competency and confidentiality and finally, consistency. The failure to control the *Shari'ah* non-compliance risk would give a bad impression of the IFIs. According to (Ginena, 2014), the potential effect of *Shari'ah* non-compliance can lead to higher costs, financial losses, liquidity problems, bank runs, bank failure, industry smearing, and financial instability.

*Figure 1. BNM Shari'ah governance framework for Islamic financial institutions*
*Source: (Malaysia, B.N, 2010) - Central Bank of Malaysia*

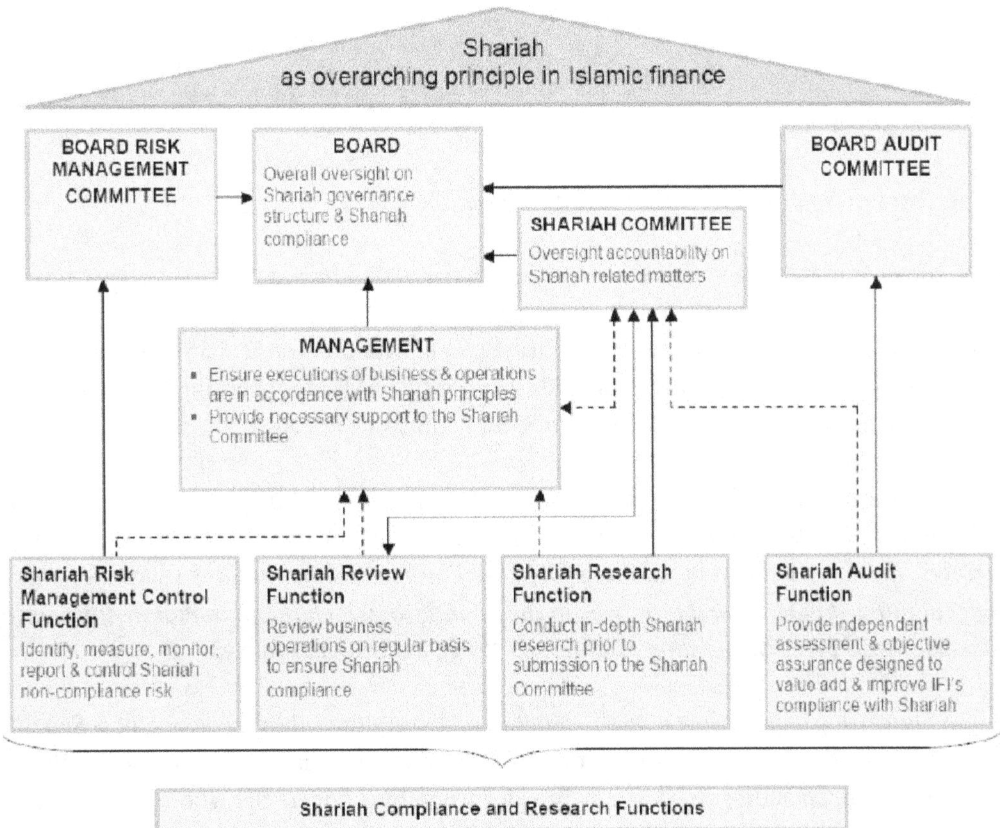


After the establishment of the SGF in 2011, BNM introduced the Islamic Financial Services Act 2013 (IFSA 2013) on 30 June 2013 that has since come into effect, substituting and repealing the Payment Systems Act 2003, the Exchange Control Act 1953, the Islamic Banking Act 1983 and the Takaful Act 1984. Among the relevant structures of this comprehensive legislation are the provisions involving the execution of *Shari'ah* Non- Compliance Risk (SNCR) and the imposition of statutory duty upon the Islamic financial institutions. These are to guarantee that their aims, operations, affairs, businesses and activities are following *Shari'ah* principles, as part of the implementation of *Shari'ah* governance in the Islamic financial system in Malaysia. According to Miskam & Nasrul (2013), the enforcement of IFSA 2013 provides a more significant authority to the *Shari'ah* Advisory Council. This is very important to ensure that their aims, operations, affairs, businesses and activities are following *Shari'ah* rules. This is one of the key areas in the evolution of the legal framework for Islamic finance in Malaysia, which aims to provide greater certainty and predictability in the Islamic financial institutions in order to build public confidence in the system. Section 28 of the IFSA 2013 ("Islamic Financial Services Act 2013," 2015) concerning *Shari'ah* compliance, states that an institution shall at all times ensure that its aims and operations, business, affairs and activities are in compliance with *Shari'ah* law.

## 2.2 Concept of the *Shari'ah* Audit

Numerous *Qur'an*ic verses and Hadiths indicate the "audit" process:

*Then as for he who is given his record in his right hand, He will be judged with an easy account, and return to his people in happiness. (Surah al-Insyiqaq: Verses 6 to 9).*

*Surely Allah takes account of all things (Surah al-Nisa': Verse 82).*

As such, the overall meaning of auditing in Islam is the *Shari'ah* audit to cover all aspects including reviewing the operations, controlling and reporting transactions and dealing for correction of what is due, stated by Islamic jurisprudence to provide trust and fair reports for decision making.

According to Auditing for Islamic Financial Institutions (AAOFI) concerning the Audit Standard for Islamic Financial Institutions No.1 (ASIFI), *Shari'ah* audit can be defined as follows:

*The objective of the an audit of a financial statement is to enable the auditor to express an opinion as to whether the financial statements are prepared, in all material respects, in accordance to Shari'ah rules and principles, the Accounting and Auditing for Islamic Financial Institutions (AAOIFI) and relevant national accounting standards and practices in the country in which the financial institutions operate. The phrase used to express the auditor's opinion is 'to give a true and fair view.*

From the *Shari'ah* perspective it is more detailed and specific within the scope of a *Shari'ah* audit that is wider than the conventional audit as it is not limited to financial statements only. It is a fact that the scope of the *Shari'ah* audit perspective is broader whereby it covers the whole institution including its objectives, processing, marketing, personnel, as well as the financial and non-financial performance. Furthermore, auditing is important for the assurance of corporate accountability and enhances the faith of the stakeholders in the economic structure. The scope of the *Shari'ah* auditors has been stated in the *Shari'ah* governance framework in which the scope of work covers all aspects of the business activities and operations of IFIs and, including but not limited to, audit and financial statements of IFIs, compliance audit on the organisational structure, people and information technology application systems and a review of adequacy of the *Shari'ah* governance process (Malaysia, 2010)

The implementation of the *Shari'ah* audit is important to IFIs due to its most important purposes by providing reasonable assurance that the business activities and operations of IFIs do not break the *Shari'ah* rules and principles. The objectives of a *Shari'ah* audit are therefore to check if the business operations and activities of an IFI are *Shari'ah* compliant, to ensure the internal control of an IFI is sound and effective whilst complying with *Shari'ah* law and to ensure the recording and reporting of incidences of *Shari'ah* non-compliant events and risks. In addition, the audit ensures the restructuring of *Shari'ah* non-compliant events and avoids any recurrence of *Shari'ah* non-compliant events and ensures the minimisation of *Shari'ah* non-compliant risks. It satisfies the *Shari'ah* auditors that everything that they examine is *Shari'ah* compliant. The stability, good performance and compliance with the *Shari'ah* rules and principles are the factors that attract public assurance and expansion of the number of investors, stakeholders and shareholders to engage in business relationships with IFIs. From the *Shari'ah* perspective, revenue and earnings derived from this investment are considered as permissible and justified (Shafii, Abidin, Salleh & Jusoff, 2013). This will assist IFIs to increase their number of customers and investors, and at the same time they can boost their deposit base and enlarge their businesses.

## 2.3 *Shari'ah* Audit and Risk

Based on the definition of the Basel Committee on Banking Supervision (BCBS), operational risk is "the risk of financial loss or damage resulting from inadequate or failed internal processes, people and systems or from external events. This definition includes legal risk, but exclude strategic and reputation risk". Ginena (2014) listed four effects from *Shari'ah* risk i.e. credit risk, legal risk, reputation risk, and market risk. Nevertheless, SNCR can occur in credit risk. Credit risk is where the stakeholders no longer trust the ability of the bank to execute the responsibilities of an Islamic financial institution in violation of *Shari'ah* principles. This arises when a customer does not pay for the financing provided because of trust issues with respect to bank compliance. This situation will lead to loss at the bank and consequently cause liquidity problems. Hence, it is important that IFIs comply with *Shari'ah* principles to gain and retain the trust of stakeholders.

Good governance will ensure that institutions are able to reduce risks, especially SNCR. Any funds obtained from non-halal resources will be segregated from the profits of the company as such monies are considered as a loss to a company in which funds derived from the mistakes incurred will be donated to certain groups. Therefore, it is important to have a *Shari'ah* audit that serves to protect IFIs from exposure to risks, especially *Shari'ah* non-compliance risks.

## 2.4 *Shari'ah* Audit Practice and Scope

The introduction of the implementation of Islamic law in Islamic financial institutions has brought great changes, especially in terms of business operations that must comply with *Shari'ah* principles. This change also affected the way in which the auditing scope became broader and more comprehensive (Kasim, Sanusi, Mutamimah, & Handoyo, 2013). According to the SGF-BNM (SGF-BNM, 2011), "*Shari'ah audit refers to a periodical valuation conducted from time to time, to provide an independent assessment and objective assurance designed to add value and develop the degree of compliance in relation to the Islamic Financial Institutions' business operations*".

*Shari'ah* audit can be defined as an audit process in IFIs that should be more comprehensive as compared to conventional audit that only takes into account the value factors regardless of the moral and ethical values set by Islam. Abbott, Daugherty, Parker, & Peters (2016) stressed that auditing is significant to assure corporate accountability and to enhance the stakeholder's confidence in the economic structure to engage in business relationships with the IFIs. (Shafii et al., 2013) mentioned that the inadequacy of proper auditing practices in IFIs is a major problem currently faced by the *Shari'ah* auditing framework. Despite that, Yussof, (2013) stated that there was no specific standard to be used as guidance and instead they are guided by their moral beliefs (binti Kasim, Ibrahim, & Sulaiman, 2013). In recent practice, the conventional auditor conducts an audit to prepare an annual statement of an IFI and a *Shari'ah* advisor provides a separate report on *Shari'ah* compliance practice of the IFI (binti Kasim, Ibrahim, & Sulaiman, 2013). The main problem faced by the *Shari'ah* audit in an IFI is the inadequacy of proper auditing practices due to no specific guidelines that can be followed by the *Shari'ah* auditors. To address these issues, a proper set of guidelines should be immediately formulated in order to meet the requirements of IFIs as well as to reduce reliance on Western accounting qualifications that may not fully meet the standards set by the country. It has been suggested to establish an Association of Chartered *Shari'ah* Accountants and Auditors (ACSAA) in addressing this issue (Najeeb & Ibrahim, 2014).

## 2.5 Professional Competency

As stated in the SGF, the internal audit unit is responsible for coordinating the *Shari'ah* audit. For each IFI, the *Shari'ah* audit is performed by an internal auditor with proficient knowledge and skills *vis-à-vis Shari'ah* law. The auditor will ensure that the internal control system is strictly in compliance with *Shari'ah* principles to achieve the objectives of the bank (Shafii, Salleh, & Shahwan, 2010). However, there is a lack of expertise in performing the *Shari'ah* review by the *Shari'ah* auditors (Besar, Abd Sukor, Abdul Muthalib, & Gunawa, 2009). Kasim & Sanusi (2013) found that only 5.9% of the respondents had qualifications both in the field of *Shari'ah* and accounting/auditing. Meanwhile, a study conducted by (Ahmad&Al-Aidaros 2015, 2015) explained that the majority of the *Shari'ah* auditors lack the expertise and human talent as well as sufficient team members to perform the *Shari'ah* audit. To ensure quality audit systems, auditors require more knowledge and expertise in order to enhance their function in *Shari'ah* auditing. In addition, (Najeeb & Ibrahim, 2014) argued that a conventional auditor will not fully understand the *Shari'ah* principles applied to IFIs. To perform an audit on *Shari'ah* related matters, the *Shari'ah* auditors must have knowledge of both *Usul Fiqh* and accounting to ensure the IFIs comply with *Shari'ah* principles. Thus, Shafii, Salleh, and Shahwan (2010); Khalid, Haron, and Masron (2018) stressed that good audits depend on efficient human resources who possess the skills and expertise in order to be capable of setting a work plan and reviewing the output. To overcome this issue, there is also a strong need for proper training in *Shari'ah* knowledge since most bank officers do not have a *Shari'ah* background (Othman, Ishak, Arif, & Aris, 2014; Sayd Farook, 2013). Therefore, the *Shari'ah* auditors in IFIs should equip themselves with the skills and qualifications needed to ensure that *Shari'ah* audit can be fully implemented and all operations in the IFI are following *Shari'ah* law.

## 2.6 *Shari'ah* Committee and Professional Competency

Another aspect that needs to be of focus is the *Shari'ah* committee. The *Shari'ah* Committee plays an important role in IFIs to ensure all the business operations and activities comply with *Shari'ah* law. A related issue for the *Shari'ah* committee is the area of independence. The fundamental concept of the audit is to be independent, where the auditors are not allowed to audit their own work (Kasim, Ibrahim, & Sulaiman, 2009). This issue is highlighted when the *Shari'ah* committee is also involved in conducting process audits. Generally, the remuneration of the *Shari'ah* committee (SC) is paid by IFIs. A conflict of interest occurs when the SC has to audit the same institution and this threatens the limitation and independence of the decision making (Malkawi, 2014). Therefore, this situation can lead to the occurrence of SNCR.

The failure of Islamic banking to meet the *Shari'ah* requirements may lead to SNCR where the risk exists only in Islamic banking and not in conventional banking. The *Shari'ah* non-compliance risk event for a certain situation cannot be avoided. Poor governance is due to a lack of qualified *Shari'ah* officers, and an inadequate internal control instrument which is the key factor that causes *Shari'ah* non-compliance events in Islamic banking. This means that the knowledge and experience of *Shari'ah* officers in managing and handling of IFIs are the main factors to place *Shari'ah* compliance of IFIs on the right track. However, according to (Najeeb & Ibrahim, 2014) it is rare to find a *Shari'ah* committee that includes a competent accountant/auditor. Therefore, the integrity, transparency, and efficiency of the *Shari'ah* committee in carrying out its responsibilities are necessary to ensure that the established *Shari'ah* corporate governance enhances quality and reduces SNCR events in IFIs.

## 3. METHODOLOGY

The objective of this research is basically to evaluate the role and qualification of *Shari'ah* Audit as an important organ of the SGF and to examine the extent the *Shari'ah* audit to help in reducing the risk exposure of Islamic banks. In order to achieve the research objective, this study surveyed five different groups of respondents who were directly involved with the *Shari'ah* compliance/auditing processes in IFIs in Malaysia comprising Bank A, Bank B, Bank C, Bank D, and Bank E. This study used the interview method to obtain detailed information to answer the objective of the study.

Three sets of bank groups were surveyed, namely a fully-fledged Islamic bank represented by Bank C, Islamic bank subsidiaries represented by Bank A, and Bank D, and lastly, Islamic foreign banks represented by Bank B and Bank E. The study was conducted using a qualitative approach and primary data was gathered through semi-structured interviews with five respondents from five Islamic banks in Malaysia and coded as RA, RB, RC, RD, and RE. The interview method was selected as the mode of collecting data as it was believed that the results from this method would be more meaningful. The researchers highlighted that human experience and uniqueness as measured by the qualitative approach, could address certain elements such as views/ideas, feelings, and intentions from the different perspectives of the respondents. The semi-structured interview technique allowed each interviewee the freedom to express their view pertaining to the research objective in which the interview conducted using an open framework allowed two-way communication to take place. Five interviews were held separately with five respondents of different backgrounds, namely the Head of Group Islamic Business Compliance from Bank A, an Executive of the *Shari'ah* Secretariat from Bank B, a Senior Manager of *Shari'ah* Risk Management from Bank C, an Executive of *Shari'ah* Review from Bank D and the Head of *Shari'ah* Audit from Bank E. As is known, the *Shari'ah* committee is assisted by four key functions which are the *Shari'ah* review function, the *Shari'ah* risk management function, the *Shari'ah* research function, and the *Shari'ah* audit function. These four functions report any *Shari'ah*-related matter to the *Shari'ah* committee, and they are also the "eyes" of the *Shari'ah* committee. It was therefore appropriate to interview officers who had such a background in relation to the *Shari'ah* committee.

The interview process continued until the number of respondents had been saturated, in the sense that no new information could be obtained, and the predetermined size of respondents had been reached. Specifically, the interviews focused on two main themes. First, the interviews focused on investigating the current practices of *Shari'ah* auditing, which were then divided into seven subsections; and the second theme was *Shari'ah* compliance that may lead to risk exposure in IFIs. The interviews were conducted for 1 hour with each respondent. An email was sent to each respondent to explain the purpose of the study and to gain permission to conduct the interview. The confidentiality of the interviews was also stated in the email. The interviews were conducted in both languages, Malay and English and were held at the offices of the respondents.

*Table 1. Summary of background of respondents*

| # | Bank | Background | Position | SGF | Experience |
|---|---|---|---|---|---|
| 1. | Bank A | BA (Hons) Accounting | Head of Group Islamic Business Compliance | *Shari'ah* Officer under *Shari'ah* Compliance Department | 5 years |
| 2. | Bank B | BA (Hons) *Shari'ah* and Islamic Studies (Islamic Economics and Banking) | Executive of *Shari'ah* Secretariat | *Shari'ah* Officer under *Shari'ah* Compliance Department | 3 years |
| 3. | Bank C | BA (Hons) Accounting | Senior Manager of *Shari'ah* Risk Management | *Shari'ah* Risk Management Function | 14 years |
| 4. | Bank D | BA (Hons) *Shari'ah* and Civil Law | Executive of *Shari'ah* Review | *Shari'ah* Review Function | 3 years |
| 5. | Bank E | BA (Hons) Accounting | Head of *Shari'ah* Audit | *Shari'ah* Audit Function | 19 years |

All interviews were audio recorded, then transcribed and manually analysed using content analysis. The data from the interviews was scrutinised for similarities and only relevant data was categorised using the specific theme. The table below shows a summary of the background of the respondents.

An interview data matrix was developed to identify commonalities and differences in the research theme (refer to Table 2).

*Table 2. Interview data matrix of Shari'ah audit committee and risk exposure*

| Category | *Shari'ah* Compliance | *Shari'ah* Audit |
|---|---|---|
| Number of employees | 8 to 30 employees based on the size of IFI, quality, and competency of the employees. | The number of internal audits is more than 15 but only 4 staff handle *Shari'ah* audit and the number of existing staff is adequate to ensure IFIs comply with *Shari'ah* principles. |
| Qualification | 1. Follows as mentioned in SGF issued by BNM.<br>2. Normally *Shari'ah* Committee and *Shari'ah* review must have *Shari'ah* background but other functions such as the *Shari'ah* risk management function, *Shari'ah* research function, and *Shari'ah* audit do not have *Shari'ah* background. | 1. Must have an accounting background.<br>2. Most staff do not have a *Shari'ah* background, but they attended training and courses related to *Shari'ah* knowledge such as Islamic Banking, *Muamalat* and Islamic Law. |
| Operational risk and *Shari'ah* non-compliance risk (SNCR) | Source of operational risk:<br>1. People risk: Lack of knowledge and expertise.<br>2. Technology risk: System parameters do not tally.<br>3. Legal risk: Staff do not follow prescribed steps during trading.<br>SNCR management:<br>1. Adoption of 3 lines of defence.<br>2. Using the *Shari'ah* parameters.<br>3. By finding a road course /solution without incurring high costs for banks.<br>Level of SNCR:<br>Ø Medium/minimum.<br>The person in charge if SNCR occurs:<br>1. The person who makes mistakes should be responsible.<br>2. Depends on who finds the issue.<br>3. The solution involves all parties. | 1. *Shari'ah* audit is 3rd line of defence. |

*continues on following page*

*Table 2. Coninued*

| Category | *Shari'ah* Compliance | *Shari'ah* Audit |
|---|---|---|
| Independence | Independence in a certain area | Independence |
| Organisation structure | 1. Respondents seem to really understand the SGF structure, function, report and process<br>2. Partially follow or not fully follow as mentioned in SGF depending on the size of the IFI. | 1. Respondents seem to really understand the SGF structure, function, report and process.<br>2. Partially follow or not fully follow SGF. |
| Guidelines and standards | Follow as mentioned in SGF issued by BNM. | 1. Follow guideline from IFI.<br>2. Regarding *Shari'ah* compliance and decisions on principles to follow the decisions of the *Shari'ah* Advisory Council (SAC), *Shari'ah* Committee, and fatwa.<br>3. AAIOFI just a benchmark and it is not used in Malaysia.<br>4. There is no proper framework to govern practice for internal *Shari'ah* audit in IFIs. |
| Roles and responsibilities | 1. Respondents seem to really understand the roles and responsibilities as mentioned in SGF issued by BNM. | 1. Respondents understand roles and responsibilities as required in *Shari'ah* audit.<br>2. Audit of financial statements.<br>3. The coverage of audit includes all aspect of IFI business operations and activities such as people, process, organisation structure and IT.<br>4. Audit frequency depends on the risk exposure, critical of issue and place. |

## 4. FINDINGS

The interviews were held from July until August 2017 at five Islamic banks in Malaysia and consisted of five respondents from different backgrounds, namely, the Head of Group Islamic Business Compliance, a Senior Manager of *Shari'ah* Risk Management, a Head of *Shari'ah* Audit, and a Senior Executive of the *Shari'ah* Review and an Executive of the *Shari'ah* Secretariat.

### 4.1 *Shari'ah* Audit

#### 4.1.1 Number of Employees

The guidelines set by SGF position the *Shari'ah* audit function under the responsibility of the internal audit unit whose role is more extensive. The research found that basically, the number of the current *Shari'ah* audit staff in IFIs is adequate to ensure that IFIs comply with *Shari'ah* rules and principles. In terms of a dedicated team, IFIs commonly have four employees who are core in *Shari'ah* audit. Generally, some of *Shari'ah* audit staff may not have a *Shari'ah* background but they have *Shari'ah* exposure by taking *Shari'ah*-related courses such as Islamic banking and Islamic law. Studies conducted by Kasim, Ain, Hashim, & Salman (2016), argued that most of the internal control team of IFIs are not qualified to fulfil the *Shari'ah* audit since they do not have a *Shari'ah* background in performing the task. As identified by the SGF issued by BNM in Section VI, *Shari'ah* audit staff should have the required *Shari'ah*-knowledge and training. However, nowadays, to seek employees who have both qualifications in *Shari'ah* and audit can be quite difficult as *Shari'ah* audit in the Islamic financial industry is still new as compared to the conventional audit system. Hopefully, in the future, there will be many qualified *Shari'ah* audit function staff available since several efforts have been made to produce suitably efficient officers.

### 4.1.2 Qualification

The results from the interview showed that the respondents who form part of the *Shari'ah* audit function of the IFIs generally do not have a *Shari'ah* background, but they have *Shari'ah* exposure by taking training and courses related to *Shari'ah* principles such as Islamic Banking, *u*, and law. All interviewees strongly agreed that *Shari'ah* understanding and knowledge are necessary for every *Shari'ah* audit member of staff to be involved in the *Shari'ah* audit process as outlined by BNM and to possess *Shari'ah*-related knowledge and training.

Since the establishment of IFIs is still relatively new as compared to the conventional system, to seek officers who are expert in both *Shari'ah* and audit is quite difficult. That is why BNM provides the flexibility whereby internal audit function staff may seek the proficiency of the *Shari'ah* officer of the IFI in carrying out the audit as long as the objective of the audit is not affected. It is suggested that the *Shari'ah* audit function staff improve their knowledge by attending courses interrelated to *Shari'ah* knowledge. *Shari'ah* knowledge is important to *Shari'ah* the audit function. Internal audit staff should possess *Shari'ah* knowledge in order to add value and understand the condition of each of the *Shari'ah* principles. This is because the *Shari'ah* audit function can then directly recognise any event of *Shari'ah* non-compliance in Islamic transactions and operations. Thus, they can ensure all the operations and businesses of IFIs comply with *Shari'ah* principles.

### 4.1.3 *Shari'ah* Audit in the Context of *Shari'ah* Non-Compliance Risk for IFIs

The *Shari'ah* audit function plays a key role in an IFI to assure the effective management of risk. It is the last line of defence in ensuring *Shari'ah* compliance in IFIs. The line of defence principle is a long and well-established concept that has been deployed in a variety of industries and situations. The second line (compliance, legal, risk management, and *Shari'ah* review) also plays an important role through effective advisory and continuous monitoring of the business. Thereafter, the internal auditors will need to monitor their work in association with the compliance and risk management team as well as assessing the work of these functions. The findings from these audits are reported to all three lines.

### 4.1.4 Independence

The *Shari'ah* Audit serves as an independent reviewer established by the IFI management to review the system of internal controls in order to be more transparent. The *Shari'ah* audit team is an independent party whereby the team reports all information obtained to the Board Audit Committee (BAC) while matters relating to *Shari'ah* non-compliance risk will be reported to the *Shari'ah* committee. Therefore, the freedom of *Shari'ah* audits refers to the freedom to audit and to report any information pertaining to the institution to a specific unit of function. According to the guidelines:

*Regarding reporting, anything that is related to audit... they will directly report it to the internal audit board. Next, they will report to the CEO. Each of the IFIs activities will be monitored by BNM. - (RB)-*

### 4.1.5 Organisation Structure

Based on the interviews, the researchers found that the interviewees understood every function, role, and process as contained in the SGF. Understanding of these guidelines is critical to strengthening the *Shari'ah* governance process and to ensure business operations in IFIs comply with *Shari'ah* law.

#### *4.1.5.1 Shari'ah Governance Framework- Impact on Shari'ah Audit Function:*

From the face to face interviews conducted, it was found that the SGF 2011 issued by BNM positively impacts the *Shari'ah* audit. Prior researchers have stressed that the guidelines issued by BNM are very useful for improving the quality and efficiency of IFIs (Hamza, 2013). The respondents stated that that the guidelines issued by BNM are very helpful at facilitating the *Shari'ah* auditing function. The team only needs to follow the principles underlying this guideline. However, the staff may have some reservations whereby the guidelines issued by the regulator are not uniform and consistent. In addition, it requires the IFIs to have their own guidelines, with the approval from the SC and the BOD. The approval by the SC and the BOD allows them to conduct their business as agreed. The problem again arises when BNM issues new guidelines causing change or to re-evaluate their policies in order to comply with the new guidelines. It is necessary to see whether the policy issued impacts their business or not. This makes it difficult for IFIs. Sometimes the *Shari'ah* matter is complied with, but in terms of guidelines, they are still evolving. Nonetheless, it is believed that the IFIs in Malaysia are still new and need to continuously improve themselves. It is suggested that the regulators should be more systematic and consistent in the future when issuing guidelines.

#### *4.1.5.2 The Current framework Implemented by Shari'ah Audit_*

In this subsection, the research investigated the framework or standards used by the audit process as part of the internal audit. The results of the interviews found that the internal audit in IFIs adopted the framework established by the Institute of Internal Audit (IIA) Standards for Professional Practice of Internal Auditing (IPPF). IPPF is the worldwide framework used for the audit process. In order to audit *Shari'ah* compliance, internal audits will follow the guidelines set by the *Shari'ah* Advisory Council (SAC) and decisions of the *Shari'ah* committee. In addition, a respondent stated that a new audit framework was not needed as the existing guidelines issued by BNM and the institution were enough to be used as a reference.

SGF together with the guidelines issued by the SAC of BNM and the decisions of the SC are more than enough. However, some other respondents argued that they need the *Shari'ah* audit framework to be different from the conventional framework. It was also mentioned that the Accounting and Auditing Organisation for Financial Institutions (AAOFFI) is a Bahrain-based standard and it is a good standard to practice but it is not suitable to be applied here. This is because IFIs in Malaysia are guided by BNM and it is not a requirement to use the AAOFFI in Malaysia. AAOIFI is the main international organisation that formulates and publishes accounting, auditing, ethics, governance and *Shari'ah* standard for IFIs. Also, it can be used as a benchmark by all IFIs.

### 4.1.6 Roles and Responsibilities

*Shari'ah* audit plays an important role in ensuring that all products and services and related contracts of Islamic instruments are following *Shari'ah* rules and principles. The research found that the respondents understood the roles and responsibilities of the *Shari'ah* audit function as mentioned in the SGF-BNM. The scope of the *Shari'ah* audit function covers all aspects of the business operations and activities of an IFI including the audit financial statement, compliance audit on the structure of the organisation, people, process, and IT and lastly it reviews the adequacy of *Shari'ah* governance. Audit frequency depends on the risk exposure and is critical of issue and place. This indicates that the functions of the *Shari'ah* audit function are more specific and cover-all aspects such as the governance structure, operation, product, etc. In managing SNCR, the *Shari'ah* audit function is located as the third line of defence whereby it is responsible for preventing *Shari'ah* non-compliance events from occurring.

## 4.2 *Shari'ah* Compliance

### 4.2.1 Number of Employees

The provision in the SGF provides for the requirement of an effective *Shari'ah* compliance function but does not specify the number of *Shari'ah* officers to perform the *Shari'ah* compliance function. The result showed that the number of staff is significant in relation to the size of the bank. This means the number of employees depends on the size of the bank and the capability of the staff. The productivity of the bank is not measured by quantity, but it is measured by the quality of the staff. The results showed that the majority of IFIs in Malaysia have 9 to 10 *Shari'ah* officers in the *Shari'ah* compliance function, and each has at least a degree in a related field. Only one bank had 30 staff members for the *Shari'ah* compliance function. The IFI had total assets of more than RM45.8 million in 2014 as compared to banks, i.e. around less than RM22 million in total assets-(RM16.3 million for Bank B, RM21.1 million for Bank D, RM13.6 million for Bank E). The investigation showed that employers will be hiring those with extensive knowledge and have good interpersonal skills such as good communication skills and versatility.

### 4.2.2 Qualification

The result indicated that basically, *Shari'ah* compliance staff must have *Shari'ah* exposure, understand the financial industry, and be fast learners. Moreover, additional knowledge, such as in economics, investment, etc., is value added. The officer added that to seek a perfect candidate is impossible right now because the Islamic financial industry is developing a system which is still new and there are several aspects that need to be improved, especially concerning people, systems, and operations.

### 4.2.3 Shari'ah Non-Compliance Risk

The result indicated that most of the respondents agreed that the level of SNCR in IFIs is minimal. The guidelines issued by the regulator are adequate in controlling *Shari'ah* non-compliance risk. Staff must strictly comply with the rules provided by BNM. Furthermore, any contract that is of very high-risk to the bank will not be taken up. This is because the objective of the establishment of a bank is to make it profitable.

The results from the interviews showed that banks are using their own methods to control the *Shari'ah* non-compliance risk and basically, the methods applied are almost the same for each bank. This includes cooperation between all parties, implementation of three lines of defence, use of *Shari'ah* parameters and lastly risks and control self-assessment (RCSA). All parties play an important role to control and monitor SNCR in IFIs. Without cooperation from all parties, it is impossible for the banks to control the risk. To control the risk of SNCR involves every level, from the business line until the third line of defence. Moreover, cooperation by the regulator, BNM, is also helpful in assisting the IFIs in managing SNCR. The respondents agreed that the three lines of defence are effective in managing the *Shari'ah* non-compliance risk in IFIs, and it is an approach for safeguarding the internal control framework as well.

Another method used to monitor SNCR is the *Shari'ah* parameters. The *Shari'ah* parameters issued by Bank Negara are to be used as a standard guide in the application of respective *Shari'ah* contracts in IFIs and to promote harmony in the Islamic financial practice in Malaysia. Lastly, a method used by the IFIs is risk and self-assessment (RCSA). Moreover, the respondents explained that the common operational risks that occur in IFIs are people, systems and legal risk. A lack of knowledge by employees is one of the 'people risks' faced by IFIs where the employees may give inaccurate information and explanation pertaining to the services and products provided to the customer. Moreover, the 'technology/system risk' occurs when the system parameters do not tally with the manual. Lastly, 'legal risk' occurs when workers do not follow the set steps during trading conducted.

#### *4.2.3.1 Parties Involved if Shari'ah Non-Compliance Occurs*

All participants strongly agreed that a person is fully responsible for his/her own actions. The *Shari'ah* review is responsible to review the business operations on a regular basis in order to ensure *Shari'ah* compliance. The team will write a report of their review. If there is a finding in the report, they will report it to the SC and follow-up action will be taken to mitigate the *Shari'ah* non-compliance risk. The *Shari'ah* compliance team will monitor the issue until it is resolved. However, sometimes the *Shari'ah* non-compliance cannot be traced. Therefore, internal/*Shari'ah* auditors undertake the action of reducing risk based on the third line of defence of the audit.

Accordingly:

*...So, the person responsible is the person who makes the mistake. - (RC)*

### 4.2.4 Independence

All participants strongly agreed that for the *Shari'ah* reviewers to function effectively, their independence is of great importance. This is because they can exercise objective judgment without any influence while performing their review. In addition, independence refers to good and quality *Shari'ah* decisions. Such decisions cannot be made without adequate information supplied by the management. Any findings and review by a *Shari'ah* officer must be directly reported to the *Shari'ah* committee. However, one respondent argued that those who are involved in the review are paid by the same institution whose review is being conducted, thus compromising their independence and resulting in a conflict of interest. Nevertheless, this person stressed that as long the reporting is not in contradiction with *Shari'ah* principles, and the reporting of SNC is submitted to the *Shari'ah* committee, there is still independence.

### 4.2.5 Organisation Structure

The interviews indicated that all banks must abide by the SGF, but the design depends on the IFIs themselves. This is because there is a compliance check before all products are launched, as well as a post-launch audit, i.e. after the product has been launched by the Islamic banks. Respondents seem to really understand the SGF structure, function, reporting, and process, although some IFIs partially follow or do not fully follow the guidelines as mentioned in the SGF. This appears to depend on the size, complexity, and nature of the business operation of the IFI. This includes enhancing the responsibilities of the related main organs in terms of accomplishing *Shari'ah* compliance and the research function to achieve a *Shari'ah*-based operating environment.

### 4.2.6 Role of *Shari'ah* Compliance Department

The interviews indicated that all the participants seemed to have an in-depth understanding of the roles and function of the *Shari'ah* compliance department, namely, to ensure *Shari'ah* compliance in all Islamic banking activities. The respondents explained that they follow the *Shari'ah* governance framework issued by the regulator.

## 5. CONCLUSION AND RECOMMENDATIONS

This study posits that the roles and responsibilities of the *Shari'ah* audit are crucial to ensure the business operations and activities comply with *Shari'ah* principles and to mitigate SNCR in an IFI. IFIs need to have a *Shari'ah* audit to provide advice, besides strictly monitoring the operations of IFIs by following the spirit of Islam. The regulators, policymakers, and market players should improve the existing governance framework for the Islamic banks to strengthen the functioning of the Islamic financial system.

In addition, in order to strengthen the *Shari'ah* audit function and *Shari'ah* compliance in IFIs, there are several methods that can be highlighted. These include improving the quality of the staff by providing adequate training for them. The quality of employees reflects the ability of an institution. Therefore, emphasis on this issue needs to be taken seriously by the institution to reduce the issue of a lack of knowledge as well as to reduce SNCR. To empower the existing framework, cooperation from all parties is needed including participation from stakeholders, regulators, and the industry. Overall, the level of SNCR in IFIs is at a minimum. This means the IFIs are still good at controlling SNCR. Moreover, the SGF issued by the regulator significantly impacts the IFIs where it enhances the role of the board, the *Shari'ah* Committee, and the management in relation to *Shari'ah* matters. This includes enhancing the relevant key organs having the responsibility to implement *Shari'ah* compliance and research functions to achieve a *Shari'ah*-based operating environment. This is because they need to comply with *Shari'ah* per the guidelines released by the regulator, and this has been proven to be quite enough in controlling SNCR in IFIs. In addition, the role and qualification of the *Shari'ah* audit staff are highly important in reducing the *Shari'ah* risk exposure of IFIs. *Shari'ah* audit staff should possess good knowledge, both of *Shari'ah* and accounting/auditing, so that they can understand the *Shari'ah* principles and execute their works without any hesitation or prejudice. The cooperation of all parties including practitioners, regulators, and academics is crucial to the enrichment of resources, ideas, and initiatives for improvement.

This chapter highlights the salient link between the roles played by *Shari'ah* audit to mitigate SNCR in IFIs. Furthermore, it expands the current literature by presenting current issues faced by *Shari'ah* audit and *Shari'ah* compliance staff and their impact on risk that can be beneficial to practitioners.

## 5.1 Recommendations for IFIs

Continuous training of employees is vital for enhancing the integrity and understanding of the employees. This is so that they will become knowledgeable and capable in delivering the right information to customers more effectively and efficiently. Meanwhile, it is important to minimise the risk especially *Shari'ah* non-compliance risk where *Shari'ah*-compliance in all activities and operations in the IFI is an important requirement to be followed.

## 5.2 Recommendations for the Regulator

The execution of *Shari'ah* audit in the IFIs significantly relies on the role of the regulators. The regulatory body should implement a harmonisation of *Shari'ah* rulings. The diversity of differences of thought by the scholars on the same issue can cause confusion in the minds of the public. If there is a set of rules specific to the whole country it can be a source of great strength for the development of Islamic financial institutions. Additionally, it will also benefit the IFIs in their compliance with *Shari'ah* principles. This will be a starting point for the *Shari'ah* audit, and the industry should be moving towards the right path.

## Classifications

JEL Classification: G28, M42, M48
KAUJIE Classification: L22, L23, L24, L33

## REFERENCES

Abbott, L. J., Daugherty, B., Parker, S., & Peters, G. F. (2016). Internal Audit Quality and Financial Reporting Quality: The Joint Importance of Independence and Competence. *Journal of Accounting Research*, *54*(1), 3–40. doi:10.1111/1475-679X.12099

Abdelsalam, O., Duygun, M., Matallín-Sáez, J. C., & Tortosa-Ausina, E. (2014). Do ethics imply persistence? The case of Islamic and socially responsible funds. *Journal of Banking & Finance*, *40*, 182–194. doi:10.1016/j.jbankfin.2013.11.027

Ahmad & Al-Aidaros. (2015). (2015). The Need of Independent *Shari'ah* Members in Islamic Cooperative Banks: An Empirical Study of Professional Accountants in Malaysia. *International Review of Management and Business Research*, *4*(1), 110–120.

Ahmed, M., & Khatun, M. (2013). The Compliance with *Shari'ah* Governance System of AAOIFI : A Study on Islamic Banks Bangladesh Introduction : *Journal of Islamic Economics. Banking and Finance*, *9*(3), 15.

Besar, M. H. A., Abd Sukor, M. E., Abdul Muthalib, N., & Gunawa, A. Y. (2009). The Practice of *Shari'ah* Review as Undertaken by Islamic Banking Sector in Malaysia. *International Review of Business Research Papers*, *5*(1), 294–306.

Binti Kasim, N., Ibrahim, S. H. M., & Sulaiman, M. (2013). Emerging issues for auditing in Islamic Financial Institutions : Empirical evidence from Malaysia. *Journal of Business and Management*, *8*(5), 10–17.

binti Kasim, N., Ibrahim, S. H. M., S. (2009). *Shari'ah* Auditing in Islamic financial institutions: Exploring the gap between the "desired" and the "actual." *Global Economy and Finance Journal*, *2*(2), 127–137.

Endaya, K. A., & Hanefah, M. M. (2013). Internal Audit Effectiveness: An Approach Proposition to Develop the Theoretical Framework. *Research Journal of Finance and Accounting*, *4*(10), 92–102.

Endaya, K. A., & Hanefah, M. M. (2016). Internal auditor characteristics, internal audit effectiveness, and moderating effect of senior management. *Journal of Economic and Administrative Sciences*, *32*(2), 160–176. doi:10.1108/JEAS-07-2015-0023

Ghani, N. L. A., & Rahman, A. R. A. (2015). An analysis of *Shari'ah* audit practices in islamic banks in Malaysia. *Jurnal Pengurusan*, *43*, 107–118. doi:10.17576/pengurusan-2015-43-10

Gheeraert, L. (2014). Does Islamic finance spur banking sector development? *Journal of Economic Behavior & Organization*, *103*, S4–S20. doi:10.1016/j.jebo.2014.02.013

Gheeraert, L., & Weill, L. (2015). Does Islamic banking development favor macroeconomic efficiency? Evidence on the Islamic finance-growth nexus. *Economic Modelling*, *47*, 32–39. doi:10.1016/j.econmod.2015.02.012

Ginena, K. (2014). *Shari'ah* risk and corporate governance of Islamic banks. *Corporate Governance: The International Journal of Business in Society*, *14*(1), 86–103. doi:10.1108/CG-03-2013-0038

Grassa, R. (2016). Corporate governance and credit rating in Islamic banks : Does Shari'ah governance matters? Springer US. *The Journal of Management and Governance*, *20*(4), 875–906. doi:10.100710997-015-9322-4

Hamza, H. (2013). *Shari'ah* governance in Islamic banks: Effectiveness and supervision model. *International Journal of Islamic and Middle Eastern Finance and Management*, *6*(3), 226–237. doi:10.1108/IMEFM-02-2013-0021

Hashim, F., Mahadi, N. D., & Amran, A. (2015). Corporate Governance and Sustainability Practices in Islamic Financial Institutions: The Role of Country of Origin. *Procedia Economics and Finance*, *31*(15), 36–43. doi:10.1016/S2212-5671(15)01129-6

International Monetary Fund. (2017). *Ensuring financial stability in countries with Islamic banking. IMF Country Report.*

Islamic Financial Services Act 2013. (2015).

Karim, R. A. A. (1990). The independence of religious and external auditors: The case of Islamic Banks. *Accounting, Auditing, & Accountability Journal, 3*(3), 34–44.

Kasim, N., Ain, N., Hashim, B., & Salman, S. A. (2016). Conceptual Relationship between Corporate Governance and Audit Quality in Shari ' ah Compliant Companies Listed on Bursa Malaysia. *Modern Applied Science, 10*(7), 106–114. doi:10.5539/mas.v10n7p106

Kasim, N., Mohamad Ibrahim, S. H., & Sulaiman, M. (2009). *Shari'ah* Auditing in Islamic Financial Institutions: Exploring the Gap between the "Desired" and the "Actual.". *Global Economy and Finance Journal, 2*(2), 127–137.

Kasim, N., Sanusi, Z. M., Mutamimah, T., & Handoyo, S. (2013). Assessing the current practice of Auditing in Islamic Financial Institutions in Malaysia and Indonesia. *International Journal of Trade, Economics, and Finance, 4*(6), 414–418.

Khalid, A. A., Haron, H., & Masron, T. A. (2018). Competency and effectiveness of internal *Shari'ah* audit in Islamic financial institutions. *Journal of Islamic Accounting and Business Research, 9*(2), 201–221. doi:10.1108/JIABR-01-2016-0009

Malaysia, B. N. (2010). *Shari'ah Governance Framework for Islamic Financial Institutions*. Kuala Lumpur, Malaysia: Bank Negara Malaysia.

Malkawi, B. (2014). A Bright Future: Towards an Enhanced *Shari'ah* Supervision in Islamic Finance. *The European Financial Review*, 14–16.

Mallin, C., Farag, H., & Ow-Yong, K. (2014). Corporate social responsibility and financial performance in Islamic banks. *Journal of Economic Behavior & Organization, 103*, S21–S38. doi:10.1016/j.jebo.2014.03.001

Miskam, S., & Nasrul, M. A. (2013). *Shari'ah* Governance In Islamic Finance. *The Effects Of The Islamic Financial Services Act, 2013*(November), 455–463.

Najeeb, S. F., & Ibrahim, S. H. M. (2014). Professionalizing the role of *Shari'ah* auditors: How Malaysia can generate economic benefits. *Pacific-Basin Finance Journal, 28*, 91–109. doi:10.1016/j.pacfin.2013.10.009

Omar, N., & Bakar, K. M. A. (2012). Fraud prevention mechanisms of Malaysian government-linked companies: An assessment of existence and effectiveness. *Journal of Modern Accounting and Auditing, 8*(1), 15–31.

Othman, R., Ishak, I. F., Arif, S. M. M., & Aris, N. A. (2014). Influence of Audit Committee Characteristics on Voluntary Ethics Disclosure. *Procedia: Social and Behavioral Sciences, 145*, 330–342. doi:10.1016/j.sbspro.2014.06.042

Platonova, E., Asutay, M., Dixon, R., & Mohammad, S. (2018). The Impact of Corporate Social Responsibility Disclosure on Financial Performance: Evidence from the GCC Islamic Banking Sector. *Journal of Business Ethics, 151*(2), 451–471. doi:10.100710551-016-3229-0

Rafay, A., & Farid, S. (2018). *Shari'ah* Supervisory Board Report (SSBR) in Islamic Banks: An experimental study of Investors' perception and behaviour. *International Journal of Islamic and Middle Eastern Finance and Management, 11*(2), 274–296. doi:10.1108/IMEFM-07-2017-0180

Safiullah, M., & Shamsuddin, A. (2018). Risk in Islamic banking and corporate governance. *Pacific-Basin Finance Journal, 47*(2), 129–149. doi:10.1016/j.pacfin.2017.12.008

Sayd Farook, M. O. F. (2013). *Shari'ah* governance, expertise and profession: Educational challenges in Islamic finance. *International Journal of Islamic Finance, 5*(1), 137–160. doi:10.12816/0002761

Shafii, Z., Abidin, A. Z., Salleh, S., Jusoff, K., & Kasim, N. (2013). Post implementation of *Shari'ah* governance framework: The impact of *Shari'ah* audit function towards the role of *Shari'ah* committee. *Middle East Journal of Scientific Research, 13*(SI), 7-11.

Shafii, Z., Salleh, S., & Shahwan, S. H. (2010). Management of *Shari'ah* Non-Compliance Audit Risk in the Islamic Financial Institutions via the Development of *Shari'ah* Compliance Audit Framework and *Shari'ah* Audit Programme. *Kyoto Bulletin of Islamic Area Studies, 3–2*(3), 3–16.

Ullah, S., Harwood, I. A., & Jamali, D. (2018). 'Fatwa Repositioning': The Hidden Struggle for Shari'a Compliance Within Islamic Financial Institutions. *Journal of Business Ethics, 149*(4), 895–917. doi:10.100710551-016-3090-1

Yussof, S. A. (2013). Prospects of a Sharīᶜah Audit Framework for Islamic Financial Institutions in Malaysia. *Islam and Civilisational Renewal, 4*(1), 80–102. doi:10.12816/0009724

Zakaria, N., & Ariffin, N. M., N. Z. A. (2016). Construct of *Shari'ah* Audit Effectiveness in Islamic Financial Institutitons. In *6th IIUM International Accounting Conference Oct. 28-29, 2015 Kuala Lumpur, Malaysia.*

## ADDITIONAL READING

Bakar, D. (2016). *Shari'ah Minds in Islamic Finance: An Inside Story of a Shari'ah Scholar (book).* Amanie Media.

Hanefah, M. M. (2012). *Governance and Shari'ah.* Audit in Islamic Financial Institutions.

Hasan, Z. (2014). In search of the perceptions of the *Shari'ah* scholars on *Shari'ah* governance system. *International Journal of Islamic and Middle Eastern Finance and Management, 7*(1), 22–36. doi:10.1108/IMEFM-07-2012-0059

## KEY TERMS AND DEFINITIONS

***Shari'ah*:** The code of law derived from the *Qur'an* and from the teachings and example of Prophet Mohammad (May peace be upon him); "*Shari'ah* is only applicable to Muslims".

***Shari'ah*** **Audit:** Refers to the periodical assessment conducted from time to time, to provide an independent assessment and objective assurance designed to add value and improve the degree of compliance in relation to the IFI's business operations, with the main objective of ensuring a sound and effective internal control system for *Shari'ah* compliance (*SGF-Section IV, Principle 7 (ii); 7.7)*.

***Shari'ah*** **Review:** Refers to regular assessment on *Shari'ah* compliance in the activities and operations of the IFI by qualified *Shari'ah* officer(s)12, with the objective of ensuring that the activities and operations carried out by the IFI do not contravene with the *Shari'ah (SGF-Section IV, Principle 7 (i); 7.3)*.

***Shari'ah*** **Risk Management:** Refers to systematically identify, measure, monitor and control of *Shari'ah* non-compliance risks to mitigate any possible of non-compliance events. The systematic approach of managing *Shari'ah* non-compliance risks will enable the IFI to continue its operations and activities effectively without exposing the IFI to unacceptable levels of risk (*SGF-Section IV, Principle 7 (iii); 7.15*).

# Compilation of References

Abbas, M., Azid, T., & Hj Besar, M. H. A. (2016). Efficiency, effectiveness and performance profile of Islamic and conventional banks in Pakistan. *Humanomics*, *32*(1), 2–18. doi:10.1108/H-09-2015-0058

Abbas, S. Z. M., Mahmud, R., & Manan, N. S. A. (2017). Foreign ownership and performance of Islamic banks. *Journal of Computational and Theoretical Nanoscience*, *23*(8), 7594–7596.

Abbott, L. J., Daugherty, B., Parker, S., & Peters, G. F. (2016). Internal Audit Quality and Financial Reporting Quality: The Joint Importance of Independence and Competence. *Journal of Accounting Research*, *54*(1), 3–40. doi:10.1111/1475-679X.12099

Abd Razak, A. H. (2018). Centralisation of corporate governance framework for Islamic financial institutions: Is it a worthy cause? *ISRA International Journal of Islamic Finance*, *10*(1), 36–51. doi:10.1108/IJIF-08-2017-0020

Abdalla, M. A. D. (2016). *Converting Conventional banks to Islamic: A Study on Influencing Factors and the Role of the Central bank, legislation and laws banking in Libya*. (Unpublished doctoral dissertation) Universiti Sains Islam Malaysia.

Abdalla, M. A. D., Aziz, M. R., & Johari, F. (2015). Analyzing the Impact of Banking laws and Legislations on the Converting of Conventional Banks into Islamic in Libya. *International Journal of Management and Applied Research*, *2*(4), 156–171.

Abdalla, M. A. D., & Ridhwan, M. A. Bin, Johari, F. B., & Musbah, A. R. (2015). Human Requirements for the Success of the Islamization of Conventional Banks. *Asian Journal of Management Sciences & Education*, *4*(January), 82–91.

Abdelsalam, O., Dimitropoulos, P., Elnahass, M., & Leventis, S. (2016). Earnings management behaviors under different monitoring mechanisms: The case of Islamic and conventional banks. *Journal of Economic Behavior & Organization*, *132*(1), 155–173. doi:10.1016/j.jebo.2016.04.022

Abdelsalam, O., Duygun, M., Matallín-Sáez, J. C., & Tortosa-Ausina, E. (2014). Do ethics imply persistence? The case of Islamic and socially responsible funds. *Journal of Banking & Finance*, *40*, 182–194. doi:10.1016/j.jbankfin.2013.11.027

Abduh, M., & Omarov, D. (2013). Muslim's Awareness and Willingness to Patronize Islamic Banking in Kazakhstan. *Journal of Islamic Banking and Finance, July-Sep*(January 2013), 16–24.

Abduh, M., Kassim, S. H., & Dahari, Z. (2013). Factors Influence Switching Behavior of Islamic Bank Customers in Malaysia. *Journal of Islamic Finance*, *2*(1), 12–19. doi:10.12816/0001113

Abdul Alim, E. (2014). *Global leaders in Islamic finance*. Singapore: John Wiley & Sons.

Abdul Razak, L., & Saupi, M. N. (2017). The concept and application of ḍamān al-milkiyyah (ownership risk): Islamic law of contract perspective. *ISRA International Journal of Islamic Finance*, *9*(2), 148–163. doi:10.1108/IJIF-06-2017-0002

Abdullah, W. A. W., Percy, M., & Stewart, J. (2014). Corporate governance disclosure practices of Islamic banks: the case of Islamic banks in the Southeast Asian and the Gulf cooperation council region. In *Journal of International Accounting Research (JIAR) Conference proceedings*, The Hong Kong Polytechnic University, Hong Kong.

Abdullah, H., & Valentine, B. (2009). Fundamental and Ethics Theories of Corporate Governance. *Middle Eastern Finance and Economics*, *4*(4), 88–96.

Abdulsaleh, A. M. (2017). The introduction of Islamic finance in Libya: Capturing the opportunities for SMEs development. *Journal of Emerging Economies and Islamic Research*, *5*(1), 39–48.

Abdu, M., Jibir, A., Abdullahi, S., & Rabi'u, A. A. (2018). Can Islamic Banking and Finance Spur Financial Inclusion? Evidence from Sub-Saharan Africa. *CBN Journal of Applied Statistics*, *9*(1), 77–104.

Abdurrouf, M. A. (2011). The relationship between corporate governance and value of the firm in developing countries: Evidence from Bangladesh. *The International Journal of Applied Economics and Finance*, *5*(3), 237–244. doi:10.3923/ijaef.2011.237.244

Abedifar, P., Ebrahim, M. S., Molyneux, P., & Tarazi, A. (2015). Islamic banking and finance: Recent empirical literature and directions for future research. *Journal of Economic Surveys*, *29*(4), 637–670. doi:10.1111/joes.12113

Abrhiem, T. H. (2013). Managing Transformation And Change For The Business Leader. *Business & Management Review*, *3*(2), 14–22.

Abu-Tapanjeh, A. M. (2009). Corporate governance from the Islamic perspective: A comparative analysis with OECD principles. *Critical Perspectives on Accounting*, *20*(5), 556–567. doi:10.1016/j.cpa.2007.12.004

Acharya, V. V., Hasan, I., & Saunders, A. (2006). Should banks be diversified? Evidence from individual bank loan portfolios. *The Journal of Business*, *79*(3), 1355–1412. doi:10.1086/500679

Ada, A. A., & Dalkılıç, N. (2014). Efficiency Analysis In Islamic Banks: A Study For Malaysia And Turkey. *BDDK Bankacılık ve Finansal Piyasalar*, *8*(1), 9–33.

Adams, R. B., & Mehran, H. (2012). Bank board structure and performance: Evidence for large bank holding companies. *Journal of Financial Intermediation*, *21*(2), 243–267. doi:10.1016/j.jfi.2011.09.002

Adel, A. K. S. (2016). *The Internal Obstacles Facing Conversion Process from Conventional Banks to Islamic Banking: An Empirical Study on Libyan Conventional Banks*. (Unpublished doctoral dissertation) Universiti Sains Islam Malaysia.

African Development Bank. (2018). North Africa Economic Outlook. Retrieved from https://www.afdb.org/fileadmin/uploads/afdb/Documents/Publications/2018AEO/African-Economic-Outlook-2018-North-Africa.pdf

Ahmad & Al-Aidaros. (2015). (2015). The Need of Independent *Shari'ah* Members in Islamic Cooperative Banks: An Empirical Study of Professional Accountants in Malaysia. *International Review of Management and Business Research*, *4*(1), 110–120.

Ahmad, W., & Luo, R. H. (2010). Comparison of banking efficiency in Europe: Islamic versus conventional banks. In S. Kim, & M. D. Mckenzie (Eds.), International banking in the new era: Post-crisis challenges and opportunities (International Finance Review, Vol 11) (361-389). Bingley, UK: Emerald Group.

Ahmed, H. (2011). *Shari'ah* Governance Regimes for Islamic Finance: Types and Appraisal-I regimi di governance conformi alla *shari'ah* nella finanza islamica: tipologia e valutazione. *Economia Internazionale/International Economics, 64*(4), 393-412.

Ahmed, M. (2009, October 14). *Did Islamic banks in the Gulf do better than conventional ones in the crisis*? Retrieved May 23, 2019, from https://blogs.imf.org/2009/10/14/islamic-banking/

Ahmed, H. (2009). Financial Crisis Risks and Lessons for Islamic Finance. *ISRA International Journal of Islamic Finance*, *1*(1), 7–32.

Ahmed, H. (2014). Islamic Banking and *Shari'ah* Compliance: A Product Development Perspective. *Journal of Islamic Finance*, *3*(2), 15–29. doi:10.12816/0025102

Ahmed, M., & Khatun, M. (2013). The Compliance with *Shari'ah* Governance System of AAOIFI : A Study on Islamic Banks Bangladesh Introduction : *Journal of Islamic Economics. Banking and Finance*, *9*(3), 15.

AI-Abdullatif. S. A. (2007). *The application of the AAOIFI accounting standards by the Islamic banking sector in Saudi Arabia* (Doctoral dissertation). Durham University, UK.

Ainley, M., Mashayekhi, A., Hicks, R., Rahman, A., & Ravalia, A. (2007). *Islamic finance in the UK: Regulation and challenges. The Financial Services Authority*. London, UK: FSA.

Akın, F., & Ece, N. (2010). İslami Finans Sistemi İçerisinde İslami Bankacılığın Yeri ve Türkiye'de Katılım Bankacılığının Gelişimi. *Mevzuat Dergisi*, *13*(151), 4–5.

Al Arif, M. N. R. (2015). Impact of spin-off policy on the asset growth on Indonesian Islamic banking industry. *Journal of Islamic Economics, Banking, and Finance*, *113*(3158), 1–12.

Al Bashir, M., & Al Amine, M. (2016). Islamic Finance in Africa: Current Penetration. In *Islamic Finance and Africa's Economic Resurgence: Promoting Diverse and Localized Investment (PP 53-120)*. Palgrave Macmillan.

Al Bashir, M., & Al Amine, M. (2016). Islamic Finance in Africa: Current Penetration. *Palgrave Studies*. In *Islamic Banking, Finance, And Economics*. Islamic Finance And Africa's Economic.

Al Bashir, W.A., & Zainuddin, Y., & Panigrahi Albashir, S. K. (2018). The Acceptance of Islamic Banking Products in Libya: A Theory of Planned Behavior Approach. *International Journal of Economics and Financial Issues*, *8*(3), 105–111.

Al-Amine, M. A. B. M. (2011). *Global Sukūk and Islamic Securitization Market: Financial Engineering and Product Innovation*. Boston, MA: Brill.

Alam, N. (2013). Impact of banking regulation on risk and efficiency in Islamic banking. *Journal of Financial Reporting and Accounting*, *11*(1), 29–50. doi:10.1108/JFRA-03-2013-0010

Alam, N., Zainuddin, S. S. B., & Rizvi, S. A. R. (2019). Ramifications of varying banking regulations on performance of Islamic Banks. *Borsa Istanbul Review*, *19*(1), 49–64. doi:10.1016/j.bir.2018.05.005

Alani, O. (2017). Islamic banking challenges in Libya. *Ijtihad Journal*, *12*, 371–393.

Al-Atyat, Y. (2007). *Transforming Conventional Banks to work According to Islamic Shari'a: A Study to show the Viability of Application in Jordan. Aman*. The Arab Academy for Banking and Financial Science.

Albertazzi, U., & Bottero, M. (2014). Foreign bank lending: Evidence from the global financial crisis. *Journal of International Economics*, *92*, S22–S35. doi:10.1016/j.jinteco.2014.01.002

Al-Darīr, S. M. A.-A. (1995). Al-Gharar wa Atharuhū Fī al-'Uqūd: Fī al-Fiqhi al-Islāmiyyi (2nd ed.). Jeddah, Saudi Arabia: Dallah al-Barakah.

AL-Hersh, N. F. (2016). The Impact of Jordan's Conventional and Islamic Banking Development Factors on Economic Growth. *International Journal of Economics & Finance*, *8*(9), 148. doi:10.5539/ijef.v8n9p148

Ali, S. S. (2011). *Islamic banking in the MENA region* (The World Bank- Islamic Development Bank Islamic Research and Training Institute Working Paper). Retrieved from http://citeseerx.ist.psu.edu/viewdoc/download?doi=10.1.1.454.2588&rep=rep1&type=pdf

Ali, A. S. (2015). Islamic Micro-finance: Moving beyond Financial inclusion. *European Scientific Journal*, *11*(10), 297–310.

Ali, S. A. M., Hassan, R., & Othman, A. A. (2017). Inadequacy of Consumer Protection from Unfair Contract Terms in Musharakah Mutanaqisah Home Financing in Malaysia. *Journal of Islamic Finance*, *6*(Special Issue), 231–241. doi:10.12816/0047351

Ali, S., & Ali, N. (1994). *Information Sources on Islamic Banking and Economics: 1980-1990*. London, UK: Kegan Paul International.

Alkassim, F. A. (2005). *The profitability of Islamic and conventional banking in the GCC countries: A comparative study* (Working Paper). Retrieved from http://upnews.kbu.ac.th/uploads/files/2012/04/04/Profitability_Islamic_B anking.pdf

Alkhamees, A. (2013). The impact of *Shari'ah* governance practices on *Shari'ah* compliance in contemporary Islamic finance. *Journal of Banking Regulation*, *14*(2), 134–163. doi:10.1057/jbr.2012.12

Alman, M. (2012). *Shari'ah* Supervisory Board Composition Effects on Islamic Banks' Risk-Taking Behavior. *Journal of Banking Regulation*, *14*(1), 134–163.

Almutairi, A. R., & Quttainah, M. A. (2017). Corporate governance: Evidence from Islamic banks. *Social Responsibility Journal*, *13*(3), 601–624. doi:10.1108/SRJ-05-2016-0061

Al-Nasser Mohammed, S. A. S., & Muhammed, J. (2017). The relationship between agency theory, stakeholder theory and Shari'ah supervisory board in Islamic banking: An attempt towards discussion. *Humanomics*, *33*(1), 75–83. doi:10.1108/H-08-2016-0062

Alqahtani, F., Mayes, D. G., & Brown, K. (2017). Islamic bank efficiency compared to conventional banks during the global crisis in the GCC region. *Journal of International Financial Markets, Institutions, and Money*, *51*(1), 58–74. doi:10.1016/j.intfin.2017.08.010

Al-Rbaia, S. M. (1989). Conversion of Conventional bank to Islamic bank and requirements. *Makkah AL-Mukarramah: Umm AL-Qura*.

Al-Tamimi, H. A. H. (2010). Factors influencing performance of the UAE Islamic and conventional national banks. *Global Journal of Business Research*, *4*(2), 1–11.

Altunbas, Y., Manganelli, S., & Marques-Ibanez, D. (2011). Bank risk during the Great Recession: Do business models matter? *ECB Working Paper* 1394.

Al-Zuhaili, W. (2003). *Financial Transactions in Islamic Jurisprudence* Vol. 1-2, (M. A. El-Gamal, Ed.). Damascus, Syria: Dar al-Fikr al-Muaasir.

Al-Zuhayli, W. (2003). Financial Transactions in Islamic Jurisprudence (M. A. El-Gamal, Trans. Vol. 1). Damascus, Syria: Dar al-Fikr.

Ammann, M., Oesch, D., & Schmid, M. M. (2013). Product market competition, corporate governance, and firm value: Evidence from the EU area. *European Financial Management*, *19*(3), 452–469. doi:10.1111/j.1468-036X.2010.00605.x

Anas, M., & Zafar, F. (2018). An Overview of SME sector, Market Access, ISO Certifications and Compliance. *SME Observer*, *8*(1), 9–14. Retrieved from https://smeda.org/phocadownload/Publicatoins/SME Observer Jan - Jun 2018.pdf

Andrieş, A. M., & Căpraru, B. (2014). The nexus between competition and efficiency: The European banking industries experience. *International Business Review*, *23*(3), 566–579. doi:10.1016/j.ibusrev.2013.09.004

Angell, J. W. (1935). The 100 Per Cent Reserve Plan. *The Quarterly Journal of Economics*, *50*(1), 1–35. doi:10.2307/1882341

Angkinand, A., & Wihlborg, C. (2010). Deposit insurance coverage, ownership, and banks' risk-taking in emerging markets. *Journal of International Money and Finance*, *29*(2), 252–274. doi:10.1016/j.jimonfin.2009.08.001

AOIFI. (2015). *Shari'ah Standard*. Manama, Bahrain: AAOIFI.

Armenakis, A. A., Bernerth, J. B., Pitts, J. P., & Walker, H. J. (2007). Organizational Change Recipients ' Beliefs Scale Development of an Assessment Instrument. *The Journal of Applied Behavioral Science*, *43*(4), 481–505. doi:10.1177/0021886307303654

Arshad, M. U., Yusoff, M. E., & Tahir, M. S. (2016). Issues in transformation from conventional banking to Islamic banking. *International Journal of Economics and Financial Issues*, *6*(3), 220–224.

Asadov, A., Muhamad Sori, Z. B., Mohamad Ramadilli, S., Anwer, Z., & Shamsudheen, S. V. (2018). Musharakah Mutanaqisah home financing: Issues in practice. *Journal of Islamic Accounting and Business Research*, *9*(1), 91–103. doi:10.1108/JIABR-08-2015-0036

Ashraf, S., Robson, J., & Sekhon, Y. (2015). Consumer trust and confidence in the compliance of Islamic banks. *Journal of Financial Services Marketing*, *20*(2), 133–144. doi:10.1057/fsm.2015.8

Asian Development Bank. (2009). *Key Indicators for Asia and the Pacific 2009: Enterprises in Asia: Fostering Dynamism in SMEs*. Retrieved January 5, 2019, from https://www.adb.org/sites/default/files/publication/27727/special-chapter-06.pdf

Asian Development Bank. (2018). *Asian Development Outlook*. Retrieved from https://www.adb.org/sites/default/files/publication/411666/ado2018.pdf

Asif, M., Ahmed, U., Zahid, M., & Khan, A. (2017). Motives Behind the Transfer of a Bank From Conventional Banking to Islamic Banking in Pakistan. *Journal of Business and Tourism*, *3*(2), 225–234.

Askari, H., Iqbal, Z., Mirakhor, A., & Krichenne, N. (2010). The Stability of Islamic Finance: Creating a Resilient Financial Environment for a Secure Future. Singapore: John Wiley & Sons (Asia). doi:10.1002/9781118390450

Asutay, M., & Harningtyas, A. F. (2015). Developing Maqasid al-Shari'ah index to evaluate social performance of Islamic banks: A conceptual and empirical attempt. *International Journal of Islamic Economics and Finance Studies*, *1*(1), 5–64.

Asutay, M., & Izhar, H. (2007). Estimating the profitability of Islamic banking: Evidence from bank Muamalat Indonesia. *Review of Islamic Economics*, *11*(2), 17–29.

Athanasoglou, P. P., Brissimis, S. N., & Delis, M. D. (2008). Bank-specific, industry-specific and macroeconomic determinants of bank profitability. *Journal of International Financial Markets, Institutions and Money*, *18*(2), 121–136. doi:10.1016/j.intfin.2006.07.001

Ayachi, R. A., Saidane, D., & Mansouri, F. (2017). Potential of Islamic finance: A survey of Tunisian Northwest companies. *Journal of Emerging Economies & Islamic Research*, *5*(2), 28–42.

Ayadi, R., De Groen, W. P., & Author. (2018). Financial Development and Inclusion in Egypt, Jordan, Morocco And Tunisia. *EMNES Studies, 4*. Retrieved from http://www.euromed-economists.org/wp-content/uploads/2018/05/EMNES_Study_004-Financial_Development_Inclusion-Egypt_Jordan_Morocco_Tunisia-v2.pdf)

Ayub, M. (2007). *Understanding Islamic finance*. Chichester, UK: John Wiley & Sons.

Ayub, M. (2007). *Understanding Islamic Finance*. West Sussex, UK: John Wiley & Sons.

Azli, R. M., Othman, R., Sahri, M., Aris, N. A., Arshad, R., & Yaakob, A. R. (2011). Implementation of Maqasid Shari'ah in Islamic house financing: A study of the rights and responsibilities of contracting parties in Bai' Bithaman Ajil and Musharakah Mutanaqisah. *Journal of Applied Business Research, 27*(5), 85–96. doi:10.19030/jabr.v27i5.5595

Baej, Y. M. A. H. (2013). *A Comparison of Key Dimensions in Conventional and Islamic Banking : An International Perspective with Implications for the Bank Transformation Process in Libya*. (Published doctoral dissertation) Griffith University.

Bahari, N. F., & Baharudin, N. A. (2016). *Shari'ah* Governance Framework: The role of *Shari'ah* review and *Shari'ah* auditing. *International Journal of Management, 3*(1), 15–18.

Bahrain Economic Development Board. (2017). *Bahrain for Islamic Finance*. Retrieved June 13, 2019, from https://bahrainedb.com/app/uploads/2017/06/IslamicFinance-254x179-Insert-Jun2017.pdf

Bait Al-Mashura Finance Consultations. (2017). *Islamic finance in Qatar (Report 2017)*. Retrieved from http://b-mashura.com/wp-content/uploads/2018/10/Islamic-finance-in-the-State-of-Qatar-Report-2017-1.pdf

Bakar, M. D. (2016). *Shari'ah Minds in Islamic Finance*. Kuala Lumpur, Malaysia: Amanie Media.

Bank Indonesia. (2002). *Cetak Biru Pengembangan Perbankan Syariah Indonesia*. Retrieved June 6, 2019, from https://www.bi.go.id/id/publikasi/lain/lainnya/pages/blue%20print.aspx

Bank Indonesia. (2004a). *Indonesian Banking Architecture*. Retrieved December 10, 2017, from http://www.bi.go.id/en/perbankan/arsitektur/struktur/Contents/Default.aspx

Bank Indonesia. (2004b). *Structural Reinforcement of the National Banking System Program*. Retrieved December 10, 2017, from http://www.bi.go.id/en/perbankan/arsitektur/struktur/Contents/Default.aspx

Bank Indonesia. (2009). *Peraturan Bank Indonesia Nomor 11/3/PBI/2009*. Retrieved June 6, 2019, from https://www.bi.go.id/id/peraturan/perbankan/Pages/pbi_110309.aspx

Bank Indonesia. (2012). *Peraturan Bank Indonesia Nomor 14/8/PBI/2012 Tentang Kepemilikan Saham Bank Umum*. Retrieved December 13, 2017, from http://www.bi.go.id/id/peraturan/perbankan/Documents/015ad3f77e3846f3a2ea16e18d778ee2pbi_140813.pdf

Bank Indonesia. (2013a). *Bank Indonesia Transferring Regulation and Supervision of Banks to Financial Service Authority*. Retrieved December 13, 2017 http://www.bi.go.id/en/ruang-media/siaran-pers/Pages/SP_155613_DKom.aspx

Bank Indonesia. (2013b). SE/*BI/ No. 15/26/DPbS Perihal Pedoman Akuntansi Perbankan Islamic Indonesia*. Retrieved February, 21 2019, from https://www.ojk.go.id/id/kanal/perbankan/Pages/Pedoman-Akuntansi-Perbankan-Indonesia-(PAPI).aspx

Bank Indonesia. (2017). *Financial Stability Review*. Retrieved January 5, 2019, from http://www.bi.go.id/en/publikasi/perbankan-dan-stabilitas/kajian/Documents/FSR_28_0317.pdf

Bank Indonesia. (2018). *Halal Industry Development To Support National Economic Growth*. Retrieved June 6, 2019, from https://www.bi.go.id/en/ruang-media/info-terbaru/Pages/Pengembangan-Industri-Halal-Dukung-Pertumbuhan-Ekonomi-Nasional.aspx

Bank Negara Malaysia. (2006). *Guidelines on the Establishment of International Islamic Bank*. Kuala Lumpur: Bank Negara Malaysia Retrieved February 7, 2019, from http://www.bnm.gov.my/index.php?ch=57&pg=137&ac=54&bb=file

Barth, J. R., Nolle, D. E., Phumiwasana, T., & Yago, G. (2003). A cross-country analysis of the bank supervisory framework and bank performance. *Financial Markets. Institutions & Instruments*, *12*(2), 67–120. doi:10.1111/1468-0416.t01-2-00001

Bashir, A. H. M. (2003). Determinants of profitability in Islamic banks: Some evidence from the Middle East. *Islamic Economic Studies*, *11*(1), 31–57.

Bayramoğlu, M, F. & Başarır, Ç. (2018). Türk Katılım Bankalarının Risk Derecelendirmesi: CAMELS Tabanlı TOPSIS Modeli Uygulaması, *İşletme & Ekonomi Yazıları, 5*(2), 390-399.

Baysinger, B. D., & Butler, H. N. (1985). Corporate Governance and the Board of Directors: Performance Effects of Changes in Board Composition. *Journal of Law Economics and Organization*, *1*(1), 101–124.

Beck, T., Demirguc-Kunt, A., & Merrouche, O. (2013). Islamic versus conventional banking: Business model, efficiency and stability. *Journal of Banking & Finance*, *37*(2), 433–447. doi:10.1016/j.jbankfin.2012.09.016

Behzadian, M., Otaghsara, S. K., Yazdani, M., & Ignatius, J. (2012). A State of Art Survey of TOPSIS Applications. *Expert Systems with Applications*, *39*(17), 13051–13069. doi:10.1016/j.eswa.2012.05.056

Belal, Z., & Hassan, R. (2015). Legal and Regulatory Framework of Islamic Banking in Libya. *Al Mashalih – Journal Of Islamic Law*, 46-58. Retrieved from https://www.researchgate.net/publication/330102366_LEGAL_AND_REGULATORY_FRAMEWORK_OF_ISLAMIC_BANKING_IN_LIBYA/citation/download

Ben Bouheni, F., & Ammi, C. (2015). Banking Governance: What's Special About Islamic Banks? *Journal of Applied Business Research*, *31*(4), 1621–1630. doi:10.19030/jabr.v31i4.9341

Ben Zeineb, G., & Mensi, S. (2018). Corporate governance, risk and efficiency: Evidence from GCC Islamic banks. *Managerial Finance*, *44*(5), 551–569. doi:10.1108/MF-05-2017-0186

Berger, A. N., DeYoung, R., Genay, H., & Udell, G. (2000). Globalization of financial institutions: Evidence from cross-border banking performance. Brookings–Wharton Papers on Financial Services, 2000(1), 23–72.

Berger, A. N., & Hannan, T. H. (1998). The efficiency cost of market power in the banking industry: A test of the "quiet life" and related hypotheses. *The Review of Economics and Statistics*, *80*(3), 454–465. doi:10.1162/003465398557555

Berger, A. N., Imbierowicz, B., & Christian, R. (2016). The roles of corporate governance in bank failures during the recent financial crisis. *Journal of Money, Credit and Banking*, *48*(4), 729–770. doi:10.1111/jmcb.12316

Besar, M. H. A., Abd Sukor, M. E., Abdul Muthalib, N., & Gunawa, A. Y. (2009). The Practice of *Shari'ah* Review as Undertaken by Islamic Banking Sector in Malaysia. *International Review of Business Research Papers*, *5*(1), 294–306.

Besar, M. H. A., Sukor, M. E. A., Muthalib, N. A., & Gunawa, A. Y. (2009). The practice of Shari'ah review as undertaken by Islamic banking sector in Malaysia. *International Review of Business Research Papers*, *5*(1), 294–306.

Bhasin, B. B., & Venkataramany, S. (2010). Globalization of entrepreneurship: Policy considerations for SME development in Indonesia. *International Business and Economic Research Journal*, *9*(4), 95–103.

Bhat, G., Hope, O.-K., & Kang, T. (2006). Does corporate governance transparency affect the accuracy of analyst forecasts? *Accounting and Finance*, *46*(5), 715–732. doi:10.1111/j.1467-629X.2006.00191.x

Bhatti, E. (2018, October 29). BankIslami becomes victim of $6.5 million cyber-attack. *Pakistan Todau*. Retrieved from https://profit.pakistantoday.com.pk/2018/10/29/bankislami-becomes-victim-of-6-5-million-cyber-attack/

binti Kasim, N., Ibrahim, S. H. M., S. (2009). *Shari'ah* Auditing in Islamic financial institutions: Exploring the gap between the "desired" and the "actual." *Global Economy and Finance Journal, 2*(2), 127–137.

Binti Kasim, N., Ibrahim, S. H. M., & Sulaiman, M. (2013). Emerging issues for auditing in Islamic Financial Institutions : Empirical evidence from Malaysia. *Journal of Business and Management*, *8*(5), 10–17.

BOI. (2017). *Board of Investment Mauritius*. Retrieved from www.investmauritius.com

Boon Ka, A. N. (2009). Shari'ah and legal issues of Musharakah Mutanaqisah. *New Horizon, Oct–Dec*(173), 46–48.

Bordo, M. D. (2008). *An Historical Perspective on the Crisis of 2007-2008*. Paper presented at the Central Bank of Chile Twelfth Annual Conference on "Financial Stability, Monetary Policy and Central Banking." Santiago, Chile, November 6-7, Santiago, Chile.

Bossone, B. (2002). Should Banks Be 'Narrowed'? *Public Policy Brief No. 69*.

Bouckenooghe, D., Devos, G., & Van Den Broeck, H. (2009). Organizational Change Questionnaire – Climate of Change, Processes, and Readiness: Development of a New Instrument. *The Journal of Psychology*, *143*(6), 559–599. doi:10.1080/00223980903218216 PMID:19957876

Bourkhis, K., & Nabi, M. S. (2013). Islamic and conventional banks' soundness during the 2007-2008 financial crisis. *Review of Financial Economics*, *22*(2), 68–77. doi:10.1016/j.rfe.2013.01.001

Bransdma, J., & Hart, L. (2004). *Making Microfinance Work better in the Middle East and North Africa (English). (Working Paper NO 29657)*. Washington, DC: World Bank; Retrieved from http://documents.worldbank.org/curated/en/889971468774294069/pdf/296570ENGLISH0Microfinance0in0MNA.pdf

Brouwer, M. (2005). Managing Uncertainty through Profit Sharing Contracts from Medieval Italy to Silicon Valley. *The Journal of Management and Governance*, *9*(3-4), 237–755. doi:10.100710997-005-7420-4

Buschmeyer, A., Schuh, G., & Wentzel, D. (2016). Organizational Transformation Towards Product-service Systems – Empirical Evidence in Managing the Behavioral Transformation Process. *Procedia CIRP*, *47*, 264–269. doi:10.1016/j.procir.2016.03.224

Butt, I., Ahmad, N., Naveed, A., & Ahmed, Z. (2018). Determinants of low adoption of Islamic banking in Pakistan. *Journal of Islamic Marketing*, *9*(3), 655–672. doi:10.1108/JIMA-01-2017-0002

Canbaz, M. (2012). Katılım Bankacılığı ve Türkiye'deki gelişimi. In F. Kaya (Ed.), *Bankacılık giriş ve ilkeler* (pp. 137–198). İstanbul, Turkey: Beta Basım.

Canbaz, M. (2014). Katılım Bankacılığı ve Türkiye'deki gelişimi. In F. Kaya (Ed.), *Bankacılık giriş ve ilkeleri* (pp. 149–252). İstanbul, Turkey: Beta Basım.

Caprio, G., & Klingebiel, D. (2002). Episodes of systemic and borderline banking crises: Managing the real and fiscal effects of banking crises. *World Bank Discussion Paper, 428*, 31-49.

Casu, B., & Girardone, C. (2006). Bank competition, concentration and efficiency in the single European market. *Manchester School*, *74*(4), 441–468. doi:10.1111/j.1467-9957.2006.00503.x

Casu, B., & Girardone, C. (2009). Testing the relationship between competition and efficiency in banking: A panel data analysis. *Economics Letters*, *105*(1), 134–137. doi:10.1016/j.econlet.2009.06.018

Cebeci, I. (2012). Integrating the social *Maslaha* into Islamic finance. *Accounting Research Journal*, *25*(3), 166–184. doi:10.1108/10309611211290158

Central Bank of Libya. (2014). *Annual-report- Central Bank of Libya 2014*.

Central Bank of Libya. (2014b). *The potential risks of implementing the free - interest law No 1/2013 on the banking sector*. El-Bieda.

Central Committee for *Shari'ah* advisory (Central Bank of Libya). (2016). *Evaluating the conversion process toward islamic banking in the Libyan banking sector. Reality and Prospects.*

Chachi, A. (2005). Origin and development of commercial and Islamic banking operations. *Journal of King Abdulaziz University: Islamic Economics*, *18*(2), 3–25.

Chapra, M. U., & Khan, T. (2000). *Regulation and Supervision of Islamic Banks*. Jeddah, Saudi Arabia: IRTI.

Chapra, M., & Ahmed, H. (2002). *Corporate Governance in Islamic Financial Institution*. Occasional Paper. Islamic Research and Training Institute/ Islamic Development Bank.

Chapra, M. U. (1985). *Towards a Just Monetary system: A Discussion of Money, Banking and Monetary Policy in the Light of Islamic Teaching*. London, UK: The Islamic Foundation.

Chapra, M. U. (1988). Towards An Islamic Financial System. *IIUM Journal of Economics and Management*, *1*(2), 1–30.

Chapra, U. (2007). The Case Against *Riba*: Is It Compelling? *Thunderbird International Business Review*, *49*(2), 161–186. doi:10.1002/tie.20138

Chatti, M. A., Kablan, S., & Yousfi, O. (2013). Are Islamic banks sufficiently diversified? An empirical analysis of eight Islamic banks in Malaysia. *Islamic Economic Studies*, *21*(2), 23–54. doi:10.12816/0001557

Chen, H.-J., & Lin, K.-T. (2016). How do banks make the trade-offs among risks? The role of corporate governance. *Journal of Banking & Finance*, *72*(Supplement), S39–S69. doi:10.1016/j.jbankfin.2016.05.010

Chen, M., Wu, J., Jeon, B. N., & Wang, R. (2017). Do foreign banks take more risk? Evidence from emerging economies. *Journal of Banking & Finance*, *82*(C), 20–39. doi:10.1016/j.jbankfin.2017.05.004

Chen, N., Liang, H.-Y., & Yu, M.-T. (2018). Asset diversification and bank performance: Evidence from three Asian countries with a dual banking system. *Pacific-Basin Finance Journal*, *52*, 40–53. doi:10.1016/j.pacfin.2018.02.007

Chong, B., & Liu, M. (2009). Islamic banking: Interest-free or interest-based? *Pacific-Basin Finance Journal*, *17*(1), 125–144. doi:10.1016/j.pacfin.2007.12.003

CIBAFI. (2017). *Corporate Governance Practices in Islamic Banks 2017* (General Council for Islamic Banks and Financial Institutions and The World Bank Group). Retrieved June 04, 2019, from http://cibafi.org/ControlPanel/Documents/Library/Pdf/CorporateGovernancePracticesinIslamicBanks2017.pdf

Čihák, M., & Hesse, H. (2010). Islamic Banks and Financial Stability: An Empirical Analysis. *Journal of Financial Services Research*, *38*(2-3), 95–113. doi:10.100710693-010-0089-0

Cizakca, M. (2014). Risk sharing and risk shifting: An historical perspective. *Borsa Istanbul Review*, *14*(4), 191–195. doi:10.1016/j.bir.2014.06.001

Cole, R. A., & White, L. J. (2012). Déjà vu all over again: The causes of U.S. commercial bank failures this time around. *Journal of Financial Services Research*, *42*(1-2), 5–29. doi:10.100710693-011-0116-9

Cooper, G. (2008). *The Origin of Financial Crises: Central Banks, Credit Bubles and the Efficient Market Fallacy*. Hampshire, UK: Harriman House.

Cunningham, C. E., Woodward, C. A., Shannon, H. S., MacIntosh, J., Lendrum, B., Rosenbloom, D., & Brown, J. (2002). Readiness for organizational change: A longitudinal study of workplace, psychological and behavioural correlates. *Journal of Occupational and Organizational Psychology*, *75*(4), 377–392. doi:10.1348/096317902321119637

Daily, C. M., Dalton, D. R., & Cannella, A. A. Jr. (2003). Corporate Governance: Decades of Dialogue and Data. *Academy of Management Journal*, *28*(3), 371–382.

Dalio, R. (2019). Why and How Capitalism Needs to Be Reformed (Parts 1 & 2). Retrieved from https://www.linkedin.com/pulse/why-how-capitalism-needs-reformed-parts-1-2-ray-dalio/?published=t

Damak, M. (2018). Islamic finance 2018: slow growth is the new normal. In *Islamic Finance Outlook (5th Edition)*. S&P Global Ratings.

Dam, K. W. (2009). The subprime crisis and financial regulation: International and comparative perspectives. *Chicago Journal of International Law*, *10*(2), 581–638.

Deegan, C., & Blomquist, C. (2006). Stakeholder influence on corporate reporting: An exploration of the interaction between WWF-Australia and the Australian minerals industry. *Accounting, Organizations, and Society*, *31*(4-5), 343–372. doi:10.1016/j.aos.2005.04.001

Delis, M. D., & Papanikolaou, N. I. (2009). Determinants of bank efficiency: Evidence from a semi-parametric methodology. *Managerial Finance*, *35*(3), 260–275. doi:10.1108/03074350910931771

Deloitte. (2016). *Taxation and Investment in Malaysia 2016 Reach, Relevance, and Reliability*. Retrieved February 22, 2019, from https://www2.deloitte.com/content/dam/Deloitte/global/Documents/Tax/dttl-tax-malaysiaguide-2016.pdf

Demirgüç-Kunt, A., & Huizinga, H. (2000). Financial structure and bank profitability. *World Bank Policy Research Working Paper*, (2430).

Demirguc-Kunt, A., Klapper, L., & Randall, D. (2013). Islamic Finance and Financial Inclusion: Measuring Use of and Demand for Formal Financial Services among Muslim Adults (Policy Research Working Paper: 6642) [PDF File]. Retrieved from http://documents.worldbank.org/curated/en/611351468337493348/pdf/WPS6642.pdf

Demirguc-Kunt, A., Klapper, L., Singer, D., & Van, O. P. (2015). The Global Findex Database 2014: Measuring Financial Inclusion around the World. (Policy Research Working Paper: WPS 7255) [PDF File]. Retrieved from http://documents.worldbank.org/curated/en/187761468179367706/

Demirgüç-Kunt, A., & Huizinga, H. (1999). Determinants of commercial bank interest margins and profitability: Some international evidence. *The World Bank Economic Review*, *13*(2), 379–408. doi:10.1093/wber/13.2.379

Demirgüç-Kunt, A., & Huizinga, H. (2010). Bank activity and funding strategies: The impact on risk and returns. *Journal of Financial Economics*, *98*(3), 626–650. doi:10.1016/j.jfineco.2010.06.004

Dempsey, M. (2013). Libya in Transition: Reforming the financial sector to spur economic growth (Case Study).

Derigs, U., & Marzban, S. (2008). Review and analysis of current Shariah-compliant equity screening practices. *International Journal of Islamic and Middle Eastern Finance and Management*, *1*(4), 285–303. doi:10.1108/17538390810919600

DeYoung, R., & Roland, K. P. (2001). Product mix and earnings volatility at commercial banks: Evidence from a degree of total leverage model. *Journal of Financial Intermediation*, *10*(1), 54–84. doi:10.1006/jfin.2000.0305

DeYoung, R., & Torna, G. (2013). Nontraditional banking activities and bank failures during the financial crisis. *Journal of Financial Intermediation*, *22*(3), 397–421. doi:10.1016/j.jfi.2013.01.001

DinarStandard. (2018). *Islamic fintech report 2018 current landscape & path forward.* Retrieved May 23, 2019, from https://www.dinarstandard.com/wp-content/uploads/2018/12/Islamic-Fintech-Report-2018.pdf

Doan, A. T., Lin, K. L., & Doong, S. C. (2018). What drives bank efficiency? The interaction of bank income diversification and ownership. *International Review of Economics & Finance*, *55*, 203–219. doi:10.1016/j.iref.2017.07.019

Doumpos, M., Gaganis, C., & Pasiouras, F. (2016). Bank diversification and overall financial strength: International evidence. *Financial Markets. Institutions & Instruments*, *25*(3), 169–213. doi:10.1111/fmii.12069

Dusuki, A. W. (2006). Corporate governance and stakeholder management: An Islamic perspective. In *National Seminar in Islamic Banking and Finance,* KUIM, Nilai, Aug. 20-30.

Dusuki, A. W. (2008). What Does Islam Say about Corporate Social Responsibility? *Review of Islamic Economics*, *12*(1), 5–28. doi:10.2190/86QB-KKY1-F27L-3KHK

Dusuki, A. W., & Abdullah, N. I. (2007). Maqasid al-Shari`ah, *Maslaha*h, and Corporate Corporate social responsibility. *The American Journal of Islamic Social Sciences*, *24*(1), 25–45. Retrieved from http://irep.iium.edu.my/2209

Earnest & Young. (2016). *World Islamic Banking Competitiveness Report 2016.* Retrieved from Earnest and Yong Website: https://www.ey.com/em/en/industries/financial-services/banking---capital-markets/ey-banking-in-emerging-markets

Ebrahim, M. S., & Joo, T. K. (2001). Islamic banking in Brunei DarusSalam. *International Journal of Social Economics*, *28*(4), 314–337. doi:10.1108/03068290110357708

Echchabi, A., Azouzi, D., & Abd. Aziz, H. (2016). The future prospects of Islamic banking in Tunisia: An empirical survey. *EuroMed Journal of Business*, *11*(1), 119–131. doi:10.1108/EMJB-03-2015-0018

El-brassi, M. A. M. A., Bello, N., & Alhabshi, S. M. (2017). Libya's transformation to an Islamic financial ystem: Issues and challenges. *International Review of Management and Business Research*, *6*(3), 976–994.

El-Gamal, M. A. (2006). *Islamic Finance: Law, Economics, and Practice.* Cambridge, UK: Cambridge University Press. doi:10.1017/CBO9780511753756

Elgari, M. A. (2003). Credit risk in Islamic banking and finance. *Islamic Economic Studies*, *6*(2), 1–25.

Elsas, R., Hackethal, A., & Holzhäuser, M. (2010). The anatomy of bank diversification. *Journal of Banking & Finance*, *34*(6), 1274–1287. doi:10.1016/j.jbankfin.2009.11.024

Endaya, K. A., & Hanefah, M. M. (2013). Internal Audit Effectiveness: An Approach Proposition to Develop the Theoretical Framework. *Research Journal of Finance and Accounting*, *4*(10), 92–102.

Endaya, K. A., & Hanefah, M. M. (2016). Internal auditor characteristics, internal audit effectiveness, and moderating effect of senior management. *Journal of Economic and Administrative Sciences*, *32*(2), 160–176. doi:10.1108/JEAS-07-2015-0023

Erkens, D. H., Hung, M., & Matos, P. (2012). Corporate governance in the 2007–2008 financial crisis: Evidence from financial institutions worldwide. *Journal of Corporate Finance*, *18*(2), 389–411. doi:10.1016/j.jcorpfin.2012.01.005

Ernst & Young. (2015). *Indonesian Banking Industry: Challenging yet Promising.* Retrieved June 4, 2018, from http://www.ey.com/Publication/vwLUAssets/EY-Indonesian-banking-industry-challenging-yet-promising/%24FILE/EY-indonesian-banking-industry-challenging-yet-promising.pdf

EY. (2017). *Luxembourg: the gateway for Islamic finance and the Middle East.* Retrieved May 23, 2019 from https://www.ey.com/Publication/vwLUAssets/Luxembourg:_the_ gateway_for_Islamic_finance_and_the_Middle_East__May_2017/$FILE/Islamic%20Finance%20-%20May%202017-LR.pdf

Fama, E. F., & Jensen, M. C. (1983). Separation of Ownership and Control. *The Journal of Law & Economics*, *26*(2), 301–325. doi:10.1086/467037

Farag, H., Mallin, C., & Ow-Yong, K. (2018). Corporate governance in Islamic banks: New insights for dual board structure and agency relationships. *Journal of International Financial Markets, Institutions, and Money*, *54*, 59–77. doi:10.1016/j.intfin.2017.08.002

Farook, S., Hassan, K., & Lanis, R. (2011). Determinants of corporate social responsibility disclosure: The case of Islamic banks. *Journal of Islamic Accounting and Business Research*, *2*(2), 114–141. doi:10.1108/17590811111170539

Farook, S., Hassan, M. K., & Clinch, G. (2014). Islamic bank incentives and discretionary loan loss provisions. *Pacific-Basin Finance Journal*, *28*, 152–174. doi:10.1016/j.pacfin.2013.12.006

Farook, S., & Lanis, R. (2007). Banking on Islam? Determinants of corporate social responsibility disclosure. *Advances in Islamic Economics and Finance*, *1*, 217–247.

Farooq, M. O. (2009). The *Riba*-interest equation and Islam: Re-examination of the traditional arguments. *Global Journal of Finance and Economics*, *6*(2), 99–11.

Fischel, W. (1933). The Origin of Banking in Medieval Islam. *Journal of the Royal Asiatic Society*, *65*(2), 339–352.

Fisher, I. (2009). *100% Money and the Public Debt*. Pakthongchai, Thailand: ThaiSunset Publications. By Irving Fisher originally published without copyright notice in the *Economic Forum* Spring Number, April-June 1936, pp. 406-420.

Friedman, M. (2015). *A Program for Monetary Stability*. Renenio Books.

FSF. (2008). *Report of the Financial Stability Forum on Enhancing Market and Institutional Resilience*. Retrieved from Basel, Switzerland: http://www.fsforum.org/publications/r_0804.pdf?noframes=1

Furqani, H., & Mulyany, R. (2009). Islamic banking and economic growth: Empirical evidence from Malaysia. *Journal of Economic Cooperation & Development*, *30*(2), 59–74.

Gait, A. H. A. (2009). Libyan attitudes towards Islamic methods of finance: An empirical analysis of retail consumers, business firms and banks. (PhD dissertation), Griffith University.

GAIT, A.H. (2009). The Impact of Demographic Variables on Libyan Retail Consumers' Attitudes towards Islamic Methods of Finance. *Islamic Economic Studies*, *17*(1), 1–18.

Gamra, S. B., & Plihon, D. (2011). Revenue diversification in emerging market banks: Implications for financial performance. *CEPN Working Papers hal-00598136*, HA.

Garcia, V. F., Cibis, V. F., & Maino, R. (n.d.). Remedy for Banking Crises: What Chicago and Islam Have in Common. (Unpublished). *World Bank and IMF Staffs*.

Gelbard, E. A., Hussain, M., Maino, R., Mu, Y., & Yehoue, E. B. (2014). *Islamic finance in Sub-Saharan Africa: status and prospects*. IMF working paper WP/14/149, International Monetary Fund, Washington, DC, 1-28.

Gelbard, M. E., Hussain, M. M., Maino, M. R., Mu, M. Y., & Yehoue, M. E. B. (2014). Islamic finance in sub-Saharan Africa: Status and prospects (No. 14-149). International Monetary Fund.

Ghani, N. L. A., & Rahman, A. R. A. (2015). An analysis of *Shari'ah* audit practices in islamic banks in Malaysia. *Jurnal Pengurusan*, *43*, 107–118. doi:10.17576/pengurusan-2015-43-10

Ghayad, R. (2008). Corporate governance and the global performance of Islamic banks. *Humanomics*, *24*(3), 207–216. doi:10.1108/08288660810899368

Gheeraert, L. (2014). Does Islamic finance spur banking sector development? *Journal of Economic Behavior & Organization, 103*, S4–S20. doi:10.1016/j.jebo.2014.02.013

Gheeraert, L., & Weill, L. (2015). Does Islamic banking development favor macroeconomic efficiency? Evidence on the Islamic finance-growth nexus. *Economic Modelling, 47*, 32–39. doi:10.1016/j.econmod.2015.02.012

Gherbi, E. H. (2018). Factors of Influence in The Establishment of Islamic Banking and Finance in Algeria. *Academy of Accounting and Financial Studies Journal, 22*(1), 1–7.

Ginena, K. (2017). *Shari'ah* risk and corporate governance of Islamic banks. *Corporate Governance: The International Journal of Business in Society, 1*(14), 25–40.

Ginena, K., & Hamid, A. (2015). The Shari'ah Supervisory board. In *Foundations of Shari'ah Governance of Islamic Banks*. Chichester, UK: John Wiley & Sons.

Global Banking & Finance Review. (2013). *List of Islamic banks in Kuwait*. Retrieved May 23, 2019 from https://www.globalbankingandfinance.com/list-of-islamic-banks-in-kuwait/

Global Islamic Finance Report. (2016). Islamic Financial Policy. Islamic Project Finance: A Growing Trend International Bank for Reconstruction and Development / The World Bank (2017). Mobilizing Islamic Finance for Infrastructure Public-Private Partnerships, Report 2017.

Goetz, M. R., Laeven, L., & Levine, R. (2013). Identifying the valuation effects and agency costs of corporate diversification: Evidence from the geographic diversification of U.S. banks. *Review of Financial Studies, 26*(7), 1787–1823. doi:10.1093/rfs/hht021

Gompers, P. A., Ishii, J. L., & Metrick, A. (2003). Corporate Governance and Equity Prices. *The Quarterly Journal of Economics, 118*(1), 107–155. doi:10.1162/00335530360535162

Grais, W., & Pellegrini, M. (2006). *Corporate Governance and Shari'ah Compliance in Institutions Offering Islamic Financial Services*. World Bank Policy Research Working Paper. World Bank.

Grais, W., & Pellegrini, M. (2006a). *Corporate governance and Shari'ah compliance in institutions offering Islamic financial services*. (4054), World Bank policy working paper.

Grais, W., & Pellegrini, M. (2006b). *Corporate governance in institutions offering Islamic financial services: issues and options. (4052)*. World Bank Publications. doi:10.1596/1813-9450-4052

Grassa, R. (2013a). *Shari'ah* Governance System in Islamic Financial Institutions: New Issues and Challenges. *Arab Law Quarterly, 27*(2), 171–187. doi:10.1163/15730255-12341254

Grassa, R. (2013b). *Shari'ah* supervisory system in Islamic financial institutions: New issues and challenges: a comparative analysis between Southeast Asia models and GCC models. *Humanomics, 29*(4), 333–348. doi:10.1108/H-01-2013-0001

Grassa, R. (2015). *Shari'ah* supervisory systems in Islamic finance institutions across the OIC member countries: An investigation of regulatory frameworks. *Journal of Financial Regulation and Compliance, 23*(2), 135–160. doi:10.1108/JFRC-02-2014-0011

Grassa, R. (2016). Corporate governance and credit rating in Islamic banks : Does Shari'ah governance matters? Springer US. *The Journal of Management and Governance, 20*(4), 875–906. doi:10.100710997-015-9322-4

Grassa, R., & Matoussi, H. (2014). Corporate governance of Islamic banks: A comparative study between GCC and Southeast Asia countries. *International Journal of Islamic and Middle Eastern Finance and Management, 7*(3), 346–362. doi:10.1108/IMEFM-01-2013-0001

Guarda, P., Rouabah, A., & Vardanyan, M. (2013). Identifying bank outputs and inputs with a directional technology distance function. *Journal of Productivity Analysis*, *40*(2), 185–195. doi:10.100711123-012-0326-7

Guide to Making Federal Acts and Regulations. (2001). Government of Canada, Privy Council Office, 2nd Edition. Retrieved from https://www.canada.ca/en/privy council/services/publications/guide-makingfederal-acts-regulations.html

Gül, M., & Ak, M. F. (2018). A comparative outline for quantifying risk ratings in occupational health and safety risk assessment. *Journal of Cleaner Production*, *196*, 653–664. doi:10.1016/j.jclepro.2018.06.106

Guo, L., Jalal, A., & Khaksari, S. (2014). Bank executive compensation structure, risk taking and the financial crisis. *Review of Quantitative Finance and Accounting*, *45*(3), 609–639. doi:10.100711156-014-0449-1

Habib, F., & Shaukat, M. (2016). Shariah appraisal of the *Takaful* model based on 'tabarru' (donation). *Journal of Islamic Banking & Finance*, *33*(3), 65–83.

Hakimi, A., Rachdi, H., Ben Selma Mokni, R., & Hssini, H. (2018). Do board characteristics affect bank performance? Evidence from the Bahrain Islamic banks. *Journal of Islamic Accounting and Business Research*, *9*(2), 251–272. doi:10.1108/JIABR-06-2015-0029

Hamidi, M. L., Worthington, A. C., West, T., & Ismal, R. (2018). *The Prospect of Islamic Social Banking in Indonesia.* Paper presented at the 4th International Monetary Economics and Finance Conference (IIMEFC), Surabaya, Indonesia.

Hamza, H. (2013). Sharia governance in Islamic banks: Effectiveness and supervision model. *International Journal of Islamic and Middle Eastern Finance and Management*, *6*(3), 226–237. doi:10.1108/IMEFM-02-2013-0021

Hanefah, M. H. (2018). *Corporate and Shari'ah governance in public listed companies and public trust entities. Bandar Baru.* USIM Press.

Haniffa, R., & Hudaib, M. (2007). Exploring the ethical identity of Islamic Banks via communication in annual reports. *Journal of Business Ethics*, *76*(1), 97–116. doi:10.100710551-006-9272-5

Haqqi, A. R. (2014). *Shari'ah* governance in Islamic Financial Institution: An Appraisal. *The Journal of Risk Finance*, *13*(1), 13–20.

Haribowo, I. (2017). The Indonesian Islamic bank's spin-off: A study in regional development banks. *Al-Iqtishad: Jurnal Ilmu Ekonomi Syariah*, *9*(1), 53–68.

Harris, L. C., & Ogbonna, E. (1998). Employee responses to culture change efforts. *Human Resource Management Journal*, *8*(2), 78–92. doi:10.1111/j.1748-8583.1998.tb00168.x

Hasan, M. M., & Dridi, J. (2010). *The effects of the global crisis on Islamic and conventional banks: A comparative study* (IMF Working Paper 10/201). Retrieved from https://www.imf.org/external/pubs/ft/wp/2010/wp10201.pdf

Hasan, Z. B. (2009). Regulatory framework of *Shari'ah* governance system in Malaysia, GCC Countries and the UK. *Kyoto Bulletin of Islamic Area Studies*, 3-2.

Hasan, A., & Sabirzyanov, R. (2015). Optimal *Shari'ah* Governance Model in Islamic Finance Regulation. *International Journal of Education and Research*, *3*(4), 243–258.

Hasan, A., & Sawari, Md., M. F. (2011). Analysis on Shari'ah governance in Islamic banking: a comparative perspective. In *International Conference on Shari'ah Governance in Islamic Banking Across Jurisdiction*, Dec. 3, 2011, Inna Garuda Hotel, Yogyakarta, Indonesia.

Hasan, M. B., Islam, S. M. N., & Wahid, A. N. M. (2018). The Effect of Macroeconomic Variables on the Performance of Non-life Insurance Companies in Bangladesh. *Indian Economic Review*, *53*(1-2), 369–383. doi:10.100741775-019-00037-6

Hasan, Z. (2009). Corporate Governance: Western and Islamic Perspectives. *International Review of Business Research Papers*, *5*(1), 277–293.

Hasan, Z. (2011). A survey on *Shari'ah* governance practices in Malaysia, GCC countries and the UK: Critical appraisal. *International Journal of Islamic and Middle Eastern Finance and Management*, *4*(1), 30–51. doi:10.1108/17538391111122195

Hasan, Z. (2012). *Shari'ah Governance in Islamic banks*. Edinburgh University Press.

Hashim, F., Mahadi, N. D., & Amran, A. (2015). Corporate Governance and Sustainability Practices in Islamic Financial Institutions: The Role of Country of Origin. *Procedia Economics and Finance*, *31*(15), 36–43. doi:10.1016/S2212-5671(15)01129-6

Hassan, R., Abdullah, N. I., Hassan, A., Ibrahim, U., Sawari, M. F., Aziz, A. A., & Triyanta, A. (2013). A Comparative Analysis of *Shari'ah* Governance in Islamic Banking Institutions Across Jurisdictions. *ISRA Research Paper*, 50, 1-63.

Hassan, M. K. (2006). The X-efficiency in Islamic banks. *Islamic Economic Studies*, *13*(2), 49–78.

Hassan, Z. (2019). Corporate governance: Western and Islamic perspectives. *International Review of Business Research Papers*, *5*(1), 2–3. Retrieved from http://industry.govmu.org/English/Documents/4_Financial%20Services_web.pdf

Holt, D. T., & Vardaman, J. M. (2013). Toward a Comprehensive Understanding of Readiness for Change: The Case for an Expanded Conceptualization. *Journal of Change Management*, *13*(1), 9–18. doi:10.1080/14697017.2013.768426

Hopener, A. G. F., Rammal, H. G., & Rezex, M. (2011). Islamic mutual funds' financial performance and international investment style: Evidence form 20 countries. *European Journal of Finance*, *17*(9-10), 829–850. doi:10.1080/1351847X.2010.538521

Humaira, M. A., & Iswusi, N. (2010). Converting conventional banks to Islamic banks: Empirical study on Jomhoryia and Trade & Development banks in Libya. *Islamic finance services conference*.

Husain, I. (2018). *Governing the Ungovernable: Institutional Reforms for Democratic Governance*. Oxford University Press.

Hussein, K. A. (2001). Operational Efficiency. In *Islamic Banking: The Sudanese Experience, Islamic Research And Training Enstitute*. Islamic Development Bank.

Hussien, M. E., Alam, M. M., Murad, M. W., & Wahid, A. N. (2019). The Performance of Islamic Banks during the 2008 Global Financial Crisis: Evidence from the Gulf Cooperation Council Countries. *Journal of Islamic Accounting and Business Research*, *10*(3), 407–420. doi:10.1108/JIABR-01-2017-0011

Hwang, C. L., & Yoon, K. (1981). *Multiple Attribute Decision Making: Methods and Applications*. Berlin, Germany: Springer-Verlag. doi:10.1007/978-3-642-48318-9

IFDI. (2018). *Islamic Finance Development Report 2018*. Retrieved from http://www.bitly/IFDatabaase

IFG-IFDI-Team. (2018). *Islamic Finance Development Indicator*. ICD-Thomson Reuters. Thomson Reuters. Retrieved from https://www.zawya.com/islamic-finance-development-indicator/files/IFDI-Rulebook.pdf?v2

IFSB. (2009). *Guiding Principles on Shari'ah Governance Systems for Institutions offering Islamic Financial Services*. Islamic Financial Services Board.

IFSB. (2017). *Islamic Financial Services Stability Report 2017*. Kuala Lumpur, Malaysia: Islamic Financial Services Board Publishing.

Ika, S. R., & Abdullah, N. (2011). A comparative study of financial performance of Islamic banks and conventional banks in Indonesia. *International Journal of Business and Social Science*, *2*(15), 199–207.

İlbahar, E., Karaşan, A., Çebi, S., & Kahraman, C. (2018). A novel approach to risk assessment for occupational health and safety using Pythagorean fuzzy AHP & fuzzy inference system. *Safety Science*, *103*, 124–136. doi:10.1016/j.ssci.2017.10.025

Indonesia Financial Services Authority. (2017). *Indonesia Banking Booklet: Volume 4.* Retrieved June 3, 2018, from http://www.ojk.go.id/en/kanal/perbankan/data-dan-statistik/booklet-perbankan-indonesia/Pages/Indonesia-Banking-Booklet-2017.aspx

Information, U. S. E. (2015). *Country Analysis Brief.* Libya.

International Monetary Fund. (2017). *Ensuring financial stability in countries with Islamic banking. IMF Country Report.*

Iqbal, Z., & Mirakhor, A. (2011) An Introduction to Islamic Finance: Theory and Practice, 2nd ed. Singapore: John Wiley & Sons (Asia). doi:10.1002/9781118390474

Iqbal, B. A., & Sami, S. (2017). Role of Banks in Financial Inclusion in India. *Contaduría y Administración*, *62*(2), 644–656. doi:10.1016/j.cya.2017.01.007

Iqbal, M., & Molyneux, P. (2005). *Thirty Years of Islamic Banking: History, Performance and Prospects.* Basingstoke, UK: Palgrave Macmillan.

Iqbal, Z., & Mirakhor, A. (2011). An introduction to Islamic finance. *Theory into Practice*, *687*. John Wiley & Sons.

Islamic Development Bank (IDB). (2017). Development Effectiveness Report 2017. Retrieved from http://idbsharedtech1.prod.acquia-sites.com/sites/default/files/2018-10/IsDB%20Develepment%20Effectiveness%20Review%202017.pdf

Islamic Development Bank (IDB). (2018). Development Effectiveness Report 2018. Retrieved from https://www.isdb.org/sites/default/files/media/documents/2019-04/IsDB_DER%202018_31Mar19_Optimized%20for%20Website.pdf

Islamic Development Bank (IDB). Annual Report. (2018). Transformation In A Fast-Changing World: A Road to Sustainable Development Goals. Retrieved from https://www.isdb.org/sites/default/files/media/documents/2019-04/usb%20Annual%20report%20English%202018_softproof.pdf

Islamic Financial Services Act 2013. (2015).

Islamic Financial Services Board. (2017). Islamic Financial Services Industry Stability Report 2017. Retrieved from https://www.ifsb.org/docs/IFSB%20IFSI%20Stability%20Report%202017.pdf

Islamic Research Institute. (2009). The Objectives Resolution. *Islamic Studies*, *48*, 89–118. Retrieved from http://www.jstor.org/stable/20839154

Islamic, C. L. R. (2016). *An Annual Publication Assessing the Key Issues and Trends in Islamic Commercial Law for the Broader Islamic Finance Industry.* Produced by ISRA & Thomson Reuters.

Ismail, F., Majid, M. S. A., & Rahim, R. A. (2013). Efficiency of Islamic and conventional banks in Malaysia. *Journal of Financial Reporting and Accounting*, *11*(1), 92–107. doi:10.1108/JFRA-03-2013-0011

Ismal, R. (2011). *Islamic banking in Indonesia: Lessons learned.* Paper presented at Multi-Year Expert Meeting on Services, Development and Trade: The Regulatory and Institutional Dimension, Geneva, Switzerland.

ISRA. (2011). Islamic Financial System: Principles and Operations. Kuala Lumpur: International Shari'ah Research Academy for Islamic Finance (ISRA).

Jaffar, M., & Manarvi, I. (2011). Performance comparison of Islamic and conventional banks in Pakistan. *Global Journal of Management and Business Research*, *11*(1), 1–7.

Jahanshahloo, G. R., Hosseinzadeh, L. F., & Izadikhah, M. (2006). Extension of the TOPSIS method for decision-making problems with fuzzy data. *Applied Mathematics and Computation*, *181*(2), 1544–1551. doi:10.1016/j.amc.2006.02.057

Jakarta Post. (2018, February 21). Government to spend Rp 404t on infrastructure projects in 2018. *Jakarta Post*. Retrieved from https://www.thejakartapost.com

Jeanne, O., & Korinek, A. (2014). Macroprudential policy beyond banking regulation. *Financial Stability Review*, *18*, 163–171.

Jensen, M. C. (2002). Value Maximization, Stakeholder Theory, and the Corporate Objective Function. *Business Ethics Quarterly*, *12*(2), 235–256. doi:10.2307/3857812

Jensen, M. C., & Meckling, W. H. (1976). Theory of The Firm: Managerial Behavior, Agency Costs and Ownership Structure. *Journal of Financial Economics*, *3*(4), 305–360. doi:10.1016/0304-405X(76)90026-X

Johnes, J., Izzeldin, M., & Pappas, V. (2014). A comparison of performance of Islamic and conventional banks 2004-2009. *Journal of Economic Behavior & Organization*, *103*(Supplement), S93–S107. doi:10.1016/j.jebo.2013.07.016

John, K., Sauders, A., & Senbet, L. W. (2000). A Theory of Bank Regulation and Management Compensation. *Review of Financial Studies*, *13*(1), 95–125. doi:10.1093/rfs/13.1.95

Jordan, C., & Jain, A. (2009, October). *Diversity and Resilience: Lessons from the Financial Crisis*. Paper presented at the Canadian Law and Economics Association Meeting, University of Toronto, Canada.

Kaabachi, S., & Obeid, H. (2016). Determinants of Islamic banking adoption in Tunisia: Empirical analysis. *International Journal of Bank Marketing*, *34*(7), 1069–1091. doi:10.1108/IJBM-02-2015-0020

Kabakova, O., & Plaksenkov, E. (2018). Analysis of factors affecting financial inclusion: Ecosystem view. *Journal of Business Research*, *89*, 198–205. doi:10.1016/j.jbusres.2018.01.066

Kabir Hassan, M. (2011). Financial development and economic growth: New evidence from panel data. *The Quarterly Review of Economics and Finance*, *51*(1), 88–104. doi:10.1016/j.qref.2010.09.001

Kahf, M., & Khan, T. (1992). *Principles of Islamic Financing: A Survey*. Jeddah, Saudi Arabia: Islamic Research and Training Institute (IRTI), Research Paper No. 16.

Kahf, M. (2006). Maqasid al Shari ' ah in the Prohibition of *Riba* and their Implications for Modern Islamic Finance. In *IIUM International Conference on Maqasid al Shari'ah* (pp. 184–203).

Kamali, M. H. (1999). "Maqāṣid al-sharī'ah": The objectives of Islamic law. *Islamic Studies*, *38*(2), 193–208.

Kamali, M. H. (2007). A Shari'ah Analysis of Issues in Islamic Leasing. *J.KAU: Islamic Econ.*, *20*(1), 3–22.

Kamali, M. H. (2013a). *Principles of Islamic Jurisprudence* (2nd ed.). Kuala Lumpur, Malaysia: Ilmiah Publishers Sdn. Bhd.

Kamali, M. H. (2013b). *The Right to Life, Security, Privacy and Ownership in Islam*. Kuala Lumpur, Malaysia: Ilmiah Publishers Sdn. Bhd.

Kamarudin, F., Sufian, F., Loong, F. W., & Anwar, N. A. M. (2017). Assessing the domestic and foreign Islamic banks efficiency: Insights from selected Southeast Asian countries. *Future Business Journal*, *3*(1), 33–46. doi:10.1016/j.fbj.2017.01.005

Kamarudin, M. F., Starr, K., Abdullah, A. N., & Husain, K. (2014). Communicating Change in Organizational Restructuring: A Grounded Theory Case Study. *Procedia: Social and Behavioral Sciences*, *155*(October), 496–501. doi:10.1016/j.sbspro.2014.10.329

Kaminsky, G. L., & Reinhart, C. M. (1999). The twin crises: The causes of banking and balance-of-payments problems. *The American Economic Review*, *89*(3), 473–500. doi:10.1257/aer.89.3.473

Kamla, R., & Rammal, G. H. (2013). Social reporting by Islamic banks: Does social justice matter? *Accounting, Auditing & Accountability Journal*, *26*(6), 911–945. doi:10.1108/AAAJ-03-2013-1268

Kammer, M. A., Norat, M. M., Pinon, M. M., Prasad, A., Towe, M. C. M., & Zeidane, M. Z. (2015). *Islamic Finance: Opportunities, Challenges, and Policy Options (No. 15)*. International Monetary Fund.

Kamran, R. (no date). *Interest (Riba) Religion and Spirituality.* Retrieved from http://www.booksie.com/all/allkamran-rifat/interest-(*Riba*)-the-myth-and-reality

Kanwal, S. (2018, October 2). The environmental issues in Pakistan. *The Frontier Post*. Retrieved from https://thefrontierpost.com/the-environmental-issues-in-pakistan/

Karimi, A. J. (2017). *Challenges facing Islamic banks*. Retrieved from https://pdfs.semanticscholar.org/6ca7/fe7cd-4303f716e0a54ea3fd5ad41e8e68aa3.pdf

Karim, R. A. A. (1990). The independence of religious and external auditors: The case of Islamic Banks. *Accounting, Auditing, & Accountability Journal*, *3*(3), 34–44.

Karim, R. A. A. (2001). International accounting harmonization, banking regulation, and Islamic banks. *The International Journal of Accounting*, *36*(2), 169–193. doi:10.1016/S0020-7063(01)00093-0

Kashyap, A. K., Rajan, R., & Stein, J. (2008). *The Global Roots of the Current Financial Crisis and its Implications for Regulation*. Paper presented at the 5th ECB Central Banking Conference, November. Retrieved from http://www.ecb.int/events/pdf/conferences/cbc5/Rajan.pdf?17bea4624be62b27d96a6a290c65da52

Kasim, N., Ain, N., Hashim, B., & Salman, S. A. (2016). Conceptual Relationship between Corporate Governance and Audit Quality in Shari ' ah Compliant Companies Listed on Bursa Malaysia. *Modern Applied Science*, *10*(7), 106–114. doi:10.5539/mas.v10n7p106

Kasim, N., Mohamad Ibrahim, S. H., & Sulaiman, M. (2009). *Shari'ah* Auditing in Islamic Financial Institutions: Exploring the Gap between the "Desired" and the "Actual.". *Global Economy and Finance Journal*, *2*(2), 127–137.

Kasim, N., Sanusi, Z. M., Mutamimah, T., & Handoyo, S. (2013). Assessing the current practice of Auditing in Islamic Financial Institutions in Malaysia and Indonesia. *International Journal of Trade, Economics, and Finance*, *4*(6), 414–418.

Kassim, S. H., & Abdulle, M. Y. (2012). Impact of global financial crisis on the performance of Islamic and conventional banks: Empirical evidence from Malaysia. *Journal of Islamic Economics. Banking and Finance*, *8*(4), 9–20.

Kassim, S. H., & Majid, S. A. (2010). Impact of financial shocks on Islamic banks: Malaysian evidence during 1997 and 2007 financial crises. *International Journal of Islamic and Middle Eastern Finance and Management*, *3*(4), 291–305. doi:10.1108/17538391011093243

Kayed, R. N., & Hassan, M. K. (2011). The global financial crisis and Islamic finance. *Thunderbird International Business Review*, *53*(5), 551–564. doi:10.1002/tie.20434

Kearney, A. T. (n.d.). *The future of Islamic banking*. Retrieved May 23, from https://www.atkearney.com/documents/10192/654853/Future+of+Islamic+Banking.pdf/27167edf-a96d-4465-b88a-83beb25ed4bd

Khalid, A. A., Haron, H., & Masron, T. A. (2018). Competency and effectiveness of internal *Shari'ah* audit in Islamic financial institutions. *Journal of Islamic Accounting and Business Research*, *9*(2), 201–221. doi:10.1108/JIABR-01-2016-0009

Khalid, S., & Amjad, S. (2018). Risk management practices in Islamic banks of Pakistan. *The Journal of Risk Finance, 2*(13), 8–10.

Khalily, M. A. B. (2016). Financial Inclusion, Financial Regulation, and Education in Bangladesh (ADBI Working Paper 621. Tokyo: Asian Development Bank Institute). Retrieved from https://www.adb.org/publications/financial-inclusion-financial-regulation-and-educationbangladesh

Khan, M. M., & Bhatti, M. I. (2008). *Developments in Islamic Banking: The Case of Pakistan*. doi:10.1057/9780230582309

Khan, T., & Ahmed, H. (2001). Risk Management –An Analysis of Issues in Islamic Financial Industry. *Islamic Development Bank-Islamic Research and Training Institute*, Occasional Paper, 91, the Islamic Research and Teaching Institute (IRTI).

Khan, I., Khan, M., & Tahir, M. (2017). Performance comparison of Islamic and conventional banks: Empirical evidence from Pakistan. *International Journal of Islamic and Middle Eastern Finance and Management, 10*(3), 419–433. doi:10.1108/IMEFM-05-2016-0077

Khan, M. A. (2005). *Islamic Economics and Finance: A Glossary (2nd editio)*. London, UK: Routledge.

Khan, M. S. (1986). Islamic Interest-Free Banking: A Theoretical Analysis. *Staff Papers - International Monetary Fund. International Monetary Fund, 33*(1), 1–27. doi:10.2307/3866920

Khan, M., & Bhatti, M. (2008). Islamic banking and finance: On its way to globalization. *Managerial Finance, 34*(10), 708–725. doi:10.1108/03074350810891029

Khediri, K. B., Charfeddine, L., & Youssef, S. B. (2015). Islamic versus conventional banks in the GCC countries: A comparative study using classification techniques. *Research in International Business and Finance, 33*(1), 75–98. doi:10.1016/j.ribaf.2014.07.002

Kim, D.-W., Yu, J.-S., & Hassan, M. K. (2018). Financial Inclusion and Economic Growth in OIC Countries. *Research in International Business and Finance, 43*, 1–14. doi:10.1016/j.ribaf.2017.07.178

Kipchillis, J. K. (2017). *Libya islamic banking strategy and action plan*. Washington, DC: World Bank Group.

Kirkpatrick, G. (2009). The corporate governance lessons from the financial crisis. *OECD Journal: Financial Market Trends, 2019*(1). Retrieved from https://www.oecd-ilibrary.org/content/paper/fmt-v2009-art3-en

Knight, F., Cox, G., Director, A., Douglas, P., Hart, A., Mints, L., ... Simons, H. (1933). Memorandum on banking reform, Franklin D. Roosevelt Presidential Library, President's Personal File, 431.

Kobayakawa, S., & Nakamura, H. (1999). A Theoretical Analysis of Narrow Banking Proposals. *IMES Discussion Paper Series 99-E-19*.

Konstans, P. (2006). Reforming Deposit Insurance. *Public Policy Brief, No. 83*.

Kontan. (2017, January 23). Setelah Bank Aceh, 3 BPD minat konversi ke Syariah. *Kontan*. Retrieved from https://keuangan.kontan.co.id

Kotlikoff, L. J. (2010). *Jimmy Stewart is Dead: Ending the World's Ongoing Financial Plague with Limited Purpose Banking*. Hoboken, NJ: John Wiley & Sons.

Kouser, R., & Saba, I. (2012). Gauging the financial performance of banking sector using CAMEL model: Comparison of conventional, mixed and pure Islamic banks in Pakistan. *International Research Journal of Finance and Economics, 82*(1), 67–88.

Kpodar, K., & Imam, P. A. (2010). Islamic banking: how has it diffused? *IMF Working Papers*, 1-29.

Kreft, S., Eckstein, D., & Melchior, I. (2017). *Global Climate Risk Index 2017: Who suffers most from extreme weather events? Weather-related loss events in 2015 and 1996 to 2015*. Retrieved from https://germanwatch.org/sites/germanwatch.org/files/publication/16411.pdf

Kumati, A. (2008). *Commercial Banking In Libya And The Potential For Islamic Banking*. (Published doctoral dissertation), Durham University.

Laeven, L. (2013). Corporate Governance: What's Special About Banks? *Annual Review of Financial Economics*, *5*(1), 63–92. doi:10.1146/annurev-financial-021113-074421

Laeven, L., & Levine, R. (2007). Is there a diversification discount in financial conglomerates? *Journal of Financial Economics*, *85*(2), 331–367. doi:10.1016/j.jfineco.2005.06.001

Lahrech, N., Lahrech, A., & Boulaksil, Y. (2017). Transparency and performance in Islamic Banking. *International Journal of Islamic and Middle Eastern Finance and Management*, *7*(1), 5–10.

Laldin, M. A., Bouheraoua, S., Ansary, R., Khir, M. F. A., Ali, M. M., & Mustafa, M. M. (2013). Islamic Legal Maxims & Their Applications in Islamic Finance. Kuala Lumpur, Malaysia: International Shariah Research Academy for Islamic Finance (ISRA).

Laldin, M. A., & Furqani, H. (2018). Islamic Financial Services Act (IFSA) 2013 and the Sharīʿah-compliance requirement of the Islamic finance industry in Malaysia. *ISRA International Journal of Islamic Finance*, *10*(1), 94–101. doi:10.1108/IJIF-12-2017-0052

Lallmahamood, M. (2014). Islamic finance in Mauritius: Prospects and Challenges. *Journal of Islamic Business and Management*, *4*(1), 25–35. doi:10.12816/0019137

Latip, M., Yahya, M. H., & Junaina, M. (2017). Factors Influencing Customer's Acceptance of Islamic Banking Products and Services. *Ikonomika*, *2*(1), 1–18. doi:10.24042/febi.v2i1.681

Lau, L. J. (2010). *Financial regulation and supervision post the global financial crisis.* Working Paper No. 2. Institute of Global Economics and Finance, Chinese University of Hong Kong.

Law No 7 - 2015. (2015). (قانون 7-2015 المعدل للقانون 1-2013 بشأن منع المعاملات الربوية.

Lee, C. C., Hsieh, M. F., & Yang, S. J. (2016). The effects of foreign ownership on competition in the banking industry: The key role of financial reforms. *Japan and the World Economy*, *37*, 27–46. doi:10.1016/j.japwor.2016.02.002

Lee, C. C., & Hsieh, M.-F. (2014). Bank reforms, foreign ownership, and financial stability. *Journal of International Money and Finance*, *40*, 204–224. doi:10.1016/j.jimonfin.2013.09.001

Lee, K., & Ullah, S. (2011). Customers' attitude toward Islamic banking in Pakistan. *International Journal of Islamic and Middle Eastern Finance and Management*, *4*(2), 131–145. doi:10.1108/17538391111144524

Lensink, R., Meesters, A., & Naaborg, I. (2008). Bank efficiency and foreign ownership: Do good institutions matter? *Journal of Banking & Finance*, *32*(5), 834–844. doi:10.1016/j.jbankfin.2007.06.001

Leon, F., & Weill, L. (2016). Islamic Banking Development and Access to Credit (University of Strasbourg Working paper, No. 2016/02). Retrieved from https://ideas.repec.org/p/lar/wpaper/2016-02.html

Lepetit, L., Nys, E., Rous, P., & Tarazi, A. (2008). Bank income structure and risk: An empirical analysis of European banks. *Journal of Banking & Finance*, *32*(8), 1452–1467. doi:10.1016/j.jbankfin.2007.12.002

Levine, R. (2004). *The Corporate Governance of Banks: A Concise Discussion of Concepts and Evidence*. World Bank Policy Research Working Paper. World Bank.

Levine, R. (1997). Financial Development and Economic Growth: Views and Agenda. *Journal of Economic Literature*, *35*, 688–726.

Levine, R. (2010). An autopsy of the US financial system: Accident, suicide, or negligent homicide. *Journal of Financial Economic Policy*, *2*(3), 196–213. doi:10.1108/17576381011085421

Lewis, M. K. (2007). Islamic banking in theory and practice. *Monash Business Review*, *3*(1), 1–8.

Libyan Civil code (1953).

Litan, R. E. (1987). *What Should Banks Do?* Washington, DC: Brookings Institution.

Loyaza, N., & Ranciere, R. (2006). Financial Development, Financial Fragility, and Growth. *Journal of Money, Credit, and Banking*, *38*(4), 1051–1076. doi:10.1353/mcb.2006.0060

Ltifi, M., Hikkerova, L., Aliouat, B., & Gharbi, J. (2016). The determinants of the choice of Islamic banks in Tunisia. *International Journal of Bank Marketing*, *34*(5), 710–730. doi:10.1108/IJBM-11-2014-0170

Lugo, L., & Cooperman, A. (2011). *The future of the global Muslim population*. USA: Pew Research Center.

Magalhães, R., & Al-Saad, S. (2013). Corporate governance in Islamic financial institutions: The issues surrounding unrestricted investment account holders. *Corporate Governance: The International Journal of Business in Society*, *13*(1), 39–57. doi:10.1108/14720701311302404

Mahdzan, N. S., Zainudin, R., & Au, S. F. (2017). The adoption of Islamic banking services in Malaysia. *Journal of Islamic Marketing*, *8*(3), 496–512. doi:10.1108/JIMA-08-2015-0064

Majeed, M. T., & Zainab, A. (2017). How Islamic is Islamic banking in Pakistan? *International Journal of Islamic and Middle Eastern Finance and Management*, *10*(4), 470–483. doi:10.1108/IMEFM-03-2017-0083

Majeed, M. T., & Zanib, A. (2016). Efficiency analysis of Islamic banks in Pakistan. *Humanomics*, *32*(1), 19–32. doi:10.1108/H-07-2015-0054

Malaysia World's Islamic Finance Marketplace. (2014). *Islamic finance ready to finance a greener world*. Retrieved 23 May, 2019 from http://www.mifc.com/index.php?ch=28&pg=72&ac=88&bb=uploadpdf

Malaysia, B. N. (2010). *Shari'ah Governance Framework for Islamic Financial Institutions*. Kuala Lumpur, Malaysia: Bank Negara Malaysia.

Malekian, E., & Daryaei, A. (2018). Islamic values forward into better corporate governance systems. *International Journal of Business and Economics*, *2*(8), 6–9.

Malik, M. S., Malik, A., & Mustafa, W. (2011). Controversies that make Islamic banking controversial: An analysis of issues and challenges. *American journal of social and management sciences, 2*(1), 41-46.

Malik, M. S., Malik, A., & Mustafa, W. (2011). Controversies that make Islamic banking controversial: An analysis of issues and challenges. *American Journal of Social and Management Sciences*, *2*(1), 41–46. doi:10.5251/ajsms.2011.2.1.41.46

Malkawi, B. (2014). A Bright Future: Towards an Enhanced *Shari'ah* Supervision in Islamic Finance. *The European Financial Review*, 14–16.

Malkawi, B. H. (2013). *Shari'ah* Board in the Governance Structure of Islamic Financial Institutions. *The American Journal of Comparative Law*, *61*(3), 539–578. doi:10.1093/ajcl/61.3.539

Mallin, C., Farag, H., & Ow-Yong, K. (2014). Corporate social responsibility and financial performance in Islamic banks. *Journal of Economic Behavior & Organization*, *103*, S21–S38. doi:10.1016/j.jebo.2014.03.001

Masruki, R., Ibrahim, N., Osman, E., & Wahab, H. A. (2011). Financial performance of Malaysian founder Islamic banks versus conventional banks. *Journal of Business and Policy Research*, *6*(2), 67–79.

Matoussi, H., & Grassa, R. (2012). Is Corporate Governance Different for Islamic Banks? A Comparative Analysis Between the Gulf Cooperation Council Context and The Southeast Asia Context. In the Economic Research Forum, 734, 2-28.

Maurer, R. (1996). Using resistance to build support for change. *Journal for Quality and Participation*, *19*(3), 56.

Mauritius National Investment Promotion Agency. (2014). *Global Assets under Management by product*. Retrieved from MCCI. (2017). *Economic Data*. Retrieved from https://www.mcci.org/en/publications/economic-data/

McLellan, D. (Ed.). (2000). *Karl Marx: Selected Writings*. Oxford, UK: Oxford University Press; doi:10.12681/grsr.651

Meera, A. K. M., & Abdul Razak, D. (2005). Islamic home financing through musharakah mutanaqisah and al-bay bithaman ajil contract: A comparative analysis. *Review of Islamic Economics*, *9*(2), 5–30.

Meera, A. K. M., & Razak, D. A. (2005). Islamic home financing through *Musharakah Mutanaqisah* and *al-bay' bithaman ajil* contracts: A comparative analysis. *Review of Islamic Economics*, *9*(2), 5–30.

Meezan Bank. (2017). *Annual Report*. Retrieved from http://www.sbp.org.pk/stats/Balance/2017/MeezanBankLtd.pdf

Mercieca, S., Schaeck, K., & Wolfe, S. (2007). Small European banks: Benefits from diversification? *Journal of Banking & Finance*, *31*(7), 1975–1998. doi:10.1016/j.jbankfin.2007.01.004

Mersch, Y. (2009). About the Role of Central Bank in Financial Stability and Prudential Liquidity Supervision, and the Attractiveness of Islamic Finance. IFSB 2nd Public Lecture on Financial Policy and Stability, Kuala Lumpur: Islamic Financial Services Board (IFSB).

Mezzi, N. (2018). Efficiency of Islamic banks and role of governance: Empirical evidence. *Managerial Finance*, *44*(5), 590–603. doi:10.1108/MF-05-2017-0171

MIAC. (2014, January). *The litmus test: challenges to awards and enforcement of awards in Africa*. Paper presented at Mauritius International Arbitration Conference, Moka, Mauritius

MIFC. (2016). *Islamic Finance : Development in Non-Traditional Markets*. Kuala Lumpur, Malaysia: Bank Negara Malaysia.

Miniaoui, H., & Gohou, G. (2013). Did Islamic banking perform better during the financial crisis? Evidence from the UAE. *Journal of Islamic Economics. Banking and Finance*, *9*(2), 115–130.

Ministry of Finance. (2017). Pakistan Economic Survey: 2016-17. Islamabad.

Minsky, H. P. (1994). Financial Instability and the Decline of Banking: Public Policy Implications. *Working Paper No. 127*.

Minsky, H. P. (2008). *Stabilizing an Unstable Economy*. New York: McGraw Hill.

Minton, B. A., Taillard, J., & Williamson, R. (2010). Do independence and financial expertise of the board matter for risk taking and performance? Working paper, Ohio State University, Oct. 14.

Mirakhor, A. (2003). *Muslim Contribution to Economics*. Paper presented at the Annual Meeting of the South-Western Economic Association, March 1983; reproduced in Essays on Iqtisad; Nur Corp. (1989); republished by Global Scholarly Publication, New York, NY (2003).

Mirakhor, A. (2010). Whither Islamic Finance? Risk Sharing in An Age of Crises. *Munich Personal RePEc Archive (MPRA)*. Retrieved from http://mpra.ub.uni-muenchen.de/56341/

Mirakhor, A., & Iqbal, Z. (1988). *Stabilization and Growth in an Open Islamic Economy (IMF Working Paper No. 22)*. Washington D.C.: International Monetary Fund.

Mirakhor, A., & Krichene, N. (2009). The Recent Crisis: Lessons for Islamic Finance. IFSB 2nd Public Lecture on Financial Policy and Stability, Kuala Lumpur: Islamic Financial Services Board (IFSB).

Mirakhor, A., & Smolo, E. (2011). Do Conventional and Islamic Finance Share Common Epistemology? *Global Islamic Finance, August,* 48-53.

Mirakhor, A. (1993). Equilibrium in a Non-Interest Open Economy. *Journal of King Abdulaziz University: Islamic Economics*, *5*(1), 3–23.

Miskam, S., & Nasrul, M. A. (2013). *Shari'ah* Governance In Islamic Finance. *The Effects Of The Islamic Financial Services Act*, *2013*(November), 455–463.

Mizen, P. (2008). The Credit Crunch of 2007-2008: A Discussion of the Background, Market Reactions, and Policy Responses. *Federal Reserve Bank of St. Louis Review*, *90*(5), 531–567.

Mohamad, M. H. (2014). The concept of "no risk, no gain" in Islamic finance. *The Star*. Retrieved from http://www.thestar.com.my/Opinion/Columnists/IKIM-Views/ Profile/Articles/2014/02/25/The-concept-of-no-risk-no-gain-in-Islamic-finance/

Mohd Nor, S., Rahim, R. A., & Senik, Z. C. (2016). The potentials of internalising social banking among the Malaysian Islamic banks. *Environment, Development, and Sustainability*, *18*(2), 347–372. doi:10.100710668-015-9651-0

Mohieldin, M., Iqbal, Z., Rostom, A., & Fu, X. (2012). The Role of Islamic Finance in Enhancing Financial inclusion in Organization of Islamic Cooperation (OIC) Countries. *Islamic Economic Studies*, *20*(2), 55–120.

Mokhtar, H. S. A., Abdullah, N., & Al-Habshi, S. M. (2006). Efficiency of Islamic banks in Malaysia: A stochastic frontier approach. *Journal of Economic Cooperation*, *27*(2), 37–70.

Mollah, S., & Zaman, M. (2015). *Shari'ah* supervision, corporate governance and performance: Conventional vs Islamic banks. *Journal of Banking & Finance*, *25*(8), 1–28.

Mollah, S., & Zaman, M. (2015). Shari'ah Supervision, Corporate Governance and Performance: Conventional vs. Islamic Banks. *Journal of Banking & Finance*, *58*(1), 418–435. doi:10.1016/j.jbankfin.2015.04.030

Molyneux, P., & Iqbal, M. (2005). Thirty years of Islamic banking: History, performance and prospect. *Islamic Economics*, *19*(1), 37–39.

Molyneux, P., & Yip, J. (2013). Income diversification and performance of Islamic banks. *Journal of Financial Management, Markets, and Institutions*, *1*(1), 47–66.

Mortuza Ali, K. M. (2006). *Introduction to Islamic Insurance*. Dhaka, Bangladesh: Research Publications.

Mubarik, M. S., Govindaraju, C., & Devadason, E. S. (2016). Human capital development for SMEs in Pakistan: Is the "one-size-fits-all" policy adequate? *International Journal of Social Economics*, *43*(8), 804–822. doi:10.1108/IJSE-02-2015-0033

Muhammad, H. F. (2015, September 10). Report on Riba Case Judgment of Pakistan. *The Lahore Times*. Retrieved from http://www.lhrtimes.com/2015/09/10/report-on-riba-case-judgment-of-pakistan/

MuscatDaily.com. (2018). Oman's Islamic banking assets jump to RO4.1bn. Retrieved May 23, 2019, from https://muscatdaily.com/Archive/Business/Oman-s-Islamic-bankingassets-jump-to-RO4.1bn-5axk

Musibah, A. S. (2014). The mediating effect of financial performance on the relationship between *Shari'ah* supervisory board effectiveness. *Intellect Capital*, *17*(10), 45–60.

Naceur, S. B. (2003). The determinants of the Tunisian banking industry profitability: Panel evidence. *Universite Libre de Tunis working papers, 11*(3), 317-319.

Naceur, S. B., Barajas, A., & Massara, A. (2015). Can Islamic Banking Increase Financial inclusion? (IMF Working Paper WP/15/31). Retrieved from IMF Website: https://www.imf.org/en/Publications/WP/Issues/2016/12/31/Can-Islamic-Banking-Increase-Financial-Inclusion-42710

Najeeb, S. F., & Ibrahim, S. H. M. (2014). Professionalizing the role of *Shari'ah* auditors: How Malaysia can generate economic benefits. *Pacific-Basin Finance Journal*, *28*, 91–109. doi:10.1016/j.pacfin.2013.10.009

Narveson, J. (1988). *The Libertarian Idea*. Philadelphia, PA: Temple University Press.

Naser, K., & Moutinho, L. (1997). Strategic marketing management: The case of Islamic banks. *International Journal of Bank Marketing*, *15*(6), 187–203. doi:10.1108/02652329710184424

Naser, K., & Pendlebury, M. (1997). The influence of Islam on bank financial reporting. *International Journal of Commerce and Management*, *7*(2), 56–83. doi:10.1108/eb047349

Nathan Garas, S., & Pierce, C. (2010). *Shari'a* supervision of Islamic financial institutions. *Journal of Financial Regulation and Compliance*, *18*(4), 386–407. doi:10.1108/13581981011093695

NathanGaras, S. (2012). The conflicts of interest inside the *Shari'a* supervisory board. *International Journal of Islamic and Middle Eastern Finance and Management*, *5*(2), 88–105. doi:10.1108/17538391211233399

Nathan, S., & Pierce, C. (2009). CSR in Islamic financial institutions in the middle east. In C. A. Mallin (Ed.), *Corporate Social Responsibility: A Case Study Approach*. London, UK: Edward Elgar. doi:10.4337/9781849802192.00022

Neaime, S., & Geaysset, I. (2018). Financial Inclusion and Stability in MENA: Evidence from Poverty and Inequality. *Finance Research Letters*, *24*, 230–237. doi:10.1016/j.frl.2017.09.007

Nienhaus, V. (1983). Profitability of Islamic Banks Competing with Interest Banks. *Journal of Research in Islamic Economics*, *1*(1), 37–47.

Nomran, M. N., Haron, R., & Hassan, R. (2017). Bank performance and Shari'ah supervisory board attributes by Islamic banks: does bank size matter? *Journal of Islamic Finance*, Special Issue (2017), 174–187.

Nomran, M. N., Haron, R., & Hassan, R. (2018). Shari'ah supervisory board characteristics effects on Islamic banks' performance: Evidence from Malaysia. *International Journal of Bank Marketing*, *36*(2), 290–304. doi:10.1108/IJBM-12-2016-0197

Noordin, N. H., & Kassim, S. (2019). Does Shari'ah Committee composition influence Shari'ah governance disclosure? Evidence from Malaysian Islamic banks. *Journal of Islamic Accounting and Business Research*, *10*(2), 158–184. doi:10.1108/JIABR-04-2016-0047

Nor, M. Z. M., Mohamad, A. M., Azhar, A., Latif, H. M., Khalid, A.-H. M., & Yusof, Y. (2019). Legal Challenges of Musharakah Mutanaqisah as an Alternative for Property Financing in Malaysia. *Journal of Legal, Ethical, and Regulatory Issues*, *22*(3), 1–8.

Obeid, H., & Kaabachi, S. (2016). Empirical investigation into customer adoption of Islamic banking services in Tunisia. *Journal of Applied Business Research*, *32*(4), 1243–1256. doi:10.19030/jabr.v32i4.9734

OECD. (2004). *OECD Principles of Corporate Governance*. OECD.

OECD. (2009). The Financial Crisis: Reform and Exit Strategies. Paris, France: Organization for Economic Co-operation and Development (OECD).

Olson, D., & Zoubi, T. A. (2008). Using accounting ratios to distinguish between Islamic and conventional banks in the GCC region. *The International Journal of Accounting*, *43*(1), 45–65. doi:10.1016/j.intacc.2008.01.003

Olson, D., & Zoubi, T. A. (2016). Convergence in bank performance for commercial and Islamic banks during and after the global financial crisis. *The Quarterly Review of Economics and Finance*, *65*(1), 71–87.

Omar, N., & Bakar, K. M. A. (2012). Fraud prevention mechanisms of Malaysian government-linked companies: An assessment of existence and effectiveness. *Journal of Modern Accounting and Auditing*, *8*(1), 15–31.

Oseni, U. A. (2017). *Fatwa* shopping and trust: Towards effective consumer protection regulations in Islamic finance. *Society and Business Review*, *12*(3), 340–355. doi:10.1108/SBR-03-2017-0016

Oseni, U. A., Ahmad, A. U. F., & Hassan, M. K. (2016). The Legal Implications of '*Fatwa* Shopping' in the Islamic Finance Industry: Problems, Perceptions and Prospects. *Arab Law Quarterly*, *30*(2), 107–137. doi:10.1163/15730255-12341319

Othman, M. A. (2013). Reflecting customers' innovativeness and intention to adopt Islamic banking in Nigeria/Ahmad Muhammad Gumel and Mohammad Azmi Othman. *Business & Management Quarterly Review*, *4*(3&4), 27–37.

Othman, R., Ishak, I. F., Arif, S. M. M., & Aris, N. A. (2014). Influence of Audit Committee Characteristics on Voluntary Ethics Disclosure. *Procedia: Social and Behavioral Sciences*, *145*, 330–342. doi:10.1016/j.sbspro.2014.06.042

Otoritas Jasa Keuangan. (2015). *Roadmap Perbankan Islamic Indonesia 2015–2019*. Retrieved February 21, 2019, from https://www.ojk.go.id/id/kanal/Islamic/berita-dan-kegiatan/publikasi/Documents/roadmap-pbs_2015-2019.pdf

Otoritas Jasa Keuangan. (2016a). *POJK Nomor 6/POJK.03/2016 tentang Kegiatan Usaha dan Jaringan Kantor Berdasarkan Modal Inti Bank*. Retrieved December 15, 2017, from http://www.ojk.go.id/id/kanal/perbankan/regulasi/peraturan-ojk/Pages/pojk-kegiatan-usaha-dan-jaringan-kantor-berdasarkan-modal-inti-bank.aspx

Otoritas Jasa Keuangan. (2016b). *POJK Nomor 10/POJK.03/2016 tentang Kewajiban Penyediaan Modal Minimum Bank Umum*. Retrieved December, 14, 2017, from http://www.ojk.go.id/id/kanal/perbankan/regulasi/peraturan-ojk/Pages/pojk11-kewajiban-penyediaan-modal-minimum-bank-umum.aspx

Otoritas Jasa Keuangan. (2016c). *POJK Nomor 64/POJK.03/2016 tentang Perubahan Kegiatan Usaha Bank Konvensional Menjadi Bank Islamic*. Retrieved February, 21 2019, from http://www.ojk.go.id/id/kanal/perbankan/regulasi/regulasi-perbankan-Islamic/Pages/POJK-tentang-Perubahan-Kegiatan-Usaha-Bank-Konvensional-Menjadi-Bank-Islamic.aspx

Otoritas Jasa Keuangan. (2017a). *Laporan Profile Industri Perbankan Triwulan II 2017*. Retrieved February, 21 2019, from https://www.ojk.go.id/id/kanal/perbankan/data-dan-statistik/laporan-profil-industri-perbankan/Documents/LPIP%20TW%20II-17%20(Publikasi).pdf

Otoritas Jasa Keuangan. (2017b). *Strategi nasional literasi keuangan Indonesia (Revisit 2017)*. Retrieved February 21, 2019, from https://www.ojk.go.id/id/berita-dan-kegiatan/publikasi/Documents/Pages/Strategi-Nasional-Literasi-Keuangan-Indonesia-(Revisit-2017)-/SNLKI%20(Revisit%202017)-new.pdf

Otoritas Jasa Keuangan. (2018a). *Indonesia Banking Statistics*. Jakarta, Indonesia: Otoritas Jasa Keuangan.

Otoritas Jasa Keuangan. (2018b). *Laporan Profil Industri Perbankan Triwulan II 2018*. Retrieved February, 21 2019, from https://www.ojk.go.id/id/kanal/perbankan/data-dan-statistik/laporan-profil-industri-perbankan/Pages/Laporan-Profil-Industri-Perbankan---Triwulan-II-2018.aspx

Otoritas Jasa Keuangan. (2018c). *Sharia Banking Statistics September 2018*. Retrieved March 5, 2019, from https://www.ojk.go.id/en/kanal/perbankan/data-dan-statistik/statistik-perbankan-syariah/Pages/Sharia-Banking-Statistic---September-2018.aspx

Otoritas Jasa Keuangan. (2018d). *Snapshot Perbankan Islamic Indonesia*. Retrieved March 5, 2019, from https://www.ojk.go.id/id/kanal/Islamic/berita-dan-kegiatan/publikasi/Documents/Pages/Snapshot-Perbankan-Islamic-Indonesia-Juni-2018/Snapshot%20Juni%202018%20(final).pdf

Ould Mohamed Mahmoud, L., & Abduh, M. (2014). The Role of Awareness in Islamic Bank Patronizing Behavior of Mauritanian: An Application of TRA. *Journal of Islamic Finance, 3*(2), 030 – 038.

P3EI-UII. (2018). *Ekonomi Islam*. Jakarta: PT Rajagrafindo Persada.

Pakistan Bureau of Statistics. (2011). *Agriculture Statistics of Pakistan 2010-11*. Retrieved from http://www.pbs.gov.pk/content/agriculture-statistics-pakistan-2010-11

Patel, I. (2010). *Islamic Banks need restructuring*. Retrieved from www.accountancy.com

Peni, E., & Vähämaa, S. (2011). Did Good Corporate Governance Improve Bank Performance during the Financial Crisis? *Journal of Financial Services Research, 41*(1-2), 19–35. doi:10.100710693-011-0108-9

Pfeffer, J. (1973). Size, Composition, and Function of Hospital Boards of Directors: A Study of Organization Environment Linkage. *Administrative Science Quarterly, 18*(3), 17. doi:10.2307/2391668

Pfeffer, J., & Salancik, G. R. (1978). *The External Control of Organizations: A Resource Dependence Perspective*. New York: Harper & Row.

Phillips, R. J. (1992a). Chicago Plan and New Deal Banking Reform. *Working Paper No. 76.*

Phillips, R. J. (1992b). Credit Markets and Narrow Banking. *Working Paper No. 77.*

Pierce, J. L. (1991). *The Future of Banking: A Twentieth Century Fund Report*. New York: Yale University Press. doi:10.2307/j.ctt1ww3v09

Platonova, E. (2013). Corporate Social Responsibility from an Islamic Moral Economy Perspective : A Literature Survey. *Afro EUrasian Studies, 2*(1&2), 272–297.

Platonova, E., Asutay, M., Dixon, R., & Mohammad, S. (2018). The Impact of Corporate Social Responsibility Disclosure on Financial Performance: Evidence from the GCC Islamic Banking Sector. *Journal of Business Ethics, 151*(2), 451–471. doi:10.100710551-016-3229-0

Possumah, B. T., Appiah, M. K., & Hilmiyah, N. (2018). Determinants of Islamic banking adoption across different religious groups in Ghana: A panoptic perspective. *Journal of International Studies, 11*(4), 138–154. doi:10.14254/2071-8330.2018/11-4/10

PricewaterhouseCoopers. (2017). *Indonesia Banking Survey 2017: Weathering the rise in credit risk. What's next for Banks in Indonesia?* Retrieved February 21, 2019, from https://www.pwc.com/id/en/publications/assets/financialservices/ibs-2017.pdf

Qaed, I. Q. M. (2014). The concept of *Wadiah* and its application in Islamic banking. *Journal of Research in Humanities and Social Science, 2*(11), 70–74.

Qureshi, S. (2017). *The challenges facing Islamic banking*. Retrieved from https://www.changeboard.com/article-details/15380/the-challenges-facing-islamic-banking/

Quttainah, M. A., Song, L., & Wu, Q. (2013). Do Islamic banks employ less earnings management? *Journal of International Financial Management & Accounting*, *24*(3), 203–233. doi:10.1111/jifm.12011

Rafay, A., Sadiq, R. & Ajmal, M. M. (2016). Fragmentation of Islamic Financial Products – An Exploratory Study of Islamic Schools of Thought. *Abasyn Journal of Social Sciences, Special Issue*, 48-61.

Rafay, A., & Farid, S. (2017). Dynamic Relationship between Islamic Banking System and Real Economic Activity: Evidence from Pakistan. *Journal of King Abdulaziz University. Islamic Economics*, *30*(2), 97–114.

Rafay, A., & Farid, S. (2018). *Shari'ah* Supervisory Board Report (SSBR) in Islamic Banks: An experimental study of Investors' perception and behaviour. *International Journal of Islamic and Middle Eastern Finance and Management*, *11*(2), 274–296. doi:10.1108/IMEFM-07-2017-0180

Rafay, A., & Farid, S. (2019). Islamic Banking System: A Credit Channel of Monetary Policy – Evidence from an Emerging Economy. *Economic Research Journal*, *32*(1), 742–754.

Rafay, A., & Farid, S. (2019). Islamic Banking System: A Credit Channel of Monetary Policy – Evidence from an Emerging Economy. *Economic Research*, *32*(1), 742–754.

Rafay, A., & Gilani, U. J. (2016). Banking Competition and Stability: Evidence from Inter-continental Markets. *DLSU Business and Economics Review*, *25*(2), 24–40.

Rafay, A., & Sadiq, R. (2015). Problems and Issues in Transformation From Conventional Banking To Islamic Banking : Literature Review for the Need of a Comprehensive Framework for a Smooth change. *City University Research Journal*, *05*(2), 315–326.

Rafay, A., & Sadiq, R. (2015). Problems and Issues in Transformation from Conventional Banking to Islamic Banking: Literature Review for the Need of a Comprehensive Framework for a Smooth Change. *City University Research Journal*, *5*(2), 315–326.

Rafay, A., Sadiq, R., & Ajmal, M. M. (2017). Uniform Framework for Sukuk-Al-Ijara – A proposed model for all *madhahib*. *Journal of Islamic Accounting and Business Research*, *8*(4), 420–454. doi:10.1108/JIABR-09-2015-0042

Rafik Al Masri. (1995). Les banques islamiques. Centre d'édition scientifique, l'université King Abdulaziz, Jeddah.

Rahahleh, N. A., Bhatti, I. M., & Nisman, F. N. (2019). Developments in Risk Management in Islamic Finance: A review. *Journal of Risk and Financial Management*, *12*(37), 10–15.

Rahman, A. A., & Bukair, A. A. (2013). The influence of the Shari'ah supervision board on corporate social responsibility disclosure by Islamic banks of Gulf Co-operation Council countries. *Asian Journal of Business and Accounting*, *6*(2), 65–104.

Rahmatullah, H., Sudarsono, R., & Komara, R. (2018). Business analysis in conversion of regional development bank into Sharia banking: Case study in NTB province, Indonesia. *International Journal of Economics, Commerce, and Management*, *6*(2), 232–339.

Ramadan, I. Z., Kilani, Q. A., & Kaddumi, T. A. (2011). Determinants of Bank Profitability: Evidence from Jordan. *International Journal of Academic Research*, *3*(4), 180–191.

Rammal, H. G., & Parker, L. D. (2013). Islamic banking in Pakistan: A History of Emergent Accountability and Regulation. *Accounting History*, *18*(1), 5–29. doi:10.1177/1032373212463269

Rammal, H. G., & Zurbruegg, R. (2007). Awareness of Islamic banking products among Muslims: The case of Australia. *Journal of Financial Services Marketing*, *12*(1), 65–74. doi:10.1057/palgrave.fsm.4760060

Rassool, N. H. (2011). Mauritius: An emerging Centre for Islamic finance. *New Horizons (Baltimore, Md.)*, *25*(180), 100–120.

Rassool, N. H. (2018). Towards establishing an Islamic retail bank in a Muslim-minority country: Prospects and challenges in Mauritius. *ISRA International Journal of Islamic Finance*, *10*(1), 35–50. doi:10.1108/IJIF-11-2017-0048

Rehman, A. A., & Masood, O. (2012). Why do customers patronize Islamic banks? A case study of Pakistan. *Qualitative Research in Financial Markets*, *4*(2/3), 130–141. doi:10.1108/17554171211252475

Report, S. A. T. P. (2019). *Datasheet of Terrorism in Pakistan*. Retrieved from https://propakistani.pk/2018/04/24/terrorism-in-pakistan-declines-by-89-in-8-years/

Reuters, T. (2016b). State of the Global Islamic Economy 2016/17 (SGIE). Retrieved from https://ceif.iba.edu.pk/pdf/ThomsonReuters-stateoftheGlobalIslamicEconomyReport201617.pdf

Reuters, T. (2017). Islamic Finance Development report 2017. Retrieved from https://islamicbankers.files.wordpress.com/2017/12/icd-thomson-reuters-islamic-finance-development-report-2017.pdf

Reuters, T. (2018). *Islamic Finance Development Report 2018: Building Momentum*. Retrieved from http://bit.ly/IFDatabase

Rosly, S. A. (2001). Iwad As a Requirement of Lawful Sale: A Critical Analysis. *IIUM Journal of Economics and Management*, *9*(2), 187–201.

Rosman, R., & Rahman, A. R. (2018). The practice of IFSB guiding principles of risk management by Islamic banks. *Journal of Islamic Accounting and Business Research*, *6*(2), 60–75.

Rosman, R., Wahab, N. A., & Zainol, Z. (2014). Efficiency of Islamic banks during the financial crisis: An analysis of Middle Eastern and Asian countries. *Pacific-Basin Finance Journal*, *28*, 76–90. doi:10.1016/j.pacfin.2013.11.001

Rothbard, M. (1978). *For a New Liberty, The Libertarian Manifesto* (Revised ed.). New York: Libertarian Review Foundation.

Rothschild, E. (1994). Adam Smith and the Invisible Hand. *The American Economic Review*, *84*(2), 319–322.

Roubini, N. (2008). Financial Crises, Financial Stability, and Reform: Supervision and Regulation of Financial Systems in a World of Financial Globalization. In J. Bilodeau (Ed.), *The Financial Development Report 2008* (pp. 33-46). New York: World Economic Forum.

Ruzlan, M. (2018). The role of law and Sharia governance in Islamic finance towards social justice in diversity. Thomson Reuters Islamic finance development report 2016. *Diponegoro Law Review*, *3*(2), 142–153.

Saaid, A., & Shafii, Z. (2013). The Obstacles Facing Conversion Process From Conventional Banks To Islamic Banking: A Review Of Literature. *The 5th Islamic Economic Conference, Malaysia. 2013. "Sustainable Development Through The Islamic Economics System,"* (September), 4–5.

Saaid, A., Shafii, Z., Shahimi, S., Academic, I., & Group, P. (2016). The Factors that Influence the Conversion Process from Conventional Banks into Islamic Banking in Libyan Conventional Banks: Proposing Conceptual Framework. *International Journal of Academic Research in Management and Business*, *1*(2), 77.

Saba, I. (2017). Islamic Finance—Local and Global Status. In Developments in Islamic Finance (pp. 1–20). doi:10.1007/978-3-319-59342-5_1

Safiullah, M., & Shamsuddin, A. (2018). Risk in Islamic banking and corporate governance. *Pacific-Basin Finance Journal*, *47*, 129–149. doi:10.1016/j.pacfin.2017.12.008

Saheeh International. (Ed.). (2010). *The Qur'an: With Surah Introductions and Appendices*. Birmingham, UK: Maktabah Booksellers and Publishers.

Saidane, D. (2010). The Regulatory and Institutional Dimension? Consolidation, Privatization, Human Resources and Good Governance. *Multi -Year Expert Meeting On Services, Development, and Trade: The Regulatory Dimension and Institutional Geneva.*

Saiti, B., Ardo, A. A., & Yumusak, I. G. (2019). Why non-Muslims subscribe to Islamic banking? *Qualitative Research in Financial Markets*, QRFM-01-2018-0005. doi:10.1108/QRFM-01-2018-0005

Salman, A., Nawaz, H., Bukhari, S. M. H., & Baker, A. (2018). *Growth analysis of Islamic banking in Pakistan: A qualitative approach. Academy of Accounting and Financial Studies Journal, 22*. Specialiss.

Samad, A. (1999). Comparative Efficiency of the Islamic Bank Vis- A - Vis Conventional Banks in Malaysia. *IIUM Journal of Economics And Management*, *7*(1), 1–27.

Samad, A. (2004). Performance of interest-free Islamic banks vis-à-vis interest-based conventional banks of Bahrain. *International Journal of Economics, Management, and Accounting*, *12*(2), 1–15.

Samad, A., & Hassan, M. K. (2006). The performance of Malaysian Islamic bank during 1984-1997: An exploratory study. *International Journal of Islamic Financial Services*, *1*(3), 1–14.

Samah, Z., & Hassan, R. (2016). Empirical study on the understanding of *Shari'ah* review by Islamic banks in Malaysia. *Intellectual Capital*, *8*(1), 8–18.

Sami, H., Wang, J., & Zhou, H. (2011). Corporate governance and operating performance of Chinese listed firms. *Journal of International Accounting, Auditing, & Taxation*, *20*(2), 106–114. doi:10.1016/j.intaccaudtax.2011.06.005

Sari, M. D., Bahari, Z., & Hamat, Z. (2013). Perkembangan perbankan syariah di Indonesia: Suatu tinjauan. *Jurnal Aplikasi Bisnis*, *3*(2), 120–138.

Sari, M. D., Bahari, Z., & Hamat, Z. (2016). History of Islamic bank in Indonesia: Issues behind its establishment. *International Journal of Finance and Banking Research*, *2*(5), 178–184. doi:10.11648/j.ijfbr.20160205.13

Saunders, A., Schmid, M. M., & Walter, I. (2014). *Non-Interest income and bank performance: Is banks' increased reliance on non-interest income bad?* School of Finance, University of St. Gallen.

Sayd Farook, M. O. F. (2013). *Shari'ah* governance, expertise and profession: Educational challenges in Islamic finance. *International Journal of Islamic Finance*, *5*(1), 137–160. doi:10.12816/0002761

Scott, K. E. (1998). Mutual Funds as an Alternative Banking System. *Journal of Institutional and Theoretical Economics*, *154*(1), 86–96.

Securities Commission Malaysia. (2007). *Resolutions of the Securities Commission Shariah Advisory Council*. Kuala Lumpur, Malaysia: Securities Commission.

Sehrawat, M., & Giri, A. K. (2016). Financial Development and Poverty Reduction: Panel Data Analysis of South Asian Countries. *International Journal of Social Economics*, *43*(4), 400–416. doi:10.1108/IJSE-04-2014-0069

Setiyono, B., & Tarazi, A. (2014). *Disclosure, ownership structure and bank risk: Evidence from Asia*. Paper presented at the 27th Australasian Finance and Banking Conference, Sydney. 10.2139srn.2395315

Shabbir, M. S., Shariff, M. N. M., & Yusof, M. S. Bin, Salman, R., & Hafeez, S. (2018). Corporate Social Responsibility and Customer loyalty in Islamic Banks of Pakistan: A Mediating Role of Brand Image. *Academy of Accounting and Financial Studies Journal*, *22*(Special Issue), 1–6.

Shaffaii, S. (2008). How *Shari'ah* Governance Empowers Islamic Finance. *Islamic Finance News*, *5*(36), 1–3.

Shafii, Z., Abidin, A. Z., Salleh, S., Jusoff, K., & Kasim, N. (2013). Post implementation of *Shari'ah* governance framework: The impact of *Shari'ah* audit function towards the role of *Shari'ah* committee. *Middle East Journal of Scientific Research, 13*(SI), 7-11.

Shafii, Z., Salleh, S., & Shahwan, S. H. (2010). Management of *Shari'ah* Non-Compliance Audit Risk in the Islamic Financial Institutions via the Development of *Shari'ah* Compliance Audit Framework and *Shari'ah* Audit Programme. *Kyoto Bulletin of Islamic Area Studies, 3–2*(3), 3–16.

Shafii, Z., Shahimi, S., & Saaid, A. (2016). Obstacles and motivation behind conversion of conventional banks to Islamic banks: An overview. *International Review of Management and Business Research*, *5*(3), 1021–1038.

Shah, S. F., Raza, M. W., & Khurshid, M. R. (2012). Islamic banking controversies and challenges. *Interdisciplinary Journal of Contemporary Research in Business*, *3*(10), 1018–1026.

Shaikh, S. A., Ismail, M. A., Shafiai, M. H., Shahimi, S., & Ismail, A. G. (2017). Role of Islamic Banking in Financial Inclusion: Prospects and Performance. In N. Alam, & S.A.R. Rizvi (Eds.), Islamic Banking. Cham, Switzerland: Palgrave Macmillan.

Shaikh, S. A. A. (2011). A critical analysis of *Mudarabah* and a new approach to equity financing in Islamic finance. *Journal of Islamic Banking and Finance*, *28*(3), 1–10.

Shanmugam, B., & Perumal, V. (2006). Governance Issues and Islamic Banking. *Islamic Finance News*, *3*(37), 12–15.

Sheikh, S. A. (2007). *Critical analysis of current Islamic Banking system.* Retrieved from www.accountancy.com.pk

Siddik, M. N. A., Sun, G., Yanjuan, C. U. I., & Kabiraj, S. (2014). Financial Inclusion through Mobile Banking: A Case of Bangladesh. *Journal of Applied Finance & Banking, 4*(6), 109-136. ISSN: 1792-6580 (print version), 1792-6599 (online) Scienpress Ltd, 2014.

Siddiqi, M. N. (1983a). *Banking Without Interest.* Leicester, UK: The Islamic Foundation.

Siddiqi, M. N. (1983b). *Issues in Islamic Banking (Islamic Economics Series 4).* Leicester, UK: The Islamic Foundation.

Siddiqi, M. N. (1985). *Partnership and Profit-Sharing in Islamic Law.* Leicester, UK: The Islamic Foundation.

Sidlo, K. W. (2017). *Islamic finance 2017: State of the art and outlook for the future.* Retrieved from CASE website: http://www.caseresearch.eu/en/islamic-finance-2017-state-of-the-art and-outlook-for-the-future-100498.

Sierra, G. E., Talmor, E., & Wallace, J. S. (2006). An Examination of Multiple Governance Forces within Bank Holding Companies. *Journal of Financial Services Research, 29*(2), 105–123. doi:10.100710693-006-5921-1

Simoes, P. M. M., & Esposito, M. (2014). Improving change management: How communication nature influences resistance to change. *Journal of Management Development, 33*(4), 324–341. doi:10.1108/JMD-05-2012-0058

Siraj, K. K., & Pillai, P. S. (2012). Comparative study on performance of Islamic banks and conventional banks in GCC region. *Journal of Applied Finance and Banking*, *2*(3), 123–161.

Siswantoro, D. (2012). A critique of Islamic banks' good corporate governance report in Indonesia. *Journal of Islamic Business and Management*, *2*(2), 10–13. doi:10.12816/0004980

SMEDA. (2007). *SME Policy*. Retrieved from https://smeda.org/phocadownload/Publicatoins/SME Policy 2007.pdf

Smith, A. (2006). *The Theory of Moral Sentiments (Dover Philosophical Classics).* Cambridge, UK: Cambridge University Press.

Smolo, E. (2010). *Al-Bay' Bithaman Ajil, Musharakah Mutanaqisah and Ijarah Sukuk: A Theoretical Comparison.* Saarbrücken, Germany: Lambert Academic Publishing AG & Co. KG.

Smolo, E. (2013). *Uvod u islamsku ekonomiju i finansije: teorija i praksa.* Sarajevo: Dobra Knjiga.

Smolo, E., & Hassan, M. K. (2011). The potentials of musharakah mutanaqisah for Islamic housing finance. *International Journal of Islamic and Middle Eastern Finance and Management, 4*(3), 237–258. doi:10.1108/17538391111166476

Smolo, E., & Mirakhor, A. (2010). The Global Financial Crisis and its Implications for the Islamic Financial Industry. *International Journal of Islamic and Middle Eastern Finance and Management, 3*(4), 372–385. doi:10.1108/17538391011093306

Smolo, E., & Mirakhor, A. (2014). Limited Purpose Banking (LPB) and Islamic Finance: Could LPB Model Be Applied to Islamic Finance? *Humanomics, 30*(2), 122–135. doi:10.1108/H-08-2013-0053

Sole, J. (2007). Introducing Islamic Banks into Conventional Banking Systems. International Monetary Fund, 1–28.

Sophia, M. (2015, March 29). *UAE's Islamic banking assets to reach $263 bn by 2019.* Retrieved June 13, 2019 from https://gulfbusiness.com/uaes-%20islamic-banking-assets-reach- 263bn- 2019/

Sori, M. Z., Abdul Wahab, S., & Yaacob, A. S. (2017). Financial Reporting of Islamic Financial Institutions – Contemporary Issues. *Journal of Islamic Finance, 4*(2), 4–8.

Spong, K. (1993). Narrow Banks: An Alternative Approach to Banking Reform. *Working Paper No. 90.*

Srairi, S. A. (2009). Factors Influencing the Profitability of Conventional and Islamic Commercial Banks in GCC Countries. *Review of Islamic Economics, 13*(1), 5–30.

Srairi, S. A. (2010). Cost and profit efficiency of conventional and Islamic banks in GCC countries. *Journal of Productivity Analysis, 34*(1), 45–62. doi:10.100711123-009-0161-7

Srairi, S. A. (2011). Productivity Growth In GCC Banking Industry: Conventional Versus Islamic Banks. *Journal of Knowledge Globalization, 4*(2), 59–90.

Stanford Encyclopedia of Philosophy. (2012). Libertarianism. Retrieved from https://stanford.library.sydney.edu.au/archives/sum2012/entries/libertarianism/

Stapleton, T. (2013). Unlocking the transformative potential of branchless banking in Indonesia. *Bulletin of Indonesian Economic Studies, 49*(3), 355–380. doi:10.1080/00074918.2013.850633

State Bank of Pakistan. (2007a). *Islamic Banking Bulletin: December 2007.* Retrieved from http://www.sbp.org.pk/ibd/bulletin/2007/Oct-Dec-Bulletin.pdf

State Bank of Pakistan. (2007b). *Pakistan's Islamic Banking Sector Review.* Retrieved from http://www.sbp.org.pk/departments/ibd/Islamic-Bkg-Review-03-07.pdf

State Bank of Pakistan. (2008a). *Instructions for Shari'ah Compliance in Islamic Banking.* Retrieved from http://www.sbp.org.pk/ibd/2008/C2.htm

State Bank of Pakistan. (2008b). *Islamic Banking Bulletin: December 2008.* Retrieved from http://www.sbp.org.pk/ibd/bulletin/2008/Bulletin-Oct-Dec-2008.pdf

State Bank of Pakistan. (2009). *Islamic Banking Bulletin: December 2009.* Retrieved from http://www.sbp.org.pk/ibd/bulletin/2009/Bulletin-Oct-Dec-2009.pdf

State Bank of Pakistan. (2010). *Islamic Banking Bulletin: December 2010.* Retrieved from http://www.sbp.org.pk/ibd/bulletin/2010/IBB-Dec-2010.pdf

State Bank of Pakistan. (2011). *Islamic Banking Bulletin: December 2011*. Retrieved from http://www.sbp.org.pk/ibd/bulletin/2011/IBB-Dec-2011.pdf

State Bank of Pakistan. (2012). *Islamic Banking Bulletin: December 2012*. Retrieved from http://www.sbp.org.pk/ibd/bulletin/2012/IBB-Dec-2012.pdf

State Bank of Pakistan. (2013). *Islamic Banking Bulletin: December 2013*. Retrieved from http://www.sbp.org.pk/ibd/bulletin/2013/IBB-Dec-2013.pdf

State Bank of Pakistan. (2014a). *Islamic Banking Bulletin: December 2014*. Retrieved from http://www.sbp.org.pk/ibd/bulletin/2014/IBB-Dec-2014.pdf

State Bank of Pakistan. (2014b). *Strategic Plan Islamic Banking Industry of Pakistan*. Retrieved from http://www.sbp.org.pk/departments/pdf/StrategicPlanPDF/Strategy Paper-Final.pdf

State Bank of Pakistan. (2015). *Islamic Banking Bulletin: December 2015*. Retrieved from http://www.sbp.org.pk/ibd/bulletin/2015/IBB-Dec-2015.pdf

State Bank of Pakistan. (2016). *Islamic Banking Bulletin: December 2016*. Retrieved from http://www.sbp.org.pk/ibd/bulletin/2016/Dec.pdf

State Bank of Pakistan. (2017a). *Green Banking Guidelines*. Retrieved from http://www.sbp.org.pk/smefd/circulars/2017/C8-Annex.pdf

State Bank of Pakistan. (2017b). *Islamic Banking Bulletin: December 2017*. Retrieved from http://www.sbp.org.pk/ibd/Bulletin/2017/Jun.pdf

State Bank of Pakistan. (2018a). *Islamic Banking Bulletin: December 2018*. Retrieved from http://www.sbp.org.pk/ibd/bulletin/2018/Dec.pdf

State Bank of Pakistan. (2018b). *Islamic Banking Bulletin: March 2018*. Retrieved from http://www.sbp.org.pk/ibd/bulletin/2018/Mar.pdf

State Bank of Pakistan. (2018c). *Statistics on Scheduled Banks in Pakistan*. Retrieved from http://www.sbp.org.pk/publications/schedule_banks/June-2018/Title.pdf

Statement Bank of Pakistan. (2015). *Shari'ah governance framework for Islamic banking institutions*. Retrieved from http://www.sbp.org.pk/ibd/2015/C1-Annex.pdf

Stiglitz, J. E. (1993). Perspectives on the Role of Government Risk-Bearing within the Financial Sector. In M. S. Sniderman (Ed.), *Government Risk-Bearing: Proceedings of a Conference Held at the Federal Reserve Bank of Cleveland*, (pp. 109-130), May 1991. Boston, MA: Kluwer Academic Publishers. 10.1007/978-94-011-2184-2_5

Stiroh, K. J., & Rumble, A. (2006). The dark side of diversification: The case of US financial holding companies. *Journal of Banking & Finance*, *30*(8), 2131–2161. doi:10.1016/j.jbankfin.2005.04.030

Stubing, D. (2014, February 22). *Oman: Islamic banking on the rise*. Retrieved May 23, 2019 from https://gulfbusiness.com/oman-islamic-banking-rise/

Suchman, M. C. (1995). Managing Legitimacy: Strategic and Institutional Approaches. *Academy of Management Journal*, *20*(3), 571–610.

Sufian, F., & Abdul Majid, M. Z. (2008). Bank ownership, characteristics, and performance: A comparative analysis of domestic and foreign Islamic banks in Malaysia. *Journal of King Abdulaziz University: Islamic Economics*, *21*(2), 3–38.

Sulaiman, M., Abd Madjid, N., & Moh Arifin, N. (2015). Corporate Governance of Islamic Financial Institutions in Malaysia. *Asian Journal of Business and Accounting, 8*(1), 65–93.

Sundararajan, V., & Errico, L. (2002). Islamic financial institutions and products in the global financial system: key issues in risk management and challenges ahead. (*IMF Working Paper No. WP/02/192*). Retrieved from https://ssrn.com/abstract=1930788

Swamy, V. (2014). Financial Inclusion, Gender Dimension, and Economic Impact on Poor Households. *World Development, 56*, 1–15. doi:10.1016/j.worlddev.2013.10.019

Sy, A. (2007). Malaysia: An Islamic capital market hub. *IMF Survey Magazine: Countries & Regions.*

Syaltut, M. (1966). *Al-Islam 'Aqidah wa Syari'ah.* Cairo, Egypt: Dar al-Qalam.

Syariah, B. T. P. N. (2018). *Annual Report 2018.* Retrieved February 22, 2019, from https://www.btpnIslamic.com/images/BTPNS_AR_2018_en.pdf

Tambunan, T. T. H. (2011). Development of small and medium enterprises in a developing country: The Indonesian case. *Journal of Enterprising Communities: People and Places in the Global Economy, 5*(1), 68–82. doi:10.1108/17506201111119626

Taylor, J. B. (2008, November). The Financial Crisis and the Policy Responses: An Empirical Analysis of What Went Wrong. *Stanford University Working Paper.* Retrieved from http://www.stanford.edu/~johntayl/FCPR.pdf

Tenekeci, M. (2017). *Katılım Bankacılığın finansal istikrara etkisi: Türkiye örneği* (Unpublished master's thesis). Karatay University, Konya, Turkey.

The Express Tribune. (2017, March 14). *FSC agrees to first define 'Riba.'* Retrieved from https://tribune.com.pk/story/1354567/25-years-fsc-agrees-first-define-riba/

The Mejelle. (2003). *Being An English Translation of Majallah el-Ahkam-I-Adliya and A Complete Code on Islamic Civil Law* (C. R. Tyser, D. G. Demetriades, & I. Haqqi Effendi, Eds.). Kuala Lumpur, Malaysia: The Other Press.

The World Bank. (2018). *World Development Indicators: World Bank national accounts data, and OECD National Accounts data files.* Retrieved from https://data.worldbank.org/indicator/NY.GDP.MKTP.KD.ZG

The world Factbook/Africa/Libya. (2019). Retrieved from https://www.cia.gov/library/publications/resources/the-world-factbook/geos/ly.html

Thomson Reuters. (2018). *Islamic Finance Development Report 2018: Building Momentum.* Salaam Gateway.

Times, K. (2008). *Islamic banks enjoy double digit growth.* Khaleej Times.

Todorovic, I. (2013). Impact of corporate governance on performance of companies. *Montenegrin Journal of Economics, 9*(2), 47–53.

Toraman, C., Ata, H. A., & Buğan, M. F. (2015). İslami Bankacılık Faaliyetlerine Yönelik Müşteri Algısı Üzerine Bir Araştırma, *Gaziantep University. Journal of Social Sciences, 14*(4), 761–779.

Triki, T., & Faye I. (2013). Financial Inclusion in Africa, *African Development Bank (AfDB).*

Tripe, D. (1998). *Cost to income ratios in Australasian banking.* Department of Finance, Banking and Property, College of Business, Massey University.

Truman, E. M. (2009). Lessons from the Global Economic and Financial Crisis. Keynote address at the conference "G-20 Reform Initiatives: Implications for the Future of Regulation," cohosted by the Institute for Global Economics and the International Monetary Fund in Seoul, Korea, November 11, 2009. Retrieved from www.iie.com/publications/papers/truman0911.pdf

Udovitch, A. L. (1962). At the Origins of the Western Commenda: Islam, Israel, Byzantium? *Speculum*, *37*(2), 198–207. doi:10.2307/2849948

Udovitch, A. L. (1967). Credit and a Means of Investment in Medieval Islamic Trade. *Journal of the American Oriental Society*, *87*(3), 260–264. doi:10.2307/597719

Udovitch, A. L. (1970a). Commercial Techniques in Early Medieval Islamic Trade. In D. Richards (Ed.), *Islam and the Trade of Asia: A Colloquium* (pp. 37–62). Oxford, UK. doi:10.9783/9781512806021-005

Udovitch, A. L. (1970b). *Partnership and Profit in Medieval Islam*. Princeton, NJ: Princeton University Press. doi:10.1515/9781400820474

Ullah, M. H., & Khanam, R. (2018). Whether Shari'ah compliance efficiency is a matter for the financial performance: The case of Islami Bank Bangladesh Limited. *Journal of Islamic Accounting and Business Research*, *9*(2), 183–200. doi:10.1108/JIABR-01-2016-0001

Ullah, S., Harwood, I. A., & Jamali, D. (2018). 'Fatwa Repositioning': The Hidden Struggle for Shari'a Compliance Within Islamic Financial Institutions. *Journal of Business Ethics*, *149*(4), 895–917. doi:10.100710551-016-3090-1

Ünal, M. (2011). *The small world of Islamic finance—Shari'ah scholars and governance—a network analytic perspective*. Retrieved from Funds@Work website, www. funds-atwork. com/uploads/media/Sharia-Network_by_Funds_at_Work_AG. pdf

Usman, A. S., & Tasmin, R. (2016). The Role of Islamic Micro-finance in Enhancing Human Development in Muslim Countries. *Journal of Islamic Finance*, *5*(1), 53–62. doi:10.12816/0027652

Usmani, M. T. (2007). *An Introduction to Islamic Finance*. Karachi, Pakistan: Maktaba Ma'rifatul Quran. Retrieved from http://muftitaqiusmani.com/en/books/PDF/An Introduction To Islamic Finance/An_Introduction_to_Islamic_Finance.pdf

Usmani, M. T. (2008). Sukuk and their contemporary applications. In Translated from the original Arabic by Sheikh Yusuf Talal DeLorenzo, AAOIFI Shari'a Council meeting, Saudi Arabia.

Uzair, M. (1955). *An Outline of Interestless Banking*. Karachi, Pakistan: Raihan Publications.

Uzair, M. (1978). *Interest Free Banking*. Karachi, Pakistan: Royal Book Company.

Vallascas, F., Crespi, F., & Hagendorff, J. (2012). Income diversification and bank performance during the financial crisis. Available at SSRN 1793232.

Venardos, A. M. (2005). *Islamic Banking & Finance in South-East Asia: Its Development & Future*. Singapore: World Scientific Publishing Co. Pte. Ltd. doi:10.1142/5751

Vinnicombe, T. (2012). A study of compliance with AAOIFI accounting standards by Islamic banks in Bahrain. *Journal of Islamic Accounting and Business Research*, *3*(2), 78–98. doi:10.1108/17590811211265902

Visser, H. (2009). *Islamic Finance: Principles and Practice*. Cheltenham, UK: Edward Elgar Publishing Limited.

Vong, A., & Chang, H. (2009). Determinants of Bank Profitability in Macao. University of Macao Working Paper.

Wallace, N. (1996). Narrow Banking Meets the Diamond-Dybvig Model. *Federal Reserve Bank of Minneapolis Quarterly Review*, *20*(1), 3–13.

Walsh, J. P., & Seward, J. K. (1990). On the efficiency of internal and external corporate control mechanisms. *Academy of Management Review*, *15*(3), 421–458. doi:10.5465/amr.1990.4308826

Wang, T. C., & Chang, T. H. (2007). Application of TOPSIS in evaluating initial training aircraft under a fuzzy environment. *Expert Systems with Applications*, *33*(4), 870–880. doi:10.1016/j.eswa.2006.07.003

Wang, Y. J. (2014). The evaluation of financial performance for Taiwan container shipping companies by fuzzy TOPSIS. *Applied Soft Computing*, *22*, 28–35. doi:10.1016/j.asoc.2014.03.021

Warde, I. (2000). *Islamic Finance in the Global Economy*. Edinburgh, Scotland: Edinburgh University Press. doi:10.3366/edinburgh/9780748612161.001.0001

Wasiuzzaman, S., & Tarmizi, H. A. (2010). Profitability of Islamic Banks in Malaysia: An Empirical Analysis. *Journal of Islamic Economics, Banking, and Finance*, *6*(4), 51–68.

Weir, C., Laing, D., & McKnight, P. J. (2002). Internal and External Governance Mechanisms: Their Impact on the Performance of Large UK Public Companies. *Journal of Business Finance & Accounting*, *29*(5&6), 579–611. doi:10.1111/1468-5957.00444

Wilson, R. (2009). *The development of Islamic finance in the GCC* (Working Paper, Kuwait Programme on Development, Governance and Globalization in the Gulf States). Retrieved from http://www.gslb.cimaglobal.com/Documents/Islamic%20finance/2011/Press%20 cuttings/ development-of-IF-in-the-GCC.pdf

Wilson, R. (1983). *Banking and finance in the Arab Middle East*. Surrey: Palgrave Macmillan UK. doi:10.1007/978-1-349-04817-5

Wooldridge, J. M. (2010). *Econometric analysis of cross section and panel data*. Cambridge, MA: The MIT Press.

World Bank Group. (2018). *Islamic Finance Bulletin*. Retrieved June 13, 2019, from http://www.tkbb.org.tr/Documents/Yonetmelikler/World-Bank- Islamic-Finance-Bulletin-Issue-37-July-2018.pdf

World Bank. (2010). *At the Tipping Point? The Implications of Kenya's ICT Revolution: Kenya Economic Update*. Retrieved March 6, 2019, from http://siteresources.world-bank.org/KENYAEXTN/Resources/KEU-Dec_2010_Power-point.pdf

World Bank. (2018). The Global Findex Database 2017: Measuring Financial Inclusion and the Fintech Revolution. Doi:10.1596/978-1-4648-1259-0

Wu, H.-Y., Tzeng, G.-H., & Chen, Y.-H. (2009). A fuzzy MCDM approach for evaluating banking performance based on Balanced Scorecard. *Expert Systems with Applications*, *36*(6), 10135–10147. doi:10.1016/j.eswa.2009.01.005

Yager, R. R. (2013). Pythagorean fuzzy subsets, In *Proceedings of the Joint IFSA World Congress and NAFIPS Annual Meeting* (pp. 57-61). Edmonton, Canada. 10.1109/IFSA-NAFIPS.2013.6608375

Yahaya, S., Yusoff, W. S. B. W., Idris, A. F. B., & Haji-Othman, Y. (2014). Conceptual framework for adoption of Islamic banking in Nigeria: The role of customer involvement. *European Journal of Business and Management*, *6*(30), 11–24.

Yanīkkaya, H., & Pabuçcu, Y. U. (2017). Causes and solutions for the stagnation of Islamic banking in Turkey. *ISRA International Journal of Islamic Finance*, *9*(1), 43–61. doi:10.1108/IJIF-07-2017-005

Yaquby, S. N. (2005). *Shari'ah* Requirements for conventional banks. Retrieved from http://www.islamic-banking.com/iarticle_7.aspx

Yellen, J. L. (2009, May). A Minsky Meltdown: Lessons for Central Bankers. *FRBSF Economic Letter No. 2009-15*. May 1, Retrieved from http://www.frbsf.org/publications/economics/letter/2009/el2009-15.pdf

Yudistira, G. (2017). OJK Dorong 62 Bank segera Tambah Modal. *Kontan*. Retrieved March 6, 2019, from http://keuangan.kontan.co.id/news/ojk-dorong-62-bank-segera-tambah-modal

Yudistira, D. (2004). Efficiency in Islamic banking: An empirical analysis of eighteen banks. *Islamic Economic Studies, 12*(1), 1–19.

Yussof, S. A. (2013). Prospects of a Sharīᶜah Audit Framework for Islamic Financial Institutions in Malaysia. *Islam and Civilisational Renewal, 4*(1), 80–102. doi:10.12816/0009724

Zafar, M. B., & Sulaiman, A. A. (2019). Corporate social responsibility and Islamic banks: A systematic literature review. *Management Review Quarterly, 69*(2), 159–206. doi:10.100711301-018-0150-x

Zaidi, S. A. (2005). *Issues in Pakistan's Economy* (2nd ed.). Oxford University Press.

Zain, S., & Shafii, Z. (2018). The impact of *Shari'ah* governance to financial and non-financial reporting in Islamic financial institutions: A literature survey. *International Journal of Islamic Business, 3*(2), 1–40.

Zainuldin, M. H., Lui, T. K., & Yii, K. J. (2018). Principal-agent relationship issues in Islamic banks: A view of Islamic ethical system. *International Journal of Islamic and Middle Eastern Finance and Management, 11*(2), 297–311. doi:10.1108/IMEFM-08-2017-0212

Zakaria, N., & Ariffin, N. M., N. Z. A. (2016). Construct of *Shari'ah* Audit Effectiveness in Islamic Financial Institutitons. In *6th IIUM International Accounting Conference Oct. 28-29, 2015 Kuala Lumpur, Malaysia.*

Zaki, F., & Hussainey, K. (2015). Conversion into Islamic banks: Jurisprudence, economic and AAOIFI requirements. *European Journal of Islamic Finance, 3*(June 2016), 1–9.

Zamer, K. Z. (2018). Islamic Banking: A New Approach for Financial inclusion. *International Journal of Economics and Finance, 10*(7), 118-124.

Zeineb, G. B., & Mensi, S. (2014). Does the PLS Paradigm Spur the Islamic Banks Vs Conventional Banks Soundness: Case of the Global Financial Crisis. *Journal of Economics and Development Studies, 2*(3), 177–192. doi:10.15640/jeds.v2n3a13

Zeitun, R. (2012). Determinants of Islamic and conventional banks performance in GCC countries using panel data analysis. *Global Economy and Finance Journal, 5*(1), 53–72.

Zulkhibiri, M. (2016). Financial Inclusion, Financial Inclusion Policy and Islamic Finance. *Macroeconomics and Finance in Emerging Market Economies, 9*(3), 1–18.

# About the Contributors

**Abdul Rafay** is a practitioner cum academician. For more than 23 years, Mr. Rafay has been working as a freelance advisor, consultant & trainer to a wide variety of public & private sector national and multinational companies in the areas of Corporate Finance, Financial Policy & Implementation, Auditing & Assurance, Accountancy, Corporate Tax Management, Financial Technology and System Consultancy. He has been providing consultancy to various industries including Textile, Auto Assembling, Footwear, Industrial/Agro Chemicals, Ice Cream/Dairies, Glass/Ceramics, Healthcare, Mining/Natural Resources, Packaging/Paper Sacking, Steel/Pipe Casting, Rice Processing, Brokerage/Co-operative Financing, Software Development, Real Estate, Printing/Publishing, and Construction/Civil Engineering etc. Mr. Rafay is a Fellow member of the Institute of Chartered Accountants of Pakistan. He is also member of various national and international professional bodies including Institute of Internal Auditors (IIA), USA; Association of Certified Fraud Examiners (ACFE), USA. Since 2001, he has been a life time member of Lahore Tax Bar Association. He has served as Co-regional Director (Founding) of Lahore-Islamabad Chapter of Professional Risk Managers International Association (PRMIA), Washington, USA (2011-2013). In 2012, he was nominated as Member: Education & Training Committee (ETCOM) of The Institute of Chartered Accountants of Pakistan (ICAP). He is also a member of ICAP's "Islamic Finance working group" which is closely in liaison with State Bank of Pakistan and other stakeholders for Islamic Finance Accounting and Auditing Standards. He is Alumni of Rausing Executive Development Center (REDC), Lahore University of Management Sciences (LUMS), Pakistan. In 2014, International Finance Corporation (World Bank Group) selected him for Training of Trainers (ToT) for Corporate Governance Action Planning for SMEs. He is also an approved trainer for Institute of Financial Markets of Pakistan (IFMP) established by Securities and Exchange Commission of Pakistan, the corporate regulator. In 2013, his name got included in the list of "Certified Directors" as per Clause (xi) of The Code of Corporate Governance 2012 issued by SECP. Since 1994, Mr. Rafay has also been associated with teaching in some of the top business schools of Pakistan. His specialized subjects of interest include: Strategic Corporate Finance, Financial Derivatives, Investments/Portfolio Analysis, International Financial Reporting Standards, Corporate Restructuring (Mergers & Acquisitions), Financial Statement Analysis & Corporate Taxation. He also served as an instructor in Civil Services Academy, Pakistan to train the CSS Officers selected by Federal Public Service Commission of Pakistan (FPSC). Currently he is a Professor of Finance & Accounting in University of Management & Technology, Pakistan. He has published more than two dozen research papers in SSCI, ESCI and Scopus indexed journals published by reputed global publishers including Emerald, Sage, Taylor & Francis and IGI Global. He contributed multiple chapters in Books edited by International Editors. In 2019, he also edited a book "FinTech as a Disruptive Technology for Financial Institutions" published by IGI Global, USA.

***

**Aisyah Abdul-Rahman** holds PhD in Islamic Banking from International Islamic University, Malaysia. Earlier she did her MBA from same university and BBA from Lehigh University, Pennsylvania, USA. Currently she is an Associate Professor at Universiti Kebangsaan Malaysia. Her research interests include Shariah Governance, Corporate Finance, and Risk Management in Islamic Banking.

**Mohammad Zoynul Abedin** is a post-doctoral fellow in management science and engineering, collaborative innovation center for transport studies, Dalian Maritime University, China. Dr. Abedin's working area on data science, machine learning, business intelligence, and computational finance. He publishes thirty peer-reviewed articles on which fifteen are on data science domain. His publications appeared on Web of Knowledge (WoK), and SCOPUS databases.

**Mahmoud A. S. Abusloum** is a PhD scholar at IIUM Institute of Islamic Banking and Finance (IIiBF), International Islamic University, Malaysia. He is Founder & Member of the board of directors of Libyan Islamic Finance Forum (LIFF) in Malaysia. Currently, he is a lecturer at Omar Al-Mukhtar University, Al-Bayda, Libya. Previously, he was head of the Shariah department in the Faculty of Law in the same university and Cooperated Lecturer in Faculty of Management & Islamic Economic at Mohamed Ben Ali Elsanossi Islamic University – Al Bayda, Libya. Beside teaching in these universities, he worked as Branch Director of Institute of Banking & Financial studies at Central bank of Libya in Al-Bayad city.

**Mohammad Adam** is currently a Professor at Universitas Sriwijaya, Indonesia.

**Nahid Afroz** is a Research Associate at Credit Rating Agency of Bangladesh (CRAB). She completed BBA and MBA, both major in Finance, from University of Chittagong, Bangladesh. Her research area focuses on Islamic finance, micro-finance, and development studies with specific interest on Islamic securities (Sukuk), Islamic micro-finance, and financial inclusion.

**Khaliq Ahmad** holds PhD from Aligarh Muslim University, India. Currently he is a Professor at the AACSB College of Business and Economics (CBE), Qassim University, Saudi Arabia. Beside teaching, supervision, research and publishing, he was Director of Graduate School of Management. He also served as Dean, Kulliyah of Economics and Management Sciences (KENMS) and Dean of IIUM Institute of Islamic Banking and Finance (IIiBF). He is the founding President of ICIFE (International Council of Islamic Finance Educators) under the Ministry of Education, Malaysia. Beside teaching, supervision, research and publication, Dr. Khaliq has worked as Dean Institute of Islamic Banking and Finance, International Islamic University, Malaysia.

**Nor Faezah Ghazi Ahmad** holds PhD in Islamic Banking from Universiti Teknologi Malaysia. Her research interests include Shariah Governance, Corporate Finance, and Risk Management in Islamic Banking.

**Serpil Altınırmak** holds PhD in Finance from Anadolu University, Turkey. Her research interests are Islamic finance, risk management, neurofinance, behavioral finance, capital markets, financial institutions, financial statement analysis and accounting.

**Alam I. Asadov** holds PhD in Islamic Finance from the International Centre for Education in Islamic Finance (INCEIF), Malaysia. Earlier, he obtained master's degree in Economics from the University of Alabama, USA and bachelor's degree in Economics from University of Richmond, USA. Currently he is an Assistant Professor at Prince Sultan University, Saudi Arabia since September 2018. Dr. Asadov has over 15 years of work experience as lecturer, researcher and practitioner. He started his career in 2001 as a Research Assistant at the University of Alabama. From 2003 to 2007 he has works as Local and Regional Manager at Capital Retail Services Ltd., USA. During 2007-2009, he was the Head of Research department and lecturer at Samarkand Institute of Economics and Service. He worked as Economics lecturer at Westminster International University in Tashkent during 2009-2010 academic years. Dr. Asadov has published chapters in edited books, articles in refereed journals and professional magazines, and participated in international conferences and took part in some project grants.

**Ambareen Beebeejaun** is a PhD scholar in International Tax Law. Currently she is a lecturer at the University of Mauritius. She teaches corporate and taxation law.

**Nabil Bello** holds PhD in Islamic Banking and Finance from International Islamic University, Malaysia. Currently he is a Lecturer at Bayero University, Nigeria. His research interests are Islamic Banking, Islamic Capital Markets, Islamic Financial Planning and Fiqh al-Muamalat.

**Naiwei Chen** holds PhD in Economics from Texas A&M University, USA. Currently he is an Associate Professor of Banking and Finance at National Chiayi University, Taiwan. Earlier he was a Professor of Accounting at Changzhou University, China. His research interests include corporate governance, corporate social responsibility, economic growth, emerging markets, Islamic banking and finance, political economy, trade, and welfare.

**Yomna Daoud** holds PhD in Finance and Accounting from the University of Sfax, Tunisia. Presently Dr. Yomna is working as an Assistant Professor in Faculty of Economics and Management, University of Sfax, Tunisia. She has published many journal articles.

**Sheereen Fauzel** holds PhD in International Economics from the University of Mauritius. Currently she is a Senior lecturer at the University of Mauritius. Her areas of expertise are International Economics, development economics and related areas. She has participated in international conferences and has publication in notable international journals of Business, Economics and Tourism. She is a reviewer for a number of refereed journals including Current issues in Tourism and Journal of Hospitality Marketing and Management among others.

**Luthfi Hamidi** is a PhD scholar at Griffith University, Australia. He is undertaking his doctoral thesis on Islamic social banking.

**Razali Haron** holds doctorate from UKM, Malaysia. Currently he is an Associate Professor at the IIUM Institute of Islamic Banking and Finance. His research covers the area of corporate finance and corporate governance.

**Aida Kammoun** holds PhD in Finance and Accounting from the University of Sfax, Tunisia. Dr. Aida is working as Professor of Finance in Higher Institute of Business Administration, University of Sfax, Tunisia. She has published many journal articles.

**Çağlar Karamaşa** holds PhD in Quantitative Methods from Anadolu University, Turkey. His research interests are fuzzy logic and applications, optimization, multi criteria decision making, data mining and multi variable statistics.

**Naji Mansour Nomran** is a PhD scholar at International Islamic University, Malaysia. Currently is a Lecturer, Department of Finance and Banking, Faculty of Administrative Sciences, Thamar University, Yemen.

**Basil Oluch Okoth** is a PhD scholar in Management and Organization at Anadolu University, Turkey. He works on subjects that deal with leadership, gender, and organizational performance, organizational culture as well as knowledge management in organizations. His work is the field of finance is mainly with regards to financial inclusion especially through mobile banking and mobile money.

**Eda Orhun** holds PhD in Finance from Vienna Graduate School of Finance, Austria. She has taught courses in Corporate Finance and served as an academic advisor for Bank Gutmann Seminars and master theses in Vienna. Her research interests include Corporate Finance, Mergers & Acquisitions, Voluntary Disclosures, Information Economics and Financial Intermediation.

**Cumhur Şahin** holds PhD in Finance from Anadolu University, Turkey. His research interests are financial markets and institutions, capital markets and applications, real estate investment trusts, financial statement analysis etc.

**Edib Smolo** holds a PhD in Islamic Finance from the International Centre for Education in Islamic Finance (INCEIF), Malaysia. He is the Founder and CEO of Saray Consultancy for Socially Responsible & Ethical Finance. He was the International Islamic Finance Manager at Tosan, Iran; Islamic Finance Manager at Indra Technology Solutions Malaysia; the Shari'ah Coordinator at International Islamic Liquidity Management Corporation (IILM); the Researcher at the International Shari'ah Research Academy (ISRA) for Islamic Finance, among others. Dr. Smolo authored a book on Islamic finance, authored and co-authored several chapters in well-renowned books and papers in refereed journals.

**Ahmad Azam Sulaiman** holds PhD in Economics from Universiti Kebangsaan Malaysia. Currently he is a senior lecturer at the Department of Shariah and Economics, University of Malaya, Malaysia.

**Muizzuddin** is currently an Assistant Professor at Universitas Sriwijaya, Indonesia.

**S. M. Sohrab Uddin** is a Professor at the Department of Finance, Faculty of Business Administration, University of Chittagong, Bangladesh. He obtained BBA and MBA from University of Chittagong, and MBA and PhD from Ritsumeikan Asia Pacific University, Oita, Japan. His research area focuses on financial market, institutions, and instruments with particular emphasis on banking sector development including Islamic finance in developing countries.

**Andrew C. Worthington** holds PhD from the University of Queensland, Australia. Currently he is a Professor of Finance in the Department of Accounting, Finance, and Economics at Griffith University, Australia. His teaching interests encompass advanced corporate finance and equity valuation. His published research includes financial and commodity markets, alternative investments, and household finance, while his research into Islamic finance covers Islamic banking and Islamic managed funds.

**Muhammad Bilal Zafar** is a PhD Scholar at the Department of Shariah and Economics, University of Malaya, Malaysia.

# Index

## T



## U



## V



## W



## Z

www.ingramcontent.com/pod-product-compliance
Lightning Source LLC
LaVergne TN
LVHW060415300926
849162LV00006B/1432